AN INTRODUCTION TO THE SOCIAL WORLD

AN INTRODUCTION TO THE SOCIAL WORLD

Study Guide Included

Edited by:

R. Jack Richardson
McMaster University

Lorne Tepperman
University of Toronto

CONTRIBUTORS

Anton L. Allahar, *The University of Western Ontario*
Maureen Baker, *Research Branch, Library of Parliament*
Gordon Darroch, *York University*
Peter Li, *University of Saskatchewan*
Nancy Mandell, *Atkinson College, York University*
Austin T. Turk, *University of Toronto*
Susannah Wilson, *Wilfrid Laurier University*
Willem H. Vanderburg, *University of Toronto*

McGRAW-HILL RYERSON LIMITED

*Toronto Montreal New York Auckland Bogotá Cairo Hamburg Lisbon
London Madrid Mexico Milan New Delhi Paris San Juan
São Paulo Singapore Sydney Tokyo*

ISBN 0-07-549458-2

3 4 5 6 7 8 9 0 THB 5 4 3 2 1 0 9

Printed and bound in Canada

CANADIAN CATALOGUING IN PUBLICATION DATA
Main entry under title:
An Introduction to the social world
One-semester version of: The Social world.
Bibliography: p.
Includes index.
ISBN 0-07-549458-2

1. Sociology. I. Richardson, R. J. (Richard John), date –.
II. Tepperman, Lorne, date –.
III. Allahar, Anton. IV. Title: The Social world.
HM51.S642 1986   301   C86-094874-9

ACKNOWLEDGEMENTS

Putting a book like this together can be difficult. However, we had a great time putting this one together because of the excellent people we worked with.

Our first thanks go to the contributing authors. They are all fine scholars and, more than that, professionals. They took our criticism and requests for revision with good humour and grace. Needless to say, the book could not have existed without their scholarship, creativity, hard work and co-operation.

We are also grateful to the editors of this book. Fred Chorley, sponsoring editor at McGraw-Hill Ryerson, conceived the project of producing this one-semester version of the original book and energetically and capably brought it through the necessary stages to fruition. Joan Blishen, Fred's predecessor, enthusiastically supported the development of the original, larger version. Alan Wain, our style editor, honed our drafts into clearer and more engaging prose, showing a large amount of "sociological imagination" along the way. He also wrote the Study Guide, which appears as an appendix in this text. Carol Soloman, the production editor, took another bash at our prose and made it more readable and consistent from one chapter to another. Finally, dozens of reviewers advised us on ways to improve our sociological content at each stage.

The resulting book is, of course, imperfect, but we accept responsibility for the flaws that remain. We hope the book will achieve the purpose for which it was written: namely, to better inform our students, a new generation of sociologists, about the history, goals and methods of this most interesting enterprise in which we share, the discipline of sociology.

EDITOR'S INTRODUCTION

This text was derived from *The Social World: An Introduction to Sociology* after a need for a condensed text, more suited to a one-semester course, was identified. The chapter selection, made after consultation with instructors across the country, covers the main core areas of sociology, along with a number of other areas that have particular relevance to today's examination of sociology.

An important and unique feature of *An Introduction to The Social World* is the inclusion of the student Study Guide as an integral part of the text instead of as a separate supplement. The Study Guide questions are found in an appendix at the end of the text and provide students with a valuable learning tool.

Thanks are due to those instructors who participated in the survey that finalized the chapter selection for this book and to those who reviewed the chapters, particularly the following: Irv Barat, Esty Bybelezer, Marion Colby, L. Comeau, J. Curtis, T.J. Derksen, H. Doughty, Diane Einblau, Fred Elkin, John Fox, W. Gilsdorf, Ed Grabb, Colin Gray, L. Greaves, Douglas Hudson, Leon Jacobs, Geoff Johnstone, Ed Kseynych, Raymond Liew, K. Parley, R. Prus, Jeff Reitz, Stanley Ryerson, E. Sanderman, Elaine Smith, R. Stebbins, Rose Tekel, and Sandra Ward.

TABLE of CONTENTS

SOCIOLOGY
and
SOCIETY

Sociology is the science that constructs theories about the social relations making up a society. Let's consider what this means.

This apparently simple definition hides some important difficulties. For sociologists, the word *science* means much the same as for physicists or biologists: namely, the construction and validation of theories about the real world. A science of social relations is more complex than one concerned with atoms or amoebae. But, in principle, the goals of all sciences are the same.

Theories are, for sociologists as for physicists, tentative explanations of observable reality and the basis for predicting future events. Every theory is judged against competing theories in terms of thoroughness and economy of explanation. A science tests and retests its theories to improve and even discard them in favour of better ones.

Social relations are any relationships between people that are somehow binding. In this sense, the subject matter of sociology is the *social bond*, which connects individuals in groups and societies.

Societies, then, are collections of social relationships. A society is made up of all the families, clubs, groups, corporations, understandings, arrangements and rules that its members share. Seeing the boundaries of a given society is sometimes difficult, for many social relationships may span an international border, like the one between Canada and the United States. Indeed, some writers have wondered whether Canada and the United States, which are certainly distinct nation-states, are really distinct societies. (Others, for similar reasons, have wondered whether the two are distinct economies, since they are so closely tied by trade and the flow of migrants.) Yet, in principle, the idea of a "Canadian society" still has value to sociologists, as to others.

The Character of Sociological Theories

The theories sociologists construct have certain characteristics. As noted earlier, they are tentative, thorough and economical. But they should also be *true*, as far as we can tell. Sociologists, being human, may become blinded to what is true and false. Our intellectual shortcomings, personal interests and values may mislead us. To reduce the risk of this, sociologists use agreed-upon methods of discovering, confirming, and communicating their findings and theories.

Sociological theories should not be circular or tautological, i.e. true by definition. A theory that "satisfied workers are happy with their jobs" is tautological if what we mean by "satisfied" is "happy with their jobs." Foolish as it may sound, many students and even professional sociologists make theories which prove tautological on inspection. A tautological theory, though true, has no value to science because it cannot be disproved.

A theory that is not tautological is open to *verification* or validation. Scientists, including sociologists, never prove a theory absolutely right; they only prove contending theories wrong. The theory that best survives multiple attempts at disproof and shows itself thorough and economical is considered the most valid.

Some of Einstein's theories in physics waited for decades until equipment was developed to test their mathematically derived predictions. Likewise, some sociological theories are not immediately verifiable because they predict future events: for example, Marx's theories about the coming of communism to industrial societies. Others cannot be validated because they assume the existence of invisible (i.e. unmeasurable) forces: for example, Freud's theory of the unconscious. How remarkable that these very theories have taken a central position in social science, despite their problems of verification. On the other hand, Marx's theoretical importance was established largely through analyses of past and present societies, and Freud's through the treatment of neuroses, not through prediction.

Whatever the difficulties, verification must always be sought. Every theorist must appeal to objective evidence and reason over intuition, emotion and good intention in promoting his/her ideas.

Two other aspects of sociological theories are worth mentioning. First, theories should be *important* or socially relevant. Sociologists aim ultimately to understand the whole social world and not simply its smallest, most readily accessible parts. To sociologists, all social relations are of interest. But, as sociologists/citizens, we should keep our eyes on the public problems of our times. Sociology's history shows the best work has been done by "middle range" researchers moving back and forth between pure theory and an active concern with on-going events. Still, sociologists should avoid promising results prematurely. Nothing undermines popular faith in any science more than false claims, even if motivated by good intentions.

Sociology that influences the way some portion of society is working is called *applied sociology*. Applied sociology is being taught in more and more North American universities, largely because sociological application is becoming a bigger part of sociologists' on-going work. Each year, more graduate sociologists take jobs outside universities, applying their sociological knowledge to government and corporate decision-making.

Finally, sociological theories should be *nonobvious* or counter-intuitive. Many accuse sociology of dressing up common sense in impenetrable jargon. This unfortunate idea, though apparently justified by many published works, is inherently wrong. Good theories do *not* just give us back what we already know. On the contrary, a good theory, by connecting previously unconnected facts, yields insights no one anticipated. The degree to which sociology succeeds in making such non-obvious theories is a measure of its maturity as a science. If sociology falls short, the failure is not for want of trying.

Like other scientists, sociologists create a conceptual language to work in: a set of terms, precisely defined, whose value may not be immediately obvious to the layperson. Like theory itself, theoretical language need not justify itself at every turn. It may not be obvious or easily penetrated, yet it will still withstand the charge of being jargon if, finally, it yields insights harder to reach in some other language. In this respect, mathematics is the prime example of a theoretical language that is not jargon; but it is not the only example. Sociology, too, has its own language.

Sociology Contrasted With Other Disciplines

Sociologist Kenneth Westhues has helped us better understand sociology by comparing it with other, similar activities. For example, sociology is different from journalism and history. Both journalism and history describe real events and to some degree base their descriptions on an interpretation or implicit theory. Sociology is different. It makes its theories explicit in order to test them. Telling a story is, for sociologists, less important than testing the interpretation on which the story is based. Sociology may be a good preparation for doing history or journalism, but it differs from these disciplines.

Sociology also differs from philosophy. Both are analytical — that is, concerned with making and testing theory. However, theorizing is quite different in these two fields. Sociology is resolutely *empirical*, or concerned with evidence grasped by the senses, and philosophy is not. This does not mean philosophy has a greater concern with the internal logic of its arguments. Sociological theories must stand up logically, but they must *also* stand up to observable evidence in a way philosophical theories need not. A sociological theory whose predictions are not supported by evidence gathered in an agreed-upon way will not be accepted by sociologists, no matter how logical the theory may be.

Finally, sociology differs from psychology, which is also analytical, reflective and empirical. The difference here lies in the units of analysis. Psychologists study the behaviour of individual humans (or, occasionally, animals) under varied experimental conditions. Sociology's subject is the social relationship or group of relationships observed in nature: the family, group, or total society. Sociology and psychology come together in a field called social psychology; but even it is defined differently by sociologists and psychologists.

To summarize, sociology is concerned with making scientifically valid theories about social relations. These theories should be "scientific" in the usual meanings of the word. But certain methodological problems make the scientific study of social relations more difficult than the scientific study of atoms, amoebae, or even individual monkeys and humans.

Some Methodological Difficulties

First, we can rarely, if ever, experiment on groups or families, let alone societies. By "experiment" we mean the random assignment of cases to experimental and control groups, the careful manipulation of the experimental group, and the comparison of the two groups before and after manipulation. (This procedure is described further in Chapter 2.) Yet experimentation is the basic method of testing theories in physical and to a lesser degree in biological sciences.

The impossibility of experimentation in sociology leads us to develop alternative methods, none completely satisfactory. The sociologist must know and use a large variety of research methods. Any sociological theory must withstand a battery of weak tests, using many approaches, since strong (experimental) tests are not possible.

The second main difficulty lies in the existence of competing paradigms in sociology. *Paradigms* are ways of thinking. Different paradigms not only define which problems are key to understanding social relations; they also define which research procedures are most appropriate and which evidence most relevant. Paradigms have multiplied in sociology for many reasons, including: a strong philosophical (deductive) tradition in European sociology and an empirical (inductive) one in America and Britain; the rising and falling popularity of particular research techniques; and fluctuating political radicalism in the public mind and in the universities. The ambiguity of sociological method also contributes. If a sociological proof *must* consist of many weak approximations, room exists for many approaches, many paradigms.

A third main difficulty lies in the reactive nature of the sociologist's object of study. Sociologists and the people being studied all hold views likely to affect research outcomes. Usually these preconceptions bias the outcomes in favour of what the investigator expects. Some researchers think this reactivity is desirable. They believe the sociologist's role is to combine study with social action: to discover, study and eliminate problems at the same

progressive   conservative   people

time. Most, however, prefer to separate these activities in the interest of scientific precision. People, unlike atoms or guinea pigs, can and do monitor what scientists say about them. Indeed, most people have their own theories about how society works. Their actual or expected reaction to scholarly analysis contributes to the climate of disagreement within sociology.

A fourth problem is the nonrepetitiveness of history. If our subject is society itself, we must study many societies under different conditions, in hopes of finding "natural experiments." But sociologists will never find two societies identical in every respect except the one of theoretical interest. Always, new kinds of societies are found in new historical contexts. Consider the Industrial Revolution. It will never be repeated. For this reason, no theory about the Industrial Revolution can be tested as a physicist or chemist might test a theory. Of course, there are many different theories about industrialization, growth and development, even theories about why the Industrial Revolution first occurred where and when it did. Yet, theories about societies industrializing today are dealing with a different phenomenon: industrial development in the midst of an already industrialized, colonized world. Sociologists can apply their understanding of eighteenth-century England to studying industrialization in twentieth-century India, but only by making a great deal of allowance for the different contexts. In this respect, sociology faces a problem similar to the one facing biologists and ecologists, among others.

The Notion of a Social System

These methodological problems which prevent sociology from using true scientific method may never be fully overcome. On the other hand, several other factors make the scientific study of social relations somewhat easier. Social relations are *systemic*: they contain arrangements of parts that sustain one another in a given pattern over time. Some theorists have argued that all sociologists study social systems, and all social systems, large and small, have common features. If this is true, an understanding of social systems in general can be used to understand a particular case that is hard to study directly. Information about smaller, more accessible social systems can be used to develop and test theories about larger, less accessible ones.

Not all sociologists would accept this view. Many reject the explicit focus on social systems; they find the concept too limiting. Yet, a compelling result of system thinking is the discovery of the "unanticipated consequence," of which Robert Merton (1910-) has written a great deal. Research demonstrates that people are often constrained by the social relationships in which they participate, despite their own plans and wishes to the contrary. People (alone or in groups) are part of a larger, complex reality beyond their easy control. They are part of a *social structure*, as discussed in the next chapter and elsewhere in this book.

This observation has led sociologists to a unique understanding of public planning. More and more, applied sociology helps planners guard against the unanticipated consequences of their actions: against plans that will inevitably fail, produce undesirable social side-effects, or even prove "fatal remedies," killing the patient in the process of curing. Only by understanding societies as social systems can planners intervene in ways that will actually work.

Unanticipated consequences prove a society is more than the simple sum of people and things, each with distinct properties that mix together. The combination of people produces complex interactions, as in chemistry and ecology. Eventually sociologists will fully understand these interesting, complex interactions.

The two chapters that follow develop some of the ideas put forward in this Introduction. "Sociology: The Science of Society" clarifies the discipline's competing paradigms and discusses their historical background. It discusses two issues central to our discipline: namely, "free will versus determinism" and the concept of "social structure." The second chapter extends our understanding of experimental and nonexperimental methods of research. These chapters come first in the book because they are the most basic. A good understanding of sociology's subject matter and purpose means, first, understanding the discipline's theory and method.

1

Sociology: The Science of Society

Anton L. Allahar

INTRODUCTION

It is exceedingly difficult, if not pointless, to attempt an exhaustive and all-encompassing definition of sociology. This is not to imply that what sociology is or what sociologists do is totally incomprehensible. Rather, it is meant to sensitize the reader to the fact that the scope of the discipline is wide-ranging, rich, complex and continually growing. For these reasons, a single definition will never suffice. It would be so broad and general that it would say very little. For example, defining sociology as "the study of social order, social disorder and social change," though essentially accurate, is so general that it has little practical utility.

As a point of departure, therefore, it seems more appropriate to talk of such things as the aims, methods and uses of sociological inquiry — in other words, what sociologists do. Generally, sociologists try to make sense of that noisy blur of human activity called "society." They try to define, describe, explain and interpret human behaviour within the contexts of social groups and institutions. Unlike the psychologist, who focuses on individual motivations and purposes underlying human behaviour, the sociologist is interested primarily in general and recurrent behaviour patterns, whether in small groups, specific social institutions, regions of a country or entire societies.

One thing that becomes immediately apparent to the student of sociology is the infinite complexity of the term "society." It is so vast and dynamic that sociologists often compartmentalize various aspects of societal relations in smaller, more manageable units. One of the traditional divisions is between *macrosociological* and *microsociological* areas. The former refers to large-scale social interactions, such as the impact of unemployment on marriages or the relationship between religion and economic development. Microsociological issues, on the other hand, are small-scale behaviour patterns within groups and institutions. For example, how is power distributed within the family, or how are decisions made and implemented in specific office settings? Both the macro- and microsociological areas of concern share fundamental characteristics that serve to define the sociological outlook or approach.

SOCIOLOGY AND HISTORY

WHY HISTORY IS IMPORTANT

Many of the essential insights of sociology are drawn from history. Most sociologists agree that individuals are not born with ideas, nor do ideas drop from the sky. Our basic modes of interaction, our social institutions, patterns of organization, communication, and conventions, in a word, our cultures, are history-laden. What occurs in any given society, therefore, usually takes history as its point of departure and builds on historical knowledge. As will be seen in the chapter on culture, the concept of society also implies language and communication.

Sociologists, then, may choose to ignore history at their own peril. For history is indispensable as a means of understanding future ways of behaving. History, understood as a social process that has generated a stock of knowledge relating to past failures and triumphs, is thus a lucrative repository of information. This does not mean, however, that understanding history alone is sufficient to understand society.

The sociologist must also realize that humans are rational, thinking beings possessed of a will. Hence, whether individually or in groups, they may choose to act contrary to the established historical pattern. In fact, they may not even know that a given pattern exists. It is the task of the sociologist to identify the pattern of social convention and then *explain* why it persists or dies out.

THE INDUSTRIAL AND THE FRENCH REVOLUTIONS AS HISTORICAL WATERSHEDS

Of the major modern historical processes, the Industrial Revolution and the French Revolution have received the most sociological attention. Indeed, several social theorists have argued that sociology as a formal discipline was born as a reaction to the events surrounding these two major social developments (Zeitlin, 1981b; Collins and Markowsky, 1984:28; Nisbet, 1966; Seidman, 1983). The Industrial Revolution, which first took hold in England in the early eighteenth century, is generally described in terms of the social and economic changes which it wrought.

Among these were: the displacement of the peasantry from the land and their replacement by agricultural wage workers; the growth of industrial towns that drew people away from the self-sufficient villages of the countryside; the widespread production of marketable commodities, which changed informal barter and simple exchange relations in the absence of a formally constituted market; and finally, the creation of huge numbers of urban dwellers (both employed and unemployed) who were totally dependent on wage labour for their survival.

If the Industrial Revolution was characterized by sweeping social and economic changes, the French Revolution of 1789 is most remembered for its social and political consequences. The watchwords of the revolution — liberty, individuality, fraternity and equality — heralded a new way of life for French men and women in virtually all aspects of society and made possible the cry for political democracy. The bourgeoisie, a relatively new class of manufacturing, commercial, and industrial entrepreneurs, rivalled the monarchy, aristocracy and nobility for power. They challenged established authority and tradition and called for new rules of conduct that would free them to pursue their economic and political goals. The destruction of French feudalism thus became the *precondition* for the rise of this class, as well as other new classes.

HISTORY OF SOCIOLOGICAL THOUGHT

ENLIGHTENMENT VERSUS ROMANTICISM

Out of the ferment created by the French Revolution, some of the major forerunners of sociological thinking were born. The eighteenth-century Enlightenment produced an unprecedented interest in science and rationality. Instead of resorting to intuition, introspection, tradition, authority and revelation as sources of truth, many philosophers and thinkers embraced a faith in science, which promised to liberate the human being from superstition and fear of the unknown.

Driven by a deep-seated humanitarianism, Enlightenment thinkers attempted to show that the universe was intelligible, that the laws governing its operation could be discovered and manipulated to the benefit of man. They criticized the divine right of kings to rule, traditional authority and privilege and religion as sources of human bondage. Taking account of the social situation in France during the eighteenth century, the forerunners of sociological thought analysed French social institutions, practices and beliefs with a view to explaining the nature and logic of the human condition. They were convinced that only by constructive social criticism and appeals to rationality could men and women create a more just and equal social order. Their concerns were eminently sociological, and these thinkers helped shape sociological thought down to the present.

But while Enlightenment thinkers such as Montesquieu and Rousseau set the tone for much present-day sociological scholarship, they also provoked a countercurrent that, too, made a significant contribution to the development of the discipline. That countercurrent has been called the romantic and conservative reaction to the French Revolution and the Enlightenment philosophy which followed in its wake. In essence, the romantic-conservatives, also deeply concerned with human behaviour and interaction, disagreed with the heavy emphasis Enlightenment thinking placed upon science and rationality. They argued that significant components of social behaviour were nonrational but nevertheless crucial for analysing social interaction.

Specifically, the romantic-conservatives reacted to the lack of respect for religion, morality and the wisdom of established tradition and custom, and the subjection of imagination, feeling and sentiment to rational ridicule. They cherished the old order and saw progress or change as something that should come about, not via revolution, but through slow and gradual reform. And herein lay their conservatism.

Out of the clash between these two major philosophical orientations, the two founding fathers of sociology forged their seminal ideas. Henri de Saint-Simon (1760-1825) and Auguste Comte (1798-1857) blended some tenets of Enlightenment philosophy with certain aspects of romantic-conservative thought to produce a *positive science of society* — a means for uniting what may otherwise appear to be two opposing currents: order and progress. Their writings deal with some of the concerns that have remained central even in contemporary sociological literature: social class, power, religion, ideology, the family, property, inequality and politics.

These themes were later seized upon by three men who are today regarded as the main pillars of the discipline of sociology: Karl Marx (1818-1883), Émile Durkheim (1858-1917) and Max Weber (1864-1920).

SOCIOLOGY'S THREE PILLARS — MARX, DURKHEIM AND WEBER

Harbouring a deep-seated humanitarian concern, Marx analysed the operations of the capitalist economic system, which he saw as inherently unjust, dehumanizing and destined to be overthrown. Employing a class analysis, he argued that the capitalist class, whose sole economic motive is the pursuit of profit, exploits the working class to a point where the latter is eventually moved to react violently. From the point of view of the working class, exploitation creates both the *objective* conditions of misery and the *subjective* conditions for the developing class consciousness which combine to make the workers revolutionary. The inevitable clash between

Marx was born and educated in Germany. He studied law and philosophy at the universities of Bonn and Berlin, but, owing to his radical views, was blacklisted and never managed to practise either. In 1842 he met Friedrich Engels, with whom he collaborated on many of his writings. Marx spent many years at the British Museum while writing **Das Kapital** *(1867), an analysis of the exploitive aspects of capitalism.* By permission of the Bettmann Archive, New York, N.Y.

Karl Marx (1818-1883)

the two principal classes of capitalist society ultimately results in victory for the workers and the establishment of a socialist society, where private property and exploitation are eliminated, social inequalities are greatly reduced, and human dignity is restored to the worker.

In Durkheim one can see some broad similarities to Marx. Both were interested in the rise of capitalism, the impact of economic changes on individuals and their communities, the origins and consequences of social inequality, and the problem of social order. But whereas Marx was more directly concerned with class and power struggles, Durkheim posed the prior question: "How are the social structures within which power and class struggle operate even possible in the first place?" (Grabb, 1984:74). Or, stated differently, "How is society possible"?

From this question, Durkheim was led to develop some of his central sociological ideas. Beginning with the concept of *solidarity*, he wanted to explain how, in spite of all the tensions and conflicts in society, human beings nevertheless are bound together in stable and enduring relationships. Depending on the society in question, solidarity or social cohesiveness for Durkheim was of two types: mechanical and organic.

He associated *mechanical solidarity* with primitive societies. It is a solidarity based on "likeness" or "sameness," for in such societies, where people are organized into

Durkheim was born in France, where he studied philosophy and history at the École Normale Supérieure and the University of Paris. In his doctoral dissertation, **The Division of Labour in Society** *(1893), he developed his core ideas concerning mechanical and organic solidarity, and in some circles this earned him the title "the father of sociology." He also wrote extensively on law, morality and religion, and his study of suicide is still regarded as a classic in sociological methodology.* By permission of the Bettmann Archive, New York, N.Y.

Émile Durkheim (1858-1917)

clans, tribes, extended families and other such units, they all share basic similarities, e.g., they are self-sufficient, employ simple tools, are deeply religious. But what binds these separate groups together, what gives them solidarity, is what Durkheim refers to as a *collective conscience* — a totality of beliefs and sentiments common to average citizens of the same society (Durkheim, 1933:79). Further, Durkheim tells us, the collective conscience, which embodies the moral rules that make solidarity possible in primitive society, is rooted in religion. For primitive religion "contains in a confused mass, besides beliefs properly religious, morality, law, the principles of political organization, and even science. . . . " (Durkheim, 1933:135). He thus argues that law is essentially religious in its origin and that legal or judicial rules gradually develop out of the collective conscience through the influence of religious beliefs. When there is a close correspondence between the laws and the collective conscience of a society, that society is a moral one (Grabb, 1984:75).

Organic solidarity, on the other hand, is linked with modern societies. For Durkheim, the principal cause of the transition from primitive to modern society was the increasing specialization of tasks and activities associated with the division of labour. As opposed to primitive society, where most people worked at similar jobs, held similar beliefs, possessed similar amounts and types of knowledge, modern society is characterized by *social dissimilarity*, the rise of individualism, and a corresponding variety of values and norms to suit the new circumstances.

Max Weber (1864-1920)

Hence, in modern society mechanical solidarity is gradually undermined, and the collective conscience is eroded by the growth of a "personal conscience." For this change to occur, Durkheim tells us, the individual must be freed from the pervasive hold which the collective conscience has on him in primitive society:

> . . . the individual personality must have become a much more important element in the life of society, and in order for it to have acquired this importance, it is not enough for the personal conscience of each to have grown in absolute value, but also to have grown more than the common conscience (Durkheim, 1933:167).

The decline of mechanical solidarity, then, is accompanied by "a growing multitude of individual differences" (Durkheim, 1933:172); and in order that society not fall apart, "another solidarity must slowly come in to take the place of that which has gone" (Durkheim, 1933:173).

The new form of solidarity Durkheim terms "organic." Stemming from the division of labour, organic solidarity refers to the fact that society, like a living organism, is made up of distinct parts that must be *integrated* if the whole is to survive. And this task of integration falls to the division of labour, which replaces the collective conscience as the glue of society because it requires that members of a society be dependent on each other (Durkheim, 1933:181). In conclusion, therefore, we can see that Durkheim, like Marx, looks to the economic structure of modern society as the source of both order and change.

Weber, finally, appears unfamiliar with Durkheim's works, but he certainly read Marx. And although he accepted some of the main tenets of Marxism regarding class inequality and conflict, he disagreed with Marx's basic two-class schema. Weber's work was largely concerned with the structures of domination in capitalist society, particularly the bureaucratic structures. Using *bureaucracy* as his principal unit of analysis, Weber reasoned that bureaucrats and managers, who are not necessarily members of the capitalist class as it is defined by Marx, nonetheless wield a great deal of *power*. They are able to issue commands and have them obeyed, owing to the type of *authority* conferred upon them by the structure of bureaucratic organization in capitalist society. Unlike the traditional and charismatic forms of authority prevalent in earlier societies, modern society is characterized by increasing bureaucratization and the rational-legal type of authority. Such authority is based on the general acceptance by people of impersonal bureaucratic laws and rules. Interestingly, also, Weber argued that even in a socialist society, bureaucratic domination is inescapable.

In a later section of this chapter, we will take another look at the contributions of Marx, Durkheim and Weber.

THE SOCIOLOGICAL IMAGINATION

THE INFLUENCE OF THE PAST

Awareness of the relationship between history and sociology and the ability to appreciate the historical context of the origins of sociological thought are indispensable to an understanding of what sociology is. Indeed it is in this precise sense that C. Wright Mills (1959:146) observed that "all sociology worthy of the name is 'historical sociology'." As one of the most celebrated sociologists of the twentieth century, Charles Wright Mills (1917-1962) left an indelible stamp on the discipline. In his now classic monograph, *The Sociological Imagination*, Mills speaks of that quality of mind which characterizes the true sociologist.

It is only by carefully cultivating "the sociological imagination," Mills argues, that one can grasp the infinite complexity of social life. Such an imagination can simultaneously comprehend history and personal biography and understand how they intersect in society. By the intersection of history and biography he means realizing how individuals live their personal lives within the context of historical sequences (Mills, 1959:6). For Mills, therefore, the sociological imagination is developed through the rigorous application of social scientific methodology to an understanding of historical and contemporary social processes.

MAN IS BOTH A CREATURE AND A CREATOR

As individuals, we are born into a world that is not of our own making. The society, norms and culture we inherit have definite histories to them, and those histories impinge on our lives, whether or not we like it, whether or not we are conscious of it. But this is a two-way street. Although we have no direct input into our societies before birth, the moment we are born we start acting as historically specific beings who influence our worlds. We are transformed from mere *creatures* of history into *creators* of history. To become aware of our personal biographies, our destinies, ourselves, then, we must understand the larger historical forces operating around us, even those forces and the particular conditions which called us into existence.

> The sociological imagination enables us to grasp history and biography and the relations between the two within society. That is its task and its promise. To recognize this task and this promise is the mark of the classic social analyst (Mills, 1959:6).

Neither individual biographies nor social histories can be understood in and of themselves. The two fields of investigation must be combined with the one informing the other. And the key to undertaking the entire project lies in the cultivation of that quality of mind referred to by Mills as the sociological imagination.

All too often in Western, liberal societies, where such emphasis is placed on the individual being self-motivated, self-supporting, self-fulfilled, self-confident and so on, the individual forgets that there is a wider social context within which he or she operates. Surely all of our behaviours and aspirations contain an element of individual or personal initiative. But the point is to recognize that such initiative is socially and culturally conditioned.

THE IDEA OF SOCIAL STRUCTURE

Saying social behaviour is somehow "conditioned" immediately suggests a "conditioner." How does the wider social context affect human behaviour? The answer lies in the concept of *social structure*, which Coulson and Riddell (1980:33) described as "a key leadoff point, and the anchorage idea of sociology."

STATUSES, ROLES AND NORMS

The concept of social structure recognizes that much of our everyday behaviour is regular and patterned. Such behaviour occurs within various social groups and generally follows set conventions. As members of society we each occupy several *statuses* and fulfill a variety of *roles*. For example, the status of student, daughter or policeman is accompanied by a series of behaviours expected of a student, daughter or policeman. These behaviours include a variety of rights and responsibilities that others associate with persons occupying such statuses and fulfilling their specific roles. According to the established *norms* of our society and culture, we have a fairly clear idea of how students, daughters and police officers should behave. In sociological terminology, we refer to these as *normative expectations*, i.e., those aspects of social interaction that can be taken for granted in a "normal" situation.

It is clear, too, that any given individual will occupy a number of different statuses. For example, one can be a daughter, a mother, an engineer and a teacher all at the same time. One's different statuses and roles often complement each other, but there is always the possibility of a conflict, as in the case of the police officer who sells illegal drugs. The statuses of police officer and drug dealer are incompatible, and hence we do not normatively expect them to be associated. But this does not mean to say they never are. Statuses also are either ascribed or achieved. An *ascribed* status is one into which we are born, for example, our gender status. It is relatively fixed and unchanging. *Achieved* status, on the other hand, is one we enter through purposive action, for example, our occupational status. It is subject to change because it can be gained or lost. Statuses and roles are important aspects of social structure.

SOCIETY AS A COLLECTION OF INTERACTING PARTS

To more clearly illustrate what is meant by this concept, Coulson and Riddell (1980: 34-46) use the analogy of a watch. A watch can only tell us the time if its parts are *arranged in a particular way*. If we take a watch apart and hold its pieces in our hand, we cannot tell the time from all the screws, springs, wheels and hands that are thrown together in a haphazard fashion. The parts of the watch only reveal the time when placed in a set relationship to specific other parts, when structured in a definite manner. And while we may be unable to physically *see* that structure or the relationship among the parts, it nevertheless is real.

The same applies to human social behaviour. Human interaction is never the mere sum of the number of people or behaviours involved, but rather the patterns, the ways in which individual behaviours are displayed in relation to the whole. Our behaviour is never quite as haphazard as it may sometimes seem. It is, as was said above, patterned, fairly regular and highly structured; and it is the task of the sociologist to uncover that structure and make sense of it. For if our behaviour were totally unstructured and left up to individuals' whims and fancies, not only would it be impossible to study it, but *social* living itself would be impossible.

FREE WILL VERSUS DETERMINISM

Since our behaviours are so conditioned by social structure, one may well wonder if individuals have any choice in the courses of action they pursue. Indeed, it may appear that we are so subject to this pervasive invisible force called social structure that we are wholly passive creatures devoid of will or initiative. Nothing is further from the truth.

Free will and determinism are not all-or-nothing phenomena. They are not either-or propositions, for human behaviour is clearly guided by elements of both. Surely we conform *generally* to group pressure, laws, norms, expectations and so on, but, as curious, thinking beings possessed of a will, we also at times, (consciously or unconsciously) resist group pressure, break laws, violate norms and defy expectations. Social life is not so tightly programmed that every facet of our behaviour can be prescribed. In fact, we are the ones who consciously make laws, collectively produce culture and determine what is appropriate and inappropriate behaviour for a given situation. The margin for social maneuverability is usually quite wide, and the various norms or social conventions are often loosely defined.

As social beings we have a need for belonging, we desire acceptance by friends and family, seek social approval and generally conform to the expectations of the group(s) to which we belong or want to belong. In this sense, social structure clearly influences us. But, as active social beings, we also drop out of groups, join others that we seek to change from the inside, or even establish our own groups with accompanying laws and norms.

Recognizing the importance of social structure for moulding behaviour does not imply a denial of free will. These are matters of degree. Human beings are, and have always been, limited to achieving those things which our physical and intellectual capacities permit. Not only are we limited by climate and geography, but also by physical strength, height, age *and* existing levels of skill, knowledge and scientific development. So a certain degree of "unfreedom" has always been with us. Freedom is relative.

To produce our basic needs — food, clothing and shelter — we have had to adapt to physical and biological limitations and overcome them with our intellects to survive. Thus, survival is a more or less constant struggle against nature, against traditionally established patterns of social organization, even against other human beings.

If we did not *actively* produce our own means of subsistence, no one would have done so for us. We would have died out, and the human species would have disappeared from the earth. In other words, we have never been free *not* to produce, *not* to become actively involved with each other, *not* to create.

In this sense, we can agree with Coulson and Riddell (1980:18), who argue that, far from being a depressing science that only shows us how we are prisoners of social structure, sociology is a liberating science. By helping us to understand the hidden constraints on our behaviour, by identifying the invisible mechanisms governing much of our social interaction, sociology lets us make meaningful choices regarding specific courses of action. And this is where free will, or *voluntarism*, enters the picture and serves to counterbalance determinism. Whether dealing with individuals in small-scale interpersonal relationships, or with groups operating at the larger societal level, sociological insight helps us avoid pitfalls hidden to the casual observer who relies primarily on common sense to guide his or her behaviour.

This does not mean there is anything inherently wrong with common sense as a mode of reasoning. But sociological insight is more systematic and rigorous. It penetrates surface appearances and gets to the underlying causes of social behaviour in a way that common sense, intuition, revelation, tradition and references to sacred and secular authorities can not. As Nisbet and Perrin (1977:10-12) point out, sociological explanation relies on the logic of verification, whereas the above-mentioned ways of arriving at knowledge do not. For example, some people believe that Canadian Indians have less respect for law than other Canadians; men are smarter than women; blacks make better athletes than whites; doctors are smarter than nurses. For such people, the so-called facts speak for themselves; the statistics do not lie. The task of sociology, however, is to question such "facts" and, as in the case of these examples, expose their falsity.

APPROACHING SOCIETY

Apart from using historical data, sociologists have also employed a number of other techniques for gathering information on relevant issues. These techniques will be discussed more fully in Chapter 2, but, for the present, a brief introduction is in order.

The types of research questions addressed by sociologists will determine, to a large degree, the types of data that they will collect. Sociological questions, as we saw, can be of a macro or micro nature. But it must not be assumed that one is divorced from the other. For example, Marx's (macro) concern with the impact of economic exploitation on the development of revolutionary consciousness among workers is directly related to Weber's (micro) interest in how individuals socially construct *meanings* of their world. Revolutionary consciousness is intimately connected to people's religious orientations and values, which are linked with their family and class backgrounds, which in turn are filtered through their personal and individual life experiences and finally balanced by their subjective assessments of the likelihood that revolution is in their best interests.

It is clear, therefore, that to determine which individuals, groups and classes are most likely to develop revolutionary ideas is no simple matter. Or similarly, if we wish to know what kinds of people move to suburbia, which segments of the elderly population will protest specific types of governmental legislation, which economic groups will be more prone to a particular type of deviant behaviour or which religious groupings will favour abortion, a wide variety of data on individuals, groups, classes, organizations, beliefs, occupations, residential location and so on will have to be collected, interpreted and analysed.

In this context, we can think of how the research on a specific group can have implications for the larger society. A case in point is a recent Toronto study of occupational discrimination against blacks in that city. The research findings pointed clearly to the existence of extensive discriminatory practices in both the private and public spheres. Apart from the psychological and economic consequences at the level of individuals, such discrimination also has serious familial, political, social, and even constitutional (human rights) implications. Clearly, no single sociological study, no one theoretical or methodological approach will suffice to capture the complexity and magnitude of the problems involved in that situation. As a result, sociologists, whether working independently or hired for example, by government, will gather relevant information using a variety of methods.

Since all members of the society, black and non-black, are affected, the sociologist in this study will be interested in *interviewing* samples of the population, administering *questionnaires* or conducting *surveys* and *participating* with people on an overt or covert basis in order to experience directly the situation, all with a view to collecting data on the extent of discrimination. After such data are scientifically analysed, recommendations are made to the proper authorities, and specific policies aimed at correcting the situation can then be implemented. These, in turn, can affect individuals, groups, organizations, communities or society as a whole.

Thus, in addition to historical methods, sociologists also collect a great deal of contemporary data on various aspects of social life through a multiplicity of methods. And it is a direct consideration of those methods and research techniques that we address in the next chapter.

SOCIOLOGY AS A SCIENCE

EMPIRICAL KNOWLEDGE

The reason sociological knowledge claims superiority to knowledge derived from common sense observations, intuition, biblical revelation and so on is that sociological knowledge is scientifically generated. But, before proceeding further, some clarification of the term "science" is necessary. Originating from the Latin verb *scire*, to know, the term "science" refers to the acquisition of systematized knowledge based on observation, study and experimentation. Scientific knowledge is thus *empirically* derived, for it comes to us via sensory perception: seeing, feeling, hearing, smelling and tasting.

Generally speaking, when we hear the word science, we think of natural or physical sciences such as botany, geology, physics or chemistry. We also think of the scientist as someone making precise and accurate predictions about his or her subject matter. In a sense, the subject matter of the natural or physical scientist — plants, rocks, metals or gases — lends itself neatly to observation, experimentation, testing, weighing, measurement and manipulation. It is relatively uncomplicated to study such things within controlled laboratory settings, where the scientist can observe the behaviour of matter in response to the careful manipulation of specific conditions or variables.

NATURAL VERSUS SOCIAL SCIENCE

The physicist studying the strength of a given physical structure, say, a bridge, may build a model to scale in her laboratory and simulate normal conditions, applying weights, calculating for wind pressure, erosion and so on. In this way she obtains a reasonably accurate idea of how much weight the bridge can support, the potentially weak points and the types of safety measures that should be implemented. This is all possible because her subject matter is always *compelled to react* in the same manner when subjected to the same conditions. For sociology, a social science, however, the situation is different. The subject matter of the social scientist is *qualitatively* different. It does not lend itself readily to controlled laboratory testing, for the subject matter of the social scientist is the human being, the human group, the human society. For the sociologist in particular, his laboratory is the society at large. And that society is so highly complex and variable that it is often difficult to predict precisely how every individual or group will behave at any given time. Such precise prediction, however, is *not* the concern of the sociologist.

What distinguishes the subject matter of the natural scientist from that of the social scientist is precisely what distinguishes natural science from social science. Whereas the subject matter of the former is devoid of consciousness and a will, the subject matter of the latter is possessed of consciousness and will. As was stated above, the structure of the bridge will *always* react in the same way to set or fixed conditions. It cannot choose *not* to buckle under too much pressure. The human being, on the other hand, if punched in the nose today, may choose to run away; but tomorrow, the same punch may elicit the opposite response — he or she may *choose* to punch back.

Because the sociologist's subject matter is comprised of rational, thinking beings with emotions, feelings, sentiments, values, morals, consciousness and will, studying it calls for different methods than those employed by the natural scientist. Further, since humans are primarily subjective beings, they interact and communicate through symbols to *interpret* and *assign meanings* to the multiplicity of phenomena that make up the natural and social universe. And this sets them apart not only from rocks and trees, but also from lower forms of animal life that do not possess the capacity for abstract thought. Nisbet and Perrin state the matter succinctly. What really serves to differentiate the social from the natural sciences, they say, is that

> only individuals assign meanings to the world around them and act in terms of such meanings. The difference between mere water and holy water, or between mere oil and anointing oil, lies in the meaning conferred (1977:4).

Sociology, then, as the science of society, seeks to make sense of those meanings, to uncover what is regular or patterned about them, to identify when and where they can be expected to influence behaviour.

As a social scientist, the sociologist specializes in generalities, whereas the natural scientist specializes in the particular. The former aims not to make precise predictions of how a given individual will react in a given situation, but rather to identify general behaviour patterns within and among groups, explain how and why those patterns emerge, how they persist, why they may break down, and under what conditions new ones may be established. This social forecasting is never aimed at one hundred percent accuracy, for the complex and variable nature of social behaviour does not permit it.

As a social science, sociology recognizes that all individuals are unique, but this does not mean that such uniqueness rules out making accurate general statements about group attributes. In fact, as Sorokin (1969:7-8) correctly points out, sociology even distinguishes itself from the other social sciences in this respect. Whereas economics, politics, religion and psychology deal narrowly with *homo economicus*, *homo politicus*, *homo religiosus* and *homo psychologicus*,

> *homo socius* of sociology is viewed as a generic and manifold *homo*, simultaneously and inseparably economic, political, religious, ethical and artistic, partly rational and utilitarian, partly non-rational and even irrational, with all these aspects incessantly influencing one another.

Therefore individual uniqueness is not a barrier to sociological explanation. Surely each individual possesses unique qualities and personality traits, but social behaviour never takes place solely on the basis of those qualities and traits that distinguish individuals one from the other. As Coulson and Riddell state:

> There is no incompatibility between a thing being unique and sharing characteristics with others . . . an individual does not respond to a situation in terms of one characteristic alone, but as a whole person. (1982:18)

Hence, while an individual's *total* combination of characteristics may make him or her unique, that individual shares many characteristics with others. And those common characteristics make it possible to identify general patterns and permit sociological explanation and prediction.

The above speaks to sociology's dual task. Firstly, we can see that, while sociology differs from the other social sciences in its scope and content, it is also related in various degrees and combinations to the other social sciences. The first challenge to sociology, then, is to explain the common elements and relationships in a given social phenomenon. The second challenge is to account for the differences. Since almost every sphere of social interaction will encompass economic, political, religious and other elements, it is evident the sociologist's ability to make informed generalizations places him or her in an advantageous situation. In sum, while the economist is narrowly concerned with considerations of prices and wages, while the political scientist studies patterns of vote distribution, and while the specialist in religious behaviour investigates how people's present-day behaviour is influenced by their views of the hereafter, only the sociologist brings them all together to render a genuinely *social* explanation of human behaviour. This is what distinguishes sociology as a separate discipline within the social sciences.

CONTENDING PERSPECTIVES WITHIN SOCIOLOGY

So far, we have been discussing the sociological outlook or perspective as being common to all practitioners of sociology. Though helpful, this may prove misleading if the reader assumes all sociologists agree on all things. As Wilson (1983:10) has argued, there is "no single all-embracing theory that has proven adequate to deal with the wide range of problems sociologists identify as theirs." Sociologists aim to understand society, critique it and suggest how it may be reformed. However, one must not assume, as was stated in the introduction to this chapter, that the variety and complexity of social living somehow indicate that sociological insight is a mere hodgepodge of inconclusive and unconnected information. Rather, instead of viewing the abundance and variety of sociological theory as a sign of sociology's weakness and ineptitude, it must be regarded as a sign of its vitality and strength (Wilson, 1983:10). For it is through the free interplay of opposing ideas that we can gain a fuller understanding of our complex social world.

Hence, sociologists, though they may agree on what constitutes a social problem or issue, do not always agree on the ways to deal with it. In essence, this is a philosophical matter concerning differences in ontology and epistemology. *Ontology* refers to a theory of essence or being — it talks about what *is* or what is real. Epistemology, on the other hand, refers to method: how do we come to *know* what is or what is real?

At first sight these differences may seem trivial. But not so, for our ontological and epistemological premises often determine which problems we deem relevant and their appropriate solutions. More crucially, if two sociologists, coming from distinct ontological and epistemological positions, study a common problem, it is highly unlikely they will ever agree on a common solution.

Consider, for example, the question of human aggression. The researcher who makes the ontological assumption that aggression is natural and *instinctual*, will clearly never agree with the researcher who thinks aggression is *learned* behaviour. This is the old nature versus nurture argument, and, depending on one's position in this argument, the epistemological questions can vary greatly.

The sociologist who assumes human aggression is natural will design a totally different plan of investigation from the sociologist who sees aggressive behaviour as the result of social learning processes. And as each delves more deeply into his or her respective study, the questions asked will become increasingly dissimilar. In the end, since the kinds of questions we ask tend to determine the kinds of answers we receive, our two sociologists will present us with two diametrically opposed sets of research findings on the same problem. The two researchers, and others within the scholarly community, must then determine which findings are more adequate. Then the process snowballs and generates all types of debates, subsidiary studies, conferences, refutations, confirmations and so on, and these collectively make up and define the stuff of sociology.

To get a clearer idea of the main contending perspectives in sociology today, however, it would be helpful to identify a specific theme and examine how it has been addressed by various sociological schools of thought. One issue of interest to all such schools is that of social order and social change. We will, therefore, examine how functionalists, Marxists and symbolic interactionists conceive of the problem of order in society.

STRUCTURAL FUNCTIONALISM

As one of the leading schools of thought in sociology, structural functionalism has had a long history. The term "function" itself, is one

> which came into the foreground of philosophic discourse in the last quarter of the nineteenth century and has maintained an increasingly strong position there ever since (Kallen, 1937: 523).

Though difficult to trace directly, its overall origins may be found in the disciplines of biology, art, law and architecture. But as far as its use in the social sciences goes, we must look to anthropology and the works of such men as Bronislaw Malinowski and A.R. Radcliffe-Brown. Among sociologists specifically, Durkheim is viewed as the first to have applied systematically functionalist principles to the analysis of society.

The structural functionalist approach has been characterized by much confusion and disagreement, both among its practitioners and its critics; and much of this confusion stems from the definitions of the terms "structure" and "function." Before discussing these terms, however, two points must be made: a) The questions addressed by structural functionalists are eminently sociological, and, like the questions of Marxists and symbolic interactionists (to be discussed next), concern the general relationship between social order and social change; and b) it is misleading to identify the structural functionalist approach exclusively with any *one* theorist, for many structural functionalists make different assumptions about society, ask different questions and employ different research procedures to answer them.

Why, then, are they grouped together in a single school of thought? The answer lies in their *teleological* approach to understanding society: They all seek to analyse social structures and practices by reference to the ends or purposes they serve. Structural functional analysis, for example, argues that specific social institutions (e.g., marriage, religion) exist because they contribute to the overall survival of the social system. Those institutions that do not function toward this end will ultimately disappear.

Structural functionalism is based on the notion that society is more than just the sum of its individual parts. For society, like an organism, has a structure of its own, over and above its constituent elements. And in the same way that a living organism

*Parsons was born in the United States and studied at Amherst College and the London School of Economics. Though initially interested in biology, he later switched to social science and came to distinguish himself internationally in sociology. For several years he held the chair of sociology at Harvard, during which time his name became synonymous with the school of structural functionalism. His book, **The Structure of Social Action** (1937), was the first of 150 books and articles that spanned a career of over 50 years.* Photo courtesy of the Harvard Office of News & Public Affairs.

Talcott Parsons (1902-1980)

has *needs* that must be met if it is to survive, so too with society. Continuing this *organismic analogy*, society's needs are seen to include such things as reproducing the species, regulating the behaviour of individuals and providing for the physical subsistence of the population.

The strategy of social inquiry adopted by this school treats society as a *system* whose various parts are organized into *structures* or institutions, each of which fulfills some *function* for the system as a whole (Grabb, 1984:71). Let us, then, examine what is meant by these terms and see how they inform this particular sociological approach.

Talcott Parsons (1902-1980) is the structural functionalist best known for his use of the concept of "social system." For him society or the social system is viewed as

a set of related and interdependent phenomena which have boundaries that are maintained; it exists in a state of equilibrium or balance with its environment and has certain mechanisms for maintaining this state (Cashmore and Mullan, 1983:180).

The "mechanisms" referred to are social institutions which are related to a number of subsystems that in turn are connected to the larger social system. Every social system or subsystem must fulfill four basic *needs* that are key to its survival: a) adaptation; b) goal attainment; c) integration; and d) pattern maintenance.

At the level of society, these *vital system needs* correspond to four subsystems of the larger social system: the economy, the polity, the community and the fiduciary. As subsystems, however, each of these contributes to the maintenance and survival of the larger whole, which is society. But subsystems are still systems, and as such must also ensure that their respective needs of adaptation, goal attainment, integration and pattern maintenance are met. For the social system, then, the economic subsystem that encompasses the economic institutions contributes to adaptation by ensuring the effective production and allocation of disposable resources. The political subsystem and its related institutions set overall goals for the society and provide for their realization. The community functions as an integrative subsystem by promoting a sense of social cohesiveness or solidarity. And finally, the fiduciary is that subsystem concerned with pattern maintenance at the cultural level. It deals with such things as promoting value commitment and shared social goals.

Hence, the idea of the social system is one of a social whole in which the various structures or institutions function in harmony to maintain it in a state of equilibrium. This is how the concept of "structure" becomes relevant to structural functionalism. For structures refer to organized patterns of relationships or practices between parts of a system. Structure also implies that there is some continuity to the pattern, that it is enduring.

Thus, if we look at the economic *structure* of society, we are concerned with the economic institutions and the specialized tasks or functions they perform in the economic division of labour: in the area of energy, for example, we can think of the oil companies that extract the oil from the ground; the processing of oil into gas; the use of gas to power cars; the use of cars in getting people to work. All of these specialized economic tasks and the adaptations and interconnections they imply constitute the *economic structure* of a society. And the same can be done for the political, juridical, educational and religious institutions.

To discuss social institutions as structures automatically implies a consideration of the people who populate them. The activities of these people are themselves structured in a hierarchy of *statuses* that cover a multiplicity of *roles*. The statuses or positions that individuals occupy in an institution correspond to the goals of the institution, and each individual has a role with its accompanying rights, duties and responsibilities. Thus, from the micro level of the individual to the macro level of the social system as a whole, one can trace the many links that integrate the society.

This then brings us to the last key concept in structural functional analysis: the idea of *function*. Here the term refers to the contributions that an institution or structure makes in relation to the whole. In other words, we are told that the function of a social institution has to be understood in terms of its contribution to the survival of the social system: The institution of marriage functions to ensure orderly procreation and the nurturing of children, which enable the society to maintain itself from generation to generation.

But as Robert K. Merton (1957), himself a structural functionalist, has pointed out, this view is conservatively biased in favour of a strict, orderly view of society. It leaves little room for considerations of change and conflict. For if all institutions function positively to promote system survival, how does change come about? Thus, while Merton acknowledged the fact that a given social structure may be functional for some, he also recognized that it will not necessarily by functional for all. And in his analysis of the political machine, he came to appreciate the existence of conflicts between competing interest groups in society, though he never dealt with how they might be eliminated. In addressing the conservative bias, however, Merton introduced the notions of *functions* and *dysfunctions* of social structures: Those structures that help the system adapt to its environment are said to be functional; those that impede such adaptation are labelled dysfunctional.

However, although Merton recognized that the same structure could have both functional and dysfunctional effects, he and other structural functionalists usually assume that a given pattern or institution would not survive unless its functions outweighed its dysfunctions (Wilson, 1983:76). And to this he added one further refinement: The functions and dysfunctions of an institution can be *manifest* or *latent*. If they are intended and recognized by members of society, they are manifest; if they are unintended and unrecognized, they are latent. For example, the institution of religion has the manifest function of giving the individual spiritual support and comfort, while it functions latently to maintain group solidarity (Cashmore and Mullan, 1983:152).

In sum, therefore, structural functionalism contributes many insights into the operations of society that are not necessarily provided by other sociological approaches. And given its conservatism, its inability to deal with questions of radical change in society, it makes for an interesting backdrop against which to examine the more radical perspective of Marxism. [For a more eleborate and systematic exposition of structural functionalism and the important criticisms of it, see Coulson and Riddell (1980) and Wilson (1983)].

MARXISM

The school of sociology that draws its main lines of reasoning from the work of Karl Marx (1818-1883) is radically opposed to functionalism. Whereas functionalists are preoccupied with the questions of order and stability in society, Marxists stress disorder and conflict as equally integral aspects of social living. Some key concepts employed by Marxists are social class, exploitation, struggle and revolution.

Like the functionalists, Marxists study social order, but they disagree with the functionalists on how social order is achieved. Instead of assuming order is automatically generated on the basis of commonly shared values, Marxists think that order is largely *coerced* — it comes about, directly or indirectly, through force. And the ability to use force or to threaten to use force belongs to certain groups and classes owing to their positions in the social structure.

In essence, Marxists argue that order is secured by one of, or a combination of, three elements (Zeitlin, 1981a:112-114). The first element is fear, pure and simple. We behave properly, obey the laws and do what is expected of us because we fear the consequences of arrest, imprisonment and punishment. Of course, some people willingly break the law and flout social conventions, but such people are few, and their collective deviance does not disrupt the general social order. The second element is more narrowly economic. In our society, the vast majority of people depend on wages and salaries to survive. Without a job many of us would be unable to feed and clothe ourselves. Hence, as Weber (1961:208-209) says, we go to work and do what is expected, for "under the compulsion of the whip of hunger" we cannot affort to risk being fired. Finally, the third element that promotes an ordered society according to Marxists is ideology. Those in power maintain control, not by force alone, but by encouraging us to view the world as they see it. Their definitions of justice, morality and propriety become our definitions. This point will be developed further in the chapter on ideology, which discusses the Marxian notion of false consciousness and the Weberian idea of the legitimation of authority.

Society, for the Marxists, is not made up simply of a variety of individuals and groups that co-operate and work together in pursuing common social ends. Quite the contrary: Society is composed of hostile and antagonistic classes pursuing incompatible ends. For example, among the many social classes, Marx focused on the two principal ones: the bourgeoisie, or the property-owning capitalist class, and the proletariat, or propertyless working class. The primary goal of the capitalists is accumulating capital in the form of money, land, livestock, factories, machinery or raw materials. And in pursuing this goal, the capitalists' interests conflict with those of the workers.

The conflict of class interests is seen to reside in the fact that the capitalists own and control the bulk of the property in society, and if the mass of the people are to survive, they must seek employment in the factories, farms, corporations and other enterprises of the capitalists. But, in pursuing profit and accumulating capital, the capitalists cannot afford to pay their workers the *full value* of everything that the latter produce. Hence, the wages paid to the workers represent what is left after the capitalist has deducted his profit and reinvested part of it, paid his rent, bought new raw materials, replaced and repaired his machinery, and put aside some for his personal consumption.

Realizing they live quite differently from the capitalists and that their lot in life does not improve over time in the same way as the capitalists', the workers become understandably upset. Some form unions to secure better wages, better working conditions, better benefits; they may even go on strike to achieve these ends. Reasoning that the factories, farms, corporations and businesses cannot work without them and that the wealth and general well-being of the capitalist are derived from their labour and the products of it, the workers start seeing their own interests as opposed to those of the capitalists. They argue that they are *exploited*, i.e., that they are giving more in labour than they receive in wages, and demand a more equal share of the profits.

Out of this situation, the Marxists say, revolutions are born. To maximize profits, capitalists aspire to pay low wages and to crush unions, since higher wages and benefits imply lower profits. When such a situation is widespread, when wages are so depressed that workers can barely afford decent food, clothes, housing, education for their children and adequate health care, society runs the risk of a working-class uprising. The Marxists insist, further, that such a risk increases when the *objective* conditions of poverty and misery combine with the worker's *subjective* awareness that they could take matters into their own hands and make things better for themselves. This is called *developing class consciousness*.

This is generally how Marxists view a breakdown of social order. There comes a time when fear of the police, fear of losing one's job and the appeal of the prevailing ideology can no longer function to preserve the social order.

To Marxists, then, capitalist industrial society represents a curious mix of order and conflict. The institutional framework responsible for preserving order and regulating conflict is called the *state*. For Marx, the state is a committee of men making decisions, developing laws and taking action *in support of the interests of the capitalist class*. The state is not an impartial body governing society in the interests of all individuals, groups and classes. Hence, Marx argues that the advent of socialism will mean the disappearance of the class-based capitalist state. In a socialist society, the workers are supposed to hold both economic and political power after over-throwing capitalism. Socialism is a transition stage between the unequal capitalist society and the final stage, communism, in which all men and women will be equal. Further insight into Marxist views of the capitalist state and society can be found in Miliband (1969) and the response to Miliband by Poulantzas (1973). Good summaries of both positions are contained in Giddens (1982).

SYMBOLIC INTERACTIONISM

While the concerns of functionalists and Marxists are macrosociological, owing to their focus on whole societies or large subsections of them, the perspective known as symbolic interactionism deals with more microsociological issues. Symbolic in-teractionists pay less attention to the impact of social structure on human behaviour, while emphasizing the moment of social interaction at the individual level.

As a separate perspective within the discipline, symbolic interaction draws its main teachings from the works of Max Weber, George Herbert Mead and Herbert Blumer. Although it would be inaccurate to characterize Weber as a symbolic interactionist and nothing more, it is clear that Weber's writings on "social action" provide the basis upon which this tradition was built. For Weber, the sociological enterprise deals with an *interpretive* understanding of human social behaviour. To correctly interpret behaviour, Weber argues, sociologists must realize that human beings are *subjective* actors who attach *meaning* to their acts. In fact, interaction is only possible if subjective meanings are shared by the participants in an interactive situation — and this is what makes it specifically *social* interaction.

According to Weber, social structure alone cannot explain the totality of behav-iour. As mentioned earlier, the subject matter of sociology is the living, thinking, acting, conscious human being. And human behaviour, though constrained by social structure, is also infused with purpose, motive and subjective intent. Hence, no accurate assessment of behaviour can ignore human choice and will, for these in-variably intermingle with social structure to produce set patterns of social action.

For Mead (1934) and Blumer (1962), however, social structure is of less im-portance in understanding behaviour. For them, social living is "symbolic" in that we communicate, co-operate and socialize using common symbols, e.g., language. As Haralambos and Heald observe:

> Symbols provide the means whereby man can interact meaningfully with his natural and social environment. They are man-made and refer not to the intrinsic nature of objects and events but to the ways in which men perceive them (1980:544).

Because human beings do not have instincts to guide their behaviour, they rely almost entirely on *learning* what is appropriate or inappropriate behaviour. Such learning, however, can only take place on the basis of shared symbols whose meanings are communicated to the actors involved in a continuous process of interaction.

Mead was born in the United States to a comfortable middle-class family. He studied philosophy and psychology at Oberlin College and Harvard University. As he came to see the influence of societal forces on the development of mind, self, and language, his work increasingly assumed a sociological orientation. In 1893 he joined the faculty of philosophy at Chicago, where he deepened his interest in sociology. Though not a prolific writer, Mead's **Mind, Self and Society** *(1932) is an authoritative statement on the symbolic interactionist dimension of human life.* The Granger Collection, New York.

George Herbert Mead (1863-1931)

Thus, to survive, make plans and develop society, men and women consciously construct and live within a world of meaning. And most importantly, at the level of interacting individuals these meanings are *negotiated* — they are defined and refined by social actors in specific situations.

For the sake of social order, therefore, actors must interpret the meanings and intentions of others and respond in an *inter-subjective* manner. To explain this, Mead developed the concept of "role-taking," whereby an individual imaginatively places herself in the position of the person with whom she is interacting. For example, if you observed someone walking briskly toward you with a stern look on his face and shouting verbal abuse, you consciously (or unconsciously) put yourself in that person's place by using your imagination in order to interpret his intention and meaning. And based on the interpretation you assign to such symbolic action, you choose to (re)act: You may run away, prepare for a fight, attempt to pacify that person, and so on. In the meantime, the person is also observing and interpreting your behaviour, for he is also role-taking; and depending on his interpretation of your behaviour, he may choose to strike you, to talk out the problem, or to threaten you verbally. Hence, we see how the symbolic interactionist, who analyses human interaction at the level of individuals, views interaction as a more or less continuous process of interpretation and reinterpretation of meanings.

In sum, then, social order is maintained when the various parties to any given interactive situation have similar interpretations and definitions of that situation. In the words of Haralambos and Heald:

It is a 'negotiated order' in that it derives from meanings which are negotiated in the process of interaction and involves the mutual adjustment of the actors concerned. The net result is the establishment of social order, of an orderly, regular and patterned process of interaction (1980:553).

For a more detailed exposition and critique of symbolic interactionism, refer to Meltzer, Petras and Reynolds (1975).

A BRIEF ASSESSMENT

While each of the sociological perspectives discussed above has its own great strengths, none is perfect. Structural functionalism, for example, has been criticized at several levels; such criticism will be discussed in greater detail in the coming chapters. For the moment, however, some of the general features can be mentioned. The most telling criticism levelled at this school concerns its inability to account for radical social change. The conservative bias inherent in this approach leads to a one-sided emphasis on questions of social order, system integration, equilibrium and consensus. Structural functionalism has also been faulted for its use of the organismic analogy. All too often, structural functionalists tend to forget that they are dealing with an analogy and treat society as if it were, in fact, a living organism with all the characteristics that living organisms share. Two other criticisms that may be noted here concern the imprecise definition of key terms and the tendency toward circular reasoning. Terms such as structure, function and system, for example, are neither clearly nor consistently operationalized, and this leads to much confusion. On the question of circularity or tautological reasoning, the structural functionalists argue that only those social institutions that function positively to maintain the social system will continue to survive. The problem here is that one cannot tell the difference between the cause and the effect: How do we know that a given institution has functioned positively? Because it has survived! Why did it survive? Because it functioned positively! We are left neatly enclosed in a circle.

Shifting our focus to the orthodox Marxist approach, three common criticisms are encountered. The first concerns the blurring of class boundaries in an advanced capitalist society. Surely we can distinguish the owners of productive property from the nonowners, but there have been very significant increases in the white collar, managerial and technical sectors that serve to confound greatly the Marxian schema. Though not owners of productive property in the direct sense, these sectors wield a great deal of power in the day-to-day operations of capitalist enterprises. And although their interests may often complement those of the direct owners, the orthodox Marxist approach has great difficulty explaining just how those interests intersect in their class model. Related to the above is the charge that the orthodox Marxist view of the capitalist state is far too mechanical. It is simplistic and inaccurate to assert that the state is nothing more than a tool in the hands of the capitalist class that can be manipulated at will. Finally, there is the oft-repeated criticism that Marx did not foresee the extent to which capitalism could deflect or even accommodate many of the contradictions which he felt would lead to its demise. Contrary to the expectation of Marx, the socialist revolution simply has not occurred in advanced capitalistic societies.

Regarding the microsociological approach of symbolic interactionism, the two major criticisms of this school concern its tendency to neglect the importance of social structure and its overemphasis on the conscious and subjective actions of individuals. Symbolic interactionists generally assume that individual behaviour is guided by inner states and personal motives that override the constraints of social structure. By doing so, they open themselves up to the charge that their work is more psychological. Also, by making the conscious, individual actor their unit of analysis, they are unable to claim objectivity, and this calls into question the scientific status of their work.

CANADIAN SOCIOLOGY

If sociology has often been described as a young science, one that is still in its infancy, then Canadian sociology will have to be described as a mere fetus. As recently as the 1960s, the only autonomous department of sociology in Canada was at McGill University. This meant, as Clark (1979:399) has pointed out, that up until around 1965 the ranks of sociology teachers in this country were very thin, and what might be called a body of Canadian sociological literature was even thinner. Apart from McGill and the University of Toronto, where sociology was but an appendage to the department of political economy, Canadians wishing to study sociology usually did so at American universities.

When one talks of the pioneers of Canadian sociology, the names of Carl Dawson, Harold Innis (an economist), S.D. Clark and John Porter immediately spring to mind. These men left an indelible stamp on the development of the discipline in Canada and served to give it a focus distinct from American sociology as it was conceived and practised at the University of Chicago. Dawson's work on Canadian ethnic communities, Innis' writings on the fur trade and metropolis/hinterland relations, Clark's research on diverse aspects of Canadian society and economy and Porter's analyses of culture and stratification in the Canadian mosaic served to define the beginnings of an indigenous sociology of Canada. Building on these pioneering efforts, contemporary Canadian sociologists have begun to develop a truly Canadian sociological literature.

Canadian sociology, however, did not develop along a single path. As a result of the French-English cleavage in Canadian society, there also emerged distinct Francophone and Anglophone sociological orientations. In French Canada, the strong links between educational and religious institutions obstructed the initial acceptance of sociology, which often challenged religious beliefs and teachings and counselled a more secular approach to life (Rocher, 1977:495). In English Canada, on the other hand, as in Britain, sociology was viewed as an upstart social science and in the early years reluctantly was attached to more traditional departments such as history, anthropology and political economy. Having to contend with the influence and opposition of the Catholic Church, Francophone sociology came to develop a more critical and activist side in comparison to its Anglophone counterpart, which was characterized by the conservative, functionalist and Chicago-based teachings of such men as Hughes and Park.

In discussing sociology in English Canada particularly, one cannot fail to take note of the "Canadianization debate" of the early 1970s. That debate, Hiller tells

Carl Dawson (left), Everett Hughes (right) and sociology graduate students at McGill, 1931. The work of Dawson and his students was the earliest in Canadian sociology and focused primarily on the development of ethnic communities in greater Montreal and the Prairies. Everett Hughes, an eminent American sociologist, taught at McGill for many years. His study of the ethnic division of labour in an Eastern Townships community influenced Quebec sociology for decades. Courtesy of Dennis William Magill.

The work of S.D. Clark has left an indelible mark on Canadian sociology. His early work incorporated historical and economic analysis into sociological explanations of the development of Canadian social institutions. He later added elements of American structural functionalism to his repertoire. One of Clark's unique strengths has been his ability to discover and explain nonobvious and often surprising relationships between economy and society.

us, can be divided into two stages: The first concerned matters of *personnel*, while the second related specifically to *content* or *perspective* (1979:126; 132). The personnel dispute accompanied a rising tide of economic and political nationalism and was especially aimed at the large numbers of foreigners, mainly Americans, who occupied key academic positions in Canadian universities. The issue over content and perspective, however, was more fundamental. It called for a genuine Canadian orientation to understanding this society and sought to reject foreign models, foreign theoretical formulations and foreign case studies. Canadian sociology, it was maintained, must be rooted in an appreciation of Canada's unique history and must address Canadian problems. According to Hiller, the Canadian sociology movement sought

> to develop different or at least additional theoretical perspectives than currently typical of sociology in Canada, and which should change sociology from an imported to a more indigenous discipline (1979:133).

As we will see in the following chapters, then, both the development of sociology in Canada and the development of Canadian sociology, though still nascent, have already generated a rich tradition upon which to build.

SUMMARY

In this chapter we have examined sociology from a wide-angle perspective, sacrificing detail for a more panoramic view of the discipline. We have seen that the laboratory of the sociologist is society at large, with all of its infinite variety and complexity. Further, sociologists are not only concerned with present-day forms of social organization, but also study history in a search for possible future trends and patterns.

Generally speaking, sociologists of all persuasions agree that society is the product of human beings interacting in social situations. Culture, norms, values, laws, religion and politics are just some of the major social conventions studied by sociologists. These make up the "stuff" of society, for more than anything else they distinguish human beings from other animals. Sociologists, therefore, concern themselves with human beings and the wide variety of behaviour people display as individuals, in groups, as members of social classes, as citizens and so on.

Sociologists want to know whether such behaviour is regular and predictable. To what extent do our groups, classes and associations influence our behaviour? This question acknowledges the pervasiveness of social structure, which largely patterns our behaviour. On the other hand, sociologists also study behaviours that occur in spite of the fact that our interactions are highly structured. This raises the question of free will versus determinism. For our society to be an ordered one, some patterned response or predictability is necessary; but the human being, as a conscious and thinking animal, is never totally passive. Hence, sociologists, as social scientists, seek to understand both social order and the factors sustaining it and social disorder and change and the factors promoting them. The active, curious, restless human being is both a creature and a creator of society, pursues both stability and change, is conditioned by social structure and possessed of free will; and out of this point-counterpoint interplay sociologists derive the subject matter of their discipline.

DISCUSSION QUESTIONS

1. In what sense are human beings simultaneously creatures and creators of society?

2. How does sociological insight differ from insight yielded by common sense, intuition and revelation?

3. How does the concept of "social structure" relate to the debate concerning free will and determinism?

4. What is the basis upon which sociology claims to be a science?

5. Though instructive as an analogy, what are some of the potential problems and/or limitations that can result from viewing society as a living organism?

2

Sociological Methods of Research

Peter Li

INTRODUCTION

Sociologists use several methods to approach social facts, the choice of which depends on the nature of the research problem, the preference of the researcher and the scope of the study. The basic objective of these methods, however, is the same. All methods accomplish two tasks: they collect accurate empirical evidence and discard incorrect explanations.

Science questions the obvious. This means questioning what has been taken for granted, re-examining facts and advancing novel explanations based on new observations and insights. To challenge what others have accepted require weeding out unreliable and irrelevant facts from voluminous evidence and building new concepts and theories from the empirical findings.

In this chapter, we shall examine the following methods of investigation: experimental design, historical/comparative research, survey method, participant observation and the use of secondary materials. The experimental design provides the framework for scientific proofs and disproofs, although its direct application to sociological problems is often not feasible. Thus, sociologists must often use comparisons to approximate the logic of experimentation. Comparing similar cases yields a general type, while contrasting different cases permits specifying typological differentiations. In a case study where explicit comparisions are absent, sociologists use detailed information gathered to refute or refine existing theories. We shall also study measurement and sampling problems which affect all types of research. But before we proceed, we must understand the logic of sociological inquiry and how to formulate a sociological question.

THE LOGIC OF SOCIOLOGICAL INQUIRY

All sciences have certain standards and rules of research practice. These standards represent coherent traditions of scientific research and are referred to as *paradigms* (Kuhn, 1970). Put simply, paradigms are examples or models representing points of view expressed in scientific schools of thought. They represent basic assumptions, philosophies and cumulative findings upon which scientists conduct their research.

Underlying scientific development is what Kuhn (1970) calls the *structure of scientific revolution*, that is, the transformation of one paradigm into another. The catalyst for a scientific revolution is the appearance of anomalies, or gaps, between facts and the theories that supposedly explain them. When the anomalies recur systematically, scientists are forced to search for new solutions which the old paradigm fails to provide. New ideas, previously rejected, may be re-examined. Questions never raised before may now be asked. Out of this confusion come new theories to explain the anomalies. Some theories survive testing, others are discarded. Through repeated experiments and trials, new ideas are advanced and gradually forged into a new paradigm which will serve as a new guideline for research and for problem-solving until anomalies surface again.

Sociology today is a multi-paradigm discipline (Ritzer, 1975) with several competing schools coexisting. Examples include structural functionalism, symbolic interactionism and dialectical materialism. One way of evaluating the validity of paradigms is to rely on empirical evidence. To understand how theories are tested, we must examine the research cycle.

The Research Cycle

The research cycle basically works on two levels: theory and facts. One goal of science is to develop more general theories that may be applied more universally. Sociologists are constantly theorizing about human interactions and relationships. In such an exercise, a sociologist checks for logical inconsistencies until he comes up with a rational explanation of the phenomena he is investigating. This exercise, however, is largely a mental construct. The way to find out whether the explanation or theory has an empirical basis is to check it against concrete facts. If the facts are inconsistent with the theory, the sociologist must re-evaluate his mental construct and modify it. After the modification, testing begins again.

As an example, let us consider a study of suicide by Émile Durkheim, a prominent French sociologist. Durkheim (1951) noted that suicide rates varied from one country to another, and he wanted to explain this variation. He suspected suicide might be related to psychological states of mind, cosmic factors (climatic and seasonal variations) and social factors. He developed measurements for his concepts and gathered data bearing on each set of factors. His analysis led him to discard cosmic factors and focus on certain social forces. He found suicide rates higher among Protestants than Catholics and higher among nonmarried people than married ones. These findings were the empirical generalizations of his study. His next step was to explain these general observations. He concluded that suicide is related to how much an individual is integrated into meaningful and cohesive groups. On the one hand are those who are overly integrated into a social group. They may commit suicide because they perceive themselves as insignificant compared to the group. On the other hand, there are those who are isolated from social groups, and the absence of goals in stressful times is also conducive to suicide. Furthermore, clearly stated goals and well-defined norms provide guidelines for people's behaviour. The absence of norms during rapid social change confuses individuals about how to behave. This, according to Durkheim, also increases the likelihood of suicide. Following this theory, suicide rates are lower among Catholics and married people because they are more integrated normatively and socially than their counterparts.

As the foregoing example shows, the research cycle usually begins with an analytical question. Hypotheses, or tentative answers, are then developed, and key concepts are *operationalized*, a process that translates abstract concepts into a set of procedures allowing empirical measurement. For example, suicide was operationalized by Durkheim (1951: 44) to mean "all cases of death resulting directly or indirectly from a positive or negative act of the victim himself, which he knows will produce this result." Data are then collected, coded and analysed. The outcome of data analyses is to arrive at summary statements about the empirical observations. Through repeated observations, these summary statements become *laws*. Although a law describes a relationship, it does not explain it. To do that we have to move to the higher level of theorization. Explanations or theories are subject to further research and verification. Figure 2-1 summarizes the steps in the research cycle. The cycle is a never-ending process, with each research project answering some questions and leaving others open for further inquiry.

Figure 2-1   The Research Cycle

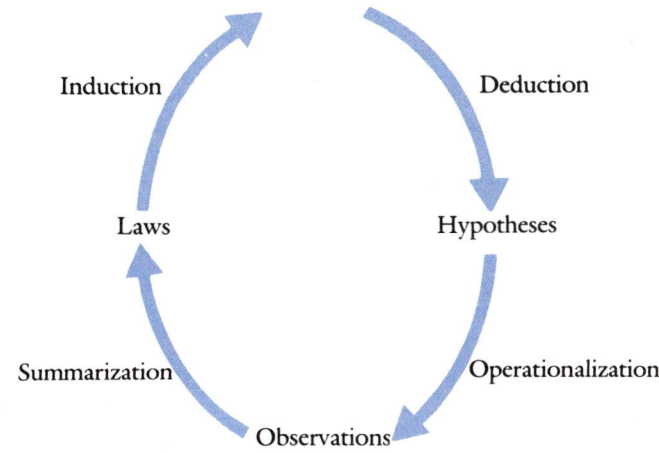

FORMULATING A RESEARCH PROBLEM

In attempting to understand society, sociologists often study a class or category of people, in the hope of discovering some regularities about the group (Li, 1981). Thus, sociologists are not so much concerned with the behaviours and attitudes of an individual person, but with how similar people would behave. There are certain implications of this approach. When a sociologist finds that people belonging to a social category have a distinct view towards a social issue, he is implying that people not belonging to the same social group do not have the same view towards the issue. For example, if one shows that those with a university education are more likely to support legalizing marijuana because education tends to liberalize people's orientation, then one should expect to find that others without a university education are less likely to support legalizing marijuana.

   The above example also shows that there has to be some variation across groups before meaningful questions can be raised. Sociologists speak of age, sex, income, education, ethnic origin and occupation as *variables* because these characteristics vary from one individual to another. The variable a researcher wishes to explain in a study is called the *dependent variable*. Variables which are used as explanations are called *independent variables*. "Explanations" here simply means relationships, in that when an independent variable varies, so does the dependent variable. For example, a sociologist may wish to explain why some wage earners are more committed to their jobs than others. The dependent variable is job commitment, and it varies from high to low from person to person. Job commitment may be related to job incentives, one of which is income. The variation in job commitment may be explained by income levels (independent variable) if the higher the income a person receives, the greater is his commitment to the job.

To think of social phenomena as variables is similar to thinking of individuals or groups as having certain characteristics. You may describe an acquaintance as tall, about twenty-five years old, Caucasian and male. If you can describe the same types of characteristics, that is, height, age, race and sex of five other people, you would have data on four variables for six individuals. The *unit of analysis*, or the unit to which the characteristics refer, may be individual or group, although the unit remains the same throughout a research project. The unemployment rate of regions and the size of the family are two examples in which the unit of analysis is a group.

Sociology is a discipline of comparison, in that sociologists are always interested in learning why some groups have certain characteristics and not others. For example, why are suicide rates higher among Protestants than among Catholics? Why are younger people more likely to move than older people? The way these questions are raised necessitates a comparison. Protestants have to be compared to Catholics to find out how these religions make a difference in suicide rates. Older people must be compared to younger people, and so on. The way a question is raised influences the answer. The question "Why do people smoke marijuana?" implies that there is a motive for smoking marijuana. The typical layperson's response is that people smoke marijuana because they are lonely. For beginners in sociology, it is frequently tempting to attribute motives to behaviour. Examples are: People go to university because they are motivated to study; people smoke because they are nervous; people are unemployed because they lack the motivation to work. However, people do many things without necessarily having a motive. Motives are hard to define and empirically test, and arguments based on loosely defined motives often produce circular explanations.

To consider marijuana smoking in a sociological way would involve comparing people who smoke regularly with those who don't smoke marijuana. The basic approach is to see how the ones who smoke marijuana differ from those who don't. One may find, for example, that the ones who smoke marijuana regularly do so as a group. They are therefore more likely to be sociable than socially isolated. In contrast, the ones who don't smoke regularly may have no group support. Social isolation from a support group explains why they do not smoke regularly. The sociological question "Why do some people smoke marijuana regularly, while others do not?" permits a much wider basis of comparison between the two groups and leads to answers not necessarily confined to commonly assumed motives.

There is often a difference between issues of public concern and sociological problems. For example, the question of the legalization of abortion is a controversial one. Sociology does not answer moral questions or pass value judgements on behaviours. Sociologists may study the beliefs of a pro-life group and how their beliefs affect their behaviour. It is quite possible to study an anti-abortion group without being an advocate of its position. This does not mean, however, that sociological findings cannot be applied to promote social causes or change social policies.

Now that we have seen how sociologists raise questions, we will be able to understand how they conduct research. But first, we must understand the logic of scientific tests through experimentation.

EXPERIMENTAL DESIGNS

Classic Experimental Design

In conducting an experiment, observations are usually taken in laboratory settings, where the conditions are artificially contrived. The researcher manipulates one variable at a time to observe its effect on another variable. The basic idea is to see whether the presence or absence of a *test variable* changes the variable being studied.

The logic of experiments is best illustrated in the classical experimental design in which two groups are exposed to identical conditions before the experiment. During the experiment, the test, or independent, variable, is introduced to one group but not the other. Subsequent comparisons are made to see how this manipulation affects the dependent variable under investigation.

For example, a researcher may be interested in studying the effectiveness of television instruction on the arithmetic performance of school children. Arithmetic performance is the dependent variable, and it may be measured by testing each child. The independent variable is exposure to television instruction. The experiment tests whether exposure to a television instruction program makes the students perform better or worse than those not viewing such a program.

There are seven steps in the classical experimental design. They are: 1. selecting a sample; 2. randomly assigning subjects to the experimental and control groups; 3. ensuring all conditions are equal; 4. pretesting; 5. introducing the treatment to the experimental group; 6. posttesting; and 7. making comparisons.

The procedure of the classical experimental design is given in Figure 2-2. Points O_1 and O_2 represent observations of the dependent variable in the experimental group during pretest and posttest respectively. Points O_3 and O_4 represent observations of the dependent variable in the control groups during pretest and posttest respectively. T represents the treatment or the independent variable.

Figure 2–2   The Classical Experimental Design

	Pretest	Treatment	Posttest	Comparison
Experimental Group	O_1	T	O_2	$O_2 - O_1$
Control Group	O_3		O_4	$O_4 - O_3$

The classical experimental design requires that both the experimental and control groups be exposed to identical conditions, except that the independent variable is introduced only into the experimental group and not into the control group. By comparing the dependent variable before and after the test, any change observed in the experimental group and not in the control group can be attributed to the independent variable.

Quasi-experimental Designs

Although the classical experimental design is a convincing method of establishing relationships, it is often not feasible to use it. It is for example, impossible to induce a revolution in one country and not another to study its effects. Thus, a researcher may have to modify the experimental design to accommodate a specific problem. As he relaxes the restrictions of the design, he is introducing a greater likelihood of errors in his research. We shall discuss three variations of the classical experimental design, called quasi-experiments, which produce less conclusive results.

The *one-shot case study* is a design in which a single group is measured on a dependent variable at one point in time, after an event that supposedly has changed the dependent variable — as, for example, the effect of a race riot on racial attitudes. The one-shot case study may be summarized as follows:

Occurence of   Posttest of

X   ⟶   Y

The main drawback of this design is that the researcher isn't sure whether Y would be at a certain level with or without the occurrence of X. Suppose a study following a riot finds a high level of racial tension. One cannot conclusively attribute such a level to the riot because tensions may already have been high before the riot.

In a *static-group comparison*, observations of the dependent variable are taken in two groups after an event has occurred in one group but not the other. For example, one may compare the centralization of government administration in a country that has experienced a coup d'etat within the past five years to the administration in another country that has not experienced such an abrupt change of government. The design may be summarized as follows:

Group 1   Occurrence of   Posttest of

X   ⟶   Y

Group 2   No Occurrence of   Posttest of

X   ⟶   Y

Without a baseline comparison, we are not sure whether it is indeed the independent variable which makes a difference in the two groups or whether the difference existed prior to the occurrence of the independent variable. If, using the above example, we find a high level of centralization in the country with the coup d'etat, we are still not sure whether the coup led to centralization because we have no measurement of centralization before the coup. Indeed, if such a difference existed before the coup, high centralization may well be a cause and not a consequence of radical political change.

The *one-group pretest-posttest design* compares one group before and after an event takes place. If we want to study the effectiveness of a media campaign encouraging birth control, we can take a survey prior to the campaign to find out what attitudes exist among the population, then administer the campaign and conduct the posttest to measure any change in attitudes. The design may be represented as follows:

Pretest on   Occurrence of   Posttest on
X   Y   X

The problem here is that there is no way of knowing whether the change would have happened with or without the occurrence of the event being studied. In the above example, something else, and not the media campaign, may have caused changes in attitudes.

Sources of Invalidity

Many factors can invalidate experimental results. Quasi-experimental designs are more vulnerable to these factors. The issue of *internal validity* refers to whether it is the experimental treatment, and not something else, that makes a difference in the dependent variable. *External validity* refers to the extent to which the experimental results may be generalized to a larger population or a different setting. The sources of internal validity include the effects of 1. history; 2. maturation; 3. testing; 4. instrumentation; 5. statistical regression; 6. selection biases; 7. experimental mortality; and 8. selection-maturation interaction (Campbell and Stanley, 1970). The sources of external validity are 1. representativeness of sample; and 2. reactive effects of experimental arrangements.

The problem of *history* refers to events, other than treatments, that occur between the pretest and the posttest of an experiment and that are competing explanations for changes in the dependent variable. The government may announce incentives for small families in the middle of a media campaign for family planning, thus confounding the effect of the campaign on respondents. *Maturation* refers to natural changes among the subjects of an experiment over time, such as becoming tired. The effect of *pretesting* refers to sensitizing the subjects to a test, making it unclear whether an improvement is caused by the experimental treatments or the subjects' increased awareness. The problem of *instrumentation* concerns the instability of the measuring instruments, so that changes in the dependent variable may be attributed to faulty instruments and not necessarily to the experimental treatment. The problem of instrumentation also includes inconsistencies of the observer, who may use different standards for recording the subjects. *Statistical regression* refers to the tendency towards the average performance when subjects are selected on the basis of their extreme scores on the dependent variable. For example, if a group of under-achievers is selected and is placed in a learning program, the students will most likely improve over time, since they have reached the lower limit in performance. *Selection biases* result from differentially assigning subjects to experimental and control groups so that the subjects are not comparable. If, for example, the subjects in the experimental group are more intelligent than the ones in the control group, then the improvement in the experimental group may be attributed to the biased characteristics of the subjects and not to the treatment. *Experimental mortality* refers to subjects dropping out of an experiment before it is completed. The remaining subjects taking the posttest may be radically different from those in the group for the pretest. *Selection-maturation interaction* refers to a complicated change produced by the joint problem of selection and maturation, as, for example, when under-achievers are bored easily during the experiment.

Even if there is internal validity in an experiment, the findings cannot be applied to a larger group if the sample is not representative of a population. This is a problem of external validity influenced by the *representativeness* of the sample. Another problem is the *reactive effects* of experimental arrangements, which must be considered when applying experimental results to real life. Although a researcher may establish the internal validity of an experiment and its external validity to people under similar experimental conditions, it is doubtful whether people react the same way in a real life situation.

The Limitations of Experimentation

Experimental designs offer a formal procedure to isolate the effects of variables, but they require a researcher to artificially manipulate the conditions of an experiment. Such manipulations are often impractical for sociological problems. For example, if a sociologist wants to study the effect of the Great Depression on the union movement, it is impossible to reproduce past events. The effect of a revolution can only be studied after the revolution has taken place. In short, historical events cannot be randomized, and their effects on behaviour are difficult to assess in laboratory settings. Cross-national studies also create insurmountable problems in applying experimental designs, as historical, cultural and social variations make laboratory control impossible. Even on the individual level, there is a potential difference between subjects' responses under contrived conditions and those in real life situations. In the following sections, we shall see how sociologists use alternative methods to pursue their scientific inquiry.

HISTORICAL/COMPARATIVE RESEARCH

Sociologists study phenomena which they themselves have not artificially induced. This requires examining situations *ex post facto*. As Durkheim (1964: 125) put it:

> When . . . the production of facts is not within our control and we can only bring them together in the way that they have been spontaneously produced, the method employed is that of indirect experiment, or the comparative method.

This sociological method involves comparing similar and different cases to show the presence or absence of a relationship. For example, why did capitalism develop in Europe and not elsewhere? This is one of the fundamental questions Weber addressed in his comparison of world religions. Weber concluded that the Protestant ethic teaches that economic accumulation in this world is consistent with salvation in the next, thus giving support to capitalist development (Weber, 1958). In contrast, none of the other major world religions promotes accumulation of capital for investment (Bendix, 1962).

The historical/comparative method is evident in Marx's analysis of various types of society. Each type, to Marx, has its own characteristics and logic of development.

To understand a particular class structure at a specific historical juncture requires studying the material conditions of society. Each productive system is characterized by a definite set of social relationships. A preclass system exists in hunting and gathering societies because there is little division of labour and a low capacity to produce more than basic needs (Marx, 1965). Ancient society, as in Rome and Greece, created a ruling class based on landed property (Giddens, 1971). Capitalism is characterized by ownership of capital and the need of workers to sell labour power as a commodity, so that capitalists and wage labourers are the two predominant classes (Marx, 1967). Accordingly, as the mode of production changes in a society, so do social relationships.

The method of comparing similarities and differences can be misleading in historical cases, as each situation is unique in terms of its occurrence in a given time and location. The comparative method sometimes requires a researcher to abstract the common grounds of seemingly different situations and to specify subtle differences in similar cases. This is how explanations are refined. For example, in Brinton's (1964) study of four revolutions — England's in 1640, America's in 1776, France's in 1789 and Russia's in 1917 — he shows certain common characteristics in all four situations, despite their historical differences. His case studies demonstrate the typical conditions before a revolution, and the assumption is that the absence of those conditions would make a revolution unlikely. Durkheim's (1951) study of suicide shows that there is more than one cause, leading him to conclude that there is more than one type of suicide. In other words, although all suicides are related to social integration, specific comparisons show the conditions under which different types of suicide are likely to occur.

The historical/comparative method basically ascertains the presence of a relationship in similar cases and the absence of a relationship in very different cases. Further comparisons may indicate how cases are similar in some ways and different in others, thus producing changes in the relationship under study. The logic is best illustrated in survey research.

SURVEY RESEARCH

Survey research is widely used in sociology. Its basic feature is the systematic collection of data from sample populations by means of questionnaires or structured interviews. A researcher approaches a group of people who are exposed to a set of events or experiences and asks them questions about these experiences. Variations in the independent variable are not controlled but statistically manipulated after the fact. For example, a researcher may study how urbanites and rural dwellers vote in federal elections. The independent variable, in this case, is statistically manipulated. Changes in the dependent variable are not observed directly over time. Instead, its variations from one individual to another are analysed in connection with variations in the independent variable.

Logic of Survey Research

Like other designs, survey research aims at discovering relationships between variables. A researcher uses survey answers to group the respondents into categories. To the extent the dependent variable changes from one category of the independent variable to another, there is a relationship. Assume, for example, that the respondents are divided by sex and that 70 percent of the males and 20 percent of the females have incomes over $35 000. As we move from one category of the independent variable (male) to another category (female), we find a corresponding change in the dependent variable (incomes over $35 000) from 70 percent to 20 percent respectively. In other words, there is a relationship between gender and income.

The problem with this type of analysis is that we do not know whether the variation in gender leads to the variation in income, or whether some other factors are operating. These competing variables are called *rival causal factors*. We have rival causal factors because, when we first group our subjects into categories of the independent variable, we have no way of controlling for other variations. The males may have different levels of education, aspiration and experience than the females.

One way of *controlling* for rival factors is to identify them and divide the categories of our independent variable into subgroups for comparison. If, for example, we suspect the education of the respondents, and not gender, may make a difference in income, then we can divide the male and female respondents further into two educational groups. By comparing the high-education-female group to the high-education-male group, we make education a constant, and gender becomes the characteristic which is varying. These subgroup comparisons then tell us what changes, if any, occur in the dependent variable. If, by varying education and controlling for gender, we do not observe a change in the dependent variable, then we know education is not a relevant independent variable. Conversely, if, by varying gender and controlling for education, we find a change in the dependent variable, then we know gender is the relevant variable, and we have eliminated education as a rival causal factor.

This process of comparing subgroups and eliminating variables can be tedious. But it reveals the relevant variables in explaining the dependent variable.

The rival causal factors have to be tested individually. After testing and eliminating several rival factors, we will still be uncertain as to whether there are other factors we may have ignored. Researchers often make assumptions about these unknown factors. One assumption is to consider the effects of these factors, if any, to be randomly distributed among the categories of our independent variable so that they do not disturb or interfere with our dependent variable.

Bivariate Analysis

One widely used method of studying survey data is *contingency table analysis* (Davis, 1971). It may be employed to study *bivariate* and *multivariate* relationships. In the simplest form, a contingency table has two variables, with two or more categories in each variable. The table has several boxes or cells. The number in each cell indicates the number of cases which have a shared attribute as determined jointly by the two variables. Each case can only appear in one cell. Table 2-1 is an example of a contingency table. It cross-tabulates two variables, attitude toward uranium development by age.

To facilitate comparisons, it is always more convenient to convert raw figures to percentages. There are two ways the percentages can run, either by row or by column. The rule to follow is to compute the percentages in the same direction as the categories of the independent variable. Thus, comparisons of percentages can be

TABLE 2-1   Attitude Toward Uranium Development by Age

"DO YOU APPROVE OR DISAPPROVE OF BUILDING A URANIUM REFINERY 100 MILES FROM YOUR COMMUNITY?"

	UNDER 30	30 AND OVER
Approve	56%	68%
Disapprove	44	32
Total	100	100
	(200)	(250)

made between categories of the independent variable. For example, Table 2-1 shows 56 percent of the respondents under 30 years of age approve of the statement, while 68 percent of the respondents 30 years of age and over approve of it. The percentages indicate that older people are more likely to approve of building a uranium refinery. In other words, there is a relationship between age and attitude towards uranium development.

A bivariate table tells us whether a relationship exists or not, but it does not explain the relationship. In the above example, it is not clear why younger people are more likely to disapprove of the building of a uranium refinery. Are younger people more concerned about environmental pollution? Do older people have something to gain by supporting a refinery? These are questions which require us either to refine or to explain the original relationship. We may suspect, for example, that property owners have more to gain from uranium development because such development would inflate property values. If we can demonstrate that older people are more likely to own property, then perhaps we can explain why they are more likely to support uranium development.

Table 2-2 cross-tabulates home ownership by the age of the respondent. It shows 30 percent of the respondents under age 30 own their home, compared to 72 percent of the respondents 30 years of age and over who own their home. In other words, the older people are more likely to own their home than the younger people. This table provides evidence to support our explanation of the uranium refinery survey.

TABLE 2-2   Home Ownership by Age

DO YOU OWN YOUR PRESENT DWELLING?

	UNDER 30	30 AND OVER
Own	30%	72%
Not Own	70	28
Total	100	100
	(200)	(250)

Multivariate Analysis

Multivariate analysis controls for those variables which we suspect may affect the relationship under study. In our example, we want to control for the variation in home ownership to see whether it affects the original relationship between attitude towards uranium development and age. Table 2-3 shows such a control table.

TABLE 2-3   Attitude Towards Uranium Development by Age and Home Ownership

	OWN		NOT OWN	
	UNDER 30	30 AND OVER	UNDER 30	30 AND OVER
Approve	75%	75%	48%	48%
Disapprove	25	25	52	52
Total	100	100	100	100
	(80)	(190)	(120)	(60)

The original sample is divided into two groups: those who own their home and those who do not own their home. Within each group, we cross-tabulate attitude towards uranium development and age. If, for example, we find no relationship between attitude towards uranium and age among the respondents who own their home, then we know that age is really not the variable which explains the attitude.

Table 2-3 shows 75 percent of the younger age group who own their homes *and* the same percentage of the older age group approve of the statement. Simply put, younger and older respondents who own homes are just as likely to approve of the statement. We notice also that younger and older respondents who do not own homes are just as likely to approve the statement as well. However, when we compare the first column to the third column, we find a change in percentages. The respondents in these two columns belong to the same age group but differ in home ownership. In other words, as we vary home ownership, holding age constant, we find home owners are more likely to support uranium development. Specifically, among home owners, 75 percent of those under age 30 favour development. In contrast, among those who do not own homes, 48 percent of those younger than 30 approve of the development. In short, home ownership, and not age, makes a difference in the response to the statement.

When we are analysing three or more variables, it is often convenient to put them into a system which allows causal relationships to be specified. Such a system is referred to as a model (Blalock, 1972). In the previous example, we find two relationships on the basis of Tables 2-1 and 2-2. The relationships may be summarized as follows:

Table 2-1   Age ———▶ Attitude
Table 2-2   Age ———▶ Home Ownership

In a subsequent analysis of Table 2-3, however, we find home ownership, and not age, affects the attitude towards uranium development. Taken together, these relationships suggest the following model:

$$\text{Age} \longrightarrow \text{Home Ownership} \longrightarrow \text{Attitude}$$

This model indicates that the original relationship between age and attitude is spurious. The way to test for a spurious relationship is to control for the intervening variable, home ownership. If, by controlling the intervening variable, the original relationship disappears, as in Table 2-3, then the relationship is spurious.

We have seen how, when statistical controls are used, survey research approximates the logic of experimentation. The inability to use laboratory controls calls for multivariate analyses to eliminate spurious relationships. Although survey results are not as conclusive, such findings are strengthened if they are replicated in other studies and supported by theories. Furthermore, survey research gives more flexibility to the study of sociological problems in real life situations. In the next section, we shall learn another sociological method that provides the greatest flexibility for the study of people in their daily life.

PARTICIPANT OBSERVATION

A *participant observer* "gathers data by participating in the daily life of the group or organization he studies" (Becker, 1958: 652). He observes the interactions of people in situations, how they behave, what they do and what they say. In addition, a participant observer also talks to the participants and finds out their interpretations of various events. He inquires about past events and about other situations he may not have a chance to observe. He also interprets events and makes decisions about what to follow up on, and whom to speak to. In short, a participant observer is an active researcher in the field.

In general, participant observation is effective in studying small groups. Historically, sociologists have successfully applied participant observation to the study of ethnic organizations, street crimes and urban ghettos. Some classic studies include *Street Corner Society* by Whyte (1955); *Tally's Corner* by Liebow (1967); *Boys in White* by Becker *et al*. (1961); *Urban Villagers* by Gans (1962).

Gaining Entry Into the Field

It is often difficult for a researcher to be accepted initially by the people he wants to study, especially if he is a total stranger. One way of gaining entry is to establish contacts with some members of the group. These contacts may be made indirectly through a friend or an acquaintance who may in turn know the members of the group. It is important to recognize at what level the contact is made. In a voluntary organization, for example, it is more useful to have the leader of the group, rather than other members, introduce the researcher to the group. The leader usually is identified more closely with the group and its accomplishments, and he may be more willing to speak to a researcher. Being introduced by the leader also suggests to the members that the researcher has been endorsed by the leader.

Depending on the nature of the group one is studying, sometimes there is a good reason to participate in disguise. For example, Griffin (1977), a white researcher, wanted to study the experience of being black. The only way he could experience being black was to hide his white identity by dyeing his skin. The researcher, however, has to resolve the ethical questions involved. Is it ethical for a researcher to lie to the people he is studying in order to obtain data? Can scientific research justify misleading the people being studied?

What the Observer is Looking For

A participant observer is looking for facts, facts that tell him about the lives of people, how they behave in various situations, how they interpret events and individuals in their daily experiences. Out of all these facts, an observer hopes to develop more general concepts that help him understand the group. As his study progresses, the researcher hopes to make summary statements about the group and to find evidence supporting these statements. Since what the observer is looking for depends so much on the concrete situation, it is helpful to study an example.

Elliot Liebow spent one and a half years studying a group of black men who congregated around a corner carry-out store in Washington, D.C. (Liebow, 1967). Before entering the field, he had only a vague idea about investigating low-income families. Shortly after he moved into the field, he found himself completely submerged in the research. We describe his experiences as follows:

> My initial excursions into the street . . . seldom carried me more than a block or two from the corner where I started. From the very first weeks or even days, I found myself in the middle of things; the principle lines of field work were laid out, almost without my being aware of it (Liebow, 1967:237).

His field observations were centred around twenty or so men. He found out what they did for a living, what they had done in the past, who their friends and relatives were, and how they felt about things. He summarized his field approach:

> Throughout this period, my field observations were focused on individuals: what they said, what they did, and the contexts in which they said them or did them. I sought them out and was sought out by them (Liebow, 1967: 248).

The final report of his field work is a brilliant analysis of the inner world of street-corner black men and its relation to the outer world. He described the marginal employment of the men, their transient relationships with wives and lovers and their phantom ties with friends and pseudo-kin. Liebow concluded that these relationships had a lot to do with the economic instability of the men, and that the inner world of these people was closely tied to the world outside, a world they had little hope of entering.

Recording and Analysing Field Notes

It is important for a field worker to take detailed notes of his experiences. These notes represent the researcher's records of what happened in the field, whom he spoke to and what they said on each occasion. In short, the field notes are the data base for subsequent analyses. They can effectively illustrate one's analysis and provide a context to the readers.

Field materials and notes are analysed throughout the field research and not just at the end of the project. In analysing the notes, a researcher is looking for concepts and statements which best summarize the empirical situation. One way of developing such concepts and statements is to search for similarities among the cases. Sometimes it is impossible to develop a concept or statement that fits all cases. A researcher may quantify his field materials by stating how many cases fit a particular pattern, while other cases fall into other patterns. These other patterns, or exceptions, are *deviations* from the dominant pattern. It is just as important to account for the deviant cases as for the major social type.

In studying a group or an organization, a researcher is frequently looking for underlying norms, relationships and structures. Often, by seeking an answer that is the opposite of what we are looking for, we find meaningful information. For example, what holds a social group together may not be readily seen. The question, however, may be answered by inquiring into the conditions under which the group breaks down (Whyte, 1955).

THE USE OF EXISTING DATA IN SOCIAL RESEARCH

Aside from collecting data first-hand, a researcher can use existing data sources such as official statistics, public documents and private records. These methods of data collection are sometimes called *unobtrusive measures* because the researcher is removed from the events being studied.

Official Statistics

All modern governments collect official statistics for planning, administration and other purposes. These statistics include unemployment figures, divorce rates, population changes, labour-force characteristics, health service records and a host of others.

Since most official statistics are not collected for research purposes, researchers must use ingenuity in applying these statistics to a particular research problem. Marriage records, for example, may contain information on the family backgrounds of the couples, which may be used to study intergenerational mobility. Birth certificates and death records may contain brief descriptions of family histories, which can be used to reconstruct genealogies. Tax returns have information on income, which can be used to study inequality. Rogoff's study of occupational mobility in Indiana (1953) was based on occupations given in marriage records, and Johnson's analysis of income inequality in Canada (1977) shows how official statistics may be applied to social research.

There are several problems in using official statistics. First, official statistics are compiled by government agencies for classifying people into the statistical categories. By changing the definitions of classification, official statistics can be manipulated. Unemployment figures are good examples. If the definition of an unemployed person is one who has been unemployed for four weeks and actively looking for a job, then the unemployment figures would not include those unemployed for less than four weeks or those not actively looking for work. Changing the definitions of statistical categories also means figures compiled at different times may not be totally comparable. Stirling and Kouri (1979) produced unemployment rates in various provinces of Canada that are almost twice as high as the official figures by using a different definition of unemployment. Similarly, crime rates as compiled by law-enforcement agencies are subject to changes in legislative bills which redefine violations of the law. An increase or decrease in drug-related convictions may reflect a tightening or loosening of laws pertaining to drug addiction and possession.

Criminologists know that official crime statistics often reflect the law-enforcement agencies' capacity to handle criminals more than changes in criminality in society. This observation suggests another aspect of official statistics. Since they are compiled by officials, government statistics sometimes reveal as much about the people compiling the figures as about the people the statistics supposedly describe. Cicourel and Kitsuse (1963), for example, discovered in their investigation of a school that the teachers' evaluations of students revealed more about the subjective standards used by teachers than about the students themselves.

Public Documents

Aside from official statistics, all government departments and agencies have correspondence, memoranda and other written documents. Many of these materials are classified for reasons of security and confidentiality. But, after a certain time, some government materials are declassified and placed in public archives. These materials provide valuable sources for studying government policies, political parties, public administration and other related topics.

Archival materials provide a context for many social events. The letters and memoranda of politicians, for example, often reveal much about their lives over and above what is evident from their public appearances and records, as the diaries of Prime Minister Mackenzie King show (Pickersgill and Forster, 1970). Internal government records often reveal why certain policies were made.

Judicial and political records provide another source of materials for social research. Both the Congress in the United States and the Parliament in Canada maintain extensive records of the bills and statutes passed, the debates that took place, the voting patterns of legislators and minutes of various committee meetings. Another type of public record are the reports compiled by congressional hearings or royal commissions. These hearings and commissions generally deal with a specific social or political issue. The reports contain interesting accounts or testimonies and briefs presented by the public, as well as recommendations and analyses by officials. They record the views of different interest groups on public issues.

Private Documents and Other Sources

Other sources of unobtrusive measures are private documents produced by private citizens or voluntary associations. Many people keep letters, diaries, biographies and essays. These materials provide insights into the private lives of people and their interpretations of events and experiences. For example, private collections can provide valuable data for studies of immigrants' experiences — their interpretations of the new world, their ties to the old one, their aspirations and disappointments. A classic study in this area is the work of Thomas and Znaniecki (1958) on Polish peasants in North America and Europe, which is based on many private documents of Polish immigrants.

Newspapers, novels, cartoons, television and radio programs are additional sources of unobtrusive measures. For example, relying largely on old newspapers, Ward

(1978) analysed anti-Orientalism in British Columbia from the 1860s to the 1940s. Haskell (1974) studied female stereotypes in movies.

In the sections that follow, we shall examine sampling and measurement problems which affect the external and internal validity of all research methods.

SAMPLING PROBLEMS

Research is always limited by the resources available. Given that we only have the resources to study a segment of the entire population, how should we select the sample so that we can speak with some confidence about the rest of the population? This is the question sampling theories try to answer.

Whenever we must rely on a sample to generalize to a population, the question of external validity becomes an issue. External validity refers to the extent to which a generalization is valid or biased because of our particular sample. Putting it another way, the external validity of research is determined by the population to which we can generalize our findings, based on a sample. Probability sampling theories provide the methods for drawing samples which have greater likelihood of accurately reflecting the characteristics of the population.

PROBABILITY SAMPLING DESIGNS

1. Simple Random Sampling. In a simple random sample, every element of the population has an equal and independent chance of being selected. To draw a simple random sample, one must have a complete list of all the elements in the population. Each element can only appear once on the list. For each element, a unique number is assigned. The students of a university campus may be seen as the population, from which a sample may be randomly selected. A complete list of student numbers is a good source from which to draw a random sample. Random numbers can be generated from a table of random numbers. A student is selected into the sample if his or her number matches with a number from the table.

2. Systematic Sampling. A systematic sample is one in which every nth case is selected from a list of all cases in the population after the first case has been randomly selected. For example, randomly pick a first case from a telephone directory and thereafter pick every nth case. A systematic sample may be treated, in practice, as a simple random sample. In general, systematic sampling is simple to use and highly practical. It is a procedure often used in selecting a sample from a telephone directory, a voters' list or other compilations of names.

3. Stratified Sampling. Instead of drawing cases from the general population, a stratified sample divides the population into various homogeneous subgroups and then randomly or systematically selects cases within each subgroup. This design increases the efficiency at a given cost level and can be more accurate than a simple random sample in estimating population characteristics. Assume we wish to study university students on a campus of 10 000 students, with 4 000 in the first year, 3 000 in the second year, 2 000 in the third year, and 1 000 in the fourth year. Also assume we have the resources to study 1 000 students. Using a simple random sample, we may not obtain an accurate representation of each of the four years because of sampling error, that is, fluctuation from one random sample to another.

If it is important to have such representation, a better way to select our cases is to divide the students into four subgroups, according to their year of registration. Within each subgroup, we can then select 250 students, using either random sampling or systematic sampling.

Stratified sampling requires prior knowledge of the population in order to stratify the subgroups. Generally, one should use a major independent variable as a criterion of stratification. In our example, the independent variable was the student's year of registration.

4. Cluster Sampling. Cluster sampling divides the population into geographic areas and then draws probability samples within these areas. A cluster sample is like a stratified sample, but instead of using the characteristics of the population to subdivide the population, a cluster sample uses *geographic locations*. Census tracts and census districts are good examples of geographic subdivisions. Cluster sampling reduces the transportation cost of interviewing. Within each geographic cluster, cases may be selected randomly by simple random sampling or systematic sampling.

NONPROBABILITY SAMPLING DESIGNS

5. Quota Sampling. Quota sampling ensures that a given proportion of the elements in the sample has certain characteristics, irrespective of how the elements are selected. For example, if we want to have 60 percent males and 35 percent Catholics in our sample, we can set these figures as quotas for sampling. In selecting the cases, we would make sure our sample had these characteristics.

6. Availability Sampling. In an availability sample, the elements in the sample are easily available to the researcher. The criterion of selection is not based on known probability, but upon how accessible the elements are. If we want to study illegal immigrants, it is not likely that a comprehensive list of names is available for sampling, and we have to select subjects as they become available. Although restrictive in terms of generalizing the results, this procedure can be very informative about the group under study.

7. Snowball Sampling. Snowball sampling relies on the subjects referring other subjects to the researcher. Its name evokes a snowball accumulating more snow as it rolls down a hill. In the same way, a researcher gathers more cases through referrals while studying available subjects. This procedure cuts down the refusal rate, especially when the subjects are somewhat apprehensive about participating. For example, criminals and social deviants may be reluctant to speak to researchers for fear of revealing their identity.

MEASUREMENT PROBLEMS

Measurement may be defined as the assigning of numerals to objects, events or persons according to rules (Stevens, 1951). In sociology, measurement involves quantifying the social properties of individuals and groups as variables. All variables have two definitions: theoretical and operational. The *theoretical* definition delineates the variable's conceptual boundaries, while the *operational* definition allows the variable to be classified into empirical categories. For example, education may be conceptualized as the formal schooling a person receives, and, operationally, it may be measured in three categories: (1) elementary; (2) secondary; and (3) post-secondary. To the extent that the categories bear quantifiable relationships to each other, a scale can be developed. In the above case, people in the post-secondary category have more education than those in the secondary, or elementary categories. Otherwise, the measurement remains at the level of classification, as, for example, the classification of respondents into 1. male and 2. female.

In developing the categories of a variable, there are two principles to follow. The first principle is that the categories must be mutually exclusive, that the boundaries of categories cannot overlap. Secondly, the categories should be totally exhaustive. All the categories taken together should account for all the empirical cases.

LEVELS OF MEASUREMENT

Although measurement involves the assignment of numbers to attributes, or categories, of variables, the meanings of these numbers may vary, depending on the variables. In some cases, as when sex is a variable, the numerals representing male and female are symbolic and are merely used to classify the subjects into two groups. In other cases, as when education varies, the numbers may represent the actual years of schooling, and so they have numeric properties. Variables may represent different levels of measurement. There are four levels of measurement to consider: nominal, ordinal, interval and ratio.

A *nominal* level of measurement can classify objects or people into categories. When numbers are used for such a classification, they are merely symbols representing the qualitative categories and do not carry any numeric properties. For example, one can use the number (1) to represent Catholics, (2) for Protestants, and (3) for other religious affiliation.

An *ordinal* level of measurement can rank-order the categories as well as classify them. The variable "education," as defined earlier, has these categories. Those in group (3) have an education that is higher than those in group (2) and group (1). There is, therefore, a rank-order among the three groups. Although we can differentiate the ones with a higher education from those with a lower education, we have no measurement of how much more or less education one group has compared to others.

An *interval* level of measurement has all the properties of a nominal and an ordinal measure. In addition, the distances separating the categories or units are equal intervals. The Fahrenheit temperature scale is an example of interval measurement. The difference between 50° and 51° is 1°, and so is the difference between 49° and 50°. An interval level of measurement, however, does not have an absolute zero, so that one cannot speak of 90° being twice as hot as 45°. An example of an interval level of measurement in social science is the intelligence quotient.

The only difference between a *ratio* measure and an interval measure is that the former has an absolute zero, as, for example, in age and years of formal schooling.

QUESTIONNAIRE CONSTRUCTION

Students constructing a questionnaire for the first time often find it difficult to decide on which questions to include or exclude and how to phrase the questions to accurately measure the sociological concepts they have in mind. Some of the difficulties are not just technical but relate to theoretical confusions. Confusion may arise from the specification of the research problem, the develoment of hypotheses and the operationalizations of variables. After all, a questionnaire is no more than a tool to be employed for a clearly stated purpose.

A questionnaire may contain both open-ended and close-ended questions. *Open-ended* questions are those which do not provide a choice of answers; the respondents are free to answer any way they wish. *Close-ended* questions, on the other hand, have a set of answers from which the respondents must choose. An example of an open-ended question is: "What is the most serious problem facing the country today?" A close-ended question is: "Last week, how many hours did you work for pay? 1. None; 2. Less than 10 hours; 3. 10 to 19 hours; 4. 20 to 29 hours; 5. 30 hours and over."

Although open-ended questions are flexible, in that they allow the respondents to answer any way they desire, they are difficult to code or to summarize. To analyse the answers of open-ended questions, a researcher must first do a content analysis and develop a set of categories for sorting the answers. Open-ended questions, however, are sometimes useful to elicit quotations from respondents, which may be used to substantiate statistical discussions. Close-ended questions produce results which are easy to code. Sequential numbers are often assigned to the categories so that they can be directly entered into a computer.

Questions should not be worded in a way that appears to support a particular choice. For example, "Do you think Canada has been harmed by immigrants coming into this country?" is a biased question because it implies that our country has been harmed by immigrants. A proper way to phrase the question is to include both sides of the issue: "Do you think this country has benefited or been harmed by immigrants coming into the country?"

Double-barrelled questions are ambiguous because there are two things contained in a single question, and answers to such questions are hard to interpret. Here is an example: "Would you or would you not support legalizing abortion and marijuana?" If a respondent answers yes, it is not clear whether he or she supports legalizing abortion or marijuana or both.

All questionnaires should be pretested before they are applied to the actual sample. To the greatest degree possible, respondents in the pretest sample should be similar to those in the actual sample. It is often necessary to pretest the questionnaire more than once. During the pretest, the researcher should see how the respondents react to the questions and determine which ones are too difficult, unclear, too lengthy and so on. The aim is to improve both the reliability and validity of the survey. A poorly constructed questionnaire not only has large measurement errors, but is also less likely to be completed by respondents.

SUMMARY

All research methods are concerned with collecting accurate empirical evidence and with discarding incorrect explanations. Sociologists, like other scientists, follow the *research cycle* in using empirical evidence to verify theories.

The *classical experimental design* provides a basis for testing the effect of an independent variable on a dependent variable in a laboratory setting. The basic approach is to expose the experimental group, but not the control group, to a treatment to see if a subsequent change is produced, while holding other experimental conditions constant. *Quasi-experimental designs* are deviations from the classical experiments and consequently subject to various threats to their *internal and external validity*.

Sociologists must often use alternative methods to approximate the logic of experimentation. The *historical/comparative* method compares similar and different cases to show the presence or absence of a relationship. This method is evident in the works of classical sociologists like Durkheim, Weber and Marx.

Survey methods also employ comparisons. Instead of artificially controlling for the independent variables, as in experimentation, survey methods statistically manipulate them after the fact. Changes in the dependent variable at different levels of the independent variable are compared, and controls are introduced statistically.

Participant observation allows a researcher to participate in the daily life of the people that he studies. This method is suitable to the study of small groups. It allows the blending of theoretical conceptualization with field research.

Besides collecting data first-hand, sociologists use *unobtrusive measures* such as official statistics, public records, private documents and other sources.

Problems of sampling and measurement affect the validity of all methods. In *probability samples*, the probability of selection is known. The four types are: *simple random sample, systematic sample, stratified sample* and *cluster sample. Non-probability sampling designs* include *quota samples, availability samples* and *snowball samples*.

Measurement involves quantifying observations. The four levels of measurement are *nominal, ordinal, interval* and *ratio* measurement.

In developing a questionnaire, a researcher should pretest the questions.

DISCUSSION QUESTIONS

1. What is the relationship between sociological theory and research method?

2. What are the sources of invalidity in an experimental design in which there is no control group?

3. How does one control for the variations of independent variables in comparative and survey research?

4. What are the major problems in using secondary data and official statistics?

5. What are the advantages and limitations of: a stratified sample; a cluster sample; and a snowball sample?

PROCESSES
of SOCIAL
ORGANIZATION

What ties people together in groups? What makes them behave in predictable ways? How are people assimilated into on-going social organizations?

These questions will all be addressed in this section of the book. The following chapters examine basic processes of social organization: acculturation, socialization, control and deviance.

To a large degree, the answers to the above questions also answer opposite questions: What severs the ties between people or prevents ties from forming? Why do people sometimes behave unpredictably? What keeps them from assimilating into on-going organizations? To understand social conflict, deviance and change is also to understand social consensus and stability. The two differ only in their emphasis, as in the question, "Is the waterglass half empty or half full?" However, theorists who approach society from the opposing standpoints of order and change differ in important ways. For this reason, this book devotes an entire section to change. (See page 321.) The related topic of social conflict is discussed throughout this text. (See, for example, the chapter on stratification and class.)

The problem of order is, for sociology, a central one. English political theorist Thomas Hobbes (1588-1679), for example, declared that, in a state of nature, lacking government, people's selfish desires would run wild; they would lead lives that were "solitary, poor, nasty, brutish and short." This was why a sovereign ruler was needed. People could not rely on "society" to protect its members: only the nation-state could do so.

The nineteenth century saw an upsurge of anarchist and utopian philosophies opposing this Hobbesian view. They held that nation-states were unnecessary and repressive and that social order could emerge naturally from people's co-operative instincts. Unlike Hobbes, utopian and anarchistic theorists believed selfishness was learned and artificial and co-operativeness and sociability, natural. In large part, their views led to the study of society as an entity distinct from the state.

The sociologists studying "community" supported this distinction. With industrialization and urbanization, social relations changed markedly. No longer were they based on tradition and blood ties but on impersonal, temporary, more limited kinds of bonds. Such changes within an enduring nation-state proved that social order was distinct from political order and that it contributed in a unique way to human well-being. This observation led toward the systematic study of social order, what establishes and what disrupts it.

Culture and Acculturation

The *culture* of the entire Western world was *modernized* in the nineteenth and twentieth centuries. By "culture" we mean the entire collection of values and behaviours that characterize life in a society. "Modernization" is complex. It grows out of industrialization, urbanization, the rise of modern science and technology, secular religion, mass literacy and a new public awareness of the world. By a "modernized" culture we mean one that accommodates these new developments. According to researchers like sociologist Alex Inkeles, such a culture produces new kinds of personalities: people who are more inclined to plan, reason, grant equality to others and interest themselves in other parts of the world. By some definitions, modernization expands human horizons beyond past and present to future, beyond narrow interest in self, family and community to an interest in nation, world and cosmos.

Other images of modernization are less favourable. Karl Marx (1818-1883) and Max Weber (1864-1920) depicted modern society as exploitive, alienating, immense and impersonal, over-organized but with insufficient concern for human beings, obsessed with technology and efficiency, faddish and overcrowded with meaningless gadgetry. Modernity, in this view, is a worldwide consumer's market characterized by the fetish for commodities— an obsession to acquire material possessions as a proof of personal value.

Whichever assessment seems more accurate, and both apply in some instances, Western culture has changed significantly in the last two centuries. Culture, like population, is an important part of the context within which a society maintains or changes its way of maintaining order. Accordingly, the social relations that make up society in the West have also changed significantly.

Acculturation is the process by which members of a society learn their culture. The process usually occurs in an unstructured, often unconscious way, the way language is learned. Babies learn to speak their society's language without knowing they are learning it. They practice, imitate, use trial and error. The learning of cultural values probably also proceeds this way. For example, research by sociologists Bernd Baldus and Verna Tribe has shown that, by an early age, Canadian schoolchildren have learned to associate good manners and morals with symbols of high social standing (for instance, a nice car, a large home).

Where and how did they learn this? Perhaps unconsciously, from the mass media portrayals of rich and poor people, or from unspoken cues provided by their parents and other adults.

Acculturation is related to two other important processes. One is *assimilation*, the process by which adult members of foreign cultural groups learn the values and behaviours of a culture into which they have immigrated. In a society like Canada's, so heavily composed of immigrants, a smooth assimilation process is crucial. Despite our commitment to multiculturalism, some consensus is necessary among Canadians of varied cultural origins.

Socialization

The second related process is *socialization*, by which people learn the social rules defining relationships into which they will enter. Socialization goes on throughout life, but in childhood the changes are most dramatic and visible. A child is born without any knowledge of social rules. Yet, by the time he or she begins school, the child has learned to follow the orders given by people in authority (chiefly adults), to co-operate (chiefly with peers), to accept certain responsibilities and to carry out assigned tasks at home.

Typically, the roles and rules learned in socialization are suited to the values learned in acculturation. For example, in our society a child is acculturated to believe that children must obey authority. They are trained to associate authority with adults, and particularly with specific adults: parents, grandparents, teachers and policemen, among others. Peers, by contrast, must establish their authority. Since none of the learned bases for authority seem to apply, obedience among peers must be established by fighting, which is the way animals accomplish this task. Once a rough hierarchy has been established, children "know their place" in the playground just as they do at home.

In some situations, no rules exist. Rules must be hammered out by the interacting group, then learned and obeyed. In other situations, participants must follow the existing rules, even if they conflict with earlier experiences. This conflict is experienced by the workman promoted to foreman, for example. As workman, he may have felt loyal to the workers and opposed management; as foreman, he *must* feel loyal to management and, equivalently, opposed to the workmen. The structure of the worker/foreman relationship creates this conflict. People must solve it through resocialization, and research shows they generally weather the transition, if not always smoothly.

Control and Deviance

Societies bring restrictions aplenty. Social life and social relationships require rules. Rules imply control, and control in turn implies authority, the right to impose and enforce rules. Differential authority creates social inequality. This suggests that no society, whether capitalist, socialist or communist, will ever be wholly egalitarian, for no society can operate without rules and authority. This theme will be developed more thoroughly in other chapters.

An early, surprising discovery by Émile Durkheim (1858-1917) is that any society needs deviance. This statement seems paradoxical, since any society also needs order, and deviance implies disorder. Yet deviance, like conflict, offers an opportunity to reaffirm order, an occasion to remind society's members of the limits of proper behaviour. Punishment of deviance, like the conduct of a war with outsiders, strengthens social solidarity and group cohesion, and thus is a process of social organization.

The question of why particular people break the rules is the object of continuing attention from criminologists. Many reasons can be given for deviance, ranging from chemical, physiological, psychological, up through social and cultural factors. What is surprising is not that deviance happens so often, given the tremendous number of reasons for its occurrence; but rather that it happens so rarely. Of course, everyone deviates in some way, at some time or another (perhaps daily). In this sense, deviance is amazingly common, the norm and not the exception in human societies. Yet most deviance is minor and hidden. Furthermore, most deviance is prevented, minimized or hidden not because of coercion but because of acculturation, socialization and an unwillingness to risk exposure to ridicule, criticism or ostracism.

The material basis of social life should not be ignored in explaining conformity. We all depend upon the good will and co-operation of others for money, information and other kinds of assistance. Without these, we find it hard to carry out our social roles, hold jobs or participate in social life. Thus, excommunication, communal expulsion, the "silent treatment" and other forms of banishment have been used with great success by religious and secular organizations to control their members. The example of an expelled member helps a great deal to pull the other group members back into line.

Having said that, we must remember the importance of formal social controls. These include laws and law enforcement agencies, which punish serious deviations. Whether informal social controls would be sufficient without formal ones backing them up, we shall never know. No societies of any complexity lack formal social controls, any more than they lack inequalities.

A Summary and Look Ahead

To summarize, people are gathered into social relationships by processes of social organization. These include acculturation, socialization, control and deviance. These processes are similar in social organizations of differing size and complexity. All social systems require smooth functioning of these processes. Yet social organizations of different sizes and complexity differ in other important ways. Thus, the science of society cannot be reduced, as some would wish, to a science of human individuals or groups. To move from individuals to groups to societies, sociologists must understand a great deal more than they do about the effects of size and complexity on social functioning.

The next section will take us from social roles, the basic building blocks of social relationships, to larger and more complex sets of social relations. The section following this one will deal with the still more complex social relations that make up society's central institutions.

3

Culture, Change and Autonomy

Susannah Wilson

INTRODUCTION

Canada's history, ethnic composition and proximity to the United States make us particularly aware of debates about Canadian culture and Canadian identity. Our sense of ourselves comes partly from appreciating cultural differences within Canada. While it may be difficult to describe what Canadian culture is, we sense we are unlike our American neighbours in important ways. In this chapter, we will explore how sociologists have approached the nebulous topic of culture and what these findings reveal about ourselves as Canadians.

Bronislaw Malinowski, (1939:588) one of anthropology's founding fathers, described culture as "the most central problem of all social science." Most sociologists would say it is one of the most, if not *the* most, central concept in sociology. The concept of culture was introduced into the English language in the 1880s by two anthropologists, Matthew Arnold and Edward B. Tylor, although its origins can be traced to the fourteenth century (Langness, 1974). Tylor (1924:1) defined culture as "that complex whole which includes knowledge, belief, art, morals, law custom and any other capabilities and habits acquired by man as a member of society." Since Tylor's time, the concept has been developed and altered (and, as Boon [1973] suggests, "obscured and misunderstood") by social scientists in many disciplines.

The major difficulty in defining culture is that it is so all encompassing. As Hall (1976:14) explains, "There is not one aspect of human life that is not touched and altered by culture." Another anthropologist, Schneider (1973) said that culture seems to refer to everything, including the kitchen sink, since the kitchen sink is part of *material culture*. Anthropologists customarily distinguish *material culture*, or cultural artifacts, from *nonmaterial culture*, which refers to values, ideas and beliefs. Edward Hall notes that when anthropologists study another culture, their focus will be influenced by what they define as important in their own culture. Nevertheless, there is general agreement that culture is learned, that aspects of culture are interrelated and that culture is shared to the extent that cultural differences define group boundaries (Hall, 1976).

Generally, discussions of culture focus on four elements: *norms, values, beliefs* or *ideologies* and *expressive symbols*. Over time, the emphasis given to these elements has changed. Now, more attention is paid to expressive symbols. The current focus of many studies is the symbolic representation or meaning of both the material and nonmaterial culture. Culture then, is "the symbolic-expressive aspect of human behavior" (Wuthrow et al., 1984:3).

MAJOR THEMES IN THE STUDY OF CULTURE

In this section, we will look briefly at the differing emphases given to the study by the major theoretical traditions in sociology. Generally, functionalists emphasize the basis and reinforcement of value consensus. The way Parsons connects the cultural and social systems to individual behaviour is an example of this. For *Marxists*, aspects of culture are part of the superstructure of society and are reflected in ideology. Ideologies serve to frame and legitimize the existing economic order. *Interactionists* focus primarily on symbolic expressive aspects of culture, such as language. Using a common language, saluting a flag or attending a religious ceremony confirms our identity as members of a culture or group. At the same time, these expressive symbols perpetuate the group's existence as new members are introduced to them.

CULTURAL VALUES AND NORMS

Talcott Parsons described culture as one of four interrelated systems of action. The other three action systems are the *social system*, the *personality system* and the *biological system*. The social system "is a way of organizing human action" (Parsons, 1973:36), the "master example" of which is society. Societies consist of individuals who interact within the framework of a common culture. Collective identity is expressed in our readiness to include ourselves in particular groups. For example, we might identify ourselves as "we" Canadians, "we" Memorial University students, "we" Roman Catholics, "we" sociologists and so on. We are all members of many such groups. Some groups will be small, but some will be large and cut across national boundaries. Over 5000 sociologists attend meetings of the International Sociological Association.

According to Parsons, values, norms and beliefs are the most important distinguishing characteristics of a social system. Institutionalized values, or value systems, "constitute relatively generalized patterns of orientation" which "focus on the normative regulation of social relationships" (Parsons, 1973:37-38). In complex, differentiated systems such as ours, subsystems, or collectivities, will have particular value systems, although Parsons assumed that these are more or less congruent with widely held values. Norms, unlike values, are situation specific. They define desirable patterns of interaction and come to be regarded as standards against which behaviour is evaluated. Beliefs are existential statements about how the world operates and often serve to justify values and norms.

Individuals learn norms, values and beliefs during socialization. For example, North Americans are taught to value equality of opportunity and personal freedom, and we believe these should be protected. Canadians and Americans may differ in the emphasis placed on core values and in the symbolic expression of these. In a classic study, Lipset (1963) found that Canadians are more conservative, more authoritarian and more oriented to tradition, hierarchy and elitism than Americans. Some values, such as the incest taboo, and norms, such as those restricting public nudity, are shared by most cultures. On the interpersonal level, our interactions with others are predictable because we have learned to accept and expect certain standards of behaviour.

Subcultures are identifiable because they share norms, values and beliefs which differ from those of the core culture. Some argue our lives are far more influenced by subcultural norms and values than by those shared by the society as a whole. In pluralistic and fragmented societies like ours, it is difficult to determine the extent of shared meanings. Our emphasis on individualism, fueled by the human potential movement of the 1970s, gives us a great deal of flexibility within the boundaries imposed by formal and informal sanctions.

In one sense, cultural values are implicit in the choice of topics covered in this textbook and the ways issues are analysed. The study of sociology in the West is carried on in a milieu which reflects particular cultural values. In China, sociology is much more directly connected to social policy than it is in Canada or the United

States. The section of this text that describes Canadian economic institutions and the mass media reveals a great deal about how cultural values in Canada have become institutionalized.

IDEOLOGY

Functionalist sociologists emphasize the integrative role of common cultural elements. For Marxists, the impression of a shared culture is the result of a complex process of social construction and legitimation, with strong ideological support. Ideologies as defined by Marchak (1981:xi) are "beliefs about realities which are by their nature held on faith . . . . The function of ideology is to direct the members of the society to a shared understanding of what their collective lives are all about." Marchak described the two major ideologies in Canada now as *liberalism* and *socialism*.

> The first describes Canada as a liberal democracy governed by representatives elected by a majority of adult citizens. The society is maintained by a stable and self-sufficient free-enterprise economy staffed by reasonably happy and affluent workers. The second describes Canada as a society ruled by an hereditary oligarchy and multi-national imperialist corporations, maintained by a large and increasingly impoverished working class (Marchak, 1981:ix. Permission granted by McGraw-Hill Ryerson Limited.)

Marchak argues that the 1980s saw the emergence of a third ideology: *corporatism*. Corporatism is an ideology of "legitimate authority, the natural hierarchy of persons and skills, and of the subordination of the individual not only to society but as well to the state" (Marchak:170).

Bourdieu and Passeron (1977) argue that the function of education is to reproduce the dominant culture. Educational success is largely determined by how well individuals internalize the dominant culture. It is, in Bourdieu's words, the most important means of accumulating *cultural capital*. Cultural capital consists of symbolic elements valued by the dominant class, including speech, rules of etiquette, knowledge and experience.

EXPRESSIVE SYMBOLS

In the postwar period, a number of social movements expressed dissatisfaction with the dominant culture and with basic structural inequalities. Youth, students, blacks, women and even middle-class professionals involved in the human potential movement criticized several generally held social values. The civil rights movement and the women's movement focused on unique and previously undervalued aspects of their own cultures. The introduction of native, black and women's studies programs in North American universities is in part a response to this kind of demand. Many groups expressed their differences symbolically, in their dress and hair styles. Peterson (1979) suggests that the attention now paid by sociologists to expressive symbolization coincided with the increased visibility of countercultures in our society.

Generally, our collective identity is represented in the symbolic expression of our cultural traditions, in language and in the countless rituals which punctuate our lives as citizens, employees, members of families and so on. In confirming our group membership, these symbols reinforce our sense of ourselves. We identify with and feel comfortable with familiar symbols. We feel we belong. When we travel, we find important cultural differences, even in such taken-for-granted aspects of social interaction as how much personal space we can claim when talking to others, eye contact and touching behaviour. And, as many of us have experienced with some frustration, different cultures attach different meanings to the notion of time and of being "on time."

Time Difference

Hall (1976) describes Westerners' orientation to time as *monochronic*. In other words, we prefer to do one thing at a time. Monochronic time emphasizes schedules and promptness. A *polychronic* orientation to time, typical of Latin America and the Middle East, is characterized by several things happening at once (1976:14). Typically, Westerners tend to compartmentalize their lives and prioritize their activities. Monochronic time is tangible: "They (Westerners) speak of it as being saved, spent, wasted, lost, made up, accelerated, slowed down, crawling and running out" (1976:15). As Hall explains, these differences are learned, but they are learned so well and are so well integrated with other aspects of culture that they are treated as natural.

The fast pace of life in North America makes it tempting to disparage the Spanish idea of "mañana." In fact, Peace Corp volunteers found that, next to language, their greatest difficulties in adjusting to a foreign culture were in dealing with "the general pace of life and the punctuality of others" (Levine and Wolff, 1985:32). Attempts to explore different meanings attached to social time cross-culturally are limited by linguistic comparisons. Cultures which place a high priority on punctuality have more specific words to describe time dimensions than cultures in which time is less important. For example, "esrerar" in Portuguese means "to hope for," "to wait for" and to "expect." (Levine and Wolff, 1985:34) To circumvent these problems, Levine and Wolff used unobtrusive measures to estimate the pace of life in six countries. These researchers found important differences in the accuracy of the country's bank clocks, pedestrian walking speed and the average time it took to buy a stamp.

Language

Perhaps the most useful expressive symbol is language. In addition to being an efficient means of communicating, language is an expression of group membership. This is obvious when we think about French and English Canadians. But language can also distinguish members of smaller groups: professionals, students, punkers or even members of families. Whether in the form of family "nicknames" or technical jargon, we all develop peculiarities of speech which symbolically differentiate members from nonmembers. At the same time, these unique ways of talking help to establish rapport between members of the group.

Several anthropologists have concluded that language also shapes our perceptions of the world. The *Sapir-Whorf Hypothesis* assumes that language helps define experience because it orients us to certain aspects of our environment. Thus, when people acquire language, they also acquire a way of organizing their experience. Cultural differences rooted in the very structure of language make cross-cultural communication difficult.

Feminists argue that language is based on male experience and therefore describes a masculine view of the world. When we use generic terms such as "he" and "man,"

Table 3-1 The Pace of Life in Six Countries

	Accuracy of Bank Clocks	Walking Speed	Post Office Speed
Japan	1	1	1
United States	2	3	2
England	4	2	3
Italy	5	4	6
Taiwan	3	5	4
Indonesia	6	6	5

Numbers (1 is the top value) indicate the comparative rankings of each country for each indicator of time sense.

Reprinted by permission from *Psychology Today Magazine* © 1985.

we are, in effect, reinforcing this masculine view. Furthermore, people who hear generic terms envision a male referent. Students asked to select pictures to illustrate an introductory sociology text chose more pictures of males when the chapter titles used generic terms such as "Urban Man" than when the chapters had neutral titles like "Urban Life" (Schneider and Hacker, 1973).

Mass Mediated Culture[1]

Although the media are the focus of a later chapter, we cannot discuss culture without considering the role of the media in the social construction of reality. The media, particularly television, are pervasive cultural influences. Continuity is preserved by the production and reproduction of cultural symbols, and the media are active in this process.

You have probably heard that by the time you graduate, you will have spent more hours watching television than in school. In fact, in your lifetime, you will spend more time watching television than doing anything else except working or sleeping. More than 98 percent of American homes have television sets, and these are turned on for an average of *seven* hours a day. Television viewing has increased steadily among all age, educational and ethnic groups in the last decade (Neuman, 1982:471)

In Gerbner's view, television is a unique medium because it is so pervasive. He feels (1978) that television has assumed the role once occupied by religion in preindustrial societies in that we are born into its symbolic environment and rarely

[1] This term is borrowed from the title of a book by Real (1977).

NOT JUST GOOD CHRISTIAN MEN REJOICING NOW
By Kelley Teahen

God is not a she, at least not in the language of churches of the Christian tradition. And ever since the first righteous monk translated the Greek word for "humanity"—anthropos—as "man" in the scriptures, it has sounded like the Holy Writ is addressed to only the male half of the Christian community.

During the past decade a sensitivity has developed to so-called exclusive language within the songs, prayers and scripture translations used in churches. Such language excludes womanhood in two ways. The community of worshippers is often described as "sons of God" or "the brethren," not taking into account the women in the congregation. And God is understood to be He Himself—the lord, king, master and father of all.

Some churches do not feel this kind of language poses a problem for the women of their communities.

"Sexist language is not a dominant issue with the evangelicals," said Rev. Brian Stiller, executive director of the Evangelical Fellowship of Canada, which represents such denominations as the Pentecostal Assembly, the Salvation Army and some Mennonite groups. "Women have been very involved in our ministry over the years and there's an implicit acceptance of women when we say 'mankind.' "

In other churches however—notably the United and Roman Catholic—women have felt set apart in worship and, during the past few years, have brought about changes in the words sung and spoken in prayer and praise. . . .

"All language about God is inadequate, but somehow we always think of God as 'He,' " she said.

Although many may fear the richness of traditional language in liturgy and in standard hymns such as Faith Of Our Fathers will be diminished by exclusive adaptations, the churches—notably the Roman Catholic, whose women are not allowed to enter into the higher callings of its ministries—feel the changes in language are needed to reflect the Church's growing awareness of women's roles in the community.

"I may not be happy, grammatically, with a word like humankind," said Father Poirier.

"But it sure is a lot fairer than saying mankind."

The Globe and Mail, Toronto, August 3, 1985.

question its cultural assumptions. "Television is the ritual that dramatizes the myths underlying American culture, it explains and justifies the major social institutions of American society and socializes individuals into their life roles" (White, 1983:286).

In a series of continuing studies begun in 1967, Gerbner and his associates have studied the cultural environment of television. They have regularly monitored television content and compared these trends with attitude studies of the television audience. The symbolic environment of television is analysed by what Gerbner calls *cultural indicators*. His focus is on the priorities, values and relationships in television drama. His studies found heavy viewers internalized a world and a value system congruent with the world of television. For example, heavy viewers who witness a great deal of televised violence see the world as more threatening than light viewers. Therefore, they are more inclined to support greater measures of social control (Gerbner and Gross, 1976). The media thus act as an instrument of social control, reinforcing and legitimizing certain kinds of social relationships. (These ideas are taken up in more detail in Chapter 12.)

This has been a brief introduction to the major concepts in the study of culture. Next we will look at some ways sociologists have found these concepts useful for understanding social behaviour.

SUBCULTURES

As described in the section above, subcultures are groups whose norms, values and expressive symbols differ from ones more generally held. In the section below, we will look at several ways of conceptualizing these groups. Lewis's analysis of the culture of poverty emphasizes value differences, whereas the description of British youth culture focuses on symbolic expressive differences.

THE CULTURE OF POVERTY

Anthropologist Oscar Lewis coined the phrase *culture of poverty* to describe

> a subculture of Western society with its own structure and rationale, a way of life handed on from generation to generation along family lines. It is a culture in the traditional anthropological sense in that it provides human beings with a design for living, with a readymade set of solutions for human problems, and so serves a significant adaptive function. This style of life transcends na- tional boundaries and regional and rural-urban differences within nations (Lewis, 1966:19).

Lewis identified 70 traits which characterize the culture of poverty. These traits describe: the relationship between the subculture and the larger society; the nature of the slum community; the nature of the family; and the attitudes, values and character structure of the individual. There is a lack of integration between the subculture and the larger community as a result of segregation, discrimination, fear, suspicion and apathy. The community itself is characterized by unemployment, underemployment, low wages and a chronic shortage of cash. Marriage is typically unstable, and families are mother centred. "The individual who grows up in this culture has a strong feeling of fatalism, helplessness, dependence and inferiority" (Lewis, 1966:23).

Lewis's solution—"slowly to raise their level of living and incorporate them in the middle class"—is typical of the 1950s and early 60s approach to social problems. The assumption was that cultural deficiencies could be identified and altered. The same assumption used to explain global underdevelopment. Thus, foreign aid in- cluded an exchange of personnel to train Third World people in the ways of Western industrial capitalism. In the 70s these ideas gave way among sociologists to more critical and radical analyses of development and underdevelopment, although the legacy of the 50s and 60s remains in some quarters. In the more radical social climate of the late 1960s and 1970s, many challenged the presumption that our middle-class, Western way of life should be a model of social development.

The term *ethnocentrism* describes this seemingly universal tendency to rate one's own group or culture more positively than any other group or culture. A Canadian study (Kehoe, 1982) found that, among grade five students, subjects who perceived themselves positively were most likely to appreciate cultural diversity, and those who most appreciated cultural diversity were least ethnocentric.

YOUTH CULTURES

A different way of looking at subcultures focuses on groups that develop around some sort of expressive symbolism. A number of studies of British youth culture have been done along these lines. As Brake (1980) explains, British youth culture arises out of a concern with masculinity, which is reflected in expressions of male superiority and disdain for homosexuality.

According to Brake, an important element of subcultures is the symbolic use of style. Style consists of: image (appearance enhanced by costume, hair-style and jewellery); demeanor (expression, gait and posture); and argot (a special vocabulary). These help to differentiate insiders from outsiders and full-timers from pretenders. In postwar Britain, there has been a discernible turnover of youth cultures, as mods replaced teddy-boys and skinheads replaced mods. Each group has had its own distinctive style. The teddy-boy dress code was a unique adaptation of upper-class style. Teddy-boys wore long, velvet-collared Edwardian jackets, tight drainpipe trousers, bootlaced ties and thick, crepe-soled shoes known as "brothel-creepers." Their heroes were James Dean and Elvis Presley. Hairstyles imitated early Elvis—sideburns and duck-tails, or DAs as they were called. Skinheads of the 60s (a group which re-emerged a few years ago) were self-consciously working-class and ardent football (soccer) fans. They focused their aggression on three groups: Asian immigrants, hippies and homosexuals.

THE TSIGOLOICOS

Professional groups might also be considered as subcultures. In 1956, Horace Miner wrote a wonderfully facetious article called "Body Ritual Among the Nacirema," which poked fun at this "backward" American tribe. Recently, an "elite clan" of the Nacirema, the Tsigoloicos, were the subject of a similar analysis. (See page 76.)

CORPORATE CULTURE

In recent years, the business community has begun to understand problems of organizational change in terms of *corporate culture*. An article in *Business Week* (October 27, 1980) describes how understanding an organization's culture can have important consequences for business decisions.

> "Culture implies values, such as aggressiveness, defensiveness, or nimbleness, that set a pattern for a company's activities, opinions, and actions. That pattern is instilled in employees by managers' example and passed down to succeeding generations of workers."

Managers are beginning to understand that company values are well entrenched and therefore difficult to change.

The *Business Week* article explains how the culture of PepsiCo Inc. changed as the company decided to become a more aggressive competitor. In an ad campaign familiar to us all, Pepsi challenged Coke's domination of the market.

> "That direct confrontation is reflected inside the company as well. Managers are pitted against each other to grab more market share, to work harder, and to wring more profits out of their businesses. Because winning is the key value at Pepsi, losing has its penalties. Consistent runners up find their jobs gone."

CULTURAL CHANGE

Cultures change because of technological innovations, economic or environmental change, the introduction of new members through migration or as a result of internal conflicts. In this section we will look at the impact of technological innovation on Canadian society, the process of cultural diffusion and some important symbolic changes.

Rosengren (1981) has described four positions to categorize theories of cultural change: materialism, idealism, interdependence and autonomy. The *materialist* position assumes that cultural changes follow structural changes; this is the classic Marxist stance. The theories of Innis and McLuhan, which describe cultural changes resulting from changes in communication technology, are also materialist. The *idealist* position is that cultural changes precede structural changes. For example, Weber's thesis, which states that the cultural values of Calvinism created an environment in which capitalism could thrive, could be called idealist. Other positions assume that culture and structure are *autonomous*, although perhaps most discussions of their relationship focus on their *interdependance*. In other words, most analysts claim that culture and structure are not related to one another holistically. Rather, various aspects of both interact at different times in the ongoing process of change.

TECHNOLOGY AND CHANGE

Innis and McLuhan, two Canadians, are called *technological determinists* because of their focus on technological innovation as a source of change. Both were primarily interested in innovations in communication technology. Innis argued that the modes of communication influence the nature of social organization. Oral cultures, where communication is by speech alone, will have a strong temporal bias and will focus on the past. These societies will emphasize tradition and have a strong moral order. Cultures with a written language will be present and future oriented and will favour the growth of science and technical knowledge.

McLuhan took from Innis the centrality of communication technology but focused on how these changes influence the way we perceive the world around us. According to McLuhan, print cultures depend on sight to acquire knowledge and confirm experience. Print organizes experience in a linear fashion. Because reading is a private

MYTH AND SYMBOL AMONG THE NACIREMA TSIGOLOICOS: A FRAGMENT

The Tsigoloicos are a large, decentralized clan distributed throughout that geographical area occupied by the Nacirema. Though nomadic in disposition, the group has recently accepted more permanent settlement as a consequence of gradual exhaustion of natural resources. The clan has a relatively short history, and has only recently claimed elite status and conceived elaborate rituals whereby this is conferred upon new members. It is thus difficult to classify the Tsigoloicos in either of the two great Nacirema phratries (i.e., the Secneics and the Seitinamuh), a fact which probably explains the disdain in which they are held by the more firmly established clans of each.

The life of the Tsigoloicos seems to pass alternately through the two distinct phases observed among the central Australian tribes by Spencer and Gillen (1904). In the first phase, economic activity is indeed the preponderating one, and the Tsigoloicos limit themselves to the two primary occupations for which they are rewarded—i.e., the production and exchange of ritual inscriptions, and the preparation of neophytes for initiation into the clan. These occupations are typically pursued with only mediocre intensity and the dispersed condition of the clan results in a life which is uniform, languishing, and dull [*EF*, p. 246]. Periodically, however, the Tsigoloicos come together at a designated location to participate in a ceremony remarkably similar to the Arunta corrobori. Here, on the contrary, the reason and will of the primitive give way to his passional faculties, and he is caught up in the collective effervescence of communal life [*EF*, pp. 246, 258]. And while the ostensive function of such gatherings remains the exchange of ritual inscriptions, it is clear that their latent function is to reaffirm the solidarity of the clan—i.e., to give it a sense of itself and to reassure its members that it does, in fact, exist [*EF*, p. 257].

Our interest here, however, is in the religious institutions of the Tsigoloicos and especially in the bizarre mythologies which underly them. These myths apparently grow out of the daily, profane activities of the Tsigoloicos themselves. As indicated above, each clan member is expected to periodically produce and exchange certain ritual inscriptions. For the most part, these inscriptions have little of the sacred about them; their utility is temporal and generally confined to the individual who produces them; and they are quickly deposited in the large vaults of Tsigoloicos temples, where they are soon forgotten.

A very few Tsigoloicos inscriptions, however, seem to have acquired and retained sacred status—i.e., they inspire collective sentiments of awe and respect, and are set aside from profane inscriptions and treated with special precautions [*EF*, pp. 56, 301]. The Tsigoloicos themselves appear confused over how this sacredness came into existence; for these are typically very old inscriptions, written in oblique, turgid styles and even strange languages (ironically, the inscription seems to gain in dignity as its meaning is more obscure). As a result, the Tsigoloicos maintain a small class of priests, called *stsiroeht*, whose functions include the interpretation of sacred inscriptions and concoction of fantastic myths to account for their special powers. The result is a set of representations which express the nature of these sacred things and the relations which they sustain, either with each other, or with profane things [*EF*, p. 56]. At the same time, the Tsigoloicos have established rites which prescribe how a man should comport himself in the presence of these sacred objects [*EF*, p. 56].

Jones, Robert; "Myth and Symbol Among the Nacirema Tsigoloicos;" *American Sociologist*; Vol. 15: 207-212; (1980).

activity, it encourages individual confirmation of experience. The electronic media develop different ways of organizing experience. Television viewing is multisensory and involves the viewer more than print does. Because television is a shared experience, it draws individuals together as members of the global village. McLuhan described the generation gap of the 1960s as a conflict between these two modes of thought. Parents who grew up in a print culture and children who grew up with television inevitably saw the world differently.

Alvin Toffler, in *Future Shock* (1971), described changes in social patterns resulting from technological and environmental change. A film explaining his main points was released soon after his book. Shortly after the film's release, many of the changes Toffler described had become "old hat." Sociology students who had grown up in the electronic age were accustomed to Toffler's formerly radical ideas and saw nothing new in his thesis.

CULTURAL DIFFUSION

The influence of the media, the ease of international travel and the multinational corporation have all contributed to a blurring of international cultural distinctions. In a way never before possible, we witness international events in politics or sports as they happen. We are surrounded by evidence of cultural diffusion. American popular culture is really a universal popular culture. One can eat Kentucky Fried Chicken in Nairobi, watch *I Love Lucy* in Scandinavia and discuss American films in Bulgaria. And even in the heart of West Africa, one need never go without Coca-Cola.

As business is increasingly conducted in an international environment, the idea of cultural diffusion has taken on a more popular meaning. For example, part of Japan's great economic success in the postwar years is attributed to that country's uncanny ability to adopt those Western business techniques which could be easily integrated into Japanese life and reject others. Indeed, many Japanese managers travelled to the United States in the 1950s and 60s to study the successful American management model. Ironically, by the 1980s the pattern was reversed. Western managers were seeking ways of adapting Japanese techniques to the North American business environment. Recently several books[2] have praised the Japanese model, which places far more emphasis on human resource development than has been typical in North America. About 35 percent of Japan's workforce will spend their entire working life with the same employer. Employees are usually reassigned or retrained rather than laid off when jobs become obsolete or the economy slumps. Management–worker relations are more apt to be collaborative than adversarial. These more egalitarian relationships are symbolized by such practices as uniform dress for all, line workers and managers alike.

According to some analysts, the success of a few exemplary American companies results from their use of management techniques similar to those employed in Japanese companies: for example, quality circles, semiautonomous work groups and job rotation.

SYMBOLIC CHANGE

Raymond Breton (1984) argues that much of the recent change in Canada is change in the symbolic order. In a society where most people share a symbol system, attempts to reinforce that system will have an integrating effect. Breton's point is that Canada is different because Canada is a binational, multicultural country. Restructuring the symbolic environment involves introducing new symbolic elements and breaking with the past to form a new collective identity.

From Breton's perspective, the symbolic environment of Canadian society until World War II was primarily British. This was reflected in Canada's social institutions, language, customs and the symbols which represented Canadian culture. Various conflicts developed as non-British groups struggled to control their own educational systems or media, but, except for the French, none of these were particularly successful. Once this symbolic environment was well established, cultural pluralism was less threatening. In the postwar years, Quebec's Francophone protest increased. "Their intense feeling was that Canadian society was not their society, its institutions not their institutions, its meanings and symbols, not their meanings and symbols" (Breton, 1984:129).

The institutional elites responded by trying to change the symbolic environment. Some of the changes involved changing the symbols themselves: The flag was changed; *O Canada* was named the national anthem; money and stamps were redesigned and the constitution (the *British* North America Act) was repatriated.

Public response to these changes was mixed. Some saw them as positive developments, but others resisted or opposed them. Those who opposed felt a sense of symbolic loss, a reaction which is understandable since symbolic change inevitably involves conflict.

In the following section, we will focus specifically on several dimensions of Canadian culture: Americanization, regionalism, ethnic pluralism and multiculturalism. Breton's discussion of symbolic change is an apt introduction to these themes.

[2] For example, William Ouchi, *Theory Z: How American Business Can Meet the Japanese Challenge* (Addison-Wesley, 1980); and Richard T. Pascale and Anthony Athos, *The Art of Japanese Management* (Simon and Schuster, 1981).

CANADIAN CULTURE

It is quite difficult to describe the cultures of complex, highly differentiated modern societies such as ours. The extent of cultural diffusion in technology and in popular culture via the mass media makes the material and nonmaterial cultures of the advanced industrial countries very homogenous. Furthermore, in countries like Canada, the United States and Australia, with large immigrant populations, distinctive elements of culture are difficult to identify. In Canada, the overwhelming presence of the United States makes it even more difficult to define our uniqueness.

It was popular in the past to describe Canadian society as a *mosaic* and the United States as a *melting pot*. This was supposed to convey the importance of ethnic pluralism in Canada, as opposed to the assimilation model in the United States. More recent comparisons found that the differences between these two countries in their policies towards immigrants are not as distinct as they once appeared. Some groups are more readily assimilated, and some groups resist assimilation in both Canada and the United States. Furthermore, the recent phenomenon of "ethnic rediscovery" is more or less universal, related more to an increased awareness of ethnic and racial inequalities than to a celebration of culture (Porter, 1979). Nevertheless, both our proximity to the United States and our ethnic composition are fundamental aspects of our sense of ourselves as Canadians. In the following sections, we will describe how Americanization, regionalism and multiculturalism have shaped and continue to shape the Canadian identity.

THE AMERICANIZATION OF CANADIAN CULTURE

In a recent article, Ogmundson (1980:1) argued that "a central aspect of the Canadian experience—Americanization—has received insufficient attention from academic social scientists in Canada, especially those involved in the study of culture and ethnicity." He thinks Canadian sociologists recognize our economic and political dependance on the United States but not that country's cultural domination of Canada. Unlike the analyses of bilingualism, multiculturalism or discrimination, Americanization has been all but ignored. Yet, American domination of our cultural industries, such as publishing, (including textbook publishers), film making, art and television means that Canadian popular culture is largely American. Thus, Ogmundson argues, we can study anglophone Canadians with the models used to study other American minority groups. In his view,

> It may well make very little sense to study Canada as a separate sociological entity. Rather it seems more sensible to study Canadian culture, and its various subcultures, in the same way that we study the disappearing cultures of the Inuit, the Indian, the Franco-Manitoban—as declining group(s) within a larger system (1980:3).

This analysis seems particularly negative to Canadian nationalists. On the other hand, it is clear that the media—the purveyors of our culture—*are* indisputably American dominated.

THE MEDIA AND CANADIAN IDENTITY

Frederick Elkin (1983) looked specifically at the question of the media and our national identity. He argues that there are powerful internal and external forces that support a strong national identity and other forces which work against it. Elkin considered those forces which stem from mass communications. He began by describing what he means by a Canadian national identity.

> We assume a close link between culture and identity. An identity that stems from any collectivity implies some distinctive cultural elements. To experience the Canadian identity implies at least a concern with some things considered Canadian, and may imply a complete absorption in Canadian institutions and Canadian problems. For most Canadians it probably includes a concern with Canada vis-à-vis other countries on the international scene; an interest in federal government politics, federal-provincial relationships, political parties, and leading political figures; an awareness of problems associated with the Arctic, Quebec, western energy resources, and the native peoples; a familiarity with a unique history and geography; an enjoyment of the popular culture associated with Canadian entertainment stars and distinctive holidays; and an interest in Canadian participation in international and professional sports such as hockey, football (including the Grey Cup), baseball, and soccer—all of which are given considerable attention in the mass media.
>
> We assume too a close link between the collective identity applied to a nation, large group or institution and the individual identity, experienced by those who make up the collectivity. For the individual, the image of the group is internalized and is part of the psychological world that enters into his or her sentiments, thoughts, and behavior. A Canadian success is experienced with pleasure and a Canadian failure with a sense of loss (Elkin, 1983:148). (This material is copyright of Addison-Wesley Publishers Ltd. and is used here by permission of the Publisher. All rights reserved.)

When Canadians are free to choose, most prefer American films, magazines, television programs and books, and the Canadian government has been disinclined to restrict the amount of American media penetration in Canada. The availability of American products "reinforces American influence and presumably weakens Canadian identity as such" (Elkin, 1983:149). The strongest internal force mitigating against a strong national identity is the French-English duality of language and culture. Separate public and private media organizations serve these two communities, and the separateness of communities is emphasized by language differences. Multiculturalism also operates against a strong national identity. For many of the 25 percent of Canadians whose cultural heritage is neither English nor French, maintaining their own language and culture has become an important concern. What we commonly call the ethnic media serve audiences which Elkin estimates number into the millions. Finally, Elkin describes how regional sentiments, particularly those expressed in separatist movements, act, in some contexts, as divisive forces. Opposing these divisive elements are the integrative forces of public institutions and regulating bodies. The Canadian Radio-Television and Telecommunications Commission, the CRTC, regulates all broadcasting in Canada. This agency controls the amount of foreign ownership (limited to 20 percent) and foreign content (30 percent of all music played on Canadian radio stations and 60 percent of all television content must be Canadian). Organizations such as the CBC and the Canadian Press have especially emphasized Canadian content.

REGIONALISM

Canadian sociologist Bernard Blishen (1978) asked a large sample of Canadians the following question: "Some people say they are (name of province of residence) first, and Canadian second, while others say they are Canadian first and (name of province of residence) second. How would you describe yourself? Canadian first, provincial first, both equally, neither, other (specify), don't know." French-speaking Quebec residents were asked the following question. "Comment vous définessez-vous *en tout premier lieu*: comme un Canadien-français, un Québecois, un Canadien tout simplement, ou autrement?" The results of this study indicate that most Canadians have a stronger national than regional identity. The two groups with strong regional identities were French-speaking residents of Quebec and non-French residents of the Maritimes. Interestingly, at the time of this survey, when separatist sentiment in Quebec was high, only 30 percent of the respondents identified themselves as Quebecois first.

If these attitudes are representative, many Canadians feel a strong regional identity. In the past, regional differences have been described in terms of economic indicators, but, as Matthews (1982:91) argues, regional disparity is also a social and cultural phenomenon. "Regionalism . . . refers to a sense of identification of consciousness-of-kind which inhabitants of a particular territorial area feel for that territorial area, and/or for their fellow inhabitants of that region" (1982:86). While the study of regional cultures has not been a major thrust in Canadian sociology, it seems that most Canadians recognize regional inequality but nevertheless prefer their own region, regardless of its economic opportunities (Schwartz, 1974).

ETHNIC PLURALISM

One important dynamic of Canada's population structure is its ethnic composition. In the early years of this century, 90 percent of Canada's population were British or French. Now these two groups account for less than 75 percent of the population. Of the remaining 25 percent, the largest immigrant groups are Germans, Italians and Ukrainians. All other immigrant groups, as well as Canada's two indigenous populations, account for 2 percent or less of the current population. In Chapter 9, you will consider Canadian ethnic and racial relations in detail. Here we will look briefly at the issue of *ethnic identity*.

Ethnic identity has been defined as "a socio-psychological process by which in-dividuals or groups subjectively include themselves in a community of their alleged ancestors or predecessors, who shared a distinct culture" (Isajiw, 1983:108). Eth-nicity is one among several social categories, including age, sex, social class, nation-ality and so on, the total of which constitutes an individual's *social identity*. In a sense, these categories help us "locate" ourselves and those with whom we interact. Sometimes these categories are based on *stereotypes*—the positive and negative images we have of ourselves and others. Depending on the nature of our social interaction, some social categories will be more important than others. In other words, some categories have greater salience than others at different times. *Ethnic salience*, as defined by Mackie and Brinkerhoff (1984:117) is "the importance an individual attaches to being ethnic," a definition which draws attention to the fact that "ethnicity is a variable, whose salience is situational" (1984:117). In other words, ethnic identity will be more important in some situations than in others.

Mackie and Brinkerhoff (1984) used a sample of University of Calgary students to investigate ethnic salience. When the students were asked how they usually thought of their own identity, 54.8 percent responded, "Canadian"; 19.2 percent named an ethnic group; and the remaining 19.2 percent gave a hyphenated response (i.e., Italian-Canadian)—if these response categories were provided. But, when asked how they would define their ethnicity, 33 percent of the students gave no response when the question was open-ended. Only 4.4 percent of the group chose ethnicity from a list of five social identities as the "most important aspect" of themselves. The other more important identities were gender (62.3 percent), citizenship (17.1 percent) and religion (12.5 percent). Ethnicity was more salient for women than for men, for working-class than for middle-class students and predictably was higher for those born outside of North America.

As noted earlier, the cross-cultural diffusion of technologies and ideas and the "internationalization" of popular culture has tended to blur differences between cultures. Within Canada, these same processes promote assimilation. In Porter's view (1979a:125), both Canada and the United States face a similar dilemma over ethnic identity. "(O)n the one hand if they value and emphasize ethnicity, mobility and opportunity are endangered, on the other hand if they emphasize mobility and opportunity, it will be at the cost of submerging cultural identity." Perhaps this dilemma is most acute for indigenous groups. Although many Native Americans remain isolated from mainstream Canadian society, Gerber's (1979) research shows that others are making some economic headway, either as individuals or through community development projects. In most cases, Gerber argues, this has not threatened the survival of reserve communities, nor does it necessarily diminish ethnic identity. "The elaborate provincial and national organizations and the proliferation of developing Indian communities indicate that assimilation and integration at one level are accompanied by ethnic differentiation at another" (Gerber, 1979:420). As Isajiw (1983:109) says: "Assimilation and retention of ethnic identity are not necessarily contradictory, zero-sum processes, that is, that the more one assimilates, the less one retains identity, and vice versa." Rather, he argues, ethnic identity will have a different meaning for each generation. Ethnic subcultures are no more resistant to change than are dominant cultures. While we all tend to romanticize the past, or in Marshall McLuhan's terms, see life in "the rear-view mirror," no modern culture remains static. For young people, ethnic identity may be more a matter of not wanting to lose sight of cultural traditions and historical roots without necessarily wanting to retain traditional life styles or life patterns.

MULTICULTURALISM

In October, 1971, Prime Minister Trudeau announced the initiation of a policy of "multiculturalism within a bilingual framework." This policy was to encourage the expression of non-English, non-French cultures in Canada. The incentive for such a policy arose out of the Royal Commission on Bilingualism and Biculturalism. Representatives of Canada's "other" ethnic groups told the commission that their interests would be overshadowed by a policy of dualism. A policy of multiculturalism, on the other hand, would better reflect Canada's ethnic diversity.

The federal government's multicultural policy supported ethnic publications, conferences, festivals and so on. Critics argue that most of the support has been for specific projects and that long term effects are difficult to determine. Isajiw (1983) has said that there are two other important conceptions of multiculturalism. The first calls for the institutionalization of selected minority-ethnic activities within the mainstream of Canadian society. For example, in academic circles, we have seen the formation of the Canadian Ethnic Studies Association. The other way of thinking of multiculturalism, according to Isajiw, is as a set of values which oppose prejudice and discrimination and which support equal opportunity. While this has not been a major thrust of Canada's attempt at multiculturalism, some initiatives have been taken to reduce interracial or interethnic tensions through public education.

Perhaps it is too soon to judge the Canadian government's policy on multiculturalism. The amount of money allocated has not been great, and the issue has been overshadowed by fundamental economic problems. Certainly, the criticisms have been strongly stated. Those on the left argue that the policy only serves to appease. Others, including John Porter (1979:133), an eminent Canadian sociologist, oppose multiculturalism because they feel that, while bilingualism may survive (given enough support), neither biculturalism nor multiculturalism are compatible with the post-industrial phase we are entering in the 1980s.

SUMMARY

Two seemingly contradictory points have been made about the study of culture. First, culture is a fundamental concept in sociological analysis. But the current generation of sociologists has neglected the systematic study of culture partly because culture is such an all-encompassing feature of social life. On the other hand, the research cited throughout this chapter shows that culture remains a key reference point in any sociological analysis.

While most sociologists agree about the importance of values, norms, beliefs, ideologies and expressive symbols, these are given more or less emphasis by different researchers. *Functionalists* tend to emphasize core values, norms and beliefs and the ways these are institutionalized. *Marxists* focus on the way dominant ideologies frame and legitimize existing social arrangements. *Interactionists* focus on the symbolic expressive aspects of culture.

In complex societies such as ours, some values and beliefs will be shared (more or less) universally. But unless these are challenged, we are usually unaware of their strength. Our day-to-day interactions are more directly influenced by the norms of the subcultures or groups of which we are members. Four subcultures were discussed in this chapter: the culture of poverty, youth culture, the culture of a professional group and corporate cultures.

The section on cultural change described the effects of the introduction of new technologies and new symbols. However, neither of these factors alone can account for the rhythms of cultural change, for their influence cannot be isolated from the myriad other factors that affect us. Perhaps the complexity of modern social life and the interdependency of modern cultures eludes traditional analysis. John Porter may have been right when he suggested:

> What of cultures? Cultures are traditionbound. Anthropologists view cultures as established ways of doing things, or of viewing the world, or as designs for living and survival passed from generation to generation, and, while for societies more simply organized than those of today, the role that cultures played and for many continue to play was important, they are less and less relevant for the postindustrial society because they emphasize yesterday rather than tomorrow. Can cultures of the past serve societies facing the coming of post-industrialism? The one recurring theme in many of the analyses of the next twenty-five years is the rapidity of change, of the shock of the future. One can almost speak of the end of culture, as some have written of the end of ideology. Many of the historic cultures are irrelevant to our futures. Opportunity will go to those individuals who are future-oriented in an increasingly universalistic culture. Those oriented to the past are likely to lose out. (From THE MEASURE OF CANADIAN SOCIETY by John Porter, p. 133. Copyright © 1979 by Gage Publishing Limited. Used by permission.)

DISCUSSION QUESTIONS

1. Describe a subculture you are familiar with. Your family might be an interesting group to focus on. What norms, values, beliefs and expressive symbols characterize this group?

2. What symbols differentiate Canadian, American and British cultures? How are these different from non-Western cultural symbols?

3. Compare stereotypes of Americans and Canadians. Think of the stereotypes you hold of other cultural groups. Where do these ideas originate? How are they perpetuated?

4. Working with a group of students from different faculties (music, arts, business, etc.) develop an inventory of style differences which characterize members of different faculties in your school. Do professors implicitly encourage these differences?

5. Observe people in a public area of your university. How do differences in dress, demeanor and argot serve as symbols of exclusion and inclusion?

6. Consider the feminist claim that language is sexist. In your next written assignment, consciously avoiding using sexist terminology (i.e., the generic "he").

7. Consider your initiation to university life as a process of acculturation. How did initiation week activities help to establish group cohesion? In what ways could this adjustment be made easier?

8. Gerbner feels that the media create a symbolic environment which defines a world view and a value system. While watching your favourite television drama, imagine what someone unfamiliar with Western culture would learn from it. Try to list some of these *cultural indicators*.

9. Discuss the issue of assimilation with a first-generation immigrant. How does he or she feel about the dilemma of maintaining cultural identity described by Porter?

10. Using Mackie and Brinkerhoff's study as a guide, do a mini-study to measure ethnic salience among your colleagues.

4

Socialization

Susannah Wilson

INTRODUCTION

Peter Berger (1975:55) called socialization the process by which we learn to become members of society. For all of us this process starts at birth an continues throughout our lives. Because much of this learning goes on in the early years of an individual's life, sociologists distinguish primary from secondary socialization. *Primary socialization* occurs from birth to adolescence. And, as Berger points out, because children have less power than adults and because they are unaware of alternatives, early socialization is largely imposed. In satisfying a newborn infant's needs—even such a basic need as food—parents respond within a framework of culturally defined expectations. If an infant is fed according to a schedule, the baby will learn to be hungry at "feeding time." "The same observation pertains to elimination, to sleeping and to other physiological processes that are endemic to the organism" (Berger, 1975:50). Consequently, while we will all develop individual likes and dislikes, even our early experiences of hunger, pain and comfort are mitigated by the social world into which we are born.

Secondary socialization is the ongoing process of learning to adjust to new situations. At key transition points, such as entering or leaving the labour force or becoming parents or grandparents, we learn new role expectations and adjust our behaviour to these. While sociologists have been most concerned with primary socialization, socialization continues throughout the life cycle. In effect, we are not talking about one, but a series of processes. Because adults bring to new situations the accumulated learning of their previous experiences, including certain preconceptions about each new role, secondary socialization differs from primary socialization.

During childhood, members of our family have the greatest influence on our socialization. But, beginning sometimes at an early age, child-care workers, teachers, friends and the mass media also help shape our basic beliefs and values.

Socialization establishes boundaries of behaviour. Because of this, there are similarities in the way individuals in certain cultural settings mature. But we are all individuals, so people react differently to similar experiences. Some children thrive on routine; others resent it. Some grow up wanting to be like their parents; others react against these models. As children mature, and their interactions outside the family increase, they recognize differences in the behaviour, speech and values of the people they encounter. Even within our families there are fundamentally different behavioural expectations for men and women, old and young. We gradually learn how our own views are relative. One interesting thing about meeting people from different cultural backgrounds is learning how their definitions of social reality differ from ours. In fact, much of social research, particularly studies using participant observation, is designed to make these differences explicit.

In the previous chapter, we called socialization the process by which we internalize cultural norms. In large part, cross-cultural differences in language, customs and values reflect differences in how we have been socialized. While recognizing that parents are individuals who have specific goals and expectations for their children, we can see that socialization is also influenced by structural variables. How we are socialized will depend on whether we grew up in Vancouver or Moncton; whether we spoke English or Ukrainian at home; and whether we worshipped at a church or a synagogue. In a sense, socialization is a restriction. "The values, beliefs, assumptions, and ways of life that come to be 'second nature' to children make it difficult for them to function effectively in some kinds of social situations involving persons who have been socialized in other subcultures" (Elkin and Handel, 1978:74). This is particularly important when we consider class and sex differences in socialization. For example, if early socialization is based on traditional assumptions about the sexual division of labour, young women will place less importance on acquiring the kind of education most likely to lead to future job security. Some of the implications of gender differences in socialization are addressed in detail in Chapter 7.

Perhaps because of the intensity and importance of early learning, much of the socialization literature has focused on children. However, socialization can also be reciprocal. The idea of mutual learning seems evident when we consider the role of peer groups in socialization. It also seems clear that much of adult socialization involves reciprocity. As Peters (1985) argues, reciprocal socialization need not be restricted to interaction between peers. For example, in many ways children influence their parents or teachers. According to Peters, parental socialization (the socialization of parents by their children) will be optimal in families where affectivity is high, respect is good and where excessive parental power is not exercised. He also believes that parents' self-image will be influenced by their children's reactions to them as parents. Peters used a sample of parents of undergraduate students to test how adolescents socialize their parents. While several parents responded to questions by saying "I learned nothing from my adolescents," others said that their children influenced them. The area of greatest influence was sports, although adolescents also influenced parental involvement in politics, leisure and personal care. They also influenced their parents' attitudes to sexuality, handicapped persons, minorities and drugs.

In summary, we can make four general points about socialization. First, socialization continues throughout the life cycle. Secondly, it is a reciprocal process. Thirdly, how we are socialized will depend largely on our social class, our ethnicity, our sex, our religion. Finally, although we normally refer to parents, the media, education and peer groups as the most important agents of socialization, socialization involves all of our interactions, whether formal or informal, conscious or not.

THEORIES OF SOCIALIZATION

As you become more familiar with sociology, you will see sociologists often disagree about the best way to analyse any social situation. This, of course, is not unique to sociology, although it has been argued that sociology differs from some other sciences in that no one perspective dominates. In the first chapter of this book, you read about several theoretical points of view within sociology and learned that the question sociologists ask and often the research methods they use depend on their theoretical orientation. Not all sociologists make the same distinctions when categorizing the extensive body of theoretical and empirical work done in their field.

Some sociologists begin with social structure as the unit of analysis, and others begin with individuals. The difference between them largely depends on what assumptions are made about human nature and the nature of social organization.

Dawe (1970:214) called these two approaches (1) the sociology of social system and (2) the sociology of social action. "One views action as the derivative of system whilst the other views system as the derivative of action."

In the past, some sociologists viewed socialization as more or less imposed on individuals. Others (likely most sociologists today) understand individuals are actively engaged in the process of socialization.[1]

In the following section, we will describe more specifically two contrasting views of socialization. The "action as derivative of system" approach is best represented in the work of American sociologist Talcott Parsons. The other way of understanding socialization, which focuses on individual actors creating meaning while involved in myriad social interactions relies most heavily on the perspective described in Chapter 1 as symbolic interactionism. George H. Mead (1863-1931) and Charles H. Cooley (1864-1929), two American sociologists, were key influences in developing the symbolic interactionist perspective. Perhaps more than any other theorists, these two men have influenced the way most sociologists understand socialization.

Socialization is a fundamental concern of sociologists because it provides a link between the individual and society. "From the point of view of the individual, interaction with other people is the means by which human potentialities are actualized. From the point of view of society, socialization explains how commitment to the social order is maintained over time" (Mackie, 1982:83).

PARSONS' FUNCTIONALIST VIEW

For Parsons and for other functionalist sociologists, socialization is the process whereby individuals *internalize* socially approved norms and value. When individuals are properly socialized, they develop into "normal, conforming, socially acceptable and socially approved adults" (Boughey, 1978:104). Deviants have failed to internalize accepted codes of behaviour. Thirty years ago, deviants were assumed to have been improperly socialized. Now it seems simplistic to assume that, even within certain social groups, there are established and generally agreed upon rules of behaviour. Critics of this "top-down" view of socialization point out that the meanings we attach to social behaviour are not universal but are situated in many social contexts. The emphasis on individual conformity to group norms amounts, as Wrong (1961:183–193) pointed out, to "an oversocialized view of man" and presumably of women as well. To say that we are all socialized does not, however, imply that we have been completely moulded by the norms and values of our culture.

THE SYMBOLIC INTERACTIONIST PERSPECTIVE

Symbolic interaction focuses on the *processes* of socialization and the ways individuals actively participate in this process. Both Charles H. Cooley and George H. Mead were interested in how individuals develop a sense of self and the importance of family interaction in this process. Cooley believed children were born with an instinctual capacity for *self* development and that this matured in interactions in primary

---

[1] On the other hand, empirical studies of socialization seem to be dominated by the determinist viewpoint, perhaps because of the strong influence functionalism has played in the professional socialization of most academic sociologists.

groups. For Cooley, primary groups are "characterized by intimate face to face association and cooperation" (1909:23). These interactions Cooley called *nursuries of human nature*. Once infants have gained control over their immediate environment, they begin to develop a sense of self, or what Cooley called an *I-feeling*.

Adults communicate their attitudes and values to their children primarily through language, and children understand themselves based on these interactions. In other words, we begin to see ourselves as we imagine others see us. This feeling, "I feel about me the way I think you think of me," Cooley called the *looking-glass self*, which he said has three elements. This awareness involves: "the imagination of our appearance to the other person; the imagination of his judgement of that appearance; and some sort of self-feeling, such as pride or mortification" (1902:184). Cooley was pointing out the importance of the *perceptions* of others' reactions to us in determining how we feel about ourselves. No doubt we can all think of instances where our intentions were misread or when we have misunderstood the approval or disapproval of others.

One important problem raised by Mead deals with how we become sensitive to the responses of others (Campbell, 1975:10). How do we learn to present ourselves in different social situations? According to Mead, we learn symbolically, through role-taking. At first, a child's behaviour is a combination of instinctual behaviour and imitation. This Mead called the *pre-play stage*. Later, during the *play stage*, children learn to assume the roles of others and to objectify that experience by seeing themselves from the others' point of view. In the next stage, the *game stage*, children learn to handle several roles at once and thus to anticipate the behaviour of others. Finally, children learn to internalize general social expectations by imagining how any number of others will act and react. At this *generalized other stage*, the child has a sense of self and can react in a socially approved way.

As young children experience the approval and disapproval of those around them, they begin to understand what is expected of them. This more conventional, controlled and socially conscious part of self Mead called the *me*. The *I*, on the other hand, is more impulsive and individualistic.

The concepts of the self introduced by Cooley and Mead are difficult to substantiate with empirical investigation and have been criticized for this reason. However, two studies of students' self-concepts tested the idea that the self is developed through social interaction. Miyamoto and Dornbusch (1956) asked students to rate themselves and other members of their group in terms of intelligence, self-confidence, physical attractiveness and likeableness. Each student was also asked to rate how they thought each other group member would rate them. The researchers found more similarity between the students' ratings of themselves and their *perceptions* of how others would rate them than between their perceptions and the actual ratings given by their peers. In a more recent replication of this study, Quarentelli and Cooper (1966) followed a panel of dental students from entrance to graduation. This second study found that the correspondence between self-concept and the perceptions of others' opinions remained the same for the duration of the study, indicating that this relationship is not transitory. Their general conclusion supports Mead's theory. The *perceived* views of others, not their actual opinions, influence our self-concepts.

The views of Erving Goffman will be discussed in a later chapter. However, he added an important twist to the understanding of socialization which bears mentioning here. Goffman agreed with Mead that the self is created in social interaction. As we have seen, for Mead, this involved a relatively straightforward process of role-taking. Goffman, on the other hand, saw social interaction as something individuals learned with difficulty. He called this process *impression management*.

CLASS AND SOCIALIZATION

In the previous chapter, we described Oscar Lewis's ideas about a culture of poverty. Lewis argued that poor children in Western countries are socialized to respond to their environment in certain ways. "By the time slum children are six or seven they have usually absorbed the basic attitudes and values of their subculture" (Lewis, 1966:21). Lewis's critics say that the behavioural patterns he observed are just adaptations to a particular set of circumstances. Whether or not one agrees with Lewis, there do seem to be class differences in socialization.

A series of sociological studies done in the United States has found consistent differences in parental values which seem related to the occupations of parents. "White-collar occupations are characterized by low supervision, an emphasis on people or ideas rather than objects, and a relatively high degree of self-reliance" (Ellis, Lee and Petersen 1979:387). Consequently, white-collar parents tend to place a high value on self-reliance in their children. In contrast, the occupational experiences of blue-collar parents mean they will place a high value on conformity in their children. Anthropologists studying cross-cultural patterns of socialization have found similar differences. It seems that self-reliance is valued in hunting and gathering societies, whereas conformity is valued in agricultural societies. Thus, research in both disciplines suggests that "where adults are closely supervised in their economic, political or family roles, they tend to value conformity in their children; where they are more autonomous in these roles, self-reliance becomes a primary socialization value" (Ellis, Lee and Petersen, 1979:390). Ellis, Lee and Petersen tested this idea with data from 122 different cultures and found a universal relationship between autonomy for adults and the value of self-reliance in children.

Another study (Alwin, 1984) found that parents now place a higher value on autonomy than they did a generation ago. Public opinion surveys done in Detroit in 1958, 1971 and 1983 revealed some interesting differences. Parents were asked:

If you had to choose, which thing would you pick as the most important for a child to learn to prepare him for life?
a) to obey
b) to be well-liked or popular
c) to think for himself
d) to work hard
e) to help others when they need help

Respondents were asked to rank their top four choices. Alwin found "To think for himself" was the most preferred quality and that the number of parents citing this as most important increased over time. Being well-liked was the least preferred and this became less important over time. Obedience decreased in importance, but hard work increased. The number of parents who valued being helpful remained stable. Since the change was due primarily to shifting attitudes among Roman Catholic respondents, Alwin concluded that the differences were due to the increased assimilation of ethnic group members who were Roman Catholic.

Another way to look at the relationship between class and socialization is to focus on children's perceptions of social class differences and the ways these are legitimized. An American study (Lauer, 1974) discovered that even children in grade two could rank occupations by prestige. Furthermore, the children's ranking closely resembled the rankings established in national studies, and the accuracy of the ranking increased with the ages of the children. "By the time we reach grade six, the rank correlation is nearly .9 and the children are quite capable of legitimating the ranking by reference to occupational functioning, prerequisites, and rewards. . . . Thus, beginning in the home and continuing in the school, these children have been socialized to accept the inequalities implied in the ranking and to perpetuate them through legitimating reasons (Lauer 1974:179, 181).

In a study of Toronto-area children, Baldus and Tribe (1978) used pictures and stories to assess young children's perceptions of social inequality. The pictures were presented in sets. The first set showed two men, one well dressed and one casually dressed. The children were also shown pictures of two houses (one taken in a high-income area of the city, one in a working-class area), two different living rooms, and two cars (one old and one new and expensive). Children in grades one, three and six played a game matching the sets of pictures. Children's ability to match correctly increased with age but was not affected by the children's sex, their school environment or their parents' social class. The children also provided ready evaluations of the two men. The well-dressed man was described as cheerful, nice, intelligent and well liked. They described the casually dressed man as tough, lazy, likely to swear, steal or drink and not caring much about his family.

The researchers felt one of their most important findings was the similarity of response despite social class differences among the children, for these evaluations are keys to the children's self-concepts as well as to their evaluations of others.

There are, however, important social class differences in the socialization of boys and girls. Research evidence (summarized in Weitzman, 1984) concludes that working-class and lower-class families are more concerned about cultivating differences between boys and girls. Middle-class parents seem more concerned with developing a range of behavioural traits in their children, whether boys or girls. In the following section, we will look more specifically at these kinds of differences.

SEX-ROLE SOCIALIZATION

Three main determinants of status in most cultures are age, sex and social class. The preceding section described how social class differences are related to differences in socialization. While many sociologists do not agree with Lewis, accumulated research findings describe social class differences in socialization *practices*. Later in this chapter, we will describe how socialization changes throughout the life cycle. This analysis assumes that as we learn new roles, we internalize society's expectations about *age specific* behaviours. In this section, we will focus on sex-role socialization, a topic which has received a great deal of research attention.

Traditionally, differences between men and women were assumed to be based on natural or biological differences between the sexes. Much research was devoted to specifying the nature of these differences. In the 1970s this presumption was carefully scrutinized. Analysis of previous research findings by Maccoby and Jacklin (1974)— who reviewed over 1400 studies—and others, revealed that many behavioural and attitudinal differences once thought to be based on biological propensities were, in fact, learned capacities. Recently, biological determinism has received a new lease on life. However, when we encounter determinist views, we should keep in mind that scientific discoveries have a political context. The current swing back to determinism should be seen as a reflection of deep-seated resistance to change (Oakley, 1981). Feminists like Rossi (1984) also argue that some sex differences are influenced by biology, and that at certain points in time (i.e., during puberty or pregnancy), biological processes are more important than at other times. Rossi feels that if we correctly identify these differences, they can be the basis of conpensatory socialization for both females and males. Chapter 7 will describe these findings in greater detail.

Research evidence suggests that *gender* (learned) differences are much more significant than *sex* (biological) differences. Gender differences refer to psychological traits such as intuition, dependance or aggression usually associated with masculinity or femininity.

Most societies attach importance to both sex and gender differences. Some expectations will be more or less universal (usually those related to childrearing and economic roles); others will vary from culture to culture. In every society, these expectations are based on stereotypes. Sex stereotyping begins before birth. The size, the activity and the position of the fetus are presumed to be related to its sex. While prenatal sex differences may largely be based on folklore, it is clear that strong reinforcement of gender stereotypes takes place almost from the moment of birth. Rubin, Provenzano and Luria (1974) interviewed parents of newborn children within 24 hours of the birth. Although the babies were similar in size and other physical characteristics, they were described very differently by their parents. Daughters were described as "softer, finer featured, weaker, smaller, prettier, more inattentive, more awkward, and more delicate." Sons, on the other hand, were described as "firmer, larger featured, better co-ordinated, more alert, stronger and hardier." Thus, the stage is set within the first hours of life. Furthermore, the male children are still seen as more desirable than female children. Oakley (1981:95) asked London women expecting their first child what sex they preferred. Fifty-four percent said boys; 22 percent said girls and the rest didn't care. After the children were born, 93 percent of those who had boys were pleased, but 44 percent of those who had girls were disappointed. When my own daughter was born in 1979, I was stunned when one of the nurses remarked, "Oh well, maybe you'll have better luck next time."

Cooley and Mead identified the importance of early interaction with family members, or *significant others*, to use Mead's phrase. They did not, however, explore the process of developing a sexual identity. The following paragraphs describe several psychological theories of personality development as they relate to gender identification. (More detailed descriptions are found in O'Connell, 1979; and Mackie, 1982.)

PSYCHOANALYTIC THEORY

Freud identified several stages of psychological development: oral, anal, phallic, latent and genital. Sexual differences in development began, for Freud, with the phallic stage, when both boys and girls resolve their early attachment to their mothers. A boy sees his father as a rival for his mother's affection, but fears this rivalry will lead to castration—as he assumes it has for girls. Fear of castration is the mechanism for resolving a boy's Oedipal complex. Resolving the Oedipal complex by identifying with his father develops a strong superego in a boy. A girl's discovery that she is missing a penis leads her to blame her mother and desire her father. For a girl, however, the Oedipal complex is not easily resolved. Consequently, female superegos are weaker. Thus, for Freud, personality differences are rooted in physiological differences, specifically, in the awareness of having or not having a penis. Such biological determinism was strongly criticized by Freud's contemporaries and by others who agree with other tenets of his psychoanalytic theories. The theories of penis envy and fear of castration simply do not have empirical justification.[2]

IDENTIFICATION THEORY

Many psychologists have pursued the idea that normal development depends on identification with the same-sexed parent. However, it is difficult to demonstrate that young children will identify with a parent before they are aware of themselves as either male or female. Nor is it clear why boys would necessarily identify with fathers when, in most cases, they have more contact with mothers. For most children, parents are but two of many people they encounter, including, of course, the ever-present models on television.

SOCIAL LEARNING THEORY

Social learning theory says gender roles are learned through *reinforcement*. The process of gender learning presumably begins at birth, when children are labelled according to sex, and is reinforced throughout childhood. This reinforcement encourages children to generalize some behaviours and to avoid others. However, research has not found a strong association between the behaviour of children and the behaviour of their same-sexed parent. Children learn sex-specific behaviour, but it is not clear that they learn it exclusively, or even primarily, from their same-sexed parent, as the theory suggests.

COGNITIVE DEVELOPMENT THEORY

Cognitive development theory assumes that gender identity begins when children categorize themselves as either a boy or a girl. Usually this occurs late in the child's

[2] I cannot resist countering Freud's anecdotal evidence of penis envy with an observation made by my five-year-old daughter. As she said when she noticed her young brother pulling his penis in the bath: "Maybe he wants to pull it off so he can be like me."

Changing gender roles have blurred the rigid distinctions of the 1950s.

second year. After this, children are moved to behave in ways consistent with the gender label, and their attention is focused on same-sexed models. So for Kohlberg, the main proponent of this theory, social reinforcement is far less important in learning gender roles than cognitive development. While the social learning and cognitive development theories seem to correspond to our sense of how gender identity is acquired, both focus on *differences* in male/female behaviour.

Some recent approaches to sex-role socialization move beyond dichotomizing gender roles. For example, a series of studies (Bem, 1974) have focused on individuals who appear to have a balance of masculine and feminine characteristics. Bem calls such individuals *androgenous* and reports that one-third of those she has studied fit this description. Recent recognition of the restrictive nature of traditional male and female roles make alternative conceptualizations such as this attractive. Changes in women's roles, particularly in labour force participation, and the consequent increased involvement of men in domestic tasks have blurred the rigid sex-role distinctions of the 1950s. Even 20 years ago, it would have been impossible to imagine that, by the mid-1980s, thousands of young boys would be caring for their own Cabbage Patch dolls.

The women's movement has been responsible for many changes in what is expected of women and men. Both structural and ideological changes challenge traditional sex-role socialization, although some people will always prefer the "good old days." Kimball (1975) feels that there is some ambivalence in the messages young girls are receiving. They still seem to be presented with two choices: to be feminine *or* to be competent. The conflict this ambivalence produces, particularly in the face of the adolescent desire to be popular, may cause young women to make choices that will not maximize their future economic security. When journalist Ann Pappert (1980) visited a Toronto high school in 1979, she found that the main goal of most young women was marriage. They expected, perhaps like their mothers, to be gainfully employed for a short time before they had children. Lindell (1982) found that *working-class* high-school women were realistic about their probable future in the labour force (although they had no specific career plans) and so accepted the inevitability of day-care for their children. *Middle-class* students expected to leave the labour force when children arrived, an expectation which current labour-force trends suggest may not be realistic.

THE MASS MEDIA

The media has been strongly criticized for contributing to the stereotyping of gender roles. The results of hundred of studies of media content support this conclusion. Women are underrepresented, stereotyped and trivialized by the media. In an extensive study of sex-role socialization, Fischer and Cheyne (1977) concluded that the media are far more consistent in stereotyping women than either parents or the educational system. And children spend more time watching television than they do at school.

The role of the media in establishing similar stereotypes about social class differences has been less extensively studied. We know that the media exaggerate the number of professionals in the population. Younger "middle-Americans" are the most numerous protagonists in media drama. Nonwhites, like women, are underrepresented and stereotyped.

George Gerbner, whose studies of American television content were described in Chapter 3, feels strongly about the influence of television in socializing young people.

> Television is the central and most pervasive mass medium in American culture and it plays a distinctive and historically unprecedented role. Other media are accessible to the individual (usually at the point of literacy and mobility) only after the socializing functions of home and family life have begun. In the case of television, however, the individual is introduced virtually at birth into a powerful flow of messages and images. The television set has become a key member of the family, the one who tells most of the stories most of the time. Its massive flow of stories showing what things are, how things work, and what to do about them has become the common socializer of our times. These stories form a coherent if mythical "world" in every home. Television dominates the symbolic environment of modern life.(From Gerbner et al. "The Mainstreaming of America," *Journal of Communication* 30(3) p. 14.)

ADOLESCENT SOCIALIZATION

Some have suggested that adolescence was a creation of advertisers who "discovered" that young people had money to spend. Others have argued that the identification of this age group as distinct from others accompanied the latter stages of industrialization and the introduction of compulsory education. Whatever its origins, adolescence is clearly a social construct and not a natural stage of development.

In North America, we see adolescence as a period of change and ambivalence, growth and experimentation, in which young people gain independance from their families and prepare for adult reponsibilities. Simmons (Mortimer and Simmons, 1978) suggests that childhood socialization is primarily concerned with regulating biological drives, whereas adolescent socialization focuses on values and self-image. Because the period of economic dependence is prolonged in our society by increased education (and high youth unemployment), adolescence stretches well into the 20s.

Lyell (1973) argues that adolescent feelings of ambivalence and low self-esteem occur because, until people enter the labour force, their activities are not generally highly regarded. She used a *semantic differential scale* to test this assumption. She asked young people to score themselves on 25 adjective pairs (i.e., active-passive, strong-weak, good-bad), first, as they would like to be and second, as they really are. A high correspondence between these two ratings was taken to indicate high self-esteem. The four groups in the study were: young adult working males; young female adults who were not working; female adolescents who were not working; and male adolescents who were not working.

She found that working adult males felt more positively about themselves than the other three groups, all of whom showed considerable evidence of low self-esteem. Thus, Lyell argues, when adolescents are aloof, indifferent or apathetic, we should understand that these feelings result from their subordination to and exclusion from the formal occupational system.

The socialization theories described earlier relate specifically to childhood socialization and to the development of the self. Childhood socialization is presumed to be closely tied to interactions within the family, whereas adolescence, as Campbell (1975) describes it, involves a period of *unlearning*, as young people develop a sense of autonomy and independence. According to Campbell, the most significant experience of adolescence is "the demise in *relative* influence of the family as a reference group and the central emotional pillar" (1975:34). This does not mean that the family becomes unimportant. But the influence of peers, the media and the school is greater than ever before.

Parsons (1942) introduced the term *youth culture* over 40 years ago. Since then, sociologists and psychologists have debated whether adolescence is a transition period or whether this age group has a distinct culture. In Chapter 3, the study of British youth culture was described from the point of view of expressive symbols. North American studies of adolescent culture have usually adopted the framework of more traditional studies of subcultures as groups with distinct norms and values. In his study of Illinois high schools, Coleman (1961) described students as sharing an adolescent culture. Because adolescents spend a lot of time at school, or in school-related activities, many of which are unrelated to their formal education, and because most of their interactions involve others of the same age group, Coleman concluded that these young people have a distinct adolescent subculture. In this environment, popularity and athletics were valued above academic achievement, a finding Campbell sees as convincing evidence of a strong youth culture. "Only a youth culture of considerable strength could sustain antieducational and antiintellectual values in the very setting of an institution established to serve educational purposes!" (Campbell, 1975:40).

Tanner (1978) studied youth culture in five secondary schools in Edmonton, Alberta. Based on the findings of an earlier British study (Murdock and Phelps,

1973), Tanner hypothesized that "commitment to school is inversely associated with the two main variants of 'youth culture,' namely pop-media culture and street culture" (1978:91). The British study found that working-class boys with low commitment to school were likely to be oriented to a street culture, whereas middle-class students with low commitment (mainly girls) chose the pop-media culture as an alternative. Tanner's study tested this relationship in a Canadian setting.

Tanner operationally defined street culture as self-reported delinquency. He found that low commitment to school was related to high involvement in self-reported delinquency, that this was inversely related to socioeconomic status and that the relationship was stronger for boys than girls. In other words, working-class boys were the most likely to be involved in delinquent behaviour—if their commitment to school was low—and middle-class girls were least likely. No such straightforward relationship emerged concerning student commitment to school and their interest in popular music. School-rejecting boys were more involved in music than school-rejecting girls, but this was unrelated to social class. Tanner suggested that music *may* provide a more acceptable form of revolt for girls and middle-class school rejectors—although the two aspects of youth culture are not mutually exclusive.

Other sociologists are skeptical about the notion of a distinct youth culture. As Elkin and Handel (1978:231) argue, "With regard to fundamental values, the continuity of adolescent socialization with adulthood outweighs the discontinuity." Campbell's (1975:41-2) point is that there is considerable correspondence between parental and adolescent values. Because parents want their children to be well liked and because they want good relationships with their children, they are unlikely to strongly oppose too many aspects of the youth culture. In addition, the peer group's influence is tempered because parents control "scarce and valued resources," including their approval. Furthermore, Campbell says that early socialization has created important *cultural boundaries*. "By virtue of membership in a family, one is *assigned* to a social class, to a residential area, to a race, to a moral system, to a religion, to an ethnic tradition, to a social space" (1975:43). As children mature, they increase their contacts and experiences, but these will not be random events or associations. By and large, they will be compatible with previous experiences. It is, therefore, unlikely that the school environment will be very different from the environment the child already knows. Middle-class children will attend a high school with other middle-class children, who will likely value school achievement. Certainly, some students will rebel, but usually their defiance will not pose a significant challenge to parental values.

ADULT SOCIALIZATION

In the introductory paragraphs of this chapter, we noted that socialization is a life-long process. While this assumption meets with little argument, adult socialization has not been a major focus of research. Adult socialization differs from childhood socialization because children are more malleable. The accumulated learning of adults makes them more resistant to change. Nevertheless, as we change our jobs, marry, have children, cope with middle-age and so on, we are continually being socialized. Many of these changes are life-cycle changes, although the fact that we can predict

Rituals like graduation or marriage ceremonies help to signal changing status.

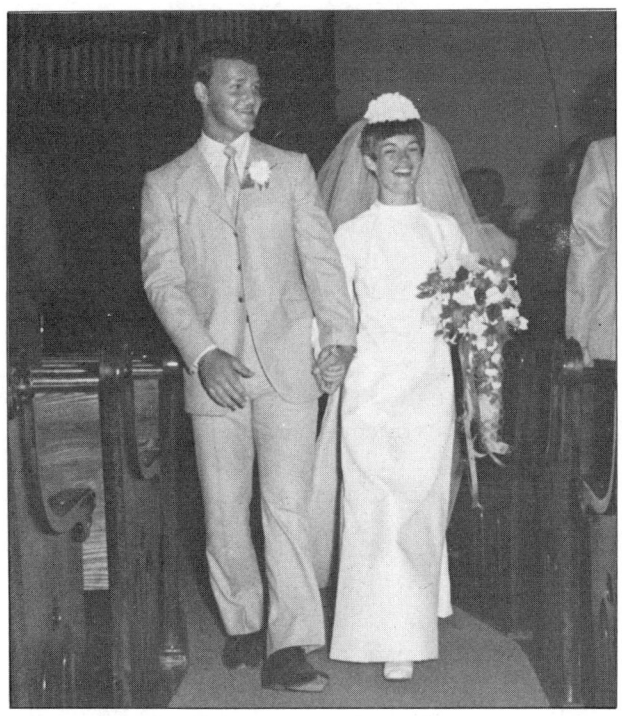

childbirth, retirement or widowhood does not mean that the adjustment will be easy. When these changes occur, individuals go through a period of *disengagement* as they change roles. The idea of disengagement has been used to describe the experience of widowhood and divorce, although it can describe any role change (Mortimer and Simmons, 1978). Rituals like graduation or marriage ceremonies help to signal changing status.

Some socialization is formal, as in the training we receive in professional schools or in work-related courses. Increasingly, formal training is available in areas previously left to the family, the schools or to other agents of socialization, or for which socialization was once taken for granted. Thus, new parents may feel inadequate without training in childbirth and later in child-care, and people anticipating retirement sign-up for courses in retirement training. In many ways, adult socialization is informal. Without being told, we quickly learn what standards of behaviour are expected in new social or work situations. Students, for example, are adept at cataloguing these kinds of differences in behaviour and using them in comparing universities.

In some cases, we can learn to adjust to new situations because our previous experiences gave us the capacity to imagine what new experiences will be like. Sociologists call this preparation *anticipatory socialization*. "Anticipatory socialization refers to training in skills and values that is oriented toward a new role that one will enter at some future time" (Campbell, 1975:47). The effectiveness of anticipatory socialization will depend on how ambiguous the new situation is and how similar to our previous experience.

Professional schools are important socializing agents for adults, and medical schools in particular have been studied in this regard. What students learn during these years goes beyond acquiring technical skills. They are learning how to behave like doctors. Some researchers have questioned whether professional schools play an important role in socializing students. They argue that the similarity of attitudes and values results from selective recruitment of middle- and upper-class students rather than socialization. In their panel study of Canadian medical students, Chappell and Colwill (1981) found that medical schools effectively change some attitudes. But they also found that students recruited to medical schools shared certain attitudes at the outset. Interestingly, these seemed unrelated to social class or sex. Although these researchers do not describe their findings in terms of anticipatory socialization, it seems that a medical student's orientation to the profession begins long before she enters medical school. If so, she will enter medical school with an orientation which is reinforced during her prolonged training period.

In most cases, we cannot anticipate what it will mean to our sense of self to experience the sudden death of someone we love, our parents' divorce or being fired. When we encounter these situations, we have to learn new rules. There are, however, occasions when people choose to, or are required to, change their behaviour in rather dramatic ways. This process is called *resocialization*. For example, when families or individuals relocate for school or work, they may find that their previous world view is fundamentally challenged. Wives of men who go to work in Arab countries find it extremely difficult to adjust to the many social restrictions placed on women there. Companies often expand considerable energy preparing employees for this culture shock. Sometimes, resocialization is occasioned by social changes that individuals cannot control, as when the nature of a job is completely altered by technology.

Generally, the term "resocialization" applies to the kind of learning that goes on in what Goffman (1967) called *total institutions*. Total institutions, like prisons, boarding schools or mental hospitals, make considerable effort to alter existing values and self-concepts. Because individuals are removed from familiar surroundings and because their daily routines are altered to conform to the goals of the institution, the changes in behaviour can be dramatic.

Seiber and Gordon (1981) introduced the idea of *socializing organizations* as a way of understanding socialization. Socializing organizations include total institutions, as well as schools, job-training programs, counselling centres and voluntary associations. These organizations are formally chartered to bring about some change in their members, but often the explicitly stated aims are less important than the latent messages they send. "As recruits participate in the organization they learn its social and speech etiquettes, modes of self-presentation, rituals, routines, symbolic codes of deference, and other patterns of social relations" (Seiber and Gordon, 1981:7). Sometimes, there is a formal period of orientation designed to facilitate this kind of learning. An extreme example is the introduction to military training usually referred to as "boot camp." Universities customarily hold orientation weeks, where "recruits" are introduced to the informal side of university life.

Much of adult socialization is self-initiated. When adults join organizations like Weight Watchers, Parents Without Partners or homophile groups, for example, they do so because they seek the social support these groups provide. It is during transition periods that this support is most needed. The consciousness raising groups that characterized the women's movement in the 1960s provided forums for women to discuss the changes they were experiencing. The human potential movement of the 1970s also had a significant impact on changing values and beliefs. One social analyst (Yankelovich, 1981) estimated that as many as 80 percent of Americans were involved in a search for self-fulfillment in the 1970s. He estimated that 17 percent were deeply committed to the search. Whether adults change as a result of these experiences will depend on the extent of the changes sought and the other kinds of demands placed upon them (Mortimer and Simmons, 1978).

SUMMARY

In this chapter, you have been introduced to several concepts used by sociologists to better understand socialization and also to a number of studies that develop these concepts. Generally, sociologists view socialization as a process that continues throughout life and that is influenced by all of our social interactions. Social class and sex differences in socialization were related to behavioural differences among adults.

In the past, some sociologists described socialization as if it were imposed on individuals. Some argued that different personality types developed in different cultural settings. In contrast, Cooley and Mead helped to shed light on ways in which individuals are actively engaged in their own socialization process. Socialization is not something that simply happens to us. The messages we receive during socialization are inconsistent and sometimes contradictory, and we all draw our own conclusions from these competing influences as we establish our own life course. Individual life chances are strongly affected by structural variables, the most important of which are sex, race and social class.

DISCUSSION QUESTIONS

1. Talk to your parents about what they considered to be important values for your early development. What differences do you anticipate in the raising of your children?

2. Some people have argued that the entertainment media provide lessons in "who counts" in our society. The next time you are watching television, think about what power relations are implied in the program.

3. Interview a foreign student in one of your classes to find out what resocialization he or she experienced in coming to a North American university.

4. Is Alwin correct in assuming that the socialization values of immigrants are changing? What aspects of traditional socialization remain?

5. Feminists object to the use of the generic "he" or "man" because they argue that people hearing these terms envision a male referent. The study by Alwin (page 93) contains examples of such usage. Would Alwin's results have been different if a nonsexist term had been used? What if "she" was substituted for "he" in the questionnaire? Would more parents have cited being helpful as most important?

6. The underrepresentation of women in educational materials is an important socializing experience. Compare this text to other sociology texts and to introductory texts in other disciplines to see if women are underrepresented in them. Consider such things as the number of pictures and other references to women.

5

Control and Deviance

Austin T. Turk

INTRODUCTION

THE SOCIAL CONSTRUCTION OF RIGHT AND
WRONG
Moral Boundaries and Social Order: The Functions of Stigma
Intragroup vs. Cross-group Stigmatization: Labelling Processes

COPING AND IDENTITY: THE INDIVIDUAL AS
DEVIANT
Anticipation and Experience: Responses to Labelling
Deviant Worlds and Straight Ways: Subcultures, Evasions and Holidays

COMPETITION AND POWER: THE ORGANIZATION
AS DEVIANT

SOCIAL CONTROL AND SOCIAL CHANGE

SUMMARY

INTRODUCTION

We are not born knowing right from wrong. This is the basic premise from which the sociology of deviance and its control begins. Against theological or biological determinism, social and behavioural scientists have accumulated an enormous fund of empirical evidence. This chapter will introduce some of the main findings and examine their implications.

As in any developing science, there has been lively controversy among proponents of different theories and research methods. However, most specialists in the study of deviance and social control agree on several issues and are increasingly concerned with complementarity more than conflict among diverse lines of investigation. The following discussion will focus upon 1) the social construction of right and wrong, 2) sources and varieties of deviant behaviour, 3) organizational deviance and 4) changing patterns of social control.

THE SOCIAL CONSTRUCTION OF RIGHT AND WRONG

There is a very human tendency to take for granted whatever has become familiar, including norms covering the full range of behaviour patterns and nonbehavioural attributes. Furthermore, the familiar tends to become valued so much that we may even begin acting as if the familiar is somehow *right* and better than possible alternatives. Our capacity to accept diversity and change in right-wrong distinctions varies from *absolutism* to *relativism*. Some people find it hard to accept any normative standards other than those which they themselves hold. They consider themselves morally superior because of their beliefs and behaviour, and so may be called *moral absolutists*. Examples include the members of various Christian, Jewish, Islamic and other religious groups. Other people (a far smaller number) think that no one conception of right can legitimately evaluate human ideas or conduct. Such *moral relativists* typically condemn (at least in the abstract) using coercion to prevent, eliminate or punish even harmful conduct. Most people are neither total absolutists nor consistent relativists. Rather, they are absolutist about some things, accept diversity of opinion about other things and are fairly indifferent toward most normative issues.

If most people "live and let live" without concerning themselves too much with questions of morality, how are particular moral boundaries and orders established? To say that moral limits are "natural" or "inevitable" does not explain their existence, but it does remind us that every human relationship generates its own characteristic pattern of normative expectations, failures and controls. No two people can automatically meet each other's expectations. For them to have a relationship (as lovers, parent and child, employer-employee, leader-follower) they must read each other's signals, agree on meanings and priorities and commit themselves to making the relationship work in terms of that agreement. None of this happens automatically; any social relationship is an on-going process. When more people are involved, we speak of "structures" in trying to comprehend their links to one another and the

Is this sidewalk salesman a social deviant or a respectable member of society? On what do you base your judgement? Photo courtesy of Catherine Jolly, Toronto.

task of describing and explaining the relationships involved becomes more complex. Insofar as social order is achieved, it tends to become moral order as well.

The boundaries of social relatedness are moral ones to the extent they are used to decide who is subject to the agreed-upon norms of belief and behaviour. Participation in some relationships requires only a limited and perhaps temporary commitment, so that interaction failures produce little sense of outrage or moral indignation. The stronger the commitment, the greater the emotional impact of failures. In both low-commitment and high-commitment relationships, the connection between deviant behaviour and moral boundaries is symbiotic and problematic.

MORAL BOUNDARIES AND SOCIAL ORDER: THE FUNCTIONS OF STIGMA

When bad, illegal, improper, anomalous and in general disturbing human behaviour began to be studied scientifically in the nineteenth century, investigators assumed that deviation was pathological and conformity was healthy. The aim was to learn how to eliminate deviation, especially in its most disturbing forms, as then perceived: violence, insanity, perversion, dishonesty and idleness. Research since then has led to the startling conclusion that definitions of "deviant" and "normal" are largely subjective and that deviance is "essential to the very organization of society . . . [functioning] to establish and maintain behavioural boundaries and to affirm the value of conformity" (Farrell and Swigert, 1982: 27).

Concepts of deviance vary among individuals and change over time. There is a generalized antipathy toward deviants but considerable variation in the images of them and their attributes. In Simmons's (1969: 25–38) survey research on public stereotyping, respondents were asked to use five words each to characterize "marijuana smokers, adulterers, homosexuals, beatniks, and political radicals." The term "deviant" was not used in presenting the categories. Analysis revealed a fair degree of stereotyping, but the inclination to stereotype was significantly correlated with low education. All categories were seen as "irresponsible," and all except the radical were described as "lonely and frustrated." The more specific images were as follows: marijuana smoker—"an insecure escapist, lacking self-control and looking for kicks"; adulterer—"immoral, promiscuous, and insecure"; homosexual—"perverted and mentally ill"; beatnik—"a sloppy, immature nonconformist"; political radical—"ambitious, aggressive, and dangerous" (Simmons, 1969: 28).

One might suggest that public stereotyping is beside the point. Given that more educated people are less likely to stereotype, maybe the most highly informed, i.e., the social control professionals, accurately identify "real" deviants on scientific, not stereotypical, grounds. Studies of the classification and processing of the mentally ill and criminals do not support this argument. Numerous studies "demonstrate that the behaviour or 'condition' of the person alleged to be mentally ill is not usually an important factor in the decision of officials to retain or release new patients from the mental hospital" (Scheff, 1984: 105). From a flood of research on the criminalization process, "sufficient evidence has accumulated to reject the traditional assumption that distinguishing crime from not-crime merely involves the fitting by competent specialists of legal concepts to observed facts" (Turk, 1984: 319). Deviance, as professionally and officially defined, is the outcome of a complex series of problematic interpretations and discretionary actions.

Historical and comparative studies show that perceptions and assessments of specific forms of deviance are not constant. Demon possession, witchcraft and other once commonly acknowledged phenomena have vanished for more and more people, despite periodic revivals. Conceptions of the nature, causes, types and symptoms of mental illness have become increasingly controversial as the "medical model" has been challenged from within and without the "psy-professions" (Ingleby, 1983; Scheff, 1984). Such crimes as blasphemy, mopery (exposing one's genitals in the presence of a blind man!), abortion and lottery gambling(!) no longer exist, while new crimes such as opium trafficking (since 1908 in Canada, 1914 in the United States) and, most recently, improper disposal of toxic waste are constantly being defined.

How Deviance Contributes to Social Organization
Though variable and discretionary in its specifics and constantly the target of control efforts, deviance always exists in some form. Moreover, it contributes in several ways to social organization (Cohen, 1966: 6–11).

First, deviance is not necessarily even disapproved of if it is used to circumvent "red tape" (an organization's own rules) to accomplish organizational purposes. Finders, operators and expediters are sometimes legendary for their ingenuity in overcoming military and other bureaucratic constraints to "get the job done." Their wheeling and dealing may be officially condemned and sometimes punished, but it is unofficially tolerated most of the time. Another, rather more serious, example of approved deviance is illegal or ethically questionable behaviour by control agents, such as political security police, which is not merely tolerated but frequently encouraged and even required (Turk, 1981).

Second, deviance may be a *safety valve* for a group or society. The more restrictive and demanding the norms of participation, the more pressure there is upon members to subordinate their personal desires to collective interests. To defuse potentially destructive tensions, social relationships have *norms of patterned evasion* by which usual normative expectations are suspended. Prostitution is a classic example of functional deviance, in that it constitutes an understood though disparaged alternative (for men) to the dissolution of insufficiently gratifying marriages (Davis, 1971). Keeping a mistress or concubine has, in many cultures, been a more accepted, though not fully approved, extramarital solution to the problems generated by traditional (especially arranged) marriage systems. *Moral holidays* (e.g., Mardi Gras and New Year's Eve) and *time outs* also reinforce established relationships by permitting ordinarily disallowed behaviour on the clear understanding that a return to conformity is expected when the party is over.

Third, until moral boundaries are overstepped, they remain abstractions with little or no power to induce conforming behaviour. From vicarious and personal experience, one learns the real meaning of a rule by seeing what happens (and to whom) when it is broken. The meaning of malingering, for example, is clarified when an employee is reprimanded for absenteeism or a soldier sent back to combat. Being physically or psychically fatigued may explain performance failure, but only up to the point where authoritative others, such as employers and military psychiatrists, consider it an acceptable excuse (Daniels, 1970).

Fourth, deviance helps to maintain group solidarity by providing a tangible threat. Much like an external enemy, the deviant is a common enemy against whom others can unite. Child molesting is almost universally despised; a reported incident tends to stimulate "great fear and hysteria in the family, outrage in the neighbourhood, and excitement and vengefulness among the police" (Thio, 1983: 150). Private justice organizations such as neighbourhood patrols and watch committees are a frequent outcome. Demanding more stringent laws, applauding vigilante or police violence against suspected molesters and tolerating the brutal degradation of convicted molesters ("rapos") by other prisoners are other common responses.

Fifth, it is strange but true that deviance can sometimes unite a group *for* rather than *against* the deviant. Though not really approving the deviance, people are often protective of "their" deviant and may go to great lengths to cover for the incompetent, the shirker or the outlaw folk hero (a Robin Hood or John Dillinger, for example). Shielding the deviant has been observed in many settings—families, work units, and military training squads (Dentler and Erikson, 1959: 105).

Sixth, badness and abnormality provide reference points for measuring goodness and normality. The greater the contrast, the more readily people can understand what being good or normal means. This insight may have led to the invention of the traditional Tahitian village *mahu*—a male who, as a child, is selected to spend his life as a woman (Levy, 1971). A village has only one *mahu*, who is expected to have sexual relations with the other men. In a culture marked by the minimal differentiation of gender roles, the *mahu* reminds everyone of their appropriate roles as men and women.

And lastly, deviance indicates that there may be a cultural or organizational problem that needs attention. The *anomie* theory of deviance, as formulated by Merton

The appearance of this punker draws stares, but its very outrageousness helps to define what is normal in dress and hairstyles. Photo courtesy of Catherine Jolly, Toronto.

(1957: 131–144), locates the source of deviance in *means–ends discrepancy*—contradictions between culturally encouraged goals and structurally available means for their achievement. A society that teaches people to value themselves and others according to degree of material success but maintains class and racial barriers to legitimate opportunities for success can expect the disadvantaged to seek illegitimate opportunities, such as robbery, theft and fraud. "Double failures," denied illegitimate as well as legitimate oppportunities, may retreat into alcoholism, drug addiction, sexual deviance, mental illness or suicide. Despite its many limitations (Clinard, 1964), there is obvious merit in the proposition that deviance may signal defects in social organization and possibly lead to needed social changes.

Observing that deviance can be functional does not imply that it is always functional. The harmful consequences of some forms (e.g., mass terrorism, sadistic murder) may outweigh their functional payoffs, and less harmful forms of deviance may serve just as well to determine moral boundaries. The amount of deviance required to establish and sustain particular norms is also debatable.

Erikson (1966: 181) has speculated that "societies somehow 'need' their quotas of deviation and function in such a way as to keep them intact." His study of the seventeenth-century New England Puritans examined the three "crime waves" the Massachusetts Bay Colony experienced: the Antinomian (1636) and Quaker (late 1650s) theological challenges to Puritan orthodoxy and later, in 1692, the Salem witchcraft outbreak, which simultaneously violated the normative demands of the theocratic state and provided occasions for brutally but clearly asserting its supreme authority. Erikson's evidence does not directly support his interpretation of it, and his idea of some distinct quota of deviance being needed has been severely criticized. The particular forms and amounts of deviance identified and processed by control institutions are enormously variable, depending heavily upon political-legal policies and economic contexts (Connor, 1972; Turk, 1982; Currie, 1968).

INTRAGROUP VS. CROSS-GROUP STIGMATIZATION: LABELLING PROCESSES

The drawing of moral boundaries is accomplished by *stigmatizing*, or *labelling*, particular individuals, not merely or necessarily by formulating explicit rules. Variations in the labelling process and in its impact upon the individuals being labelled are associated with the scale and formality of the social order. There are significant differences as well as similarities in labelling within small groups and across group boundaries. In each, the process occurs in a *prior normative context* and has "five analytically distinct but empirically blended phases or dimensions: *identification, justification, negotiation, enclosure*, and *disposition*" (Grimes and Turk, 1978: 41).

Though deviance is a socially constructed reality, it is not constructed on the spot. Through time, a framework is established within which later interpretations and responses occur. Because members of a group share understandings of their own ways, norms are generally tacit. In contrast, where people from different backgrounds and groups are involved, the relevant norms are likely to be explicit agreements or laws.

Criteria for identifying cases of deviance include all sorts of observed or imputed behavioural, anatomical, mental or spiritual attributes. Initial or preliminary definition (*typification*) of deviance is based on little information, which is interpreted largely in accord with stereotypes. Again, the criteria for identification are usually generally understood within groups but must be specified ("reasonable grounds for arrest") in cross-group situations. For the other members of a group, it is enough to sense that something is wrong, but the police officer's hunches must be further substantiated if legal proceedings are to begin.

When a case of deviance is identified, those who must deal with it marshal empirical and theoretical grounds for their actions. Intragroup justification relies upon the commonsense knowledge people have of reality and one another. There are no technical restrictions upon the gathering of evidence. Labelling across groups is a potential source of intergroup conflict, and commonsense understandings cannot be relied upon. Therefore, more limited formal procedures and appeals to legality are ordinarily used to build cases in the absence of intimate knowledge and shared understandings.

Accused persons are pressured to participate in confirming the accuracy of their deviant labels. Negotiation is typically unequal, involving not whether but how the alleged deviant is to be classified. Within groups, the controlling members exert pressure by appealing to group *participation* as a shared value. Across groups, control agents are much more prone to appeal to the suspect's sense of expediency with the inescapable fact of *membership* in the collectivity (usually the state) that binds different groups together.

As the fact and nature of the deviant case are established, controlling others enclose the deviant within physical, social and/or symbolic barriers. Opportunities for normal interaction are closed off and pressure to accept a deviant identity becomes increasingly hard to resist. Enclosure is more often symbolic and social in intragroup labelling (e.g., ostracism, transfer to a lower position, stripping of medals and insignia), more often physical in cross-group labelling (e.g., pretrial detention, confinement to quarters).

The outcome of a case may be rehabilitation, termination, or institutionalization (in a social sense, i.e., demotion to a lower rank). Rehabilitation to normal participation in social interaction is more likely to be a goal within than across groups, and it is far more likely than the other alternatives to be achieved. At the other extreme, termination of social existence by exile or execution is generally decided upon later in intragroup situations and with greater moral indignation, which is heightened by failure to elicit confession and/or achieve rehabilitation. Authentic concern about the individual deviant occurs far less often in cross-group labelling, where "population control" is ultimately more important than personalized control. Consequently, deviants are more often relegated to a permanently inferior status (socially institutionalized) than terminated or rehabilitated. *Career deviants* may even be needed in greater numbers in multigroup collectivities because more bad examples and providers of illicit goods and services may be required to preserve the social order (if not the moral order) of such large organizations.

COPING AND IDENTITY: THE INDIVIDUAL AS DEVIANT

As we have seen, from an analytical perspective, deviance sometimes helps to construct moral boundaries and maintain social order. Nonetheless, negative labelling (stigmatization) is nearly always intended to eliminate or minimize deviance. And deviance is usually understood as conduct near or beyond a group's *range of tolerance*. Nonbehavioural attributes (such as skin colour, height, weight, mental or spiritual conditions), observed or imputed, are ordinarily of concern only because they are presumed to correlate with or cause unacceptable behaviour. Accordingly, most theorists and researchers have concentrated upon explaining deviant *behaviour*.

The search for explanations of deviant behaviour has led scientists to examine myriad biological, psychological, and social factors as possible causes. Certain behaviours have typically been assumed deviant without much concern about the origins of such assumptions or the problematic nature of labelling processes. *Deviance* has been equated with *variance*, and the specific effort to account for deviant conduct has tended to dissolve into the general effort to explain all human behaviour. One influential attempt to give deviance research a theoretically meaningful focus has been that of Edwin Lemert over the past 35 years.

Lemert's (1972: 62–92) proposal is that we concentrate on the task of explaining secondary rather than primary deviation. He sees *primary deviation* as an essentially unpredictable, polygenetic occurrence

> arising out of a variety of social, cultural, psychological, and physiological factors, either in adventitious or recurring combinations. While it may be socially recognized and even defined as undesirable, primary deviation has only marginal implications for the status and psychic structure of the person concerned (Lemert, 1972: 62).

Secondary deviation refers to the patterned responses of individuals to being subjected to labelling processes. The personal problems created by societal reactions to their deviance "become central facts of existence for those experiencing them, altering psychic structure, producing specialized organization of social roles and self-regarding attitudes" (Lemert, 1972: 63). The eventual outcome is the secondary deviant, whose life and identity are organized around the experience of being a deviant in his own and others' eyes.

ANTICIPATION AND EXPERIENCE: RESPONSES TO LABELLING

Becoming a secondary deviant is neither inevitable nor easy. Learning who one is and coping with that awareness are as hard for the deviant as for the conformist. Many contingencies affect whether an initial deviant act will lead to a deviant identity. We may adapt Lofland's (1969) model of *defensive deviance* to trace the progression from the point where the (primary) deviant feels threatened (by actual or feared control efforts), through *psychosocial encapsulation* (becoming obsessed with "the problem"), to *closure* upon a pattern of action resulting in public and self identification as a (secondary) deviant.

At any time, the individual may stop the progression. The likelihood of going on always depends upon the factors pushing the person on or simply making it easier to go on than to drop out (the *opportunity structure*). These factors include the characteristics of 1) the surrounding others, 2) the places where activities are possible, 3) the "hardware" needed to behave in particular ways and 4) the individual involved.

The Opportunity Structure: Four Factors Affecting Deviants

1. Other people may inhibit or facilitate secondary deviance. This seems obvious enough until the researcher tries to determine which kinds of behaviour by others will be inhibiting and which facilitating. Does negative labelling deter or produce further deviance? The question has provoked fierce debates (Gove, 1975). The answer, of course, is that labelling may have either effect, so that the real issue is not whether but *when*. Thorsell and Klemke (1972) have suggested that labelling is more likely to deter when certain conditions are met: It occurs early in the deviant career. The deviant is nonprofessional (i.e., not a secondary or socially institutionalized deviant). The labeller's opinion matters to the one who is labelled (as in intragroup labelling). The label is easily removed when deviance stops (i.e., labelling is reversible). Negative labelling results in significant rehabilitative and supportive activities being made available to the deviant. Positive labels are emphasized instead of negative ones. Insofar as such conditions are more often found in intragroup settings, deterrence is more likely to result from intragroup than from cross-group labelling.

Besides *controlling others*, there are also *facilitating others*—people whose behaviour toward the deviant makes secondary deviance more probable. Friends and strangers, accomplices and victims, followers and guides all may facilitate more than inhibit the progression to secondary deviance. Lofland (1969: 212–242) distinguishes between deviant-smiths and normal-smiths. *Normal-smiths* are people who, as supporters (including experienced secondary deviants), deliberately or inadvertently deny that the individual is really or culpably deviant and thereby blur the distinction between normal and abnormal, right and wrong. The individual may then have little reason *not* to be deviant. *Deviant-smiths* are typically controllers who are clearly skeptical about the deviant's being or becoming anything else. They may cut off the deviant from opportunities to escape the progression to secondary deviant. When both normal-smiths and deviant-smiths are present, the deviant is least able to avoid moving on to where deviance is a "master status" overriding all else.

2. Places vary greatly in the extent to which they inhibit or facilitate deviance. It is easier to carry on many forms of deviant behaviour in private than in public, or else in places formally or tacitly set aside for deviant activities. "The strip" is found in cities all over the world. In the 1960s, Toronto's Yorkville ("hippies, weekenders, bikers, and greasers") and Rochdale "free university" were widely known examples of such places (Mann, 1970: 109–128, 207–217). A person living in a small town, known to everyone and expected to be in particular places at specific times, has little chance to experiment or persist in violating local standards. Conversely, people living anonymously in large cities have many opportunities to be deviant and are more likely to encounter both normal-smiths and deviant-smiths. In addition, as the Yorkville and Rochdale examples suggest, cities offer many more and varied "deviant places" (bars, clubs, massage and tattoo parlors, hotel rooms, underground garages) where various forms of deviant activity are possible and even expected. Every private, secluded, dark area is a facilitant, especially if people can come and go without anyone's noticing or caring.

Beyond the opportunity structures found in private and public spaces, facilities for enclosing and "correcting" deviants are themselves places where deviants are pressured to accept deviant identities. In one controversial study (Rosenham, 1973), pseudopatients feigned "hearing voices" to gain admission to the psychiatric wards of 12 hospitals on the east and west coasts of the United States. All were admitted for observation, then immediately ceased to feign any abnormality. Eleven were diagnosed as schizophrenic, one as a manic-depressive psychotic (with a more favourable prognosis, given by the only private hospital in the sample). The phony patients were never detected and the initial diagnosis stuck, no matter what they did. Observation periods ranged from 7 to 52 days, averaging 19 days, and were determined by the staff. Despite the absence of any unusual or symptomatic personal history information (all true, excepting names and occupations) and of any observed symptomatic behaviour, all the pseudopatients were discharged with a diagnosis of "in remission" (i.e., still perceived as having been and continuing to be insane).

3. The less a deviant act requires in the way of hardware (weapons, tools, computers, vehicles, costumes, substances, sales records), the more likely it is to occur and recur. Many forms of deviance (e.g., casual promiscuity, disorderly public conduct and incidental assault) require no hardware and so are easy options available to anyone. But to become a professional prostitute, drug dealer, thief, robber, fence or assassin, one must acquire the necessary equipment and learn how to use it. "Road hustlers" (card and dice cheats) advance from the haphazard, crude operations of "rough" hustling to professional standing only after surviving a hard apprenticeship (Prus and Sharper, 1977: 47–59). Much like a professional musician, the road hustler uses hardware (dice, cards, cash, appropriate clothing) and develops extremely complex skills until "the ability to manipulate cards or dice is rather commonplace and taken more for granted" (Prus and Sharper, 1977: 47). Only a true virtuoso is considered a "mechanic," and few reach this level.

4. Not all individuals subjected to labelling accept the deviant identity imputed to them. Contrary to some ambiguous formulations and misinterpretations of labelling theory, stigmatization is not always traumatic, deeply and negatively affecting the deviant's self concept. Though exaggerated, Matza's (1969: 144–180) image of the deviant's virtually unquenchable capacity to "mediate the process of becoming" a secondary deviant reminds us that labelling (especially cross-group) may be necessary but is not causally sufficient to produce a secondary deviant. Studies of the impact of official labelling indicate that it is probably *least* traumatic for those people against whom it is most often directed: "maximal for first offenders, the middle-class, and whites, and minimal for prior offenders, the lower class, and blacks" (Liska, 1981: 132).

Some individual deviants may even accept labels without accepting all their negative connotations. Indeed, becoming a "professional" typically involves learning rationalizations (or ego defenses) that discount the "badness" of being a call girl, hustler or hired killer. Call girls, for instance, learn to justify their behaviour on grounds such as counter-exploiting exploitative and cheating men, servicing deserving but deprived men, preventing rapes and murders and keeping marriages and families intact (Bryan, 1965, 1966).

Many prostitutes and ex-prostitutes have organized to seek, not rehabilitation, but improved working conditions, medical services, legal protection, fringe benefits like unemployment compensation and greater public respect for their contribution to society. Acronyms emphasize the message: COYOTE ("Call Off Your Old Tired Ethics") in the United States and BEAVER ("Better End All Vicious Erotic Repression") in Canada.

In some instances, deviants have organized movements to abolish legal and non-legal definitions which label them and their behaviour as deviant. The gay liberation movement is unquestionably the most celebrated example. What was once a largely secretive and fearful subculture has, over the past 20 years, become the increasingly open gay community. The organized gay populace is a growing political force in many cities, such as San Francisco and Toronto, "which may be on its way to becoming the homosexual capital of North America" (Johnson, 1971: 380). Beginning with the decriminalization of private consensual acts between adults, the movement achieved perhaps its most fundamental breakthrough when the American Psychiatric Association voted in 1974 to redefine homosexuality as not, per se, a psychiatric disorder, though the degree of actual change in diagnostic practice remains questionable (Conrad and Schneider, 1980: 204–211).

DEVIANT WORLDS AND STRAIGHT WAYS: SUBCULTURES, EVASIONS AND HOLIDAYS

Efforts by deviants to find optimum or tolerable combinations of others, places and hardware frequently result in the emergence of *deviant subcultures*. Social scientists, journalists, novelists and other observers have documented the infinite variety of such social constructions. These worlds of deviance are usually pictured as alien, exotic or erotic islands cut off from the rest of society. However, though by no

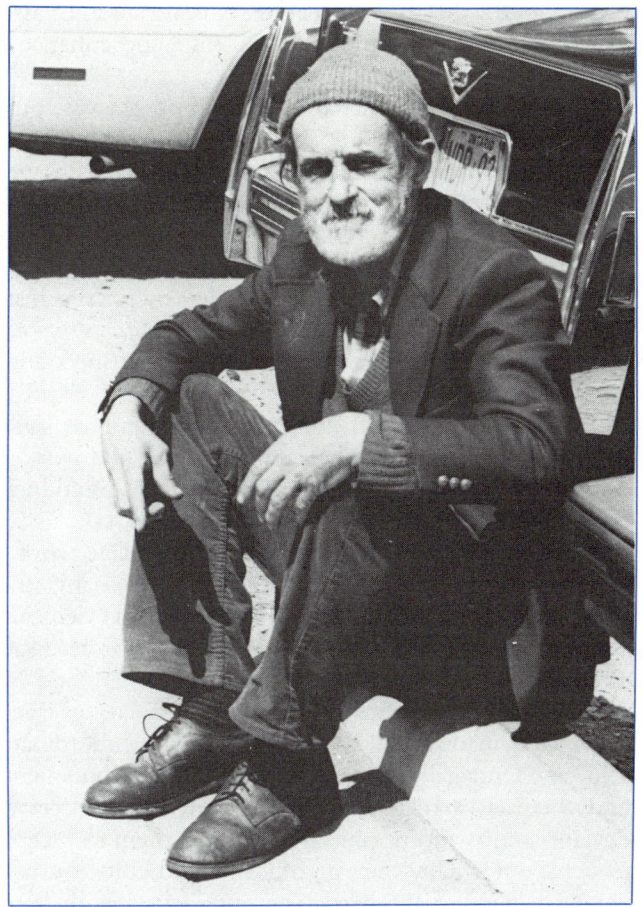

Inhabitants of the underside world openly deviate from the prevailing norms of prosperity, appearance, competence and hopefulness.
Photo courtesy of Catherine Jolly, Toronto.

means commonplace to most of us, deviant subcultures are integral (if not necessarily functional) to the straight world of moral evasions and holidays.

Deviant subcultures may centre around a particular form of deviance, but usually incorporate several forms that exist in a symbiotic relationship with one another and the straight world. Such "vices" or "morality offenses" as illicit drug dealing and use, pimping and prostitution and illegal gambling tend to go together, along with theft, mugging and various hustles. The *underworld* is the habitat of institutionalized deviants. These live partly off one another but mostly off the "straights" who visit them seeking fun, relaxation, adventure, information or for other, more sordid reasons. In this uncertain and often dangerous world, few total commitments are possible; interpersonal relationships are usually ephemeral and expedient.

Violence is never far away in the world of institutionalized deviance. For some inhabitants and visitors, violence itself becomes a *focal concern* with its own subcultural meanings. Among biker outlaws, such as the Hell's Angels, violence is routinely used to defend territorial claims ("turf") and discourage business competition, especially in the illegal drug market. It is also used to assert status, demonstrate tough masculinity, maintain internal discipline and enhance sexual gratification (Thompson, 1967).

Overlapping the underworld of pimps, thieves, pushers and other criminal elements is the *underside world* of the assorted "bums, dropouts, freaks, and losers" who openly deviate from the prevailing norms of prosperity, appearance, competence and hopefulness. They are "the disreputable poor . . . who remain unemployed even during periods approaching full employment and prosperity" (Matza, 1975: 198). As the cast-offs of society, they are an affront to "decent people"—who attribute failure to moral shortcomings, blaming the victim instead of society.

Adjacent to the losers' world is the *fringe world* of the semi-respectable, whose occupations or other activities make them suspect and who are in varying degrees excluded from participating in straight society. Carnival workers, circus performers and those who perform the more gruesome and unpleasant services for society deviate from norms of stability, appearance, odour and work (productive, honest, clean, as commonly defined). Denigrated occupations often include gravediggers, executioners, "night soil" (human feces) removers in Asia, as well as surgeons in times past and policemen at all times! An irony of police work is that the implicit threat of police action is disturbing or frightening to many straight people (and, of course, to all deviants), leading them to ostracize and demean police officers for engaging in such "dirty work"—even as it is recognized as necessary. (For representative studies of the police and their problems, see Blumberg and Niederhoffer, 1985.)

Though not ordinarily recognized as such, a large part of the fringe world of deviance is made up of those afflicted with "abominations of the body" (Goffman, 1963:4). Unusually proportioned, blind, deaf and mentally retarded people typically find themselves relegated to discredited and inferior statuses. An abundance of deviant-smiths and normal-smiths press them to accept deviant identities. Attempts to behave normally may be officially and consciously encouraged but are not ultimately facilitated. In particular, interaction with "normals" tends to be carefully monitored and restricted. Intimate relationships (friends, lovers, spouses, adoptive parents) with normals are generally discouraged and sometimes legally prohibited. The more stringent the standards defining normalcy are, the less able abnormals are to meet them and to count upon continued acceptance in society (Mercer, 1973).

"Respectability" and "normalcy" presumably mean the absence of deviant behaviour in other than exceptional circumstances (moral holidays and time-outs, for example). However, mounting evidence shows that deviance is often hidden within the most sacred bastions of the straight world. Alcoholism and other drug abuse, sexual deviations, mental aberrations and role failures, stealing, fraud, and/or violence characterize the lives of many families. Bryant (1973: 396) has even concluded that "a family may be considered a social collusion system for the maintenance of internal secrets and the concealment of stigma, scandal, and inappropriate behaviour on the part of its members." Other observers have found similar deviant patterns in businesses, factories, schools, government agencies, hospitals, churches—virtually every part of the straight world. This leads many analysts to question whether moral boundaries really differentiate straights and deviants or whether they only signal the relative power of people in a society.

COMPETITION AND POWER: THE ORGANIZATION AS DEVIANT

Legal and moral boundary construction has long been viewed by many analysts as a "conflict process" or "conflict game" (Lofland, 1969: 13–25). Different categories and groups of people are seen to be openly or implicitly competing for "the means and opportunities to realize their respective visions of the good life" (Turk, 1982: 12). Yet, most studies have examined only individual deviance. The definitional and methodological problems raised by the concepts of structural and organizational deviance have only recently been seriously confronted.

Many researchers (and students) find it hard to think of *collective* behaviour as something other than the sum total of *individual* acts. While it is relatively easy to imagine individuals as deviant, the deviance of organizations and other collectivities—up to and including whole societies—is not as readily visualized. A little thought, however, shows the only real problem is one of scale. Governments, armies, corporations and even social classes and ethnic populations are frequently regarded as acting units and blamed (stigmatized) for "their" actions. In fact, since the Middle Ages, churches, towns and kings ("the crown") and even commercial corporations have been legally considered "juristic persons" rather than 'natural' ones" (Coleman, 1974: 13–31).

Ermann and Lundman (1982: 9–11) observe that corporate entities can produce deviant behaviour in at least three ways. First, leaders may deliberately use their positions to bring about illegal or unethical collective actions. Second, administrative coalitions and compromises may lead to unintended deviant collective behaviour. Third, organizational complexity itself may result in deviant behaviour, even though no individual deviance occurred.

Illegal manipulation of organizational resources by leaders has been described in several studies of corporate and governmental deviance. The Lockheed Corporation, for instance, was recently prosecuted for bribing officials in several countries (Boulton, 1978). Top executives, including the chairman of the board, decided to unload the Starfighter jet, which the American Air Force had rejected as unsafe. The defective plane was sold to various foreign air forces, and a spate of fatal crashes ensued. Probably the best known and documented recent example of governmental deviance in the United States is Watergate, the crimes (breaking and entering, obstructing justice, perjury and others) engineered by then President Nixon and his top aides (Roebuck and Weeber, 1978).

The Ford Pinto story illustrates how administrative procedures can result in organizational deviance (Ermann and Lundman, 1982: 10, 17–18). Lee Iacocca succeeded in pushing for a crash program to develop a small, fuel-efficient car to meet the foreign competition. The Pinto was rushed through design to production in record time. When evidence of a potentially hazardous fault in the fuel tank was found, it was ignored because the design engineers were keenly aware of Iacocca's decree that the car could not exceed 2000 pounds in weight or $2000 in cost. (It was later calculated that the cost of correcting the problem would have added about 11 cents per unit!) Over the next several years, the Pinto fuel tank ruptured in numerous crashes, and several people died in the resulting fires. Ford tried to deny responsibility but lost many suits. In 1978, the company was ordered to repair the nearly 2 000 000 Pintos it produced and became the first corporation ever indicted for homicide. No one at Ford wanted an unsafe vehicle, but organizational policies and hierarchical division of responsibilities produced one.

It is not easy to find concrete examples of entirely inadvertent organizational deviance. Still, many researchers have found that such deviance is often better explained as a product of insensitivity or ignorance rather than intent. Clinard and Yeager's (1980) monumental study of corporate lawbreaking indicates that it varies with the cultural, economic and political-legal environment. Both executives and workers are socialized to be dedicated "organization men" who do not look past the "bottom line" and their particular assignment. Responsibility is diffused through a complex and dehumanizing system, and any lingering personal doubts are discounted as irrelevant to doing business.

Given such findings, it is not surprising that many people see bureaucratic organizations as inherently deviant. Anarchists have developed a political ideology that condemns all varieties of formalism, legalism and hierarchy. Critics of *bureaupathology* and *bureaucratic justice* advocate dismantling organizations and replacing them with informal and egalitarian associations. Social theorists have uncovered dysfunctions and insoluble dilemmas that are characteristic of all formal organizations. And attitude surveys have consistently revealed high levels of hostility toward bureaucracies and a readiness to cheat, attack and otherwise "punish" them (Smigel and Ross, 1970).

Whether complex, necessarily formal organizations of diverse people and groups can ever be fully normal and respectable (*legitimate*) seems doubtful. As long as collective demands and goals take precedence over individual wishes, organizations must deviate from normative expectations developed mainly in interpersonal relationships. Cross-group norms can never be as readily understood and accepted as intragroup norms.

In any case, to explain organizational deviance as simply what organizations are and do is equivalent to imputing original sin to all human beings. We are left with no way to differentiate better from worse, much less to account for the difference. That organizations, like people, *vary* in their deviance indicates a better way: Learn more about the sources of that variation. As was learned in the long search for the causes of individual deviance, the causes of organizational deviance are most likely to be found in the *interactions* between organizations and their social environments.

SOCIAL CONTROL AND SOCIAL CHANGE

Environments are not constant. It follows that the sources of organizational and individual deviance will change as environmental conditions change. Technological innovations, discovery or depletion of natural resources, economic development or decline, internal and international political realignments—all such factors generate pressures upon whatever social and moral orders have been constructed. Established normative expectations are altered as their social and cultural foundations shift as a result of environmental changes. Whether change is revolutionary or evolutionary, people experiencing it will have to revise or recreate the normative understandings

Christian morality was a strong force in medieval Europe and continued to be important during the sixteenth and seventeenth centuries. Some say that the morality of the twentieth century is a technological morality, which defines "good" as that which serves the collective interest. Photo courtesy of Catherine Jolly, Toronto.

by which they relate to one another. The alternative is to lose all sense of meaning in life. In short, structural pressures upon social orders produce pressures upon moral orders.

Jacques Ellul (1969) discerns three great historical transformations in the basic moral order of the Western world. *Christian morality* was a strong force in medieval Europe and continued to be important during the sixteenth and seventeenth centuries. It extolled an other-worldly orientation over this-worldly, material concerns like politics and economics. The inner soul of the individual was the only significant reality, its salvation the only important goal. *Bourgeois morality*, which originated in the Reformation, was an adaptation to the industrial and commercial revolution. It retained the preoccupation with an individual's inner state but developed a new conception of the soul's relationship to the material world. This-worldly success became the outward sign of inner virtue. Attending to one's proper business and rejecting idleness, unproductive pleasures and undue levity became the mark of a good man or woman. Industriousness and propriety were assumed to be the moral preconditions of success, and so they were. Material success in competition with others became the measure of one's worth as a human being. People were responsible for themselves; failure to succeed was a sign of moral weakness.

Today, says Ellul, the once prevailing bourgeois morality is crumbling as individualism is made meaningless by the collectivization of social life. Entrepreneurial skills are irrelevant as individuals become subordinate to massive and complex organizations. What is emerging is a *technological morality*, the morality of the fully collectivized person. Whatever is normally and situationally required to perform one's assigned role is "good." Normalcy and morality are defined not by other-worldly or inner criteria or by any personal standard but by collective interests and demands. "In the last analysis, it appears as a suppression of morality through the total absorption of the individual into the group" (Ellul, 1969: 198).

One does not have to agree entirely with Ellul. The demise of individualism may not be as imminent as he believes. Resistance to governmental and corporate collectivization is widespread, even in totalitarian societies. Individualistic, this-worldly orientations and other-worldly religious movements have acquired new vigour. Everywhere, it appears, people keep trying to construct *moral* as well as social order; everyone hopes to find a "symbolic balance" that will enable them to achieve personally meaningful identities (Klapp, 1969). We are beyond 1984, and no fully effective and eternally unshakeable social structure or control technology is yet on the horizon. Deviance and the need to control persist, as they must, for they are but the two sides of any human relationship.

SUMMARY

Conceptions of right and wrong are developed in the on-going process of constructing social relationships. Variations beyond what has come to be expected tend to be regarded as not just different but somehow *wrong*. At the extremes, *absolutists* reject anything new or different, while *relativists* are characterized by an indiscriminate tolerance. In time, social orders tend to become moral orders.

Images of deviance are largely subjective, varying among individuals and groups and changing over time. Nonetheless, deviance in some form is always present and may contribute to social order by 1) helping to get around red tape, 2) providing a safety valve, 3) making abstract norms concretely meaningful, 4) uniting groups against a common threat, 5) fostering group solidarity against outsiders, 6) providing reference points for measuring goodness and normality and 7) signaling organizational or cultural problems.

Moral boundaries are drawn by stigmatizing specific individuals. The basic phases of the labelling process, which always occurs in a *prior normative context*, are *identification, justification, negotiation, enclosure,* and *disposition*. Intragroup, compared to cross-group, labelling occurs in a less explicit context and is more subtle, unrestricted, informal and concerned with rehabilitating the individual.

Because *primary deviation* is largely unpredictable and has only marginal social and psychological significance, research on individual deviant behaviour has focused mainly on explaining *secondary deviation*. The process of becoming a secondary deviant is highly problematic, and individuals may halt it at any time. The progression is contingent upon: what kinds of others are involved (controllers vs. facilitating deviant-smiths and normal-smiths); the availability of appropriate or necessary places and hardware; and the capacity of the individual to accept or resist a deviant identity.

Deviant worlds (or subcultures) are integral to the straight world, varying only in the degree to which they are clearly a part of it. The worlds of deviance include the underworld of socially institutionalized deviance, the world of "losers," the fringe world of the semi-respectable and the hidden deviant world within the straight world.

While most studies have focused upon individual deviance, at some point the scale and complexity of social relationships generate *organizational deviance*. Collectivities from groups to corporations and nations may violate legal and other norms. Organizational deviance may be the intended result of elite manipulation, the unintended consequence of policy decisions and administrative procedures or the inadvertent outcome of sheer organizational complexity. Individuals within complex organizations are under pressure to become organization men and women, for whom collective interests and demands override personal moral and other concerns. Awareness of such pressures and their frequent consequences leads many people to see complex organizations as inherently *bureaupathic*. This is equivalent to seeing natural persons as innately sinful. Thus both individual and organizational deviance should be understood as the products of *interactions* between the acting unit and its social environment.

As environments vary, so does the interaction. It follows that patterns of deviance and control shift as people adapt to the changing conditions of their lives. Jacques Ellul suggests that the basic moral order of the Western world has changed from the *Christian morality* of other-worldly, spiritual individualism to the *bourgeois morality* of this-worldly materialistic individualism. Today, he says, the new *technological morality* of the fully collectivized individual is emerging. Yet, people still seek meaning in their lives, despite the pressures of our large, complex society. The human dialectic of control and deviance goes on.

DISCUSSION QUESTIONS

1. What are some examples of moral absolutism and relativism?

2. How can we know when deviance is functional?

3. In what ways is the social order of a university class also a moral order?

4. Can primary deviation be explained? Why or why not? Give an example of primary deviance.

5. Are all places deviant places?

6. What is insanity? Who is insane?

7. Is it possible to differentiate between organizational and individual deviant behaviour?

8. How can collective deviance be controlled?

TYPES of SOCIAL ORGANIZATION

All societies consist of social organizations: small and large ones, simple and complex, temporary and permanent, informal and formal.

Some societies are very small and organizationally simple. The earliest human societies, hunter-gatherer groupings, may have numbered mere dozens of people. They were really just extended families, with everyone related to everyone else by birth or marriage. In this sense, early societies could be viewed as a large family, and what was good for the family was good for society. Kinship exchanges bound extended families together through marriage and the exchanges associated with it (dowry, bride-price). Thus, marriage was a more central process of social organization than it is today.

But even today, the family is a fundamental social organization. The modern nuclear family is a small, relatively simple social organization containing three main relationships: parent and child, spouse and spouse and sibling and sibling. A less temporary social organization than some (say, a school class), it is also self-dissolving with the passage of a generation. In time, the parents die, leaving their children to marry and establish new families.

True, some families are very temporary, dissolving because of divorce (or early death) and reconstituting through remarriage. Others may contain many generations, and so be more complex. Grandparent/grandchild alliances tend to undermine and complicate child/parent relationships. Some households may also contain aunts, uncles and other extended kin. Such additional relationships also add complexity to the family and household.

To a larger degree, family complexity is increased by remarriage. More and more households today are nontraditional, containing unmarried or temporarily married spouses and children of different parents. Conflicting rules and role expectations that result complicate matters further.

Much of this is due to the easing of divorce laws, a result of changing ideas about gender and *gender relations*, the relations between men and women. Male and female rights and responsibilities, though far from equalized, have changed enough to modify family roles a great deal. Women are more able, economically and socially, to maintain their own households. Thus, household forms and composition come to vary more. These changes in gender relations, their causes and consequences, will be discussed at length in a later chapter.

Roles and Interactions

"Role" is a word in common use. However, it has a special meaning for sociologists that is spelled out in the chapter on roles and interactions (Chapter 6) in relation to the so-called *dramaturgical view of society*. This sociological view assumes that "all the world's a stage,/And all the men and women merely players./They have their exits and their entrances,/And one man in his time plays many parts/His acts being seven ages." (Shakespeare, *As You Like It*, Act II, Scene VII, lines 139–143).

Shakespeare's lines suggest the changeability of human identity, the many difficult transformations that come with aging, until finally we are "sans teeth, sans eyes, sans taste, sans everything" (line 166). Sociologists holding the dramaturgical view see human beings in terms of the parts they play on the "stage" of life. People are supposed to move smoothly from one role to another and to retrain themselves as often as necessary to play their assigned parts. This view, though provocative, suggests a disturbing uniformity among us and denies that some of us, at least, may be intent on expressing our "real" selves. Some might also find this view cynical: Individuals ("actors") have real personalities or sincere beliefs that determine how they enact their roles. The dramaturgical view supposes that people are guided more by the immediate prospects of reward and less by scruples, ethics or life purpose. This view also fails to separate the self from the role. What people "really" are when not on stage (how they see themselves, how they view their lives) is ignored.

From a dramaturgical standpoint, interactions between people are determined by the agreed upon "script." The ways a doctor and patient interact, for example, will be largely prescribed in the roles "doctor" and "patient," which are learned by doctors in medical school, by patients in the mass media. Some interactions are complicated by role-conflict, or cross-cutting roles. For example, imagine I am the child of a wealthy family, passing the time with a poor gardener come to rake leaves at our family mansion. By following the rule that age accords the gardener authority, I violate the equally strong norms according me superior authority on the basis of my social standing. How such confusions are resolved is far from clear.

Top-down, Bottom-up

Yet, even under the simplest, least ambiguous conditions, interactions are not simply determined by social roles. People must frequently respond to new situations by creating new roles and rules. This process particularly interests the sociologists known as symbolic interactionists and phenomenologists, who hold that social organization typically proceeds from "the bottom up", not from "the top down." Unlike those who argue that people come into a pre-existing world in which they must learn to play assigned parts, "bottom-up" theorists claim that social order is constantly created or negotiated by interacting people. What is problematic for sociology, in this view, is how people make sense to one another, reach agreements and manage (however provisionally) to make their agreements work.

This approach can be criticised on several grounds where the alternative "top-down" theory seems more appropriate. First, top-down theory is more consistent with a view of society that emphasizes persistent inequalities of power. Such inequalities favour certain roles and interactions over others. The distribution of power, to be discussed at length below, controls the social processes that organize social relationships. But since the distribution of power in a society is rarely renegotiated, neither are the most important social relationships.

Second, top-down theory fits the observed persistence of social order. Though change and conflict are everywhere, they are clearest against a strong backdrop of order. And, to explain the maintenance of order, we need theories that focus on the processes that maintain on-going social organization with little change. Bottom-up theories do not fill the bill. On the other hand, the creativity and spontaneity described by bottom-up theory can be seen in evolving social movements, in the formation and revitalization of ethnic communities and in movements of protest against social inequality.

Power is always exercised from above *and* from below. Indeed, the distribution of power between those at the bottom and those at the top helps to account for social movement formation. As well, the resurgence of neighbourhoods, networks, informal communities and other new forms of social life in modern cities all show the creativity of human beings facing the supposed "death of community." These social organizations display both "top-down" socialization and "bottom-up" creativity as well as responsiveness to external pressures for change.

Creativity can be seen clearly in kinship relations. New kinds of families and households create new kinds of relationships, and these relationships demand new social roles: roles that tell us what to expect of step-siblings, of the "spouses" mommy or daddy brings home for a year or a month, of "grandparents by a second marriage." What should a second wife expect of her spouse in relation to what the first wife might have received (in consideration, gifts) and what should she expect of her spouse's children by his first marriage? Should she expect to be called (and treated as) "Mommy"? How should we refer to the people living with us conjugally for a month or two? What should other people call them? What is our relationship with their friends, or parents? These questions, asked more frequently all the time, demand creativity from everyone. In time, we all create new social roles, new names for relationships and new forms of interaction in response to a world that has already changed.

Large Organizations and Small

How are large organizations related to smaller ones? At first glance, many similarities are evident. All organizations arise out of similar social processes. All organizations are composed of roles, interactions and relationships which are similar. Just as all physical objects are composed of similar, though not identical, atoms and are distinguished by how these atoms are aggregated (as solid *versus* liquid, or large object *versus* small), so social organizations are composed of similar, though not identical, social building blocks, gathered together in somewhat different forms.

Secondly, large social organizations are composed of smaller ones. For example, social classes, ethnic groups and urban communities all contain families, genders and roles. In many cases they also include social movements and formal organizations. Thus, smaller organizations are the building blocks of larger ones.

Thirdly, just as large organizations contain smaller ones, so formal organizations include informal ones; permanent organizations, temporary ones; and complex organizations, simpler ones. Thus, a large, complex organization is, in a sense, merely the sum of its small, informal, transitory organizations. For example, the Toronto Jewish community, which has existed for well over a century, comprises many large, formal organizations (schools, synagogues, newspapers, clubs). But it also includes all Jewish individuals, families and temporary groupings who, though organizationally unaffiliated, have some other basis of identification or interaction with the community.

In modern societies, more and more social life is lived under the umbrella of ever larger, more enduring and complex social organizations. Of these, the modern welfare state, the international trade union and the multinational corporation are good examples. Their size, complexity and permanence and the protection afforded them as distinct entities under law enable them to amass greater resources than smaller organizations and individuals. In the end, the power these resources command clearly distinguishes the large, complex organization from the small, simple one. The role of power in social life will be discussed at length in the next section.

Roles and Interactions

Nancy Mandell

INTRODUCTION: SOCIAL ORGANIZATION

OVERVIEW

Sociologists investigate problems on either the macro or the micro level. *Macro level analyses* examine major institutions and large structures, both as separate parts of the whole society and as interdependent phenomena. Often the connections between these institutions and structures are not readily discernible. Research studies reveal their complex relationships. For example, the close connection between the activities of factories producing essential parts for nuclear power plants, corporate lobbies in Parliament asking for favourable tax breaks and the desire of the military to increase the defense budget is an example of the way the military-industrial complex functions.

While macro studies examine institutional arrangements, *micro-order analyses* expose the unspoken rules of social interaction which make orderly social life possible. How people behave, the groups they form and the rules they live by all shape our society. Micro analyses focus on social interaction, revealing how individuals act out of awareness of others and how they adjust their behaviour according to the perceptions of others.

Both macro and micro studies examine social organization, a term which refers to the variety of interactional patterns found in society. Interactional patterns include structural or institutional relationships (universities, corporations, prisons), group formations (political, leisure and ethnic associations) and interpersonal bonds (friend/friend, neighbour/neighbour, husband/wife). Within each structure, consistent and normative patterns of behaviour guide people's day to day interactions. These arrangements help unify and stabilize the social system, while other stresses and tensions within social organizations promote change.

Canada's health care system is a social organization containing both large- and small-scale behaviour patterns and elements of harmony and discord. Some groups, such as government ministries of health and provincial medical societies, are permanent, formal organizations. Other groups, such as holistic health centres and feminist health collectives, are new, evolving medical alternatives. How these groups interrelate shows the overall character of the health care organization.

Groups within the health system contain distinct interactional configurations. These informal lines of communication are less conspicuous than the formal structure of the organization. But they reveal patterns of power, influence, co-operation and antagonism among the participants. For example, any community health centre produces power struggles between physicians and social workers over clinical areas of responsibility. Within any formal organization, informal relationships mould the character of the system. As these relationships alter, the form and nature of the social unit also changes.

Individuals, then, have an interactive relationship to groups and institutions. Individuals both produce social organizations and are acted upon by them. The family is an example. Couples who establish a joint residence, have children and both contribute financially to the household have created a social unit called a nuclear family. Yet, once in existence, this organization can affect the behaviour of its members. Most people with families insist on fidelity, nurturing of children and financial provision for dependents. Organizations are thus objective entities determining our behaviour. They are also subjective arrangements arising out of the day-to-day interactions of their members. Macro-order analyses reveal how large organizations shape our behaviour. In contrast, micro-order studies examine the interpersonal bonds among organizational participants.

THE MACRO LEVEL OF ANALYSIS

The macro-order level of analysis includes the systemic or structural organization of a social unit. The term *social system* is interchangeable with *social unit*. Social systems are the actual practices and behaviours of individuals in relationship to each other in particular organizational settings.

Macro level analyses of organizational settings focus on institutions, the conceptual bridge between what people do and what people believe. Institutions include the stable cluster of values, norms, roles and expectations that decide how the needs of a society should be met. Through socialization practices, institutions transfer cultural beliefs, norms, values and roles to each new generation. For example, Canadian studies show how the socialization of doctors (Shapiro, 1978) and chiropractors (Kelner et al., 1980) in formal, institutional settings ensures that students will graduate showing similar behaviour toward their patients, their colleagues and the public.

Within macro analysis, the key concepts are role, status, group and institution. All four are involved in the web of relationships that makes societies possible and predictable. Given the importance of these concepts, they are dealt with in more detail on pages 136–154.

THE MICRO ORDER OF ANALYSIS

The macro approach is called *structuralist* or *determinist*, meaning that it focuses on how social organizations constrain and determine human activity. In contrast, the micro approach is associated with *interactionists*, who concentrate on the daily exchanges among individuals, which weave the fabric of social life. How determinists and interactionists study social class illustrates their differences. For structural determinists, particularly Marxists, an individual's social class is determined by his relationship to the means of production. Hence, the upper class, or bourgeoise, own the factories, and the working class, or proletariat are employees. Social class is a static concept, defined according to one's relationship to the means of production.

For interactionists, social class is a status designation, but it is also a process. How we eat, talk, maintain friendships, join social clubs, organize our children's after-school activities and monitor their educational progress are but a few examples of the myriad ways we create social class.

Micro-order studies concentrate on this *social construction of reality* (Berger and Luckmann, 1966), or the way individuals and groups create social structure. Situational definitions are called perspectives and are a co-ordinated set of ideas and actions a person or a group uses in dealing with some problematic situation. Perspectives refer to a person's ordinary way of thinking, feeling and acting in such a situation (Becker et al., 1961).

These perspectives constitute patterned behaviours which vary historically. For example, current perspectives about the appropriate behaviour for children differ substantially from medieval ideas on the subject. Situational definitions also vary according to the individual's location in the social structure. Traditionally, upper-class parents have defined children as needing less direct parental stimulation and supervision than have middle-class parents. Upper-class children are likely to have full-time nannies and to be sent to boarding school at an early age.

Within any social situation, there exist rival perspectives. In a study of under-graduate college life, Becker, Geer et al. (1968) concluded that students are most interested in their social life, professors are most concerned with teaching and ad-ministrators are preoccupied with the college making a profit. Within any organi-zation, situational definitions may conflict. College teachers may not, for example, appreciate the perspective of their students. In this situation, as in every other one, the group with the ability to control the actions of others exercises power. Power is a central element in our interpersonal relationships. It affects how we behave and how others manage us. Those who exert power can make their definition of a situation stick. Day-care workers may have the authority to control two-year-olds. But if the children disobey, the teachers must alter their tactics.

Situational definitions are constantly changing. Rules of conduct, agreements and bargains shift, requiring participants to adjust. This behavioural fluctuation is called *negotiation*.

The notion of perspectives as definitions of a situation is rooted in seeing social organizations as negotiated orders. Symbolic interactionists and other negotiation-order theorists outline how interaction patterns are initiated and maintained. Re-search has examined negotiation processes among teachers and students, (Stebbins, 1975), skid row alcoholics (Wiseman, 1979) and professional wrestlers (Turowetz and Rosenberg, 1978). In a classic study, Glaser and Strauss (1965) analysed the emergence of *awareness contexts* among terminally ill patients and the hospital staff. (Awareness contexts describe how patients and the medical staff treat one another. See insert on page 136 about this study.)

Other negotiation-order studies focus on the interactional processes between and among institutions. In a study of the American liquor industry, Denzin (1977) reveals a five-tier economic structure which establishes market policies. In a critical look at health care in the United States, Freidson (1975) illustrates how adminis-trative and political activities affect, but do not determine medical practices. In both studies, the emphasis is on institutional negotiations and their effects on particular social units.

In summary, the macro approach sees the social structure as a self-perpetuating, static arrangement that limits individual behaviour. To a certain extent, social or-ganizations do determine our actions. However, social organizations would not exist without networks of individual and group relationships. Sociologists try to show how individuals co-ordinate their activities and construct group situational defini-tions. The focus of the micro order on interactional activities and the analytic frame of negotiated orders reminds us of the interdependence of institutions and conscious human activity.

AWARENESS OF DYING

The phenomenon of awareness is central to the study of interaction. Barney Glaser and Anselm Strauss (1965) introduced the concept of awareness contexts. Any act of communication contains varying degrees of understanding or awareness between the participants. *Awareness context* refers to the combination of what each person knows about the identity of the other and his own identity in the eyes of the other. Any interaction contains four possible types of awareness. An *open awareness context* occurs when each participant knows his own and the other's true identity. In a hospital, an open awareness context prevails when a patient knows he is dying, identifies himself this way and is defined and treated by the hospital staff as dying. The patient might finalize his will, take care of business and financial matters and settle personal scores. The medical staff, in turn, makes no attempt to disguise the diagnosis.

The complete opposite to this is the *closed awareness context*. In such cases, the patient does not know he is dying and is not aware that the hospital staff has identified him in this way. As Glaser and Strauss state, "The hospital is magnificently organized, both by accident and design, for hiding the medical truth from the patient." Records are not available for scrutiny, the staff conceals information, medical discussion about the patient's condition goes on outside his room and the family makes constant reference to future events.

The third context, the *suspicion awareness context*, is a modification of the closed awareness context. One participant suspects the true identity of the other or the other's view of his own identity or both. For example, the patient may suspect he is dying, yet the physician may believe the patient does not know.

Finally, in the *pretense awareness context*, both participants realize that the patient is dying but pretend not to know.

SOCIAL ROLES AND SOCIAL IDENTITIES

SOCIAL ROLES

Roles and Everyday Life

Both macro- and micro-order studies examine the connection between roles and interactions. By participating in collective activities, human beings learn how we behave in particular social situations. *Roles* provide normative expectations and standards for anticipating how strangers will act and for judging how we should adjust our responses.

The smooth transaction of society's daily affairs is greatly facilitated by role playing. In fact, we often do not realize how much we rely on roles to predict others' behaviour until the role prescriptions are violated. Confronting "out of role" behaviour confuses and frustrates us. Harold Garfinkel (1967), an American ethnomethodologist, demonstrated how much humans rely on roles by having his sociology students deliberately break norms in familiar social settings. By breaching customary and unspoken expectations, Garfinkel and his students were scraping below the surface of social behaviour to discover how people understand daily routines. One of Garfinkel's more popular experiments was to have his students act as guests in their parents' home. They asked permission to use household facilities and equipment, addressed their parents formally as Mr. and Mrs. and displayed impeccable manners. This behaviour so violated the norms of usual family interaction that neither the students nor the family members could tolerate it for very long.

The Structuralist Approach to Roles

All sociologists, it seems, want to know about the origin and transmission of social roles. Macro-order role analyses take a structuralist approach, which stems from the work of Talcott Parsons (1951), Robert Merton (1967) and Ralph Linton (1936). These sociologists viewed society as organized according to a system of roles. The concept of social role became the conceptual link between individual activity and social organization. All individuals have scripts to enact. These scripts are organized into systems of roles. Hence, we have family roles, workplace roles and friendship roles. Social organizations are often analysed by examining their role structure.

The structuralist sees roles as the prescribed pattern of behaviour expected of a person in a given situation by virtue of his position in the transaction. Roles refer to observable behaviour, to what the individual actually does in a given social situation. All roles are socially defined according to the position or status an individual occupies in the social structure. Every social status carries with it a set of norms and expectations that specify how the role it defines ought to be played. The status of doctor suggests a set of behaviour, obligations and privileges that we can all agree upon. Doctors should always act in their patients' best interests. They are obligated to prolong and save lives. In exchange for their dedication and long working hours, they receive the societal privileges of professional autonomy, elevated prestige and high wages.

Roles involve both prescribed behaviours and reciprocal claims and obligations specifying what activities the actor is entitled to expect from others. Patients expect doctors to make every effort to heal them. Reciprocally, doctors expect patients to contribute to the healing process by following their orders. While the patient role specifies ideal role behaviour, our actual role performance often deviates from the norm. For example, studies indicate that over half of all patients ignore their doctor's advice. It is the nature and extent of such deviation that the interactionists study.

We are not always free to choose the parts we play in society. Some scripts, called *ascribed roles*, are assigned to us whether we like it or not. These ascribed roles are given to us at birth on the basis of biological characteristics like race and sex and on the basis of some characteristics of our parents, such as religion, caste or social class. Other parts, called *achieved roles*, require individual choice or talent before they are assumed. Occupational, marital and friendship roles are achieved.

"Let's play you're a guest, and I'll think of ways of trying to get rid of you."

Drawing by Whitney Darrow, Jr.; © 1947, 1975. The New Yorker Magazine, Inc.

Both ascribed and achieved roles can be ones we accept but do not enjoy. The role of mental patient may be partially ascribed and achieved and is not likely to be a role we joyfully accept. Other roles are less clearly differentiated according to their voluntary or involuntary assignment. For example, are sex and gender ascribed or achieved? Sex is usually seen as an ascribed status, while gender role behaviour is achieved. *Gender* refers to the cultural, social and psychological characteristics assumed appropriate to one's sex. Thus, gender represents learned behaviour that is acquired over a lifetime. *Sex*, on the other hand, refers to biological features.

Merton (1967) outlined how roles are systematically organized. Each social status involves, not a single associated role, but an array of roles. Physicians play the roles of primary care consultant, scientific researcher, hospital administrator, government consultant and medical school teacher. Upon entering a new status, individuals are confronted with a *role set*, an array of roles to be played in order to meet the expectations of a variety of people.

Role sets differ from multiple roles. *Multiple roles* refer to the fact that each person simultaneously enacts many different roles throughout her life. Hence, the physician is also a mother, a wife, a daughter, a professional weightlifter and a community worker.

Anxiety and stress are pervasive experiences in twentieth-century life. This pressure to succeed, achieve and conform can be analysed as *role strain* or *conflict*. Our actual behaviour does not match our definition of the normative expectations contained in our role prescriptions. We often feel pulled apart by the competing demands within role sets. The role of primary care consultant, for example, may make time claims on a physician that make it difficult for her to fulfill her teaching and research commitments. Peer discussion regularly revolves around strategies for coping with the pressures of role-set demands.

Another source of role strain is the attempt to fulfill multiple roles. Individuals often play two or more roles, each governed by conflicting norms. Consider the working mother. The norm of a wage labourer may periodically conflict with the norm of a domestic labourer. Which norm do women adhere to when their children are sick? Do they stay home and care for the child or go to work? Conformity to one role (staying home) may require deviating from another (going to work). The role overload chart indicates how women respond to role set and multiple role conflicts.

How individuals perform their roles provides another source of potential strain. Role performance can produce conflict when we disagree with others about how we or they ought to behave. Often the norms associated with roles are merely blueprints providing general behavioural guidelines. There are many ways to father, for example. Most of us will find that our definitions of good parenting are sometimes in contradiction to others' definitions. Prolonged discrepancy between actual and situational expectations can cause guilt feelings, frustration and anger. One way to cope with this is to recognize that these feelings result, not from personal inadequacies, but from competing role definitions.

Role performance can also produce strain when the role itself requires inconsistent and diverse conduct. The role of teacher contains a potential conflict in that it requires satisfying both administrators and parents. Educational administrators want teachers to cover all the material outlined by the Ministry of Education for their grade level. Parents may expect a more individualized program tailored to meet the academic and social needs of their child. Teachers sometimes "burn-out" as a result of the frustration they experience in juggling conflicting role demands.

Ambiguous roles create role conflict. The more unclear the role requirements, the more likely it is individuals will disagree over how to play the role. Typically, newly created roles and changing roles are unclear. Alice Rossi (1968) has discussed how women are prepared, through anticipatory socialization and gradual acquisition, to take on occupational and marriage roles. In contrast, transition to the parenting role

ROLE OVERLOAD AND WOMEN'S ROLE PERFORMANCE

People have a variety of ways of adjusting to overload situations (Miller, 1960). These common overload reactions are defined below. Each is accompanied by an illustration of the way in which an overworked housewife-mother might cope with role overload in her daily life.

Overload Reaction

1. Omission: Temporary nonprocessing of demands.

2. Queuing: Delaying response during high overload period.

3. Filtering: Neglecting to process certain types of information while processing others.

4. Cutting categories of discrimination: Responding in a general way to a number of demands.

5. Employing multiple channels: Processing information through two or more parallel channels at the same time.

6. Errors: Processing demands incorrectly.

7. Escape from the task.

Mother's Response

1. Forgetting to pick up the cleaning; or not hearing a child's request while talking on the phone.

2. Promising a child that Mother will talk about their problem after dinner; telling someone to call back after the children are asleep.

3. Neglecting household tasks or elaborate food preparation in order to take care of children's needs.

4. Preparing common meals that disregard the food preferences of different family members; having a common bedtime hour for children of different ages; not responding to the unique personality needs of each child.

5. Talking to children or husband while cooking or ironing; changing a diaper while talking on the phone.

6. Confusing the date of a meeting or social engagement; burning the dinner; yelling at a child for something that she/he had gotten permission to do.

7. Going to a movie; falling asleep; leaving home.

Frieze, Irene; J. Parsons; P. Johnson; D. Ruble and G. Zellman. *Women and Sex Roles*, Norton, 1978, p. 161.

occurs abruptly with the birth of a child. Isolated, fatigued and suddenly immersed in 24-hour child care, the caretaking role often feels overwhelming to new mothers.

The structuralist perspective employs the *blueprint* approach when discussing roles and interactions. Individuals are perceived as learning a set of roles in the course of their socialization, which determines their interactional behaviour. Roles are conceptualized as standard, rule-governed actions that individuals automatically and appropriately enact in various settings. Since other organizational members have internalized the same rules, predictable relationships occur. This unified and orderly pattern of interaction becomes codified into characteristic structures.

The Interactionist Perspective on Roles

While the structural perspective views roles as passive constructions, interactionists emphasize the dynamic aspect of activity formation, performance and conflict. The concept of role was originally employed by George Herbert Mead (1938) to explain co-operative behaviour and communication. Today, symbolic interactionists are reluctant to use the term "role" in analysing micro-order activities because of its structural connotations. Interactionists argue that social interaction cannot adequately be explained by role analysis. Instead, the more inclusive concepts of social acts and situational definitions or group perspectives are used to capture the diverse, situational dimensions of human action.

Interactionists do not analyse events in terms of roles. Rather, they concentrate on the type of experience individuals are having at a particular moment, in a particular place in their social lives. Interactionists ask "What is it that's going on here?" (Goffman 1974:8) and "How are these situational definitions different for various groups in this setting?" Discerning group perspectives means understanding what social acts individuals engage in to create distinct activities, how these activities coalesce into regular patterns and what external or internal forces lead to behavioural changes.

In understanding perspectives, researchers find that *nonverbal behaviour* is as significant as verbal expression. Infants, for example, rely on nonverbal behaviour to communicate.

In conversation, adults use nonverbal cues to tell their partners to continue, repeat, elaborate, hurry up, become more interesting, less salacious, give them a chance to talk. These messages are transmitted by nodding the head, eye contact, raising of eyebrows, slight movements forward and small postural shifts. (Ekman and Frieson 1969:82).

Interactional investigations involve more than ascertaining a set of roles. Individuals and groups are constantly interpreting events. People are always acting on their understandings and responding to the demands and expectations of others. How people mesh together their perspectives constitutes the *analytic focus*.

ROLE ENACTMENT

Interactionists discuss role enactment as an active, reflective process in which individuals try to figure out what their part in the social exchange is and how others expect them to behave. In his discussion of role enactment, Mead (1938:8–25) identified four phases individuals go through in carrying out any social act.

The first involves an *identification with self*. The individual asks who he is or ought to be in that particular situation. Secondly, an individual must then *behave in a manner appropriate* to this identification. We do not simply play roles as puppets; we explore possibilities and choose those most suitable. These decisions are relatively simple when the social norms governing action are clearly defined. Our interactions with shopkeepers and post office workers are based on distinct rules. However, choosing an appropriate stance becomes difficult in ambiguous situations. When we are unsure of someone's sex, considerable confusion results. People greeting new babies always want to know the child's sex because this information determines how they will treat the child.

Thirdly, individuals *use the behaviour of others* as cues to guide their own behaviour. Through their actions, other people convey to us what they expect us to do. By symbolically communicating their expectations, people create a collective definition of the situation. In devising any role performance, we consider the expectations of others. These shared expectations provide countless regulations that we hardly ever think about.

The final element integral to the enactment of roles is an *evaluation* by us and by others of our performance. An individual's part in an exchange provides him with a distinctive position from which to evaluate his own performance and those of others.

The late Erving Goffman (1963, 1967), an American sociologist, analysed the *interaction rituals* people employ in daily life. These rituals include all the taken-for-granted cues we use in dealing with others. *Access* rituals (1967:41), for example, refer to how we greet and take leave of others. The rules governing greetings between intimates differ from those regulating the greetings of boss and employee. Strangers, of course, do not greet one another but rather engage in the ritual of *civil inattention* (1963:84). This ritual can be seen in elevators, where individuals glance at each other only long enough to acknowledge the other's presence. Excessive eye contact is considered inappropriate in such public places. Children, as nonpersons, are permitted to stare.

Interactionists conceptualize roles as negotiable social acts. Social acts are the basic unit of human behaviour, on which all communication is established. By focusing on the social actions among individuals, interactionists can describe the wider dimensions of human exchanges.

Role Playing and Role Taking

Role enactment is similar to role playing. *Role playing* consists of living up to the obligations of the role one assumes and insisting that others meet your expectations. However, role playing, and indeed all social interaction, would be impossible without role taking. To play a role, you have to understand how others might react to you. You gain this understanding by imaginatively projecting yourself into the point of view of others. A patient, for example, imagines how her complaints will sound to the physician and states her situation vigorously or diffidently, depending on the length and severity of her illness. Mead called this "taking the role of the other toward self" (1938:374). *Role taking* refers to empathizing with others by symbolically assuming their point of view. We observe their behaviour, learn how they think and feel and, simultaneously, see how they are interpreting our behaviour.

We take the roles of others into account so naturally that we never reflect upon this process unless an interactional problem arises. A problem, according to Mead, is some action, word, gesture, thought or physical obstacle that stops the smooth flow of interaction and causes us to think about our situation. When problems arise, we realize that we must put ourselves in the other's shoes and imagine their thoughts and feelings. Greeting friends is done with no reflection, unless one of them snubs you. Most daily exchanges occur on this customary, habitual level. Life would be too exhausting and stressful otherwise. The role of tourist in a foreign country is often tiring because we have to work so hard at comprehending the new cultural system. Similarly, one reason new students at university feel so lost and anxious is the alarming array of new problems they confront. Meeting the demands of professors, finding student hangouts, making new friends and securing dates are all difficult in a strange situation. For the most part, students behave as most people do in new situations. They appear nonchalant, remain silent and closely follow the ways of more experienced students. Often neophytes find people to inform or coach them on how to behave in an unfamiliar setting.

For the interactionists, social change is a gradual, continual and consensual process of mutual realignment of perspectives. Mead (1938:79) outlines exactly how change occurs. In the course of interaction, confusions and misunderstandings between people often arise, effectively ending the exchange. One cannot continue to act until these problems are solved. Resolution occurs when individuals reflect on their situation and come up with alternative ways of behaving. This reflection can occur within minutes or take several years.

Interpersonal negotiation is central to problem-solving. In most situations, degrees and types of bargaining can be identified. Anselm Strauss (1963) has suggested that each situation contains working agreements that broadly outline how individuals should interact. These general agreements do not take on the specificity or the constraining nature of rules. Rather, any agreement can be "stretched, negotiated, argued, ignored and applied at convenient moments" (Strauss 1963:153). Understanding this situational negotiation is essential in analysing social settings.

Wilfred Martin (1976), in a recent Canadian field study of the schooling process, employed the concept of negotiation to explain how teachers view students. Martin (1976:6) defined negotiation as the " . . . total set of processes whereby actors, in pursuit of common interests, try to arrive at a settlement or arrangement with each other or with a third party." The teachers Martin observed classified student role performance according to three categories. The "nonnegotiable" students were those the teachers viewed as problems. Hence, the teachers refused to bargain with them and instead issued explicit directives and stated explicit consequences of disobeying these directives. The second group was labelled "continuously negotiable." These "teachers' pets" joined in open negotiation with the teachers and were often successful in gaining their ends. The third group, the "intermittently negotiable" students, represented the silent majority, whose participation in open or closed negotiation depended on how legitimate their demands were seen to be.

The work of Martin and Strauss demonstrates that role bargaining is a pervasive feature of role enactment. As originally conceived, role taking is falsely based on a model of interaction between equals within neutral settings and leading to mutually satisfying alignments. Interactionists use the concept of negotiation to account for the varying degrees of power which individuals exercise. Negotiation-order theorists acknowledge that most relationships are unequal. Individuals do not have identical power and ability to determine outcomes, and situational definitions are often imposed by those with the most control.

Roles and Self Identity

Sociologists have linked the concepts of self and role. Through social interaction, we develop a self-identity. Our self-image is closely linked to the roles we enact and reflects how we imagine others characterize us. Just as we perform many diverse roles during our lifetimes, we also have many selves or ways of viewing ourselves.

A classic field-work study by Erving Goffman (1959b) dramatically reveals how roles and situational expectations affect self-behaviour and the behaviour of others. Goffman analysed the effect of being labelled mentally ill and treated as such within the institutional setting of a mental hospital. Mental patients go through a regular sequence of changes in their self- and other definitions. In the first stage, as pre-patients, they typically feel betrayed and skeptical of those who committed them. Once committed, patients are stripped of their rights and liberties. Tension arises between the patients and the staff and family who try to convince the patients that this help is "for their own good."

In the second stage, as inpatients, the patients' self-definitions undergo a transformation. Confronted with unacceptable views of themselves and with isolation, humiliation and stark living conditions, patients present favourable explanations for their past and current behaviours. Patients suggest they were misdiagnosed, overworked or suffer from bad nervous systems. However, the staff and other patients create a social environment that denies these agreeable self-images and forces the patients to constantly review who they are. Over time, patients take on the selves the others present to them. Adopting these self-images is also a more efficient way of coping with their demoralizing situations.

How, then, do we define the self? The self is a social product, an outgrowth of our interaction with others. According to Lindesmith et al. (1977:324), the self is an organization or integration of behaviour imposed upon individuals by themselves and by societal expectations and demands. Selves do not exist except in a symbolic environment from which they cannot be separated. As we move through life, we acquire a succession of selves. William James (1890:294), the noted American social psychologist, first commented on the social and multi-faceted nature of self-identity:

> The individual has as many different social selves as there are distinct groups of persons about whose opinion he cares. Many a youth who is demure enough before his parents and teachers, swears and swaggers like a pirate among his "tough" friends.

Given the situational and changeable nature of self-concepts, is there one true or real self, a unique identity which persists despite the variety of experiences we encounter? Sociologists disagree on this question. But the majority have used role enactment as an explanation for multiple selves. Role enactment allows for a wide variety of acts within a permitted range. Despite individual differences in personality, temperament and life experiences, sociologists emphasize the similarities in role performance. What role variations do exist are seen as resulting from an individual's prior experience or from immediate situational pressures.

Not only do we appear to others as many different people, but often the performance of one role is interrupted by the encroachment of other roles. Given this role diversity, what unifies an individual's behaviour is her controlling conception of what she is doing. This self-direction comes from the ongoing, private dialogues an individual has with herself. By talking with herself, reviewing her behaviour in different situations and evaluating her diverse performances, the individual maintains a consistent sense of self.

Recognition of the *situational self* has led to research on how various environments affect individual and group behaviour. Philip Zimbardo (1971), a social psychologist, demonstrated the effect of the situation on the self in his Stanford County Prison experiment. Zimbardo designed a realistic mock prison in the basement of one of Stanford's buildings. Through a newspaper advertisement, he solicited volunteers who were willing to spend two weeks playing the role of either a prisoner or a guard. The experiment had to be abandoned after six days due to the emotional strain the prisoners were under. Five prisoners had to be released, four because of severe emotional depression or acute anxiety attacks, one because he developed a psychosomatic rash. The prisoners were behaving like "servile, dehumanized robots who thought only of escape, of their individual survival and of their mounting hatred of the guards" (Zimbardo, 1971:3). This happened because, soon after the experiment started, the guards began abusing their power. They made the prisoners obey petty and meaningless rules, forced them to do tedious and useless work, demanded that they laugh and sing on command and ordered them to publicly humiliate each other. In less than a week, ordinary, mature, emotionally stable, middle-class college students became caught up in the traditional prisoner and guard roles.

How do we reconcile an individual's controlling sense of self with his presentation of various and often unpleasant selves? An individual resolves this tension by talking to himself about his seemingly discrepant behaviours, assessing their origin and evaluating their impact on others. This private self-reflection allows an individual to explain current behaviours within the context of his own historical account of past and present acts.

IMPRESSION MANAGEMENT

In all sorts of exchanges, people employ interactional strategies designed to help them control and impose their definition of the situation on the group. Since group definitions become self-fulfilling prophecies, we recognize the importance of controlling how others interpret events and act on these constructions.

Erving Goffman investigated how people manage their self-impressions. *Self-impressions* include impressions the self makes on others and impressions that others make on the self. (In the course of interaction, selves act, others respond, and selves incorporate these responses into their next act. People are constantly monitoring and evaluating their own behaviour and that of others.) Goffman's approach is thus called *dramaturgical*, based on the idea expressed by Shakespeare as "all the world's a stage and all the men and women merely players."

Building on Mead's notion of role taking, Goffman suggested that actors both empathize with their fellow participants in creating joint social acts and actively strive to manage and control how these others will interpret their behaviour. In all interactional exchanges, we consider our audience expectations and characteristics and attempt to present ourselves favourably. In the *Presentation of Self in Everyday Life* (1959a), Goffman outlined two ways an individual manages impressions. He deliberately gives some impressions. These consist of the information or sign activity an actor wants the audience to receive. An individual also gives off some impressions unwittingly. Both behaviours occur within structurally defined limits. Goffman calls attempting to convey a specific impression *front-stage behaviour*. Deliberately concealing information from our audience is called *back-stage behaviour*. Goffman uses a waiter in a restaurant to illustrate. The front-stage scene for waiters is the formal dining area of the restaurant. Waiters try to convey a sense of sincerity in serving their customers. As in any successful front-stage performance, the actor stages a good performance by acting in role and by manipulating the situational props (the setting and lighting, the food). In some social encounters, such as those that take place in a restaurant, performance teams co-operate in staging a successful and convincing routine for the audience.

Raven and Rubin photo. Permission granted by John Wiley & Sons, Inc.

However, according to Goffman, if we really wanted to know what the waiter was like, we would also have to observe his back-stage, or out of role, behaviour. Kitchens, for example, are back-stage areas for waiters, since that is where the audience does not normally enter. The information a waiter discloses about himself in the kitchen when discussing his customers or arguing with the chef is far more instructive in providing us with a well-rounded picture of this person.

GENDER DISPLAYS

While we do sometimes willfully manage gender-type impressions, many gender behaviours are not consciously manipulable. Learning appropriate gender displays is a central lesson in childhood socialization, so these behaviours become habitual.

LANGUAGE AND THE INTERACTION BETWEEN MEN AND WOMEN

Interactionists have studied conversations between men and women. Somehow, in their everyday communications, both sexes reinforce their unequal status. To alter gender inequality, we must understand how, through interaction, men are encouraged to assume positions of dominance and women to fill submissive roles.

One way to tackle this methodological problem is through conversational analysis. People widely believe that women talk much more than men and that they talk about trivial matters. However, there has not been one study to support this notion. In mixed-sex conversations, men talk more than women. In 1972, Jessie Bernard analysed television sitcoms and found that men talked more often than women. In 1977, Nancy Henley noted that it was often impossible for women to talk when men were present, particularly if the males were their husbands. If women wished to talk, they talked to each other. Henley thinks that the stereotype of the talkative woman arises from the role of women in a patriarchal order, where they are required to be submissive and silent. Men wish to dominate and give orders to women. Any amount of talk by a woman is considered excessive.

In a conversational-analysis study, Zimmerman and West (1975) and West and Zimmerman (1977) suggested that the speech behaviour of women interacting with men resembled that of children talking to adults. They found that 98 percent of interruptions in mixed-sex conversations were made by men. Interruptions prevent women from talking and ensure female silence by allowing men to "gain the floor."

Men also denied equal status to women as conversational partners by not pursuing topics of interest to women and by not allowing women an equal number of turns to talk during a conversation. Women maintained longer silences and used a childlike intonation pattern when talking by raising their voices at the end of an exclamation ("I told you so!") instead of dropping their voices, as adult men do.

Pamela Fishman (1978) recorded the daily conversations between three couples who were white, professional and between the ages of 25 and 35. Five of the six were in graduate school. Two of the three women were avowed feminists, while all three men described themselves as sympathetic to the women's movement.

Despite these protestations of gender equality, there was an unequal distribution of work in conversation. The women asked three times as many questions as the men. The women used conversational attention-getters, such as "Do you know what?" or "This is interesting." Women used "yeah," "umm" and "huh" to show they were constantly attending to what was being said. The men also produced over twice as many statements as the women, and they also got responses. The women introduced a number of topics. When they hit one the men wanted to pursue, often the men did so by interrupting and assuming control.

Fishman concluded that women are the "shit workers" of routine interaction. Shit work includes sitting and being a good listener, filling silences and keeping the conversation going, developing others' topics and presenting and developing topics of their own. Women who deviate from this role and successfully control interactions are considered domineering, castrating and aggressive.

Jack Sattel (1982) has analysed "male inexpressiveness" as a strategy men use to maintain their dominant interactional position. Male inexpressiveness refers to behaviour that does not indicate affection, tenderness or emotion. It also includes behaviour that is not supportive of the affective expectations of a wife or female intimate. Sattel suggests that men are inexpressive only when they want to be. From an early age, boys learn that inexpressiveness is a means of assuming and maintaining positions of power. Giving off an affectively neutral impression convinces others of one's rational and calm decision-making ability. By being silent and inexpressive, especially in tense situations, men consolidate their power and "make the effort appear as effortless, to guard against showing the real limits of one's potential and power by making it all appear easy." Sattel further suggests that men are situationally expressive when they see expressiveness as a useful way to exercise control. For example, one way for a man to "come on" to a woman is to show his weaknesses and frailties. Such behaviour is to be read by the woman as a sign of authentic interest in her.

However, in one of his last works (*Gender Advertisements*, 1979), Goffman suggests several ways individuals deliberately use specific strategies to control and manage social encounters involving gender behaviours.

Gender displays are the culturally established gender behaviours that are so stereotypical they can be recognized in almost any social context. Gender displays include the smile, the leer, the seductive posture and the feminine touch. Each display represents typically masculine and feminine behaviour. These displays are part of our everyday life and are easily recognized in television and magazine advertisements.

Using Goffman's analytical frame, Posner (1982) has examined sex-role stereotyping in Canadian magazine advertisements. By examining body postures, facial expressions, eye contact and relationship to physical objects, Posner shows how these advertisements reinforce stereotypical images of women and men. Women are portrayed as childlike, tactile, mentally drifting and passive. Men are aggressive, active, alert and in control. Our uncritical acceptance of these images indicates that we agree that men and women present themselves to others in fundamentally different ways.

SOCIAL GROUPS AND INTERACTIONS

THE INDIVIDUAL

Individuals in Groups

Throughout this chapter, we have stressed the social character of interaction. People have always formed associations and most social interaction occurs within groups. Our behaviour, personality and character are moulded by the groups to which we belong. Moreover, most changes in our lives result from alterations in our group membership. Entering university, working in our first job, getting married, having children and aging are experienced as group events. How we interpret our university life varies tremendously according to our group participation. Women's studies, athletic teams, debating societies, chess clubs and musical societies are examples of different groups in which students can become involved and which can colour their university experience.

What is a Social Group?

But what is a social group? What, for example, distinguishes a random collection of people at a hockey game from a neighbourhood street gang? Generally, a social group is any collection of two or more people interacting together in an orderly way on the basis of shared understanding about how they and other group members ought to behave. Just because people are together in the same place does not mean that they constitute a social group. Collective behaviour is not group behaviour. For the hockey-game crowd to be regarded as a social group, its members must interact. Instead, crowd members react individually to a central stimulus (the game) and subliminally to each other. In contrast, neighbourhood gangs develop group consciousness and a sympathetic identification with similar groups. Social groups vary in size, organization, durability and flexibility of action.

Sociology contains two distinct approaches to studying group behaviour. The first, a *structuralist* interpretation, focuses on the structural characteristics which distinguish groups from nongroups. Often, only stable aggregates are studied, including ones with a readily identifiable membership, a clearly defined central activity and the binding of one member to another in well-established relationships (Shibutani, 1961:33). This definition of groups includes everything from small peer groups to all members of the Moslem faith.

The second approach, the *interactionist* perspective, defines groups according to their central activity. Interactionists focus on group process, on how the group members work together. A group is thus more than a collection of individuals who happen to be at the same place at the same time. Social groups are units of interacting individuals who have a common sense of identity and a "capacity for common endeavour" (Shibutani 1961:33).

Incorporating both the structuralist and the interactionist views, groups can be said to have the following characteristics:

1. Group members share a sense of identity, co-operation and consciousness of themselves as a group.

2. This identity is established through repeated patterns of interaction, in which group members evolve stable and predictable ways of accomplishing group goals.
3. These interactional patterns are based on shared understandings about definitions of situations, expected situational responses, goals, plans of action and rules of appropriate conduct.
4. Interactional patterns are further differentiated according to the division of labour within the group. The allocation of various group tasks creates a degree of member interdependence and integration within the collective enterprise.
5. Interactional patterns are further differentiated according to the degree of ongoing negotiation, in which group members adjust to situational demands.

Each group has its own norms, roles, status arrangements, rules, shared beliefs, negotiation limits and lines of action. Sociological investigation reveals the internal dynamics of group processes and explores the group's external relationships to other social organizations.

TYPES OF GROUPS

Primary Groups

Three main elements significantly affect group interaction. These are group size, the tasks of the group and the nature of the interpersonal relations within it. Based on these three characteristics, groups are classified as either primary or secondary.

Charles Horton Cooley (1909:23), a founder of American sociology, introduced the concept of primary groups to refer to those groups "characterized by intimate face-to-face association and cooperation." Primary groups are based on what Cooley called the primary relation. *Primary relationships* are those small, intimate, co-operative contacts which provide emotional support and teach us our culture. The most common forms of primary bonding are emotionally intense, such as parent-child relationships, love attachments and friendships. In these close primary relationships, we interact by responding to others as unique and whole personalities. These personally satisfying relationships are essential early in life if a person is to learn how to form close relationships with others. Later in life, we participate in primary groups such as families and peer networks.

These primary associations provide affection and security and facilitate personal growth and self-esteem. Given the emotional closeness of these relationships, primary-group members are not interchangeable. The loss of a member through death, divorce or other circumstances requires considerable readjustment. While most primary relations are happy and personally satisfying, others are intensely antagonistic. For example, our experiences within the family are crucial to developing our self-identity, yet, because of child abuse and wife-beating, family relationships are often brutally violent.

Almost any small group can develop primary relations. As Simmel (1955), a German sociologist, pointed out in his brilliant work on *triads* (interactions among three people) and *dyads* (interactions between two people) the size of a group determines its quality and type of interaction. Only small groups can ripen into personal and intimate relationships.

Within any larger organization, such as an army, a college, a factory or a business corporation, small, primary groups may develop. This usually occurs when the members are together for a long time, confronting joint problems and undergoing similar experiences. Friendship networks link the individual to the wider society. The closeness and commitment to other primary group members ultimately sustains small groups and enables their members to accomplish the larger goals of society. William Foote Whyte's classic field work study (*Street Corner Society*, 1961) is perhaps the most thorough treatment of the effect of the primary group on individual behaviour. Whyte graphically details the primary relations among a group of men in the north end of Boston. By living in the area and befriending the group, Whyte discovered how these Italian men, who congregated together on certain street corners, evolved their sense of self-esteem and identity from their gang membership.

Secondary Groups

While Cooley never discussed the concept of the secondary group, it is a term widely used in sociology today. *A secondary group* is any collection of people who communicate sporadically on an impersonal basis. Often these groups are formed to accomplish a specific purpose. Hence, the group members respond to one another in terms of the limited roles they have taken on to carry out the group's task. Participation in political campaigns, fund-raising organizations, neighbourhood committees or an introductory sociology class are all secondary-group activities. All tend to be unsentimental, instrumental, limited and specific attachments.

Unlike primary groups, secondary-group members are not often emotionally committed to one another. Because of the larger size of secondary groups, it is impossible for all members to know each other personally. Also, the size of the group necessitates specialization of roles and responsibilities. A formal system of decision-making is used to organize the group's tasks. While most social organizations fall somewhere between primary and secondary groups, the distinguishing element between the two types is the relative strength of the sense of identity and attachment to the group which the members feel.

Business organizations are secondary groups that shape workers' behaviour. In a detailed examination of corporate life, Kanter (1977:3) concluded, "Organizations make their workers into who they are." Corporations typically recruit, as managers, people they think will fit into the company. The more individual discretion managerial jobs require, the more likely it is that other managers will hire men they feel they can trust to make responsible decisions. One way of guaranteeing trust is to recruit men from similar educational and social backgrounds. Once in place, "good" managers are defined as those who are good team players, who fit into the organization, who have strong peer acceptance and who make others feel comfortable. In short, good managers evince *general* skills and knowledge which can be adapted to organizational demands.

GROUP INFLUENCE ON OTHERS

Reference Groups

Groups modify behaviour, attitudes, character, identity and emotions, and reference groups are particularly influential. *Reference groups* are associations to which individuals refer when formulating and evaluating their own beliefs and actions. The concept stems from interactionist work, which maintains that co-ordinated group action emerges from sharing perspectives.

Reference groups are powerful organizing influences in shaping individuals. They are groups to which people aspire. Thus, individuals do not necessarily belong to their reference group. For people undergoing anticipatory socialization, their reference group is often the group to which they expect eventually to belong. For example, university students enrolled in nursing school may look to nurses who have already graduated for professional standards rather than to other nursing students. Similarly, social climbing and marginality, in which individuals are caught between two social groups with no clear commitment to either, are explained in terms of reference groups.

An early major study of reference groups was undertaken by Theodore Newcomb (1943), who examined the changing attitudes and values of students at the all-female Bennington College in New England. Most of the 250 women came from conservative families. Thus, their family values conflicted with the liberal orientation of the faculty and administration. Following one cohort through their four undergraduate years, Newcomb noticed that the longer the students stayed at the school, the more liberal they became. All but a small minority switched their primary reference group from their conservative families to the liberal faculty. A follow-up study done 25 years later (Newcomb, Koenig, Flacks and Warcick, 1967) indicated that these value changes had persisted. The more liberal students remained committed liberals in their adult life, as measured by their career choices, periodical subscriptions and voting behaviour.

Distinctions are usually drawn between the normative and the comparative functions of reference groups. The *normative function* refers to individuals assuming, either through direct or vicarious participation, the perspectives of the group. The group's norms, values and attitudes are behavioural guides. Teenage friends who dress alike and march in peace demonstrations are examples of the normative influence of groups.

The *comparative function* is exercised when individuals use the beliefs of their reference groups as standards by which to judge the beliefs and actions of others. During the process of assimilation, immigrants gradually acquire the perspectives of the dominant cultural group. Shaffir (1974) studied how religious converts (Jews joining the Montreal Lubavitcher Jewish chassidim movement) adopted the standards and actions of their new reference group.

Why we choose one reference group over another is unclear. From their research on ethnic assimilation, Haas and Shaffir (1978:16) concluded that we are more likely to select groups if we have favourable feelings toward their members and if we are treated in a friendly and sincere manner. Other important factors include the

Following the horrors of World War II concentration camps and the mass extermination of Jews, gypsies, leftists and homosexuals, North American social scientists became fascinated with the phenomenon of people hurting other people. Was the German compliance with Nazi demands a result of some national characteristic? Or was it a result of group influence, which would suggest that such horrors could be carried out by any nation?

To explore these questions, Stanley Milgram (1963) carried out a series of experiments to test to what extent people would obey authority. Milgram assigned the subjects the role of teacher, in what they thought was a study of learning and memory. As the teacher, the volunteer was to administer an ever increasing voltage of electric shocks to a "learner" every time the learner answered a memory question incorrectly. The learner was presumed to be strapped to an electrode, which conducted the electric current. Opposite the learner and separated from him by a wall, the teacher sat in front of an electric shock generator from which he could administer the shocks.

The teacher was told that the experiment would test the effect of punishment on learning. In fact, the real purpose was to ascertain when the teachers would refuse to participate in the experiment despite the researcher's insistence that they continue to administer apparently extremely painful shocks to a learner. Twenty-six of the 40 adult males tested went all the way, administering the most extreme shock of 450 volts to what they thought were real learners.

Milgram explained his results by noting that all of us have spent years being taught to obey those in authority. Most social groups demand conformity to their rules as a condition of membership. Experience in internalizing rules of conduct and obedience in certain group situations increases the likelihood we will "live by the rules" in other group situations.

perceived status and rewards to be gained from membership, individual rates of social mobility (upwardly mobile people choose higher status groups as reference groups) and the individual's own personality and view of himself. We tend to choose groups that seem similar to us in some way (Merton, 1957:288–92).

Reference group theory emphasizes the significance and power of the group in defining and evaluating definitions of social situations. It helps explain behavioural inconsistencies as individuals change groups and make choices between alternatives. (Reference group theory encouraged a wealth of studies that examine the influence of groups on the behaviour of those outside. The issue of social conformity has received special attention and is discussed in the inserts above and opposite.)

SUMMARY

In this chapter, we have discussed the differences between macro and micro analyses and their approaches to the study of roles and interactions. *Macro-order* studies stress

JONESTOWN

Reference group theory encouraged a wealth of studies examining the influence of groups on the behaviour of those outside the group. The issue of social conformity has received special attention. Humans conform to and obey others, often in a seemingly blind and unthinking fashion. The following excerpt explains the 1978 Jonestown mass suicide of over 900 people in terms of the types of power exerted in the commune:

Coercion
It is true that armed guards surrounded the group and some people may have felt that if they didn't drink the poison, they would be killed anyway.

Informational Power
Jones told them that because of the murders of the congressman and some of those with him, the commune would very soon be attacked either by the Guyanese army or the CIA. There was talk of torture and concentration camps. "When they start parachuting out of the air, they'll shoot some of our innocent babies. Can you let them take your child?" ("Hurry, My Children, Hurry," 1979).

Referent Power
Jones was a beloved leader for most of his followers. The group, which was composed of many poor blacks, had given up all their possessions, cut off ties with their families, and followed him to the jungles of South America to start a new society. The fact that he felt it was time to "die with dignity" must have motivated many who wanted to emulate him. "To me death is not a fearful thing," Jones said that day. "It's living that's cursed. It's not worth living like this. . . . I like to choose my own kind of death for a change. I'm tired of being tormented to hell. Tired of it." (Applause) (Ibid.). Jones's referent power for one of the members is evident in this statement heard on the tape: "Like Dad (the cultists called Jones "Dad") said, when they come in, they're going to massacre our children. And the ones that they take captive, they're gonna just let them grow up and be dummies. And not grow up to be a person like the one and only Jim Jones." (Applause) ("Hurry, My Children, Hurry," 1979).

Expert Power
Jones was clearly the expert on what should be done. He controlled everything that happened at Jonestown, and had directed the members' activities for years. Jones's statements to the group emphasize his expertise. "I've tried to keep this thing from happening. But I now see it's the will of the sovereign Being that we lay down our lives in protest against what's been done." As one man said, "I'm ready to go. If you tell us we have to give our lives

now, we're ready; all the rest of the sisters and brothers are with me" ("Hurry, My Children, Hurry," 1979).

Legitimate Power

Jones used many techniques to reinforce the feeling that he was the group's legitimate leader and that they were obligated to obey him. By insisting that they call him "Dad" and call his wife Marcellne, "Mother," he likened his role to that of a parent. Children must obey their parents. At meetings of the commune, he sat on a chair on an elevated platform almost like a king. He laid the groundwork for his legitimacy during the years preceding the tragedy. He had carried out an extensive program of socialization in which group members were called upon to declare, verbally and in writing, how much they loved him and how important he was to them. There were rewards for acceptable behavior and punishment, often in the form of brutal beatings, for unacceptable behavior (Winfrey, 1979).

In addition to this vast store of personal power available to Jones, there was the equally vast force of *peer pressure among the followers themselves*. Seeing their friends and relatives killing their children and then taking their own lives undoubtedly convinced many members that suicide was the only alternative for them.

In summary, by analyzing the influence process of Jonestown, an unbelievable, bewildering event becomes an understandable tragedy.

the objective conditions that influence the interpersonal bonds which develop. The social structure or environment within which interaction takes place encourages some types of interaction more than others. The *micro-order* focuses on interactional activities in which individuals learn new behaviours, express their interpretations and adjust to the demands of others.

The *structuralist,* or *blueprint*, approach to roles and interactions sees individuals as passive; they merely learn prescribed patterns through the socialization process. Successfully socialized individuals perform in situationally appropriate ways. Thus, *role sets, multiple roles* and *role strain* are defined according to normative standards of role enactment.

In contrast, the *interactionist*, or *process*, perspective emphasizes the dynamic quality of social structure. Individuals are seen as active agents who bring their own meanings to social encounters. Within a general framework of consensus, individuals continually *negotiate* definitions of legitimate behaviour. Roles and interactions are negotiable social acts, patterns which coalesce into group perspectives.

Social groups are an intermediate level of social organization linking the macro and the micro orders. *Primary relations* are the most intimate interpersonal bonds. It is from these affiliations that we derive our sense of identity, and in them we experience relationships most intensely. The influence of *reference groups*, one type of primary group, as a source of values and actions attests to the significance of primary relations.

However, most of our behaviour occurs within larger, more impersonal *secondary groups*. We co-operate with larger numbers of people in institutions to accomplish group goals. Analyses of secondary groups reveal the influence of the organizational setting in delineating interactional processes. Focusing on roles and interactions within group settings uncovers the interdependent and reciprocal relationship between individual acts and institutional arrangements.

DISCUSSION QUESTIONS

1. Devise an experiment to see if the findings of Zimmerman and West and those of Sattel can be replicated *OR* in what conditions might their findings *not* be replicated.

2. Choose a primary and a secondary group to which you belong. Analyse and contrast the roles, norms, status relationships and level of cohesiveness in both groups.

3. Can you recall an awkward social situation you have recently been in? Explain why you felt uncomfortable by analysing the role requirements you were attempting to fulfill.

4. Apply Goffman's ideas of impression management to some social situation you are familiar with.

5. Using the theory of reference groups, discuss some of the changes that have occurred in your life.

Gender and Gender Relations

Maureen Baker

INTRODUCTION: MAINTAINING GENDER DIFFERENCES

From the moment a human baby is born, we treat it according to its sex. Wrapping newborns in pink or blue blankets symbolizes this distinction. As soon as people hear a child's name, they usually know whether it is a girl or a boy. Differences in dress, in mannerisms, in personality, in toys and interests are carefully cultivated by parents, who fear they could harm their children by blurring these distinctions. Children themselves are often offended if they are mistaken for a member of the opposite sex.

Segregation of the sexes used to be common in schools, clubs, the workplace and in political life. Until the 1970s, schools usually maintained separate entrances for girls and boys and did not allow the sexes to play together at recess. In some provinces, taverns had one entrance for "ladies and escorts" and one for men only. Private clubs for business and professional men did not admit women. Until just before World War II, a woman was expected to quit her job when announcing her marriage, and until very recently she was expected to leave when she became pregnant. Expectant fathers were not allowed in the delivery room with their wives until a few years ago.

Recently there has been a concerted effort to minimize the differences in the opportunities presented to the sexes in the workplace and to blur the physiological differences. Unisex hairstyling and clothing are fashionable among some segments of the population, yet others exaggerate sexual differences in appearance. Some people tenaciously adhere to the idea that males and females are different in abilities, interests and personality. Others argue that differences between the sexes are "natural," should be respected and accentuated to enhance the quality of life.

BIOLOGY OR SOCIALIZATION?

How much of the behavioural and attitudinal differences between males and females is caused by physiology? How much is developed through different social treatment? This has been a controversy for many years. Because of the ethical problems involved in doing research on human infants, studies of the innate differences between the sexes are usually performed on animals. These studies, however, have been inconclusive.

Although the origins of gender differences cannot be easily discovered, it is apparent that behavioural differences exist between male and female humans from childhood on. Especially in early adolescence, the aptitudes, personalities, interests and achievement levels of North American girls and boys become more distinct. Males and females develop different verbal abilities by age ten. Girls tend to do better in spelling and boys in mathematics. Girls show less independence in decision-making, less assertiveness and self-confidence and more of an interest in helping people and maintaining relationships. While boys play competitive games with carefully laid-out rules in teams and groups, girls are more likely to play co-operative games in smaller groups.

Many studies of sex differences have had their methods and basic concepts challenged. For example, research on aggressiveness has often considered only physical

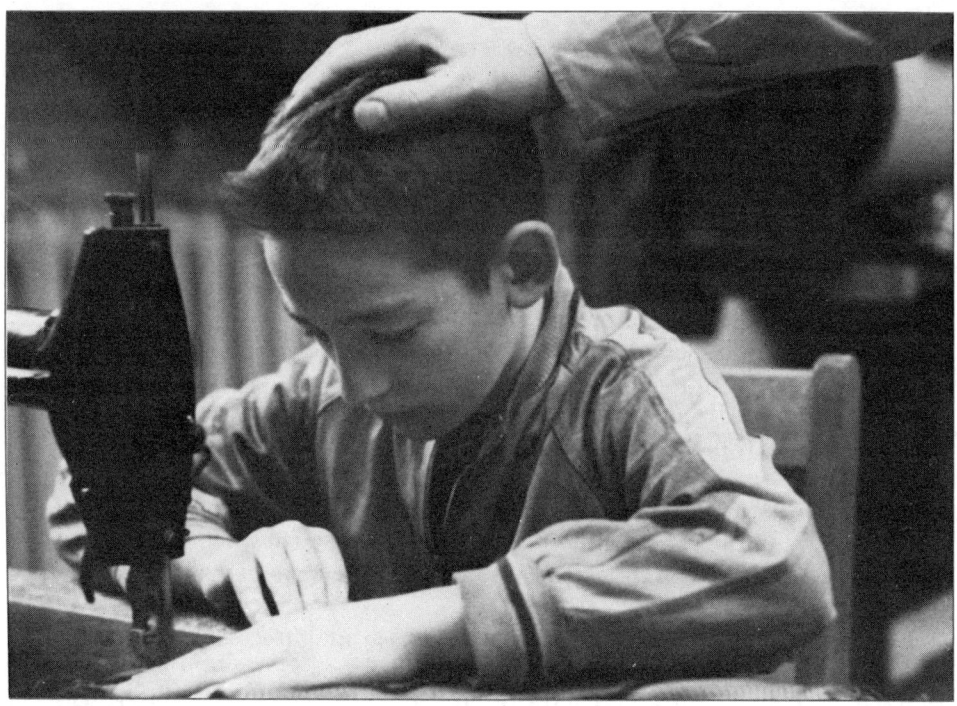

In the summer of 1956, this young boy was learning to use a sewing machine in Ontario.
Walter Curtin, Public Archives Canada/PA-137104.

fighting, and not verbal abuse, as evidence of aggressiveness. In studies using children from different cultures, results have varied. In the 1930s, the American anthropologist Margaret Mead found tribes in New Guinea with quite opposite ideas from each other and from North Americans about masculinity and femininity and appropriate activities for the sexes. Even when similar gender distinctions are found in cross-cultural research, the origins of these differences are not easily analysed.

The controversy about innate versus socially induced gender differences reappeared in recent research on the human brain. Some researchers found that the two different sides, or hemispheres, of the brain are developed differently in males and females. One side seems to control language development and the other side spatial relations and analytic abilities. But we do not know whether these developmental differences are innate sex differences or whether they simply result from different training. Since we cannot experiment on human infants or young children, we cannot separate the effects of physiology from the effects of socialization.

The influence of hormones on levels of aggression has also been debated for years, but because experiments have been done on animal primates rather than humans, we do not know if hormone levels influence aggression in humans. We are also unsure if certain hormones are released when we feel anger or whether they cause us to feel anger and to act aggressively.

Without rejecting the thesis of instinctual or innate differences between the sexes, it is clear that North American males and females are socialized very differently. Without realizing it, mothers and fathers talk to and cuddle baby girls more and treat them with more gentleness. Little boys are granted greater independence and personal freedom in decision-making, and they are permitted to stray farther from home than girls. Girls tend to be coddled and protected more and are taught to be neater, cleaner and more obedient. Physical activity is encouraged in boys and curbed in girls by verbal reprimand and by the way they are dressed.

Within the family, girls see their mothers performing most of the child-care and housework while their fathers are away at work. Once small children learn which sex they are, they often imitate the same-sex parent and so develop rigid ideas about sex-appropriate behaviour.

At school, children see that women are the secretaries, nurses and teachers of young children, while men teach older students and become principals. Their guidance counsellors have encouraged them to prepare for sex-appropriate jobs. This occupational segregation is also apparent on the television programs they watch and the glimpses they get of the division of labour in the community. As children spend more time away from home—at school, with their friends, at community functions and later in part-time work—they learn that men and women are expected to behave differently and to perform different jobs.

The physiological differences between the sexes are certainly reinforced by social customs and traditions of gender-related behaviour. Although attitudes toward sexual equality are changing, behaviour has changed less. Inconsistencies between attitudes and behaviour are still apparent: Adolescents *say* they believe in equality yet are often afraid to violate social convention.

Treating boys and girls differently affects their status, income and power as adults. Let us look at male and female participation in education, work and politics as illustrations of the implications of differential socialization and opportunity.

STATUS AND POWER DIFFERENTIALS IN CANADA BETWEEN MEN AND WOMEN

THE EDUCATIONAL SYSTEM

The quality and length of education has always varied considerably by sex and social class. In the early 1800s, poorer children received only a rudimentary education. Girls were considered to need formal schooling less and were expected to acquire domestic skills as well as reading and writing. Among the higher classes, young men were often trained in the professions, but young women were excluded from Canadian teachers' colleges until 1849, from universities until the late nineteenth century and from professional schools until well into the twentieth century (MacLellan, 1971:6). In the nineteenth century, many people felt that higher education would make women unfit for their domestic role. Allowing males and females in the same classroom was expected to lead to sexual immorality.

As women's paid labour became more important to the burgeoning factories and businesses of nineteenth-century England and North America, the case for higher education for women became stronger. If women were allowed to work in unskilled jobs, why could they not train for the professions? But the number of women who entered university peaked in the 1920s and tapered off somewhat during the 1930s, when families could not afford to send their daughters to school. Priority was often given to the son's education.

Since 1951, the proportion of females aged 18 to 24 in postsecondary educational institutions has risen from 4.6 percent to 21 percent in 1982–83 (Statistics Canada, 1983). However, the professional schools are still dominated by males, despite the dramatic increase in female students in medicine, law and dentistry in the past decade (Boulet and Lavallée, 1984:30; also see Table 7–1). At the same time that a higher proportion of postsecondary students are female, unemployment rates have soared. The value of education on the labour market has declined, especially for those with undergraduate degrees in general arts, education and law.

Males and females with the same education cannot always find comparable jobs. Because women are more likely to work part-time and to be hired in female job ghettoes, men and women with similar education generally do not make the same wages. The average yearly salary for a woman with a university degree or college diploma is about $2000 less than the average salary for a male graduate (Statistics Canada, 1981).

TABLE 7-1   Proportion of Women Among Full-Time University Students, By Specialization and Level of Study (1972-73 and 1981-82)

	UNDERGRADUATE LEVEL		MASTER'S LEVEL		DOCTORATE	
	1972-73	1981-82	1972-73	1981-82	1972-73	1981-82
Medicine	22.5%	38.0%	29.2%	40.7%	20.3%	33.6%
Law	18.0	39.9	7.7	37.0	33.3	15.9
Education	49.7	57.7	43.7	57.7	29.9	48.4
Humanities	51.9	59.5	42.5	53.6	34.2	41.4
Engineering	1.7	8.5	2.9	7.3	2.9	6.3
Physics	8.2	11.3	5.7	9.6	4.4	7.2
Sociology	57.0	67.3	36.8	51.9	32.7	46.4
Dentistry	8.3	22.7	16.7	26.7	–	–
Social Services	72.4	81.4	53.7	69.2	32.7	46.4

Derived from *The Changing Economic Status of Women* by Jac-André Boulet and Laval Lavallée for the Economic Council of Canada, Ottawa, 1984, p. 30, Table 3-3.

Despite employment inequalities, women have relatively high educational ambitions. In a national study sponsored by the Canadian Advisory Council on the Status of Women in Canada, Baker (1985) found that a similar proportion of adolescent girls and boys (over 75 percent) wanted to go to college or university. Although

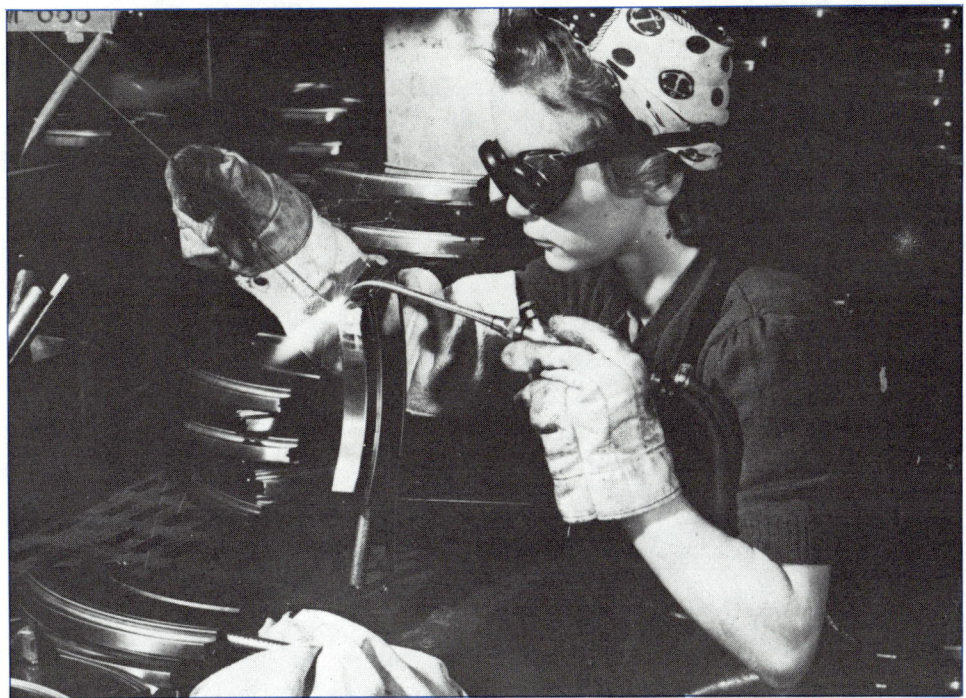

During World War II, many women took jobs outside the home, often in war-related industries. This girl was a welder at a plant that manufactured Bren guns.
National Film Board, Public Archives Canada/C-7481.

not all the girls planned to work for pay continuously throughout their adult lives, they realized the importance of higher education.

While an increasing proportion of females are enrolling in higher education in the Western world, illiteracy (especially among women) is still a problem in developing countries (see Table 7-2 on page 166).

GENDER AND WORK

In the last two decades, the proportion of women in the labour force has risen dramatically. While higher education has kept more young people out of the full-time labour force, more married women have been returning to work or remaining employed throughout their childbearing years. Although only 4 percent of married women were in the labour force in 1941, over 50 percent worked in 1981. This increase has been attributed to an expansion of the service sector of the economy, inflation and the need for two incomes, women's higher education and their increased desire to use this education on the job, lower birth rates and changing attitudes about women's role.

TABLE 7-2   Illiterate Population 15 years and Over by Sex (1980)

	PERCENTAGE OF ILLITERATES	
COUNTRY	MALES	FEMALES
Afghanistan	66.8%	94.4%
China (1982)	20.8	48.9
Cuba (1979)	4.3	4.9
Hungary	0.7	1.5
India (1981)	53.3	75.1
Saudi Arabia	65.5	87.8
Yemen	82.4	98.5
United States	—*	—
U.S.S.R.	—	—
*—less than 0.5%		

UNESCO, *Statistical Yearbook 1984*, Paris, 1984.

Although it used to be uncommon for mothers with young children to work outside the home, women are increasingly staying in the labour force and taking short-term maternity leaves. Table 7-3 looks at labour force participation rates since 1901, and Table 7-4 looks at participation rates in 1981 by age.

Recent controversy over equal pay legislation shows that men and women seldom do the same kind of work. While "men's work" covers a broad spectrum, from manual labour, skilled labour and commissioned sales to professional and managerial positions, women are clustered in fewer occupational categories. Most working women are in clerical or service positions, although there are also high proportions in food processing and lower-level professional jobs, such as teaching, nursing and social work (sometimes called the "semiprofessions").

Clerical and service jobs are low paying, have few promotional opportunities and are often temporary or part-time. Regardless of the education achieved by women workers and regardless of their occupational category, women tend to receive lower wages than men. Even women with postgraduate education often start at lower salaries and do not advance as quickly as their male counterparts. Table 7-5 (on page 168) shows the discrepancies between the salaries of males and females two years after graduation.

Men are more likely to graduate from fields which command higher salaries (such as medicine, law, dentistry and engineering). Men are also more likely to work overtime. After age 25, women are much more likely to work part-time. Twenty-two percent of working women aged 25 to 64 work part-time, compared to 1.6 percent of working men (Wallace, 1983:50). Women workers are less often protected by unions. Although the percentage of women union members is increasing, only about 20 percent of women workers and 33 percent of men workers are union members (Boulet and Lavallée, 1984:14). Unions traditionally have been reluctant

TABLE 7-3   Labour Force Participation Rates of Men and Women, Canada (1901-1981)

	MEN	WOMEN
1981	79.4%	52.9%
1971	76.4	39.9
1961	81.1	29.3
1951	84.4	24.3
1941	85.6	22.9
1931*	78.4	19.4
1921*	80.3	17.7
1911	82.0	16.6
1901	78.3	14.4

* Includes 10-13 year olds

Derived from Statistics Canada, *Historical Statistics of Canada*, 2nd ed., Minister of Supply and Services, Ottawa, 1983, pp. D107-122; 1971 and 1981 figures from J.-A. Boulet and L. Lavallée, *The Changing Economic Status of Women*, Economic Council of Canada, 1984, p. 7.

TABLE 7-4   Participation Rates of Men and Women in the Canadian Labour Force By Age Group (1981)

	WOMEN	MEN
Age group:		
15-19	51.2%	55.0%
20-24	78.2	92.0
25-34	66.2	95.8
35-44	64.6	95.6
45-54	55.9	92.7
55-64	35.4	77.8
65 and over	5.3	17.1
All age groups	52.9	79.4

Derived from *The Changing Economic Status of Women* by Jac-André Boulet and Laval Lavallée for the Economic Council of Canada, Ottawa, 1984, p. 7, Table 2-4.

to include part-time workers and have seen them as unfair competition and cheap labour. More recently, they have realized that, unless part-time workers and women full-time workers are recruited, the gains of the union movement will be eroded.

Generally, women workers are better educated than their male counterparts. Measures of productivity have not revealed consistent differences between the sexes,

TABLE 10-5   Average Annual Salary Two Years After Graduation
(June 1978)

	MALES	FEMALES
University Degree	$15 900	$14 400
Master's or Ph.D.	$21 800	$17 700
Bachelor's	$15 400	$14 200
College Diploma	$13 600	$11 700

Derived from Statistics Canada (W. Clark and Z. Zsigmond), *Job Market Reality for Postsecondary Graduates, Employment Outcome by 1978 Two Years After Graduation*. Ottawa: Statistics Canada, Cat. 81-572E, 1981, pp. 141, 142, 144.

Workers solder fuses during World War I in the British Munitions Company Ltd. at Verdun, Quebec. Public Archives Canada/C-18734.

PROMOTE WOMEN, WELCH URGES
By Duncan McMonagle

Deputy Premier Robert Welch has called on private employers to practice "enlightened self-interest" and remove barriers to women's advancement.

Promoting people solely on merit would, in addition to giving women a better chance at advancement, make companies more efficient, he said in a speech yesterday to a conference of the Ontario Human Rights Commission.

Mr. Welch, the minister responsible for women's issues, has been pressing public bodies such as hospitals and boards of education to hire and promote more women, but he has resisted opposition calls to impose affirmative action on private industry.

In a recent annual report on affirmative action in the Ontario public service, Mr. Welch urges private employers to follow the Government's example—promote women and pay them more.

The report noted that the pay for women working for the Ontario Government has crept forward, and they now earn on average 76.8 per cent of what the average man is paid—one percentage point more than a year ago. They continue to do much better than women in private industry, who earn only 63 per cent of what men do, no gain at all from a year ago.

The annual report shows big differences in the way the various Government ministries treat women.

The ministry that paid women best was Correctional Services, at 87.8 per cent of men's salary. But only 27.2 per cent of the ministry's almost 5 000 employees were women.

Women in the Energy Ministry fared worst compared to their male colleagues: They earned only 58.1 per cent of the men's salary. Eighty of the ministry's 164 employees were women, and the ministry is encouraging their promotion to economists' jobs, the report said.

The lowest average salary for women is the $20,250 of the Consumer and Commercial Relations Ministry. By far the highest is the $31,319 paid by the Management Board secretariat.

The men's averages range from $24,569 in Health to $46,301 at the Management Board secretariat.

The Globe and Mail, Toronto (February 8, 1985).

except that mothers of preschool children show some decline in productivity because of the extra workload at home.

Studies show that married women working for pay retain most of the routine household tasks (Meissner et al., 1975; Luxton, 1980). Childcare, housecleaning, cooking and shopping have remained women's responsibilities, even when they also work for pay. This double burden of paid and unpaid work interferes with some women's desire for extra hours or responsibility at work. But for other women, who work long hours and wish to be promoted, stereotypes and myths about women workers or women's role may interfere with their opportunities.

The female participation rate in the labour force varies in different countries, depending on the availability of work, child-care facilities, inflation and attitudes about women's role. While less than 30 percent of women over 14 worked for pay in Italy in 1981, over 60 percent of women over 16 were in the labour force in Sweden (Boulet and Lavallée, 1984:49). For many years, Sweden has supported a publicly funded child-care system and a government policy of equality between the sexes.

In the Soviet Union, nearly all adult women work for pay. Marxist ideology supports the idea that participation in production and financial independence are essential for equality between the sexes. But labour has been in demand in the Soviet Union since the industrialization of the 1930s, and the shortage of men in the population (due to wars and civil unrest) required the acceptance of women as workers.

Women are more widely and evenly distributed in the Soviet economy (Heitlinger, 1979) than in Western industrialized countries. They are extensively employed as manual workers in productive industry, as skilled workers and in the professions (especially medicine).

POLITICAL RIGHTS AND POSITIONS OF POWER

Women's Rights in the Nineteenth Century

Feminism is an ideology that argues that women should have legal, educational and occupational opportunities that are equal to men's, that women's contribution to public life has historically been downplayed and that the status of women should be raised. If we accept this definition, we could argue that feminism as an ideology has existed for thousands of years. At certain times, women (and some men) have tried to promote feminist goals through government lobbies, demonstrations, public lectures, consciousness-raising groups, publications and individual achievement. The women's movement has never really been a unified social movement but rather a collection of groups with similar goals but different strategies and priorities. Sometimes these groups have worked in tandem and sometimes at cross-purposes.

There has always been a split in the women's movement between *liberal feminists*, who have focused on reforming the existing system, and *socialist feminists*, who want to abolish inequalities based on class along with those based on gender. The socialist feminists have seen gender differences as an example of the inequality of a society organized around profit, where those most vulnerable are exploited. They have argued that equality between men and women is not possible without first eliminating inequalities between rich and poor, the powerful and the powerless. In this chapter, we will refer to both groups of feminists but concentrate on liberal feminism, which has had more impact on government legislation and policy changes in Canada.

Membership in Feminist Groups

Historically, those who join feminist groups are middle-class women, who have leisure, verbal skills and access to the press. Men affiliated with these women have often been peripherally involved as well, with greater involvement in the nineteenth

THE RIGHTS OF INDIAN WOMEN

After travelling 30,000 kilometres and talking to 300 chiefs and native councils, Indian Affairs Minister David Crombie has struck what he thinks is a fair balance between the rights of Indian women and the rights of bands to self-determination.

Mr. Crombie introduced long-promised legislation in the Commons yesterday under which Indian women would no longer lose their status and associated rights when they marry non-Indians. The estimated 16,000 women who have lost their status and band membership could apply to have it automatically restored.

At the same time, however, the country's 579 Indian bands would retain the right to determine, by majority vote, whether to bestow band membership on the first-generation children of those women who lost their rights.

In the meantime, those 46,000 children would be eligible for registration as status Indians, which would give them access to services now available to Indians living off reserves.

The Globe and Mail, March 1, 1985. Full credit to The Canadian Press.

than in the twentieth century. Members of the women's movement have also been active in other social reform or radical movements, such as socialism and the temperance, abolitionist, trade unionism, antiwar and civil rights movements. In fact, the impetus for involvement in feminism sometimes has been a reaction against an experience in another social movement. For example, after helping black American men get the vote in the 1870s, American, British and Canadian women expected blacks to help women win the vote. When it became apparent that black men had no such intentions, the women's suffrage movement gathered strength.

Issues and Priorities

Since the 1790s, feminist writers such as Mary Wollstonecraft, John Stuart Mill and George Sand have expressed concern about women's lack of public roles, legal rights and education and the double standard of sexual morality. Both the French and the American Revolutions inspired demands for equality for women. But it was the influx of working-class women into the mines and factories of England that led to a widespread public debate about the conditions of work and their potential impact on women's reproduction, the family, morality in the workplace, women's access to higher education and political office and the role of women in general.

Once women began working in factories, the demand for their labour dramatically increased in other areas. The expansion of education in the 1840s and 1850s led to an influx of women teachers, who were usually paid about half the wage of a man because "men supported families" and had teacher's training in "normal school." When women tried to enroll in Canadian teachers' colleges, they met with strong opposition until 1849, when the first woman enrolled in a college in New Brunswick.

In Canada, the fight for coeducation at the postsecondary level lasted over 30 years. While Mount Allison University in New Brunswick admitted women in 1858 (MacLellan, 1971:6), the more prestigious universities, like the University of Toronto, kept women out until 1884, for fear of "lowering their standards." Generally, coeducation was resisted until it was proven financially necessary. The need for more students was often the major motive in allowing women to enter universities. For women, acceptance into professional schools and associations was not accomplished, in some cases, until the twentieth century (MacLellan, 1971:8–12).

Although women were working for pay, they still had no legal rights to keep and administer their own money or to own property. These matters were in the hands of a woman's husband, a fact that put her in a dependent position similar to that of a child. The English *Married Women's Property Act* of 1870 became the impetus for similar laws in Canada. These laws gave married women the right to maintain property they owned prior to their marriage and administer their own finances and property during marriage. Ontario was the first province to legislate this change in 1872.

Leaders of the nineteenth-century women's movement were also concerned with protective legislation, minimum wages and women's and children's working conditions. Dress reform was also an issue, since women's long dresses were cumbersome in some factory jobs and for the new fad of the 1890s—cycling. The right to use birth control was advocated by Margaret Sanger, but little progress was made on this issue until the next century. Generally, women were rebelling against their severely restricted role in society (Kealey, 1979:15).

Focusing on Voting Rights

Despite interest in improving women's status in several areas, leaders in the movement began to focus on the right to vote, or women's suffrage. They felt that if women could vote and hold public office, women would change the world by abolishing war and human suffering, since women were spiritually and morally superior to men.

The antisuffrage lobby was worried about the alliance between members of the women's movement and temperance groups. They also felt that the husband, as head of the household, voted on behalf of his wife, and she, therefore, had no need for a separate vote. Granting voting rights to women might destroy the harmony of the home and lead to a decline in the birthrate. Since the family was seen as the basic unit of society, anything which threatened it was a serious problem.

In Britain, the lobby for women's suffrage was very controversial from 1905 to 1914. There were demonstrations, and the Pankhurst sisters and other members of the Women's Social and Political Union were imprisoned. But in Canada, the movement was tamer. The first suffrage group, founded in 1876, actually called itself the Toronto Women's Literary Club. By 1883, they had become bolder and renamed themselves the Toronto Women's Suffrage Association. The movement was founded by Emily Howard Stowe, who fought long and hard with the medical association to become Canada's first female doctor. By the turn of the century, there were suffrage groups all across the country, with headquarters in Toronto (Nunes and White, 1973:29–30). Nellie McClung, from Manitoba, was also a prominent leader

The Women's Canadian Club

Ottawa

The boys at the front need socks.   Can you knit a pair ?

This sign was part of the war effort campaign in 1917. As a result of the government's eagerness to pass a bill that would allow military conscription, the vote was extended to nurses overseas and the wives and mothers of servicemen in 1917. The next year, it was extended to all women over 21. Public Archives Canada/PA-125232.

YOU MUSTN'T ASK TO VOTE
You may be our close companion
Share our troubles, ease our pain,
You may bear the servant's burden
(But without the servant's gain;)
You may scrub and cook and iron
Sew the buttons on our coat,
But as men we must protect you—
You are far too frail to vote.

You may toil behind our counters,
In our factories you may slave
You are welcome in the sweatshop
From the cradle to the grave.
If you err, altho' a woman
You may dangle by the throat
But our chivalry is outraged
If you soil your hands to vote.

Courtesy of L. Case Russell and *The Globe and Mail*, Toronto (September 28, 1912).

in the fight for suffrage. She used tactics such as an all-female mock parliament in 1896, lecture tours and publications. The suffragists were supported by western farmers' organizations, organized labour in British Columbia, a substantial number of Protestant clergy, influential sectors of the press and national women's groups such as the Women's Christian Temperance Union, the National Council of Women (established in 1893) and the Women's Institutes (MacLellan, 1971:15). However, the counter lobby was also very strong, strengthened by the brewers and distillers of alcoholic beverages, prominent businessmen and many women.

It was not until 1917 that women could vote in Canadian federal elections (although Australian women could vote in 1902 and New Zealanders as early as 1893). In Canada, the Conservative government of Robert Borden wanted to pass a bill that would allow military conscription for the war raging in Europe. Borden assumed that women who were nurses overseas would support the bill, as would women whose husbands and sons were fighting. So he proposed the extension of the vote to these women in 1917 (and his bill was passed). The next year, in 1918, the vote was extended to all women 21 and over. American women won the right to vote in 1919, and British women in 1921. Women in the Canadian provinces received the vote as early as 1916 (in Manitoba, Saskatchewan and Alberta), but in Quebec, there was no female suffrage until 1940 (Report of the Royal Commission on the Status of Women in Canada, 1970:338).

As early as 1917, Soviet women gained equal rights legislation. Although they are much more likely than women in Canada to be in the labour force and to be represented in politics, only 27.4 percent of Communist party members are women. Although more than 50 percent of the lower echelons of the party structure are held by women, reaching the highest positions in the labour force is easier for men.

In Yugoslavia, which had a woman as president in the late 1970s, women were well represented in both local and national politics. In Albania, one-third of the people's assembly seats were held by women. Generally, in Eastern Europe (as in Western European and North American) countries, women have been elected more often to local rather than national politics (Heitlinger, 1979). Yet, in socialist countries that encourage women to hold office, women's representation is much higher.

After the Vote

The first woman, Agnes Macphail, was elected to the Canadian House of Commons in 1921 but it was 14 years before the next woman won a federal seat (Cochrane, 1977:10). Several women were elected to the provincial legislatures, but none were appointed to the Senate until a lengthy court case (initiated by five Alberta women) was brought to determine whether or not women were "legal persons." It was decided they were. After the negative decision was appealed by the Judicial Committee of the Privy Council in 1929, women were declared eligible to sit in the Senate. Cairine Wilson was then appointed in 1930 (Royal Commission on the Status of Women, 1970:340).

During the 1920s, some major changes in social legislation occurred that could be attributed to women voters or members of Parliament or may have been just a sign of the times. For example, by 1928, most provinces had passed legislation on mothers' allowances, maintenance for deserted wives, protection of children and

TABLE 7-6   When Women Won the Right to Vote in Federal Elections

New Zealand	1893
Australia	1902
Finland	1906
Norway	1907
Denmark	1915
U.S.S.R	1917
Canada	1918
U.S.A.	1919
Britain	1921
Spain	1931
Rumania	1935
Italy	1945
Greece	1952
Switzerland	1971
Liechtenstein*	–
Kuwait	–
Saudi Arabia	–

* Women won the right to vote in communal elections in 1976.

equal guardianship of children by both parents. At the federal level, divorce law was equalized for the sexes, and old age pensions were introduced.

From 1920 until the 1970s, the proportion of women MPs did not rise above 1 percent, and the influence of women voters did not produce dramatic changes in political issues. Few women had the educational or occupational background to run for Parliament. Women were also hampered by their domestic responsibilities and by the widespread belief that women belonged in the home. Yet women made inroads into other areas during the 1920s. By the 1930s, more women were enrolled in university undergraduate programs than in the early 1950s. And a greater proportion of postgraduate students were female during the 1920s than throughout the next four decades (Royal Commission on the Status of Women, 1970:168). Because there were fewer men in Canada during and after World War I, new jobs were opened to women, and other jobs were created by an expansion of manufacturing and the service industries. But women's organizations after the 1930s became more concerned with social service than with widening the scope of women in society. The alignment between the women's movement and labour declined as women became more oriented toward issues such as child welfare, juvenile delinquency and mothers' allowance, which were an extension of women's maternal role (*maternal feminism*).

During the 1930s, economic hard times led to legislation that kept married women out of government jobs. Politically, there was little agitation for women's rights, as many people were more concerned about the rising unemployment and increasing number of bread lines. The Great Depression focused on male unemployment, and women were expected to run the households, care for dependent relatives and try to earn some money on the side to assist male breadwinners.

RECENT ATTEMPTS TO CHANGE WOMEN'S STATUS

During World War II, women again entered the labour force in increasing numbers to work in offices and munitions factories and to fill jobs vacated by men who went to fight overseas. The provision of day nurseries indicated strong government support for women who worked outside the home. Yet, when the war ended in 1945, day-care services were cut back and returning soldiers expected their jobs back. Social pressure forced many women back into the home. The 1950s saw the postwar baby boom, and was a time of high marriage rates and relatively low participation of women in public life. But the proportion of married women in the workforce actually increased from 4.5 percent in 1941 to 11.2 percent in 1951 to 20.8 percent in 1961 (Armstrong and Armstrong, 1978:52). Expansion of the service and industrial sectors of the economy created new jobs, and the demand for labour increased. Despite the popular ideology, which called for mother at home, caring for the children, more working-class wives entered the labour force because of financial pressures caused by inflation.

It was not until the 1960s that the women's movement was revitalized. Simone de Beauvoir published *The Second Sex* in 1949, but her ideas had influenced few North Americans. However, with the expansion of colleges and universities in Canada and the United States, an increasing number of women entered postsecondary institutions and began to aspire to intellectual achievement and paid employment. Rising expectations were also created among American blacks and among native peoples in Canada and the United States. With the expansion of the economy, minority groups and women expected a greater share of the jobs, higher wages and more opportunities for leadership in society. Trade unionism, civil rights, "red power," socialism and protests against American involvement in Vietnam all coincided with the renewal of activism for women. Breakaway groups of women from the "new left" formed the women's liberation movement in the United States and Canada, and these small, leaderless "consciousness-raising" groups spread quickly throughout North America. Reform-oriented lobby groups were formed in many countries. One of the best known was Betty Friedan's National Organization of Women (NOW), formed in 1966 to express dissatisfaction with the results of President Kennedy's Commission on the Status of Women in 1961 (Freeman, 1975:449). Friedan's book, *The Feminine Mystique* (1963), became a best seller because it so clearly identified the problem of so many American women, who were excluded from meaningful social and political participation.

The Canadian Movement

In Canada, the Committee for Equality for Women was formed in 1966 by Laura Sabia, then president of the Canadian Federation of University Women. This collection of women's groups lobbied for a royal commission on the status of women. With the help of the secretary of state, Judy LaMarsh, the commission was established in February, 1967 (Wilson, 1982:127). Its report was published three years later.

In 1972, a conference to follow up the report gave birth to a new women's group called the National Action Committee. As an umbrella group for 170 women's organizations across the country, it has acted as an important pressure group (Wilson, 1982:127). But smaller and more radical groups also arose out of the Student Union for Peace Action. The Voice of Women, an organization promoting world peace, has also been influential. Other feminists have been involved in organizing women's centres, rape crisis centres, transition houses for battered wives and other specialized counselling services for women. The Women's Press, in Toronto, and women's bookstores across the country have helped transmit feminist ideas and served as a meeting place for like-minded women.

In the 1970s, the Canadian and provincial governments set up advisory councils on the status of women for policy advice, research and publicity on women's issues. The establishment of the Canadian Advisory Council on the Status of Women (CACSW) in 1973 was one of the recommendations of the Royal Commission on the Status of Women. Status of Women Canada and the Women's Bureau of the Department of Labour were set up to initiate and implement government policy related to women. But critics of the advisory councils say they are a diversionary tactic to make it appear that the government is doing something to improve the status of women. While the publications of the CACSW are widely distributed to the public, to schools and to universities, some say they are preaching to the converted. Costly public relations work, political appointees and more conferences than actual changes have been the results of the councils according to critics, who say that the councils carefully avoid anything that is controversial or that approaches socialist feminism.

The Feminist Party of Canada has also been a product of the women's movement. Formed in 1979 by women who had been active in NAC and other women's groups, the party is meant to give a political voice to feminists. Disappointed with women's inroads into the three major political parties, these women assumed that only by creating a new political party could women become more active, gain experience in political office and voice their feminist views without jeopardizing party policy. Although a party with such specialized interests can never hope to win an election, it can provide a strong voice for feminist concerns.

Women's groups all over the world have been heavily involved in antinuclear protests and demonstrations for disarmament. A large portion of protesters in England, Germany and Canada have been women. The effectiveness of these demonstrations against international policy remains to be seen. Women's interest in peace may be an offshoot of maternal feminism. Making military policy and fighting wars have been primarily male activities. Women, as creators of life, do not want to give birth to children who will be killed in war or who will have to live under the threat of nuclear destruction.

Considering that women in Canada could not vote or hold office before 1917, it is not surprising that they do not yet have equal representation in the House of Commons and the Senate. The move toward equality has been extremely slow. From 1920 to 1970, 0.8 percent of elected representatives to the House of Commons were women (Kopinak, 1980:445). In 1984, 9 percent of those elected were women, although 15 percent of the candidates were women. Four of the twenty-two new senators appointed in 1984 were female, which brings the percentage of women senators to 11 percent (Terry, 1984:1).

Why are men overrepresented in politics? One reason relates back to our earlier discussion of education and work. Most members of Parliament have a background in law or business, fields in which women have traditionally been underrepresented. Although only 5 percent of lawyers were female in 1971, this had increased to 15 percent by 1981 (Statistics Canada, 1983a). The recent influx of female law students indicates that this figure may increase dramatically within the next decade. In 1982–83, 42 percent of Canadian law students were female (Statistics Canada, 1983:60). Women have also substantially increased their proportionate enrollment in business and commerce courses over the last few years.

Running for office takes a lot of money, and involves long hours of work, trips away from home, and a single-mindedness that married women with children are seldom able to manage because of their domestic duties. While married men can often count on their spouses to look after the children when they are away in Ottawa, married women seldom can. Consequently, most women who have made their mark in politics have been unmarried, divorced, widowed, married and childless or beyond the years of childrearing.

Other important factors in running for office are confidence, assertiveness and feelings of political effectiveness. We suggested earlier that girls are often socialized to be less assertive and independent than boys and to have less confidence in their abilities.

CHANGING RELATIONS BETWEEN THE SEXES

A few years ago, a cigarette company that made slim "feminine" cigarettes advertised their product by the slogan "You've come a long way, baby!" How far have women really progressed toward equal opportunity and equal rewards for their efforts? In answering this question, we take on the difficult task of comparing life styles and goals. Whether or not a change is actually a move toward equality or a backward step is often unclear. Even comparing government statistics from one decade to the next can be difficult, since definitions of terms and composition of samples change.

Certainly, dramatic changes have occurred in higher education. In 1951, 5 percent of females aged 18 to 24 were enrolled in postsecondary institutions (Statistics Canada, 1980:81). In 1982–83, this figure had increased to 21 percent (Statistics Canada, 1983:65). However, educational segregation at the university level is still a pattern, in that men tend to specialize in general and applied science, engineering, law, medicine, dentistry and business to a greater extent than women. Most women still study general arts, applied arts, nursing, dental hygiene, physiotherapy and

These young women attended the Young Women's Christian Association School Girls Camp in 1917. Adelaid McDonald, Public Archives Canada/PA-124245.

home economics (although there has been an increase of women in law, medicine, veterinary science and pharmacy in recent years).

In the workplace, there has been a dramatic increase in the proportion of women working for pay. In 1941, 23 percent of women were in the labour force and 86 percent of men. In 1984, 95 percent of men between 25 and 44 years of age worked for pay, while 70.7 percent of women did (Statistics Canada, 1984). However, despite this influx of women, the gap between the incomes of men and women has changed only slightly. Women have entered the lower echelons of the labour force and have progressed less rapidly than men.

We have already noted that party politics are still dominated by men and that the proportion of women members of Parliament is only 9 percent. However, in the past ten years, there has been more change than in the previous 50 years. Because women are absent from official positions of power, this does not mean that women have no influence in decision-making. The wives and female associates of members of government and business often have some input into political and business decisions. However, those who are in power are not compelled to listen to their comments or advice, and women receive no direct payment or prestige unless they have official positions.

The status of women within the family has also changed in the last two years as a result of reform of laws affecting matrimonial property and divorce settlements. Several provinces now presume that matrimonial property is owned by both spouses, regardless of who paid for it. This gives some financial recognition to the childrearing and housework of the nonearning wife. Marriage is now more likely to be seen as an equal partnership, rather than as a unit headed by a husband, who has a dependent.

The rising labour force participation of married women may have only marginally changed the division of labour in household tasks, but it seems to have given women increased power in their relationships. Some studies suggest that the earning wife has more say in financial decisions and in where the family lives, and she can ultimately leave the relationship if she has her own money. At the same time, she may have given up some control over routine decisions in the home (such as what to eat or how to decorate the house) and some control over the children (who may now be cared for by a sitter).

There is still research evidence that men expect women to defer to them in conversation. For example, men interrupt women more than women interrupt men. People still see men as more authoritative, and women experts are often not trusted by clients or students. Sexual harassment is still a problem in the workplace, and being viewed as "sex objects" still interferes with occupational mobility for many women. Etiquette is still based on the outmoded notions that women are helpless and need protection from men and that women deserve special respect simply because they are women. Perhaps in the past, this respect was intended to make up for women's lower wages and powerlessness in society.

What seems clear from a number of studies is that attitudes toward the equality of the sexes have changed. It is no longer socially acceptable to tell sexist jokes in front of women, to pat bottoms, to admit publicly that a person was not hired *because* she is a woman, to create separate pay scales for men and women or to fire a woman because she is pregnant. Most adolescents believe in equal education for women, in equal pay for equal work and equal promotional opportunities for the sexes. But what people *say* they believe and how they behave are not always consistent.

WHY ARE WOMEN SUBORDINATED?

FOUR EXPLANATIONS

The reasons behind the widespread subordination of women have been the subject of many books and articles. Four groups of theories will be briefly discussed here: They are biological, psychological, idealist and economic theories.

Biological Theories

These explanations of women's subordination focus on the relationship between body size, strength, biochemistry, women's childbearing capacity and social roles and status. Some have argued that male dominance originated in man's larger size and greater strength. This gave him not only a protective role over woman, but also the ultimate power of the threat of physical violence. Theorists such as Lionel Tiger have drawn parallels between primate and human behaviour, referring to men's tendency to group together in hunting, the protection of women by men and the development of a male-oriented culture. Others have focused on dominance hierarchies in animals, which are based on size and strength, and possible parallels with human behaviour. Relationships between male sex hormones, high energy levels and more aggressive behaviour have also been used to explain male dominance.

The biological theorists sometimes claim that pregnancy and lactation have limited women's political and economic contributions to society and led to their more domestic role (Shulamith Firestone, 1970). During pregnancy and lactation, women need greater male protection. But, as a radical feminist, Firestone proposes ways to overcome biological inequalities and sexual dependancies.

Menstrual mood changes, postpartem depression and menopausal problems have also been used to explain women's lack of presence and responsibility in public life. However, childrearing itself has served as an alternative (and equally important) contribution by women to society. Women's so-called maternal instincts and ability to breastfeed have made them more appropriate caretakers of children than men.

Critics of these theories say that there is no necessary relationship between smaller body size and lower status, especially in industrialized society. After all, both Hitler and Napoleon were short. Nor does pregnancy necessarily imply an exclusion from paid work or childrearing by women only. Many women now work until their eighth month of pregnancy, and children are frequently raised by sitters or nonrelated caretakers. In hunting and gathering societies, women continue their work until childbirth and are often cared for and protected by other women during and after birthing. Male and female children are often raised by parents or community members of the same sex.

Although sociologists have tended to downplay the role of biology in social life, sociobiologists think that genes, hormones, body size, ability to reproduce and physical strength may strongly influence patterns of social behaviour. However, physical differences between the sexes have been accentuated by differences in diet, exercise and fashion. And the variations within each sex are greater than the differences between them. Some differences, real and imagined, are presumed to exist, and cultural patterns formed around them. For example, women on many Caribbean islands carry very heavy loads on their heads, because of the presumed strength of the female neck. In North America, many precision factory jobs requiring manual dexterity rely on female labour (whereas brain surgeons, requiring similar skills, are almost always men).

Psychological Theories

According to Sigmund Freud and others influenced by him, the basic nature of men and women is determined by their psycho-sexual development. Because males and females differ sexually, they react differently to their physical maturation, develop different personality characteristics and consequently play different roles in adult life. Some psychoanalysts focus on women's receptive sexuality and supposedly passive personalities, as well as the role of maternal instincts in shaping their abilities and ambitions. Others have argued (Karen Horney, Simone de Beauvoir) that passivity, desire for children and the lack of motivation to compete in the political and economic world are more the result of the way girls are brought up, i.e., passivity and domesticity are rewarded in girl children, while independence and competitiveness are punished. Learning theorists focus on the role models provided for children, the linguistic labels that parents attach to certain behaviours and the ways children imitate and identify with same-sex parents.

What the psychological theories cannot easily explain are the structural barriers to equality of the sexes: the unequal laws, the effect of the economy on equality and why some societies have made more progress toward gender equality than others.

Idealist Theories

With an emphasis on socialization and cultural tradition, the idealist theories argue that ideas about appropriate behaviour for the sexes are passed down from previous generations. Young children are raised to fit in with these ideas. But where do these ideas come from? When Kate Millett discussed the tradition of patriarchy in *Sexual Politics* (1970), she could not adequately explain the origin of this male dominance. Thus, idealist theories are often ahistorical and usually assume that if people become conscious of the inherent sexism of their attitudes, they will change.

Since women are the main caretakers of children, why do they raise their female children to accept an inferior status? If children were raised to believe that the sexes are equal, would inequalities disappear? Some say that vested interests still encourage men to cling to their advantage by preventing women from gaining more power, jobs or money. After all, if the status of one group is raised, does this not imply that another group is going to have to give up something?

Economic Theories

Some economic theorists (Friedrich Engels, for example) refer to earlier stages of society and argue that the relative status of the sexes has changed as societies moved from hunting and gathering to agricultural, preindustrial, industrial to postindustrial economies. In hunting and gathering societies, women usually gathered while men hunted. The food gathered formed over half of the diet, and this gave women an important economic and political role. When people became farmers, several social, political and demographic changes occurred. The concept of private property and inheritance became more significant. Consequently, knowledge of paternity became essential, and monogamous marriage was institutionalized. With the increased food supply from farming, the birth rate rose; this kept women in a more domestic role. Gradually, women's role in production shrank until, after the Industrial Revolution, most middle-class women were expected to stay at home to raise their children.

Some theorists argue that capitalist industrial society exploits anyone who is vulnerable. Child and female labour was used at the beginning of the Industrial Revolution to save money, and an ideology was created to provide reasons for

STUDY DISCOVERS ADVERTISERS FAILING TO ELIMINATE SEXISM

By Dorothy Lipovenko

Self-policing by the Canadian advertising industry is not working because sex-role stereotyping of women persists, a national watchdog group warns in a report to the federal Government.

"Woman continues to be cumulatively portrayed in ways that suggest her place is in the home, her interests do not include issues of the world or public affairs but are limited to interests in other people and her own appearance. Her primary roles are those of caretaker of men and children and sexual object of men," says MediaWatch, a women's group that monitors images of women in the media.

Among the findings of MediaWatch:
• Female characters are more passive and use seductive non-verbal behavior;
• Men outnumbered women more than two to one in voice-overs for commercials;
• Men exclusively pitch products such as cars and financial services while women are more likely to present cosmetics and health care products;
• Women were more likely to be partly or provocatively clothed;
• Men are shown to be more interested in their careers or business, while women are shown to be more interested in clothes and their appearance.

The Globe and Mail, Toronto (June 6, 1985).

paying these new workers less. Later, when laws prevented the use of child labour and protected women workers, and there was a surplus of labour, a new ideology was created to justify a more domestic role for women.

The work of housewives was not regarded as real work, since it was not paid. Women's domestic activities were denigrated in a money-oriented society (Eichler, 1973).

The socialist feminist theorists, such as Dorothy Smith and Juliet Mitchell, argue that what women and men do in their work lives affects the way they are valued. If they work at home with children for no direct pay, they are viewed as less important than those who have more public and remunerated positions. If they make an important, visible contribution to the economy, they are seen by others, and see themselves, as more important.

Authors like Blumberg (1978) and O'Kelly (1980) use an economic argument but supplement it with points from psychological, biological and idealist theories. They conclude that women have historically fared better in noncompetitive and nonmilitaristic societies with lower birth rates. Especially in hunting and gathering societies, where women's role in production is significant and birth rates are low, equality between the sexes is more likely. In modern socialist countries with a policy of gender equality, more progress has been made in equalizing laws and participation in public life.

Of the four groups of theories outlined above, the economic explanations seem to be the most persuasive. While the biological and psychological theories focus on the origin of women's subordination, they cannot adequately explain the social structures created to perpetuate male dominance. The idealist theories can account for the continued existence of female subordination but not the origin of patriarchy. Only the economic theories are historical and cross-cultural and deal with both the origin and perpetuation of female subordination.

DEBATES IN WOMEN'S ISSUES

Now that women's issues have become politically more important, several major issues have surfaced. These include pornography, abortion, sex segregation, pensions for homemakers, divorce laws and affirmative action. Is pornography a form of exploitation of women, or are censorship and sexual freedom more important issues? Should women have the ultimate say over whether or not they will reproduce or do husbands and fetuses have rights that should take precedence? Should women be allowed to work and fight side-by-side with men in all situations, or is some sex segregation still justifiable? Will the problem of poverty among elderly women be partially solved by pensions for homemakers, or will this simply perpetuate a domestic role for women? Who would pay for these pensions? Should women be expected to be self-supporting soon after divorce, or is this an unfair expectation, since many ex-wives lack job experience, and discrimination against women exists in the work-place. Is preferential treatment for qualified female candidates for a job or a promotion a form of reverse discrimination?

Within the women's movement, the divisions between heterosexual and lesbian women, between liberal feminists and socialist feminists and between those who argue that segregation is more productive than integration continue. The questions of whether sex overrides class, of the importance of motherhood and women's traditional roles, of whether children need their mothers at home and whether those who are fighting for equality have just adopted male values continue to be debated. At the same time, many traditional women are arguing that women's status was higher when they concentrated on motherhood and childrearing; they believe that women's maternal contributions should be more highly valued by society. Clearly, the 1960s to the present has been a period of debate and changing relations between the sexes, but with each change there have been voices raised to question the wisdom of disturbing tradition.

Sexism within the educational system continues to be under attack. Many studies have shown that teachers assume males are more serious students and gear classes to them. Textbooks have been found to contain a disproportionate number of examples of male characters and activities. Girls and women have been portrayed as less exciting and powerful characters. Social science courses have been accused of focusing on male activities and ignoring women's less public roles. Women's studies classes have been created to counteract this bias but have often been perceived as ghettoes for female students and faculty.

BARRIERS TO EQUALITY

The tradition of women having responsibility for childrearing and housework is still a major stumbling block to equality between the sexes. As long as women do most of this unpaid or low-paid work, they will have little motivation and energy to

What motivation will there be for men to take on a greater share of housework? National Film Board, Public Archives Canada/C-84798.

increase their responsibilities in public life. Low-paid work stigmatizes the work and the person doing it. Either higher wages could be paid for domestic labour, or both sexes could equally share the unpaid or poorly paid jobs. But what motivation will there be for men to take on a greater share of housework or to work as child-minders or cleaners?

The reasons given for not organizing society to promote equality between the sexes often seem very practical (lack of money for equal pay for work of equal value, lack of washroom facilities to enable the boss to hire women as well as men). But these are often merely excuses. Prejudices and stereotypes still prevent women from being accepted as equals. But guilt feelings, lack of confidence and fear of conflict and controversy keep women from insisting on their right to be treated equally. Without laws to protect their interests or a supportive group to stand up for them, many women accept inequality. Since organizations have a vested interest in maintaining the status quo, women will have to be strong to overcome the barriers that stand between them and equality.

SUMMARY

Distinctions between males and females are carefully cultivated in North American society and in many other cultures. Although some research suggests that sex differences in aptitude and personality are innate, conclusive evidence is difficult to find because of the ethical problems involved in studying infants and young children and the inability to disregard socialization or upbringing when studying adults.

From birth, parents encourage different traits and interests in their children, depending on their sex, and this socialization continues in school and in the community.

Attitudes about the value of the different roles of and opportunities for the sexes and the division of labour in the family lead to status and power differentials between the sexes in public life. In this chapter, we examined the educational system, paid employment and politics to compare the status of men and women. Although women are approaching equality in education and have dramatically increased their participation in the paid labour force within the last decade, more changes have been apparent in attitudes than in actual behaviour. Structural and psychological barriers still prevent women from attaining equality with men in public life.

DISCUSSION QUESTIONS

1. Why is it so difficult to determine whether gender differences are cultural or innate?

2. How do television programs and magazines contribute to stereotyped thinking about males and females? How do they blur gender distinctions?

3. What is meant by "women's double day?" Why do married women continue to do most of the housework, even when they work outside the home?

4. Has there been more change in attitudes or behaviour with respect to equality between the sexes?

5. What barriers still exist to gender equality in the workplace and in politics?

8

Families

Maureen Baker

INTRODUCTION: THE IMPORTANCE OF THE FAMILY

Despite the publicity about rising divorce rates, over 85 percent of Canadians marry at least once, and most of these couples produce children. Nearly 75 percent of those whose marriages dissolve soon move into new relationships, and second marriages are becoming common. Nonetheless, more Canadians live alone now than ever before. Young people are more likely to live away from their parents and separation and divorce produce more people who are between relationships, choose to live alone or cannot find a new partner. Many women outlive their husbands by ten years or more (considering they marry men older than themselves). Rather than move in with relatives, more widows and widowers choose to live independently. But living alone does not indicate a rejection of family living. Rather, it is for many a temporary stage—before marriage, between marriages and after divorce or the death of a spouse.

Pressure to marry remains high in the 1980s. Especially for lower-income single parents, who find it difficult to pay the bills on their own, pressures for economic and emotional security are strong. High rates of unemployment and job insecurity make shared accommodation essential for many. The desire for regular sex, companionship and love remains strong, as does the urge to reproduce. Although the number of middle-class women choosing to have children out of wedlock has increased slightly, most women find this alternative emotionally and financially stressful. Many more couples now have sex before marriage and live together, but living together often leads to marriage.

The preference for legal marriage is especially strong among religious and older people. Many legal impediments to common law relationships have been removed. Children of such relationships are no longer classified as illegitimate, and both parents must support their children. But social pressures to legalize a relationship in the traditional religious ceremony remain, even for people who are not church-goers.

Employers often see the married man as more emotionally and geographically stable and as a more reliable worker. The unmarried man may pay higher insurance rates because he is thought to be more reckless and carefree. In fact, a prejudice against unmarried people has existed in our culture for hundreds of years. Unmarried people of both sexes are considered less mature, more selfish and less experienced than married people; the unmarried woman over 40 is a "spinster" or an "old maid," both terms which have pejorative connotations.

FAMILIES AND HOUSEHOLDS

The term "family" refers to the relatives with whom we live or used to live and the larger group to whom we consider ourselves related by blood or marriage. There are different types of families. The husband-wife, or *nuclear family*, has been the most usual arrangement in Canada, yet one in six Canadian families has only one parent (Boulet and Lavallée, 1984:39). A "one-parent family" implies that only one parent raises the children. In actual fact, two parents may participate and even co-operate, although they live apart.

The term "household" refers to all those sharing a dwelling, whether they are related or not. Gib Milne, Public Archives Canada/PA-128761.

The *extended family* involves several generations, such as grandparents, parents and children, living together. The *census family* used in government documents involves at least one parent living with his or her dependent children. Most definitions of "family," then, involve children, and a distinction is often made between a "childless couple" and a "family." A journalist recently wrote that it has been a long time since we have had a "real family" at 24 Sussex Drive, implying that the former prime minister and his children are not really "a family." Letters to the editor in response to this remark showed that many people today live in one-parent families, and this arrangement is an increasingly acceptable way for a child to be raised (*The Globe and Mail*, December 8, 1984).

The term *household* refers to all those sharing a dwelling, whether they are related or not. Technically, it would be more accurate to call one-parent families one-parent households to avoid the assumption that the absent parent is not involved. The Canadian government gathers statistics on households and families and uses these to plan schools, hospitals and social services. Businesses also use the statistics for future market strategies. Academic researchers often rely on family statistics gathered for other purposes, but they also gather their own information on how families live.

Increasingly, the state is taking over the functions of the family. Educating the young, caring for the sick and assisting the unemployed is now the job of government. Yet family members still provide valuable services for each other. Cleaning houses and caring for preschool children are usually unpaid jobs performed by wives and mothers. Relatives provide accommodation, interest-free loans, child-care, nursing care and other services which are invaluable and would cost millions of dollars if provided by private industry or the state. As long as families provide all these services, they do not have to be organized and financed by the state or employers. Marxists argue that this is one reason the family is such an important social institution.

CULTURAL VARIATIONS IN FAMILIES

THE STRUCTURE OF THE FAMILY

In the 1980s, diverse cultures still organize their families differently. However, there is a trend towards a *nuclear* or *conjugal family* with increasing industrialization and urbanization. In the conjugal family, husband and wife live with their children and place more importance on the marital relationship than on ties with their own parents.

The extended family also remains an important unit in some cultures. For example, many Eastern Europeans, Southern Europeans, Latin Americans and Chinese maintain close ties with siblings and parents after they marry. Relatives may provide companionship, child-care or financial assistance; they may be employment partners or simply help out with a problem or crisis. They may visit daily or weekly and, especially in North America, telephone frequently. Close ties with the extended family are also apparent among working class-people and among women of all social classes.

It is unclear whether the extended family used to be more prevalent than the nuclear family. American sociologists such as Talcott Parsons say that the American family of the 1960s was more isolated from kin than in past centuries and that this placed increased pressure on marriages. However, historians have discovered that nuclear families were more prevalent than extended ones even in mid-seventeenth-century Europe (Leslie, 1979: 179). Neither has it been common for married couples to live with their parents at any time in Canadian history. Geographic mobility and short life expectancies encouraged nuclear families, except for short periods during a couple's marriage (Nett, 1981).

In Canada and in most industrialized countries, *monogamy*, or having only one spouse at a time, is the social custom and the law. Yet many Canadians have several spouses throughout their lifetime through divorce and remarriage or consecutive nonmarital relationships. This has led some sociologists to label our current marriage pattern as *consecutive monogamy* or *sequential polygamy*.

Having more than one spouse at a time (*polygamy*) is illegal in all Western developed countries. This is due to the assumed difficulties of providing adequate emotional and financial support to more than one partner and to religious ideas of sexual exclusivity. However, polygamy is practised in some Moslem countries. *Polygyny*, or allowing more than one wife, is the more common arrangement, but it is usually reserved for wealthier men who can afford to pay bride prices and to support more than one woman. For this reason, polygyny is sometimes a status symbol. However, this form of marriage is also prevalent in societies with more females than males, usually where there is a high number of male deaths in hunting accidents and warfare.

Polyandry, or marriage with more than one husband, is very uncommon. Confusion about paternity may explain why it is less acceptable. Another reason may be that there are often fewer males than females in any population because it is the men who engage in high-risk activities. But perhaps the most important reason is that males often have a higher status and have organized social life to suit their preferences. Sharing their females may neither suit their sexual nor social needs.

In countries where women's education is low and their labour force participation restricted, such as in Morocco and rural India, dowries are sometimes used as insurance for a woman. She is given money, household goods or land by her parents, and her husband cannot dispose of this property. If they divorce, the ex-wife keeps this dowry to live on or to assist her to find another husband. The larger the dowry and the wealthier the woman's family, the more desirable a marriage partner she is (especially if she is also physically attractive). But providing a dowry is sometimes a financial strain on a woman's family, and this makes it less desirable to have a female child. As women become more educated and enter the paid workforce, they can support themselves and need a dowry less. Yet newspaper reports from India, where the dowry system is declining among the middle-classes, claim that mothers-in-law sometimes want their sons to divorce undowried wives to remarry those with dowries (which would improve the mother-in-law's standard of living). Numerous murders of daughters-in-law were attributed to this motive in New Delhi in 1980.

In countries such as Morocco, it is also very important that the bride (but not the groom) be a virgin on the wedding day. Loss of virginity lowers the reputation of the bride and her family and could cause problems with inheritance if she were pregnant by someone else. Ceremonies surrounding consummation of a marriage (relatives stand outside the bedroom waiting for proof of virginity) are still performed in some Moslem countries. However, in societies with a greater public role for women (higher education, greater participation in politics and the labour force), virginity, dowries and polygyny tend to fade away, at least among middle-class or urban young people.

Population growth has led to policies limiting family size in some developing countries. For example, government policy encouraging one-child families in China has led some rural families to kill female babies in the hope that they will have a male next time. The preference for male children is still strong in many parts of the world: Female children require expensive dowries, and if a daughter becomes pregnant before marriage, she will disgrace the family. In addition only male children perpetuate the family name in many societies. Since women often cannot support themselves or their aging parents, parents prefer male children. Even when females are educated and self-supporting and the need for dowries no longer exists, the preference for male children lingers, since cultural traditions may lag behind their utility.

MATE SELECTION

Marriages are still arranged in some societies, especially where the extended family is the norm and the new marriage partner affects the functioning of the larger family unit. Parents or aunts and uncles are often involved in negotiating arranged marriages, but marriage brokers may be used if the family has insufficient connections. If status is ascribed by increasing age, older family members may select marriage partners for younger members. The decision is based on family reputation and financial status, the young person's personality and his or her education. But a previous relationship between the new couple would not be necessary. Societies which practise arranged marriages often feel that romantic love is an unsound basis for marriage.

When status is achieved through education and occupation and people live in nuclear families, marriage decisions are usually left to the couple involved. While most of these young people say that they marry because they are "in love," many patterns can be noted in love choices. Several different theories have tried to explain these choices. The *theory of complementary needs* suggests that people fall in love with someone whom they *think* will best fulfill their psychological needs. Their personalities are expected to complement each other. The *theory of social homogamy* proposes that we are attracted to people who are similar to us in life experience, ethnicity, race, religion, age, education or social class. These two theories are sometimes combined to suggest that, from a pool of eligibles who are socially similar to us, we choose someone who seems to satisfy our psychological needs.

Perhaps, though, we become involved with people similar to ourselves simply because those are the people we most often meet. Sociologists have noticed that North Americans often marry someone who lives very close to them (*residential propinquity*). Travelling far from home to visit a potential mate may require too much effort. People sometimes meet by accident and become involved through a process of misunderstanding, conflict, resolution and shared experience. This developmental theory suggests that the process of involvement may be like an escalator that carries us toward marriage. Social pressure to marry is strong at certain times in life, especially after graduation, around the ages of 22 to 24, after a relationship of a few years or when a pregnancy becomes visible.

Sociologists have also found patterns in the relationship of mate selection to marital stability. Marriages that are most likely to be stable take place between the ages of 20 and 30, are not precipitated by premarital pregnancy and are between mature and religious people from similar social backgrounds, whose families approve of the relationship.

THE BASES OF FAMILY LIFE

During the last century, much of the behaviour of people in families was attributed to human nature. Before cross-cultural studies were done in the early 1900s, we were not aware of the range and variety of human behaviour. People thought that instincts governed behaviour and that "civilized" people behaved in one particular way. The discovery that marriage and family patterns are related to economic and political systems rather than to biology led to relativism in social science. For example, in some societies men have more than one wife not because they like frequent sex, but because wives are status symbols and sound economic investments (because they produce food, services and children).

Of course, there are some biological bases to family life. The human infant needs physical care and a long social-learning period. Living in a family provides some continuity of care. Marriage also provides for regular sex, although this can be and is obtained outside the marriage. Incest taboos prevent genetic abnormalities, but they also maintain the social group. In fact, most of our social customs about whom we can marry and when, and how we should organize our sexual lives have more to do with maintaining social harmony and protecting dependents than with biology. Elaborate wedding ceremonies celebrated with expensive dinners create bonds between families and contribute to the stability of the larger community. Cultures all over the world want to organize personal and sexual life to create a unit in which emotional and material security are maintained and reproduction can take place.

HISTORICAL CHANGES IN THE FAMILY

The idea that "a man's home is his castle" has become far less true over the centuries. A Roman law called *patria potestas* gave a father the right of life or death over his children and considerable power over his wife. Under English medieval law, men were guardians of their children and their wives. Parents in the eighteenth century had three duties: to maintain, to protect and to educate their children. A man could beat his children or his wife. The wife had no legal rights; instead her husband exercised rights on her behalf (such as the right to administer her own money or property). But gradually, the power of men over family members was reduced as the state intervened more in family life.

ECONOMIC AND LEGAL CHANGES

In preindustrial society, men, women and children produced goods and services for the family. Early Canadian farms usually operated at a subsistence level, with the husband acting as the representative to the outside world. With the building of factories, many young men left the rural areas to seek wage labour, since it was difficult to make a living from the land. Daughters were usually expected to stay with their parents and do housework until they were married, to enter convents or work as servants in wealthier homes.

With large-scale industrialization in southern and eastern Ontario, wage labour became preferable to personal service or farm work. Many working-class families moved to towns or cities and took factory jobs; children and women worked for a lower wage than men and all family members pooled their financial resources. Gradually, as factory-made goods replaced home-made goods, the family became a unit of consumption rather than one of both production and consumption.

The poor working conditions for women and children in the early days of industrialization led to international controversy about women's role, child labour and the decline of the family. Legislation limiting the labour of children under six years old was introduced in England in 1833, and gradually, with the assistance of trade unionists and women's groups, conditions were improved for women and young workers. These benefits were later extended to men.

Not until 1870 in England and 1872 (or later) in Canada could married women retain their own wages or property without their husbands' permission. Until the

At one time, a man did his own washing only if he didn't have a wife. Public Archives Canada/PA-32425.

laws were changed in the provinces (from 1910 to 1922), a husband could also insist on custody of the children if a marriage dissolved. Women were obliged to live where their husbands wanted and they had sole responsibility for child-care and running the home.

The care of children and housecleaning are still the responsibility of women, and these household duties have often been used as a reason to keep women out of paid work and to justify hiring priority for men and lower wages for women. Although both sexes often contribute financially to the family, men are expected to support their wives and children. Thus, unemployment has been considered more of a blow to a man than to a woman.

Family members working for pay outside the home gradually reduced patriarchal authority within the family and public concern about working conditions for women and children led to state intervention in both work and family life. When family members no longer worked together, the husband/father could not supervise them closely, and this eroded his authority. When children were apprenticed, or worked as servants in someone else's house or were in school, parents relinquished some control over them. Protective laws gradually specified the hours and conditions of work for children and women, as well as the laws increasing women's individual rights and requiring compulsory education for children.

Of course, these changes in the structure of the family affected the way family members treated each other. Children became valued more for emotional reasons than for what their labour contributed to the family income. Wives became more confident in asserting their own needs and interests and began to expect more from life than childrearing. Families became protective of their privacy but at the same time grew to expect state assistance with family problems and crises.

The economic changes affecting society have formed the basis of Marxist and political economy theories of the family. For example, Engels thought that monogamy arose when nomadic people became more sedentary and concerned with private property. Knowledge of paternity became important to ensure that this property could be passed on to heirs. Monogamy and private property also led to women's lower status in society, as they became the "property" of men and were restricted to domestic roles.

Anthropologists recently discovered that birth rates often rise when a formerly nomadic people settle on a piece of land and develop large-scale agriculture (O'Kelly, 1980: 80, 156). Rising birth rates tend to keep women in a more domestic role. Recognizing the role of high fertility in lowering the public participation of women has provided motivation for the family-planning movement and direction for feminist strategists.

DEMOGRAPHIC CHANGES

Since the turn of the century, many demographic, economic and social changes have altered the family structure. In industrializing countries such as Canada, infant mortality and maternal death rates gradually fell as a result of improvements in nutrition, sanitation, housing and health care (see Table 8-1). Life expectancy rose, especially for women. While the average life expectancy at birth was 60 years for males and 62 years for females in 1921 (Urquhart, 1983: B65-74), it increased to 72 years for males and 79 years for females in 1981 (Statistics Canada, 1983: 2).

Birth rates have fallen in most industrialized countries with urbanization, modernization, improved methods of birth control and women's increased participation in the labour force. In the cities, a large family became difficult to accommodate, and children were no longer a financial asset, since they attended school instead of working for pay. With increasing education, women began devoting their time and energy to activities other than childbearing.

Birth rates have generally declined since 1900, but there have been fluctuations (see Table 8-2). During the 1930s, birth rates declined, but they rose again after World War II. The postwar baby boom (from 1945-65) was a time of high marriage rates, high fertility and increasing emphasis on family values. Yet, throughout this period, women's labour force participation gradually rose, as did their level of education.

Birth rates also vary provincially. Quebec, with its large Catholic population and traditional family structures, had a high birth rate until the 1960s. But by 1981 its birth rate was 14.8, compared to the national average of 15.3 (Statistics Canada, Vol. I, 1983: 2). Ontario has the lowest rate (14.2) and the Northwest Territories the highest (28.5), which reflects the higher birth rates among native people.

The age of marriage gradually declined until the early 1970s. With student loans, rising wages, lots of jobs for married women, birth control and more personal freedom, young people had fewer reasons to postpone marriage. Fewer pregnancies and freedom from childrearing enabled women to further their education or enter the labour force. The age of marriage stabilized in the later 1970s and then began

TABLE 8-1   Infant Mortality and Maternal Death Rates from 1921 to 1981 (Canada)

	INFANT MORTALITY RATE (PER 1 000 LIVE BIRTHS)	MATERNAL DEATH RATE (DEATHS DURING CHILDBIRTH) (PER 10 000 LIVE BIRTHS)
1921	102*	4.7*
1931	86	5.1
1941	61	3.6
1951	39	1.1
1961	27	0.5
1971	18	0.2
1981	10	0.2

* Excludes the Yukon and Northwest Territories

Urquhart, M.C. (editor). *Historical Statistics of Canada*, 2nd edition, Ottawa: Statistics Canada, 1983, p. B51-58.
Statistics Canada, *Vital Statistics, Births and Deaths*, Ct. 84-204, 1983, p. 2. Reproduced by permission of the Minister of Supply and Services Canada.

TABLE 8-2   Changes in Birth Rates from 1921 to 1981 (Canada)

	LIVE BIRTHS (PER 1 000 POPULATION)
1921	29.3*
1931	23.2
1936	20.3
1941	22.4
1946	27.2
1951	27.2
1956	28.0
1961	26.1
1966	19.4
1971	16.8
1981	15.3
1982	15.1

* Excludes the Yukon and Northwest Territories

Urquhart, M.C. (editor). *Historical Statistics of Canada*, 2nd edition, Ottawa: Statistics Canada, Ottawa, 1983, p. B1-14.
Statistics Canada, *Vital Statistics, Births and Deaths 1981*, Vol. I, Cat. 84-204, Ottawa, 1983, p. 2. Reproduced by permission of the Minister of Supply and Services Canada.

A habitant family poses with its spinning wheel. Associated Screen News Ltd., Public Archives Canada/PA-112729.

rising again as couples postponed marriage by living together or rejected marriage altogether.

In 1981, the average age of a woman at the birth of her first child was 24.8 years and at the birth of her second child, 27.2 years (Statistics Canada, 1983, Vol. I: 17). Recently, more single women in their thirties have been having babies. This reflects changing norms about unmarried pregnancy and an increasing number of couples living together outside legal marriage. However, it may also be a reflection of the high proportion of couples in their thirties in the population as the baby-boomers approach middle-age. An important long-term change is that childbirth and childrearing take less of a woman's life today than in the past. Since women, on average, live nearly 80 years, they now have over fifty years for other activities after having a family.

SOCIAL CHANGES

In the early twentieth century, new jobs in manufacturing and office work, with fixed hours and greater personal freedom, made domestic servants scarce and costly. While large houses with servants' quarters were built for the middle-classes until about the 1920s, smaller houses were built for smaller households after that date. After the 1920s, middle-class wives were expected to devote their time to child-care, volunteer activities, needlework or domestic duties. While poorer wives took in sewing, laundry or boarders to help make ends meet, wealthier wives remained out of the labour force. But postwar inflation and the expansion of the service sector of the economy gradually pushed even middle-class women with young children into the work world. As more women entered the labour force, laws and social practices encouraging male dominance declined. Laws equalizing pay, grounds for divorce, division of property after divorce and custody of children have been legislated since the 1920s, and there has been a greater emphasis on marriage as an economic partnership in recent years.

Whether the economic changes led to the women's movement or whether the ideas about liberation arose out of revolutions, such as the French and American Revolutions, the Vietnam War protests or socialist thought has been a controversy for many years. The political economists have argued that ideas are generated from people's material existence—the work they do and the lives they are forced to live. In explaining the division of labour in society and the family, biological determinists and learning theorists have focused on women's reproductive ability and experience and the fact that they are socialized to be passive and domestic. Women's increased interest in education and paid labour and their attempts to become more independent from domestic concerns have certainly influenced the structure of the family and preoccupied family studies for the past two decades.

Marriage has gradually become a less sacred bond and more an institution for personal fulfillment. Increasingly, unsatisfying marriages are dissolved and new liaisons are initiated, combining children from former marriages and creating more complex kin relationships. As divorce and remarriage rates rise, marriage is no longer a permanent bond. More people now go through different marital statuses and living arrangements in their adult lives, moving from single to married to divorced to living together to remarried. These long-term trends in family structure and interaction could be related to Weber's idea that society is moving from traditional to rational-legal authority. We no longer rely simply on tradition and morality but have allowed our family life to be rationalized and demystified.

RECENT ISSUES IN THE CANADIAN FAMILY

Several family issues have been controversial recently. These include maternal employment and child-care, divorce and remarriage, legal changes in the division of matrimonial property and child custody and increased reports of family violence. Each of these will be discussed in this section.

CHILD-CARE FOR WORKING PARENTS

Since 47.2 percent of women with children under the age of six were in the labour force in 1981 (Eichler, 1983: 248), many mothers need child-care assistance. Estimates of day-care need are usually based on the number of mothers in the labour force (because researchers assume that women, and not men, care for children). According to the Department of Health and Welfare, most parents make private arrangements for the care of their children. Nearly half of children under the age of six years are cared for by their parents (usually the mother). Only 5.8 percent of children under six attend day-care centres, and 22.3 percent are in a nursery or

Adolescents' Views of their Future Child-care and Housework Arrangements

"I'll take the kids to nursery school and hopefully go to work. I'll be a child psychologist in a clinic . . . This is hard, because I want to work and I want to have kids. But I don't like the idea of day care. After lunch, I'd drop them off at Grandma's house or it would be nice to work half-days . . . "

Faye: 18 years old, Winnipeg

(At age thirty)"I'm married. I have one child aged one or two. I work and my baby-sitter comes to my home every day. She's a woman I know very well . . . " (translation)

Lise: 15 years old, rural Quebec

"One child will be in school, and the other two will have a sitter . . . but I want six children. I'll take off three months after the birth of each child."

Rhonda: 16 years old, Montreal

"It really wouldn't bother me to do all the housework, because my husband would have a job that involves a lot of work, and he would be tired when he got home."

Betty: 15 years old, rural Nova Scotia

"My wife would work, but if there was no day care she would stay home to look after them (the children) . . . I'll help my wife with the housework, but it'll depend how tired I am when I get home at night." (translation)

Laurent: 17 years old, Montreal

"I go home (at age thirty), pick up my kids, make dinner half the time . . . My wife gets home same time as me—maybe a little later . . . "

Jim: 15 years old, Vancouver

"I would have two children—nine and seven—(at age thirty). The children would be at school . . . I would be reading and watching soap operas, and cleaning a little . . . I'm trying to remember what my mother does . . . "

Joanne: 15 years old, rural Ontario

"I have to get my kid ready for school (at age thirty). I'll watch the kid go off to school. As soon as everbody's out, I'd clean up and go back to bed. I'll get up around lunchtime . . . "

Wanda: 15 years old, rural Manitoba

Excerpts from *What Will Tomorrow Bring . . . ? A Study of the Aspirations of Adolescent Women.* Maureen Baker for the Canadian Advisory Council on the Status of Women, Ottawa 1985.

kindergarten. 18.6 percent are looked after in their own homes by someone other than a parent, and 18.6 percent are cared for in another private home (Eichler, 1983:249). These figures indicate that most preschool children are cared for in shared child-care arrangements. Even though baby-sitters are now frequently used, more parents would take their children to day-care centres if they were available (Johnson, 1977).

TABLE 11-3   Numbers of Children under 6 Requiring Day-care and Licensed Spaces Available, Canada, 1975-1982

YEAR	ESTIMATED NUMBER OF CHILDREN UNDER 6 WITH MOTHERS IN THE LABOUR FORCE	NUMBER OF CHILDREN UNDER 6 OCCUPYING LICENSED FAMILY AND DAY CARE CENTRE SPACES	PERCENTAGE OF CHILDREN UNDER 6 WITH ACCESS TO LICENSED DAY CARE	NUMBER OF CHILDREN UNDER 6 NOT ACCOMMODATED WITHIN THE FORMAL SYSTEM
1975	562,000	64,589	11.49%	497,411
1976	620,000	75,330	12.15%	544,670
1977	656,000	73,865	11.26%	582,135
1978	695,000	73,475	10.57%	621,525
1979	721,000	86,780	12.03%	634,220
1980	760,000	92,423	12.16%	667,577
1982	950,000	110,573	11.63%	839,427

Health and Welfare Canada, National Day Care Information Centre, Status of Day Care in Canada, 1975-1980; Day Care Spaces in Canada—1982. (Figures for 1981 are not available.) Reprinted from Day Care in Canada: A Background Paper by L. Johnson and N. McCormick, Canadian Advisory Council on the Status of Women, Ottawa, August 1984, Page 20.

The federal government shares day-care costs with the provinces. Despite cuts in other social programs, day-care funding levels have not been altered. However, there is still a shortage of day-care space.

A recent report by the Department of Health and Welfare (1984) claimed that the number of day-care spaces in Canada for children under two is steadily declining despite the influx into the workforce of mothers with children of that age. Of the 123 000 spaces in commercial and nonprofit centres in 1983, less than 7 percent were allocated for children under two years. This is a decrease of about 1200 spaces from 1982 and a decrease of 1600 spaces from 1979. In fact, day-care serves only 10 percent of children under two in families where parents are students or work at least 20 hours a week.

Most working parents rely on baby-sitters. But the high turnover of baby-sitters (many families go through four or five a year) may not be good for children. In fact, weak social support for publicly funded infant day-care may be a result of a previous controversy about the role of the mother in the child's early development. Research from the 1950s and 1960s emphasized the importance of maternal bonding and emotional stability in the child's early years and stressed that all young children are best cared for by their mothers. However, recent comparisons between infants raised within their own families and infants cared for in child-care facilities indicate that many variables affect the development of children (for example, the quality of care and the socioeconomic background of the child).

The number of day-care and family-care spaces (a place allotted to one child in day-care) peaked in 1983 (Lipovenko, 1984). But infant day-care is particularly underfinanced and has not kept pace with the growth in demand. The Health and Welfare study (1984) indicated that when parents must rely on informal child-care arrangements, they are more likely to obtain mediocre and even negligent services.

By April, 1985, 61.4 percent of mothers with children under 16 were in the labour force. Since childbearing benefits *society*, child-care services for employed parents are essential. But recent cutbacks to social programs mean that parents will have to continue to rely on relatives, neighbours or hired sitters to care for their children. Considering that women earn less than two-thirds of men's wages, few female single-parents can afford unsubsidized child-care. The child-care tax deduction (now $2000 per child to a maximum of four children) seldom covers the entire cost of child-care (estimated at $3000 per child per year in 1982). A more realistic tax deduction and increased numbers of day-care spaces are needed.

DIVORCE AND REMARRIAGE

Although the divorce rate has been rising since World War II, it has soared in Canada since divorce law was liberalized in 1968. Divorce rates are also rising in other industrialized countries, and this has been attributed to increased personal freedom from family and religious tradition, more opportunity for husbands and wives to meet new partners, greater opportunities for women to support themselves if they leave their husbands, less commitment to duty, more emphasis on personal fulfillment in marriage, fewer children (which means that the consequences of a divorce are less complex) and more liberal grounds for divorce. Although Canada's divorce rate has risen dramatically in the past 15 years, the United States and most Eastern European countries have higher divorce rates. Restrictive divorce laws, a traditional role for women, and emphasis on the sacred bond of marriage are often found in Catholic countries. But all societies allow couples to break out of unhappy marriages, even if they are not allowed to remarry. Annulments, separations and desertions took place long before divorce was legalized. However, leaving an unsatisfactory marriage has always been easier for men than for women. Men have been less encumbered with the care of dependent children and more able to support themselves.

Canadian divorce rates fluctuate considerably by province, with higher rates in the West. Frontier areas with a highly mobile labour force and a high proportion of young workers (25-to-40-year-olds) have higher divorce rates, as do large urban centres. Rural areas with a stable population have lower rates. But divorce rates record only a fraction of the number of dissolved or "unsuccessful" marriages. Many people separate with no legal agreement and therefore do not come to the attention of authorities. Others live apart with a separation agreement but without legal divorce. After all, divorces usually involve lawyers and cost money. Other people live in the same household but live separate lives. They stay together to avoid the embarrassment of divorce or because they are afraid to live alone, for financial reasons, for religious reasons or "for the sake of the children." However, research suggests that it may be more harmful for children to live with estranged or hostile parents than to live in a one-parent household (Ambert, 1980: 166-167). Still, some children *are* hurt by divorce, especially if it results in a drop in standard of living or continued parental conflict.

TABLE 8-4   Divorce Rate in Canada By Year
(per 100 000 population)

YEAR	DIVORCE RATE
1921	6.4
1931	6.8
1941	21.4
1951	37.6
1961	36.0
1968	54.8
1969	124.2
1970	139.8
1981	278.0
1982	285.9
1983	275.5

Statistics Canada, *Vital Statistics, Marriages and Divorces*, Vol. II, 1981, 1982, 1983, Cat. 84-205, Table 1, p. 2; M. Baker (editor), *The Family: Changing Trends in Canada*. Toronto: McGraw-Hill Ryerson, 1984, p. 85.

A decade ago, people without children were more likely to divorce. But increasingly, divorce affects families with children, and 53 percent of divorcing couples in 1983 had one or more children (Statistics Canada, 1985: 26).

The one-parent household is usually headed by the mother. Despite new laws that say custody should go to the parent who is best able to care for the child, 74 percent of children are awarded to the mother, 17 percent to the father and 9 percent to others (Statistics Canada, 1985: 24). Fathers are only slightly more likely to gain custody in 1983 than they were in 1971 (see Table 8-5 on page 204). The non-custodial parent is expected to pay child support but often defaults on these payments after the first year. This means that most separated or divorced women must live on government assistance, their own income or sporadic support payments. Social workers and women's groups recently expressed concern about the high proportion of one-parent families headed by females on welfare. Some provinces, such as Manitoba, automatically garnishee the wages or government benefits of the defaulting parent without action being taken by the custodial parent. But most provinces expect the custodial parent to initiate action.

About three-quarters of divorced men and two-thirds of divorced women remarry. Reasons for this difference in remarriage rates have been debated. Without child

TABLE 8-5   Divorce Rates in Several Industrialized Countries 1981
             (per 1 000 population)

Japan	1.3
France	1.6
Sweden	2.6
Canada	2.8
United Kingdom	2.9
U.S.S.R.	3.3
United States	5.1

Statistics Canada, *Marriages and Divorces, Vital Statistics*, Vol. II, 1983, Cat. 84-205, Table 21, p. 32, Ottawa, 1985. Reproduced by permission of the Minister of Supply and Services Canada.

TABLE 8-6   Percent of Children Awarded to Mothers, Fathers, or
             Others in Custody Cases After Divorce

	FATHER	MOTHER	OTHER	NO AWARD
1971	15.2	74.2	0.4	10.1
1976	15.0	78.9	0.4	5.7
1980	16.0	78.2	0.2	5.5
1983	17.0	73.8	0.2	9.0

M. Eichler, *Families in Canada Today*, Gage, 1983, p. 215; Calculated from Statistics Canada, *Marriages and Divorces 1983*, Cat. 84-205, Ottawa, 1985, p. 24. Reproduced by permission of the Minister of Supply and Services Canada.

custody and with higher disposable incomes, most divorced men have greater opportunities to meet new partners; they may also have a greater emotional need to recouple. While women rely on their mothers, sisters and female friends for assistance and companionship after separation, men are less likely to have close emotional bonds with their relatives or with other men (Baker, 1983). They often date widely within the first year after separation and often marry within two years of the legal divorce.

American statistics indicate that remarriages have a higher probability of divorce than first marriages. It may be that people in first marriages simply do not believe that divorce is a possible alternative to an unhappy marriage and would not divorce under *any* circumstances. Those who seek a divorce are less likely to be religious and are more likely to have come from a divorced family. But apart from this, remarriages have different strains and problems than first marriages. Bringing together two sets of children, who may not get along, could certainly cause controversy between the new partners. The husband may be supporting his new family, his former wife and his children from the first marriage, which may result in financial

JUDGE CONCERNED OVER FATHERS' RIGHTS
By Marina Strauss

Ontario Judge David Steinberg says he is concerned that men who father children as a result of a casual sexual relationship are often not told about the birth and the subsequent adoption.

Legislative amendments are needed to ensure that the biological father is made aware of the birth of his child. The father should have the opportunity to present to a court an alternative plan for his child's upbringing where this is reasonable and practical before the child's placement for adoption, Judge Steinberg of the Unified Family Court in Hamilton said in a recent ruling.

Judge Steinberg nevertheless approved the adoption of a child who was born Jan. 4, 1984, in unusual circumstances after a casual, one-time sexual encounter between the parents.

The mother said in an affadavit that she did not know she was pregnant until the day before the baby's birth.

"No one except my parents knows of my pregnancy or of the baby's birth," the mother's affadavit says.

Her family and the biological father's family have been friends for many years and she knew the father of the baby all her life but they did not have a romantic relationship.

Under the Child Welfare Act, the biological father technically is not a parent because the law defines a parent as a mother of a child or a person who has filed a legal declaration affirming that he is the father, or other provisions—none of which the father qualified for in this case.

The child was placed with the adoptive parents 13 days after his birth and has done well there, the judge found.

"What concerns me is the total withholding of any information concerning the pregnancy and birth of the child from the biological father," Judge Steinberg said.

"The biological father in this case, notwithstanding its unique features, is however in no different position from many other men who have had casual sexual relationships with women who are deliberately excluded from any knowledge of the pregnancy or the birth of their children."

Judge Steinberg acknowledged that most men in that situation would welcome the decision of mothers to place the children for adoption.

Still, he said, "there are some who would cherish the opportunity to care for and raise their offspring."

Under existing laws, the judge said, these biological fathers have no way of getting information about the children or to present a plan prior to their placement in adoptive homes.

The Globe and Mail, Toronto (February 8, 1985).

strain and be resented by the second wife. Former marriage partners sometimes continue to plague each other or reappear to dredge up old memories. Relatives may compete with each other to see the children. Arrangements for visiting children or parents may become a problem. All these factors may disrupt the stability of remarriages. Although remarriages have higher rates of dissolution, those who stay together *claim* to be happier and to have matured and learned from their previous marital relationship.

Recent American studies have also suggested that wives with a university education and paid work, whose husbands do not share the housework, are more likely to *consider* divorce than other women (Huber and Spitze, 1980). The fact that women have taken over a part of the traditional male role (earning income) while men are generally not sharing women's traditional role (doing housework) may also be increasing dissatisfaction in marriage.

FAMILY LAW REFORM

Since 1978, most Canadian provinces have changed their family law. The most publicized changes relate to the division of matrimonial property. After the 1971 Murdoch case, many groups lobbied for change because they felt that women were receiving a smaller share of matrimonial property and that their unpaid contributions to households were not being considered. In the Murdoch case, the wife ran the family farm for several months of each year while her husband worked out of town at another job. The 25-year marriage broke up after he physically assaulted her, but the court gave the farm to the husband because his name was on the deed and most of the money used to purchase it came from him. The wife was given $200 a month alimony and was allowed to continue to live in the farmhouse (Dranoff, 1977: 52). After 25 years, her contributions to the farm and her running of the family household were judged inconsequential.

In Ontario, the property or possessions used within a marriage (i.e., house, car, furniture) are now considered "family assets" and are divided equally if the marriage breaks up. Even if the wife is not working outside the home for pay, she is entitled to one-half of the family assets. But there remains some dispute about whether spouses are entitled to money invested in business ventures. If a woman frees her husband from domestic labour and therefore allows him to work overtime to make extra money, is she entitled to a share of that money? It appears that the answer, so far, is no.

In Quebec, a woman is no longer expected to take her husband's surname at marriage. She may keep her own name or hyphenate her name and her husband's. In other provinces, too, more married women are keeping their own names. Children from the marriage may be given a hyphenated name that includes the surnames of both parents.

The custody of children in a divorce action is no longer automatically given to the mother. The new laws state that each parent has an equal *right* to custody, and each parent is expected to support the children. Yet, in reality, women still usually receive custody, especially of young children.

Since 1978, most Canadian provinces have changed their family law to recognize the unpaid contributions women make to households. Graetz, Andy, *Weekend Magazine*, Public Archives Canada / PA-115226.

In some provinces, several courts have been consolidated to deal with all family matters (divorce, custody of children, child support and juvenile delinquency). Lawyers defend the child's interests if the parents disagree, are deemed to be negligent or are absent.

A backlog of divorce petitions has led to a new divorce bill that would shorten the separation period to one year (from three or five). Some people think that this would make divorce too easy and not provide adequate support for unemployed wives and dependent children. Initially, this bill cited "marriage breakdown" as the only valid reason for divorce, but amendments added adultery and cruelty as separate reasons that did not require any waiting period. The new divorce bill makes divorce cheaper for the government, eliminating red tape and shortening time spent in the courts. Although spouses are expected to be self-supporting within a few years, allowance will be made for those with no job experience or prospects.

Family Violence

The recent Badgley Report (1984) on sexual abuse of children was widely publicized because it claimed that one-half of all women and one-third of men had experienced some sexual abuse in their lives. Most incidents occurred when they were children or adolescents, and they often involved male relatives. The growing reports of sexual and physical abuse indicate that it is no longer acceptable to treat children as property and that the state will intervene if a child is deemed to be in danger. However, all studies of child abuse state that reported incidents represent only a small portion of the actual number of cases. Fear of reprisals, lack of knowledge about whom to tell or feelings of guilt discourage many children from reporting incidents. Sexual abuse especially goes unreported.

At least one wife in ten is beaten by her husband at some point. Wife battering is often related to the husband's need to exert his dominance and is often unrelated to the wife's behaviour. In fact, it often occurs when she is sleeping and he returns home drunk. Concern about the inability of the police to deal with domestic violence has led to the creation of temporary shelters and transition houses for battered women, feminist counselling services and a series of government reports investigating the problem. Since 1981, the police in London, Ontario, have been laying charges against abusive husbands wherever possible and the Crown Attorney's office has taken a firm stand against dropping charges. So far, 70 percent of the charges laid have been heard in the courts, with a conviction rate of almost 100 percent (McGraw, 1983). Yet women are often abused many times before they go to the police. A recent Canadian study suggests that abused wives are beaten an average of 35 times before they seek outside help (McGraw, 1983). As with child abuse, fear of reprisals and guilt discourages women from going to the authorities. But in addition, many women lack the financial resources to leave an abusive husband and have nowhere to go. They remain in the situation while deciding what to do, often hoping that things will change

Cohabitation vs. Legal Marriage

Fifty years ago, a sexually experienced man expected to marry an inexperienced woman. Gradually, this double standard disappeared, and women now have more nonmarital sexual experience. However, women are still more likely than men to have sex with only those they are "in love with" or whom they plan to marry.

Widespread premarital pregnancy and a desire for independence probably led to the earlier marriages of the 1960s and early 1970s. Yet, with improved contraception and changing attitudes, the age of marriage has risen slightly in recent years as more people cohabit without legal marriage. Some believe that this is a new "courting" pattern—living together to see if you are compatible for marriage. Cohabiting is particularly common among divorced people and those worried about the impermanence of marriage.

Studies have found that people who live common-law are less concerned with tradition, organized religion and socially acceptable behaviour and are therefore less likely to oppose the dissolution of the relationship. In other words, although more people cohabit for long periods of time, common-law relationships are even less likely than marriage to be viewed as permanent.

SUMMARY

Over the last two decades, the age of marriage in Canada has declined and then risen slightly, the birth rate has continued to decline, the divorce rate has risen and levelled off and the labour-force participation of married women (especially young mothers) has increased dramatically. Fewer people live in two-parent families, but more two-parent families have two earners. Mothers are less likely to stay home with their children until they are school-age or adolescents and they are more likely to simply take a maternity leave from work or to stay home for a few years. As women become more educated and jobs become more financially necessary and harder to find, wives and mothers become more committed to paid work. This has led to major changes in family structure and stability.

Although fewer babies are born to each woman now, there has been only a slight rise in childlessness among women. While childlessness by choice is facilitated by effective birth control and the greater availability of abortion, involuntary child-lessness has also been successfully medically remedied so that more people *can* have children. Some unmarried women choose to have children without legal marriage. But having children no longer means an exclusively domestic role for women. Men are slightly more involved in infant and child-care than they were two decades ago, and couples are more likely to hire baby-sitters or to take their children to day-care centres.

Marriage is no longer seen as a life-long commitment, and the remarriage rate after divorce is higher than a few decades ago. The stigma attached to divorce is lessening, and more children live in reconstituted families. The variety of family types, even in a country like Canada, is so great that we can no longer talk about "the family" but of "families." Yet variety always existed within Canadian families. Not only did we experience ethnic variations among immigrant groups and native peoples, but immigration, migrant labour, maternal deaths and high accident rates in the frontier made one-parent families, adoption, boarding and remarriage quite common in the nineteenth century.

In recent years, the sociology of the family as a field of study has been broadened by social historians and feminist scholars. Sociologists such as Jessie Bernard and Margrit Eichler have emphasized that the marital experience is different for males and females. We can no longer assume that couples go through a life cycle together but must acknowledge that individual people experience changes in their lives and marriages which may occur at different times. We no longer become engaged, marry, have children, rear our children and grow old according to the patterns defined for us mainly by American sociologists of the 1950s and 1960s. People sometimes raise other people's children as well as their own. Men sometimes have two sets of children—one from their first marriage and one from their second. Family life has become more complex, with increasing divorce and two-earner families.

Only recently have the laws allowed people to live outside the family with greater ease and protection. It is no longer socially and financially necessary for women to be legally married to reproduce. It is not even necessary to have sexual intercourse to reproduce, as a result of the technology of artificial insemination. Despite the available alternatives in relationships and family life, most people follow social custom rather than create their own alternatives. This is the path of least resistance. Yet enough people have opted out of traditional patterns to force legal and social changes in family life. Now more egalitarian and open to individual preferences and rights, the family continues to be an important institution to both the individual and the state.

Over the past century, the Canadian family has changed as more mothers work for pay and fewer children are born. Children today are cared for by baby-sitters, and divorce and remarriage rates are high. These trends are the consequence of widespread economic and legal changes that began in the late eighteenth century (increasing industrialization, urbanization and demand for labour). In the nineteenth century, families began to produce less for their own consumption, and family members started to work for wages outside the home. As a result, the authority of the father was weakened, and eventually, state regulation of family life increased. Greater participation in public life led to more legal and political rights for women and less emphasis on childbearing. Despite these changes in the family, marriage has remained popular.

DISCUSSION QUESTIONS

1. Is there a maternal instinct? Discuss the evidence for and against.

2. Why is child abuse and wife battering so underreported?

3. What do we mean when we say there has been social pressure to marry? What evidence is there for this?

4. Why do so few divorced men receive custody of their children?

5. Is there a trend towards the nuclear family with increasing industrialization? Why or why not?

9

Race and Ethnic Relations

Peter Li

INTRODUCTION

With the exception of native people, Canada is made up of immigrants. To the extent that it consists of different races and ethnic groups, Canada is a mosaic. Its society is pluralistic in origin. Roughly speaking, this mosaic is composed of the aboriginal peoples, the two charter groups of English and French Canadians and other immigrants.

The emergence of Canadians as a people was marked by conflict between racial and linguistic groups, although the bases of disputes were frequently not language or culture. Historical examples include: the conquest of Canada's native people in the eighteenth and nineteenth century (Patterson II, 1972); the Riel Rebellion and the execution of Louis Riel in 1885; the colonization of Quebec after the British conquest of 1760 (Milner, 1978); and the antiorientalism of British Columbia around the turn of the century (Ward, 1978). These sad events in our history are a reminder that racial and ethnic problems exist in Canadian society, despite the fact that contemporary Canada did not have a civil rights movement in the 1960s, as the United States did, nor the kind of race riots that hit the United Kingdom in the 1970s. News reports also remind us that racial and ethnic divisions are features of Canadian society. The subject matter of these news items ranges from land claims and demands for self-government by native peoples to discrimination against black taxi drivers in Montreal; from the compensation claims of Japanese-Canadians interned in Canada during World War II to antisemitism in the classroom.

This chapter will provide a sociological basis for understanding race and ethnic relations. Before we discuss how racial and ethnic distinctions operate in Canadian society, we must study some sociological perspectives on this subject.

THEORETICAL PERSPECTIVES

WHAT ARE RACE AND ETHNICITY?

There are basically two ways to define race and ethnicity.

Traditionally, sociologists have used *subjective identity* as a basis for defining ethnicity and race. Accordingly, ethnicity is ascribed at birth. Members of an ethnic group share a sense of peoplehood, or identity, based on descent, language, religion, tradition and other common experiences (Weber, 1968:385-398). Ethnic identity allows members of an ethnic group to develop *closures* (Weber, 1968:388), or boundaries, within which ethnic institutions, neighbourhoods, beliefs and cultures are developed and maintained. The members of a racial group also have observable physical traits in common.

More recently, some sociologists have defined race and ethnicity in the context of intergroup relations. For example, according to Wilson, "Racial groups are distinguished by socially selected cultural traits" (1973:6). Physical and cultural traits define social groups only in so far as they are socially recognized as important. In other words, race and ethnicity take on a social meaning only when physical and cultural traits are paired with social attributes, such as intellectual, moral or behavioural characteristics. Whether such associations are alleged or real is often irrelevant. Attaching a social meaning to the physical or cultural characteristics of a group implies that rewards and resources in society are, to some extent, divided along racial and ethnic lines and that the dominant or privileged group can use physical and cultural features of people as a basis of stratification. Some sociologists (van den Berghe, 1984:216-218) use the term *social races* to suggest that they are not genotypical subspecies. Indeed, there is indisputable evidence to indicate that *phenotypes* (superficial physical traits such as skin colour) provide little ground for a scheme of genetical classification (Rex, 1983). The meanings of race and ethnicity, therefore, have to be understood not in terms of phenotypes, but as social constructs based on unequal relations. For example, in South Africa, every person is legally defined in a racial category. However, a person may have fair skin and be classified as black because one of his parents is legally black. This shows that there is no direct correspondence between skin colour, genetical grouping and social classification.

How ethnicity and race are defined affects the questions sociologists ask about ethnic groups and race relations. For example, defining ethnicity as subjective identity raises questions of identity change and persistence in the process of assimilation. In contrast, defining race and ethnicity as products of unequal relations leads to questions about dominant and subordinate groups.

ASSIMILATION AND PLURALISM

The theme of assimilation dominated race and ethnic studies up until the 1960s. *Assimilation* is the process whereby people of diverse origins conform to a single or amalgamated culture. This concept has been applied to the study of immigrant groups in North America to see how, over time, they become incorporated into the culture of the dominant group.

There are many different versions of assimilation theory. Park (1950) develops the notion of a *race relations cycle*, which takes the form of contacts, competition, accommodation and assimilation. Through migration or conquest, people of different origins meet. After the initial contact, the second stage of the cycle is characterized by conflicts arising from competition over scarce resources. Over time, conflicts are resolved as the competing groups accommodate each other. The final stage is assimilation, out of which a single indistinguishable cosmopolitan population emerges. According to Park, this process is progressive and irreversible. Immigration restrictions and racial barriers may slow down this process, but they can neither stop nor reverse it.

The concept of assimilation has been refined by many sociologists, notably Milton M. Gordon (1964). He distinguishes several versions of the assimilation model as applied to the United States. *Anglo-conformity* refers to the process by which immigrant groups and racial minorities are to conform to the language, behaviours and institutions of the dominant Anglo-Saxon group. A more liberal version of assimilation is the *melting-pot thesis*, which sees all groups as contributing to American culture, as people of every stock are amalgamated into a new nation. Other sociologists (Kennedy, 1952; Herberg, 1955) have proposed a *triple melting pot* to suggest that assimilation in America takes place within the three major religious groups of Catholics, Protestants and Jews.

Pluralism, the third assimilation model, refers to both the persistence and assimilation of ethnic groups. In a pluralistic society, ethnic groups may share some aspects of a common culture and participate collectively in economic and political life while retaining unique cultural aspects in their social networks, residential enclaves, churches and languages. Gordon (1964) distinguishes between two types of pluralism: cultural and structural. Cultural pluralism is the retention of ethnic traditions in primary group relations while participating with other ethnic groups in secondary group relations. Structural pluralism, on the other hand, refers to the existence of separate subsocieties along with a massive trend of acculturation to a common culture.

The assimilationist perspective has been criticized on several grounds (Price, 1969; Li and Bolaria, 1979). Park's race relations cycle is simplistic and mechanical. Its prediction of irreversible assimilation is too rigid and is not supported by the experiences of many racial and ethnic groups. A more fundamental objection to assimilation models is that assimilation is loosely defined. Assimilation implies a standard of behaviour and values that immigrant groups have to acquire to become assimilated, yet such a standard is often absent. For example, what does it mean if a person eats spaghetti more often than hamburger? Does it mean that an immigrant is less assimilated if he works and lives like his neighbours but maintains his ethnic friends? Unfortunately, the concept of assimilation is more an ideology calling for Americanization or Anglicization than a realistic description of immigrants' experiences. Thus, the assimilationist perspective has been branded ethnocentric (Rex and Moore, 1967).

The single melting-pot thesis has been challenged by pluralists who argue that racial barriers and ethnic revival have produced persistent ethnic cleavages along religious and racial lines, despite assimilation in some areas (Glazer and Moynihan, 1963). For example, different racial and ethnic groups may have to participate in the same economic and political system, but ethnic distinctiveness is maintained through religious ties and informal social networks. Critiques of pluralism, however, maintain that pluralists downplay the problem of ethnic and racial inequality and that their view of a plural society often assumes a basic equality for all groups (Steinberg, 1981). In a society that is structured on systematic inequalities, pluralism can only be an ideal for some ethnic members, as there is no tenable basis for permanent ethnic preservation (Steinberg, 1981). Even among the upwardly mobile groups, who have the resource base to preserve ethnic pluralism, ethnicity remains expressive or symbolic (Gans, 1979). In other words, there is little support for preserving one's ethnic distinctiveness while participating in the mainstream economic and political life, which is structured unequally, not pluralistically.

The pluralist perspective has also been criticized for unduly emphasizing the transplanted culture from the old country as the principal antecedent and defining characteristic of ethnic groups (Yancey, Ericksen and Juliani, 1976). In doing so, cultural pluralists overlook the importance of the structural conditions of the host society in shaping ethnicity in urban life. Ethnicity is an emergent phenomenon, in that transplanted ethnic cultures may die and new ones evolve, being constantly influenced by the exigencies of survival. Valentine (1968) argues that there is a difference between the material preconditions under which people live and the cultural responses they develop. Culture and ethnicity are variables and not ascribed attributes. The key question is not so much whether immigrants maintain their old-world culture, but under what conditions does ethnicity become particularly salient (Yancey, Ericksen and Juliani, 1976). Hence, the establishment of certain types of businesses among some ethnic groups may have more to do with the conditions and restrictive opportunities in the host society than with a cultural propensity to engage in certain lines of work (Ward and Jenkins, 1984; Bonacich and Modell, 1980; Li, 1979). Differences in historical and structural conditions help to explain why divergent achievements are found even among ethnic groups with similar cultural backgrounds and physical appearances (see insert).

DOMINANT AND SUBORDINATE GROUPS

A different approach to race and ethnic relations is to examine them as unequal relationships, produced and maintained by power differentials between a dominant group and a subordinate one. In this sense, the terms majority/minority groups in the context of ethnic and race relations are defined by unequal power, and not numeric differences. This approach treats race and ethnicity as relational concepts and not descriptive categories. The focus is on the institutional framework within which groups are defined as racial or ethnic and how social interactions are organized (Bolaria and Li, 1985).

There is a close relationship between labour exploitation and racial categorization (Cox, 1948; Thompson, 1975; Rex, 1983; Miles, 1982), which refers to giving phenotypical traits social meanings. This relationship is best illustrated by colonial and capitalist economies under which labour cost is kept as low as possible in order to maximize profit. The basic structural dilemma in such societies is how to confine a pool of subservient labour to menial tasks when economic accumulation inevitably leads to increased economic activity and opportunities for mobility. Physical and cultural attributes provide the rationale for assigning a group of socially defined undesirables to undesirable jobs. Over time, the cultural and physical characteristics of a subordinate group become inseparable from its work role and its subservient position (Bolaria and Li, 1985).

Colonial Model

One institutional framework under which race and ethnic relations must function is colonization. The most significant aspect of colonial economies is the massive deployment of nonwhite labour (Rex, 1983). European colonizers transformed previously public resources and brought about economic development in some regions of their colonies at the expense of other sectors. Importing slaves or indentured labourers and inviting in white settlers gradually replaced the indigenous social structure of the colony with a new social order in which race became a dominant feature of stratification (Bolaria and Li, 1985).

The colonization process has seven parts (Frideres, 1983). These are: (1) the incursion of the colonizing group; (2) the social, economic and cultural destruction of the colonized people; (3) the taking of external political control by the colonizers; (4) the establishment of the economic dependence of the colonized people; (5) the provision of low-quality social services for the colonized people; (6) the emergence of racism; and (7) the development of a colour line.

Different aspects of the colonial model have been applied to explain race relations in advanced capitalist societies. For example, Rex (1973, 1983) argues that immigrants from ex-colonies to metropolitan societies such as Great Britain carry the

The historical facts show, for example, that prior to the end of the Second World War, the Chinese were subjected to a discriminatory immigration system which sought to exclude them (see Li, 1979a). One of the consequences of such exclusion was to produce a highly unbalanced sex ratio among the Chinese, even long after the legislative control was removed in 1947. This largely delayed the birth of a second generation which did not begin to emerge in sizable numbers until the sixties (Li, 1979d). In contrast, the immigration system permitted the Japanese to bring their wives as early as 1908 (see Adachi, 1976), and this resulted in a much more balanced sex ratio among the Japanese community as compared to the Chinese (Li, 1979d, Table 3). Furthermore, the experience of relocation and subsequent repatriation of the Japanese in Canada resulted in a large drop in population among the Japanese in Canada (Adachi, 1976). The small volume of Japanese immigration to Canada in the postwar years greatly altered the demographic and social characteristics of the Japanese community (Ujimoto, 1976). These historical factors, and not cultural adaptability, are important in understanding the present demographic structures of the Chinese and the Japanese in Canada.

Historically too, the Japanese and the Chinese entered different occupations in Canada, in part because of different opportunities available to the two groups. The heavy concentration of the Chinese in the service industry as laundrymen and restaurant workers, for example, was largely a result of restricted opportunities in the non-ethnic sector (Li, 1979a). The damage to the Japanese ethnic business during the relocation of the Second World War (see Adachi, 1976) probably resulted in many Japanese having to seek employment in other sectors after the war. These historical experiences must be considered in explaining the differences of the two groups in the occupational structure of today.

What is understood as the adaptive capacity of minority groups then, may be no more than different responses under various constrained situations. Ethnic differences in economic achievements in many cases are probably more related to unequal opportunity structures to which these groups are subjected, than to the adaptive capacity of their old world cultures.

Peter S. Li "Income achievement and adaptive capacity: an empirical comparison of Chinese and Japanese in Canada," in K.V. Ujimoto and G. Hirabayashi (eds.) *Visible Minorities and Multiculturalism: Asians in Canada*.

stigma of colonial workers, which places them in a disadvantaged position. Many immigrants constitute an *underclass*, a bottom stratum below the working-class (Rex and Tomlinson, 1979). Another extension of the colonial model argues that racism facilitates the superexploitation of immigrants and workers in peripheral countries as advanced capitalist countries extend their investments to peripheral markets and transform these countries to neocolonies (Portes and Walton, 1981; Castles and Kosack, 1973). Finally, the concept *internal colonies* has been used to describe the situation of some racial groups in America [the blacks (Blauner, 1972), the Mexicans (Moore, 1970), and the native peoples (Frideres, 1983; Patterson II, 1972)] because of their similarity to colonized people. Internal colonization refers to the political and economic domination of minorities within a country, such that the minorities suffer from exploitation and oppression similar to that endured by indigenous people under classical colonization. For example, Frideres (1983) shows that the native peoples in Canada suffer from colonial status. Such controls as the Indian Act and native reserves produce experiences like those of second-class citizens in colonies and result in lower opportunities and poorer quality of life for native people in Canada.

Split Labour Market Model

The *split labour market model* is developed by Bonacich (1972, 1979) to explain racial and ethnic conflicts. The source of antagonism is not race and ethnicity, but differences in the price of labour between two groups that are often divided along racial and ethnic lines. Historically, this economically based antagonism surfaced as racial conflict between nonwhite and white labour. The real issue, however, had to do with white workers resisting their replacement by the cheaper labour of nonwhite workers as capitalists tried to lower their labour costs. Depending on the resources of various classes, racial antagonism may be "resolved" by excluding nonwhite workers or by assigning labour by race or ethnic group, as in a caste or near-caste system. The split labour market refers to the price differentials between two groups performing the same task, or in a submerged form in which the higher-paid group monopolizes certain positions, and the lower paid group is restricted to marginal participation.

The emergence of a split labour market is related to two conditions, both of which arose from the development of capitalism in Western Europe (Bonacich, 1979). The first was the rise in the cost of the labour of white workers and the second was the availability of nonwhite labour from the peripheral countries as imperialism accelerated their underdevelopment. The theory of split labour market has been applied to explain racism against blacks in the United States (Bonacich, 1975, 1976) and antiorientalism in Canada (Li, 1979) and Brazil (Makabe, 1981).

The split labour market implies that there is a relationship between class and race. Bonacich's theory also suggests a close tie between labour recruitment and capitalist expansion. Indeed, there are grounds to suggest that Canadian immigration policy, like that of other advanced capitalist countries, is designed to regulate the volume and type of immigrants to suit the country's labour needs. Historically, Canada has favoured immigrants from Britain, the United States and Northern Europe and excluded others from nonwhite countries except in times of severe labour shortage (Li and Bolaria, 1979). A preferential system based on country of origin was maintained until 1967, when a universal point system was introduced (Hawkins, 1972). The change facilitated the recruitment of skilled labour from nontraditional source countries as the economic prosperity of the postwar years increased the demand for technical labour. Despite these changes, postwar Gallup polls show that native Canadians most prefer immigrants from the United Kingdom and northeastern Europe, and least prefer immigrants from Asia (Tienhaara, 1974). According to another study, native Canadians are more willing to accept the services of immigrants in lower-prestige occupations than high-prestige occupations (Jones and Lambert, 1965). During economic hard times, immigrants are often seen as competitors who take away jobs from native Canadians (Li, 1979). These findings give further credence to the split labour market theory. In a later section, we shall examine more closely the relationship between ethnic origin and class in Canada.

So far, we have covered two major approaches to race and ethnic relationships. We can now discuss some empirical studies that use these theoretical positions. The problem of language maintenance and shift represents one aspect of ethnic persistence and assimilation, whereas the question of racial and ethnic inequality is central to the dominant-subordinate group relationship. Before we discuss the empirical findings, we shall examine racial and ethnic patterns in Canada.

RACIAL AND ETHNIC PATTERNS IN CANADA

Race and ethnicity are important features of Canadian society because: (1) Canadians came from different origins; and (2) racial and ethnic lines cross other cleavages in our society. Canada has seen a decline of the British ethnic group over the past 85 years and an increase in the non-British and non-French population. People of British origin, however, remain the single largest group in Canada. In 1901, for example, 57 percent of the total population were of British origin, and by 1981, they were down to 40.2 percent. The non-British and non-French population increased from 8.5 percent in 1901 to 33.1 percent in 1981. The number of people of French origin declined slightly from 30.7 percent in 1901 to 26.7 percent in 1981.

Canada's ethnic diversity can be seen from Table 9-1. In 1971, the non-English and non-French population (23 percent) came from 31 different backgrounds. The majority of these ethnic minorities were European, with Asians, native peoples and blacks constituting the racial minorities.

Most of the population increase among the ethnic and racial minorities has resulted from changing immigration patterns, especially in the postwar years of industrial expansion. The demand for technical manpower led the Canadian government in 1967 to begin a wider recruitment of skilled labour from nontraditional sources (Hawkins, 1972). Historically, the United Kingdom, northern continental Europe and the United States had been the major sources of immigrants to Canada. The demand for skilled labour from these countries as a result of the postwar economic boom meant that Canada had to compete with other industrial nations for immigrants with professional and technical skills. Third World countries became the main suppliers of skilled labour in what some call the "brain drain" (Parai, 1965). Table 9-2 shows the changing sources of immigrants to Canada. Before 1961, the ten leading sources of immigrants were European countries and the United States, with the British Isles accounting for nearly 30 percent of all immigrants. Between 1971 and 1981, however, the ten leading countries included India, the Philippines, Jamaica, Vietnam, Hong Kong and Guyana. The British Isles, still the largest supplier of immigrants to Canada, accounted for only 13.8 percent of all immigrants entering the country between 1971 and 1981. More recently, the federal government has trimmed the volume of immigrants in response to high unemployment in Canada,

TABLE 9-1   Population by Ethnic Group, 1951, 1961 and 1971

ETHNIC GROUP	1951		1961		1971	
	No.	%	No.	%	No.	%
British Isles	6 709 685	47.9	7 996 669	43.8		
English	3 630 344	25.9	4 195 175	23.0		
Irish	1 439 635	10.3	1 753 351	9.6	9 624 115	44.6
Scottish	1 547 470	11.0	1 902 302	10.4		
Welsh and other	92 236	0.7	145 841	0.8		
French	4 319 167	30.8	5 540 346	30.4	6 180 120	28.7
Other European	2 553 722	18.2	4 116 849	22.6	4 959 680	23.0
Austrian	32 231	0.2	106 535	0.6	42 120	0.2
Belgian	35 148	0.2	61 382	0.3	51 135	0.2
Czech and Slovak	63 959	0.5	73 061	0.4	81 870	0.4
Danish	42 671	0.3	85 473	0.5	75 725	0.4
Finnish	43 745	0.3	59 436	0.3	59 215	0.3
German	619 995	4.4	1 049 599	5.8	1 317 200	6.1
Greek	13 966	0.1	56 475	0.3	124 475	0.6
Hungarian	60 460	0.4	126 220	0.7	131 890	0.6
Icelandic	23 307	0.2	30 623	0.2	27 905	0.1
Italian	152 245	1.1	450 351	2.5	730 820	3.4
Jewish	181 670	1.3	173 344	1.0	296 945	1.4
Lithuanian	16 224	0.1	27 629	0.2	24 535	0.1
Netherlands	264 267	1.9	429 679	2.4	425 945	2.0
Norwegian	119 266	0.8	148 681	0.8	179 290	0.8
Polish	219 845	1.6	323 517	1.8	316 425	1.5
Portuguese	—	—	—	—	96 875	0.4
Romanian	23 601	0.2	43 805	0.2	27 375	0.1
Russian	91 279	0.7	119 168	0.7	64 475	0.3
Spanish	—	—	—	—	27 515	0.1
Swedish	97 780	0.7	121 757	0.6	101 870	0.5
Ukrainian	395 043	2.8	473 337	2.6	580 660	2.7
Yugoslavic	21 404	0.2	68 587	0.4	104 950	0.5
Other	35 616	0.2	88 190	0.5	70 460	0.3
Asiatic	72 827	0.5	121 753	0.7	285 540	1.3
Chinese	32 528	0.2	58 197	0.3	118 815	0.6
Japanese	21 663	0.2	29 157	0.2	37 260	0.2
Other	18 636	0.1	34 399	0.2	129 460	0.6
Other	354 028	2.5	462 630	2.5	518 850	2.4
Eskimo	9 733	0.1	11 835	0.1	17 550	0.1
Native Indian	155 874	1.1	208 286	1.1	295 215	1.4
Negro	18 020	0.1	32 127	0.2	34 445	0.2
West Indian	—	—	—	—	28 025	0.1
Other and not stated	170 401	1.2	210 382	1.2	143 620	0.7
Total	14 009 429	100.0	18 238 247	100.0	21 568 310	100.0

Canada Year Book, 1980-81, p. 137. Reproduced by permission of the Minister of Supply and Services Canada.

TABLE 9-2 Ten Leading Countries of Birth of Immigrants for Each Period of Immigration, Canada, 1981

Before 1961

Country of birth	Number	% of total
Great Britain	524 900	29.8
Italy	214 700	12.2
United States	136 900	7.8
Poland	118 000	6.7
U.S.S.R.	112 600	6.4
Netherlands	112 400	6.4
Federal Republic of Germany	107 200	6.1
Yugoslavia	39 100	2.2
German Democratic Republic	28 400	1.6
Austria	28 300	1.6
Ten leading countries as a percentage of all immigrants who arrived before 1961		80.8

1961-1970

Country of birth	Number	% of total
Great Britain	195 300	21.1
Italy	141 000	15.2
United States	67 000	7.2
Portugal	57 300	6.2
Greece	40 700	4.4
Yugoslavia	33 200	3.6
Federal Republic of Germany	31 400	3.4
India	28 200	3.0
Jamaica	23 600	2.5
France	19 100	2.1
Ten leading countries as a percentage of all immigrants who arrived during the 1961-1970 period		68.7

1971-1981

Country of birth	Number	% of total
Great Britain	158 800	13.8
United States	97 600	8.5
India	75 100	6.5
Portugal	66 400	5.8
Philippines	55 300	4.8
Jamaica	49 900	4.3
Socialist Republic of Vietnam	49 400	4.3
Hong Kong	42 200	3.7
Italy	29 100	2.5
Guyana	27 500	2.4
Ten leading countries as a percentage of all immigrants who arrived during the 1971-1981 period		56.6

1981 Census of Canada, Catalogue 99-936, *Canada's Immigrants*. Reproduced by permission of the Minister of Supply and Services Canada.

but it encourages the immigration of entrepreneurs, who, it is hoped, will create more jobs. In 1982, for example, 449 immigrants entered Canada as entrepreneurs out of 55 472 immigrants destined to enter the labour force.

The immigrant population in Canada is statistically overrepresented in skilled, professional and technical occupations. Figure 9-1 shows the occupational distribution of male immigrants compared to male nonimmigrants. There is a higher percentage of male immigrants in the managerial, professional and technical category and in the processing, machining and assembling group. Figure 9-2 compares female immigrants and nonimmigrants. Female immigrants are clearly overrepresented in the skilled occupations of processing, machining and assembling. These statistics support the earlier claim that the changing immigration pattern is a result of increased demand for technical and skilled labour.

Figure 9-1   Percentage Distribution by Occupation Major Groups of the Immigrant and Non-immigrant Male Labour Force 15 Years and Over Not Attending School Full-time, Canada, 1981

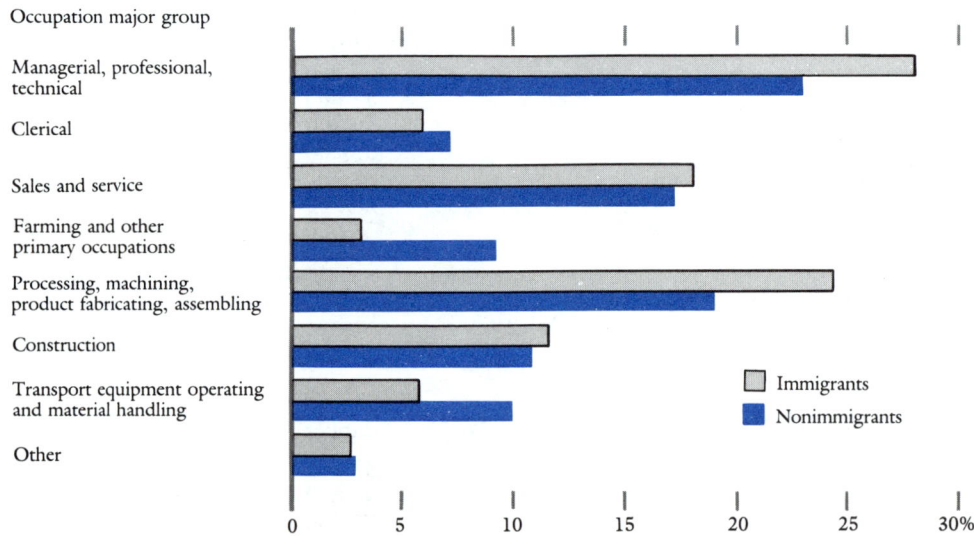

1981 Census of Canada, Catalogue 99-936, *Canada's Immigrants*. Reproduced by permission of the Minister of Supply and Services Canada.

In addition to ethnic diversity, there is linguistic variation in Canada. The 1981 census shows that English is the mother tongue for 60 percent of Canadians. A quarter of all Canadians are of French mother tongue, 85 percent of whom live in Quebec. More than 2 million people speak a language at home that differs from their mother tongue. About 3.7 million Canadians are bilingual, but bilingualism is more common among those whose mother tongue is French. Table 9-3 shows

Figure 9-2   Percentage Distribution by Occupation Major Groups of
the Immigrant and Non-immigrant Female Labour Force
15 Years and Over Not Attending School Full-time,
Canada, 1981

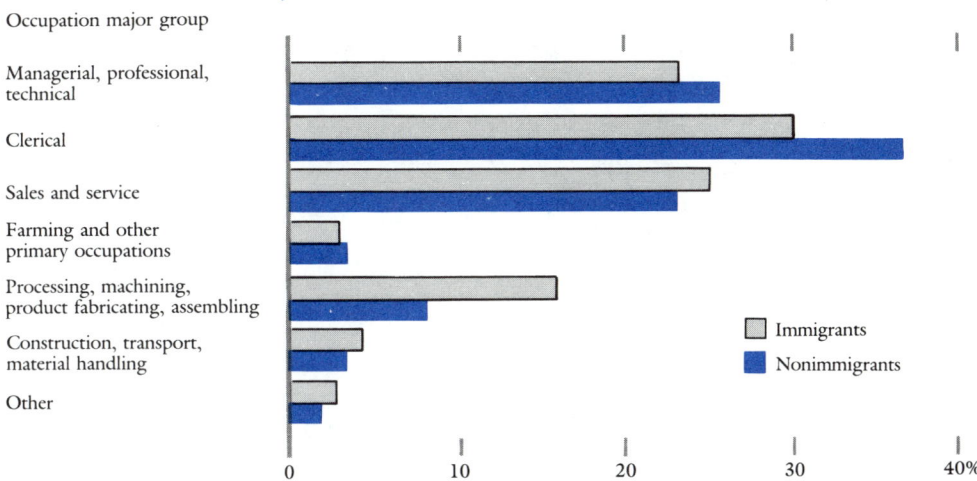

1981 Census of Canada, Catalogue 99-936, *Canada's Immigrants*. Reproduced by permission of the
Minister of Supply and Services Canada.

the linguistic distribution of Canadians by provinces and territories. The figures
show that those whose mother tongue is English are the majority of the population
everywhere in Canada except Quebec and the North West Territories. Compared
to eastern Canada, western Canada has a larger percentage of non-English and non-
French population.

There are marked regional differences in the linguistic patterns in Canada. The
importance of language regions is well summarized in Joy's *bilingual belt* thesis
(1972), according to which the bilingual belt of Soo-Moncton separates the unilingual Francophones of Quebec from the unilingual Anglophones of the rest of Canada. Using 1971 census data, Beaujot (1982) shows that 82.7 percent of the population
in the French zone can speak French only, and 33.5 percent of the population in
the bilingual zone is officially bilingual. This belt has less than one-quarter of Canada's population but over 60 percent of our bilinguals. In the English zone, only
5.8 percent can speak French. The 1981 census indicates that those who are officially
bilingual represent 15.3 percent of the total population. About one-third of those
whose native tongue is French are bilingual, in contrast to 8 percent of the English.
Bilingualism is less common among the English in Quebec than among the French
in the rest of Canada. Figure 9-3 shows the bilingual population as a percentage of
each region. About one-third of the population in Quebec and one-quarter of the
population in New Brunswick are bilingual.

The problem of linguistic and economic inequality is central to understanding
the British/French relationship in Canada. The basis of hostility between the two

TABLE 9-3   Percentage Distribution by Mother Tongue of the
             Population, Provinces and Territories, 1981

MOTHER TONGUE	NFLD.	P.E.I.	N.S.	N.B.	QUE.	ONT.	MAN.	SASK.	ALTA.	B.C.	YUKON	N.W.T.
	%	%	%	%	%	%	%	%	%	%	%	%
English	98.8	94.0	93.6	65.1	10.9	77.3	71.7	79.7	81.1	81.9	87.4	54.1
French	0.5	4.9	4.2	33.6	82.4	5.5	5.1	2.6	2.8	1.6	2.3	2.7
Other	0.7	1.1	2.2	1.2	6.7	17.2	23.1	17.7	16.2	16.5	10.3	43.2

1981 Census of Canada, Catalogue 99-935, *Language in Canada*. Reproduced by permission of the
Minister of Supply and Services Canada.

Figure 9-3   Bilingual Population as a Percentage of the Total
              Population, Canada, Provinces and Territories, 1981

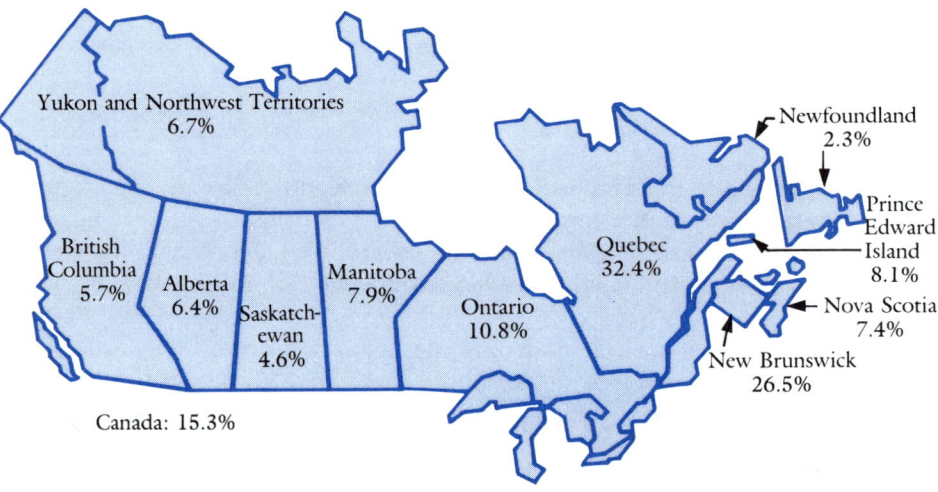

1981 Census of Canada, Catalogue 99-935, *Language in Canada*. Reproduced by permission of the
Minister of Supply and Services Canada.

groups is frequently economic, although ethnic antagonism frequently manifests
itself in linguistic and cultural terms. To better understand this feature of Canadian
society, we shall examine the historical roots of French Canada and its relationship
with English Canada.

HISTORICAL ROOTS OF FRENCH CANADA

Before the British conquest of 1760, New France was a French colony. Although
the language of the 90 000 inhabitants was French and their religion was Catholic,

the life style in the colony was distinct from that of France (Milner, 1978). Under the *seigneurial system*, land titles were granted by the French crown to *seigneurs*, or land owners, who in turn, parcelled out land to the *Canayens*, or French settlers. The social structure reflected the colonial rule. Fur trade was monopolized by the French regime, and the *habitants* of New France were engaged in subsistence farming. The Catholic Church provided both spiritual and administrative stability to the French settlement.

The conflict in the colony between Great Britain and France was over control of the fur trade; it was not a result of linguistic differences between the French and the British settlers. The French defeat resulted in the Treaty of Paris of 1763, which gave Great Britain control over New France. With the immigration of English-speaking merchants, the English Protestants gradually assumed power in Montreal and Quebec. The French population remained almost exclusively rural. Although the Quebec Act of 1774 recognized the religious and linguistic rights of the French, it also upheld the feudal legacy of the colonial system and the authority of the Church.

The American Revolution of 1776 brought thousands of British Loyalists to Canada. In Montreal, the English Protestant minority became the elites of a unified financial, transportation and staples cartel that dominated subsequent economic development (Milner, 1978). By the time of Confederation, the English oligarchy based in Montreal was well entrenched. Although the British North America Act of 1867 recognized the status of French as an official language in the Parliament of Canada and the legislature of Quebec, commercial enterprises were virtually all in the hands of the English.

The dominance of the Protestant English in Quebec persisted through the first half of the twentieth century. A high birth rate, low education and submission to clerical authority were characteristic of the French population in rural Quebec. The Roman Catholic Church perpetuated a rural mythology that was conservative, fatalistic and passive.

The victory of the Parti Québécois in 1976 indicated the strength of French nationalism in the province, but changes really began during the Quiet Revolution of the 1960s. Industrial expansion after World War II, the increased migration to cities as a result of a high birth rate and the reform of the educational and welfare systems contributed to a new consciousness among the young French intelligentsia (Milner, 1978). Quebec nationalism was a response to the historical inequality between the British and the French and to the exploitation of labour by English capitalists. Consequently, the independence movement in Quebec was closely tied to labour politics and the political Left (Milner, 1978).

In many ways, the language struggle of the French-Canadians resulted from their economic and political oppression (Jackson, 1977). Generally, when language serves to maintain group boundaries, language conflicts, as Jackson puts it, "also become the focus of class, status and power conflicts" (1977:63).

LANGUAGE MAINTENANCE AND SHIFT

There is much research available on language use among Canadians. This interest arises partly from the multilingual background of Canadians and partly from the historical rivalry between Francophones and Anglophones. The Official Languages Act of 1969, which made Canada officially bilingual, and the subsequent inclusion in the census of questions on language use also stimulated language research.

The 1981 census found ten major *home languages* of Canadians. A home language is the language spoken by the respondent at home at the time of the census. English is the home language for 68 percent of Canadians and French for 25 percent. The remaining 7 percent speak a home language other than English or French.

Language maintenance has to do with whether an ethnic or racial group retains its language over time. *Language shift* refers to a change from the use of one language to another. A study by de Vries and Vallee (1980) distinguishes two types of shifts: ancestral and current. *Ancestral shift* occurs when the mother tongue of a person, or the language he learned in childhood, does not correspond to his ethnic origin, as in the case of a Ukrainian who speaks English as his mother tongue. *Current shift*, refers to the use of a language other than the mother tongue at his present home, for example, a person whose mother tongue is French and who now speaks mainly English at home. *Anglicization* refers to the extent of adopting English as the language used at home by linguistic minorities (Castonguay, 1979). The Language Continuity Index, calculated as the ratio of persons speaking a particular home language to the number of individuals who have the same language as a native tongue, indicates how much a native tongue is gaining or losing in its use as a home language (1981 Census of Canada, Language in Canada).

The data from the 1981 census (Table 9-4) indicate that the English language group has a score of 111.4 percent on the Language Continuity Index, suggesting there are more people speaking English as a home language then there are people whose native tongue is English. Other language groups have varying tendencies to shift to another home language. Although the French have the highest index score among the linguistic minorities, language maintenance is strongest for French in Quebec and New Brunswick and weakest in the Prairies. Vallee (1969) has postulated that the influence of Quebec on French language retention diminishes the further away a region is from Quebec. With respect to other linguistic minorities, the Chinese have the highest score (83.5 percent) on the Language Continuity Index, followed by the Portuguese (79.5 percent). In contrast, language retention is weakest among the Dutch and Ukrainians.

The ability of linguistic minorities to maintain their languages is affected by the demographic-ecological structure of each region, which imposes varying constraints on the linguistic minority (Lieberson, 1970). In regions where the minority is small relative to the majority population, there is greater pressure for minority-group members to learn the language of the majority. For example, the relatively low degree of residential segregation among those of German origin (Richmond and Kalback, 1980:189) may explain their weak language retention.

Language maintenance is sometimes seen as an aspect of ethnic identity (Isajiw, 1976) and language shift as an indication of assimilation (Anderson and Frideres, 1981). Ethnic communities vary according to what Breton (1964) calls their *institutional completeness*, or the extent to which they can offer their members various services through their own separate institutions. In a recent study, Reitz (1980) found a substantial variation in ethnic group cohesion. Similarly, Lieberson (1970)

TABLE 9-4 Language Continuity Index for English, French and Nonofficial Languages Canada and Provinces, 1981

	ENGLISH	FRENCH	ITALIAN	GERMAN	UKRAINIAN	CHINESE	PORTUGUESE	NETHERLANDIC LANGUAGES	ABORIGINAL LANGUAGES	POLISH	GREEK
	%	%	%	%	%	%	%	%	%	%	%
Canada	111.4	95.9	68.6	31.7	33.1	83.5	79.5	16.8	78.0	43.7	77.0
Newfoundland	100.5	67.5	37.5	26.9	33.3	84.8	65.8	—	58.5	—	50.0
Prince Edward Island	102.7	63.0	60.0	24.1	50.0	69.0	55.6	31.6	—	—	—
Nova Scotia	102.7	68.5	33.5	24.4	14.2	68.4	62.3	10.9	90.5	24.0	78.9
New Brunswick	104.4	93.4	44.0	31.5	27.6	81.8	83.8	17.6	85.0	34.3	59.6
Quebec	116.4	100.2	75.1	36.5	54.9	84.3	82.2	23.8	88.0	50.3	85.8
Ontario	111.2	71.2	69.1	34.2	41.6	86.1	81.1	15.8	76.0	48.2	74.0
Manitoba	119.9	59.7	59.3	42.5	34.0	85.9	78.2	20.5	78.8	34.7	67.4
Saskatchewan	116.4	39.8	43.8	21.9	32.4	76.1	57.0	16.5	76.6	23.2	67.2
Alberta	113.1	48.5	51.8	30.4	26.0	85.7	70.8	16.2	70.5	36.3	62.3
British Columbia	112.0	34.6	48.4	25.0	17.9	80.1	66.4	17.9	47.0	31.6	60.4
Yukon	110.0	44.2	16.6	22.4	7.0	78.6	—	—	27.3	12.5	100.0
Northwest Territories	117.4	51.2	69.6	12.2	7.1	85.7	60.0	9.5	85.6	22.2	44.4

1981 Census of Canada, Catalogue 99-935, *Language in Canada*. Reproduced by permission of the Minister of Supply and Services Canada.

has suggested that highly segregated ethnic minorities have a greater chance of maintaining their languages. The degree of ethnic segregation and cohesion may be measured by in-group interaction, ethnic identification, endogamy (or in-group marriage), ethnic language retention, ethnic neighbourhood residence and ethnic church affiliation (Reitz, 1980).

RACIAL AND ETHNIC INEQUALITY

Sociologists are interested in why some racial and ethnic groups do better than others socially and economically. Obviously, there are various ways of comparing the performances of racial and ethnic groups, for example, by occupational status, income and membership in the elite. The *explanations* of inequality, however, are more complex. To varying degrees, historical, cultural and institutional factors account for why certain ethnic groups occupy privileged positions in a society, while others are deprived of equal opportunities for advancement.

THE VERTICAL MOSAIC

John Porter (1965), in *The Vertical Mosaic*, offers several explanations of how ethnicity and class intersect in Canadian society. The title of his book refers to the intimate relationship between ethnicity and class. First, he compares the *charter status* of the British and French with the *entrance status* of later immigrants. The charter group retains many privileges and prerogatives and lays down the conditions and rules under which other groups are admitted. Entrance status implies lower occupational status. Over time, some groups may improve their entrance status, while others may not. The concepts of charter group and entrance status are useful in understanding the privileged positions enjoyed by the English throughout the history of Canada, as compared to the disadvantaged status of the later immigrant groups that were recruited for various economic developments, as in the case of the Irish, who built canals and railways in Upper Canada, the Asians, who opened mines and constructed railroads in the West and the Ukrainians, who homesteaded in the Prairies.

Porter's second point is that, within the charter groups, the British are doing much better occupationally than the French. His analysis of the 1931, 1951 and 1961 censuses shows that the French were underrepresented in professional and financial occupations and overrepresented in the agricultural and primary occupations. By comparison, the English were increasingly overrepresented in the professional and financial occupations. The occupational inequality between the English and French has been shown by many other studies. For example, Hughes (1943), in his ethnographic study of an industrial town in Quebec, found a general pattern of ethnic stratification typical of Quebec, with the English occupying the management positions and the French composing the rank and file. In a study of Francophones and Anglophones in the federal public service in 1965 and 1973, Beattie (1975) reports that Francophones received less pay and had a lower chance of promotion than Anglophones. More recently, Milner (1978) has shown that in

Quebec, the *grande bourgeoisie*, or owners of multinational corporations are still largely Americans and English-Canadians.

Perhaps Porter is best known for his analysis of the economic elite of Canada, in which he shows that the English have overwhelming control. The economic elite are defined as those who hold directorships in dominant corporations in Canada. In 1951, for example, Porter found that, of the 760 individuals in the economic elite, 92.3 percent were British, 6.7 percent were French and 1 percent were from other backgrounds, mainly Jewish. In 1951, the British represented 47.9 percent of Canada's population, the French, 30.8 percent and other ethnic groups, 21.3 percent. The British were clearly overrepresented in the upper echelons of corporations. Porter's findings are supported by Clement's more recent study of the Canadian corporate elite (Clement, 1975). Clement's data show that in 1972, 86.2 percent of the 775 individuals in the economic elite were English, 8.4 percent were French and 5.4 percent were of other origin. The underrepresentation of the French goes back, as we have seen, to the British conquest of 1760, after which the British took over the economic and political insitutions of New France. Subsequent generations of English-Canadians maintained an economic empire in Quebec, largely by relying on the British market and British capital and, more recently, through ties with industrial capitalists in the United States (Clement, 1975).

The fourth point of *The Vertical Mosaic* deals with the relationship between ethnic origin and occupation. Porter suggests that "immigration and ethnic affiliation have been important factors in the formation of social classes in Canada . . . (and) ethnic differences have been important in building up the bottom layer of the stratification system in both agricultural and industrial settings" (1965:73). His analysis of the 1931, 1951 and 1961 censuses showed that people of English and Jewish origin were persistently overrepresented in the professional and financial occupations and underrepresented in agricultural and unskilled jobs. All other racial and ethnic groups were underrepresented in the professional and financial occupations, with the exception of Asians in 1961. Porter's conclusion is that, over this 30 year period, the British maintained their overrepresentation in the white-collar sector, while the French could hardly retain their position relative to other ethnic groups. With the exception of the French, the rough occupational ranking of various groups had remained the same, with the Germans, Scandinavians and Dutch close to the occupational levels of the English, and Italians, Poles and Ukrainians near the lower end of the occupational structure.

More recently, this *blocked mobility thesis* of Porter's has been questioned (Darroch, 1979) because a reanalysis of Porter's data indicates a trend of decreasing occupational dissimilarity among ethnic groups. However, using a more detailed analysis, Lautard and Loree (1984) have shown that, despite declines since 1931, occupational dissimilarity among ethnic groups remains large. Lautard and Loree argue that, although the average, or mean, ethnic inequality declined, the relative ranking of ethnic groups over the three decades remained stable. In other words, the ethnic groups at the top and the bottom of the occupational structure basically retained their positions relative to each other throughout this period. On the basis of their reanalysis, Lautard and Loree conclude that the "relationship between ethnicity and occupation remains a durable feature of Canadian society (1984:342).

INEQUALITY, RACISM AND VISIBLE MINORITIES

In recent years, it has become fashionable among policy makers and academics to use the term "visible minorities" to refer to nonwhite racial groups (Ujimoto and Hirabayashi, 1980). Evidence suggests that these minorities experience a double jeopardy in the labour market because of their recent immigrant status and racial origin. The 1981 census indicates that, with the exception of people of Japanese origin, a high proportion of other visible minorities in the labour force is foreign born (Abella, 1984). For example, 88.9 percent of black males and 91.5 percent of black females in the labour force were born outside of Canada. Over 90 percent of Indo-Pakistani, Indo-Chinese, Korean, Pacific Islands and Central and South American origin in the labour force are foreign born. Many of them immigrated to Canada after the 1967 change in the Immigration Act. In a recent Royal Commission Report entitled *Equality in Employment*, Abella (1984) found a definite concentration of some racial groups in certain job categories. For example, Indo-Chinese males were largely employed in blue-collar and service occupations, and close to 50 percent of Indo-Pakistani women were in clerical and service jobs. Native people had the highest

TABLE 9-5   Participation Rates and Unemployment Rates of Selected Ethnic Groups by Gender, 1981*

	MALES		FEMALES	
	PARTICI-PATION	UNEMPLOY-MENT	PARTICI-PATION	UNEMPLOY-MENT
British	77.8%	5.6%	51.4%	7.7%
French	76.2	9.7	47.9	12.4
Other European	80.9	3.9	54.0	5.9
Indo-Pakistani	85.7	4.5	60.3	10.0
Indo-Chinese	77.6	8.3	58.9	12.3
Japanese	82.4	3.1	58.6	5.0
Korean	82.2	4.9	63.7	6.6
Chinese	79.0	4.2	61.0	5.4
Pacific Islands, including Philippines	84.8	3.4	75.3	4.3
Black	83.0	7.3	65.2	9.5
Native People	60.7	16.5	36.7	17.3
Central/South American	86.2	6.9	57.9	7.1
Total Labour Force	78.2	6.5	51.8	8.7

* Single ethnic origin only.
Royal Commission Report on Equality in Employment, p. 82. The original source is from Statistics Canada, unpublished data from the 1981 Census. Reproduced by permission of the Minister of Supply and Services Canada.

unemployment rate (see Table 9-5). Other groups with high unemployment rates were French females (12.4 percent), Indo-Chinese females (12.3 percent) and Indo-Pakistani females (10 percent).

Table 9-6 shows the income levels of various ethnic and racial groups from the 1981 census. The income level of each group is expressed first as a gross deviation from the grand mean, or national average, and then as a net deviation controlling for sex, nativity, occupation, age, number of weeks worked and education. In other words, the net effect measures the amount of income inequality associated with an

TABLE 9-6   Gross and Net Effect[1] of Racial and Ethnic Origin on Annual Income

	N	GROSS EFFECT AS DEVIATION FROM GRAND MEAN ($)	NET EFFECT, CONTROLLING FOR SEX, NATIVITY, OCCUPATION, AGE, NUMBER OF WEEKS WORKED AND EDUCATION ($)
Jewish	159 250	+ 6 261.6	+ 2 936.0
Scandinavian	176 650	+ 1 859.8	+ 1 034.6
Portuguese	104 200	− 2 001.9	+ 626.5
Croatian & Serbian	71 600	+ 458.6	+ 378.3
German	708 750	+ 652.4	+ 274.6
Ukrainian	325 350	+ 794.7	+ 212.7
Italian	443 100	− 509.4	+ 148.5
British	5 365 250	+ 355.8	+ 103.7
Dutch	251 800	+ 311.3	+ 76.6
Czech & Slovak	42 500	+ 2 136.9	+ 62.9
Hungarian	71 750	+ 1 901.6	+ 20.4
Polish	161 500	+ 720.8	− 222.7
French	3 333 800	− 501.1	− 240.3
Other[2]	1 610 400	− 1 113.3	− 277.9
Greek	83 750	− 1 893.9	− 796.3
Chinese	168 100	− 1 294.6	− 931.1
Black[3]	85 900	− 1 588.0	− 1 679.5
Canada (all groups)	13 163 650	14 044.9	14 044.9

[1] Gross and net effects are measured as deviations from the grand mean income, using Multiple Classification Analysis (Andrews et al., 1976).
[2] Includes other single responses and multiple responses of ethnic origin.
[3] Includes African, Caribbean, Haitian, and other Black
Compiled from 1981 Census of Canada Public Use Sample Tape, Individual File. Calculations were based on those 15 years of age and over, who were employed in the Canadian labour force, excluding inmates.

origin when variations in other factors are controlled for. The table indicates that lowest income groups were French, "Other," Greek, Chinese, and black. Their low-income positions did not change, despite controlling for other factors, and this suggests market discrimination on the basis of origin.

The Canadian "vertical mosaic" suggests that structured inequality is associated with ethnic and racial origin. Structured inequality refers to the institutional arrangements by which rewards and privileges are distributed and maintained. The idea of structured inequality contradicts the notion of an open society in which everyone has the same opportunities. One aspect of structured inequality is *institutional racism*, by which racial inequality has become part of social institutions. Wilson (1973:34) says that institutional racism exists "when the ideology of racial exploitation gives rise to normative prescriptions designed to prevent the subordinate racial group from equal participation . . . ." This form of racism differs from individual racism, which may be manifested in various prejudiced dispositions of individuals.

MULTICULTURALISM IN CANADA

On October 8, 1971, the then prime minister, Pierre Trudeau, announced in the Canadian parliament the policy of multiculturalism within a bilingual framework. The purpose of the policy, according to Trudeau, was "to break down discriminatory attitudes and cultural jealousies . . . (and) form the base of a society which is based on fair play for all" (House of Commons Debates, October 8, 1971:8545). Despite such good intentions, there is little indication that racial prejudice has been less prevalent or ethnic inequality less evident in Canada. The policy has failed to effectively combat racism and discriminatory practices.

Roberts and Clifton (1982) argue that most ethnic groups in Canada do not have the structural resources to promote their cultural heritage, and the policy of multiculturalism simply reinforces the concept of *symbolic ethnicity*, which provides the *appearance* of pluralism. For example, with the exception of French, most minority languages are not recognized in the school system as languages of instruction, and multiculturalism, in practice, mainly means the preservation of ethnic music, crafts and dance. As Li and Bolaria put it, "The irony of multiculturalism is that it furnishes Canadian society with a great hope without having to change the fundamental structures of society. Multiculturalism is the failure of an illusion, not of a policy" (1983:1).

With the Canadian Constitution and the Charter of Rights and Freedoms, there are better prospects for implementing the individual and collective rights of Canadians. However, Evelyn Kallen has suggested that "individual human rights will take precedence over collective (ethnocultural) rights, except in the case of securing the linguistic and religious (cultural) rights of the English and French charter groups" (1982:230).

SUMMARY

There are two ways to define race and ethnicity: as cultural groups and as conflict groups. The first definition leads to questions of assimilation and pluralism, whereas

SOUTH AFRICA: THE PLURALIST EXTREME

In many ways, South Africa is clearly at one extreme . . . among most contemporary multiethnic societies. The economic, political, and social inequalities among ethnic groups, specifically, between whites and nonwhites, are unmatched. What is perhaps most peculiar about the South African system in comparison with the others is the officially proclaimed justification of these inequalities and the openly declared intention of dominant whites to sustain them. In none . . . of course, is equality among diverse groups realized; dominant groups in each seek to maximize and protect their disproportionate power. But in contrast to South Africa, there is official acknowledgment in Brazil, Canada, Northern Ireland, and the United States of the desirability of reducing interethnic disparities. Equally anomalous is the shape and degree of institutional separation among South Africa's ethnic groups. In none of the other four societies is the segregation of groups so rigid, and nowhere is it so legitimized. The overwhelming issue of South Africa is thus unambiguous: how will the ethnic disparities in power and privilege be transformed?

Despite the resolve of dominant whites to preserve their supremacy, the forces of change today are drawn unmistakably in South Africa. The end of European colonialism and the assertion of self-determination on the part of indigenous African peoples after World War II marked a power shift in which black political elites replaced white. South Africa has tenaciously resisted this historical drift. Although white South Africans at this point may quite reasonably claim to be indigenous Africans, their objectives and policies seek the perpetuation of white supremacy. Thus, they find themselves portrayed by black Africans as well as Third World peoples everywhere as the sole anachronism of a past colonial era. In a very broad sense, the South African case represents symbolically the confrontation of white and nonwhite peoples globally. The ethnic issues of South Africa today, therefore, have implications not only for South Africa itself or for the larger African continent but also for the entire world.

CANADA: BUILDING CORPORATE PLURALISM

The Canadian case illustrates most clearly the fact that physical distinctions among groups are not an essential ingredient in the emergence and maintenance of ethnic conflict. Ethnic boundaries can be shaped in a number of ways and, once established, adamantly sustained generation after generation. In Canada, cultural differences, especially language, have served as an effective barrier between its two major ethnic groups. Here is a society, then, that forces us to recognize that ethnic conflict in the modern world is not limited to racially diverse societies.

Another aspect of the Canadian case that distinguishes it from the other four societies is the territorial factor. One of the major ethnic protagonists maintains a territorial base that solidifies its collective consciousness and reinforces its social and economic differences from the larger society. This is unlike the American, Brazilian, or Northern Irish cases, in which ethnic groups are relatively dispersed geographically, or even the South African case, despite attempts by the dominant group there to impose such territorial lines.

The roots to English-French discord in Canada are, as we have seen, historically deep and abiding. But this is a conflict that, by comparison with the black-white conflict in South Africa or even the United States, is subdued. Whatever the nature of its resolution, it is not likely to degenerate into warfare, as is so probable in South Africa, or to erupt periodically in violence, as in the United States. The democratic context of Canada makes ethnic conflict apparently amenable to political solution.

From RACE AND ETHNIC RELATIONS: AMERICAN AND GLOBAL PERSPECTIVES by Martin N. Marger 1985 by Wadsworth, Inc. Reprinted by permission of the publisher.

the second is mainly concerned with domination and subordination. Many views of assimilation and pluralism have been developed by sociologists, including the *melting-pot thesis*, *Anglo-conformity* and *cultural and structural pluralism*. The assimilationist perspective has been criticized for being mechanical and evolutionary, and in particular, pluralists are unduly accused of emphasizing the transplanted ethnic cultures. From the vantage point of the second definition, race is not a genotype and ethnicity is not primordial. Superficial physical traits, such as skin colour, are only meaningful when social meanings are attached to them. The relationship between a dominant group and a subordinate group is developed in the *colonial model* and the *split labour market model*. Both models relate race and ethnic relations to the process of production.

Race and ethnicity are important features of Canadian society because: (1) Canadians came from different origins and (2) racial and ethnic lines intersect with the class structure. The Canadian population has increased its ethnic and racial diversity as a result of postwar immigration. In addition, linguistic variations in Canada are associated with ethnic origin and geographical region. The linguistic conflicts between the British and the French, however, have historical roots that go back to the conquest of New France and the subsequent economic domination of Quebec by the British.

In *The Vertical Mosaic*, John Porter raised several major points about the relationship between social class and ethnic origin. (1) The charter group retains many privileges and lays down the rules under which other immigrant groups are to be admitted. (2) Within the charter groups, the English are doing much better occupationally than the French. (3) The English have overwhelming control among the Canadian corporate elite. (4) There is a close relationship between ethnic origin and occupation.

Evidence suggests that visible minorities (mostly recent immigrants) encounter a double jeopardy in the labour market because of their immigrant status and racial origin. Despite the multicultural policy and its stated goals to accomplish greater equality, achievements in this area remain limited.

DISCUSSION QUESTIONS

1. Why is it meaningful to consider the dominant/subordinate group relationship and not just physical traits as defining characteristics of race and ethnicity?

2. What are the similarities and differences of the following models: melting-pot; cultural pluralism; and Anglo-conformity?

3. Why are some ethnic groups more able to maintain their home language than others?

4. How do the concepts of charter and entrance status help us to understand ethnic inequality in Canada?

5. To what extent does institutional racism impede the achievements of visible minorities in Canada? How successful has multiculturalism been in combating racism?

10

Class and Stratification

Gordon Darroch

INTRODUCTION

"Order is Heaven's first law; and, this confessed,
Some are, and must be, greater than the rest."
   —Alexander Pope, *Essay on Man* (1733)

Stephen Jay Gould, in his perceptive *The Mismeasure of Man* (1981), cites Pope to illustrate the argument that "appeals to reason or to the nature of the universe have been used throughout history to enshrine existing hierarchies as proper and inevitable. The hierarchies rarely endure for more than a few generations, but the arguments, refurbished for the next round of social institutions, cycle endlessly" (1981:30).

This chapter has three main objectives. First, it will consider the basic traditions of social thought that continue to inform thinking about contemporary social hierarchies or social inequality. Three basic theoretical perspectives will be reviewed. Secondly, it will show how social hierarchies are sustained or reproduced by specific social processes; they do not merely continue of their own accord nor are they "in the nature of things." On the contrary, social class and stratification are historical phenomena, and an understanding of the historical processes is essential to understanding contemporary forms.

Thirdly, the chapter will review some of the main patterns of inequality in conditions and in opportunities in contemporary Canadian society—distribution of ownership and wealth, of education and income and of the chances to alter one's position or that of one's family. As part of that review, we will consider the relationship between the popular notion that Canada is a middle-class society and the evidence that Canadians have experienced widespread proletarianization in this century. In fact, these are not contradictory notions. A central feature of this chapter is a specific historical interpretation of their relationship. Finally, our focus on class and socio-economic stratification ignores other important forms of inequality, for example, gender inequality and inequality among ethnic groups and regions. These questions are raised in other chapters.

TWO CONCEPTIONS OF SOCIAL INEQUALITY

There are two distinct ways of thinking about inequality. One considers differences among individuals or social groups by measuring the amount of income, education or status the individuals or groups possess. Social inequality is thought of as a ladder or set of ladders, with groups and individuals standing on different rungs. This view usually implies that people can go up or down the social ladders. This movement is called *social mobility*.

A second conception emphasizes relations between two groups, relations of dominance and subordination or of dependence or exploitation (Ossowski, 1963). This second perspective obviously implies a more explicitly political and, perhaps, moral analysis: After all, the term "exploitation" in everyday speech connotes an unfair exchange—some people getting something for nothing.

This general distinction corresponds broadly to the distinction between the analysis of stratification and the analysis of social class: *stratification* is concerned with forms of social ranking, or relations of order; *class* is concerned with exploitation and relations of dependence. Class analysis and, in particular, Marxist theory, has set the terms of reference historically for discussions of inequality. Stratification theories challenge class analysis—or, as Albert Saloman puts it, "debate with Marx's ghost" (cited by Zeitlin, 1981:127).

PERSPECTIVES ON INEQUALITY
THE MARXIST THEORY OF CLASS

Marxist theory of social class is the most elaborate, challenging and radical perspective on social inequality. It is provocative because it carries a political and, ultimately, revolutionary message. It commands attention because it is a complex theoretical system built from detailed historical analyses of the rise and expansion of Western capitalism.

Marx did not formally define class, though there are clarifying remarks at the end of his major work, *Capital*. The term appears in his work in varying contexts, conforming to usage familiar in the nineteenth century. In this, Marx drew from the writing of such English classical political economists as Adam Smith, David Ricardo and Thomas Malthus. Although Marx was German, he fled to London for political reasons in 1849, and he lived there until his death in 1883.

Marx, like David Ricardo, considered the three great classes of English society to be landlords, capitalists and wage-labourers (Zeitlin, 1981:114). These three groups are distinguished by their sources of income, that is, rents for land, profits from production and wages. But Marx looked for a more fundamental difference. What most divides these groups is their relationship to and control of the basic economic resources of the society. Landowners control major blocks of land, capitalists control industrial production and wage-workers' livelihoods depend entirely on selling their skills and their capacity to work. Pressing the analysis further, Marx recognized an even more fundamental division: the division between groups with a proprietary interest in the basic economic resources of society and those who were excluded from ownership and control. In this respect, landowners and manufacturers shared common interests and were sharply divided from the workers. Marx did *not* suggest that the real social world was divided neatly into two competing classes. Rather, there are many class interests and many segments of classes—there are miners and dockworkers, clerks and professionals, small farmers and artisans, financiers, merchants and industrialists and so forth. What he did recognize was that, within this social hierarchy of occupational, income and political groups, there was the more fundamental division between the propertied and nonpropertied.

It is often said that Marxist theory defines class in terms of the ownership of the means of production. The *means of production* include those basic economic resources—land, capital and labour—referred to earlier. This latter definition requires elaboration.

The relations between the private ownership of property and wage labour are only a specific historical form of exploitation in the process of production. "Exploitation" in Marxist theory means a process of extracting *surplus value* from a population. Though these terms are not familiar outside of Marxist theory, the *idea* of exploitation through the extraction of surplus value is quite familiar, for example, when we think of slave-based or feudal societies.

Consider slavery. Slave owners claimed the products of the slaves' labour as a right of their ownership of the slave. The slave-owners still had to deduct from total production the cost of maintaining their slave population. In general, the difference between the value of slave production and the cost of maintaining the slaves was the owners' surplus value. Minimizing maintenance costs, of course, helped to maximize profits.

In the feudal society of medieval Europe, surplus value tended to be extracted from the main producers—the peasants—in the form of surplus products. The peasant gave up a portion of his harvest in return for services from the landowner, for example, protection from marauders and some assurance of help in lean years (Moore, 1969).

Another concept requires clarification. In Marxist analysis, the conventional sociological notions of types of societies are replaced by another concept: the mode of production. *Modes of production* are different historical ways of organizing productive activities by which people develop and maintain a whole way of life. A mode of production is also a specific mode of exploitation. Thus, there are slave, feudal and capitalist modes of production.

Note that a mode of production is an abstract concept and does not actually exist in a pure form. A society (or social formation), in Marxist analysis, is a mixture of modes of production, although a particular mode is usually dominant at any given time. Contemporary Western societies, like Canada are a mixture of a predominantly capitalist mode and a petit-bourgeois, or small property-owning mode. That mixture greatly influences current political debates and social institutions.

What is the core of the Marxist analysis of exploitation in capitalism? The answer lies in an analysis of two capitalist institutions: private ownership of the means of production and the free labour market.

In Marx's words, in capitalism " . . . two very different kinds of commodity-possessors must come face-to-face and into contact; on the one hand, the owners of money, means of production, means of subsistence, who are eager to increase the sum of values they possess, by buying other people's labour-power; on the other hand, free labourers, the sellers of their own labour-power and therefore the sellers of labour" (Marx, *Capital*, vol. I, 714, cited by Zeitlin, 1981:110).

Private property is not simply the ownership of things but a social institution, entailing enforceable claims or rights to use. As C.B. MacPherson says, "What distinguishes property from mere momentary possession is that property is a claim that will be enforced by society or the state, by custom or convention or law" (1978:3). In contemporary society, both social convention and the state enforce property rights. In Marxist analysis, the capitalist class, or bourgeoisie, is composed of those who privately own and effectively control the main means of society's production; the raw materials, energy, land, factories and offices, machinery and equipment. In so doing, they also own, control or influence the main means of making a living of virtually everyone in the society.

Capital is necessarily accompanied by *wage labour*. The class of people dependent on selling their capacity to work—their labour power—is the working class, or *proletariat*. In this theoretical sense, the working class includes all those who are the nonowning class and who are legally "free" to sell their labour power to the owning class. It will be important later to note that this definition includes most of those who consider themselves middle-class, for example, salaried professionals and other white-collar workers. Note, too, that labour power and labour are distinguished. The former is the intrinsic human capacity to work or to create. The latter, in capitalism, is a commodity and is bought and sold on the market. The key to understanding capitalism in Marx's analysis is to recognize that the relationship between classes is exploitative, first, because only in the labour process can value be added to production and, secondly because private ownership means that the owning class can appropriate this additional value in the form of profit. Owners also privately determine the uses of this additional value in investment decisions.

Finally, since the basic relationship between capital and labour is exploitative, it involves a fundamental conflict of interests in the long run. This conflict causes various forms of class struggle and, ultimately, social revolution. There is not space here to outline Marx's political analysis, although it is as important as the theory of exploitation on which it is founded.

In subsequent sections, we will discuss the process of proletarianization in Canada over the last 130 years and what that concept contributes to an understanding of class and stratification in Canada.

We will not attempt a major evaluation of Marx's theory of class and class conflict. However, the major changes in capitalist societies over the last century have important implications for Marxist class theory. A variety of interpretations of Marx's work have emerged. In some cases, there are deep divisions and lively debates among Marxist authors (Althusser, 1969; Poulantzas, 1978; Thompson, 1979). Some critics of Marx have used capitalism's changes to revise or reject Marx's core ideas (Dahrendorf, 1959; Nisbet, 1959; Bell, 1961; Porter, 1965). For example, widespread stock ownership and the growth of a managerial sector, it is said, means that those who own capital don't necessarily control it. The growth of social services and state welfare systems prevents widespread hardship, even during the periodic economic downturns to which capitalism is prone. The general increase in productivity has raised the standard of living of all classes, and, perhaps above all, the growth of middle-class occupations (white-collar jobs)—technicians, bureaucrats, office workers — has increased opportunities for upward mobility for all. Many argue that these changes render obsolete the ideas of progressive proletarianization, a society divided

---

If we stop history at a given point, then there are no classes but simply a multitude of individuals with a multitude of experiences. But if we watch these men over an adequate period of social change, we observe patterns in their relationships, their ideas and their institutions. Class is defined by men as they live their own history, and, in the end, this is its only definition.

Reprinted from THE MAKING OF THE ENGLISH WORKING CLASS, by E.P. Thompson, by permission of Victor Gollancz Limited, England.

By class I understand an historical phenomenon, unifying a number of disparate and seemingly unconnected events, both in the raw material of experience and in consciousness. I emphasize that it is an *historical* phenomenon. I do not see class as a "structure," or even as a "category," but as something which in fact happens (and can be shown to have happened) in human relationships.

More than this, the notion of class entails the notion of historical relationship. Like any other relationship, it is a fluency which evades analysis if we attempt to stop it dead at any given moment and anatomize its structure. The finest-meshed sociological net cannot give us a pure specimen of class, any more than it can give us one of deference or of love. The relationship must always be embodied in real people and in a real context. Moreover, we cannot have two distinct classes, each with an independent being, and then bring them *into* relationship with each other. We cannot have love without lovers, nor deference without squires and labourers. And class happens when some men, as a result of common experiences (inherited or shared), feel and articulate the identity of their interests as between themselves, and as against other men whose interests are different from (and usually opposed to) theirs. The class experience is largely determined by the productive relations into which men are born—or enter involuntarily. Class-consciousness is the way in which these experiences are handled in cultural terms: embodied in traditions, value-systems, ideas, and institutional forms. If the experience appears as determined, class-consciousness does not. We can see a *logic* in the responses of similar occupational groups undergoing similar experiences, but we cannot predicate any *law*. Consciousness of class arises in the same way in different times and places, but never in just the same way.

There is today an ever-present temptation to support that class is a thing. This was not Marx's meaning, in his own historical writing, yet the error vitiates much latter-day 'Marxist' writing. "It," the working class, is assumed to have a real existence, which can be defined almost mathematically—so many men who stand in a certain relation to the means of production. Once this is assumed it becomes possible to deduce the class-consciousness which "it" ought to have (but seldom does have) if "it" was properly aware of its own position and real interests. There is a cultural superstructure, through which this recognition dawns in inefficient ways. These cultural 'lags' and distortions are a nuisance, so that it is easy to pass from this to some theory of substitution: the party, sect, or theorist, who discloses class-consciousness, not as it is, but as it ought to be.

But a similar error is committed daily on the other side of the ideological divide. In one form, this is a plain negative. Since the crude notion of class attributed to Marx can be faulted without difficulty, it is assumed that any notion of class is a pejorative theoretical construct, imposed upon the evidence. It is denied that class has happened at all. In another form, and by a curious inversion, it is possible to pass from a dynamic to a static view of class. "It"—the working class—exists, and can be defined with some accuracy as a component of the social structure. Class-consciousness, however, is a bad thing, invented by displaced intellectuals, since everything which disturbs the harmonious co-existence of groups performing different "social roles" (and which thereby retards economic growth) is to be deplored as an "unjustified disturbance-symptom." The problem is to determine how best "it" can be conditioned to accept its social role, and how its grievances may best be "handled and channelled."

If we remember that class is a relationship, and not a thing, we cannot think in this way. "It" does not exist, either to have an ideal interest or consciousness, or to lie as a patient on the Adjustor's table. . . .

The question, of course, is how the individual got to be in this "social role," and how the particular social organization (with its property-rights and structure of authority) got to be there. And these are historical questions. If we stop history at a given point, then there are no classes but simply a multitude of individuals with a multitude of experiences. But if we watch these men over an adequate period of social change, we observe patterns in their relationships, their ideas, and their institutions. Class is defined by men as they live their own history, and, in the end, this is its only definition.

Reprinted from THE MAKING OF THE ENGLISH WORKING CLASS, by E.P. Thompson, by permission of Victor Gollancz Limited, England.

between owners and workers and the likelihood, (or certainty) of class conflict and revolutionary change.

Others recognize that the changes are fundamental but argue that they do not render Marx's work irrelevant. Marx was not, after all, trying to set up a simple model of a class society with universal application; what he did want to establish was a method of analysis that revealed the basic contradictions within capitalism and lent itself to the analysis of actual, historical tendencies.

THE WEBERIAN THEORY OF STRATIFICATION

Max Weber was aware of Marx's conception of class and worked out his more formal theoretical discussion as a critique of, or at least, as a response to it. Weber bridged the nineteenth and twentieth centuries, so he saw the beginning of many of the aspects of contemporary capitalism that challenge Marxist theory. In fact, Weber's understanding of the central institutions of capitalism was much like Marx's: He emphasized the concentration of the means of production in the hands of a few and the growth of a labour market of legally free individuals who hire themselves out to employers (Weber, 1968: vol. I: 300ff.; Gerth and Mills, 1958:180–181).

Despite these common points, two positions clearly distinguish Weber's perspective from Marx's. First, Weber argued that proletarianization was not, as Marx had suggested, creating a homogeneous class of industrial workers with shared conditions of life and political orientations. For Weber, a variety of *class situations*, determined by differing relations to property and by differing positions in the labour market, characterized twentieth-century capitalism. In effect, Weber was reflecting here on the emergence of the propertyless but nonmanual workers, that is, the new middle-classes. As a consequence, Weber doubted that capitalism's development would entail a polarization between bourgeoisie and proletariat. Secondly, Weber analysed forms of power or domination, rather than forms of production and social class. Weber is perhaps best known as the master theorist of the growth of modern bureaucracy. It is this concern with bureaucratization that led him to focus on the growth of the "white-collar" sector of propertyless workers. Office and salaried work increased rapidly in the first decades of this century with the growth of both state and private bureaucracies. This growth of bureaucracy led Weber to reject the Marxist focus on the separation of workers from the means of production as a specifically capitalist phenomenon. Rather, this proletarianization was only one example of a general concentration of power in the hands of the few (Weber, 1968:980ff). Finally, although Weber treated ownership of private property and the existence of a labour market as defining characteristics of capitalism, they were not the key to domination in contemporary society. Their elimination, he argued, would only give way to other forms of bureaucratic control: "Also (and especially) every rational socialist economy would retain the expropriation of the workers and would only complete it by expropriating private owners" (Weber, 1956:79, cited by Mommsen, 1977:381). In other words, the state would replace private ownership, deepening and extending the loss of control by individuals over their work and over the means of production.

His concern with forms of power led Weber to clarify the concept of class (Weber, 1968: vol. II: 926ff). He begins with the claim, "Now: 'classes,' 'status groups' and 'parties' are phenomena of the distribution of power within a community" (Gerth and Mills, 1958:181). These are not different dimensions of stratification but different ways in which the interest of individuals and social groups may be pursued in market societies. It is characteristic of Weber not to assert that any one of these ways is necessarily dominant; their relationship varies under different historical conditions.

For Weber a *class* is a group that shares the same economic relationship to markets either in commodities or labour. Class situations, then, result from similar kinds of control over goods or skills that produce income. Weber accepts that possession of property is one, but only one, determinant of class position, i.e., of one's chances on the market and, therefore, of one's life chances (Gerth and Mills, 1958:181–82).

But property ownership is only one among many relations to the market; there are many other forms of marketable skills and resources and, indeed, more than one type of property. For example, ownership may be of natural resources, of money or investment funds, of warehouses, stores, mills, factories, corporations. Each generates a significantly different class situation for the owner.

Thus, in the Weberian tradition, class is a strictly descriptive term; it entails no underlying theory of power, exploitation or value. In fact, Weber sees a class, first of all, as a collection of individuals who happen to be in similar market situations but who by no means share common political orientations. In direct contrast to the Marxist tradition, Weber viewed the transition from a common class situation to a common awareness of interests, organization and class action as a rare occurrence (Giddens, 1973:43).

For Weber, *status groups* are also understood as interest groups, but in contrast to social classes, they are based on shared styles of life, forms of consumption and on prestige or honour accorded by the larger community. They stand in contrast to social class groups, and Weber thought that status groups might sometimes oppose class interests. For example, groups whose power stems from landed or "old" family wealth might oppose the industrially based wealthy or the *nouveau riche*. Another case would be status groups whose claim to privilege is based on ethnic, racial or religious grounds. In each case, the social group marks itself off by its style of life and system of values. These serve as entrance requirements that debar the unworthy.

Weber distinguishes between class and status group to stress that forms of stratification do not rest alone on property or position in economic markets. As Giddens has written: "The theorem informing Weber's position here is his insistence that power is not to be assimilated to economic domination—again, of course, a standpoint taken in deliberate contrast to that of Marx" (1973:44). Weber realized that control of economic resources is one way to maintain status distinctions, as in the case of institutional racism. But he did not think that social interests could be reduced to economic ones (Weber, 1968: II: 935).

Finally, in contrast to the rare conditions under which Weber believed that shared class or market situations generated real social communities of interest, status groups are true communities: They are founded on social criteria of exclusive membership and, as a result, reflect shared ways of life, social interaction and shared values (Gerth and Mills, 1958:186–87). Again, Weber contrasts status groups with class, emphasizing that class consciousness and class politics are historically rare and fragile.

Parties, the third phenomenon noted above, are a form of planned political action. Parties are discussed by Weber as phenomena of the "modern" world, in that they require a staff and modern organizational apparatus. However, Weber's definition of a party includes a range of political organizations, including unions, and formal pressure or lobby groups for professional and manufacturers' associations. For Weber, parties may either represent class interests, status interests or both (Gerth and Mills, 1958: 194–95).

Weber did not formulate a systematic theory of class and stratification. Nor did he attempt to provide an integrated theory of social stratification. His careful discussion of class and status groups tried to separate the two as historical aspects of the way power is distributed in society. There is, however, a theoretical core to the definitions developed elsewhere in his work, and it centres on the process he called *social closure* (Weber, 1968: 342). Social closure has been defined as any social process by which a group restricts access to social resources and opportunities. A group may do this by turning almost any characteristic into a criterion of membership, thereby " . . . restricting access to resources and opportunities to a limited circle of eligibles" (Parkin, 1979: 44). In effect, closure is a social strategy to monopolize social and economic positions.

Forms of social closure may also be developed as a collective means of advancing a group's position in a stratification system. For Weber, property is a form of social closure, since it lets owners monopolize access to the means of production and to their rewards on the market. Status groups are also based on closure strategies, as they are set apart by socially constructed criteria (race, religion, ethnic origin, language).

The central criticism of the Weberian tradition is that the conceptual distinctions are too formal and arid; what they gain in theoretical precision, they may lack in depth of understanding of capitalist society. They have led to a simplistic notion of the multiple dimensions of stratification, without a theory of the relationships among these dimensions. Critics have found Weber's formal distinctions to be of little help in understanding the rise of class consciousness (Giddens, 1973: 79) or in accounting for the realities of class exploitation and power (Stedman Jones, 1976).

THE FUNCTIONAL THEORY OF STRATIFICATION

A third perspective on class and stratification is supplied by functional theory (see page 23 in Chapter 1). It has two distinguishing features. First, it is founded on the notion that social class divisions and conflict are largely irrelevant in contemporary, industrial societies, although some inequality is both universal and useful (functional).

Secondly, this theory shares basic assumptions with contemporary Western political culture and ideology.[1] The core of that culture is a version of classical liberalism, which emphasized the moral value of rewarding personal merit and individual attainment.

The first, often implicit, assumption of functional theories of stratification is that social class divisions of an earlier era have been dissolved in the more complex society of the mid- and late twentieth century. Usually, functional theorists acknowledge that there was a deep and visible conflict of interests between the working families of the mines, mills and factories of early industrial capitalism and the owners and operators of industrial and commercial property.

But the functionalists assume that these conflicts disappeared as the modern industrial economy spawned four main trends: greatly increased real incomes and purchasing power for working and middle-sector families; a broad increase in the specialization and complexity of jobs; increasing opportunities for upward educational and occupational mobility; and finally, progressive sharing out of capital in the form of a dispersion of stock ownership among many shareholders and a widening gap between owners and managers of firms. Thus, the material and social circumstances of nonowning classes have greatly improved and the power of capital, as a class, has diminished.

It should be obvious how commonplace these functionalist assertions are in contemporary journalism, political rhetoric and in everyday conversation. Familiarity does not make them accurate, of course, but they undoubtedly raise basic questions about the nature of class and stratification in our society.

A second key assumption of functionalist theory is that social inequality is an *essential* feature of any efficient human society. Kingsley Davis put it this way: "Social inequality is, thus, an unconsciously evolved device by which societies insure that the most important positions are conscientiously filled by the most qualified persons" (1949: 367).

[1] By ideology is meant a relatively articulate set of political ideas that serves to justify existing institutions or their change by interpreting the past and prescribing future action. Each of the theoretical perspectives discussed here contains ideological elements.

Davis's central idea contains three separate theoretical tenets. First, certain positions in society are essential to its orderly functioning; it follows that some positions are more important than others, that they require more skill and they impose more onerous responsibilities. This could be called the "demand" side of the division of labour. Secondly, of those able to work, only a limited number have the talent and are willing to pay the costs of being trained to accomplish society's essential tasks. That is, there is a scarcity in the "supply" of talented and trained personnel. Thirdly, there must be inducements, or *differential rewards*, to operate as motivating factors for just enough talented and trained people to fulfill the needs of the economy. In this respect, functional theory is essentially a theory of motivation—it presents social stratification as a system of motivation which fills society's demand for labour from a limited supply of talent (Tumin, 1953; Wesolowski, 1962). The theory relies largely on a market metaphor for its persuasiveness.

Advocates of functional theory insist that the needs of the whole society, not just those of any one interest group, are served by stratification; they say that the theory does not predict any particular level of inequality but just states that some is necessary. Despite such qualifications, the criticisms have been pointed and numerous.

One criticism questions the assumption that positions in the occupational world can be ranked by importance. By what criteria do we compare, say, the importance of farmers and army generals, of lawyers and nurses, of teachers and politicians, of baseball players and bus drivers? Yet these occupations differ widely in the amount of prestige they are accorded, in income and in various "perks" of the job. The point is a telling one, for, despite the wide appeal and the simplicity of functional theory, no adequate response has been offered to this question (Tumin, 1953; Stinchcombe, 1963). In a blunt form, it asks: Why is it that in our society, physically hard, dirty and dangerous work is usually much less well rewarded than safe, clean and physically undemanding work (Wesolowski, 1962); or, why is the work women do (including unpaid domestic labour) less functional for society than men's work? Certainly, it is less well rewarded.[2]

Regarding Davis's second central assumption, that there is a scarcity of skilled and trained labour, there is a question about whether Western society may not be more wasteful of potential human talent than efficient in recruiting it (Tumin, 1953). Critics point to the relatively few women recruited to managerial positions or to the professions. Others cite the barriers faced by visible minorities in all Western countries as further evidence of a restrictive rather than "functional" system of stratification.

Finally, there is the assumption that stratification helps motivate and recruit the right people for the right jobs. The central criticism here is that there are many ways to motivate individuals in their work beyond material or symbolic rewards (Tumin,

[2] It may be objected that some physically demanding and dangerous work is paid at very high rates, for example, oil rig workers or transport truckers. But a closer look reveals that almost all blue-collar workers have high earnings for a relatively few years of their working lives, when they are young and most healthy. They do not look forward to increasing earnings over a career, nor do they usually enjoy the employer-supported pensions, health, dental and investment plans that are part of the lifetime earnings of many white-collar workers (see the discussion and evidence for England of Westergaard and Resler, 1975: Ch. 5).

1953). To argue otherwise implies, that *our* culture, with an emphasis on tangible, individual rewards, represents a universal form and, that people are not motivated by the intrinsic rewards of work itself or by social, humane or altruistic considerations.

Despite pointed criticism since the 1950s, functionalist theories still hold a central place in contemporary social thought. They do so partly because of the sheer simplicity of the theory and because its main assumptions correspond to core values of Western society, emphasizing the significance of occupational mobility and monetary compensation for individual skill, diligence and self-discipline.

CLASS FORMATION IN CANADIAN HISTORY

An analysis of class is an analysis of social change. Both the Marxist and Weberian perspectives view class as an historical phenomenon: Class relationships and structures are maintained and changed through specific historical processes.

An analysis of the development of social class relations rests on an analysis of proletarianization, which is a feature of Marxist thought. Recently, however, it has become central to both Marxist and non-Marxist analyses of the rise of capitalism in Western Europe (Tilly 1981; Levine, 1984).

Specifically, what we want to know is how a society dominated by small property-owners—on the land or in their own shops and homes—is transformed into a society divided between big capital and wage labour. As Greer neatly puts it for the Canadian case: "If most producers in early Canada worked 'for themselves,' how and when did the practice of 'working for anyone but themselves' come to be the norm?" (1985:21). We do not yet have an answer, but this section will examine the most widely proffered explanation.

THE CONVENTIONAL VIEW

Most of the historical and sociological writing on proletarianization in Canada relies on a single interpretation of the changes that took place between 1840 and the decades immediately after Confederation, in 1867.

The Canada of Confederation consisted of three major regions: the Maritimes and Upper and Lower Canada, or Quebec and Ontario, as they are now called. The West was still in an early stage of colonial exploration, settlement and exploitation by the fur-trading companies. It was in central Canada, especially in the major cities (Montreal, Toronto, Hamilton) that industrialization began (Burgess, 1977; Palmer, 1979; Kealey, 1980).

What led to this fundamental turning point in class relations in Canada? Three factors are most often cited (Palmer, 1983: Ch. 2; Pentland, 1981; Teeple, 1972:43–66; Rinehart, 1975).

First, there was the growth of the railways. The railways expanded the market for goods and helped assure regional economic integration. A mere 115 km of track could be counted in all of Canada in 1850; there were over 3200 km in 1865, centred on Montreal and Toronto (Palmer, 1983:61). Secondly, hundreds of small producers—the owners and operators of saw and grist mills, iron forgers, brewers, cabinetmakers, boot- and shoemakers, carriage-makers and tailors—took advantage of the expanded market and began consolidating into larger mechanized factories.

Only a few emerged as major capitalists, of course; the growth of industry was very uneven. Many small shops continued alongside a relatively few large factories. The urban and town industries employed both migrants from rural areas (especially in Quebec, it seems [Robert, 1982]) and recently immigrated skilled workers from Britain (Pentland, 1981). They formed the first Canadian industrial labour force.

Thirdly, and most significantly, the land previously available to immigrants and native Canadian families to farm was, after 1840, more and more restricted. Land policies, it has been argued, reduced access and forced the growth of a class of landless labourers in Ontario (Johnson, 1971): Land speculators held much good land, and the state and the church each had been granted one-seventh of the acreage of the province. In addition, after mid-century, the best land in rural Ontario was already owned and successful farmers were expanding their holdings at the expense of newcomers (Gagan, 1978). In Quebec, after the 1840s, whole families as well as many young, single men and women left rural Quebec to seek city work in Lower Canada and in New England as a result of the over-exploitation of land and the lack of funds for agricultural diversification (McCallum, 1980).

CRITICISMS OF THE THEORY

In moderately varying versions, this interpretation has influenced virtually every historical account of capitalist class formation in Canada. It is central to both historical (Teeple, 1972; Kealey, 1980; Palmer, 1979; Johnson, 1972) and sociological accounts (Rinehart, 1975; Hunter, 1981: Pt.IV). Important as it is, this perspective causes several problems. Many of the accounts are based heavily on the work of one pioneering scholar, Clare Pentland. His early work was remarkably insightful, but its weaknesses and misconceptions have only recently been given careful attention (Akenson, 1984; Greer, 1985). The questions raised are likely to affect all of the work relying on Pentland's interpretation.

For example, some recent historical evidence for Ontario seriously questions the extent of proletarianization by the time of Confederation. Community studies show that family farming *expanded* in the 1860s and 1870s (Gagan, 1981) and that land speculation, crown and clergy reserves and land policy posed few barriers to acquiring farmland (Akenson, 1983). Table 10-1 presents evidence recently collected for a large area of central Ontario for two census years, 1861 and 1871 (Darroch and Ornstein, 1984). This mobility table shows the percentage of men who stayed in an occupational category or who changed groups between 1861 and 1871.[3] The rows of the table show the proportion who stayed or moved for each group. The main diagonal of the table indicates the occupationally stable groups: For example, 53.4 percent of the merchants, manufacturers and other commercial and industrial property owners stayed in that category over the decade, while 59.3 percent of the professionals and 29.8 percent of the clerks and other white-collar workers were occupationally stable.

---

[3] These are data for individuals in the labour force. They are available for the 1881 census and earlier censuses only. Individual data for censuses after 1881 are still confidential, though aggregate data, of course, are available in census volumes and disseminated by Statistics Canada.

TABLE 10-1 Occupation in 1871 By Occupation in 1861, For Men, in Central Ontario

OCCUPATION IN 1861	PERCENTAGE DISTRIBUTION OF OCCUPATIONS IN 1871								NUMBER WITH OCCUPATIONS IN CENSUS OF 1871	TOTAL NUMBER IN 1861
	MERCHANT ETC.	PROFESSIONAL	OTHER NON-MANUAL	ARTISAN	LABOURER	FARMER	FARMER'S SON	TOTAL		
Not present in 1861	5.2	3.9	3.3	20.5	20.5	30.0	16.8	100.2	6729	
Merchant manufactuers, etc.	53.4	2.5	4.9	17.8	6.1	14.7	0.0	100.0	163	452
Professional	12.4	59.3	2.5	8.6	2.5	14.8	0.0	100.1	81	270
Other non-manual (clerks, etc.)	27.7	17.0	29.8	4.3	8.5	10.6	2.1	100.0	47	165
Artisan-craftsmen	8.4	1.7	1.3	65.3	7.9	14.5	0.9	100.0	533	1591
Labourer	4.3	1.1	1.4	13.6	36.3	39.7	3.6	100.0	705	2505
Farmer	2.3	0.4	0.1	4.3	6.1	86.4	0.6	100.0	1406	2962
Farmer's son (living with fathers)	3.2	1.9	0.9	7.2	6.8	39.9	40.1	100.0	531	1365
Total, for men with occupations in 1861	6.8	2.7	1.4	16.7	12.6	52.7	7.3	100.0	3466	9310

From Darroch & Ornstein, 1984: Manuscript Censuses of 1861 and 1871.

There are two main findings of interest here. First, there is a great deal of occupational change. Large numbers of men changed work categories during the ten years. The job changes are major, since jobs are grouped in large and quite different categories. For example, about 18 percent of the merchants and manufacturers and other owners of shops and property became artisans, and fully 15 percent moved into farming. One in three clerks (27.7 percent) or white-collar workers became merchants and manufacturers. And nearly 40 percent of labourers became farmers (most farmed their own land). There is really no evidence of class barriers to the movement between farming, labouring and the work of artisans, merchants or manufacturers. This was a very permeable occupational structure. And there is no obvious class barrier between the distinctly wage-labouring jobs (classified as labouring, which includes semiskilled workers) and nonproletarian work (property owners, including farmers and artisans).

Secondly, most movement was into farming, the one category that people did not leave. Undoubtedly, the predominant ambition and achievement of Canadians in this period was to become a family farmer.

These findings certainly call into question the notion that, by the 1870s, access to Ontario farmland was restricted and a class of landless labourers was established as the core of an emerging capitalist society.

That the vast majority of the population was on the land and the number of farmers was still growing does not imply that this was an egalitarian society. Stratification was startling in Canada and the United States. The best evidence indicates that, in both countries, over 50 percent of adult males owned *no* property whatsoever in 1870 or 1871, including farmland or a home (Soltow, 1975). In the cities, moreover, the inequalities were stark. In Toronto between 1861 and the turn of the century, the richest 10 percent of families owned at least 50 percent of *all* the assessed wealth in each decade; the poorest 20 percent of families never owned more than 2 percent (Darroch, 1983: table III). In addition to being characterized by rapid urban industrialization and marked stratification, nineteenth-century Canadian society was dominated by the values of the petite bourgeoisie, the owners of small businesses, tradespeople and professionals.

It is not yet possible to say how long this social formation persisted. Table 10-2 shows changes in Canada's occupational structure between 1891 and 1961. The data include both men and women in the labour force.

It can be seen that, in 1891, 45.7 percent of the labour force was in farming. Less than a third were industrial workers ("others and operatives").[4] By 1921, one-third of the labour force was still in the farming sector (the majority were small-farm owners). It is not until after 1941 that less than a quarter of the labour force is in farming. It appears that the Depression of the 1930s and the demands for industrial production during World War II contributed to the waning of this sector. The actual number of farms continued to increase from about 370 000 to over 730 000 between 1871 and 1941. But during the 1940s the number of farmers begins to decline. By 1971, it had dropped sharply to fewer than the 370 000 of

[4] The "Other and operatives" is a catch-all category that includes all members of the labour force not classified in the other categories. (See Leacy, 1983, comments on Tables D86–106.)

TABLE 10-2   Work Force by Occupation, Canada, 1891-1961
(Percentages)

YEAR	OWNERS & MAN- AGERS	PROFES- SIONS	CLERI- CAL & SALES	FARMERS & FARM WORK- ERS	LABOUR- ERS	OTHERS & OPERA- TIVES	TOTAL	TOTAL WORK- FORCE
1891	4.9	3.4	5.3	45.7	6.8	32.9	100.0	1 607 945
1901	4.7	4.7	6.2	40.1	7.1	37.2	100.0	1 782,621
1911	8.0	3.1	8.3	34.1	12.2	34.3	100.0	2 275 148
1921	8.3	5.5	12.3	32.8	9.7	31.4	100.0	3 173 169
1931	5.7	5.9	11.9	28.7	11.6	36.2	100.0	3 927 230
1941	5.4	6.7	12.4	25.8	6.3	43.4	100.0	4 195 951
1951	8.1	7.3	16.3	15.9	6.7	45.7	100.0	5 218 596
1961	8.6	10.0	19.7	10.3	5.0	46.4	100.0	6 305 630

From F.H. Leacy (ed.), *Historical Statistics of Canada*, 1983 (Ottawa: Statistics Canada): Table D86-106. Reproduced by permission of the Minister of Supply and Services Canada.

100 years earlier (Leacy, 1983: Table M12–22). Of course, in this century, popu-lation, the size of the labour force and production have grown rapidly.

We focus on farming because it has remained the most important segment of the petite bourgeoisie, although it has been shrinking in the last few decades. Farmers may only recently have been replaced as the core of the modern petite bourgeoisie by small businesspeople and self-employed professionals.[5]

CLASS AND STRATIFICATION IN CONTEMPORARY CANADA

Theoretical debates about inequality in contemporary Western societies are more often debates about root assumptions than about social structure and social expe-rience. Are class divisions and conflict dissolved with the growth of the service industries, white-collar work, rising standards of living and increased individual mobility? Or is contemporary capitalism more deeply divided by the concentration of big capital and the parallel growth of wage and salary work at the expense of

[5] In a national survey in 1981, 13 percent of the employed labour force were self-employed, including farmers and professionals. Nearly twice this number (25 percent) were employed directly by government agencies or by crown corporations, and 6 percent were owners or part-owners of companies with five or more employees (that is, the capitalist class proper). The other 56 percent were distinctly working-class, the salaried and wage employees of private firms (Ornstein, 1983: Table 1). Of course, this class structure is not the same as the subjective identification of class membership: Most Canadians think of themselves as being middle-class.

small businesses? Is our society mainly characterized by individual equality of opportunity or by structural inequality of condition?

THE CONCENTRATION OF CAPITAL AND WEALTH

That the Canadian industrial system is dominated by a relatively small number of large capitalist enterprises will come as no surprise. For the past 20 years, Canadian political and economic writing has shown that Canadian industry is *controlled* by major corporations and that these are *foreign owned* (Grant, 1965; Levitt, 1970; Naylor, 1972; Clement, 1977). Controversy has largely focused on foreign ownership rather than on the concentration of economic power itself. Evidence shows that foreign interests in major sectors of the economy have increased throughout this century—especially in manufacturing and in the petroleum, natural gas and mining and smelting industries. Fifty-two of the 100 largest industrial firms in Canada were foreign owned in 1979 (*Financial Post*, 1979, cited by Osberg, 1981: 27). In the 1985 report of the largest 500 firms in Canada, 46 (9 percent) were wholly foreign owned and another 87 (17 percent) partly foreign owned, with many of these among the very largest firms (*Financial Post 500*, 1985, May 25).

But despite the prominence of the foreign ownership issue in the press and in academic circles, other analyses do not indicate that foreign-owned industries have disproportionate economic power in Canada. For example, detailed studies of the interlocking directorships of corporate boards in Canada reveal a tight centre of Canadian-owned financial and industrial firms (Carroll, Fox and Ornstein, 1982). Other studies have questioned the prevailing account of the nineteenth-century roots of foreign control, arguing that a Canadian bourgeoisie emerged during the economic expansion between 1896 and the depression of the 1930s and that it still controls the major investments in Canada's economy (Noisi, 1981).

The issue of concentration of economic power receives less attention but the problem is easier to demonstrate. Economic power in Canada is concentrated in the hands of those few families and individuals who control a small number of dominant firms. By economic power, we mean the capacity to affect the livelihoods of large numbers of people through decisions on investment, economic production strategy and expansion or closure of plants. The 100 largest industrial firms in Canada, cited by the *Financial Post* in 1979, had total sales exceeding the combined sales of all other businesses, which made up 97 percent of all firms in Canada (Osberg, 1981: 27–28). Considering the distribution of economic power another way, the 3655 manufacturing firms with 100 or more employees reporting to Statistics Canada in 1978 made up less than 12 percent of all manufacturing firms but produced 76 percent of the *value added in production* (value of production less costs of plant and energy) and employed 68 percent of the labour force in manufacturing (*Manufacturing Industries in Canada: National and Provincial Areas, 1978*, Ottawa; Statistics cited by Ornstein, 1983; Table 4). Those who determine corporate policy clearly affect the lives of a great many people, either directly, as their employers, or indirectly, through the general effect of corporate policy on the economy.

But who controls these major firms? Is stock ownership widely dispersed? Do nonowning managers largely control major firms? These questions have been hotly debated for years. For Canada, however, there is a neat consensus: Raw economic power in Canada may be constrained by a variety of conditions (union organization, the state of the market, legal arrangements), but it is heavily concentrated in the hands of a few families.

In 1970, for example, nearly 90 percent of all Canadian families reported owning no publicly traded stock at all; only about 3 percent owned stocks worth $5000 or more (1970 dollars). However limited the data may be, there can be little doubt that stock ownership is the preserve of a very few families (Osberg, 1981: 36).

John Porter's (1965) pioneering study has been followed by those of Clement (1975), Niosi (1982) and others (Carroll, Fox and Ornstein, 1982; Newman 1975). Porter and Clement established that fewer than 1000 men held the key directorships in dominant corporations and financial institutions in the 1950s and again in 1970s. The avenues into this select circle altered somewhat during the 20 years, but it remained an exclusive and largely self-perpetuating group. Despite some important differences in interpretation, there is no doubt that the economic elites and interlocking directorates that Porter, Clement and others have traced in Canada are a sufficiently closed and powerful social group to be called the bourgeoisie, a small, dominant economic and social class.

What does the power and cultural closure of a bourgeoisie imply for the Canadian system of stratification, especially for the distribution of wealth? Evidence is not readily available on this question. The holdings of the very wealthy are not recorded in national surveys. However, Table 10-3 shows one estimate of the distribution of wealth measured as family assets (deposits, cash, bonds, stocks, mortgages), total assets, (financial assets, business equity, real estate, automobiles) and net worth (total assets minus debts).

The table shows the proportion of total assets and net worth in 1970 and 1977 that accrues to each 10 percent (deciles) of the family units, starting with the poorest decile and ending with the richest. The poorest 10 percent of families had no measurable assets and a small negative net worth, i.e., debt (−1.0 and −0.6 in 1970 and 1977). The wealthiest 10 percent of families were exceedingly wealthy: They had about 69.1 and 67 percent of all financial assets, just less than 50 percent of total assets and a little over 50 percent of net worth in the two years. To recognize how much inequality this represents, consider that the less wealthy half of Canadian families (first to fifth deciles) together had just over 5 percent of the net worth of all families in 1977 and only 3.6 percent in 1970. The inequality is even more extreme for people not living in family units.

We can be sure that these patterns of inequality exclude the very wealthiest families, for reasons cited earlier. We can also be fairly certain that the pattern is very stable, though there are no definitive trend studies. If there has been change, it has been at a glacial pace and it is as likely to have increased inequality as to have reduced it since World War II. As we shall see, inequalities in earned incomes, which are distinct from wealth-holding *per se* have also been very stable for several decades.

How can we evaluate these wealth inequalities? They seem extreme: A tiny group owns a huge slice of the whole pie. Marxists and neo-Marxists might ask: Is a just, humane and democratic society compatible with such inequalities? Weberians and neo-Weberians find the inequalities unjustified but acknowledge that they reflect the great differences among the abilities of individuals and social groups to organize and act in their own interests in a market-based and liberal society: Inequality is

TABLE 10-3   The Wealth Distribution of Canada (As Measured by the Survey of Consumer Finance) 1970 and 1977

	FAMILY UNITS RANKED BY WEALTH					
	FINANCIAL ASSETS		TOTAL ASSETS		NET WORTH	
Decile (Share of) poorest	1970	1977	1970	1977	1970	1977
10%	0.0	0.0	0.0	0.0	−1.0	−0.6
2	0.1	0.1	0.2	0.3	−0.0	0.1
3	0.3	0.4	0.6	0.9	0.3	0.6
4	0.7	0.9	1.4	2.3	1.3	1.7
5	1.2	1.5	3.2	5.0	3.0	3.6
6	2.2	2.6	6.3	7.4	5.4	6.0
7	4.0	4.5	9.6	9.6	8.3	8.6
8	7.3	8.0	12.7	12.2	11.8	12.0
9	15.1	15.0	17.5	16.8	17.6	17.5
(Share of) richest						
10%	69.1	67.0	48.5	45.6	53.3	50.6

Financial assets = deposits, cash, bonds, stocks, mortgages, etc.
Total assets   = financial assets, business equity, real estate, automobiles
Net Worth   = total assets − debts

Adapted from Gail Oja, "Inequality of Wealth Distribution in Canada 1970 and 1977," in *Reflections on Canadian Incomes*, L. Tepperman and J. Richardson et al., Economic Council of Canada, 1980, p.352. Reproduced by permission of the Minister of Supply and Services Canada.

one result of economic and political pluralism. Moreover, they will note, the inequalities in wealth are either unknown to or ignored by most people; they are tolerated, if not accepted as legitimate. Functionalists and other neo-conservatives seldom address the question of inequalities of wealth, focusing instead on occupational and income opportunities. Extreme inequalities present something of a dilemma, since nothing in functional theory suggests that extremely unequal distributions are functional. However, there is a version of the theory invoked increasingly in recent years to suggest that great inequality of wealth is a reasonable consequence of maximizing the efficiency of the economy by rewarding entrepreneurial activity. Michael Wilson, the minister of finance, said in the spring of 1985 that Canada had too few wealthy people for the good of the economy. In fact, recent changes in tax legislation give Canada's wealthy the lightest taxes in the Western world: They are unique in being exempted from both inheritance taxes and capital gains taxes (*Globe and Mail*, 1985, May 30).

Courtesy Jaguar Canada Inc.

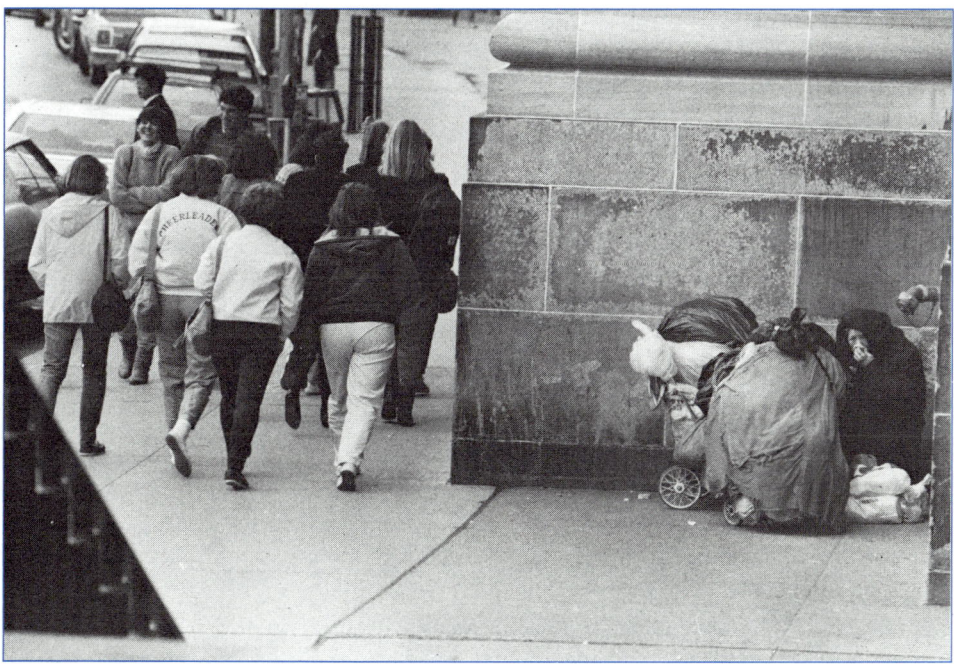

The Globe and Mail, Toronto.
Canadian society is characterized by marked inequalities in the distribution of wealth.

How does the unequal distribution of wealth in Canada compare to the distributions in other Western countries? In fact, comparisons are hazardous because of the lack of adequate evidence. So far as the data can be compared, Canada's pattern of wealth concentration is similar to that of other countries, though less unequal than Great Britain's and perhaps slightly less unequal than that of the United States (Atkinson, 1975: Ch. 7 and Table 3).

THE OCCUPATIONAL DIVISION OF LABOUR

Despite limited evidence, it is clear that a deeply stratified society is generated by the two central institutions of a class society: private ownership of the means of production and the labour market. The ownership of substantial property and of saleable wealth obviously confers opportunities for accumulating assets through investment and choice in life style, residence, and leisure activities, opportunities and choices that the great majority of people simply do not have. But this is not the whole story. Many commentators direct attention to changing occupational patterns, to widespread gains in real family incomes and to increased consumption and leisure. In this context, we should remember that class divisions and experiences are distinct from stratification. It is not unusual in our society to own and control no property (except, perhaps, a little, by mortgage), to be powerless (except for the right to a vote), to work for and be responsible to others and yet to be relatively well educated, moderately well paid and adequately housed. In modern Canadian society, individuals and families experience the (different) processes of class and stratification simultaneously. We saw from Table 10-2 that the change from a largely rural economy of farm families and small craft enterprises to an urban, manufacturing, white-collar economy became clear in the early part of this century and was quite dramatic after 1940. This was a fundamental change in the relationship of class and stratification. Table 10–4 provides another perspective on occupational changes.

The data appear in the conventional categories that distinguish office-oriented, white-collar work from that involved in the direct production of commodities (primary and blue-collar work). Blue-collar work has been stable or has actually *declined* slightly in the labour force. As we saw earlier, the proportion of primary workers, mainly in farming, declined precipitously, especially after 1940. The decline in the primary sector has been mainly offset by the growth of the white-collar sector, notably in professional, technical and clerical jobs.

These data reveal again the extent to which wage and salary work has replaced self-employment and small-property owning as the dominant labour processes and sources of income. In terms of the tripartite division of Marxist analysis, recent estimates (based on census and survey data) classify 5 or 6 percent of the labour force as major productive property-owners, 8 to 13 percent as small-property owners and self-employed and the rest of the employed 81 to 86 percent as working-class (Johnson, 1979 and Ornstein, 1983).

Various wealth, ownership, employment and occupational distributions do not just support different interpretations. It is a key argument of this chapter that they reflect different but simultaneously experienced changes in social conditions, that is, conditions of class and of stratification. Proletarianization has been the dominant

TABLE 10-4 Percentage Distribution of Labour Force 15 Years and Over by Occupation Division, for Canada: 1901, 1921, 1941, 1961, 1971 and 1981

OCCUPATION DIVISION	PERCENTAGE					
	1901[a]	1921	1941	1961	1971[c]	1981[d]
White Collar	15.3	25.3	25.3	37.9	42.3	49.8
Proprietary, managerial	4.3	7.3	5.4	7.8	4.3	6.8
Professional	4.6	5.4	6.7	9.8	12.6	15.1
Clerical	3.2	6.9	7.2	12.7	15.9	18.3
Commercial, financial	3.1	5.7	6.0	7.6	9.5	9.6
Blue Collar	27.8	25.8	27.1	26.6	24.3	23.9
Manufacturing, mechanical	15.9	11.4	16.1	16.1	17.7	17.5
Construction	4.7	4.7	4.7	5.2	6.6	6.4
Labourers[b]	7.2	9.7	6.3	5.3	–	–
Primary	44.3	36.2	30.5	12.8	7.5	5.8
Agricultural	40.3	32.6	25.7	10.0	5.9	4.2
Fishing, hunting, trapping	1.5	0.9	1.2	0.6	0.3	0.3
Logging	0.9	1.2	1.9	1.2	0.7	0.7
Mining, quarrying	1.6	1.5	1.7	1.0	0.6	0.6
Transportation, communication	4.4	5.5	6.4	7.7	3.9	3.8
Service	8.2	7.0	10.5	12.4	11.2	11.9
Unknown	–	0.2	0.2	2.6	10.3	4.8

[a] 10 years and over in 1901.
[b] Except those in Primary.
[c,d] Divisions not identical to previous years

Derived from Ostry (1967: 50-51); Hunter, 1981: 79; *Census of Canada 1981, Highlight Information on Labour Force*, March 1, 1983, pp. 29 & 30. Reproduced by permission of the Minister of Supply and Services Canada.

structural trend in this century. For many people, this has meant a move into white-collar jobs which entail less physical risk, some promise of shorter hours and greater security, the possibility of greater income and certainly a widely shared sense of increased social status.

STATUS, EDUCATION AND THE MIDDLE-CLASS

The major occupational shifts in this century have been interpreted as evidence of an "upgrading" of the work process, of job skills and the education and training they require. These assumptions have only recently come under study. There is reason to doubt that industrial work is more skilled than farming and other primary occupations, which often demand mastery of a wide variety of skills (Braverman, 1974: 430ff). Recent studies in the United States indicate that the complexity of many white- and blue-collar jobs may have actually decreased since the turn of the

In the nineteenth century, Canada had a largely rural economy of farm families and small craft enterprises. Photos courtesy of Mrs. Dorothy Wilmot, Hamilton, Ontario.

century (Dubnoff, 1978, cited by Hunter, 1981: 83; Horowitz and Herrenstadt, 1966; Spenner, 1979). Clerical and other forms of office work are subject to routinization and supervision. A Canadian survey conducted in 1981 revealed that, although such work was not closely supervised, a great deal was routine. Seventy percent of Canadian workers in all occupations reported that they were completely excluded from planning in their daily work (Ornstein, 1983: Table 6). Contrary to expectations, mobility into white-collar work has not meant increased responsibility or skill on the job, though higher educational credentials are required.

The employment of women warrants a special note. The number of women in the labour force (paid employment) has always been fairly high, but in the 1980s rose for the first time to over 50 percent of women aged 15 and over. Although women work in all sectors of the labour force, they are concentrated in a very few occupations. In 1981, over 50 percent were in clerical, service and related occupations, (Statistics Canada, 1984), and these are jobs with little responsibility, few educational requirements and low pay.

What about education? Since the 1930s, Canadian parents have increasingly invested in the formal education of their children. After World War II, especially, it was widely believed that completing high school and getting some postsecondary education were necessary to compete in the modern work world, and sufficient to ensure a well-placed job and high life-time earnings (Lennards, 1980). The belief

The shift to an urban, manufacturing, white-collar economy became clear in the early part of this century and was quite dramatic after 1940. T.M. Wathen/Quadrant.

was as widespread among educational authorities as among the public. The constricted job market of the last few years has had a sobering effect on the public and on authorities alike.

Despite some change in attitude toward education, as a result of the recent recession, enrollment in postsecondary institutions and levels of educational attainment have steadily increased (Lennards, 1980: Table 13–4). Table 10–5 shows the recent trend.

In 1981, 8 percent of the population aged 15 and over had a university degree, an increase of just 3 percent since 1970. Completion of some postsecondary education increased by just over 10 percent in the decade, although a stable 44 to 45 percent completed high school. In 1940, just a little over 30 percent of those over 15 had completed high school (Cuneo, 1980: Table 7–4).

Again, international comparisons are hampered by lack of data, but in the 1970s in the United States, over 40 percent of children obtained a college education (including junior colleges and a wider range of state colleges and universities than there are in Canada). The proportion of children attaining a university education in Great Britain in the 1970s was reported as 9 percent, rather higher than in Canada for the same period (Worsley, 1977: 235–36).

Although access to education has increased in this country and elsewhere, this increase has done little to reduce inequality in educational opportunity, even in the

TABLE 10-5 Educational Stratification, Population Fifteen Years Old and Over, Canada, 1971-1981

HIGHEST LEVEL OF SCHOOLING COMPLETED	1971	1976 (PERCENTAGES)	1981
Less than Grade 9	32.3	25.4	20.7
Grades 9 to 13	45.9	44.1	43.6
Some Post-Secondary*	17.1	24.1	27.6
University Degree	4.8	6.4	8.0

* Some differences in definition among census years.

Statistics Canada, *1981 Census, Population, Historical Tables for Census Education Data*, June 1984: Table 1. Reproduced by permission of the Minister of Supply and Services Canada.

United States. There were more children from lower-income and working-class backgrounds in institutions of higher education in the 1960s and 1970s, but as a group, they remain as underrepresented as ever. The growth in university attendance by children from middle- or upper-status families has matched or exceeded that of the less privileged in Canada, the United States and Great Britain (Lennards, 1980: 496; Pike, 1980: 124–32; Worsley, 1977: 235–36). As Michael Katz put it, referring to an earlier era, those from lower-status backgrounds have "to run harder than ever just to keep from falling behind" (1975: 284, cited by Pike, 1980: 115).

In addition to questions of access and inequality, is the question of the seeming lack of fit between educational upgrading and the demand for specific occupational skills and training over the last three decades (Berg, 1970; Harvey, 1974; Lennards, 1980). A number of studies have suggested that, rather than teaching knowledge and skills, schools primarily teach the values and attitudes appropriate to an industrial capitalist society (for example, work discipline and respect for authority; see Bowles and Gintis, 1976; Willis, 1977). Others argue that the diplomas awarded for successful school completion serve mainly as devices by which employers can sort out applicants for employment (Collins, 1971). These critical questions arise from both Marxist and Weberian perspectives and have come to undermine the simpler functionalist assumptions regarding rewards for training for skilled work in contemporary society.

Status, Prestige and Middle Class

The attitude of functionalists toward occupational and educational stratification remains firmly grounded in the view that the occupational division of labour has a distinct and stable status, or prestige order. One of the longest traditions of empirical research in stratification has been that of assessing the prestige rankings of occupations (National Opinion Research Center, 1947; Hodge et al., 1966; Pineo and Porter, 1967; Treiman, 1978). Occupations have been ranked in a similar way in several national studies in the United States, Great Britain, Germany, Japan, the Philippines and some socialist countries of Eastern Europe (Treiman, 1978). But there are important differences, especially for Eastern Europe, where skilled, manual work has come to be rated higher than certain white-collar positions (Parkin, 1971: 156–58). Moreover, the similarity in rankings may result from agreement on the relative prestige of very general categories of work rather than specific positions (Nosanchuk, 1972). Nevertheless, functionalist theory gathers some support from the tendency toward consistent occupational prestige rankings. For Canada, a national study by Porter and Pineo (Pineo, 1981: 617) asked about 800 people to group some 200 occupations into categories that reflected the occupations' general social standing. Table 10–6 shows the results of this survey.

It is readily apparent that the classification of primary, blue- and white-collar jobs given in Table 10–4, closely matches the general social standing accorded occupations by the public. The highest standing was given to the job of provincial premier and the lowest to garbage collectors and newspaper pedlars (Pineo and Porter, 1967, reprinted in Curtis and Scott, 1979: 205–220). Even this selective listing reveals that self-employed professionals command the greatest occupational prestige. A fuller listing would show that owners, managers and officials are accorded less status than the self-employed professional. Although farming is now accorded little prestige—scoring barely above manual work and somewhat below skilled clerical, sales and service work—there is a hint in these data that petit-bourgeois values centered on self-employment still carry a great deal of weight in contemporary Canadian culture.[6]

The general social standing of occupations has been of concern mainly in studies of occupational mobility. We will consider some implications of these studies in a moment. But the prestige rankings also raise questions about a most ambiguous concept—the middle-class.

The concept of the middle-class arose with the growth of white-collar work (Mills, 1956), that is, with the growth of employment in the bureaucracies of corporations and the state. The ambiguity of the concept reflects the ambiguity of the economic, social and political circumstances of this group. They are "middle" only in the obvious, but important, sense that they stand between the upper and lower groups on the scales of wealth, income and life style.

---

[6] These occupational prestige rankings have been generalized to a much larger set of occupations given in censuses by estimating "status" scores for all occupations from their relationships with other factors, such as education and income. These estimates provide socio-economic status scores widely used in research on social mobility (Blishen, 1967 and Blishen and McRoberts, 1976).

The ranking of occupations has seemed stable over time and among countries. This observation lends itself to a functionalist interpretation: The ranking does, indeed, reflect a social consensus on the functional importance of various jobs and on the origins of the stratification of rewards. Marxists have generally ignored this issue. Some Weberians have argued that the ranking of occupations is not the *source* of stratification but the *result* of the differential power of occupational groups, such as professionals, to maintain legal and social exclusivity, thus perpetuating their status and income through social closure (Parkin, 1974). Hence, the ranking simply reflects a public awareness of the realities of stratification. Parkin, for one, also notes that those with relatively low-ranked occupations tend to rank their own occupation more highly then general survey results. This suggests that they recognize the general view but resist its application to their own work (Parkin, 1971: 94).

TABLE 10-6 Occupational Prestige Rankings, Canada 1971

MAIN STRATA	PRESTIGE OF MAIN STRATA	SUBSTRATA	PRESTIGE OF SUBSTRATA
Professional	63.8	Self-Employed Professionals	78.6
		Employed Professionals	68.0
		Technicians	67.2
		Semiprofessionals	56.7
Managerial and Supervisory	59.5	High-level Management	67.7
		Middle Management	64.8
		Foreman	51.0
		Supervisors	46.3
Clerical, Sales, Service	37.2	Skilled	47.7
		Semiskilled	34.2
		Unskilled	29.7
Farming	35.0	Farmers	40.9
		Farm Labourers	23.3
Manual	33.4	Skilled	40.3
		Semiskilled	32.4
		Unskilled	24.7

Pineo, Peter, John Porter, and Hugh McRoberts. "The 1971 census and the socioeconomic classification of occupations." *Canadian Review of Sociology and Anthropology*, 14(1), 1977, p. 98. Based on the 193 Pineo-Porter-McRoberts titles that matched the 1971 Census Unit Groups.

The concept of the middle-class is poorly developed in both social theory and historical and sociological analysis. In this respect, social and historical research has been badly out of phase with cultural and political reality. Since early in this century, perhaps beginning in the 1920s, Canada, like other Western societies, has been regarded as middle-class as a result of the modestly increased disposable incomes of nuclear families, reduced working hours and an increasingly market- and consumer-oriented society. These developments are accompanied by a pervasive respect for individual effort, competitive educational and occupational opportunities, property and political order.

In fact, we have exceedingly little information about the relationship between the material and historical basis of middle-class consciousness. There are, however, some useful studies of the self-identification of social classes in Canada. Table 10-7 shows the distribution of responses on two related questions from two surveys, a national survey in 1965 and a survey of four major cities in Ontario and Quebec in 1971 (Goyder and Pineo, 1979). The differences between the two survey results suggest that any interpretation of survey questions on this topic requires caution, since results are heavily influenced by the wording of the questions and the nature of the survey (Goyder and Pineo, 1979). In any case, between 60 and 70 percent of the populations surveyed consider themselves "middle-class" or "upper-middle-class," although other studies show that manual workers tend to have a rather more politicized view of Canadian society than nonmanual workers (Rinehart and Okraku,

TABLE 10-7   Distribution of Responses to Class Identification
Questions, (National Survey 1965; Four Cities, 1971)

OPEN-ENDED QUESTION: "WHAT SOCIAL CLASS DO YOU CONSIDER YOURSELF A
MEMBER OF?"

	UPPER	UPPER MIDDLE	MIDDLE	WORKING	LOWER	N/A
	%	%	%	%	%	%
1965	1.1	3.9	63.3	10.5	4.4	16.8
1971	0.8	5.9	53.7	16.4	1.2	22.0

CLOSED QUESTION: "IF YOU HAD TO PICK ONE, WHICH OF THE FOLLOWING FIVE
SOCIAL CLASSES WOULD YOU SAY YOU WERE IN—UPPER CLASS, UPPER MIDDLE
CLASS, MIDDLE CLASS, WORKING CLASS, OR LOWER CLASS?"

	UPPER	UPPER MIDDLE	MIDDLE	WORKING	LOWER	N/A
	%	%	%	%	%	%
1965	2.0	12.9	48.9	30.4	2.1	3.7
1971	1.0	13.4	46.9	27.4	0.3	11.0

Curtis J. and Scott, W. *Social Stratification in Canada*, 2nd edition, p. 434, J. Goyder and P. Pineo, "Social Class Self-Identification," Table 1. Permission granted by Prentice-Hall Canada, Inc.

1974: 200). One cannot place too much emphasis on these studies, but they indicate that the popular notion of a broad middle-class also needs to be subjected to class analysis.

REAL INCOMES, INCOME INEQUALITY AND OCCUPATIONAL MOBILITY: THE MAKING OF THE MIDDLE-CLASS

The 1920s brought an important historical turning point to Canada. Not until the late 1920s were the wages of the average manufacturing worker sufficient to raise a family on one income. And only in the same decade were the wages of women workers high enough to allow some women to be independent of their own or other families (Palmer, 1983: 192). In the last century and early in this one, ordinary families survived by pooling several sources of income and even then they were often threatened by economic crises.

The Depression of the 1930s cut incomes for many families, but steep declines in the prices of commodities also meant that wages increased in purchasing power. In any case, the 1940s and 1950s saw greater gains in real incomes and in consumer expenditures. These trends continued until the 1970s with important regional variations. This economic expansion brought well-known changes in suburbanization, transportation, radio and television; it produced a general widening of consumer culture (Palmer, 1983: Ch. 6). Figure 10-1 shows the general pattern of rising real incomes.

Figure 10-1   Average Income of Canadian Families and Unattached Individuals

Average income of families and unattached individuals

Charting Canadian Incomes, 1951–1981, Ottawa: Statistics Canada, March 1984: p.s. Reproduced by permission of the Minister of Supply and Services.

Figure 10–1 plots the average incomes of families and unattached individuals from 1951 to 1981 and and distinguishes *actual* dollar income from *real* income, measured in 1951 dollars. Incomes include earnings form employment and from investments, as well as money from social benefits and pensions.

Actual incomes rose throughout the entire period and grew steeply from about 1965, though inflation accounted for a huge portion of the growth over the last 20 years. But still, real average incomes grew until 1976; they have stagnated since. The recent stability of average real incomes (and hence, declines in income for some segments of the population) is a reversal of historic patterns. Whereas in 1951, 60 percent of all families were one-earner families, that proportion was reduced to 57 percent in 1961, 41 percent in 1971 and just 29 percent in 1981 (Statistics Canada, 1984a: 11). The return to multiple earners for each family has been a response to economic stagnation and higher unemployment and a means of sustaining purchasing power and middle-class standards of family living. One important economic implication of this trend is the shrunken pool of potential workers, or surplus labour supply, especially of women, as compared to the 1940s, 1950s and 1960s.

The proportion of *married* women in the workforce has grown tremendously, even since 1967, from 35 to 63 percent. Moreover, women have doubled their contributions to family income. Nearly 70 percent of those in the low-income groups in 1981 were unattached people, mainly women under the age of 25 and over 65 who had no earned income. The other 30 percent are mostly single-parent families (Statistics Canada, 1984a: 15).

Given the origin of the middle-class in rising incomes and purchasing power from the 1920s to the 1970s, it would be more accurate to refer to the growth of the *middle-income society* (Porter, 1965: Part I).

Conceptual niceties apart, the growth of the numbers of people who consider themselves part of a Canadian middle-class almost certainly accompanied higher incomes, suburbanization and increased consumption; these trends have been sustained in recent years by the return to multiple family-income earners. What about inequality in income throughout this period? Has the increased purchasing power of family incomes and spreading commodity markets reduced actual stratification of incomes? In a word, no.

Table 10–8 gives a distribution similar to that for wealth distributions above (see Table 10–3). In this case, five income groups (as defined in the table) are compared; each represents 20 percent of the population (quintiles), ranged from the fifth of the population with highest income to the fifth with the lowest. The distributions over the postwar period are virtually unchanged. The great stability in income distributions comes as some surprise. After all, it flies in the face of all the rhetoric about the expansion of the middle-class and the claims that the Canadian government has been responsible for redistributing income from the upper- to the lower-middle classes and the poor through progressive taxation, social benefit and unemployment insurance programs and the welfare net. This is, as Gillespie aptly called it, one of the great myths perpetuated from the popular podium and in popular literature (Gillespie, 1980).

TABLE 10-8   Income Stratification: Percentage Distribution by Quintiles, Canada, 1951-1981

FAMILIES AND UNATTACHED INDIVIDUALS	1951	1961	1971	1981
Poorest Quintile (20%)	4	4	4	4
Second Quintile	12	12	10	11
Third Quintile	18	18	18	18
Fourth Quintile	23	25	25	25
Richest Quintile	43	41	43	42

Statistics Canada, *Charting Canadian Incomes 1951-1981*, March 1984: 6. Reproduced by permission of the Minister of Supply and Services Canada.

It is valuable to dwell on the fact that the increase in real incomes in the postwar period and stability of income inequality were simultaneous. Individuals and families today experience rising incomes and yet remain in the same *relative* position in the structures of income stratification. In effect, the entire income structure has shifted without losing shape: on average, the rich gained as much as those in the middle or the relatively poor income categories. Recognizing this difference between individual and *structural* conditions is essential to understanding the culture and politics of the middle-class in contemporary capitalist societies like Canada.

The Role of Cultural Capital in Social Mobility

Perhaps the most important element of a middle-class culture is the value placed on meritocratic principles, i.e., on the rewarding of individual effort and capabilities in a fair and open competition. Historically, these principles were central to the bourgeois and liberal democratic revolutions that assaulted the privileged position of European aristocracies. In our society, these values seem to have taken on a particular importance for middle-class families that are trying to protect and improve the life chances of their children. This adherence to competitive, individualistic principles may be one response to proletarianization, on the one hand, and to the growth of white-collar occupations, on the other. Most Canadians no longer expect to ensure their children's futures through property inheritance or by establishing them in a craft or small business. But they may hope to give their children *cultural capital* in the form of the credentials and social graces of the educated.

Middle-class aspirations and values are founded on a belief in an open and competitive society. Probably no question has attracted as much attention in sociology as that of social mobility in Western countries. The research has relied heavily on the studies of occupational prestige discussed above and on the measurable socioeconomic scales of occupations that have been built from them. Increasingly, the research has focused on a specific question in the larger mobility picture. Given that inheritance of property is now so limited and that educational credentials are thought to be so important, the research has asked how parents' statuses are translated into the statuses of sons and daughters. Specifically, it asks how family background and educational attainment are related to a person's occupational status and income (Goyder, 1984).

A major Canadian study conducted in 1973 compared Canadian and United States status attainment processes (Boyd et al., 1981; McRoberts, 1982). In the context of this discussion, the key finding of this study is that education is, indeed, the crucial link between generations in the transmission of occupational status. In contemporary Canada, most parents can do little to directly determine the careers of their children, but both the educational attainments of parents and their occupational status slightly influence their children's education. And, as almost everyone has come to believe, a person's educational attainment is his or her most important (measurable) characteristic when it comes to determining the status of a first job and of subsequent jobs. Whether the weight given to education results from the demand for application of skills on the job or from the use of credentials to screen job applicants cannot be determined from the research (McRoberts, 1982). Another important finding is that the occupational status of women is less closely tied to their family backgrounds and is affected more by educational credentials than is the status of men (Boyd et al., 1981: 662–63). Further, the study showed that status attainment processes are very similar in Canada and the United States (McRoberts and Selbee, 1981).

With respect to the historic growth of the middle-class in Canada and to current patterns of inequality, a particularly useful study is one based on a national survey in 1974. It examines occupational mobility over four generations (Goyder and Curtis, 1977). Table 10–9 shows the correlations between the occupational status scores of the survey respondent, his father, his grandfather and his eldest son (only males were surveyed and "main" occupations recorded; all sons over age 25 were included in these data).

TABLE 10-9 Occupational Mobility: Four Generations, Canada

INTERCORRELATIONS OF OCCUPATIONAL STATUS SCORES AMONG GRANDFATHERS, FATHERS, RESPONDENTS, AND SONS

GENERATION	G	F	R	S
Grandfather (G)	1.00	.49	.22	.05
Father (F)	.50	1.00	.38	.13
Respondent (R)	.27	.33	1.00	.26
Sons (S)	.03	.09	.22	1.00

* Figures above the diagonal are for the total sample; those below the diagonal are for farmers excluded in each generation.

Goyder and Curtis, 1977: 308.

The correlations measure the degree of association between the socioeconomic scores assigned to occupational titles.

There is a quite rapidly decreasing influence (correlation) of the grandfathers' status on the occupational status (as measured on a socioeconomic scale) of each succeeding generation. As in the national study discussed above, the effect is modest even in the first generation, as the correlation of .49 between grandfathers and fathers indicates. (Statistically, this number can be translated as meaning that 25 percent of the occupational statuses of the fathers is predicted by a knowledge of the grandfathers' statuses.) In other words, the occupational status of a person's grandfather or great-grandfather is almost entirely irrelevant to that person's own job status. This indicates a very open or mobile society. On the other hand, these results are not entirely surprising, since the *structure* of occupations has altered so greatly over these generations.

Structural Explanations of Social Mobility

Recently there has been much attention paid to the attempt to separate occupational mobility resulting from changes in the distribution of available jobs—called *structural* changes—from changes due to other factors. The task is very difficult, perhaps impossible (Hauser et al. 1975; Sobel, 1983). Studies that undertake the separation indicate that structural changes in the labour force account for a great deal of the individual mobility in Western societies. The study reported in Table 10–9 makes it clear that many of us had grandfathers who were farmers, but few of us have any chance to follow in their footsteps. This is intergenerational mobility due to structural change. There are, of course, many other structural changes. In studies of the United States, England and Wales and Canada, it is suggested that once the structural changes in the economies over time have been accounted for, no other changes in mobility patterns are detected (Hauser and Featherman, 1977: 15; McRoberts and Selbee, 1981). This is a particularly important argument. It means that the *relative* mobility of individuals starting from lower, middle or higher occupational origins has not changed with time, except for the changes resulting from shifts in the occupational structures themselves.[7]

In the present context, these results show again the difference between social structural changes and individual experiences. The transition from farmwork to blue-collar work to white-collar work in three generations tends to be culturally defined as significant upward mobility, given the widely accepted ranking of occupations. However, much of this observed mobility is a direct result of changing labour-force patterns, which are slightly modified by individual aspirations and achievements, job-search strategies, social contacts, employer preferences and other labour-market factors.

Since the early part of this century, and especially after World War II, many Canadians have experienced rising standards of living and the development of a consumer society. At the same time, they have experienced personal and family mobility, moving from rural to urban occupations and, particularly, from farm and manual work to white-collar jobs. These occupational changes have been accompanied by a general upgrading of educational credentials. A sociological understanding of these processes must recognize that individual experiences have been shaped by particular structural changes. The changes in the economy and the division of labour have powerfully moulded the mobility experience. Largely unchanged structures of income and educational inequality have been masked by the widespread sense of intergenerational material gain and personal achievement. It was C.W. Mills (1959) who some years ago insisted that the "sociological imagination" required

---

[7] Although occupational status attainment research finds that the most important individual characteristic influencing occupational status is educational attainment (years of schooling), it is important to recognize that even education has relatively weak effects. That is, there are enormous differences in occupational status and in income among people with the same educational credentials (Jencks et al., 1972). Here, too, one must separate structural effects from individual experience. The whole educational system has expanded over time. Everyone is getting more education. The structure of educational inequality, rather like that of income, remains largely unaltered, though individuals seek and attain additional credentials. Hence, the *relative* position of groups with different starting points is unchanged. Students with lower family income, say, have not much, if at all, improved their representation in higher education relative to those from middle- and higher-income groups (Pike, 1980: Richardson, 1977; Lennards, 1980).

an understanding, not just of personal experiences or of structures and their history, but of the connections between these two realities.

UNFINISHED BUSINESS: THE TWO FACES OF CLASS EXPERIENCE

Make no mistake, what is described here as the emergence of middle-class patterns of income, consumption, life style and values also describes the growth of the modern working-class. This is not a contradiction. There are two faces to contemporary class experience—proletarianization and the rise of a middle-class life style and culture.

To reiterate, proletarianization is the historic process by which people have experienced increasing dependence on wages and salaries as a sole source of livelihood and loss of control of the means of production and of autonomy in the labour process. A provocative extension of this thesis focuses directly on the labour process (work and the workplace), arguing that, in this century, both manual and white-collar workers increasingly have been subject to supervision and to routinization of their work (Braverman, 1974; Rinehart, 1975). This thesis has not been taken up here, but it has generated an important literature (see Paul Thompson, 1984).

Other recent studies have tried to determine the boundaries between classes and class segments in contemporary Western societies, for example, between working-, middle- and capitalist classes and gradations of those classes. (Poulantzas, 1975; Wright, 1976). This Marxist work has already drawn a biting Weberian response (Parkin, 1979: Ch. 1–3). Again, these issues have not been pursued here, though this chapter argues that, in understanding contemporary Canadian society, it is fruitful to focus on the simultaneous experience of proletarianization and the rise of middle-class culture.

There are, of course, many different labour markets and many visible differences in wealth, education, income and life style among them. But there are also two unifying threads of experience: the dependence on wages and the salience of middle-class aspirations and values. It may be that the common experience of proletarianization is so fundamental that it has the potential to give rise to a modern, mass political movement (Westergaard and Resler, 1975: 401ff). However, it is also possible that the social divisions, relative affluence, individualism and emphasis on family security that are part of middle-class culture will effectively inhibit a working-class movement in the foreseeable future (Runciman, 1966; Parkin, 1974: Ch. 2 and 3; Mann, 1973).

Changes in working conditions and the rise of the modern labour movement in Canada have not been analysed in this chapter, but they are central topics of class analysis. They are addressed elsewhere in this text in reference to economic institutions. But it is essential to recognize that the increases in real incomes and the extension of social services, from unemployment insurance to Medicare and pensions, are gains for wage and salary workers and are very much the result of their own political responses and of an active labour movement. They are political gains, that is, they did not come about as natural consequences of economic expansion, the growth of the state or of modernization (Roberts and Bullen, 1984; Heron, 1984).

Thus, central economic features of middle-class life in Canada can themselves be understood as responses to proletarianization.

SUMMARY

Much research on class and stratification in Canada is recent and scattered, with few works attempting an integrated assessment. From the point of view of class analysis, proletarianization has received little attention, although it is a key to understanding the emergence of advanced, industrial capitalism in Canada. The process appears to have moved forward unevenly from the middle of the last century into the early years of this one and then quickened after 1920 and again after World War II. Whatever the timing of the transition or the crucial turning points, the last three decades or so have seen both an increasing concentration of capital and of wealth, and the growth of wage and salary dependence.

We have argued that the more obvious and immediate experiences of Canadians over the postwar period have been those of increased real incomes and consumption and occupational and educational mobility. These experiences have sustained the strong sense of Canada as a middle-class society and have underwritten the attachment to distinctive middle-class values (social order, the sanctity of property and rewards for individual effort and talent). We have concluded that economic gains and expanded mobility have mediated the processes of property concentration and proletarianization in Canada.

Social class and stratification theory have not been particularly adept at dealing with the concept and the reality of the middle-class. In Marxist theory, the issues have often been treated as distractions from the central concern with conflict between capitalists and the working-classes. Recent research has addressed the topic but has emphasized problems of categorization at the expense of analysis of historical processes (Wright, 1976). Weberian theory contains an implicit analysis of the middle-class in its focus on variations in market positions, life-chances and bureaucratic employment in contemporary societies. But Weber left the analysis unformulated, and it has been developed by very few (Mills, 1956; Parkin, 1979). Functionalists have taken the concept and the reality for granted.

In part this failure is accounted for by the complex and unstable nature of the middle-class as a social, political and cultural amalgam. Even its composition is in need of analysis. Arno Mayer (1975) argues that this social and cultural amalgam (the middle-class) has, in a sense, replaced the older petite bourgeoisie in contemporary Western societies, but we have yet to address adequately its historical implications as a social and political force. For Canada, as for other Western societies, the need for analysis of the middle-class is pressing, since some of the major structural changes lying behind the individual experiences that define the middle-class (economic gain and status attainment) have run their course, especially the historic transition from a rural, petit-bourgeois economy to an urban, industrial one.

DISCUSSION QUESTIONS

1. The concepts of class and stratification refer to different social phenomena. What is the significance of the distinction?

2. Both Weberian and functionalist theory focus on occupational stratification. Discuss how one is concerned with power and the other with societal needs.

3. Why is the question of the size and character of the small-property-owning class (petite bourgeoisie) so important to understanding the emergence of the Canadian class system?

4. It has been claimed that the two central institutions of capitalism, private property and the labour market, generate deep inequalities in the ownership of productive property and in wealth. Why is this so? How might it be disputed?

5. Canada is often called a middle-class society. What does this mean? How can it be argued that most Canadians are both middle-class and proletarianized?

CENTRAL INSTITUTIONS of SOCIETY

This section is about institutions, sets of values, activities and resources used to meet important social needs. It builds on what we have covered earlier, illustrating how basic social processes come together to produce order and change. Here, within the central institutions of society, larger structures contain smaller ones; formal structures, informal ones; complex structures, simpler ones; and permanent structures, temporary ones.

The *central* institutions include the economy, the political system, legal system, mass media and educational system; we will discuss only the economy and the mass media in this text, for reasons of brevity. While central institutions differ in important respects, they also share many similarities. For this reason, sociologists typically ask similar questions about them.

That is not to deny that here, as elsewhere in this book, opposing paradigms compete for our attention. These paradigms, especially the Marxist, Weberian and functionalist, define which parts of the central institutions will interest us most.

Yet, within all the main paradigms, the sociological analysis of central institutions means studying *linked, interdependent parts*, the character of these linkages and the ways the parts and the whole system change over time. As well, all are concerned with the place of the institution in society, its relation to society's values, activities and power structure.

Institutional Outputs

The sociologist's first concern is with what Anthony Giddens calls *structuration* and Paul DiMaggio and Walter Powell call *institutional definition*. Their work suggests that the study of any central institution should, first, specify the institution's parts, or member organizations; then, it should analyse interactions among them, interorganizational control and co-operation, information flow and communication and mutual awareness. The chapters in this section address these issues and others as well.

The focus on structural linkage ignores only the institutional *output,* an identifying feature of any institution and the most important factor in institutional definition. An analysis may begin by asking what the institution is *supposed* to accomplish. What are its *stated* goals and the expectations of its members? Are they met, and if not, why not? Is the institution achieving some other unstated, unintended or hidden purpose? If so, what is it?

How do the *actual* outputs of the institution—programs, laws, decisions, degrees—affect people? How, for example, do television programs influence family life, peer group relations, literacy, mass behaviour? Or how do government policies influence public life, good citizenship, belief in the state, trust among countrymen? How do economic decisions shape material prosperity, class conflict, technological development? Or how does the educational system affect intellectual development, character building and the acquisition of job skills?

The *stated* goals of an institution are usually rooted in a society's dominant values. Every institution claims a strong cultural foundation and, therefore, the right to command large numbers of people and massive resources.

However, an institution's *actual* goals and practices often threaten this right. It must be continuously repaired and regenerated. To do this, central institutions support one another against attack. For example, the media support the political system; the educational system supports the economy; and the legal system supports all of these. How this co-operation comes about and how it is maintained is the subject of much current sociological research.

Institutional Co-operation

The polity, or political system of a society, includes the state, which plays a major role in protecting and controlling other institutions. The state, as Weber pointed out, enjoys a monopoly of legitimate force or authority. It has the right to give or take away freedoms, to confiscate property, to tax and redistribute wealth and to force compliance with rules by punishing deviance.

For example, the state spells out the conditions under which economic organizations may operate, buy and sell, hire and fire labour. And from the state, educational institutions get the largest part of their operating revenue. At the primary and secondary levels, provincial governments give strong direction to curriculum and other schooling policies. Not surprisingly, all institutions want to control, co-opt or win the favour of the state.

The economy also plays a major part in protecting and controlling other institutions. Indeed, Marxists assert that all social and political institutions rest on an economic base: All are ultimately controlled by the relations of production. People's relations to the means of production determine their opportunities for health, security and self-fulfillment. And an institution's linkages to the economy determine its "life chances" too. One should therefore ask of any institution what its economic foundations or relations with the economic system are. This question has led to an interest in economic elites and the ways they dominate the economy and other institutions. However, elite domination is not limited to the economy. In studying any institution, we want to know who makes up its elite: What group, class, tribe, region or other social unit is in control, and how do they use that control?

This question, in turn, raises a variety of interesting issues: How does the institution further or protect the interests of its controlling group? How does the elite keep control? Who else is contending for control, and how are they kept out? Finally, to what degree does the institution promise change, perhaps even greater equality, yet actually reproduce the existing order of class relations? The success controlling elites enjoy in holding on to and even extending their power as time passes has led to much research on power elites, upper classes and the relations between the two.

The Institutional System and Its Maintenance

However, too narrow a focus on elites may mislead us. The structure of central institutions is not created by individuals or groups of individuals, all of whom are, in time, replaced. Society is none the better or worse since Conrad Black took E.P. Taylor's place as one of Canada's most powerful and wealthy men; and Black's passing from the scene will probably make as little difference. What sets the pattern is the distribution of power, wealth and legal right that characterizes a modern capitalist, industrial society. Private property, a grossly unequal distribution of wealth and a nominally free market in capital, political decision-making and ideas, all of which benefit the powerful, define such a society. Given these features, strongly interlinked central institutions that reproduce the existing order are bound to result, whoever the elite may be.

Some hold that the key actors are neither elites nor institutions, but dominant organizations within institutions: within the economy, banks; within the polity, political parties; within the media, networks and publishing chains. From this perspective, organizations compete to dominate their own fields as much to ensure their own survival as for the benefit of institutional elites (owners, board members) or dominant social classes.

Power is the enjoyment of and the ability to protect an advantage. We must investigate how a given institution or organization exercises its power. How does a controlling elite or dominant organization control those subordinated to it: its workers, or students, or consumers, or clients, or viewers, or voters? How does the same elite or organization dominate other institutions and *their* elites, workers, clients, and the like? If such control is not exercised—if, instead, institutions co-operate and ally with each other—

how are such arrangements made and enforced? What social structures are protected and helped by a given institution and will, in turn, protect that same institution, thereby serving to maintain the established order?

Again, we must listen to the dialogue between Marx and Weber: Does one institution and one elite, or class, dominate society, as Marx holds; or, as Weber says, do many sources of domination co-exist and compete? If we accept the former, we would expect society to change through conflict between the dominant and subordinate classes; if the latter, through shifting power relationships within the dominant class.

In both paradigms, achieving legitimacy is important. Controlling society is easier if the public co-operates. What, then, structures public awareness of, participation in and perceptions about the institutions in question and their right to control? Is it ignorance? Or what Marx called "false consciousness"? Or even, as Orwell suggested with his Doublethink and Newspeak in *1984*, a distortion of our ability to tell truth from falsehood? Or are people genuinely committed to the goals of the institutions: to educational "excellence," political "good citizenship," media "awareness," and so on? Nothing is harder than trying to sort out such questions from inside a society, yet this is precisely what sociologists try to do. How, then, can we see what an institution is really doing for, or to, a society?

The Value of Comparative Analysis

Comparative analysis may help us understand. By definition, each central institution is an intimate part of its social environment. To see the unique contribution a particular institution is making, a variety of strategies must be tried.

One strategy is to study how the same kind of institution (for example, a capitalist economy, multiparty political system or adversarial legal system) works in a different cultural, social and economic setting. Another strategy is to study how a given institution has changed historically, relating changes to earlier (therefore, potentially causal) changes in other institutions. A third is to compare institutions within the same society, to see how they adapted differently to the same historical changes in cultural, social and economic contexts.

Still, we cannot minimize the importance of understanding a central institution *within* its own time and place: for example, in Canada, in the late twentieth century.

Many of the generalizations we make will hold good for all western, capitalist, industrial societies. But some will need modifying in the light of Canada's peculiar history: its economic dependency, the dominant role of multinational organizations, regional conflict, the twin British and French cultural traditions, high rates of immigration and the resulting multiculturalism, and so on.

The sociologist may want to complete the analysis by considering proposed alternatives to present arrangements, especially after discovering discrepancies between actual and intended outputs. What, the sociologist may ask, are the prospects for future change, and what dynamics are likely to bring such changes about?

Together, these questions and the answers they receive make up the study of central institutions in society.

11

Economic Institutions and Power

R.J. Richardson

INTRODUCTION

What are economic institutions? How are they related to other types of social institutions and to society in general? How do they affect our daily lives? Furthermore, what is economic power and who wields it? This chapter will examine the significance of economic institutions to society and to ourselves as individuals. We will move from general theories of economic institutions and their relationship to society to focus more specifically on North American and then Canadian issues of economic influence and power.

WHAT ARE ECONOMIC INSTITUTIONS?

Societies consist of people, their relationships with one another, their activities and their values. But the groups people form are not randomly created, nor are their activities or the values they develop arbitrary. In fact, these all are shaped by the central elements of social organization in any society. We call these *institutions*.

More specifically, institutions are collections of organizations or groups that mobilize people and resources in ways consistent with the values of a society. Institutions, in turn, disseminate and reinforce these values. Every society contains familial, political, religious, educational and economic institutions in one form or another. In some societies, these institutions are highly integrated. For example, the Bushmen of the Kalahari subsume virtually all of them under the institution of family and kinship. In others, such as modern Canada, these institutions are highly differentiated. Although they are interrelated in various ways, they each take on a concrete form of their own.

This chapter will focus on economic institutions, which we may define as *the set of organizations, groups and processes by which people in a society produce and distribute goods and services*. Between societies, these economic institutions may vary substantially, depending on:

— the society's basic mode of existence (e.g., hunting and gathering versus manufacturing);
— the technology available (e.g., Stone-Age tools versus nuclear power and the microchip);
— the central values of the society (e.g., co-operation versus competition and the primacy of the individual versus the primacy of the group).

Nevertheless, despite this diversity, economic institutions in any society provide the basic social organization for satisfying the material wants of the society's members. These wants include the necessities of life such as food, clothing and shelter and all of the goods and services that form part of the society's culture.

Economic institutions perform two basic material processes—production and distribution. The production process combines land, labour, capital, technology and organization to produce goods and services. The distributive process recognizes the claims of the members of the society to a share in the benefits of production. In other words, economic institutions produce and distribute a society's wealth.

Economic institutions are the central focus of the discipline of economics, so one might ask: Why should sociology study them too? Is it just empire-building on the part of sociologists? To this, we can answer with a firm "No!" Just as war is too important to leave to the generals, so is the economy too important to leave to the economists. We will see in this chapter that economy and society are intimately related and that economic sociology tends to focus on relationships that cross the boundaries of disciplines. For example, economists tend to study market and sociologists *non*market relationships in economic enterprise.

Marxist sociology looks primarily at the economic base of society and holds that all other institutions are merely superstructure (Marx, 1970). But one need be neither a Marxist nor an economic determinist to recognize that how goods, services and wealth are produced and distributed profoundly affects all the central institutions of any society and, therefore, the quality of human existence. Of course, economic processes are affected by other social institutions as well.

ECONOMIC POWER

When we think of power, we often think in terms of personal characteristics, as in "He is a powerful man." So, to many of us, power is perhaps merely an abstract form of physical strength. But to sociologists, power is a *relationship*, not an attribute. Weber, for example, defined power as "the probability that one actor in a social relationship will be able to carry out his own will despite resistance . . . " (1968:53). Since power is a relationship, it can also be the inverse of dependence (Emerson, 1962). Thus, your power over me depends on how much I am dependent on you.

Power can be wielded within any of society's institutions, and *economic power* is, of course, wielded in economic institutions and originates in economic relations. It is an aspect of the economy that economists tend to ignore because of their focus on competitive markets and the impersonal laws of supply and demand. But power arises in the economic realm wherever an individual or group controls a significant share of a particular resource. This creates dependence in others who want or need that resource.

Weber (1958) proposed that the distribution of benefits in an economic exchange depends on the relative market power of the parties involved. Market power, in turn, rests on two interrelated factors in Weber's analysis. The first is how much the control of a commodity is concentrated in a few hands. The second is how effectively one party to an exchange can *withhold* a commodity from the market.

We can see these principles at work in the labour market and the wheat market, for example. The labour market contains few capitalists and many workers. Thus, individual workers cannot affect wages by withdrawing their services. A major reason for the rise of unions has been the unionized workers' ability to collectively use the strike to try to reduce this imbalance in economic power.

Canadian wheat farmers, from the 1880s to World War II, participated in a competitive world market containing millions of independent producers. Throughout this period, wheat prices fluctuated violently because no individual farmer (or group of farmers) could affect the price by withholding wheat from the market. The central Canadian suppliers of their agricultural equipment and machinery, on the other hand, were few in number. Consequently, these suppliers could maintain a substantial degree of price stability by reducing production in times of falling demand. This vast difference in market power between the wheat farmers and their suppliers has been an important element of Prairie society ever since the opening of this Canadian agricultural frontier.

While Weber analysed economic power mainly in terms of the relations of exchange, Marx focused on the relations of production. Marx (1954) proposed that those who control the means of production (the bourgeoisie) dominate and exploit those who do not (the proletariat). Nevertheless, these different analyses of economic power are complementary, not incompatible. For both, the distribution of economic power is determined by economic structures. The complementarity of the analyses by Marx and Weber is not accidental. Much of Weber's work can be seen as a debate with the ghost of Marx (Zeitlin, 1968), or as a positive critique and extension of Marx. (See Chapter 10 for an explanation of some important aspects of this relationship.)

TYPES OF ECONOMIC INSTITUTIONS

The types of economic institutions that have existed throughout human history are virtually endless, ranging from the primitive communism of many tribal societies, through agricultural societies based on slavery and serfdom to modern industrial capitalism and socialism. Here, we will examine only a few examples to demonstrate the principal variables that differentiate types of economic institutions. These are the technologies employed, the division of labour, the ownership or control of the means of production, the principles under which a society's wealth is distributed and the degree to which economic institutions are separate and distinct.

Tribal societies based on hunting and gathering or primitive agriculture employ restricted technologies suitable to producing what they need. Production is usually based on the kinship unit, which is relatively self-sufficient. The unit contains a rudimentary gender- and age-based division of labour. Yet, there may still be some in the society who specialize in producing specific items, like weapons, and so there is a limited amount of exchange. However, this exchange is based on *who* is involved and what roles they play, unlike the universal and impersonal exchange of commodities. Property, such as the land used for hunting, gathering and tilling, is usually communal and regarded as the property of the group as a whole. Distribution of the products of the society's labour is relatively egalitarian. Any surplus produced tends to be distributed on the basis of noneconomic criteria, such as military prowess and tradition. In these societies, economic activity is densely interwoven with kinship obligations and religious belief, and so economic institutions are indistinct.

Tribal and industrial societies differ in all of these dimensions. Industrial society uses an extremely diverse application of machine technology. This is associated with an intensive division of labour that produces a formalized occupational structure. Whereas in tribal societies, the choice of what to produce is severely restricted by the technology, this choice is virtually unlimited in industrial societies. Yet, since resources are not unlimited, choices must be made and how these are made varies between capitalist and socialist industrial societies.

Under capitalism, there is private ownership of the means of production. Those who own or control these means will make productive choices aimed at maximizing their profits. Profits, in turn, are partly determined by the forces of supply and demand, so production is generally geared toward the goods and services in highest demand. Distribution of wealth generated by economic activity is determined by

A bushman of the Kalahari brings home a porcupine. Tribal societies based on hunting and gathering meet their needs (often very effectively) by employing restricted technologies. Irven DeVore/Anthro-Photo.

economic criteria—by the ownership of the means of production, by the commodity value of specific types of labour, expertise and technology and by Weber's "market power." Clearly, in capitalist industrial society, economic activity is secularized, rationalized and distinct from other activities. Economic institutions are much less interwoven with other institutions, such as religion, the family and the political order.

Socialist industrial societies substitute public for private ownership. Productive decisions are based, not on profit maximization, but on centralized planning that aims to meet consumer demand and political objectives, such as development and defence. Economic wealth is distributed (at least in part) according to people's needs rather than according to their position in the economic structure. Although there may be more links between political and economic institutions here than in capitalism, the economic institutions are distinct and well developed.

We have seen that economic institutions can take many forms. But what shapes them? Clearly, they are affected by technology, but we have seen important differences between capitalist and socialist economic institutions that share similar technologies. Furthermore, the Greek, Roman and Chinese civilizations developed many important technologies that were never widely used for economic purposes. Perhaps, then, technology both affects and is affected by the economy. On a broader scale, we might ask: Does the economy shape society, or is it the other way around?

In industrial societies, the diversity of technology permits an almost unlimited choice of what to produce. Here, oil and gas are extracted from tar sands. NFB, Chris Lund/Permission of Miller Services.

ECONOMY AND SOCIETY

THE TRANSFORMATION OF ECONOMIC INSTITUTIONS

Marx, Weber and Durkheim all addressed the relationship of economy to society and the transformation from one set of institutions to another. A brief and somewhat oversimplified summary of their analyses follows, working from the simplest to the most complex.

Émile Durkheim (1965) proposes that economy shapes society but that economy, in turn, is shaped by the demographic variable of population density. Primitive societies, he argues, have a sparse population and a rudimentary division of labour. All social institutions, including economic ones, are closely intertwined, and nearly everyone fills similar occupational roles. Because of this common economic base, the members of society behave alike and share a set of beliefs or a *collective conscience*. Hence, there is an idealistic basis for maintaining social order. However, the economic base of self-sufficient production fosters little interdependence among people. Therefore, there is no structural basis for social integration. The collective conscience, then, must be maintained and reinforced by *repressive and punitive laws*, because the society will lose its identity if it tolerates deviance or even individuality. Durkheim calls the economically determined basis for this type of social order *mechanical solidarity*.

If and when the population density increases to the point where a simple division of labour no longer allows the society's members to survive, Durkheim believes that a much more complex division must develop. This high degree of specialization produces a similarly high degree of interdependence among a society's members. Consequently, a new structural basis of social order develops, which Durkheim calls *organic solidarity*. This new, stronger basis of social integration no longer requires repressive law to maintain the collective conscience. In fact, the individualism and uniqueness of personality resulting from specialization are now desirable. So repressive law is replaced by *restitutive law*, which grows out of the new int~rdependent economic base. Hence, in Durkheim's view, economy shapes society and economic institutions change in response to population pressures.

Marx (1970, 1978) also holds that the economy shapes people and society. "The nature of individuals thus depends on the material conditions determining their production" (1978: 150). In his analysis, not only human nature, but also human ideas, laws, religion and social institutions arise from how people conduct their economic activities. These, in turn, occur within a specific *set* of economic institutions, which he terms a *mode of production*.

This mode of production is the foundation of Marx's conception of history, and changes in it represent distinct historical epochs. It comprises two elements: the *forces of production*, which represent the interaction between human producers, tools, technology and the material environment; and the *relations of production*, which are the class, property and power relationships in a society (Zeitlin, 1968). Marx proposes that to reproduce both themselves and their society, humans enter into social relations of production. These relations are relatively static in any given epoch. The *forces* of production, however, are dynamic. They change with population pressures, the division of labour, technological developments and so on. The friction between these dynamic forces and the static relations of production causes class conflict, which eventually becomes severe enough to produce the objective conditions for social change (that is, change from one mode of production to another). For change to actually happen, these objective conditions must also be accompanied by subjective class consciousness (Zeitlin, 1968). (For a much more comprehensive account of Marx's conception of history, see Cohen, 1978).

Marx's analysis of economic institutions and the relationship of economy to society is much more complex and conditional than Durkheim's. Nevertheless, they agree that economy shapes society. In Weber's analysis, the causal direction is unclear.

Some of Weber's analyses suggest that the change from one set of economic institutions to another is the result of economic processes and that a society is shaped by its economic base. For example, Weber (1976) analysed the decline of the slave-based economy of the Roman Empire and the evolution of that empire into a feudal society. He concluded that the disintegration of the empire was an inevitable political consequence of the decline of commerce. Elsewhere, Weber (1961) proposed that the structure of agricultural societies and their systems of land tenure depend on their economic institutions.

On the other hand, he argued that military and religious motives affect economic developments. For example, he cited the need for large armies in continental Europe as a factor favouring peasant agriculture, which maximized population per acre.

England, on the other hand, was protected by the Channel, and its navy and had much more modest military needs. This favoured capitalist agriculture, which maximized *production* per acre, rather than population. It also permitted the expropriation of peasants to meet the labour demands of the Industrial Revolution. Elsewhere (1974, 1958) Weber focused on values as the "switchmen" directing social and economic change.

Having examined the classical perspectives on the transformation of economic institutions generally, we will now look at Marx's and Weber's analyses of the emergence of capitalism as the dominant economic institution in the modern western world.

The Emergence of Capitalism

How and why did capitalism arise when and where it did? These questions were central to the sociology of both Marx (1954) and Weber (1958, 1961). There are many similarities in their conclusions as we should expect, but also some important differences.

Both held that an essential precondition for capitalism was the separation of the labourer from the means of production. This was first seen to occur with the expropriation of the English agricultural producer as feudal tenure was phased out between the sixteenth and eighteenth centuries. It was accompanied by new laws that created a class of labourers free to, indeed *compelled* to, sell their labour power on the market. Labour power, then, became a commodity, like potatoes.

Both Marx and Weber attributed the rise of the prosperous capitalist farmer to European inflation, which was induced by Spain's importation of gold from the New World. Both saw the manufacturing capitalist emerging via two routes. One was a slow process, where independent artisans employed more and more wage labourers; the other, a faster one, where merchants and financiers expanded into manufacturing. Hence, both agriculture and manufacturing increased commodity production for an expanding market.

Marx (1954) concentrated on analysing capitalism as an economic system producing commodities and surplus value (defined in Chapter 10) and continuing to reproduce the relation between the capitalist and the wage labourer.

Weber's analysis was more diverse. For one thing, although Marx certainly did not ignore the emergence of a market, Weber focused much more on it. To Weber, the rise of the mass market was as essential to the emergence of capitalism as the decline of commerce was to the end of the Roman Empire. He also extended Marx's analysis by placing it within a broader sweep of historical dynamics (Zeitlin, 1968). The first of these dynamics was the rise of rationality, which became institutionalized through technology, the marketplace, economic enterprise and the law. The second was the coincident development of bureaucracy, which separated the producer from the means of production, administration, science and war. Thirdly, Weber (1930) examined the influence of religion on the rise of capitalism. He proposed that early Protestantism encouraged the self-discipline, hard work and individualism that fostered competition and investment. This, along with a prohibition against conspicuous consumption, produced the investment in and growth of industry that were the dynamic elements of capitalism.

From Laissez-Faire to Corporate Capitalism

As capitalism emerged in England, so did the doctrine of *laissez-faire*. This doctrine was taken from the philosophy of Adam Smith (1894) who proposed that the greatest good for the greatest number was served when individuals pursued their own selfish objectives, constrained only by the "unseen hand" of competition. So government, other than acting to bolster capitalism *as a system*, left business alone.

It was from observing laissez-faire capitalism that Marx (1954) formulated his laws of capitalist competition. Marx believed that competition forced capitalist enterprise to continually adopt the latest technology. Firms that did prospered; those that did not failed. Thus, there is a tendency for the economy to be dominated by ever fewer and ever larger firms. Not only is capital concentrated in fewer and fewer hands, but employment is also increasingly to be found only in the few large establishments. Dense concentrations of impoverished wage labourers then provide the conditions for developing the class consciousness and cohesion necessary to overthrow capitalism. Thus, ultimately, "the expropriators are expropriated" (1954: 715).

Although Marx correctly forecast the increasing concentration of capitalist enterprise, the inevitable revolution by the working class that he predicted has not occurred because of several factors he could not have foreseen. Small-scale enterprise survives to this day in labour-intensive sectors of the economy and in new industries where the entry of small, new firms offsets, for a while, the process of concentration. We have also seen that the increased productivity accompanying new technology has reduced living costs, resulting in a higher standard of living for the working class than Marx forecast. Furthermore, concentration has reduced price competition among the few large firms in each industry. This has permitted wages to rise, because the cost of higher wages can be recovered by raising prices. Finally, laissez-faire capitalism has gradually given way to the welfare state.

The modern welfare state evolved out of the massive depression of the 1930s, with the result that—until the advent of President Reagan and Prime Minister Thatcher, at least—there has been ever-increasing government involvement in the economy. The welfare state reduces the economic impact of unemployment, becomes a major employer in its own right and sets minimum wages for the working class. It also provides welfare for businesses through tax breaks and subsidies.

Large modern corporations have immense power. However, their power is not unfettered, as it was in the days of laissez-faire, for they are subject to significant constraints imposed by governments and the judiciary.

HOW ECONOMY SHAPES MODERN SOCIETY

The massive unemployment of the current decade shows the effect of economic institutions on society. In fact, some claim that robotics and the microchip will make chronic unemployment endemic in future decades as well. Although the unemployed are protected from complete financial ruin by unemployment insurance and other social safety nets, they are robbed of their raison d'être. If work is central to life, as many sociologists conclude, is it any wonder that unemployment breeds psychological disorders, marital breakup, drunkenness, violence, crime and suicide? Truly, private troubles are public issues (Mills, 1959) as the economy affects so many private lives.

The economy affects us all as consumers, as well. The dramatic growth in consumer credit since World War II has induced us to buy more and sooner than we otherwise would. This has produced economic growth and material prosperity. But it has also made us more dependent than ever on economic institutions as we struggle to pay later for what we buy now. As we saw in Chapters 8 and 10, the extension of credit is also a factor in the dramatic growth of the number of families having both parents working outside the home.

Why should so many get caught in the credit trap? Duberman and Hartjen (1979) attribute this largely to the effectiveness of modern advertising. We are bombarded with images of the *affluent society* dozens of times every day. The cumulative result may not induce us to buy a specific product, but it makes affluence seem desirable and achievable. So—we buy our way into it. In a closely related argument, Vance Packard (1960) and Alvin Toffler (1970) state that economic institutions, through advertising, lobbying, influence on the school system and the book publishing industry and so on, have created the *throw-away society*. One element of this tinsel world is planned obsolescence. Industries design products—anything from light bulbs to pantyhose—that have deliberately limited life spans. Or they persuade consumers that their clothes are outmoded and must be replaced, even though still

In order to "keep up with the Joneses," North Americans contribute to Alvin Toffler's "throw-away society." Yet, what would happen to unemployment if planned obsolescence were eliminated? R. Harrington/Permission of Miller Services.

perfectly functional. Many of us with a closet full of clothes still claim we have nothing to wear.

The North American automobile (up to the late 1970s, at least) is an excellent example of industrial success in promoting Toffler's throw-away society. European cars have an average life span of about 12 years, as the Volvo ads proclaim, and they rarely undergo superficial changes in styling. North American car manufacturers, on the other hand, make major style changes about every two years, with enough trim changes in the intervening years to make last year's car out of date. Because of this successful planned obsolescence, it has become essential for people—if they are going to keep up with their neighbours—to trade in their cars about every two years. This has had two results, just as the automakers planned. First, it has increased the demand for cars. Secondly, cars can be built a lot more cheaply because they are only expected to last a few years.

In the last few years, the throw-away ethos seems to be declining. Perhaps this is a result of changing values. If so, it suggests that society can affect economy, just as we have suggested the reverse. On the other hand, sales of paper plates and drinks in nonreturnable cans continue to grow exponentially, and the ubiquitous, long-wearing blue jeans are threatening to become outmoded. Perhaps the process is circular: Recent hard economic times have affected our values, which has reduced the influence of the throw-away ethos, which has made times even harder by reducing demand and thus employment.

> ### ECONOMIC ORGANIZATIONS AND SOCIETY
> Society is adaptive to organizations, to the large, powerful organizations controlled by a few, often overlapping, leaders. To see these organizations as adaptive to a "turbulent", dynamic, ever changing environment is to indulge in fantasy. The environment of most powerful organizations is well controlled by them, quite stable, and made up of other organizations with similar interest, or ones they control. Standard Oil and Shell may compete at the intersection of two highways, but they do not compete in the numerous areas where their interests are critical, such as foreign policy, tax laws, import quotas, government funding of research and development, highway expansion, internal combustion engines, pollution restrictions, and so on. Nor do they have a particularly turbulent relationship to other powerful organizations such as the auto companies, the highway construction firms [and] the Department of Defense. . . .
>
> "Complex Organizations: A Critical Essay," by Charles Perrow. Permission granted by Random House, Inc.
>
> The excerpt illustrates one of the basic arguments Perrow makes in his influential book: Societies adapt to economic organizations more than organizations have to adapt to societies.

ISSUES OF ECONOMIC POWER
ECONOMIC POWER, CLASS AND THE STATE

Not only does the economy affect society, but many scholars have noted the pervasive economic base of social conflict. Peasants struggling against landowners, workers against employers, the poor against the rich; even racism and wars contain elements of such conflict. World War I can perhaps best be seen as a struggle for access to markets, materials and food—in short, for world economic dominance. From this viewpoint, World War II was merely the second round.

To Marx (1978), the essence of history is the class struggle. This economically based struggle is over the control of property—whether that property is human beings, land or capital. Today, this conflict is most clearly seen in the form of strikes. Class—an economic relationship—is also described as the fundamental element of social stratification in Chapter 10.

The relationship between economic power and the state has been the subject of intensive debate. To Weber (1958) and modern Weberians, it is a complex relationship in which each element affects the other. On the other hand, Marx (1978) held that all struggles within the state are class struggles for political power to represent the economic interests of one class as the general interest. It does happen, of course, that *segments* of a particular class struggle for political power (Marx and Engels, 1950).

Modern, neo-Marxist theory is split between the *instrumentalist* (Miliband, 1969) and the *structuralist* views (Poulantzas, 1978). The former proposes that a cohesive capitalist class (or its dominant element), through formal and informal ties to the polity, is able to manipulate the state into supporting its economic interests. The latter view gives limited autonomy to the state, which can respond to working-class demands while maintaining the long-term economic interests of the capitalist class. For excellent reviews of these positions, see Gold, Lo and Wright (1975) and Cuneo (1979).

However, in a critique of these views, Brym (1985) grants further autonomy to the state. He argues that one source of this autonomy is the simple fact that politicians and bureaucrats want to keep their jobs. To do so, they must not offend any class or group to the point that their re-election or re-appointment is jeopardized. In sum, "States are social structures which reflect the distribution of resources, organization and support—in short, of power—among classes and other groups at given points of time" (Brym, 1985:15). Although economic power greatly influences the state, Brym persuasively argues that it is not the only influence.

MULTINATIONAL ENTERPRISE

An important recent controversy about economic power concerns the emergence of multinational enterprise as the paramount economic fact of the present epoch. Many sociologists argue that these giant conglomerates, which operate in many countries, cannot be effectively controlled by any government. Vernon (1971) points out that a mere 187 American multinational corporations account for one-third of all sales in the United States. The international operations of these giants, he argues, are so vast that they have become a power unto themselves, defying the attempts of their own government to prevent them from exporting jobs while at the same time exporting American economic and political power around the world. As a result of the rapid growth and incredible power of multinational enterprise (MNE), "suddenly, it seems, the sovereign states are feeling naked. Concepts such as national sovereignty and national economic strength appear curiously drained of meaning" (Vernon, 1971:3).

The pervasiveness of MNE has concerned many Canadian sociologists and economists. Since World War II, well over half of Canadian manufacturing and other key industrial sectors have become foreign controlled (see Table 11–1). Although the degree of foreign control has declined slightly in the past decade, it is still the highest among the world's industrialized economies. This has prompted serious concern about the nature of our economy, our society and even our national sovereignty. Scholars such as Clement (1975), Watkins (Canada, 1970) and Brym (1985) have identified the "branch plant" nature of the Canadian economy, which has consequences as diverse as: the serious drain dividend payments place on our

TABLE 11–1 Foreign Control of Canadian Industry Selected Years, 1926-1975

Sector	% FOREIGN CONTROLLED					
	1926	1939	1948	1958	1967	1975
Manufacturing	35	38	43	57	57	56
Petroleum and natural gas[1]				73	74	74
Mines and Minerals	38	42	40	60	65	60
Railways	3	3	3	2	2	1
Utilities	20	26	24	5	5	4
Total of these industries plus commerce	17	21	25	32	35	33

[1] included in mines and minerals prior to 1958

Statistics Canada, Catalogue 67-202, various years. Adapted from Jorge Niosi, *Les Multinationales Canadiennes,* Montreal, Boreal Express, 1982.

foreign exchange; the retardation of Canadian industrial research; and the barriers to Canadian social mobility created by foreign-controlled branch plants.

A second aspect of the relationship between MNE and Canadian society has, until recently, gone unnoticed. Niosi (1982) points out the startling fact that Canada ranks sixth among the nations which are *home countries* for MNE. In fact, on a per capita basis, it ranks first! So, in two ways—as a host country for foreign MNE and as a home country for our own multinationals abroad—Canada is intimately linked to the world economy. And, to the degree economy shapes society, we are more a world than a national society.

Two further issues involving MNE are important to the relationship between economy and society. These are the questions of extraterritoriality and of values.

Extraterritoriality concerns the application of the home country's laws in the host country. Since the laws of the countries involved often conflict, they can generate a "catch-22" situation for MNE. To obey the law of one country requires breaking the law of another. The Royal Bank of Canada was placed in such a situation when it refused to break Panamanian banking law by releasing banking records of an important client to a Canadian tribunal. The Bank of Nova Scotia found itself in an even more complex and painful situation when it refused to break Bahamian law by releasing client records to a federal grand jury in Florida. It was hit with a $25 000 per day fine. Ford of Canada and M.L.W. Worthington both risked breaking Canadian law and offending Canada when they declined to fulfill orders for trucks to China and locomotives to Cuba respectively. To do so might have resulted in jail terms for the top executives of their American parent firms for breaking the United States' Trading with the Enemy Act. The questions here, of course, are: first, how can nations protect their integrity; and second, how can MNE avoid the catch-22?

Should a multinational firm be guided by the values of its home society or of the society in which it is operating? Bata finds itself in this dilemma in South Africa, where the position of the legally constituted government and the values of the dominant white society concerning blacks are diametrically opposed to the values and laws of its home country, Canada. So does Northern Telecom, as it restricts the employment of women to the most menial of jobs in Saudi Arabia, in keeping with that country's values and laws concerning gender relations but not our own. Both of these Canadian companies followed the values and laws of their host country, to the chagrin of many Canadians. But an American multinational, ITT, followed the values of its strongly anti-Communist American *home* country by participating in overthrowing the democratically elected Marxist President Allende of Chile (Bosk, 1974). This, too, offended many Canadians.

WHO CONTROLS ECONOMIC INSTITUTIONS?

We have seen that economic power is wielded, not only within and between economic institutions, but also over other sectors of society. In the early days of capitalism, this power was wielded by the owners of capital and of firms. Many of these were *nouveau riche*, and the rise of this new and powerful class of capitalists was a revolutionary development in rigidly stratified societies. We need only recall the names of Rockefeller, Carnegie and Morgan, for example, to comprehend the extent to which those controlling the rapidly consolidating American corporations wielded economic power. Gradually, this control passed to the descendants of the economically powerful through inheritance, and capitalism became more of a conservative than a revolutionary influence on social stratification. And so, a self-perpetuating capitalist class wielded increasing power from the command posts of the economy.

Then, Berle and Means (1967) argue, this power began to break down because of the very growth in size and power of the major corporations. This growth required massive infusions of new capital, which produced a wide dispersion of stock ownership and loss of control by the original owners. Management now acquired control of (i.e., was able to direct the activities of) the economy's largest corporations and so effected a separation of ownership and control. Berle and Means found that 58 percent of the top 200 American corporations were management controlled in 1929. This proportion rose to 85 percent by 1963. Several other studies supported Berle and Means's proposition that, as a corporation grows, the likelihood of management control also grows, not only among American corporations, but among Canadian and European ones as well.

Many social scientists applauded this development. They believed that management control of the economic power wielded by these dominant corporations would benefit society at large. It would break down the rigid class system and replace it with a new, more flexible, system of stratification. Economic power would now be based on achievement and occupation, not inheritance, and social mobility would be enhanced.

Then, in the 1970s, many sociologists began to refute Berle and Means's findings. They argued that a family can retain control of a corporation with even a small minority ownership, if the remaining shares are widely dispersed. In a reanalysis of

Berle and Means's data, Zeitlin (1974) claimed that roughly two-thirds of the top American corporations were retained under ownership control.

In a 1985 study, the Canadian Bankers Association concluded that nine families control 46 percent of the 300 most important companies on the Toronto Stock Exchange. If valid, this study indicates the strength of family control of the economy in contemporary Canada and an incredible concentration of economic power.

CANADIAN ECONOMIC INSTITUTIONS
THE NATURE OF CANADIAN SOCIETY

Are all industrial capitalist societies about the same, or is Canadian society unique? If so, how is it unique?

Canadian sociologists asking these questions see Canadian society as very wealthy, with a per capita production of goods and services among the top half-dozen in the world and not far below that of the United States. Furthermore, they note the flood of American television programs, movies, books and magazines across the border and wonder if a distinct Canadian culture is possible.

On the other hand, several interrelated characteristics of our society distinguish Canadian society from others. These include: the degree of foreign control of our economy; the effect of the regionalism that fragments our society; our unique (and even contradictory) combination of bilingualism and multiculturalism; and our weak sense of national identity. Even Canadian sociology differs from American sociology in its emphasis and approach. An important focus of Canadian sociology is the attempt to explain the nature of our society by determining the effect of our economic institutions on the rest of our social institutions. American sociologists put less emphasis on exploring the uniqueness of their society. When this *is* the topic of their investigations, there is an understandable urge to explain their dominance in terms of the desirable psychological traits of Americans. They contrast these characteristics with the less desirable traits they ascribe to the members of less "advanced" societies, and, *voilà*, the reason for the uniqueness of American society is made clear (Lipset, 1970). Other societies, such as Canada, are naturally less than receptive to explanations based on the shortcomings of their own members. Hence, rather than looking for psychological explanations, we seek institutional ones, such as those developed by economic sociology and political economy.

Innis and the Staples Perspective

The staples perspective was developed by Harold A. Innis (regarded by many as Canada's greatest scholar) to explain the nature of Canada's economic and social development. He developed his perspective by intensively studying Canada's staples trades (i.e., primary industries), such as the cod fisheries, the fur trade, lumber, wheat and minerals, within the context of the world market.

In essence, Innis (1930, 1956) proposed that the Canadian economy was driven by the demands for raw materials of the metropolitan markets of France, then Britain and then the United States. Canadian exploitation of these raw materials stimulated manufacturing in Europe and the United States, but not in Canada. Indeed, the entire energy of the Canadian economy has been expended in producing raw materials and in providing the infrastructure necessary to process, transport and market them. Furthermore, the demands of other countries for these staples has been highly erratic and beyond our control. This has produced a "boom-bust" economy, as the demand for these staples develops, peaks and then declines. Since different staples are produced in different regions of Canada, regional economic peaks and valleys are even more pronounced than national ones.

Why did Canada not diversify out of its concentration on staples production? Because of the *staples trap*. During good times, there is capital to diversify, but not the will to do so. After all, why meddle with prosperity? In bad times, the will to diversify is present, but not the capital.

Innis and others have used this staples perspective to explain many characteristics of Canadian society. Regionalism is seen to be the result of the different economic interests of Canadian regions and the fact that they are all tied more strongly to foreign economies than to each other. If the lifeblood of British Columbia is the American market for lumber and the Japanese demand for coal, is it not natural that British Columbians are more concerned with political and economic developments abroad than at home?

The boom-bust nature of the Canadian staples economy has historically influenced the Canadian pattern of immigration. As the demand for a particular staple in a specific region boomed, it attracted a flood of immigrants, often from a particular part of Europe. These waves of immigrants could settle together in blocks large enough to develop their own institutions and maintain their own culture. Thus, the Canadian multicultural society can be seen as an outgrowth of our staples economy.

So, too, can our weak sense of national identity. Identity, like culture, is passed on by *tradition carriers*—those who have acquired the identity and the culture of the society. However, the staples perspective suggests that the nature of our economy not only influences Canadians to focus outward, but it also draws a flood of new arrivals during boom periods. Then, as boom turns to bust, there is a surge of emigration. For example, during the last quarter of the nineteenth century, 500 000 more people left Canada than arrived here. This erratic population pattern has produced one of the lowest ratios of tradition carriers to new arrivals of any nation in the world (Bell and Tepperman, 1979). Even had we begun with a strong national identity (and many argue that we did not), this low ratio would tend to weaken it over the course of our history.

The staples perspective, then, attempts to explain the particular nature of the Canadian economy (and of our demographic structure as well). It suggests how Canadian economic institutions have affected other elements of our society. It has had, justifiably, a strong influence on Canadian scholarship, both directly and by influencing the development of subsequent approaches. However, we must be careful to neither oversimplify nor exaggerate its message. There are other persuasive explanations for Canadian regionalism, multiculturalism and weak national identity that draw on a variety of approaches (Bell and Tepperman, 1979; Hiller, 1976; Marsden and Harvey, 1979). Nor are Canadians all hewers of wood and drawers of water in contrast to our highly industrialized American cousins, as the staples perspective suggests. In fact, the contribution of manufacturing to the gross national

TABLE 11–2 Value Added in Manufacturing as a Percentage of Gross National Product, Canada and the United States, Selected Years 1870-1970

| | MANUFACTURING VALUE ADDED: % OF G.N.P. | | RATIO— |
YEAR	UNITED STATES	CANADA	US : CANADA
1870	23.0	20.5	1.1:1
1880	23.2	21.9	1.1:1
1890	27.2	25.4	1.1:1
1900	26.4	23.2	1.1:1
1910	24.6	24.6	1.0:1
1919	28.3	27.0	1.1:1
1929	29.7	27.9	1.1:1
1933	25.2	26.2	1.0:1
1939	27.1	27.1	1.0:1
1947	32.1	26.2	1.0:1
1950	31.5	33.0	1.0:1
1960	32.6	28.6	1.1:1
1970	30.7	25.4	1.2:1
1979	30.0	24.6	1.2:1

United States Department of Commerce, 1975: 201, 203, 224, 231, 666, 667; 1984: 431, 746.
Urquhart and Buckley, 1965: 130, 141, 463.
Statistics Canada, various years.

product has been nearly as high in Canada as in the United States ever since Confederation (see Table 11–2). On the other hand, Canadian industry has traditionally emphasized the production of semiprocessed goods for export and the assembly of imported components.

Political Economy: Beyond the Staples Perspective

As political economy became eclipsed by econometrics within the discipline of economics, it began making a major contribution to sociology. Innis set the initial agenda for this research by analysing the divisive effects of the new staples (e.g., minerals, newsprint, petroleum) on Canadian society. He concluded that, in moving from the orbit of British to American imperialism, "Canada moved from colony to nation to colony" (1956: 405). Canadian sociologists then began trying to explain this return to colonial status.

The staples perspective assumed that Canada was a passive hinterland unable to control its own destiny. The political economy of the 1970s, however, produced a

Canadian ruling class that was an active agent in the takeover of Canadian industry. The most influential analysis was developed by Naylor (1972) and Clement (1975). It proposes that the Canadian staples economy fostered the development of merchant capital to finance the production, transport and export of staples to Britain and the United States. It was not in the interest of the descendants of the early import-export merchants to divert capital from the staples trades into domestic manufacturing. American manufacturers filled this void by expanding into Canada with the blessings of the Canadian merchant capitalists. Perhaps the most forceful proponent of this view is Clement, who declares: "Canadian manufacturers could not survive because the commercial ruling class would not allow them to" (1975:80).

The sociological implications of this analysis are enormous. First, it implies that a small group of merchant capitalists operating in the fields of finance, trade, transportation and utilities shaped Canadian economic development to serve its own selfish ends. This, in turn, suggests that this group wielded enormous economic and political power. In fact, studies have shown that the economically powerful have had close ties to the political system and held many important political posts ever since Confederation (Smith and Tepperman, 1974; Clement, 1975). Secondly, the resulting invasion of American manufacturing enterprises ultimately led to the establishment of American economic power in Canada. Thereafter, the power of Canadian governments was constrained by the economic power of American MNE and the need to maintain good relations with the United States (Levitt, 1970; Marchak, 1979). In all this we can see the influence of the Marxist perspective, which argues that economy shapes society and economic power affects other institutions.

However, this explanation of Canadian economic development (known as the *merchants-against-industry argument*) has not been universally accepted. One study finds, on the contrary, that, historically, there was no cleavage between Canadian merchants and industrialists, for they were often the same people (Richardson, 1982). This same study also contests the supposed dominance of merchants over industrialists.

Another extensive analysis compares industrialization in Canada and several other nations. It finds, in all but Canada, that the landholding and agricultural classes helped shape the political and financial institutions to promote industrialization. To a significant degree then, this study suggests that the Canadian economy was shaped by the defeat of elements of the Canadian farmers in the rebellions of 1837 (Laxer, 1985). On the other hand, Carroll (1985) proposes looking beyond internal class dynamics, and even beyond the relationships between Canadian and American capital to explain the degree of foreign control of Canada's economy and society. Adequate explanation, he contends, will only come within the context of a Marxist theory of imperialism.

There have been several objectives in outlining these contending explanations of the development of Canadian economic institutions. First, the foregoing illustrates the dynamic nature of these institutions. Secondly, it presents, within the Canadian context, the contending views of the classical sociologists concerning the interaction of economy and society. We can see that some explanations give primacy to the economy and others, to the polity. And finally, it gives an idea of the complex and fascinating national and international relationships between the economic and political institutions of society.

ECONOMIC INSTITUTIONS AND REGIONALISM

Innis's staples perspective partly explained the high degree of Canadian regionalism in economic terms. More recently, Canadian sociologists have built upon Innis's theory to significantly extend our understanding of Canadian regionalism.

"The most significant feature of Canadian social organization is not its unity, but its regional diversity" (Matthews, 1980:51). Why should this be? Why should Canadian society be more regionally divided than the societies of Britain, France and the United States? The most persuasive explanations focus on the development of Canadian economic institutions.

There are many objective indicators, such as income and educational attainment, of profound regional differences in Canada. For example, Ontario's per capita personal income has remained almost exactly double the personal incomes in Prince Edward Island and Newfoundland over the past 50 years (Matthews, 1980). These dissimilarities are the result of the different economies of our provinces and regions. The economy of central Canadian society is based on foreign-controlled manufacturing. In fact, nearly three-quarters of all Canadian manufacturing is located within the narrow Montreal-Windsor corridor (Brym, 1985). On the other hand, the Atlantic provinces base their economies on fishing and other primary industries; the Prairies depend on agricultural products and oil for export and British Columbia on forestry and mining.

Regional specialization is partly the result of geography, of course. But it is also partly the result of political action, such as the National Policy of the late nineteenth century and the Crows Nest Pass agreement of 1897. These policies helped open Canada's western agricultural frontier as an internal economic colony of central Canada. Why? Largely because of the need for a new market for central Canadian industry, which was facing bankruptcy at the time.

It should be easy to understand that a wheat farmer, an autoworker, a fisherman and a banker all see the world differently. They earn their daily bread in very different ways, they live in different types of communities and the institutions they are connected with take different forms. Thus, Canadian regionalism is both an economic and a social phenomenon (Matthews, 1980). But, in the tradition of both Marx and Durkheim, it can be seen as ultimately derived from economic activity.

Canadian regionalism can, perhaps, be analysed best in terms of dominance and dependency. Canada itself is dominated by the United States, and this limits our ability to forge stronger interregional ties (Marsden and Harvey, 1979). Within Canada, the economic dominance of the central provinces has been reflected in, and reinforced by, the political dominance of Ontario and Quebec. Those occasions where the location of economic and political power did not coincide, such as the period of rising Quebec nationalism and the Albertan oil boom, have been turbulent times of regionally based social change.

SUMMARY

This chapter has shown that economic institutions produce and distribute the wealth of a society. Although these functions are common to all societies, they have been fulfilled in very different ways throughout human history. Sociologists are interested in the different forms economic institutions may take, of course. But most of all, sociological curiosity seeks to learn how economic institutions relate to the other institutions of a historically specific society. In other words, sociologists differentiate themselves from economists by setting out to explain the relationship between economy and society. This has been the major objective of this chapter.

Readers may, perhaps, be discouraged by the lack of agreement among Canadian sociologists on a topic as important as the development of the Canadian economy. But actually, this controversy only shows that sociologists are willing to search for answers to extraordinarily complex puzzles. Indeed, it is disagreement that provides excitement in any developing science.

DISCUSSION QUESTIONS

1. Marx, Weber and Durkheim all studied the conditions under which one form of economic institution will be transformed into another. What are the key elements of the explanations developed by each of these classical sociologists?

2. Using the development and the possible decline of the "throw-away" society as an example, show how economy and society affect each other.

3. Why should Canadians study the impact of multinational enterprise on societies?

4. Does it matter who controls the major economic institutions of a society? If so, why? If not, why not?

5. How does the study of Canadian economic development help us to understand regionalism in Canada?

12

Mass Media and Influence

Susannah Wilson

INTRODUCTION: MASS MEDIA AND MASS COMMUNICATION

As part of our daily routines, many of us wake up to the radio, read the paper over our morning coffee and read or listen to the radio en route to school or work. During the day we may discuss the news, the game or the soap with our friends or colleagues. Later, in the evening, we may relax by flipping through a magazine or watching a little television. Some of our media consumption will be active and purposeful, as when we make a point of watching *Dallas*, the Leafs or *The National*. At other times, we use the media more as background or company. Yet, whether we use the media as entertainment or as a source of information, we North Americans are avid media consumers.

The mass media are a fundamental part of the social environment. They punctuate our daily routines and fill much of our leisure time. They provide information and interpret world events. In many ways, the media both reflect and shape our definitions of social reality. In this chapter, we will look at some ways sociologists have analysed the mass media and the process of mass communication. Generally, sociologists assume that the media are social institutions which operate within particular cultural and historical contexts. The implications of this assumption will depend on the researcher's particular theoretical orientation. We will begin by looking at two theoretical traditions that have guided research in this field. The first is the empirical tradition, which developed in North America; the second is the European critical tradition. Within the last 10 to 15 years, critical theory has had a considerable influence on North American studies of mass communication.

PERSPECTIVES ON MASS COMMUNICATION

THE EMPIRICAL TRADITION

The study of mass communication has been influenced by the introduction of new media and changing images of human nature and the nature of mass society. A major preoccupation has been the media's influence on the attitudes and behaviour of individuals. The effectiveness of wartime propaganda indicated that the mass media were indeed powerful social forces since they apparently played a big part in mobilizing public opinion in support of the war effort. Later, when other tests of the direct effects of the media on behaviour proved inconclusive (see Klapper, 1960), this stimulus-response model was largely abandoned. As researchers began to discover how our families, friends and colleagues (i.e., our social networks) influence media consumption, the social context of mass communication was given greater emphasis. Currently, the influence of the media is seen primarily as shaping definitions of social reality. Effects are now understood to be indirect and cumulative, although no less powerful.

Lasswell's Model

Lasswell (1948) described the process of mass communication as "who says what, through what channel, to whom, with what effect." This simple statement is no doubt the most frequently quoted definition in the field. It draws attention to three continuing concerns: 1) the social organization of mass communications; 2) content and 3) effects. Lasswell's model also makes assumptions about the nature of mass communication that are no longer accepted. It assumes a one-way causal relationship and pictures members of the audience as passive recipients. As Carey (1975) describes it, the North American approach to mass communication has been based on a transportation model. In other words, messages are carried from communicator to audience.

The Functions of the Media

According to Wright (1975), mass communication specialists are engaged in: surveillance of the environment (gathering and distributing information); correlation of the parts of the society (interpreting information and prescribing conduct); transmission of the social heritage (communicating information, values and norms) and, finally, entertainment. Some messages may serve only one of these functions, or the functions may be combined in a single message. Certain messages serve different purposes for different audience members. Because of this, programs such as soap operas or situation comedies, which seem to offer nothing more than fantasy or escape, may also serve the functions of surveillance of the environment and correlation of the parts of society. For example, some evidence suggests that the entertainment media are a source of both normative behaviour and advice in coping with everyday problems. Later in the chapter we will look at a study that suggests that soap opera suicides may trigger imitative behaviour in some members of the audience.

Wright (1975) suggested a framework for the analysis of the media which focuses on these four funtions. This framework provides an inventory for organizing research questions and findings. For Wright, the basic question is:

	(1) manifest	(3) functions	
What are the	and	and	of mass-communicated
	(2) latent	(4) dysfunctions	

(5) surveillance (news)	for the (9) society
(6) correlation (editorial activity)	(10) individual
(7) cultural transmission	(11) subgroups
(8) entertainment	(12) cultural systems?

McQuail (1983:79) has added a fifth purpose to Wright's list (5 through 8 above): mobilization. "Nearly everywhere, the media are expected to advance national interests and promote certain key values and behavior patterns, but especially so in times of war or other crisis."

The sociology of mass communication in North America until the 1960s was characterized by an accumulation of research findings generated by models like Wright's and Lasswell's. The field was fragmented and lacked a unifying body of theory. Most of the studies were based on large-scale audience surveys or quantitative content analysis and were preoccupied with the question of effects.

THE CRITICAL CHALLENGE

In Europe, communications studies developed very differently. European studies shared a critical tradition informed by the humanities as much as by the social sciences. This orientation paid more attention to the political, cultural, economic and historical context of communication than was usual in North American research.

Many articles in a special issue of the *Journal of Communication* (Summer, 1983) entitled "Ferment in the Field" dealt with the differences between these two approaches. Some authors saw the rift as a fundamental one. Others identified areas of cross-fertilization. Differences between the empirical and critical approaches are reflected in the selection of problems, the methods used and the ideological orientations of the researchers (Melody and Mansell, 1983; Smythe and Van Dinh, 1983). As Smythe and Van Dinh (1983:117) argue: "All of us have our predispositions, either to criticize and try to change the existing political-economic order or to defend and strengthen it." The first position describes critical research; the second, the empirical (or administrative) tradition.[1] *Administrative research* raises questions that relate to models like Lasswell's and Wright's and uses quantitative methods of analysis. *Critical research* (which includes Marxist analyses) seeks "sharp critical analysis of communications phenomena in their *systemic* context" (Smythe and Van Dinh, 1983:123).

THE IDEOLOGICAL ROLE OF THE MEDIA

The major difference between administrative research and critical analysis is the "rediscovery of ideology" by critical theorists (Hall, 1982). Critical theorists consider the ideological role of the media in its broadest sense. The media create definitions of reality and thereby shape perceptions of the social world, perceptions that frame and legitimize existing social arrangements.

But the media (except publicly supported media) are also business enterprises and operate under a system of economic constraints. On one level, economic constraints will determine the *range and type* of media available in any community. On another level, economic constraints will determine *budget allocations* within media organizations (Golding and Murdock, 1979). Smythe described the main function of the media as creating audiences for advertisers. "The information, entertainment and educational material transmitted to the audience is an inducement (gift, bribe or 'free lunch') to recruit potential members of the audience and to maintain their loyal attention" (Smythe, 1977:5). Pressure to maximize audience size has a neutralizing effect on content.

The general concern with the ideological role of the media is expressed by researchers in several ways. Some focus on the nature of the content; others, on the protection of class interests by those who own or control the media. The Centre for Contemporary Cultural Studies at Birmingham, England, has developed a unique interdisciplinary approach to media studies. Hall, one of the most influential members of this group, is interested in the meanings attributed to content by members

---

[1] These two terms (critical approach, administrative approach) are used interchangeably by contributors to the symposium, although some (including Smythe and Van Dinh) prefer one or the other term.

of audiences. His method is to concentrate on the *encoding* and *decoding* of media messages. Encoding is the process whereby the media gives meaning to events by putting them in a context that supports dominant interests. Audiences, composed of a number of different groups, decode media messages in terms of their own definitions of reality. In other words, we cannot assume that all members of the audience will interpret media events in the same way.

The Glasgow Media Group (1977, 1980) has approached this issue from a different angle. *Bad News* (1977) studied news coverage of industrial disputes in Britain. The study argues that the way news is handled (i.e., the criteria of news-worthiness and the placement of news items) reflects an antiunion bias. News reports focus on certain key industries, particularly the automotive industry, and disputes that cause the most public inconvenience. Newscasters imply that industrial disputes are not in the public interest. This study also argued that the structure and placement of interviews implicitly supports management's view, although the fact that both views are presented gives the impression of impartiality. For example, interviews with managers were typically conducted in surroundings, such as executive offices, that reinforced management's authoritative role. Interviews with union represen-tatives were conducted out-of-doors or on picket lines, against a background of disorder. Interviewers typically began by asking the union representative to *justify* the union's action. The authors concluded that television news distorts the nature of industrial disputes.

In the following section, we will turn to a second important focus of analyses of the ideological role of the media: the issue of increased concentration of media ownership.

Media Ownership in Canada

In Canada, the study of media ownership has been addressed in two major studies of the Canadian elite: *The Vertical Mosaic* (Porter, 1965) and *The Canadian Corporate Elite* (Clement, 1975). Two federal commissions have also documented the increased concentration of media ownership in Canada. The Special Senate Committee on the Mass Media—usually called the Davey Report, after its chief commissioner, Senator Keith Davey—was published in 1971. Ten years later, the Kent Commission (The Royal Commission on Newspapers) was published.

Clement has argued that in capitalist societies, control of the media, "whether by the state or big business, places them squarely in the realm of the dominant interest groups already powerful in other fields" (Clement, 1975:280). The ideology artic-ulated in the media supports and maintains existing institutions and social arrange-ments, and thus acts as an effective agent of social control. "The ideological system must provide the justification for the economic system, the political system, and so forth, and this it does by attempting to show that the existing arrangements conform with the traditional value system (Porter, 1965:460)." The danger of increased concentration is that there are fewer and fewer independent interpretations of the Canadian value system in the mass media.

Privately owned media will only survive if they are financially viable. Newspapers particularly have been hard hit by the introduction of television in Canada (in 1952), by the rising costs of new technologies for typesetting and editing and by the increased costs of raw materials and distribution. These costs make it increasingly difficult for independent owners to survive. Large corporations whose properties are concentrated can more readily take advantage of economies of scale.

When the Davey report was published in 1970, it drew attention to the extent of corporate concentration in the Canadian media. In the 103 communities that supported either a daily newspaper or a primary television station, there were 485 units of mass communication (daily newspapers, radio or television stations). Of these, over half were controlled or partially owned by groups. This included 66 percent of Canada's daily newspapers, 49 percent of our television stations and 47 percent of our radio stations. Furthermore, media control was being concentrated in the hands of fewer and fewer large corporations. The Davey commission rather tentatively concluded that this situation could have the effect of reducing the number of diverse and antagonistic sources from which we derive our view of the social world.

When, on August 27, 1980, a day subsequently referred to in the press as "Black Wednesday," the Winnipeg *Tribune* and the Ottawa *Journal* shut down, concentration became a public concern. Black Wednesday followed a series of takeovers and closings that included the demise of *The Montreal Star*, which ceased publication following a long strike. What made these two closings so contentious was that the closing of the *Tribune* (a Southam paper) and the *Journal* (a Thomson paper) created, in both cases, a monopoly for the other party (for Thomson in Winnipeg and for Southam in Ottawa). Not surprisingly, there were accusations of collusion, and the two companies were charged with conspiracy to reduce competition.

In what many would call a "typical Canadian reaction," the response to increased public concern was the Royal Commission on Newspapers. The commission report, which was tabled in 1981, concluded that concentration of ownership is "entirely unacceptable for a democratic society." Some of its recommendations were that acquisitions be restricted, that ownership of different media in the same city by one person or group be banned and that financial incentives be introduced to encourage independent ownership.

The growth of media conglomerates (see Figure 12–1 on page 310), close connections between the media and corporate and government elites and the extensive use of cost-effective measures, such as wire services, as a source of news make it hard to argue that the view of the world presented in the media will be a diverse one. Although the effects of increased concentration of ownership on media content are difficult to measure, critics generally claim that the media have "tended to become bland, undoctrinaire, unlikely to disturb the status quo" (Kesterton, 1983:13).

MEDIA CONTENT

In Chapter 4 we talked briefly about the media as agents of socialization: The media reinforce social behaviour and definitions of social reality. In other words, by focusing on some groups and not others or by stereotyping social characteristics, the media provide important lessons about power and influence. For this reason, those concerned about sexual and racial inequality identify the media as major contributors to stereotypes. For example, in a classic study of the portrayal of majority and minority Americans in magazine fiction, Bereleson and Salter (1946) found that

Figure 12-1 Everywhere in Chains

Enlargement of area indicated left.

Share of English-Language Newspaper Circulation by Ownership			
	1970 % Share	1980	Share Change
Independents	40.79%	25.8%	14.9%
Southam	21.5	32.8	+ 11.3
Thomson	10.4	25.9	+ 15.5
Sun Group	—	8.3	+ 8.3
Irving	2.7	3.0	+ 0.3
Others	2.9	4.3	+ 1.4
FP Publications	31.8	—	− 31.8

Share of French-Language Newspaper Circulation			
	1970 % Share	1980	Share Change
Independents	51.0%	10.1%	− 40.9%
Quebecor	11.0	40.5	+ 29.5
Desmarais	38.2	28.8	− 9.4
Unimedia	—	14.7	+ 14.7

- 1 Chatham
- 2 Leamington
- 3 Windsor
- 4 Sarnia
- 5 Hanover
- 6 Owen Sound
- 7 Collingwood
- 8 Midland
- 9 Orillia
- 10 Barrie
- 11 Peterborough
- 12 Belleville
- 13 Trenton
- 14 Oshawa
- 15 Toronto
- 16 Orangeville
- 17 Brampton
- 18 Georgetown
- 19 Guelph
- 20 Cambridge
- 21 Woodstock
- 22 St. Thomas
- 23 Simcoe
- 24 Brantford
- 25 Hamilton
- 26 Dunnville
- 27 Welland
- 28 Niagara Falls

Permission by *MacLean's* Magazine

native, white Protestant Americans were the most numerous, the richest and most highly approved characters in the stories. In underrepresenting minorities, the media reinforce our views about who counts in our society.

Certainly, we see little evidence of the rich diversity of Canada's cultural heritage in our daily media diet. In part, this is because of our overwhelming dependence on American television and magazines. However, the fact that we can now readily identify black television heroes and heroines, newscasters and models suggest that there has been considerable progress in this area over the last two decades. Yet, in the Canadian media, the underrepresentation of members of Canadian ethnic or racial minorities persists.

Pierre Berton's book, *Hollywood's Canada* (1975), is full of examples of stereotypes of Mounties, French Canadians, native Canadians and of Canada's geography and climate, as the following exerpt shows.

HAPPY-GO-LUCKY ROGUES IN TUQUES

The impression still persists in some parts of the world and, indeed, in some parts of neighbouring United States, that almost every Canadian speaks French. I have even met, in the course of various travels, some people—again including Americans—who assume that French, and only French, is the mother tongue of Canada. (Others, equally misinformed, believe that Canada is actually a part of the United States. That view is especially prevalent in eastern Europe, where little distinction is made between the two countries.)

That idea could come from one medium only: the movies. In Hollywood's Canada the forest people were almost always French-Canadians, although they weren't confined to Quebec. Actually there appear to have been more French-Canadians outside of Quebec than in the ancient province. As we'll see, Hollywood made several pictures set in Quebec which are remarkable for the absence of French-speaking Canadians. But elsewhere, from southern British Columbia to northern Manitoba, from the Yukon border to the Cypress Hills, they turned up in picture after picture, speaking a kind of pidgin tongue ("Dees Canada, she's lak beeg woom-man!"), sporting their colourful tuques and sashes, smoking their clay pipes, indulging in broad gestures, grimacing and capering, seducing willing women, raping unwilling ones, filching deeds for lost gold mines or simply sitting around in the virgin wilderness scraping away on fiddles.

There were only four classes of forest dwellers who were not French-Canadians: prospectors, mounted policemen, lumbermen, and Hudson's Bay Company factors.

The prospectors were usually Americans, invading Canada in order to strike it rich before retreating to warmer climes. Most were amateurs, such as Clark Gable in The Call of the Wild, while others were really cowboys, like Randolph Scott in The Cariboo Trail or James Stewart in The Far Country.

The mounted policemen tended to be Irish, with names like Moran, Callaghan, O'Rourke, and Shaughnessy. Eleven of the twenty names of policemen which appear in motion-picture titles, for instance, are Irish. O'Malley of the Mounted turns up three times.

The lumbermen were mostly Anglo-Saxons and they came in two models: the Roistering Lumberjack and the Villainous Timber Magnate. The roistering image was indelibly established in 1918 by William S. Hart, the pioneer western star, in the title role of Blue Blazes Rawden, a man with an apparently hollow leg and a legendary reputation ("The boss one time he keel a bear weeth hees hands!").

"Going to hit that Hell hole, Timber Cove, like a blaze of glory!" Rawden shouts at the beginning of the picture as he and his men, firing their pistols into the air, advance upon the little lumber town for an evening of sport. In the saloon Rawden swallows his liquor neat, smashes the empty glasses on the floor, beats up the bartender, one La Barge ("the best rough and tumble fighter in the Cove"), calls for more booze ("Whisky, you frog-eater or I'll swab your own bar with you"), guzzles it straight from the bottle, plucks a half-breed girl, Babette DuFresne, from the arms of the monocled proprietor, Ladyfingers Hilgard, and finally in a *mano a mano* gun-fight shoots Hilgard dead.

It is an exhausting movie—almost as exhausting for the audience as it must have been for Hart, who appears to be engaged in calisthenics to the very end of the picture when, striken by remorse (and also by a bullet), he stumbles off into the storm to Die Alone. No one, certainly not George Brent or even Barton MacLane, who were pitted against each other two decades later in another hard-fisted lumbering yarn, God's Country and the Woman, equalled Hart's portrayal.

From *Hollywood's Canada* by Pierre Berton. Used by permission of The Canadian Publishers, McClelland and Stewart Limited, Toronto.

THE MEDIA IMAGE OF WOMEN

The media were a particular target of the women's movement in the 1970s. Critiques focused on three interrelated issues: stereotyped portrayals of women in the media; the underrepresentation of women in decision-making positions in media organizations,[2] and the media's trivialization of the movement itself.[3] Literally hundreds

[2] Betty Friedan (1963) pointed out two decades ago that even in the world of women's magazines women have had little impact. The image of the "Happy Housewife Heroine" of 1950s magazine fiction was the creation of *male* writers and editors.

[3] In the 1980s, the number of these kinds of studies dropped. There are several possible explanations for this. Perhaps feminists have turned their attention to violence and pornography in the media, although the change could also be part of the antifeminist backlash.

of studies have documented the numerical underrepresentation and sterotyping of women in the media. These studies have looked at all types of media and all age groups. The results are consistent (although advertisements seem to be the worst offenders and soap operas an exception). Women are underrepresented and trivialized in media content, and they appear in a limited range of roles.

Butler and Paisley (1980:148–169) developed a *consciousness scale* to classify images of women in advertising. They describe the scale as:

Level 1	"Put her down"	(Women portrayed as sex objects, props or decorations)
Level 2	"Keep her in her place"	(Depicts women in the home or in traditional working roles)
Level 3	"Give her two places"	(Shows women as concerned with both career and family)
Level 4	"Acknowledge that she is equal"	(Shows men and women as equally competent in the same roles)
Level 5	"Nonstereotypic"	(Indicates that women and men are able to be superior according to their own talents, motivations and interests, not according to their sex)

When this scale was tested with magazine advertisements and television commercials, most ads were categorized as at levels 1 or 2.

Gerbner (1978) is very pessimistic about what he sees as the increasingly repressive image of women in the media. This image, he argues, is indicative of the part played by the media in cultivating resistance to change. In Gerbner's view, the media do not reflect changes in women's lives; rather, they are staging a counterattack on the women's movement and its aims. Coining the phrase "women's lib" is one example of such symbolic annihilation (Tuchman, Daniels and Beret, 1978, 1979), for it makes light of the aims of the movement and the fundamental inequalities the women's movement has tried to rectify. In part, the media's response to the women's movement has to do with definitions of what is newsworthy. Legal, political or educational reforms do not make headlines. Bra-burning (if, in fact, this *ever* occurred) does. News is defined in terms of *events*, not *issues*, and reporters make distinctions between "hard" or "soft" news. Hard news receives immediate coverage; soft news can be held over. The founding of the largest and most influential women's group in America, the National Organization of Women, was treated as soft news by *The New York Times*. It was reported on the women's page, several days late, placed between a recipe for turkey stuffing and a fashion bulletin (Tuchman, 1978:201–02).

CULTIVATION ANALYSIS

The cultural indicators study of Gerbner and his associates was described in Chapter 3 (on page 72). This ambitious research project relies on two sources of data. 1) *Message system analysis* is based on a periodic content analysis of American television drama. 2) *Cultivation analysis* is the investigation (by survey research) of viewer perceptions associated with the recurrent features of television content. The content studies have revealed consistent distortions of a number of aspects of American life. For example, in the world of television, men outnumber women three to one; most of the characters are professionals and law enforcers; and over half of all leading characters are involved in acts of violence. It is Gerbner's contention that "the more time spent 'living' in the world of television, the more likely one is to report perceptions of social reality which can be traced to (or are congruent with) television's most persistent representations of life and society" (1980:14).

While Gerbner's work is not without its critics, some consider it a breakthrough (Van Poecke, 1980). Perhaps the most widely read of Gerbner's studies are the violence profiles (Gerbner et al., 1980). These profiles show a relatively stable pattern of violence and victimization in American television drama from year to year. An average of 70 percent of all prime time programs and 92 percent of all children's programs contained some violence (Gerbner et al., 1980). Surveys found that heavy viewers were more apt to express feelings of mistrust, apprehension and danger.

Gerbner et al. (1980) introduced two additional concepts—mainstreaming and resonance—to clarify the cultivation effect. *Mainstreaming* refers to the common outlook cultivated by television among heavy viewers, which seems to override whatever differences exist among them. In other words, despite differences in race, income or education, heavy television viewers tend to share a relatively homogenous outlook. "*Resonance* may occur when a feature of the television world has special salience for a group, e.g., greater fear among city dwellers, or perceived over-victimization of the elderly" (Gerbner et al., 1980:23).

A Canadian study by Doob and McDonald (1979) found a relationship between heavy television viewing and an expectation of being a victim of violence for residents of Toronto. However, when area of residence was controlled, there was little difference between light and heavy viewers. People who lived in high crime areas were more afraid. *But*, they also tended to be heavy television viewers and to watch more violent television. Doob and McDonald concluded that television was not a direct cause of fear of victimization. Gerbner interprets the findings of the Toronto study in terms of *resonance*. People who live in high crime areas "receive a 'double dose' of messages that the world is violent, and consequently show the strongest association between viewing and fear" (1980:20).

Two American researchers (Beurkel-Rothfuss and Mayes, 1981) tested the cultivation effect of television for soap-opera viewers. People who watch "soaps" are typically young, and a large number are students. They watch them for several reasons, including boredom, escape, companionship, relaxation and advice on problems. Since the soaps usually dramatize many personal and social problems (divorce, infidelity, serious illness, nervous breakdown and criminal involvement), the researchers predicted that heavy viewers would exaggerate the prevalence of these problems in the real world.

Their sample consisted of 290 students, 71 percent of whom watched at least one episode a week. Their findings confirmed their theory. Increased exposure was positively related to exaggerated estimates of the number of people who have been in jail, committed crimes, been divorced and so on. That there was a statistically significant difference between viewers and nonviewers supports the cultivation theory.

CONTENT ANALYSIS AND SEMIOTICS

Because of its accessibility and consistent form, media content has been widely used for a number of different research purposes. The method typically employed is *content analysis*. In content analysis, the researcher creates a coding scheme, much as the survey researcher creates a questionnaire. Strictly speaking, content analysis cannot be used to make inferences about communicators' intentions or the effects of the message on the audience, although these are often implied.

In the last decade, some sociologists have been influenced by new directions in linguistics and have begun to apply these linguistic models to the study of media content. This approach, known as *semiotics* (the science of signs), is concerned with media messages as structured wholes rather than as fragments of messages that are usually analysed by content analysis. For example, a sign is assumed to have meaning, not because of the number of times it occurs but because of its relational qualities or the context in which it occurs.

McQuail (1983:130–33) has drawn a comparison between this approach and traditional content analysis. Unlike content analysis, semiotics does not comply with the accepted criteria of scientific research. In other words, it is not quantitative, nor are the results generalizable. Semiotics concentrates on the latent meaning of messages, and so is useful for uncovering consistent structures in particular genres of communication, such as detective novels or popular romances. Furthermore, unlike content analysis (which assumes that the meanings of media content are more or less universally perceived), semiotics assumes that communicators and audiences attach different meanings to message systems.

MANUFACTURING THE NEWS

Several studies have focused on the process of "creating" news. Some (Fishman, 1980; Gans, 1980; and Tuchman, 1978) have approached this research as participant observers. Their interest is in how the news is chosen, covered, produced and disseminated. Others (Glasgow Media Group 1977, 1980) focus on the cultural meaning of news stories and the *methods of signification* used in television news. For example, an impression of impartiality is created by the use of actual footage of events or by on-location interviews, coupled with the "neutral" voice of the newscaster. As described earlier, these signifying conventions disguise underlying biases in the selection and placement of news items.

One interesting conclusion of studies of media content concerns the stability and predictability of news coverage (McQuail, 1983:144–46). This consistency has led some to conclude that news coverage can be described as a particular genre. One of the consistent elements is the regularity of structure. For example, the amount of time devoted to items reported in television news varies little over time or across cultures. "What is striking is the extent to which a presumably unpredictable universe of events seems open to incorporation, day after day, into much the same temporal or spatial frame" (McQuail, 1983:145).

The consistency of news content can be explained in part by the needs of the production process, cost considerations and credibility concerns. Some groups and institutions will have greater access to reporters because they are considered more credible or because they have the resources to package their message in usable form. Consistency is also the result of the way gatekeepers select the news. Gatekeeping includes "all forms of information control that may arise in decisions about message encoding, such as selection, shaping, display, timing, withholding, or repetition of entire message components" (Donohue et al., 1972:43). The consistency of the final product reflects the journalists' professional training, which engenders a particular understanding of the needs of the news organization and the nature of the audience. Journalists see their role as a powerful one. American journalists rank themselves as having less power than business elites but more than other groups, including labour, consumer groups or intellectuals. When asked who *ought* to have power, they rank themselves first (Lichter and Rothman, 1981).

MEDIA EFFECTS

A key preoccupation in the study of the mass media has been the question of the influence of the media on social behaviour. Early studies of the media assumed that it had a strong influence on social behaviour. Later, this assumption gave way to a more cautious view. Increased skepticism about the media's power was reflected in Bereleson's assessment: "Some kinds of communication, on some kinds of issues, brought to the attention of some kinds of people under some kinds of conditions have some kinds of effects" (1949:500). This shift in thinking resulted from a changing conceptualization of "effects." Early studies looked for *direct* effects of *specific* messages. Now effects are understood to be both *long term* and *indirect*.

As Katz recently proclaimed, "The best thing that has happened to communications research is that it has stopped frantically searching for evidence of the ability of the media to change opinions, attitudes and *actions* in the short run" (1983:52).

On the other hand, many critical theorists object to the separate study of media effects. As Gitlin (1978) argues, trying to measure the impact of a particular media stimulus is like expecting a fish to discover the effects of water. "How can we 'measure' the 'impact' of a social force which is omnipresent within social life and which has a great deal to do with constituting it?" (Gitlin, 1980:9).

In the following sections, we will look at four ways of identifying media effects. Together they suggest the range of concern. The first two, agenda setting and the spiral of silence, describe the role of the media in creating public opinion. The concluding section addresses the issues of the effects of media violence and imitative behaviour.

AGENDA SETTING

Agenda setting refers to the process whereby social issues are brought to the public's attention. "Audiences not only learn about public issues and other matters from the media, they also learn how much importance to attach to an issue or topic from the emphasis the media places upon it" (McCoombs and Shaw, 1976:18). Issues that get more media attention will become increasingly familiar and important to us. Issues that are not identified in the media will decline in importance. Much of the research on agenda setting has concentrated on political campaigns. McCoombs and Shaw (1976) used the media's portrayal of Watergate as an example of agenda setting. The issue of Watergate did not attract public attention until press exposure was accelerated by the televised Senate hearings. Public opinion surveys showed that only 52 percent of Americans knew about Watergate in September, 1972. By June, 1973, 98 percent knew about it.

THE SPIRAL OF SILENCE

German sociologist Elisabeth Noelle-Neuman (1984) described the media's influence on public opinion as a *spiral of silence*. Her theory rests on the assumption that our opinions depend on what we *perceive* to be the opinions of others. The media help to establish our perceptions of prevailing opinion. Noelle-Neuman argued that most people try to avoid voicing unpopular beliefs. The assessment we make of public opinion will determine our willingness to express our own opinions. It follows that opinions perceived to be unpopular will be less frequently voiced. "The appearance of strength becomes a self-fulfilling prophesy; those who think they are in the majority are more willing to speak out, those who think they are in the minority have an extra incentive to remain silent" (Taylor, 1982:311). This spiralling process establishes *one* opinion as the prevailing one. An example of how this process works is found in the media portrayal of the political climate at election time. During the 1980 presidential campaign, Glynn and McLeod (1984) found that those who believed the political climate *favoured* their candidate said they were more willing to enter into political discussions. Others preferred to remain silent.

MEDIA VIOLENCE

Questions about media effects reach their most controversial when they deal with the possible negative effects of violence or pornography. This is not a recent concern. Although most attention today centres on television violence (particularly in rock videos), movies, comics and magazines have all been considered potentially dangerous sources of influence, especially for young people. There is a strong feeling among the general public that the negative effects of violent media content are self-evident, that the sheer amount of violence in the media speaks for itself. When this feeling is coupled with anxiety about the increasing number of incidents of violent or antisocial behaviour seemingly triggered by the media, concern is understandably heightened. Gerbner's research (referred to earlier in this chapter) found that people who viewed a lot of television violence had exaggerated feelings about the amount of violence in American society and so were more inclined to favour increased social control.

For the sociologist, this issue presents a particular challenge, for it involves an analysis of content creation, the roles of regulators, cultural autonomy and technological innovation as well as the obvious concern about the effects of media violence. Much of the disagreement among academics has centred on whether or not violent portrayals cause subsequent deviant or antisocial behaviour. This might occur in several ways. Very infrequently, the effect might be direct or imitative, as in the case of *copycat crimes*. A second, more subtle and more pervasive problem is the media's role in creating definitions of social reality. For example, we may tolerate high levels of violence because we have come to think "that's the way life is."

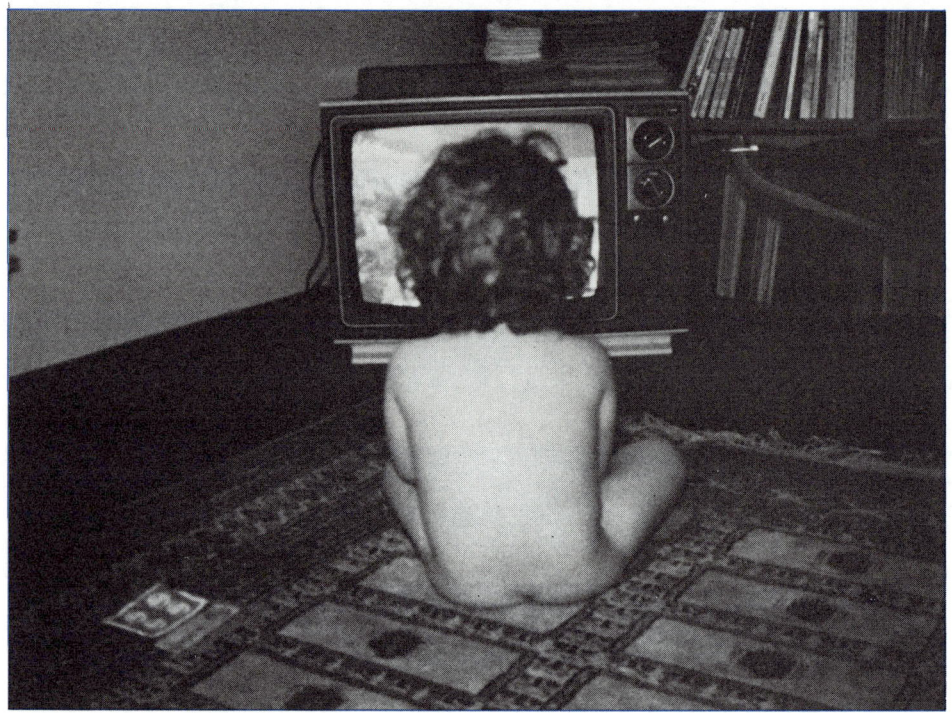

Ninety-two percent of all children's programs contain some violence.

Some of the difficulties researchers have faced in sorting out the effects of television violence are methodological. Most effects studies have been done by psychologists in the laboratory. Under laboratory conditions, subjects display more aggressive behaviour than control groups when exposed to television portrayals of violence. It is not clear, however, whether the kinds of imitative behaviour that occur in the laboratory also occur in normal settings. Experiments may confidently conclude that the response (aggressive behaviour) was triggered by the stimulus (violent media portrayals) but not that this will also occur outside of the lab. In natural settings, the difficulty lies in controlling extraneous variables. In other words, how can we be sure that the behaviour we observed was, in fact, triggered by the media and not something else? In methodological terms, experiments have the advantage of control, whereas field studies have the advantage of being able to be generalized. The greater the control, the less the generalizability.

IMITATIVE BEHAVIOUR

Strong support for the idea that the media plays an important role in triggering imitative behaviour comes from a series of studies done in the United States. These studies looked at the relationship between rates of suicide and violent death and the reporting or fictionalized representation of similar behaviour in the media. Phillips (1979, 1982) and Bollen and Phillips (1982) found that the incidence of suicide rose following newspaper reports of suicides and that the increase was related to the amount of publicity given the suicide story. The effect was greater in the geographic area where the story received greatest coverage. The researchers also investigated accidental deaths, on the assumption that some suicides will be disguised as such. Motor vehicle fatalities and noncommercial airplane crashes also increased following front-page suicide or murder-suicide stories. Increases in accidental deaths were also greatest following highly publicized accounts and were greatest in areas where the stories were most publicized. Similar results occurred whether the stimulus was television news stories or newspaper accounts. "Taken together, all of these findings support the hypothesis that publicized suicides trigger imitative behavior; sometimes this behavior is overt (in the form of an explicit suicide) and sometimes covert (in the form of automobile or airplane accidents)" (Bollen and Phillips, 1982:807).

Phillips looked at this same question using soap-opera suicides. These are relatively easy to track, as they are reported in weekly newspaper plot summaries. Phillips felt that "because they attract large, devoted audiences, soap operas may have the capacity to influence the attitudes and behaviour of many people" (1982:1343). His results showed that his reasoning was correct. The number of suicides, motor vehicle deaths and nonfatal motor vehicle accidents increased in the period following soap-opera suicides. Furthermore, the numbers peaked on the first and sixth days after the soap-opera suicides, which Phillips felt indicated impulsive versus planned reactions.

While it is clear that there are methodological problems in these studies because we cannot determine a causal relationship, it is also clear that the implications are serious. We know that the media influence us in countless insignificant ways, including our consumer behaviour, styles of dress, fads and so on. This research suggests that some people may be predisposed to imitate media behaviour in far more important ways as well.

SUMMARY

This study of the mass media has been approached from two distinct points of view: The North American empirical tradition has focused on quantitative studies of content and large-scale surveys of audiences; the European critical tradition draws on an interdisciplinary analysis of the ideological role of the media. Both types of analysis are concerned with the social organization of the media and the meaning and influence of media content, although they phrase their questions concerning these issues differently.

The discussion of the image of women and minorities in the media illustrates how media portrayals stereotype certain groups. Gerbner's cultivation theory postulates that media characterizations of behaviour or social groups engenders a view of reality consonant with these portrayals in people who watch a lot of television. Because media portrayals are distortions of reality, heavy viewers develop an unrealistic view of American society. While we understand that television drama is not the real world, we usually have different expectations of news broadcasts. It seems, however, that there is a temporal and cross-cultural consistency in the structure of news reporting, which imposes itself on whatever events are being reported.

Critical theorists define the power of the media as their ability to frame and legitimize a certain view of social reality. In many ways, the role of the media in agenda setting or in creating impressions of public opinion is not incompatible with this view. However, as Gitlin has observed, the omnipresence of the media make it difficult to isolate their effects.

DISCUSSION QUESTIONS

1. Compare the empirical approaches to the study of mass communication.

2. The Glasgow Media Group study, *Bad News*, described how methods of signification, such as the placement of news items, bias news coverage. Focus on a particular news event and systematically follow its coverage over several days to see if you agree with their finding.

3. Analyse the structure of your favourite news program for several days. Note the length of the broadcast and the length of each report. What proportion of the broadcast is devoted to local, national and international stories? Do you find other consistent elements? If you live in an area where you can watch both American and Canadian news broadcasts, compare their structure.

4. Althouth Ethiopia and other African countries have suffered serious famines for many years, in 1984 famine in Africa became an international issue. Consider the media's coverage of this issue and the overwhelming response it generated as an example of the agenda-setting function of the media.

5. Gerbner found that 70 percent of prime-time television drama and 92 percent of children's programming contain some violence. This proportion has remained relatively stable for the past 15 years, since her study started in 1967. As a member of the audience, how do you explain this preoccupation with violence? How would you imagine it is explained by writers and other communicators?

PROCESSES of CHANGE

Processes of social change deserve a separate section because they are a key to understanding social organization. Many see sociology's central role as the construction of theories about social order; many others see the construction of theories of change as the central task.

Theories of change are usually either evolutionary or revolutionary. Theories of social evolution first appeared in sociology over a century ago. Here the early work of Émile Durkheim (1858-1917) and Herbert Spencer (1820-1903) is most important. They focused on continuity in change, on how things stay the same while changing and how early changes lay the ground work for later ones.

Durkheim examined the social change from primitive, preindustrial to modern, industrial conditions. He noted two main correlates of this process: (1) work and all aspects of life associated with work become specialized, and a division of labour develops; and 2) with a division of labour, the basis of social cohesion changes from *mechanical* to *organic solidarity*.

With mechanical solidarity, people lead similar lives and tend to hold identical views and values. Violation of their values is punished harshly. Conversely, organic solidarity permits many different roles. People lead very different kinds of lives and therefore develop different views and values. Deviance is harder to define, and punishment is less uniform, harsh and automatic. Without moral uniformity, new ways of integrating people must be found. Otherwise, a state of *anomie* (normlessness) exists, which leads to psychological distress and even to higher rates of suicide.

The institutions of a society characterized by mechanical solidarity are typically undifferentiated. Religion, science, law and government may be jumbled up together in a small body of received wisdom, perhaps a holy book, legends or folktales. No mechanisms exist for developing or rejecting this wisdom and such a system has a limited capacity for change.

The emergence of a society based on freedom to contract, rather than on tradition or kinship, is a major development. Yet contractual relations are actually based on *noncontractual elements of contract* rooted in tradition or kinship. These "primitive" elements provide the trust without which rational, voluntary economic activity is impossible. Only later, with the use of strong state protections, do such traditional elements become unnecessary. Thus, modern practices rise on the shoulders of older ones.

Theories of dialectical change, or revolution, are theories of discontinuity. They are about radical shifts in social organization. Georg Hegel (1770-1831) and Karl Marx (1818-1883) first used the notion of the dialectic in social analysis. For Marx, the dominant characteristic of a society is its class structure, which arises out of relations of production. Accordingly, the change from one type of society to another involves a change in relations of production and class structure. This fundamental change is accomplished only through the revolutionary overthrow of a ruling class and its replacement by a new ruling class. Such change gives birth to a new order, but not without upheaval and revolution. As Mao said, there is no omelet without broken eggs.

A variety of theorists, of whom Max Weber (1864-1920) is the most eminent, have attempted to combine these two approaches. According to Weber, certain social forms, such as bureaucracy or the city, may radically shift the course of later social development. In that sense, they are revolutionary changes. Yet what typically follows is a return to some kind of routine, or evolution at a new level of complexity. A new social order emerges, then begins to differentiate and integrate again.

Weber gives us the example of a charismatic social movement. A fiery, persuasive leader gathers his followers and proclaims new values, smashing tradition and its guardians. Followers are swept forward by their excitement and the conviction that their leader is right. They risk and share and suffer in ways quite out of the ordinary. Eventually, especially after the prophet dies, this charismatic phase passes. People return to more ordinary lives, although their lives are transformed by their experience. Disciples organize to administer the ideals promoted by the prophet. Both revolutionary (sectarian) religious and political movements follow this pattern, despite their different goals.

Social differentiation is an apparently universal process. By "differentiation" we mean that all social organizations, from roles up through central institutions, tend to become more specialized, more different from one another, over time. This process is speeded up immensely by social and technological breakthroughs: by the invention of tools, writing and engines that use artificial sources of energy, among others. The changes associated with modernization show social differentiation in its most dramatic light.

Differentiation proceeds through the specialization of subsystems. Economy, polity, the legal system and other central institutions become more distinct from one another. They develop their own operating rules, agendas, resource bases, patterns of socialization and the like. In turn, they become internally differentiated. The law, for example, is simultaneously a business, a system of courts, a body of knowledge and rules and a self-maintaining culture, with schools, students and a particular "legal" outlook.

Differentiation is only one of the apparently universal processes of social change. Another is *integration*, or co-ordination. Without integration, differentiation leads to confusion and a waste of organizational resources and whatever benefits specialization would otherwise provide.

As social systems differentiate, their goals and interests diverge increasingly. Conflicts between them increase as interests clash. Such conflicts among on-going social units and the kinds of negotiation they lead to produce *dialectical* change. In dialectical change, the force and counterforce (or thesis and antithesis) combine in a synthesis. Thus, for example, conflict over uses of new computerized technology will probably change both the labour movement and management. Each will be thrown off its evolutionary path; new relationships between the two will, eventually, be hammered out. Then, each will return to an evolutionary path of differentiation and integration at a new level of complexity.

Where Does Change Begin?

In a certain sense, all theories of social change are variations on these few themes. Yet, theories differ in what they see as the cause of change. If all the parts of a society are tied together, it follows that they will tend to keep one another from changing much. This is precisely why many planned attempts at social change fail. An intervention in one subsystem may be offset by counterforces or shifts in an adjacent subsystem. So what kinds of change can break this pattern?

On a descriptive level, the question is easily answered. We know, for example, that capitalism transformed the social life of Western societies from what it was 500 years ago. As well, we can relate the rise of capitalism to changes in religion, warfare and colonization, monetary and economic theory, political organization and other factors. If anything, we have too many explanations but no widely accepted, single theory about the rise of capitalism in the West and its effects on society.

Likewise, we know that technology has significantly affected social life throughout history. People today are feeling the effects of microelectronics and computerization in all parts of their lives. The so-called "information revolution" grows out of the long development of science and technology in the West, associated, like the rise of capitalism, with Protestantism, warfare, the development of nation-states and other factors. In addition, certain new ideas, like efficiency, become new social goals. Where did these new ideas and goals, discussed below by Willem Vanderburg come from? How do they relate to the other social changes we have mentioned? Again, there are too many explanations of innovation and no widely accepted, single theory of technical innovation and its effect on society.

In historical analyses, theorists tell their story from many different starting points; some begin with the economy, others with religion, still others with the nation-state. A Marxist theory typically sees economic conflicts as basic and value conflicts (e.g., in religion) as superficial or secondary. A Weberian analysis, by contrast, may consider value conflicts as basic as economic or political ones. We can only judge these theories by their thoroughness, economy and agreement with the evidence. Theories of societal change, especially theories aimed at explaining the past, can rarely be verified by prediction and testing. However, not all theories of societal change focus on the past. Increasingly, theories of change aim to predict the future.

Theories about the future are not confined to sociology. They make up a new, interdisciplinary field called *futurology*, to which sociologists contribute both methods and substance. A major work in this area, *The Coming of the Post Industrial Society* (1970), is by sociologist Daniel Bell. It describes a society that, in Bell's view, is already in sight, though far from completion, a society in which knowledge is the most important social resource. To simplify, it predicts that knowledge workers, information technology and educational institutions will have even more importance than they do today.

Other theorists, like Alvin Toffler, whose ideas are similar in many respects to Bell's, predict that technological changes will continue to alter society dramatically. Our lives will supposedly become more prosperous, varied and secure as new microelectronic gadgets revolutionize our homes and workplaces. Of course, our lives have already been improved enormously by modern appliances, electricity, automobiles and the like. More of the same is predicted. Yet, this approach to prediction is missing something important.

Power and Belief

Amid all the competing sociological theories about past and future, two major concerns emerge time and again: they are power and belief. They come together in the study of ideology and its effect on social change and order.

Changes to a society are largely determined by who controls technology, knowledge and the other agents of change already mentioned. No valid theory of change can limit itself to considering *possible* effects of a change agent while ignoring the way power is actually used. For example, the fact that computers *could* free people from mindless toil tells us little. To predict the future, we must know who controls the computers and what they plan to use them for. Similarly, the fact that knowledge is becoming an evermore important social resource does not ensure that the educated will become more powerful, only that the powerful will make more use of the educated.

Yet, the mere fact of power is not everything. We need to know what people in power are thinking, how they understand the world and what their goals are. Also, how do they exercise their power: To what degree can they project their goals and world view into the minds of people they rule? Power is and will always be exercised as much by persuasion as by force.

Max Weber directed our attention to the continuing contest between power and belief: to the attempts those in power make to control the thinking of the masses; the tendency for disaffection; the rise of prophets with a power to unite and inspire trust, and the ability of disciples to consolidate the achievements of the leader and become new, powerful rivals to the existing order.

Under what conditions will those in power be able to keep control over the thinking of the masses? Will ordinary people become disaffected and rebellious? Will charismatic leaders emerge and succeed in challenging those in power? Some of these questions have already been asked and answered in earlier chapters on social movements and social class. Some will be answered in this section.

Sociology is a science of social relations. But much more preliminary work is needed before we can succeed in that enterprise. This introductory volume is no more than an outline of the sociologist's aims, tools and achievements to date.

13

Technology and Social Change

Willem H. Vanderburg

INTRODUCTION

Before reading this chapter, make a list of all the technologies and their products that you directly or indirectly depend on during a typical day. Do many of your interactions with individuals, groups and institutions involve a technology or its products? What is the overall effect of technology on us as individuals and on our society? Who controls this technology and to what ends is it used? How many of the major problems now facing humanity relate to the growing power our technology give us over our social and natural environments? Do our responses to these problems make sense? (Think, for example, of our attempts to avoid war by developing evermore powerful weapons; or the efforts to remedy our economic problems by improving productivity through automation.) It is important to reflect on your own experiences in light of our attempt here to understand the influence technology is having on individual and collective human life.

From a historical perspective, the role played by modern technology in our present world is highly unique. Technology today is increasingly widely used. Together with science, it is helping to create a knowledge base that is no longer exclusively linked to any society, that is utilized by a growing number of nations as a basis for similar ways of life aimed at economic development. For the first time in history, all the nations of the world can be classified in terms of their degree of success in achieving similar goals. They are now all underdeveloped, developing or developed nations. The growing importance of computers and the associated techniques for accessing, processing, applying and transmitting information will undoubtedly reinforce these trends.

Many aspects of the transformation of the relationship between technology and society have been studied. It has been noted, for example, that before a traditional society can utilize modern technology, it must fundamentally change its culture and organization (Goulet, 1977; Pelto, 1973; and Richardson, 1975). This is evident from the literature on the transfer of technology to Third World societies and indigenous peoples. Some authors argue that intermediate or appropriate technologies must be designed which require fewer and less substantial changes in the recipient societies (Jéquier, 1976; Rybczynski, 1980). Societies already far advanced along the road of economic development appear to acquire very similar social, economic and political structures, although the degree of similarity has been disputed (Aron, 1967; Bell, 1973; Ellul, 1977; Richta, 1969; Touraine, 1971; Winner, 1977). There is also a considerable literature on the implications of individual technologies for specific human activities. Less work has been done on using these studies to establish a comprehensive theory on how modern technology as a whole contributes to social and cultural change (Badham and Davies, 1984). It has also been recognized that technology undergoes profound changes when it begins to play a new role in society (Galbraith, 1978; Noble, 1979; Touraine, 1965). All these aspects of technology in our modern world must be accounted for in a perspective on technology and social change.

THE INDUSTRIAL REVOLUTION

Most theories of the Industrial Revolution focus on the mechanization of human work and the accompanying proliferation of machines throughout society. This overemphasis on machines obscures the fact that the technical approach and orientation to material production was also part of a general technical orientation in the cultures of many Western European societies.

In the political domain, for example, the state emerged as a product of the French Revolution. In France, the state developed its military technique by taking a rational approach to strategy, organization, logistics and recruitment. It also developed rational methods of administration to harness the resources and energies of the nation for the transformation of society. The state's attempts under Napoleon to systematize and rationalize the legal system, which led to the Napoleonic Code, are well known. It sought to suppress or alter laws based on custom. These legal transformations were quickly adopted by other Western European nations, except for England. Weights and measures were standardized. A systematic approach was adopted for the planning of roads. Science also was rationalized in the eighteenth century. This chapter will argue that the Industrial Revolution was but one facet of a larger technical revolution that manifested itself in a technical mentality concerned with rationality, efficiency, power and profits.

Many people at the time of the Industrial Revolution clearly understood that machines were only one aspect of a new society in which everything would become rational and efficient. Ths conception is manifested, for example, in the Encyclopaedia of Diderot. It clearly showed that people wished to master the world with reason by making things clear and precise, by quantifying the qualitative and by bringing rational order to chaos (Ellul, 1964). The technical orientation was most strongly embodied in the social classes and institutions that spearheaded the Industrial Revolution. They greatly enhanced their social position and power by applying it.

It should be remembered that the technology of a society contains much more than just machines. It is constituted of many elements that may be arranged along a spectrum ranging from the *hardware* on one end to *software* on the other. In other words, on one end we find instruments, machines, tools, bridges and so on, while on the other we find concepts, processes, theories, organizations, institutions, attitudes, ways of conceptualizing, values and so on. Complex machines had been invented and applied earlier in history, but never were they used in the context of a widespread technical orientation in the culture, which included a mechanistic world view, a rational conception of human life and society and a sense of the possibility of human progress. The development of each element of a technology is often a response to the conditions prevalent in a society. The technology is then made workable through innovation and finds its way into the mainstream of society by application. It diffuses into and becomes a part of the way of life of a society and, finally, is displaced from that society. All these processes are an integral part of the fabric of a society.

The failure to see the Industrial Revolution as only one aspect of the larger technical revolution can perhaps be explained by the fact that the transformations of various areas of society by the technical approach did not come together in a relatively coherent pattern until the mechanization of human work and the proliferation of machines began. This could not have happened, however, without the rationalization of the entire fabric of society. To explain this, we will first look at the *structural* characteristics of industrialization. We will examine a case study of the chain reaction of events set off in England by the mechanization of textile production—a process that completely transformed English society. Remember that each technology, from its invention until its displacement, is embedded in the fabric of a society. It both affects and is affected by the structure of the society.

THE TECHNICAL REVOLUTION

The highly interrelated character of a society is partly reflected in the network of its flow of goods. The nodes of the network represent a process in the production, transportation, consumption or disposal of some commodity. Each node is connected to others by its inputs and outputs. Societies generally organize themselves so that the output of one process is practically identical to the input of the next process a commodity undergoes. For example, in the putting-out system, where the technical revolution probably began in England, the preparation of raw materials—spinning this material into yarn, weaving yarn into cloth and finishing the cloth—was done by rural families under contract to an entrepreneur. The system was like a decentralized factory, with a technological division of labour in which families worked at home using a simple, inexpensive device such as a spinning wheel or handloom to complete a single stage of production. The system had become an integral part of rural life, where it complemented subsistence farming, particularly during times when the land required relatively little attention. The four stages of production formed a chain, with outputs of cloth on the other end, which may, in turn, have constituted the inputs for the manufacturing of clothes or other goods. Processes of transportation interposed themselves everywhere. Each process in the chain also required other goods that were often produced elsewhere, such as spinning wheels, handlooms, bleaches and dyes. In other words, the network of the flow of goods in the putting-out systems was only a small part of a much larger one. The putting-out system did not respond well to a sudden increase in the demand for textiles, which occurred, for example, when a war ended and overseas markets opened up once again. As entrepreneurs looked for ways of better controlling the work process to increase profits, the technical orientation, including the mechanistic world view of the time, brought to the fore the idea of mechanizing human work.

> The flying shuttle of 1733 made a greater production of yarn necessary. But production was impossible without a suitable machine. The response to this dilemma was the invention of the spinning jenny by James Hargreaves. But then yarn was produced in much greater quanitities than could possibly be used by the weavers. To solve this new problem, Cartwright manufactured his celebrated loom. In this series of events we see in its simplest form the interaction that accelerated the development of machines. Each new machine disturbs the equilibrium of production; the restoration of equilibrium entails the creation of one or more additional machines in other areas of operation.
>
> Production becomes more and more complex. The combination of machines within the same enterprise is a notable characteristic of the nineteenth century. It is impossible, in effect, to have an isolated machine. There must be adjunct machines, if not preparatory ones. . . . The need for organization of machines is found even in the textile industry. A large number of looms must be grouped together in order to utilize the prime mover most effectively, since no individual loom consumes very much energy. To obtain maximum yield, machines cannot

be disposed in a haphazard way. Nor can production take place irregularly. A plan must be followed in all technical domains (Ellul, 1964: 111-112).

Landes also recognizes the patterns that draw together many events of the time when he writes:

> In all of this diversity of technological improvement, the unity of the movement is apparent: change begat change. For one thing, many technical improvements were feasible only after advances in associated fields. The steam engine is a classic example of this technological interrelatedness: it was impossible to produce an effective condensing engine until better methods of metal working could turn out accurate cylinders. For another, the gains in productivity and output of a given innovation inevitably exerted pressure on related industrial operations. The demand for coal pushed mines deeper until water seepage became a serious hazard; the answer was the creation of a more efficient pump, the atmospheric steam engine. A cheap supply of coal proved a godsend to the iron industry, which was stifling for lack of fuel. In the meantime, the invention and diffusion of machinery in the textile manufacture and other industries created a new demand for energy, hence for coal and steam engines; and these engines, and the machines themselves, had a voracious appetite for iron, which called for further coal and power. Steam also made possible the factory city, which used unheard-of quanitites of iron (hence coal) in its many-storied mills and its water and sewage systems. At the same time, the processing of the flow of manufactured commodities required great amounts of chemical substances: alkalis, acids, and dyes, many of them consuming mountains of fuel in the making. And all of these products—iron, textiles, chemicals—depended on large-scale movements of goods on land and on sea, from the sources of raw materials into the factories and out again to near and distant markets. The opportunity thus created and the possibilities of the new technology combined to produce the railroad and steamship, which of course added to the demand for iron and fuel while expanding the market for factory products. And so on, in ever-widening circles (Landes, 1969:2,3).

Clearly, all these events could not happen without larger amounts of capital. To accomplish this required that existing financial institutions develop a variety of new techniques. In fact, capital became the scarcest and therefore most crucial input into the new system of production. The accumulation of capital produced by machines and also necessitated by them led to a national and later international financial organization. It also required a new legal invention, namely the corporation, with limited liabilities. Marketing of the growing quantities of goods also needed to be rationalized, and this led to a range of commercial techniques. The development of improved transportation systems, such as railroad systems, required better organizational techniques for scheduling trains. The failure of any of these techniques to rationalize a variety of other activities could have produced a major bottleneck in the technical revolution.

Because of the size and expense of the new textile machines and their need for more power than human beings could supply, work could no longer be done at home along with subsistence farming. As the mechanization of work spread, the concentration of machines in factories in the industrial centres grew, requiring the uprooting of a growing portion of the rural population. The change from a rural to an urban society intensified as industrialization advanced, with obvious social consequences. As people began leaving their families to find work in the industrial centres, their lives were totally transformed. The conditions under which they worked were different, as exemplified by factory discipline. They became wage-earners who bought the basic necessities for life as opposed to producing most of them themselves. They had escaped the social control of their families and villages and had to rely on their own individual resources. No longer was their traditional morality, which was essentially the normalized behaviour of their own group, of much use. Under these circumstances, an individualistic morality slowly emerged over many generations. The new social fabric that began to constitute itself in the industrial centres was based on greatly weakened family units, which were no longer the context for most human activity. We see here the beginning of a reconstitution of the social fabric of traditional societies, which would eventually produce a mass society. The growing importance of capital as the most crucial input into the process of industrialization made the owners of capital increasingly influential and powerful. They soon began to constitute the dominant class, controlling the capital on which everything else depended. They built the new society for their own profit. In other words, the fundamental reconstitution of the social fabric of these societies was accompanied by, and depended on, major economic, political and moral transformations.

The massive relocation of the population from the countryside to the new industrial centres created large cities.

> At the beginning, the big city engendered no particular technique; people were merely unhappy in it. But it soon appeared that megalopolis represented a new and special kind of environment, calling for special treatment. The technique of city planning made its appearance. At first, urban planning was only a clumsy kind of adaptation which was little concerned, for example, with slums (despite the efforts of the utopian planners of the middle of the century). Somewhat later, as big city life became for the most part intolerable, techniques of amusement were developed. It became indispensable to make urban suffering acceptable by furnishing amusements, a necessity which was to assure the rise, for example, of a monstrous motion-picture industry (Ellul, 1964:113,114).

The transformation of technology and society during the technical revolution created a period of immense human and social dislocation. There was massive exploitation of the workers who laboured for long hours under inhumane conditions. Each new problem created by applying new techniques required the development of further techniques. The proliferation of techniques itself raised still other problems. Human beings do not adapt easily to the rational order of machines, factories and industrial towns. The state had to constrain the individual in several ways. External constraints were not sufficient. The individual had to be adjusted to the new society, and thus the techniques of education, propaganda and psychological manipulation began to develop. As the techniques of production became more developed, human techniques became necessary. Each new technique required still others, whose development in turn permitted the further extension of the technique. It is the ensemble of techniques present in almost every sphere of human life that eventually began to characterize the new societies. We will define technique as the totality of methods rationally arrived at and having maximum possible efficiency for a given stage of development, in every field of human activity (Ellul, 1964:xxv).

The structure of the patterns of events we have described occurs in every society regardless of where mechanization is initiated. Mechanization will produce a local disturbance in the fabric of a society that can only be resolved by a further mechanization and rationalization. This in turn produces new disturbances in adjacent areas of the sociocultural fabric, and so on. These changes gradually transform the daily lives of the members of a society. As the new patterns of life are internalized by each new generation, they affect human consciousness as well as the culture of the society. We will turn now to these cultural aspects of the technical revolution.

CULTURAL TRANSFORMATIONS

The description of some of the changes in the fabric of society as a result of the technical revolution would be incomplete without considering the retroaction on the individual and on the culture of the society. By growing up in a particular society, we acquire language, and along with it, the images and stereotypes by which we think and apprehend reality. Socialization also furnishes us with a mode of behaviour and a life style. It also provides the structures for our emotional life and our memory. These are individually unique and yet culturally typical. In other words, the members of a society interpret their experiences and shape the relationships between themselves and the world by means of what we shall call a culture, following the tradition of American sociology.

Babies and children acquire the culture of their society by internalizing experiences. They thus develop their minds, which function as a kind of mental map, permitting them to live in reality in a way that is individually unique and yet typical of their culture and time. The culture integrates the lives of the members of a society into a social order based on a hierarchy of values absolutized by means of a sacred set of myths. In this way, the culture of a society permits the members to live together on the basis of a unique way of life.

The massive changes in people's daily lives implied in the above description of the technical revolution thus gradually altered not only individual consciousness but also the very foundations of the traditional cultures. Thus, a new set of values and a new morality emerged, while the myths of progress and happiness helped constitute a new ultimate value or sacred belief. This may explain, for example, the appearance of liberal Christianity, as well as changes in the art, music and literature of society. The transformations in the culture that underlie these and other phenomena are extremely slow, lasting many generations. They helped in laying the foundation for a new epoch in the history of Western civilization and, increasingly, in many other societies.

Once completed, the cultural transformation further reinforced and accelerated the technical revolution. It reunified society in a fundamental way, although it did not end exploitation. During its early phases, industrial society was built up by a social class, the bourgeoisie, who shaped it to further their own interests and power. They did so by exploiting other social classes. The bourgeoisie incarnated the spirit of the new age, while the other classes still largely lived according to the values and

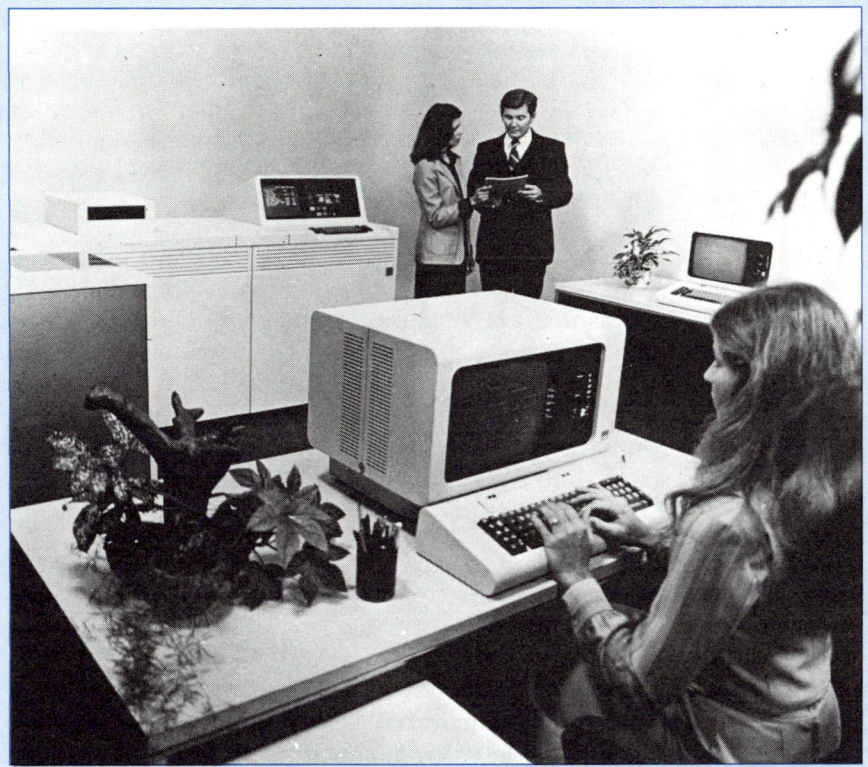

Courtesy of IBM Canada Ltd.

Because of the high value industrially advanced societies place on technology, there is a tendency to play down or ignore the losses that accompany the gains. This promotional photograph shows one side of the so-called information revolution. However, the human costs are substantial. The new electronic assembly lines, where the keystrokes and other operations of each worker can be monitored, are considered by some observers to be more oppressive than the early factories. The new information technology is integrating institutions and society in new ways, based on information flows rather than on human interaction, and this fundamentally affects the social fabric. While creating many new jobs, the new technologies appear to eliminate an even greater number. They are also speeding up military activities, leaving less time for human decisions and interventions, which, in a nuclear age, is a very serious matter. The new "postindustrial industries" may lack smokestacks, but they do produce significant quantities of dangerous chemical wastes. The industrially advanced nations will not be very successful in solving their problems if they do not treat technology more realistically. The strategy of divide and conquer applied to separating the positive from the negative implications of technology is a dangerous one.

ways of preindustrial culture. Through the processes described earlier, the other classes eventually also embraced the myths of progress and happiness through technology. Thus, the social classes were transformed into social strata of the emerging industrial societies. All these strata increasingly agreed on the desirability of the promises offered by technology, but conflict over the distribution of the benefits of technology continued, along with much exploitation.

The Third World

The massive transformation of society that we have described requires many resources. These were largely present in Western European societies due to the historically unique conditions that prevailed on the eve of the technical revolution. Since these conditions do not exist in most Third World societies, the chain reaction of transformation tends to get stuck for lack of resources of one kind of another. As a result of colonialism, the transfer of technology, the operation of the multinationals, the education in the West of their elite and so on, this process of transformation has been started in many sectors in these societies. Once the process of transformation stops, these societies can neither move forward nor return to their traditional way of life. They become societies literally divided against themselves, comprising modern and traditional elements that are incompatible with one another. This is at the heart of the problem of so-called "underdevelopment."

Some Additional Facets of the Technical Revolution

Our critique of the concepts of the Industrial Revolution and of industrial society is, of course, made with the benefit of hindsight. It permits us to place the transformation of Western Europe in the eighteenth and nineteenth centuries in a broader historical context, which reveals new patterns and thus sheds new light on the events of that time. For the people who lived during this great change, it was a challenging intellectual task to make sense of what exactly was happening. It is instructive to briefly look at these efforts, because some of them continue to profoundly influence sociology.

Henri de Saint-Simon (1760–1825) published a journal, *L'Industrie*, in 1816, in which he developed a vision for an industrial society when Europe was still mostly agricultural. He largely shared this vision of what lay ahead with Auguste Comte (1798–1857): Human and social progress could be achieved through developing and applying scientific and technical reason. As a result, society was on the threshold of the most fundamental transformation in human history, namely, the passage from a military and theological past to a scientific and industrial future. To ensure this future, Comte saw the need for a new science of society that he called sociology. Social evolution was seen to be inevitable, but by discovering its laws, social and political activity could speed up the process by preparing the prerequisites for tomorrow and by making the changes as orderly as possible. All thought and action were to be directed toward establishing an industrial society. These visions contained many ambiguities about the dynamics of industrialization and its regulation, in part because the central roles of both scientific ideas and social classes were emphasized (Comte, 1974).

When we turn to thinkers who experienced much of the actual transformation and who were therefore *analysing* what was going on, we find that what they were describing was much more than what can be covered by concepts such as industrialization, Industrial Revolution and industrial society. Their interpretations have had a great influence on the development of sociology, including the perspective presented in this chapter.

Karl Marx (1818–1883) created the concept of capital as the key to understanding what was happening at that time. Everything was directly or indirectly structured to preserve and accumulate capital. This was true in two essential ways. The social class that was building the new system required ever larger amounts of capital to build the machines, factories and the vast infrastructure of roads, canals, railroads, mines, houses and so on. Secondly, the lives of those who worked in the factories became equally determined by capital. They had to sell their capacity to work for a wage and it was with this "capital" that they had to procure all the necessities of life in the market. The workers became appendages to machines. They could no longer depend on themselves. They became totally dependent on the capitalist system. Their only resource was their ability to work—an ability that had value only if someone was willing to buy it because it was profitable, and this in turn was determined by world markets. Thus, workers totally depended on a system that they were unable to control. Because of long working hours, the lives of the workers were dominated by work, which reduced them to a mere commodity to be bought and sold.

The workers were alienated, which for Marx had a two-fold meaning: to be possessed by someone or something (like a master possesses the body and soul of a slave) and to be self-alienated by being transformed into another and not being oneself. To characterize the condition of the workers as alienated is therefore to suggest much more than simply that they were exploited. The workers had become less than human, possessed by a system over which they had no say and which did not allow them to be themselves. The descriptions of some European travellers of life in the industrial centres leave little doubt as to the accuracy of Marx's characterization of the condition of early industrial workers.

There was an additional component of economic alienation resulting from the central role capital played in society. It applied to both rich and poor. Marx showed that the amount of money possessed became the only essential quality of people in the capitalist system. Money became the common measure of all things, and virtually everything could be obtained with money. Relations between people and between people and nature were determined by money, which became an active power. One was what one had, and this is a negation of what it is to be human.

Alienation in capitalism also included an ideological and religious dimension. The new human venture based on the exploitation of human beings and nature could not be seen for what it was. People therefore had to perceive everything by means of a false consciousness and create an ideology that concealed the true situation. It is here that people were most deeply divested of themselves. The accuracy of Marx's description of the human condition (Marx, 1972, 1977) during the time of the Industrial Revolution is in no way negated by the fact that today the causes of alienation have changed. This is a matter to which we shall return.

Émile Durkheim (1858–1917) did not think that industry was the primary determinant of social change or that it could constitute a goal for future development. The characteristics of the new societies had their root in the growing division of labour in all spheres of human life under the pressure of population growth. For Durkheim, earlier societies were characterized by a measure of *mechanical solidarity*. Individuals largely shared the same experiences, emotions and values; they were therefore similar enough to give society a great deal of coherence.

The increasing social differentiation that came with a complex division of labour greatly accelerated the trend toward the opposite of mechanical solidarity, which Durkheim called *organic solidarity*. It is based on a relationship of complementarity between very different individuals analogous to that between organs of the human body, which are all different yet all indispensable. In a society where mechanical solidarity is very strong, the individual consciousness is largely coextensive with the collective consciousness. In a highly differentiated society, this is not the case. Individuals have more choice and are much more conscious of their uniqueness but this also makes them less well integrated into society, so that the collective consciousness may be weaker. The absence or disintegration of norms, often accompanied by a weakening of the moral order and religion creates *anomie*. The individual senses a lack of meaning and purpose resulting from his or her insufficient integration into the collectivity. Durkheim thought that most of the important problems of his time could be understood in terms of fundamental social processes that made a greater division of labour necessary. For him, industrialization could not provide a meaningful sense of individual and social purpose. As members of a mass society, we are no strangers to these problems, and Durkheim's work continues to be of interest (Durkheim, 1964).

Max Weber (1864–1920) did not think that industry was the key phenomenon in terms of which all the new social realities could be understood. For him, industrialization was a part of the more general phenomenon of the rationalization of social life. The rationalization of one or more areas of human life had occurred in earlier societies and took a variety of directions, depending on the culture. Rationality, for Weber, must be understood in relation to the individual actor as a social being and not in relation to the observer. However, most action in the past was largely based on internalized custom and tradition.

What was historically new at this time and significant for Weber was the widespread application of logical, systematic thought and calculation in the pursuit of conscious goals. He observed this in a growing number of areas: the economy, politics, public administration, law and culture. He examined the spread of machine technology, the rise of bureaucracies, rational capitalism, the rationalization of intellectual life and the rise of science. This rationalization led to a whole range of new problems that could not be resolved by further industrialization. As Weber put it: "Together with the machine, the bureaucratic organization is employed in building the houses of bondage of the future, in which perhaps men will one day be like peasants in the ancient Egyptian State, acquiescent and powerless, while a purely technical goal, that is, rational, official administration and provision becomes the sole, final value, which sovereignty decides the direction of their affairs" (Weber, 1974: 181). He feared that rationalization had become an end in itself by undermining all other goals that might have given it meaning. The means was becoming an end, thus profoundly alienating the people subjected to it. This was the new, harsh reality of human life as Weber masterfully portrayed it in his work (Weber, 1968).

Marx, Durkheim and Weber each gave a systematic and internally coherent interpretation of what was happening in the nineteenth century. All three saw the extraordinary coherence in the patterns of events of that time. Although they interpreted very differently the origin, nature and future of these developments, they all recognized that no simple or piecemeal solutions existed to the enormous problems posed by the technical revolution. The problems and dislocations experienced intensely by Germany, probably the most technically advanced society around the turn of the century, would be a significant factor in shaping the conditions that led to two world wars and, indirectly to the Russian Revolution. There were several new developments in the making, however, of which Marx, Durkheim and Weber experienced only the beginning. It is to these that we will now turn.

THE TRANSFORMATION OF THE TECHNICAL KNOWLEDGE BASE

We have thus far described how introducing industrial technology into Western European societies fundamentally disturbed the social, economic, political, legal, moral and religious dimensions of society; massive restructuring was required, which forced the various efforts at rationalization (until then largely piecemeal) into a chain-reaction transformation. Out of this emerged a diversity of societies that shared many important features and which resembled each other much more than they resembled earlier societies. They are often called *industrial* societies, but this is an oversimplification that will become particularly evident when we examine the so-called advanced industrial, or *postindustrial* societies. The transformation that produced the latter is rooted in a fundamental change in the technical knowledge base. This change, beginning ever so slowly toward the end of the nineteenth century (after the death of Marx) became sociologically significant only after World War II. It radically changed society once again by means of a new chain reaction. The new patterns of social change were less driven by industrialization and machine technology than those of the nineteenth and early twentieth centuries.

Until the late nineteenth century, the development and application of the various techniques was largely empirical. They were passed on from one generation to the next by apprenticeship arrangements, in which one learned a technique by working with someone who had a great deal of experience. Formal education played an almost insignificant role until the end of the nineteenth century. Take technology as an example. The increasing precision and complexity of machines, as well as the growing pressure from competition to eliminate any inefficiency, required a technological knowledge base that was as much as possible scientifically founded. The Germans were far ahead of the English in this respect, and as a result, Germany began to overtake England in its technological and industrial capacity toward the end of the nineteenth century.

This was the beginning of a complete transformation of the way technological knowledge is transmitted, developed and applied. There is clearly a discontinuity between knowledge acquired from experience and knowledge acquired by formal education. No amount of experience and on-the-job training can lead to a knowledge of the applied sciences. These can only be learned in the classroom. As a result, the knowers and the doers are more and more frequently different people.

By way of example, consider a welder with many years of experience erecting high-rise buildings. One day, as the crane is bringing up another beam for the twenty-sixth floor structure, the welder may alert the crane operator and the foreman by saying, "I've never seen such a light beam being used on this large a span. Are you sure we aren't making a mistake?" The foreman may then decide to call the engineer in the field office to check the calculations. On the basis of many years of experience, the welder has obtained a certain knowledge of the strength of beams. Yet he will never learn to calculate the strength of a beam by means of stress analysis, because this is not learned from experience but from books or classroom instruction. Without it, all the welder can say is that a beam does not look strong enough to him. It should be remembered, however, that virtually all the technical accomplishments of the past were based on a body of knowledge built up from the experience of many generations.

The changes in the knowledge base of technology were accompanied by similar changes in other areas. A greater precision of one technique necessitates similar developments in other techniques. By the end of World War II, changes in the technical knowledge base had necessitated the restructuring of a variety of institutions in society. Galbraith (1978) has examined the restructuring of large corporations after World War II. Since Galbraith did not sufficiently appreciate the interdependence of industrial technology with a whole range of other techniques, we will briefly reinterpret his findings.

At the core of the large, modern corporation, we find what Galbraith has called its *technostructure*, essentially the brain of the enterprise, in which most activities are based on knowledge acquired by the formal education of its members. Together they have an expertise in the techniques necessary for the efficient running of all parts of the corporation, such as marketing, production, engineering, management, personnel and public relations. Thus, the latest technical knowledge is applied to all aspects of the corporation. Since the expertise of each member of the techno-structure is highly specialized, each task must be so subdivided that every part is coterminous with a particular body of specialized technical knowledge. A knowledge of metallurgy, for example, cannot be applied to the design of a whole automobile. It can be applied only to the selection and design of appropriate materials for its parts. Thus, technical knowledge is applied to each and every part of the task, then to each subpart in combination with another, and then in combination with still others to ensure a coherent synthesis of the whole task. All aspects of the problem must be considered at the same time. For example, an automobile manufacturer does not spend millions of dollars on designing a new car only to discover that it cannot be produced economically or that, during the years spent designing the car and building the production facilities, substantial market changes have taken place. It is by means of a technostructure, therefore, that a large corporation takes advantage of the latest formal, technical knowledge.

The technostructure is surrounded by the body of the corporation, in which most tasks can be performed without any advanced formal education. Most tasks can be learned on the job (such as those of assembly-line workers), while others require some technical training (such as those of the operators of word processors). In all these tasks, knowledge acquired from experience plays an essential role.

The gradual restructuring of large corporations during the first half of the twentieth century was, therefore, in part a response to the emergence of the new technical knowledge base. Without this restructuring, large corporations would not be able to take advantage of the latest developments in the natural, applied and social sciences. All corporate operations became extremely effective. The development of any new product, for example, now required the collaboration of a great many people with complementary types of expertise relevant to the task. Since these people must be paid, provided with support staff, have offices and so on, the capital investment needed to bring any new product to market skyrocketed. A competitively priced product could be produced only if this investment could be written off over a large number of units manufactured. In other words, restructuring the technical knowledge base necessitated a further acceleration in the trend toward mass production. This trend in turn, required highly specialized production facilities. It was no longer possible to economically mass produce a product using general purpose machines, which were typically used for only one or two operations, although they were capable of doing many more. Production costs could be lowered by designing specialized production facilities, but this greatly added to the investment necessary to bring a new product to market.

All these factors greatly increased the risk involved in developing a new product. During the considerable length of time it took to design and develop a new product and prepare the production facilities, market conditions could change. If sales fell far below the projected figures, however, the investment in design and development of the new product and the highly specialized production facilities could not be transferred to another product. In order to protect themselves from such risks, companies diversified, so that the losses in one division could be offset by profits in another and not endanger the survival of the firm.

The corporations that exploited the new technical knowledge base, therefore, required a much greater concentration of capital than did the entrepreneurial firms of the nineteenth century. This made it virtually impossible for a family or a small group of shareholders to own these new firms. A modern corporation is usually owned by a large number of shareholders, who each own only a small part of the corporation. At shareholders' meetings, they tend to approve the plans put forward and prepared by the technostructure, which essentially controls the operation of the firm as long as it earns sufficient profits to pay reasonable dividends to the shareholders and to generate enough capital to finance its own internal operations. The greatly weakened link between ownership and control also affects the economic behaviour of the large corporation, whose goals are now much more complex than a simple profit maximization. Its relationship with the market also undergoes a profound transformation. No longer can it rely on the market to supply the specialized materials and machines that may be unique to one of its products. On the output side, the corporation attempts to manage consumer demand through a variety of techniques, including advertising. It relies on the state to create the educational institutions necessary to graduate specialists for its technostructure.

The growth and development of the new technical knowledge base required an expansion in the role of the modern state. It alone could create the educational system necessary to ensure that the nation would produce specialists in the various areas of technical expertise. Before the development of the new technical knowledge base, access to higher education was typically restricted to the upper-classes of society. In order to advance the development of the new technical knowledge base, access to the educational system had to be based not on social status, but on the intellectual capability of the individual. Hence, a person's position in the social hierarchy was increasingly determined not by his or her social status at birth, but by the amount of education he or she had received. Particularly when there was a scarcity of technical experts, equality of educational opportunities became a necessity. The result was that children from the same family could rise to very different social positions. This greater social mobility contributed to the birth of a mass society.

To provide the large corporation with a stable economic environment in which it could plan new products that would not come onto the market until years later, the state had to regulate the economy. It did so by creating a large public sector that it expanded or contracted to offset the fluctuations in the private sector. In the most advanced industrial nations, this public sector is in part occupied by projects not directly affecting the mainstream of society, such as defence, space programs and the development of nuclear energy. To ensure the development of the new technical knowledge base, the state also became involved in scientific and technical research. In order to efficiently carry out its new tasks, as well as to improve its effectiveness in more traditional domains, the state began to depend on the technical knowledge of experts. They brought their expertise to bear on these tasks, using patterns of collaboration very similar to the ones found in the technostructures of large corporations.

Developing the new technical knowledge base and the techniques derived from it did not only affect large corporations and the state, however. A growing number of activities in society were increasingly structured and restructured in accordance with the latest technical knowledge. In fact, all the characteristics of "postindustrialism" or "advanced industrialism" derive directly from the proliferation of techniques throughout society. We have already suggested that modern technology could not have emerged without a whole range of developments in other industrial techniques. Similarly, industrial techniques could not have been refined without the restructuring of many other areas of society. The transformations of technology and society are interdependent and reciprocally determine one another. The concepts of the Industrial Revolution and industrial society have obscured the many-faceted technical developments and necessitated the concepts of postindustrialism and advanced industrialism.

Courtesy of Ontario Hydro

Beginning with the Industrial Revolution, the proliferation of machines and the associated societal restructuring helped create an evergrowing demand for energy. Nuclear energy was initially thought to solve this problem once and for all. However, more and more people are becoming convinced that we have too often trusted technology to solve its own problems. In return for the electricity produced by a nuclear power plant during its lifetime (a maximum of 25 to 30 years), society is left with a vast quantity of highly dangerous radioactive waste, tailings from mining uranium and the radioactive housing of the reactor. How can we ever be totally sure that the methods proposed for storing these wastes will not be found inadequate 50, 100 or 200 years later? This raises fundamental moral questions about our responsibility to future generations. Some analysts have estimated that the total energy involved in all the activities associated with the production of electricity from nuclear energy exceeds the quantity of energy produced. The construction of some 70 nuclear power plants in North America has been stopped at varying stages. The photo shows Canada's first full-scale nuclear power station at Douglas Point, on Lake Huron. It came on line in 1967 and is now permanently out of service.

THE PHENOMENON OF TECHNIQUE[1]

It would appear that, in the debate over the nature of modern society (whether it is industrially advanced, postindustrial, technological or something else) an important point has been overlooked. Surely, one thing that sets modern societies apart from all others is that a wide range of activities is no longer based on custom or tradition grounded in a culture. They systematically research virtually every sphere of human activity in order to render it more effective, rational and efficient or to eliminate problems. They do this on the assumption (and this is a cultural hypothesis that underlies modern societies) that the quality of life can be improved by making all facets of our existence more efficient. Research takes the form of what we will call the *technical operation*, which is constituted of four stages.

The first stage involves studying some area of human life for a particular purpose. The study's results are used in the next stage to build a model that can range from a precise mathematical theory to a theory that is largely qualitative. In the third stage, the model is examined to determine what happens when its parameters are altered, in order to discover when it functions optimally. The technical operation concludes with the reorganization of the area of human life studied originally, to achieve the highest efficiency and rationality demonstrated to be possible by the model. It is by means of this pattern of events that modern societies seek to improve the productivity of a plant, the running of a large office or hospital, the effectiveness of classroom instruction, the performance of a professional athlete or hockey team, the functioning of a group and even the satisfaction derived from a sexual relationship. As a result, the technical operation deeply permeates the fabric of technologies or techniques. The French sociologist Jacques Ellul first drew our attention to this fact.

Increasingly in modern societies, almost every sphere of human activity is organized not on the basis of custom or tradition, but on the basis of a variety of techniques that ensure that everything is done as effectively as possible. Technology is only one part of the larger phenomenon of technique.

The reason the "industrially advanced" nations began to generate a mass of information at a certain point is now evident. When techniques increasingly began to replace tradition as the basis of human activities, much information was generated as a result of the technical operation. As these developments gained momentum, new technologies or techniques became necessary to deal with the mass of information. The computer and associated techniques were developed to meet this challenge and immediately found a wide range of applications. This in turn greatly accelerated the patterns of development described above.

The information economy, the proliferation of theoretical services, the rise of new intellectual techniques, the emergence of a new class of technical experts, the growth of the service sector and other phenomena taken to be signs of the "post-industrial age" (Bell, 1973) are simply the result of the proliferation of techniques in society.

[1] The following is largely based on W.H. Vanderburg, "Some Implications of Modern Technology for Culture and Knowledge", presented at the 1983 AAAS annual meeting in Detroit, later published under the same title in *Man-Environment Systems*, Vol. 13, no. 5, Sept. 1983.

Speculation on what the computer could perhaps make possible is often voiced in total disregard of the sociocultural context in which the computer was invented and applied. This leads to a serious misunderstanding of the forces behind its diffusion throughout society. The new utopias predicted for tomorrow do not take into account the continuity in the patterns of development of modern societies made possible by the computer.

THE CONSEQUENCES OF THE TECHNICIZATION OF LIFE

When we reflect on the above description of the technical operation, we see that techniques are not neutral; they do not merely make an activity more effective. An area of human life is studied not holistically but for a specific purpose. As a result, certain aspects of the situation will be externalized (i.e., excluded from consideration) in the technical operation. Although a greater efficiency will be achieved in some area, this will be at the expense of significant *externalities*. Furthermore, the techncial operation separates knowing from doing, knowledge from experience and the knower from the doer. Consider a simple example.

Around the turn of the century, as machines in factories became increasingly efficient, the operations carried out by human beings caused a bottleneck. It made no sense to further improve the efficiency of the machines when the workers could not keep pace. In this context, studies were done on how to rationalize human work to make it more efficient. Some of the most famous studies were done by Gilbreth (Giedion, 1969: 102-105). By fastening a small electric light bulb to the wrist of a worker performing some task, it was possible to record the trajectory traced out by the bulb with three cameras mounted along three perpendicular axes. From the photographic records, wire models were constructed that showed exactly how the worker moved his or her hand. By analysing these models, it was possible to optimize the movements, and once this was accomplished, the worker was taught to perform the task more efficiently.

Gilbreth's technique perfectly illustrates the technical operation. As expected, rationalizing traditional work by this or other techniques creates an important externality. It can readily be identified when we compare traditional with technicized work. If we observe a traditional craftsperson at work, the gestures reflect a variety of things, such as the person's state of mind, personality, previous experience (including apprenticeship training) and culture. Once the "one best way" was determined by means of the technical operation, all this had to be suppressed as much as possible by the worker. This led to the well-known consequence of physical fatigue largely being replaced by nervous fatigue in technicized work. Normally, even in the most routine movements, something of our personality comes through, as is evident in the characteristics of our handwriting. This can be explained if we recall what we said earlier about the role of culture (Vanderburg, 1985). Since the relationship between human beings and reality is not predetermined genetically, the limited organization of the brain present at birth is expanded by experience. The mind that thus emerges in relation to the brain is the symbolic basis for mediating all relationships with reality. Since the mind is first shaped during socialization into a culture, it functions as a kind of mental map that the members of a culture use to interpret their experience and relate to one another and reality. While the mental map of each member of a culture is unique, it is sufficiently similar to those of other members to make communication possible. In traditional work, this mental map is the symbolic basis on which the craftsperson performs his or her operations.

Once work is technicized on the basis of the technical operation, the situation changes fundamentally. When workers are taught the one best way of moving their hands, they are being asked to suppress as much as possible their personality, state of mind, past experience and culture. Of course, this is not entirely possible, since their cultural mental map continues to play a role, although it is a reduced one. In a nontechnicized relationship, the mind makes it possible for each moment to be lived holistically, that is, in the context of and in relation to a person's whole being. This is not to say that alienation is impossible. In technicized relationships, on the contrary, a person must constantly suppress the way he or she would spontaneously act on the basis of his or her mental map. In technicized work, a person's mind must make a special effort to suppress his or her subjectivity. The result is nervous fatigue, which generally characterizes technicized work, as physical fatigue did traditional work. We must not absolutize these findings but remember that we are building an ideal type following Max Weber. As far as knowledge is concerned, it follows that traditional workers knew their work differently than people engaged in technicized work.

Technique as Milieu

The illustration of the technicization of work can now be generalized to determine some implications the phenomenon of technique has for individual and collective life. There is a long tradition of thinking about technology as a means to accomplish human ends. This is true, of course, but it is only a part of the picture. Technology and techniques also mediate relationships between human beings or between human beings and anything in their environment. Consider the telephone. It mediates between many people who may never meet face-to-face. This is obvious, but we often forget that this mediation is not neutral. It fundamentally transforms the relationship, since many sociocultural dimensions of a typical face-to-face relationship are stripped away, requiring a change in the relationship. The culture's facial expressions, gestures and body language (Hall, 1977) are not transmitted by the telephone. Yet these dimensions play an important part in face-to-face conversation, to the point that many people are uneasy talking to a blind person face-to-face because he or she typically does not respond to or transmit all the nonverbal dimensions of conversation. Young children using the telephone for the first time will also behave as though it were a face-to-face encounter. They quickly learn, however, that the telephone does not mediate in a neutral fashion.

What is true for the telephone is equally true for television. It mediates between producer and consumer, between the politician and the voter, between events around the globe and the viewer, and so on. These mediated relations are also transformed in a nonneutral way. A politician may come across well in person but may have to rely on a media consultant to ensure that she projects the right image. Advertising is not a neutral diffusion of information about products. By linking a product to certain symbols alive in the minds of people, it affects them subconsciously on the level where these symbols have become a part of their being, thus partly displacing the culturally mediated and conscious process of choice. All this is well known and need not be elaborated upon. What we have said thus far is equally true for computer-mediated relationships.

Techniques do not necessarily mediate relationships on the basis of some device. Many relationships are technically mediated with devices playing little or no essential part. Take a large office, for example. Here organization theory is applied to large numbers of people collectively performing a variety of tasks as effectively as possible. Here again, organizational techniques have been developed to find the best way of identifying, executing and interconnecting the functions of the organization. By making use of job descriptions and organizational charts, an optimal model is created that specifies how the relationships between the people in that office are to be technically mediated. People no longer primarily behave spontaneously, on the basis of their cultural mental maps. The relationships have been transformed, as the studies of bureaucracy by Max Weber and others have shown. We are not suggesting that mediation on the basis of culture is totally eliminated in a modern office, but technically mediated relationships predominate. If the cultural mediation entirely disappeared, we would find the human and social transformation described by Aldous Huxley in *Brave New World* (Huxley, 1932) or what Lewis Mumford calls the *megamachine society* (Mumford, 1970). Human beings would be completely adapted to society as mere pieces in a social mechanism. Such a transformation is far more radical than the one we are describing, and there is little sociological evidence of the possibility of that situation coming about. In fact, many problems of contemporary societies are the result of tensions between their technicized and nontechnicized elements.

A society changes fundamentally once most of the relationships in which its members are engaged become technically mediated. At this point, technique becomes the primary milieu for its members. It is in relation to this milieu that life evolves. This means much more than that the members of these societies live in an urban technical environment. Human existence has known only three primary milieus: nature in prehistory, society during much of our history and technique for the "industrially advanced" nations during the past two decades. In other words, it is in relation to the primary milieu that human life evolves. The milieu completely permeates all experience and presents human beings with almost everything they need to maintain their way of life, but it also threatens their existence. It fundamentally affects how people symbolically mediate their relationships with reality. This is evident when we recall that the mind develops by expanding the genetically established organization of the brain on the basis of internalized experiences. Hence, the characteristics of the resulting mental map (and thus, human consciousness), is decisively influenced by the primary milieu.

In prehistory, human beings lived in small groups totally dominated by nature. The natural milieu provided them with everything necessary for life, but it also posed the most serious threats in the form of droughts, wild beasts or storms, for example. Nature permeated almost every experience, producing a unique type of consciousness characterized by a certain kind of mental map.

When human beings began to live in societies at the dawn of history, the im-

Courtesy of R. Vanderburg

Courtesy of R. Vanderburg

Industrialization has also transformed war. Mass production made large armies possible. This totally transformed the nature of war, which in the past was fought with armies that were small by modern standards and which often left much of the population of warring societies relatively unaffected. War based on high technology will almost certainly destroy life on our planet. Rather than dealing with the root causes of war, however, nations are pushing expenditures on arms to unprecedented levels. If even a fraction of these resources were spent on peaceful pursuits, the world would be a safer place. The arms race is a good example of technology out of control. Here are some chilling statistics from the *UNESCO Courier* (March, 1982):

Number of persons directly or indirectly involved in military activities worldwide: 50 million

Global military industrial production costs: $100 billion

Global military consumption of aluminum, copper, nickel and platinum exceeds total demand for these materials in Africa, Asia and Latin America

Global land use for military purposes: 500 000 square kilometres

Percentage of world's scientists and engineers involved in military work exceeded 20 percent in the 1970s

Percentage of global research and development expenditures in 1980 used for military purposes: 25 percent

Per capita military expenditures for every man, woman and child on earth in 1980: $110 (US)

portance of the natural milieu became overshadowed by the social milieu. The latter interposed itself between the individual and nature. This made it possible for a society to better defend itself against natural dangers, but the new primary milieu also introduced a new series of dangers, such as war and economic or political instability, that could lead to the collapse of a society or civilization. Once the social milieu became the primary and nature the secondary milieu, a new type of consciousness emerged with correspondingly different mental maps.

When the phenomenon of technique began to transform a growing number of relationships, structures and institutions within a society, the first steps toward another transition commenced. It may well be as sweeping as the one from prehistory to history. Technically mediated relationships eventually dominated culturally mediated ones, and technique displaced society as the primary milieu. Society now constituted the secondary milieu and nature moved to third place. Life in a modern society, and particularly in its large urban centres, is impossible without a variety of technical support systems, while at the same time technique presents all societies with new ultimate threats: nuclear holocaust, the destabilization and poisoning of the ecosystem and the growing inability to provide meaningful work for all people. Again, a new consciousness emerges as techniques permeate almost every experience.

SUMMARY

The following selected references examine the effects technique and/or technology are having on various areas of contemporary society. See the bibliography at the back of this text for complete references. For an introduction, see *Perspectives on Our Age: Jacques Ellul Speaks on His Life and Work,* edited by W.H. Vanderburg. In art, see *Art and the Industrial Revolution,* by F.D. Klingender; *The Voices of Silence,* by A. Malraux; *Art and Technics,* by L. Mumford. In music, see *The Tuning of the World,* by R.M. Schafer, and *Music-Society-Education-Literature,* by C. Small. In literature, see *Literature Against Itself,* by G. Graff; *Language and Silence: Essays on Language, Literature and the Inhuman,* by G. Steiner; and *Literature and Technology,* by W. Sypher. On language, see an article by T.B. Farrell and G.T. Goodnight, "Accidental Rhetoric: The Root Metaphors of Three Mile Island," in *Communication Monographs; The State of the Language,* by L. Michaels and C. Ricks; and *The Technological Conscience,* by M. Stanley. On *weltanschauung,* see *Ways of Seeing,* by J. Berger et al.; *Mechanization Takes Command,* by S. Giedion; and *Technology and the Canadian Mind: Innis/McLuhan/Grant.* For thoughts on the effects of technique and/or technology on religion, see *The Orwellian World of the Jehovah's Witnesses,* by H. Botting and G. Botting; *The New Demons,* by J. Ellul; and by J.S. Glen, *Justification by Success.* On morality and values, see *The Collective Definition of Deviance,* edited by F. James Davis and Richard Stivers. Also, *Culture Against Man,* by J. Henry and "Values in Engineering," by M.W. Thring, in *Science and Public Policy.* In education, see *Education and the Cult of Efficiency,* by R.E. Callahan; *Deschooling Society,* by I. Illich; and *Education and the Rise of the Corporate State,* by J. Spring. On technique and/or technology and leisure, see *Of Time, Work and Leisure,* by S. de Grazia; *Leisure and Work,* by S. Parker; and *Sport and Work,* by B. Rigauer. On sexuality, see *Sex and Dehumanization,* by D. Holbrook; and an article by R. Stivers entitled "A Festival of Sex, Violence and Drugs: The Sacred and Profane in our World," which appeared in *Katallagete.* On agriculture, see *The Unsettling of America,* by W. Berry; *Food for Nought,* by R.H. Hall; and *Dry Cereals,* hearings held by the U.S. Senate Committee on Commerce, Consumer Subcommittee. And finally, on war, see *War and Industrial Society,* by R. Aron; *The Baroque Arsenal,* by M. Kaldor; and *War and Human Progress,* by J.U. Nef.

The proliferation of technicized relationships in modern societies has a profound influence on human life. The separation of knowing from doing and knowledge from experience causes us to depend on experts in almost every domain of life. Since we have devalued daily life knowledge that is embedded in experience, we need to turn to experts who supposedly know much more about the various aspects of our lives than we can know ourselves. If we are responsible and know what is good for us, we live in accordance with the objective body of technical experience. Experts make their living by giving us access to that knowledge, which is believed to be vital for our existence. They do this personally or via the multitude of how-to-do-it books that tell us how to treat our babies, how to talk to our teenage children, how to save a marriage, improve our sex life, sleep better, eat a balanced diet, organize a good vacation, cope with stress and so on. Apparently, we cannot be trusted to do these things ourselves anymore.

We are not saying, of course, that in the past, people did not rely on experts, we are saying that the phenomenon was on a completely different scale. We have created a society in which all of us, including the experts, must rely on others in important matters to the point that we have become spectators of much of our own lives. This phenomenon is taking on new proportions as a result of the proliferation of information services accessed through personal computers. It is fundamentally alienating, whether we are exploited or not. The fact that the control over one's own life has become largely external is a threat to human freedom, and it is also very stressful. The difficulty of participating in technicized relationships and the loss of control over one's life leads to the reification of the human subject—a fact powerfully portrayed in modern abstract art, which developed as the phenomenon of technique began to manifest itself. The human subject disappeared from art.

The technicization of life produces a new kind of alienation that is superimposed on economic alienation.

Consider the average man as he comes home from his job. Very likely he has spent the day in a completely hygienic environment, and everything has been done to balance his environment and lessen his fatigue. However, he has had to work without stopping and under constant pressure; nervous fatigue has replaced muscular fatigue. When he leaves his job, his joy in finishing his stint is mixed with dissatisfaction with a work as fruitless as it is incomprehensible and as far from really productive work. At home he "finds himself" again. But what does he find? He finds a phantom. If he ever thinks, his reflections terrify him. Personal destiny is fulfilled only by death; but reflection tells him that for him there has not been anything between his adolescent adventures and his death, no point at which he himself ever made a decision or initiated a change. Changes are the exclusive prerogative of organized technical society, which one day may have decked him out in khaki to defend it, and on another in stripes because he had sabotaged or betrayed it. There was no difference from one day to the next. Yet life was never serene, for newspapers and news reports beset him at the end of the day and forced on him the image of an insecure world. If it was not hot or cold war, there were all sorts of accidents to drive home to him the precariousness of his life. Torn between this precariousness and the absolute, unalterable determinateness of work, he has no place, belongs nowhere. Whether something happens to him, or nothing happens, he is in neither case the author of his destiny. . . . But amusement techniques have jumped into the breach and taught him at least how to flee the presence of death. He no longer needs faith or some difficult asceticism to deaden himself to his condition. The movies and television lead him straight into an artificial paradise. Rather than face his own phantom, he seeks film phantoms into which he can project himself and which permit him to live as he might have willed. For an hour or two he can cease to be himself, as his personality dissolves and fades into the anonymous mass of spectators. The film makes him laugh, cry, wonder, and love. He goes to bed with the leading lady, kills the villain, and masters life's absurdities. In short, he becomes a hero. Life suddenly has meaning (Ellul, 1964:376-377). This and all other excerpts from THE TECHNOLOGICAL SOCIETY, by Jacques Ellul, translated by John Wilkinson. Copyright © 1964 by Alfred A. Knopf, Inc. Reprinted by permission of the publisher.

During its initial phases, the web of techniques was built up in the self-interest of a specific social class. As more and more techniques linked together during the technical revolution, they became increasingly difficult to control, due to the technical alienation produced. Such alienation was experienced even by the powerful and wealthy.

The patterns of development of the "industrially advanced" world are those of the growth of technique. Many of the problems faced by present-day societies derive from these very patterns of development, yet we continue to seek new techniques in an attempt to solve the problems created by earlier ones. It is impossible, however, to solve problems by simply doing more of the kinds of things that created these problems in the first place. This approach merely replaces one problem with another, inevitably leading to a top-heavy and unstable technical order. Yet, because of the way technique as milieu influences human consciousness, societal values and myths, we continue to turn to technique to solve the problems created by it. There can, however, be no security in evermore powerful weapons, and there can be no real solution to our economic problems without addressing the challenge technique poses to human life and society. We need to create a civilization that includes technique but is based on a culture not permeated by it. This will determine the kind of world we will leave for future generations.

DISCUSSION QUESTIONS

1. When a society faces certain problems, it attempts to solve them by extending its institutions, way of life and means of existence. During the beginning of a new epoch in the history of a society, this makes a lot of sense since its problems become an opportunity for expanding and strengthening the basis on which its members live together. There soon comes a point in its development, however, when this approach becomes counterproductive because it often amounts to solving problems by doing more of the kinds of things that helped to produce them in the first place. This "inertia" in a society is not just a matter of powerful vested interests; it is, more importantly, the consequence of the myths and values that orient the members of a culture in a certain direction by valuing certain options and thereby devaluing others. Our modern society greatly values science and technology, and we consequently look for technical solutions to the challenges we face. We have difficulty seeing that technique is useful for certain things but useless for others. Critically assess the approaches that modern societies are taking to the following challenges:

    (a) *Our approach to defense*. Beyond a certain point, the application of modern science and technique to defense and weapons development creates a threat to human survival. Is the new Star Wars research an example of attempting to solve a problem by doing more of the kind of thing that helped to produce that problem in the first place? What alternative options are available to us? Do the Canadian, American or Russian people freely decide who their enemies really are, or is this all decided for us?

(b) *Our approach to underdevelopment.* Is this a problem with a technical solution, i.e., can it be solved by the transfer of techniques of all kinds?

(c) *Our approach to unemployment.* Is a strategy of ongoing economic growth based on scientific and technical development able to solve the problems of unemployment and the need to find meaningful ways for the members of a society to participate in its way of life? What about the problems of depleting resources and environmental pollution?

(d) Can the ongoing development of technique deal with the reification of modern life?

2. At international conferences it is common to hear delegations of so-called underdeveloped nations say that they wish to acquire the science and technology of the industrially advanced world but not the materialistic, consumer-oriented culture of the democratic nations or the bureaucratic and authoritarian state of the socialist countries. Do you think that this is possible, and, if so, what has the analysis presented in this chapter overlooked?

3. We have argued that in a culture permeated by technique, the minds of the members of each new generation acquire values which essentially define "the good" as everything that directly or indirectly advances technique and the power of the institutions that are the primary agents for applying, developing and transmitting techniques. Can this be explained in Marxist terms as being a part of the ideology created by the ruling class to justify and defend its power and position? If the mind is formed by internalized experiences, to what extent do you think such arguments are plausible? Can these values be explained from a functionalist-structuralist perspective, and, if so, how do we account for such problems as: environmental pollution and its threat to human health; the increased power of our weapons and the threat it poses to human survival; and the alienation and reification of human life?

4. Who or what controls modern technique and for what purpose? Who gains and who loses? Illustrate your argument with some examples.

14

Ideology, Social Order and Social Change

Anton L. Allahar

INTRODUCTION

Social scientists use several terms which, though widely employed, generate a great deal of controversy as to their precise meanings. Ideology is such a term. One often hears of ideological debates, ideological presuppositions, ideological biases and so on, but there is little agreement as to what ideology is or what it does. The concept is at best a contentious one. It is applied generally to those whom we wish to discredit, for, whatever other meaning the term may convey, it is usually employed in a negative or pejorative sense. In everyday parlance, for instance, when someone is accused of "being ideological" in a discussion, it implies that he or she is deliberately distorting the "facts," concealing the "whole truth" or being overly narrow in outlook.

In one respect, ideology is like charisma. While it is difficult to define charisma, most people can recognize it. We say, for example, that former prime minister Pierre Trudeau has it—he has that "something special" that former prime minister Joe Clark lacks. But exactly what that something special is, is difficult to pinpoint; so too with ideology. As Marchak (1975: 1) observes, ideologies "are seldom taught explicitly and systematically."

This chapter has two goals. The first is to move toward a definition of ideology that can be agreed upon by social analysts. This will entail considering numerous statements about the nature and essence of ideology and the process by which it is acquired. Our second goal is to assess the social and political functions of ideology. In other words, once we understand what it is, we will examine what it does. Nevertheless, it must be borne in mind that, although the questions of definition and function may be separated for analytical purposes, they will not be that clearly distinguishable in actuality.

CLASSICAL VIEWS ON IDEOLOGY

KUHN'S VIEW

The basic theme of this chapter concerns the relationship between ideology, order and change. To develop this theme we will use the concept of *revolution*, which implies both order and change, as a point of departure. For the moment, however, revolution will not be understood in the political sense. Rather, we will talk more philosophically, in the manner that Thomas Kuhn (1970) spoke of *scientific revolutions*.

When discussing revolutionary changes in the realm of scientific knowledge, Kuhn contended that the process involved the "rejection of one time-honored scientific theory in favour of another" (1970: 6). But such a process is not without considerable struggle and resistance, for the scientist who practises "normal science" has a commitment to the established methods of his or her trade. "Normal science" is thus seen as inherently conservative:

> Normal science, for example, often suppresses fundamental novelties because they are necessarily subversive of its basic commitments (Kuhn, 1970: 5).

Revolutionary breaks with past practice and the acceptance of new methods and knowledge are thus conceived of by Kuhn as "tradition-shattering complements to the tradition-bound activity of normal science" (1970: 6). This commitment of a scientific community to a well defined and coherent set of established practices and beliefs is referred to as a *paradigm* (1970: 176-81). And science is replete with examples of outmoded, current and emerging paradigms. In fact, the basic "stuff" of scientific revolutions and progress entails conflicts between paradigms, between communities of scholars, their ideas, and their findings.

Kuhn's observation that changes in the dominant paradigm "cause scientists to see the world of their research-engagement differently" and that "after a revolution scientists are responding to a different world" (1970: 111) is crucial to the student of ideology and social change. For, as Hagopian has pointed out:

> Scientists are, after all, opinion makers and their views ultimately affect the general state of beliefs in society. . . . And it is quite likely that the new world harbours many aspects that are not in keeping with the view of the world associated with the traditional society (1974: 140).

Building on the insights of Kuhn, we can discuss some of the classical views on ideology. If normal science is conservative and scientific revolutions are radical, we can expect each to have its own ideological justifications of and defenses for its right to exist. The conservatives, those associated with the traditional society, will argue for the wisdom and correctness of tradition; the radicals, who have no stake in the existing order, will insist on the need for change.

MARX'S AND WEBER'S VIEWS

For Marx, ideology is viewed negatively as a set of beliefs that serves to justify and legitimize the rule of the few over the many. He sees the economic structure of capitalism, the system under which commodities produced by workers are appropriated by capitalists, as the basis for the development of class conflict and ideology. By ideology he means the moral codes, philosophies, art, law, religion and even literature that comprise a society's *superstructure*, the glue that binds together the economic base or *substructure* of that society. For example, the religious injunction, "Thou shalt not steal," clearly serves the interests of those who own property. When the propertyless worker who is compelled to sell his labour power to the capitalist internalizes and abides by this religious exhortation, potential conflict is minimized, and both worker and capitalist can go about their daily affairs.

Because Marx gave primacy to economic dealings and how they colour the greater part of all social interactions, and because he linked ideology with domination and the class structure of society, he underestimated the autonomous role that ideas and ideology can play in everyday life. His use of the term "ideology" is very general, and it was left to other scholars, most notably Max Weber and Karl Mannheim, to attempt a more complete treatment of it. We must point out, however, that neither Weber nor Mannheim managed completely to divorce ideology from class (Gerth and Mills, 1958: 61-63; Abercrombie et al., 1980: 30-36).

From Weber's point of view, it is not that Marx was wrong to emphasize the economic basis of domination, for on that score he applauds many of the insights of Marx. As Zeitlin says:

He was not concerned with refuting Marx . . . nor did he see himself as having bested Marx. On the contrary, he looked upon Marx's analytical concepts and methodological principles as extraordinarily fruitful (1981: 28).

Weber's main quarrel with Marx, however, was that he did not go far enough to take account of the noneconomic bases of human action. For Weber, human behaviour is informed largely by meanings, subjective perceptions and personal assessments of goals. Psychological states, he felt, are as important as material interests in guiding that behaviour. This is a central theme in his *Protestant Ethic and the Spirit of Capitalism* (1958). In that study, he shows how the Calvinist doctrine of predestination rendered believers psychologically anxious: There was no way of knowing whether one was saved or damned. Hence, literally to preserve their sanity, members of the faith sought to do things to convince themselves that they were worthy of salvation. They worked hard, saved their money, led ascetic lives and so on, all of which complemented the ethos of early capitalism. Weber's point, then, is that the religious ideas and teachings of Calvinism had a definite impact on how Calvinists conducted their economic lives. It was not that capitalism as an economic form came into existence and later gave rise to the ideology of ascetic Protestantism.

Weber, therefore, was concerned with "rounding out" the Marxian thesis, with demonstrating the nonmaterial bases of action and showing how, under certain circumstances, "ideas become effective forces in history" (Weber, 1974: 90). Thus, "with Marx he shares the sociological approach to ideas: they are powerless in history unless they are fused with material interests" (Gerth and Mills, 1958: 62). But where Marx emphasizes an almost one-to-one correspondence between ideas and interests, Weber is also eager to recognize possible tensions between them. In other words, though ideas and class interests are often linked, Weber leaves the door open to the possibility of a conflict between ideas and material interests.

Applying the concept of *elective affinity* to ideology, Weber would argue that human beings are not total prisoners of social or class structures. They have some freedom to choose and discard ideas as they suit their purposes:

> Ideas do gain an affinity with the interests of certain members of special strata; if they do not gain such affinity, they are abandoned (Weber, 1974: 63).

In linking the views of Weber and Mannheim on ideology, Abercrombie et al. are quick to point out their connection to Marxism. Marx's contention that the dominant ideas of every age are the ideas of the dominant class, the *dominant ideology thesis*, represents his attempt to reduce ideas to concrete economic and political interests. But for Weber and Mannheim also, class is a crucial variable:

> The sociology of knowledge tradition of Weber and Mannheim attempts to show how beliefs can be reduced to social groups . . . . the sociology of knowledge which tries to develop a non-Marxist theory of ideology in fact arrives at similar class-theoretical conclusions to the dominant ideology tradition with Marxism (Abercrombie et al., 1980: 30).

And as far as Mannheim himself is concerned, writers like Wolff (1969: 508) and Remmling (1975: 44) show that his sociology of knowledge is firmly rooted in the

Marxian tradition. This much Mannheim would not deny, for he often acknowledged his intellectual debts to Marx (Mannheim, 1936:75-77).

MANNHEIM'S CONTRIBUTION

But Mannheim, like Weber, rejected Marx's overly economic definition of class. As Coser tells us,

> Mannheim did not limit himself to a programme of study inherited from Marxian class analysis. He included a variety of other social factors such as status groups and occupational categories as existential determinants of ideas (1977: 433).

The important point, however, is that Mannheim, though sensitive to the non-material bases of thoughts and actions, nevertheless constantly referred back to the class (or what he called *group*) origins of ideas and actions. Nowhere is this made more clear than in his discussion of *ideology* and *utopia*.

For Mannheim, the everyday conditions of existence and the conflicts that they generate between various groups and classes lead to two opposing kinds of ideas. Such ideas he termed *situationally transcendent*, or unreal, for they do not fit into the prevailing order (Mannheim, 1936: 194). Situationally transcendent ideas are of two types: they are either ideological or utopian, depending on the *social location*, or *perspective*, from which they are viewed. The rulers, oppressors or members of the upper strata, who have a vested interest in maintaining the status quo, dismiss the claims of the ruled or oppressed strata as unrealistic, or *utopian*. The oppressed, conversely, see the oppressors' defense of the status quo as *ideological*: The appeal to divine law, the sanctity of tradition or the natural order of things are all deemed ideological, for they are inherently conservative and defend the existing order (Hagopian, 1974: 256).

In elaborating on his ideas, Mannheim separates the *particular* conception of ideology from the *total* conception. The first deals with the micro situation and operates at the psychological and individual level: "Since the particular conception never actually departs from the psychological level, the point of reference in such analyses is always the individual" (Hagopian, 1974: 58). The particular conception also refers to the scepticism we feel about the ideas of an opponent whom we suspect of telling lies in order to prevent us from seeing a given situation in its true light. Supposedly, it is in the interest of our opponent that we do not see the situation as it really is. Hence, at the level of individuals, the *particular* conception of ideology concerns the conscious distortion of the truth.

The *total* conception of ideology concerns the thoughts of whole classes, epochs, civilizations and ages. The ideologies of democracy and liberalism are instances of the total conception. For example, when Prime Minister Mulroney talks of his commitment to democratic principles, he speaks a language that all of Canada, North America and the Western world can understand. But in rounding out his discussion, Mannheim makes one further qualification.

The total conception, we are told, can further be divided into two types: special and general formulations. Quite simply, the *special* formulation of the total conception of ideology involves our ability to identify our opponent's ideas as ideologically and situationally determined. The *general* formulation, conversely, concerns our "courage to subject not just the adversary's point of view but all points of view, including [our] own, to ideological analysis" (Hagopian, 1974: 77).

We will now look at some contemporary views on and uses of ideology, beginning with an attempt to provide a comprehensive definition of that term.

DEFINING IDEOLOGY

THE PRIMACY OF FAITH IN IDEOLOGY

Ideology is a body of systematic beliefs and ideas. By systematic, however, we do not mean that the beliefs and ideas are necessarily *logically* interconnected in a scientific and empirical manner. The central doctrines in Christianity, for example, include belief in the Holy Trinity, belief that there is one God and that Christ is both God and the son of God, belief in the virgin birth, and belief in the resurrection. Of course, to converts who unquestioningly accept that "miracles do happen" and who accept on faith the existence of an all-powerful and all-knowing God, these beliefs are not problematic. But sociology is a social science concerned with empirical proof, and such beliefs are nonscientific and cannot be proved empirically.

We know that the virgin birth, for instance, is a logical and biological impossibility. But even if we accept that it happened, there is a further problem. In biological reproduction, the female carries the XX chromosome while the male contributes the XY chromosome which determines the sex of the offspring. Now, even if the Virgin Mary became pregnant without sexual intercourse, if the male XY chromosomal contribution were absent, her child (Jesus) logically would have had to be female. Similar logical and biological arguments could be made about the resurrection and the Holy Trinity.

The point is, nonetheless, that as an ideology, Christianity consists of a series of beliefs that are connected, though not necessarily *logically*. And what is more, Chris-. tian doctrine is accepted by hundreds of millions of people around the world as an integral part of their lives. The strength with which the ideology is embraced and its persistence in light of scientific evidence to the contrary, however, leads us to consider another feature of ideology.

The earlier observation that ideology is a body of systematic beliefs and ideas should be modified to stress that it is *primarily* a body of beliefs and *secondarily* a body of ideas. The distinction is more than semantic. For ideas are open to scientific testing and verification; beliefs are not (Rejai, 1971: 3). Hence, ideologies, as systems of beliefs, are difficult and maybe even impossible to refute or challenge on empirical grounds. Scientifically speaking, one can neither prove nor disprove the existence of God. It is purely a matter of faith: Either one believes or does not believe.

This raises a third consideration in defining ideology: the relationship between ideology and science or ideology and truth. Ideologies are like dogmas. They claim to be true but do not propose a method to substantiate their claim. Science, on the other hand, pursues knowledge and truth in a demonstrable fashion. Scientific truth can be questioned, tested, refuted, upheld or disproven. As Bergmann suggests, an ideological statement is "a value judgement disguised as, or mistaken for, a statement of fact" (1951: 210). McCain and Segal equate ideology with dogma:

You are being too ideological so let's now examine this whole matter OBJECTIVELY from MY point of view.

One way of contrasting science and dogma is to say that a scientist accepts facts as given and belief systems as tentative, whereas a dogmatist accepts the belief systems as given; facts are irrelevant (1969: 31-32).

This does not mean, however, that certain scientific truths have not been made dogma by those who accept them as absolute. Nor does social science only deal with "facts as given." For facts are never free of theory. They are always interpreted and screened subjectively as human beings seek to impart *meaning* to them.

THE FIVE DIMENSIONS OF IDEOLOGY

Based on our discussion so far, we can clarify our understanding of ideology a bit more. An ideology usually consists of five dimensions: the cognitive, affective, evaluative, programmatic, and social (Rejai, 1971: 3-10). The *cognitive* dimension refers to the fact that ideologies embody a significant element of myth, which simplifies a complex social reality (Lasswell and Kaplan, 1950: 116-33). Such simplification is usually accomplished by using symbols (for example, the crucifix) that "package" meanings of and responses to reality:

Whether linguistic (words or speech) or nonlinguistic (flags, insignia, monuments, holidays, ceremonies, anthems), symbols capture in an economical fashion large expanses of meanings and communicate these meanings in an instantaneous fashion (Rejai, 1971: 6).

As might be imagined, the cognitive and *affective* dimensions are closely related. To the extent that ideologies elicit emotive responses, they are embraced blindly and sometimes passionately. This is clearly seen in political, religious and nationalist ideologies: "One might say, in fact, the most important, latent function of ideology is to tap emotion" (Bell, 1960: 371).

The *evaluative* dimension of ideology concerns the question of "the good society." In this context, an ideology will either criticize the existing status quo or defend it by appealing to high-sounding moral principles. Particularly in political ideology, one hears explicit references to regimes that suppress or support human rights, liberty, equality and dignity. Ideologies often involve value judgements aimed at discrediting those who do not support a particular ideology. This is accomplished by masking the truth in some cases and by exaggerating it in others.

Thus, United States' President Ronald Reagan, for example, describes the Soviet Union as an "evil empire" bent on destroying the "free world." In fact, so evil are the Soviets that their govenment oppresses its own citizens. Here one is given to understand that in the United States, there is no inequality, no racial oppression, no social barriers to limit individual mobility and success. Internationally, too, we are led to believe that American foreign policy is designed with the interests of oppressed peoples at heart, whereas Soviet foreign policy is motivated by self-interest.

Many ideologies also have a *programmatic* dimension, in that they call for action that translates specific values, norms and ideas into practice. Such actions, as was hinted above, will be aimed either at maintaining a given status quo or transforming it. The ideologies of conservatism, black power and feminism are cases in point. And, as we might expect, the call to action will also have a *social* component. Hence, ideologies are associated with social groups and classes whose members represent specific interests, ambitions, hopes, dreams, ideals and preferences. As the two fundamental units of subjective action in any society, individuals and social groups or classes are creators and carriers of ideology. This is why Daniel Bell referred to ideologies as "mobilized belief systems" that seek to

> simplify ideas, establish a claim to truth, and, in the union of the two, demand a commitment to action. Thus not only does ideology transform ideas, it transforms people as well (Bell, 1960: 372).

Later in this chapter, we will take a closer look at the relationship between ideology, social class and change. But for the moment, we may take the following as a working definition of ideology that will be refined during our discussion. An ideology is a system of mobilized beliefs that claims to represent the truth and reality but does not make any provision for assessing the veracity of those claims. To make itself accessible to the majority of the population, ideology simplifies its depiction of truth and reality by using symbols, appeals to emotions, socially accepted values and high-sounding moral principles. Finally, the values and principles embraced in an ideology usually imply some course of social action if they are to be adhered to and if they are to successfully represent the interests and ambitions of their promoters.

FUNCTIONS OF IDEOLOGY

On a practical level, ideology serves two general functions. Ideologies help to either maintain social *order* or to promote social *change*. As we saw in Chapter 1, an understanding of order and change is intrinsic to the sociological enterprise. In any society, an uneasy tension exists between forces that make for stability and forces that threaten to disrupt stability and bring about change.

Without social order, social living would be impossible. As human societies grow larger and more complex, the tasks of planning and regulation at the international, national, regional and subregional levels assume increasingly bureaucratic forms. And in the liberal democratic states particularly, those tasks are plagued by a constant dilemma: How do we strike the delicate balance between individual liberty and social harmony? In one way or another, this has been the central issue in the writings of the great political philosophers such as Thomas Hobbes, John Locke, Jean Jacques Rousseau, John Stuart Mill, Jeremy Bentham, Alexis de Tocqueville and many others. At what point does the pursuit of individual self-interest conflict with the collective well-being of society? How much and what kinds of freedom can individuals be allowed without jeopardizing the whole society? Are individual liberty and social control incompatible? Can there be social order without social control?

We will see in the next section how ideology is used for social control. Of course, control may also be effected by using overt force or coercion. But using force *alone* is both costly and cumbersome and cannot guarantee long-term stability. No social system can afford to rely exclusively on force to control its members—not even in a prison or a concentration camp.

Shifting our attention to social change, we may also note the key role played by ideology. In the same way that one may speak of "ideologies of order" (for example, conservatism), one may also identify "ideologies of change" (for example, radicalism). To the extent that social change is often (though not always) associated with social movements, it is clear that ideology will have an important part to play. For it is in the ideology of such a movement that its goals are explicitly stated. And, as was said before, since ideologies usually encompass a call to action, no social movement lacks an ideological component. The ideologies of social movements give those movements a sense of coherence, identity and purpose. These issues will be reviewed when we consider the student movement and the FLQ movement in Quebec during the 1960s and early 1970s.

IDEOLOGY, LEGITIMACY AND SOCIAL CONTROL

In this study, it is assumed that social control can either deny group and individual liberty or support it. But far from being a zero-sum phenomenon, control and freedom are multidimensional and are matters of degree. Further, they are not mutually exclusive and contradictory, for some degree of control is indispensable to freedom, both individual and collective. The central questions, therefore, are control by whom and freedom for whom? These, in turn, are questions of power and social class, for the dominant class, or a fraction of that class, in any society is advantageously placed to exact obedience or compliance from the subordinate classes.

The observation by Marx and Engels that "the ideas of the ruling class are in every epoch the ruling ideas" (1969: 39) is usually taken as those authors' summary statement on ideology. Among other things, it implies a relationship between both class and ideology and between power and ideology—the organized and structured power of a given class:

> The class which is the ruling material force of society is at the same time its ruling intellectual force. The class which has the means of material production at its disposal, has control at the same time over the means of mental production. . . . The ruling ideas are nothing more than the ideal expression of the dominant material relationships grasped as ideas; hence of the relationships which make the one class the ruling one, therefore the ideas of its dominance (Marx and Engels, 1969:39).

In this context, ruling class ideologies set limits to the consciousness of the ruled classes or, stated differently, they create *false consciousness*. Since ruling class ideologies are linked to practical political and economic interests, they will portray those interests as universal. To maintain social order and stability, it is important that those who benefit from such order and stability, those with a direct stake in maintaining the status quo, convince the less privileged that the system works to the mutual benefit of everyone in it.

The related ideologies of liberalism, individualism and free enterprise are cases in point. As essential underpinnings of the capitalist system, it is crucial for the working-class and the unemployed in that system to accept that their lots in life are arrived at fairly. The so-called "system" must not be perceived as being "rigged against them" but rather must be seen as being free and open, rewarding individual merit and ensuring the survival of the fittest. Such people, therefore, must be convinced that their apparent "failure" is due to their own shortcomings. They have only themselves to blame, since the system's integrity, its commitment to fair play and equal opportunity are beyond reproach.

Thus, as was said earlier, ideologies are the intellectual and emotional justifications used by individuals, groups and classes to organize their cultural symbols, to interpret their world and to give focus and meaning to their common actions (Gramsci, 1971: 377; Simon, 1982:58-66). But at this point, a new element in the definition of ideology must be added, for ideologies do not seek to depict social reality pure and simple. They emphasize certain aspects of reality while masking other aspects. Ideologies, therefore, in serving or legitimizing the interests of the dominant class, cannot be neutral. They actively mask or distort those aspects of social reality that do not correspond to the claims advanced by those in power.

Ideology has thus been viewed as a tool for social control which the ruling or dominant class has at its disposal. Hence, the definition of the situation embodied in the dominant ideology will reflect the concerns of that ruling class. In the previously cited example of capitalism, for instance, the ideology of equal opportunity is widely propagated and embraced by the population at large. Although individual members of the society may actually be less privileged and less mobile than others, the population as a whole believes that all people compete fairly and equally for scarce resources or rewards.

In Canada, for example, we are told that "education is a means to mobility." Further, we are told that education is free, at least up until the end of high school. Thus, those who are not mobile, those who are not "successful," have only themselves to blame. The ideology of equal opportunity, premised as it is upon the ideologies of liberalism and individualism, thus becomes accepted as true, even by those lacking the various trappings of success. Accepting the blame for their lack of mobility or success, various individuals and groups rationalize their situation by saying such things as, "I did not work hard enough"; "It's my fault for not applying myself"; "Nature dealt me a rotten hand"; "The fates are against me"; "That's the luck of the draw," and so on.

Such responses do not question whether or not there *is* equal opportunity. People channel the blame either onto themselves or remove it entirely from the realm of human control and talk about such things as fate and luck. Thus, those in control, those who promote the myth of equal opportunity, those who mask the fact that class, race, religion and sex are important determinants of mobility and success, escape unscathed. The ideology persists and social order is maintained. (This point will be reconsidered in the last section on ideology and democracy.)

Any discussion of ideology, then, will also involve considerations of social control. As a mechanism of control, it is far more efficient and less costly than physical coercion. Not only does it obviate the need for close supervision, but it also makes for more social and political stability. If a given population or specific social class can be made to act in ways that run counter to its own interests (whether immediate or long-term) without perceiving those actions to be harmful to itself, then there is no need to embark upon an elaborate program to control that population or class. It is rendered so blind to its particular interests that it fails to grasp them as class interests, while simultaneously embracing the interests of its oppressor as its own. And herein lies the question of legitimacy: The rule of the oppressor goes uncriticized.

Ideology of Nationalism as Social Control

To elucidate the above points further, we may consider the ideology of nationalism in a class-divided society, particularly during times of war or large-scale social and political upheaval. Witness, for example, the reactions of the masses of Argentine and British citizens to the conflict between those two countries in 1982 over the Malvinas, or the Falkland Islands. Putting aside the grave domestic economic and political problems in their respective countries, both populations rallied solidly behind their governments and went to war for an idea—an idea that evoked a sense of patriotism and pride in their homelands.

For a brief moment, in Argentina particularly, the government did not have to worry about local uprisings and protests against the brutal and dictatorial treatment that it had been meting out to its citizens; nor did it have to worry about the immediate consequences of an unemployment rate in excess of 40 percent and inflation that topped the 200 percent mark. All energies were channelled to uphold national pride and dignity. Opposition parties, political prisoners, the unemployed and various youth groups were all prepared to put aside local differences and were mobilized against the British. And even within Britain, also a class-divided society, where Prime Minister Margaret Thatcher was losing a large measure of her popular support, similar trends were noted. Her decisive action in sending the navy and other armed forces to the Falklands boosted her political fortunes at home so much that she called national elections soon after the war and won a resounding victory.

In such situations, public sentiments can be manipulated simply by invoking the threat of a common external enemy. Another clear example of this, though in a slightly different context, occurred during the American invasion of the tiny Caribbean nation of Grenada in October, 1983. In that case, Grenada was said to have been undermined by an enemy identified as "international communism." The citizens of Grenada were given to understand that the enemy had taken control of their leaders and their country and that the only hope of salvation lay in the American Marines. Hence, during the invasion, the Grenadian people openly embraced the Marines and thanked God for having delivered them from the hell of communist perversion.

As we were told by United States President Ronald Reagan, the "popular response" of the Grenadian people showed their firm "commitment to liberal democratic traditions and institutions." However, prior to the "communist" government's coming to power, Grenada had been ruled by Eric Gairy, a dictator who had been in office for over 30 years and whose personal reign of terror was never once questioned by the American government. Thus, the firm commitment to democracy of which President Reagan spoke must be seen as an attempt to mask the absence of democratic traditions in that country. For even before Gairy, Grenada was a colonial possession of Britain, and during colonial rule local input into political and economic decisions was restricted to the point of being virtually nonexistent.

Ideologically speaking, it was important for the American government to retain Grenada as a faithful ally. The geopolitical significance of the country was enhanced even further because the Soviet Union already had ideological and military allies in Cuba and Nicaragua. Hence, the Americans could not afford another Soviet "base" in so sensitive an area, so close to its own shores. Invading Grenada was, therefore, politically necessary in order that a government more favourably disposed (ideologically) to Washington could be reinstalled. And this has, in fact, been accomplished.

But even if we grant the political and ideological interests of Washington, how can we explain the so-called "popular response" of the Grenadians to the Marines on ideological grounds? And what does this have to do with the ideology of nationalism? The answers can be found in what was said earlier about invoking the threat of an external enemy: Communism and communists are "evil." Hence the "free world" (note the ideological content of the term) must be forever vigilant lest the enemy infiltrate and take control of our countries, ourselves and our minds. And the Grenadians were made fully aware of the dangers of communism.

As far as the American Marines in particular are concerned, Grenadians had been socialized to accept them as liberators, as "good guys" whose patriotic and unselfish duty it was to save the world from communist and other "forces of evil." Grenadians, like so many others in their circumstances, wholly identified with and revered such Hollywood heroes as Audie Murphy, John Wayne and Alec Guinness and their heroic deeds in such films as *Back to Bataan*, *The Battle of the Bulge*, *The Longest Day* and *Bridge on the River Kwai*. Generations of colonialism and cultural domination had programmed the bulk of the Grenadian population to accept Washington's definition of what was in Grenada's best interests.

As an ideology, nationalism transcends class boundaries and unites an otherwise divided population in the defense of a common idea or ideal. Nowhere is this point made more clearly than in George Orwell's classic best seller, *Nineteen Eighty-Four*. In Orwell's discussion of public rallies and reactions in the fictitious society of Oceania, we can see how the citizens were constantly mobilized by the threat of foreign invasion by Eastasia and Eurasia alternately. Living with such threats, their attention and energies were cleverly directed away from their more immediate domestic problems, and the authorities did not have to worry about local dissent, uprisings or revolts against their rule:

> All that was required of them [the proles] was a primitive patriotism which could be appealed to whenever it was necessary to make them accept longer working hours or shorter rations. And even when they became discontented, their discontent led nowhere, because being without general ideas, they could only focus it on petty specific grievances. The larger evils invariably escaped their notice (Orwell, 1984: 66, courtesy of the estate of the late Sonia Brownell Orwell and Secker & Warburg Limited).

Evidently, Oceania was a special case. It was a situation in which the ruling authorities relied heavily in the short-term on coercion to secure social order. Such coercion, however, was viewed merely as a stop-gap measure to be used *only* until the government's full program could be realized. And that program aimed at total thought (ideological) control. It was designed, as we will see presently, to eliminate all conflict, opposition or threats to the social order as defined by those in power.

Social Control and Complementarity

A final point in our theoretical treatment of social control and legitimacy concerns the issue of complementarity, which is systematically elaborated in the work of Bernd Baldus (1975, 1977). This author argues that social control can be effected in two ways: either via the deliberate intervention of some body or agency or via the manipulation of *complementary conditions*. Under the rubric of interventive control, Baldus includes both *physical coercion* and *ideological persuasion*. Our use of the term *interventive control* is slightly different. We reserve it solely for physical coercion, since it seems to imply more direct and immediate attempts at controlling behaviour than does ideological persuasion. As indicated in the above discussion of Orwell's Oceania, physical and ideological control differ in both form and content. Ideological control is slower, more subtle, less easily resisted and hence, more difficult to escape once it is established. And those subject to ideological control tend to be less aware of the fact than those subject to physical control. The former is less likely to produce protest on the part of the controlled, while those in control do not suffer the loss of legitimacy. It does not occur to the controlled to question the controllers' motives and intentions.

The manipulation of *complementary conditions* represents the specific insight of Baldus. As a strategy of control "it involves the use of already existing conditions" (Baldus, 1977: 250) within the population and society at large. In essence, it seeks to discover patterns of behaviour in the target population to see whether such behaviour *complements* the interests of the authorities or the ruling class. Where it is complementary, it will be used or exploited; and where such patterns of behaviour do not exist beforehand, the ruling class may attempt to create them.

An example of the deliberate use of complementarity is reported to us by Baldus, based on his reading of Philip Agee's (1975) *Inside the Company*. As an ex-CIA agent turned critic, Agee could give incisive insights into the daily operations of the American Central Intelligence Agency. And Baldus claims that in his devastating exposé of the CIA, Agee

> shows the planned and systematic search by the Agency for complementary conditions which can be employed to weaken leftist political movements and to prevent significant social change. The financial support of existing conservative parties, the use of local mass media to disseminate false information and to conceal its origins, or the bombing of churches in such a way that it is likely to be attributed to "radical subversives" take advantage of existing conditions which are favourable to the Agency's goals. These conditions have *not* been created by the CIA, but they represent important complements essential to the success of the Agency's operations. In the ideal case, they require only minimal efforts of guidance or exposure to have their desired effects (From the *Canadian Journal of Sociology*, Vol. 2 (3), 1977, pp. 250-51. Reprinted by permission).

In a similar vein, we may refer again to *Nineteen Eighty-Four* for another example of the use of complementarity. Among the "proles" of Oceania, who made up 85 percent of the population of 300 million (Orwell, 1984: 64, 67), Orwell tells us there existed a fairly high level of apathetic behaviour. Even the mass rallies were carefully orchestrated and had an air of superficiality about them. The proles were fatalistic and resigned to their lot in life. They were mostly apolitical and interested only in the minute irrelevant details of daily life. In fact, as Winston, the main character, remarked after an aborted conversation with one of them: "The old man's memory was nothing but a rubbish-heap of details. One could question him all day without getting any real information" (1984: 82).

Using the pervasive mood of apathy and disinterestedness, the government of Big Brother realized its program of mass control by staging certain public happenings, such as the Lottery, which further distracted the proles from the reality of their condition.

> The Lottery, with its weekly pay-out of enormous prizes was one public event to which the proles paid serious attention. It was probable that there were some millions of proles for whom the Lottery was the principal if not the only reason for remaining alive. It was their delight, their folly, their anodyne, their intellectual stimulant. Where the Lottery was concerned, even people who could barely read or write seemed capable of intricate calculations and staggering feats of memory. There was a whole tribe of men who made a living simply by selling systems, forecasts and lucky amulets (Orwell, 1984: 82, courtesy of the estate of the late Sonia Brownell Orwell and Secker & Warburg Limited).

With a largely uninformed, distracted and ignorant population, the job of social control is that much easier. If those conditions are already in existence, they will be viewed as complementary to the interests of those in control or those who wish to exercise control. If, on the other hand, such conditions do not already exist, they may be created by manipulating public education systems and the mass media. Again, the techniques of subtle ideological persuasion will be used.

Using complementarity as a strategy of social control, then, will yield two benefits to the ruling authorities. The first, according to Baldus, concerns expense, for complementarity secures the desired behaviour at costs much lower than those that would be incurred if the same behaviour were secured by interventive (coercive) control.

The second benefit is that the interests of the dominant class are protected while simultaneously permitting a wide variety of behaviours among the population at large to continue. For, as Baldus observes, "Complementary behaviour is judged primarily by its instrumentality or utility for dominant class interests" (Baldus, 1977:251). Hence, it is of no immediate importance if the proles in Orwell's Oceania, for example, attributed meanings to their behaviour that were totally different from those assigned by the dominant interests:

> So long as they continued to work and breed, their other activities were without importance. Left to themselves . . . they reverted to a style of life that appeared to be natural to them. . . . They were born, they grew up in the gutters, they went to work at twelve, they passed through a brief blossoming period of beauty and sexual desire, they married at twenty, they were middle-aged at thirty, they died, for the most part, at sixty. Heavy physical work, the care of home and children, petty quarrels with neighbours, films, football, beer, and above all, gambling, filled up the horizon of their minds. *To keep them in control was not difficult* (Orwell, 1984: 65, emphasis added).

It is thus clear that the behaviour of the proles was complementary to the interests of the Party—and they were forever distracted:

> Even the civil police interfered with them very little. There was a vast amount of criminality in London, a whole world-within-a-world of thieves, bandits, prostitutes, drug-peddlers, and racketeers of every description; *but since it all happened among the proles themselves, it was of no importance* (1984: 66, emphasis added. Courtesy of the estate of the late Sonia Brownell Orwell and Secker & Warburg Limited).

Quite apart from the subjective and personal meanings assigned to their behaviour, therefore, what really mattered was the final outcome of that behaviour—its contribution to the goals of the dominant class:

> Consequently, periphery units *often are not aware of the complementarity of their own behaviour*. Moreover, the use of complementary periphery behaviour does not require an interaction between dominant class and periphery. It is often the very absence of actions in the periphery, for instance as a result of ignorance or because internal strife weakens or preoccupies the periphery, which facilitates the realization of dominant class interests. The use of complementary behaviour therefore allows the dominant class to obtain needed means from a periphery which *appears to pursue goals of its own choice, and free of outside interference* (Baldus, emphasis added. From the *Canadian Journal of Sociology*, Vol. 2(3), 1977, p. 251. Reprinted by permission).

Again, this appearance of freedom is important from the point of view of legitimacy, control and order. The less conscious one is of being controlled or manipulated and the more one feels in charge of one's destiny, the more effective is that control and the more secure the social order.

IDEOLOGY, ROUTINIZATION AND CHANGE

Before discussing the direct relationship between ideology and change, it is important that we examine the question of *routinization*, or the process by which the extraordinary becomes ordinary. In Weber's political sociology, he paid a great deal of attention to the issues of domination and authority in society. He spoke of three basic ideal types: charismatic, traditional and legal. Here we will be concerned mainly with charismatic leadership and domination. As Bendix tells us, Weber used the term *charisma* to designate

> an extraordinary quality possessed by persons . . . that is thought to give these persons a unique magical power. . . . the man who possesses genuine charisma exercises domination, but this power of command differs from legal and traditional domination in that it is extraordinary (Bendix, 1962: 299).

The rise of charismatic leaders is closely associated with times of crisis, social unrest or revolution. When the routine of everyday life is upset and traditional or legal forms of domination can no longer restore order, the situation is ripe for the appearance of someone with that "gift of grace" called charisma. Charismatic leaders are truly revolutionary in that they challenge established practice and manipulate public sentiments in a manner that often transcends traditional class, status and ethnic divisions in society. Examples of charismatic leaders from history are Jesus, Mohammed, Napoleon and Hitler.

After the passage of the initial crisis that brings the charismatic leader to the fore, there begins a process of institutionalization of the new order that Weber refers to as *routinization*. The cooling off of extraordinary states of devotion and fervour paves the way for the development of institutions, which Weber says can lead to either traditionalism or bureaucratization (Gerth and Mills, 1958: 54). The petty and mundane issues of everyday life thus lead to the routinization of charisma, as offices, rules and regulations are put in place to handle the particular concerns and needs of ordinary citizens.

Such institutionalization and bureaucratization for Weber is a necessary evil. It is necessary in order to meet the numerous and diverse demands of individuals, especially in large and differentiated societies; and it is evil in that it leads to cold, impersonal and antidemocratic institutions. Bureaucratic organizations, as we know, concentrate decision-making in the hands of the few. And this is the context in which Weber spoke of the "iron cage" of bureaucracy. It makes for greater overall efficiency but at the expense of direct mass input.

Expressing similar sentiments, Robert Michels talks of the "iron law of oligarchy" in his analysis of *Political Parties* (1962). Along with Gaetano Mosca and Vilfredo Pareto, Michels is known as an *elite theorist*. These authors believe that democracy in the strict sense of rule by the majority is impossible. There always has to be a small, cohesive minority that will make the rules to govern the masses. This is what is meant by oligarchy: "The principal cause of oligarchy is to be found in the technical indispensability of leadership. . . . The mass will never rule except *in abstracto*" (Michels, 1962: 365, 366). Like the other elite theorists, therefore, Michels is convinced that the masses are inferior to their leaders and follow them out of blind devotion:

> Taken in the mass, the poor are powerless and disarmed vis-à-vis their leaders. Their intellectual and cultural inferiority make it impossible for them to see whither the leader is going, or to estimate in advance the significance of his actions (1962: 369).

On the basis of these observations, Michels argues for "the historic necessity of oligarchy." Oligarchy is the natural outcome of political organization (or *bureaucratization*, in Weber's terms), for "the social wealth cannot be satisfactorily administered in any other manner than by the creation of an extensive bureaucracy" (Michels, 1962: 347). Thus, in analysing political parties, even socialist ones, Michels contends that oligarchy is inescapable: "It is organization which gives birth to the domination of the elected over the electors. . . . who says organization, says oligarchy" (1962: 365).

In addressing the socialist parties particularly, Michels raises the question of the relationship between socialism and democracy. Because of the social distance between the leadership and the masses, he feels that the socialist party leaders will succumb to *bureaucratic conservatism* and place the needs of organizational survival over ideology or adherence to doctrine. "Knowing what is best for the masses," the leaders of socialist parties will thus undertake a revolution that inevitably results in a "dictatorship in the hands of those leaders who have been sufficiently astute and sufficiently powerful to grasp the sceptre of dominion in the name of socialism" (1962: 19). And once in power, institutions and bureaucracies will develop and their rule will become routinized.

Picking up this theme, Crane Brinton discusses *The Anatomy of Revolution* (1965). He identifies three phases of a revolution: the rule of moderates, the reign of terror and virtue, and the Thermidor. We are concerned here with the last of the three, *the Thermidor*, which refers to the new French calendar at the time of the French Revolution and the fall of Robespierre on July 27th, 1794. Briefly summarized, the rule of moderates, or the *moderate interregnum*, covers the first phase of the revolution when the moderate rulers are sandwiched between the ousted ruling class and the more extremist tendencies within the revolutionary movement. In the second phase, the extremists take power from the moderates and institute a *reign of terror* to stamp out all opposition and inculcate new revolutionary sensibilities (virtues) in the masses.

The Thermidorian reaction, according to Brinton, begins with the leaders of the radical movement, who, after the terror and

> once the crisis period is over, will, save for the few born martyrs, cease to be crusaders, fanatics, ascetics. Their revolutionary beliefs will be softly cushioned in a comfortable ritual, will be a consolation and a habit rather than a constant prick of the ideal (Brinton, 1965: 191).

Describing the Thermidor as "a convalescence from the fever of revolution" (1965: 205), Brinton argues that during this third phase, as the revolutionaries grow old and feeble or simply die and as the revolution becomes more institutionalized, bureaucratized and routinized, a period of conservatism sets in: Revolutionary passion wanes; strict laws are relaxed; concessions to opposition interests are made; and many of the more radical economic measures are toned down. At this point, Edwards says,

> The revolutionary government itself, as it gets older, ceases to be revolutionary and presently ceases to think of itself as revolutionary. The revolution is complete (Edwards, 1970: 200).

Marxism and Change

The ideology of change most often referred to is Marxism. The ideology of Marxism is seen to be opposed to the social and economic system of capitalism: Based on Marx's critique of the dehumanizing consequences of capitalism, the ideology of Marxism has come to represent, in general terms, the interests of those who are unhappy with economic exploitation, class inequality and political impotence, as these derive from the structure of capitalist society. Like all ideologies, Marxism has a general appeal. But as a specific ideology, it is most attractive to those who are less privileged or who have most reason to be critical about the capitalist system.

This does not imply, however, that the less privileged are automatically the most critical. People in this category are often unaware of the causes of their misery. Hence, one will find poor, uneducated and unemployed people in the United States, for example, extolling the virtues of capitalism and liberal democracy. This is a condition referred to by Marx as *false consciousness*. It occurs because the pervasive influences of early socialization, schooling, religious teaching and the mass media are able to portray social inequality in such a way that the less privileged members of society come to see their problems in personal rather than in systemic terms. They internalize the definition of themselves that is embodied in the dominant ideology. And it is precisely this false consciousness that Marxism seeks to dispel.

Because ideologies are presented in ways that have a mass appeal, many people embrace them at a very superficial level of understanding. Such is the case with Marxism. Many disadvantaged individuals and groups can identify with the general sentiments Marxism expresses and see it as championing their cause. Hence, although they may not be familiar with the precise details of the Marxian critique of capitalism, they nevertheless embrace its general thrust. Thus, we must be careful not to confuse the ideology of Marxism as it has been summarized here with Marxism as a social scientific critique of capitalism.

Let us, therefore, consider the student movement to assess how it incorporated elements of Marxist ideology and used those elements, albeit superficially, to inform its purpose.

The Student/Youth Movement

During the 1960s, Western Europe and North America witnessed a period of social upheaval that altered many of their deep-seated ways of thinking and behaving. The mood of the day was aptly captured in Bob Dylan's song "The Times They are a' Changing," which served as an impetus for the rebirth of protest music, particularly in the United States. Amidst such cries as "Power to the people," "Give peace a chance," and "Hell no, we won't go" (to Vietnam), a variety of social movements took root as people began to demand changes in governmental and other social institutions. Many adopted the slogan "Question authority" as their official motto.

In this context, one might think of the student movement, the youth or hippie movement, the civil rights or black power movement, the antiwar movement and the women's liberation movement. All shared a concern with where contemporary society was heading. All argued that elected political leaders and the men who controlled the big corporations had lost sight of their social responsibilities. In relentlessly pursuing political domination and economic profits, government and business leaders were trampling the "little man," and a genuine concern for the quality of human life took a back seat to the dictates of corporate profitability. The rich were getting richer and the poor were getting poorer.

The student and youth movements, in particular, attracted young, idealistic people, the products of the postwar baby boom, who were largely of comfortable middle-class origin and who were growing up in a time of prosperity. Hearing horror stories of the war from their parents, seeing the films and learning about the Nazi holocaust, among other things, these young people were determined to avoid the excesses of their parents' generation. They organized peace marches, love-ins, and antinuclear demonstrations, all with a view to overcoming the sense of alienation that characterized the "generation gap" between themselves and the older members of society. In the process, they embraced an anti-imperialist stance, formed organizations in solidarity with Cuban revolutionaries, the Vietnamese people, the blacks of South Africa and the victims of capitalist oppression and exploitation everywhere. To this extent, the ideology of Marxism, with its *humanistic* content, was appealing to the youth of the time and to those who wrote sympathetically about them.

Among the most influential writings of the period are John and Margaret Rowntree's, *The Political Economy of Youth* (1968) and Herbert Marcuse's, *One-Dimensional Man* (1964), *An Essay on Liberation* (1969) and *Counter-Revolution and Revolt* (1972). A common theme reflected in these and other works was the implicit, and often explicit, Marxian critique of industrial capitalism. As Marcuse observed, the popular movements of the day were inspired by Marxist ideology and sought principally to unite young people and workers in opposition to economic exploitation and political repression:

> The real interest, the attainment of conditions in which man could shape his own life, was that of no longer subordinating his life to the requirements of profitable production, to an apparatus controlled by forces beyond his control. And the attainment of such conditions meant *the abolition of capitalism* (Marcuse, 1969: 15, emphasis added).

An identification with the more humanistic content of Marxism was also revealed in the youth-as-class notion of Rowntree and Rowntree (1968). Using the general sentiments associated with Marxian "class analysis" (though ignoring the theoretical rigour of the term), these authors described students and young people in general as a separate class. Armed with statistics, they argued that in the United States, at least half of the males between the ages of 18 and 24 could be found within the ranks of students, soldiers and the unemployed. Their point was that the schools and the military functioned to keep the unemployment rate at an acceptably low level, thus diffusing the potential for mass dissatisfaction and frustration among young people: "The young are exploited as soldiers, as students, and as unemployed workers" (Rowntree and Rowntree, 1968: 13). In summarizing this point, Levitt (1984: 5) notes that students came to view themselves as a new "youth proletariat," exploited by capital and manipulated by the state:

> As unemployed they are robbed of their productive potential; as young soldiers they are underpaid and trained to kill; as students they are forced to produce and reproduce themselves as skilled labour to suit the wants of corporate capital (Levitt, 1984: 122).

As with most opposition ideologies, the student movement incorporated both a moral critique of existing society and a call to action, concerning itself with such issues as nuclear testing and disarmament, environmentalism, militarism and civil rights. In claiming to transcend narrow political and ideological positions, the students saw themselves as moral crusaders armed with Truth: "Speak truth to power and the truth shall set you free." They challenged the traditional institutions and practices of the older generation, established communes, engaged freely in premarital sex, experimented with all kinds of drugs and rejected the outer trappings of material success in their society. They grew long hair, wore beards, went barefoot and generally sought to embarrass or shock the guardians of the old order. As opposed to military and economic power, they favoured flower power.

At the ideological level, the student youth identified their social and moral rejection of established society with Marxism. For them, Marxism represented everything the older generation eschewed; hence, Marxism had to be good. This is not to say that they were totally blind or ignorant of what Marxism was, but their understanding of it was very superficial and even distorted. As Levitt tells us, among the students, very few converts to the Marxism of the New Left were won as a result of a "careful presentation and sifting of evidence, through reasoned debate, or by weighty intellectual argument" (1984: 139). Rather, the appeal was more emotional given its moralistic content and its call to action and involvement. Hence, in spite of their Castro beards, their guerrilla army fatigues, their revolutionary slogans and posters of Ché Guevara, all the student radicals needed to know was that the general sentiments attributed to Marxism coincided with theirs.

But, having said all of this, what actual changes did the movement manage to effect? Although it is not easy to answer such a question in precise terms, suffice it to say that by the time the movement died in the early 1970s, an entire generation of thinking had been changed. There was much greater social awareness about nuclear war, imperialist control of Third World countries, poverty, racism, sexism, women's rights and native rights within the leading liberal democratic countries. On many high-school and university campuses, students were able to elect their own representatives; they won a voice in determining some of the content of their curricula, in recruiting teachers and in the provision of recreational, food and housing services. Sex education clinics, campus day-care facilities and offices of ombudsmen are also among the gains. And last but not least is the political awakening of students and other youth, whose votes are now actively sought by professional politicians.

The FLQ Movement

In Canada, the *Front de Libération du Québec* (FLQ) may serve as an example of an attempt at revolutionary change that embraced the ideology of Marxism. The French-speaking people of Quebec, particularly the workers, have long complained that they are second-class citizens in their own country. They charge that the owners, managers and top executives of the large corporations and businesses are English Canadians, that the huge corporate profits are not reinvested in Quebec, that they are discriminated against in matters of language and religion and that the federal government has always worked in complicity with the Anglo-Saxon capitalist interests to the detriment of *les Québecois*. In fact, their grievances were well summed up in the title of a book written by one of their leaders, Pierre Vallieres, and called *The White Niggers of America* (1971).

Arguing that Quebec was a nation separate from Canada and that Quebec was a colony of Canada, the "white niggers of America" sought to do what the "black niggers" had been doing for many years. They began a struggle aimed at the decolonization and total independence of their country—Quebec. In the process, the FLQ emerged as the militant wing of the independence movement. They employed tactics similar to those used by other groups in various parts of the world that were struggling toward the same goal: clandestine meetings, kidnappings, terrorist bombings, urban guerrilla attacks on targets that symbolized colonial tutelage, underground press releases that denounced federalism and Anglo-Saxon capitalism and so on. They even issued a manifesto outlining the philosophy of the movement, its major goals and demands.

The use of Marxist ideology and rhetoric in the *FLQ Manifesto* is clear. Its style and content bear a striking resemblance to the *Communist Manifesto* written by Marx and Engels in 1848. But it is interesting to note that while the FLQ called for an end to Anglo-Saxon capitalism, it did not call for the abolition of capitalism per se, nor did it mention anything about socialism. This reinforces the earlier point made in connection with the student movement and the notion of a "youth proletariat": Both movements embraced Marxism as an ideology, *not* as a social scientific critique of capitalism. They both had a superficial appreciation of the humanistic content of Marxism, and that was sufficient to sustain them ideologically. An excerpt from the *FLQ Manifesto* (opposite) clearly shows the extent to which the movement adopted that ideology in its demands for social change in Quebec.

IDEOLOGY AND DEMOCRACY

In closing, it will be instructive to reflect briefly on the relationship between ideology and democracy as practised in our Western liberal societies. It is instructive because for many people, the term "democracy" has a very rigid meaning, and it is reserved almost exclusively for reference to the countries of Western Europe and North America. This point was brought home to me recently upon my return from a trip to Cuba, when someone asked me, "Is Cuba socialist or democratic?" Implicit in the question is the idea that socialism and democracy are antithetical to each other— a country cannot be both socialist and democratic at the same time. The same idea, albeit in an altered form, was reflected in President Reagan's comments following the American invasion of Grenada, which were referred to earlier. Mr. Reagan said, "We (the Marines) arrived in Grenada just in time to save democracy." Apparently,

THE FLQ MANIFESTO

The people in the *Front de Libération du Québec* are neither Messiahs nor modern-day Robin Hoods. They are a group of Quebec workers who have decided to do everything they can to assure that the people of Quebec take their destiny into their own hands, once and for all.

The *Front de Libération du Québec* wants total independence for Quebeckers; it wants to see them united in a free society, a society purged for good of its gang of rapacious sharks, the big bosses who dish out patronage and their henchmen, who have turned Quebec into a private preserve of cheap labour and unscrupulous exploitation.

. . . what is called democracy in Quebec has always been, and still is, nothing but the "democracy" of the rich. . . . Consequently we wash our hands of the British parliamentary system; the *Front de Libération du Québec* will never let itself be distracted by the electoral crumbs that the Anglo-Saxon capitalists toss into the Quebec barnyard every four years. Many Quebeckers have realized the truth and are ready to take action. . . .

We are fed up with the taxes we pay that Ottawa's agent in Quebec would give to the English-speaking bosses as an "incentive" for them to speak French, to negotiate in French. Repeat after me: "Cheap labour is *main d'oeuvre à bon marché* in French."

Workers in industry, in mines and in the forests! Workers in the service industries, teachers, students and unemployed! Take what belongs to you, your jobs, your determination and your freedom. And you, the workers at General Electric, you make the factories run; you are the only ones able to produce; without you, General Electric is nothing!

Workers of Quebec, begin from this day forward to take back what is yours; take yourselves what belongs to you. Only you know your factories, your machines, your hotels, your universities, your unions. . . .

Make your revolution yourselves in your neighbourhoods, in your places of work. . . . Only you are capable of building a free society.

We are Quebec workers and we are prepared to go all the way. . . . we want to replace this society of slaves by a free society, operating by itself and for itself, a society open on the world.

Our struggle can only be victorious. A people that has been awakened cannot long be kept in misery and contempt.

Long live Free Quebec!
Long live our comrades the political prisoners!
Long live the Quebec Revolution!
Long live the *Front de Libération du Québec!*

the government of Grenada, which had developed close relations with the Soviets and Cubans, had placed Grenadian democracy in jeopardy.

Democracy is understood to be a unique social and political attribute of countries in "the free world," itself an ideological term. But what does democracy really mean? Could one argue that the word "democracy," in spite of its apparent neutrality, has ideological functions, that it masks certain aspects of social reality, that the theory and practice of democracy do not necessarily coincide?

The answers to such questions can be found by analysing liberalism and the rise of the capitalist market economy. As far as Western countries are concerned, their form of democracy is best described as *liberal democracy*. The term "liberal" is meant to indicate that before they became democratic, before the vote was extended to all adult citizens, these countries had evolved what we know today as the liberal market economy. In Britain, France and the United States, for example, this type of economy existed long before slaves were freed or women and nonpropertied people had the right to vote.

The maturation of the market society and economy and its eventual democratization, Macpherson says, coincided with the creation of a) the society and politics of choice; b) the society and politics of competition; and c) the society and politics of the market (1965: 6). Indeed, a striking feature of these countries is that they are all capitalist. Liberal democracy and capitalism appear to go well together, for, with few exceptions, the capitalist countries of today can generally boast a liberal democratic political system.

Ideologically, freedom of choice and the freedom to compete are cornerstones of capitalism. In addition, the emphasis on these freedoms is closely linked to the idea of individualism, as was discussed earlier. We speak, for example, of *individual* free choice as a major tenet of liberalism. Freedom is defined as the *individual's* ability to choose; and the society that permits the greatest personal freedom and range of choice is seen as the best society. We are told that competition is healthy. A society that does not encourage competition does not encourage excellence. Thus, the "free" and "fair" competition among individuals for desired goods and services contributes to the overall well-being of the system. And finally, there is the market, the arena of fair play in which individual freedom of choice and competition among equals can be realized.

From the point of view of ideological control, the beauty of the free enterprise, liberal, market society is that not only is success attributed to *individual* initiative and effort, but failure also is easily explained as the result of too little *individual* initiative and effort. The key point, masked by the liberal ideology, is that the system is not necessarily free and fair and competition does not necessarily take place among equals.

We are dealing here with capitalist market society, and one thing is certain: As an economic system, capitalism is premised upon a fundamental inequality between those who own and those who do not own the major means of production. All other inequalities are derived from this one. The point, therefore, is that, by definition, capitalism is a system of entrenched inequality; and while all may be free to choose and compete, *some will always be freer than others*. And this is the crucial aspect of social reality that is masked by the ideology of liberal democracy.

SUMMARY

In this chapter, we have defined ideology as a system of beliefs and ideas that orients the patterns of thought and the actions of human beings in the world. Ideologies are rooted in society, and no person anywhere can be without them. It is generally the case that ideologies are promoted by specific groups and classes with a view to protecting their own interests. In the process, ideologies mask and distort certain aspects of social reality which, if they were not masked, would threaten the security of the dominant group's interests. Finally, to be effective, ideologies must have a mass appeal. They must also claim a higher morality, a truth, with which most people can subjectively identify. And in this respect, ideologies seek not only to distort social reality but also to simplify it by using symbols whose meanings are readily understood by the population at large.

After defining ideology, we analysed its specific social and political functions. The first function was social control. We observed that some control is essential for the preservation of social order, for as populations increase and societies become more complex, social co-ordination and planning also grow in complexity. Contrary to the utilitarian view, which holds that the surest guarantee of social order is the pursuit of individual self-interest, we argue that social order must be created deliberately. It does not come about as the automatic result of each individual doing what is best for him or her. For it is not certain that what is in one person's best interest will necessarily be advantageous to another. Hence, if we all tried to maximize our own interests, there is no guarantee that the greatest good for the greatest number would automatically follow.

Ideology can also promote social change. In this context, we examined the radical, revolutionary ideologies that inform certain social movements that are aimed at restructuring the existing society or parts of it. Ideologies of change, it was said, embrace a call to action on the part of individuals and groups who perceive the status quo as somehow working against their own interests. Ideologies of change, however, can become quite conservative once the movements that they inspire and sustain gain power. This is the case with the once revolutionary ideology of Marxism-Leninism in the Soviet Union, where the status quo appears to be very intolerant of change. In terms of the analysis presented here, therefore, the government of the Soviet Union, at least in domestic matters, acts very conservatively.

DISCUSSION QUESTIONS

1. From the point of view of ideology, why are the questions of social control and social order seen to be of paramount importance?

2. In talking about ideology, Marx once remarked that "religion is the opiate of the masses." What do you think he meant? Your answer should make reference to the social functions of religion.

3. Apart from the three examples in this chapter, give a fourth example of how the ideology of nationalism has been used by a government to further its own political or economic interests.

4. Under what conditions do ideologies of change become conservative? Provide and discuss an example.

5. In what ways does the ideology of liberal democracy complement the economic system we call capitalism?

BIBLIOGRAPHY

Abella, Rosalie S. *Report of the Royal Commission on Equality in Employment*. Ottawa: Minister of Supply and Services, 1984.

Abercrombie, Nicholas; Stephen Hill; and Bryan S. Turner. *The Dominant Ideology Thesis*. London: George Allen & Unwin, 1980.

Akenson, Donald. *The Irish in Ontario: A Study in Rural History*. Kingston and Montreal: McGill-Queen's University Press, 1984.

Althusser, L. *For Marx*. Harmondsworth: Penguin Books, 1969.

Alwin, Duane F. "Trends in Parental Socialization, Detroit, 1958–1983." *American Journal of Sociology*, Vol. 90, No. 2, pp. 359-382, 1984.

Ambert, Anne-Marie. *Divorce in Canada*. Toronto: Academic, 1980.

Anderson, Alan B., and James S. Frideres. *Ethnicity in Canada: Theoretical Perspectives*. Toronto: Butterworth, 1981.

Armstrong, Pat, and Hugh Armstrong. *The Double Ghetto*. Toronto: McClelland and Stewart, 1978.

Aron, R. *Eighteen Lectures on Industrial Society*. London: Weidenfeld & Nicolson, 1967.

Atkinson, A.B. *The Economics of Inequality*. London: Oxford University Press, 1975.

Badgley, Robin. *Sexual Offences Against Children*. Report of the Committee on Sexual Offences Against Children and Youth. Ottawa, 1984.

Badham, R., and C. Davies. "The Sociology of Industrial and Post-Industrial Societies." *Current Sociology*, Vol. 32, No. 1, pp.1-145, Spring 1984.

Baker, Maureen. "Concerns and Controversies Within Family Sociology." In *The Family: Changing Trends in Canada*, pp. 1-20. Toronto: McGraw-Hill Ryerson, 1984.

———. "Divorce: Its Consequences and Meanings." In *The Canadian Family*, edited by K. Ishwaran, pp. 289-300. Toronto: Gage, 1983.

———. *What Will Tomorrow Bring? A Study of the Aspirations of Adolescent Women*. Ottawa: Canadian Advisory Council on the Status of Women, 1985.

Baldus, Bernd. "Social control in capitalist societies: an examination of 'the problem of order' in liberal democracies." *Canadian Journal of Sociology*, Vol. 2, No. 3, 1977.

———. "The study of power: suggestions for an alternative." *Canadian Journal of Sociology*, Vol. 1, No. 2, 1975.

——— and Verna Tribe. "The development of perceptions and evaluation of social inequality among public school children." *Canadian Review of Sociology and Anthropology*, Vol. 15, No. 1, pp. 50-60, 1978.

Beattie, Christopher. *Minority Men in a Majority Setting*. Toronto: McClelland and Stewart, 1975.

Beaujot, Roderic. "The decline of official language minorities in Quebec and English Canada." *Canadian Journal of Sociology*, Vol. 9, No. 4, pp. 367-389, 1982.

——— and Kevin McQuillan. *Growth and Dualism: The Demographic Development of Canadian Society*. Toronto: Gage, 1982.

Becker, Howard S. "Problems of inference and proof in participant observation." *American Sociological Review*, 23, pp. 652-660, 1958.

———. *Sociological Work*. New Brunswick, N.J.: Transaction Books, 1970.

———; Blanche Geer; and Everett C. Hughes. *Making the Grade: The Academic Side of College Life*. New York: Wiley, 1968.

———; Blanche Geer; Everett C. Hughes; and Anselm L. Strauss. *Boys in White: Student Culture in Medical School*. New Brunswick, N.J.:Transaction Books, 1961.

Bell, Daniel. *The Coming of Post-Industrial Society*. New York: Basic Books, 1973.

———. *The End of Ideology*. London: Collier Books, 1961.

———. "The Social Framework of the Information Society." In *The Computer Age: A Twenty-Year View*, edited by Michael L. Dertouzos and Joel Moses. Cambridge, Mass.: The MIT Press, 1979.

————. "Technology and Politics." *Survey,* No. 16, 1971.

Bell, David, and Lorne Tepperman. *The Roots of Disunity.* Toronto: McClelland and Stewart, 1979.

Bem, Sandra. "The Measurement of Psychological Androgyny." *Journal of Consulting and Clinical Psychology,* Vol. 42, pp. 155-162, 1974.

Bendix, Reinhard. *Max Weber: An Intellectual Portrait.* New York: Anchor Books, 1962.

————. *Nation-Building and Citizenship.* Berkeley and Los Angeles: University of California Press, 1977.

————. *Work and Authority in Industry.* New York: Harper and Row, 1956.

Bereleson, Bernard, and Patricia Salter. "Majority and Minority Americans." *Public Opinion Quarterly,* Vol. 10, pp. 168-190, 1946.

Berg, Ivar. *Education and Jobs: The Great Training Robbery.* New York: Beacon Press, 1970.

Berger, Peter, and Brigette Berger. *Sociology: A Biographical Approach.* 2d ed. New York: Basic Books, 1975.

———— and Thomas Luckmann. *The Social Construction of Reality.* Garden City, N.Y.: Doubleday, 1966.

Bergmann, Gustav. "Ideology." *Ethics,* LX1, April 1951.

Berle, Adolphe A., and Gardiner C. Means. *The Modern Corporation and Private Property,* rev. ed. New York: Harcourt, Brace and World, 1967.

Bernard, Jessie. *The Sex Game.* New York: Atheneum, 1972.

Berton, Pierre. *Hollywood's Canada.* Toronto: McClelland and Stewart, 1975.

Beurkel-Rothfuss, Nancy and Sandra Mayes. "Soap Opera Viewing: The Cultivation Effect." *Journal of Communication,* Vol. 31, No. 3, pp. 108-115, 1981.

Blalock, Hubert M., Jr. *Causal Inferences in Nonexperimental Research.* New York: Norton & Co., 1972.

Blauner, Robert. *Alienation and Freedom.* Chicago: University of Chicago Press, 1964.

————. *Racial Oppression in America.* New York: Harper & Row, 1972.

Blishen, Bernard. "Perceptions of National Identity." *Canadian Review of Sociology and Anthropology,* Vol. 15, No. 2, pp. 128-132, 1978.

————. "A Socio-economic Index for Occupations in Canada." *Canadian Review of Sociology and Anthropology,* Vol. 4, No. 1, pp. 41-53, 1967.

———— and Hugh McRoberts. "A Revised Socio-economic index for Occupations in Canada." *Canadian Review of Sociology and Anthropology,* Vol. 13, No. 1, pp. 71-79, 1976.

Blumberg, Abraham S., and Elaine Niederhoffer, eds. *The Ambivalent Force: Perspectives on the Police.* 3d ed. New York: Holt, Rinehart & Winston, 1985.

Blumberg, Rae L. *Stratification: Socioeconomic and Sexual Inequality.* Wm. Brown, 1978.

Blumer, Herbert. *Symbolic Interactionism.* Englewood Cliffs, N.J.: Prentice-Hall, 1969.

Bolaria, B. Singh, and Peter S. Li. *Racial Oppression in Canada.* Toronto: Garamond Press, 1985.

Bollen, K.A., and D. P. Phillips. "Imitative Suicides: A National Study of the Effects of Television News Stories." *American Sociological Review,* Vol. 47, pp. 802-809, 1982.

Bonacich, Edna. "Abolition, the extension of slavery, and the position of free blacks: a study of split labor markets in the United States, 1830-1863." *American Journal of Sociology,* Vol. 81, pp. 601-628, 1975.

————. "Advanced capitalism and black/white race relations in the United States: a split labor market interpretation." *American Sociological Review,* Vol. 41, pp. 34-51, 1976.

————. "The past, present, and future of split labor market theory." In *Research in Race and Ethnic Relations,* Vol. 1, edited by C.B. Marrett and C. Leggon. Greenwich, Conn.: JAI Press, 1979.

————. "A theory of ethnic antagonism: the split labor market." *American Sociological Review,* Vol. 37, pp. 547-559, 1972.

———— and John Modell. *The Economic Basis*

of Ethnic Solidarity. Berkeley: University of California Press, 1980.

Boon, James A. "Further operations of culture in Anthropology: a synthesis of and for debate." *The Idea of Culture in the Social Sciences,* edited by L. Schneider and C.M. Bonjean, pp. 1-32. Cambridge: Cambridge University Press, 1973.

Bosk, P.G. "The Transnational Corporation and Private Foreign Policy." *Society,* J/F, pp. 44-49, 1974.

Boughey, Howard. *The Insights of Sociology.* Boston: Allyn and Bacon, 1978.

Boulet, Jac-André, and Laval Lavallée. *The Changing Economic Status of Women.* Ottawa: Economic Council of Canada, 1984.

Boulton, David. *The Grease Machine: The Inside Story of Lockheed's Dollar Diplomacy.* New York: Harper & Row, 1978.

Bourdieu, Pierre, and Jean-Claude Passeron. *Reproduction in Education, Society and Culture.* Beverly Hills: Sage Publications, 1977.

Bowles, Samuel, and Herbert Gintis. *Schooling in Capitalist America: Educational Reform and The Contradictions of Economic Life.* New York: Basic Books, 1976.

Boyd, Monica et al. "Status Attainment in Canada." *Canadian Review of Sociology and Anthropology,* Vol. 18, No. 5, pp. 657-673, 1981.

Brake, Mike. *The Sociology of Youth Culture and Youth Subculture.* London: Routledge & Kegan Paul, 1980.

Braverman, Harry. *Labor and Monopoly Capital: The Degradation of Work in The Twentieth Century.* New York: Monthly Review Press, 1974.

Breton, Raymond. "Institutional completeness of ethnic communities and personal relations to immigrants." *American Journal of Sociology,* Vol. 70, pp. 193-205, 1964.

———. "The production and allocation of symbolic resources: an analysis of the linguistic and ethnocultural fields in Canada." *Canadian Review of Sociology and Anthropology,* Vol. 21, No. 2, pp. 123-124, 1984.

Brinton, Crane. *The Anatomy of Revolution.* New York: Vintage Books, 1965.

Bryan, James H. "Apprenticeships in Prostitution." *Social Problems,* Vol. 12, No. 3, pp. 287-297, 1965.

———. "Occupational Ideologies and Individual Attitudes of Call Girls." *Social Problems,* Vol. 13, No. 4, pp. 441-450, 1966.

Bryant, Clifton D. "The Concealment of Stigma and Deviancy as a Family Function." In *Deviancy and the Family,* edited by Clifton D. Bryant and J. Gipson Wells, pp. 391-397. Philadelphia: F.A. Davis Co., 1973.

Brym, Robert J. "The Canadian Capitalist Class, 1965-1985." In *The Structure of the Canadian Capitalist Class,* edited by R. Brym. Toronto: Garamond Press, 1985.

Burgess, Joanne. "L'Industrie de la chaussure à Montréal, 1840-1870. Le Passage de l'artisan a la fabrique," *Revue d'Histoire de l'Amerique Francaise,* 31 (Sept.) 1977: 187-210.

Butler, Matilda, and William Paisley. *Women and the Mass Media.* New York: Human Sciences Press, 1980.

Campbell, Donald T., and Julian C. Stanley. *Experimental and Quasi-experimental Designs for Research.* Chicago: Rand McNally, 1970.

Campbell, Ernest Q. *Socialization, Culture and Personality.* Englewood Cliffs, N.J.: Prentice-Hall, 1975.

Canada, Government of. *Royal Commission on Bilingualism and Biculturalism.* Ottawa: Queen's Printer, 1969.

———. *The Status of Day Care in Canada.* Submission to the Federal Task Force on Day Care. Ottawa: Department of Health and Welfare, November 1984.

———. *Royal Commission on Health Services.* Ottawa: Queen's Printer, 1964.

———. *Language Use in Canada.* Ottawa: Minister of Supply and Services, 1980.

———. *Report of the Special Senate Committee on the Mass Media.* Ottawa: Queen's Printer, 1970.

———. *Royal Commission on Newspapers.* Ottawa: Ministry of Supply and Services, 1981.

———. *Cultural Tradition and Political History of Women in Canada.* Studies of the Royal

Commission on the Status of Women in Canada, Ottawa: Information Canada, 1971.

Carey, James W. "Communication and Culture." *Communication Research,* Vol. 2, pp. 176-191, 1975.

Carroll, William K. "Dependency, Imperialism and the Capitalist Class in Canada." In *The Structure of the Canadian Capitalist Class,* edited by Robert J. Brym. Toronto: Garamond Press, 1985.

————; John Fox; and Michael Ornstein. "The Network of Directorate Interlocks among the Largest Canadian Firms." *Canadian Review of Sociology and Anthropology,* Vol. 19, No. 1, pp. 44-69, 1982.

Cashmore, E. Ellis, and Bob Mullan. *Approaching Social Theory.* London: Heinemann Educational Books, 1983.

Castles, Stephen, and Godula Kosack. *Immigrant Workers and Class Structure in Western Europe.* London: Oxford University Press, 1973.

Castonguay, Charles. "Exogamie et anglicisation chez les minorités canadiennes-françaises." *Canadian Review of Sociology and Anthropology,* Vol. 16, pp. 21-31, 1979.

Census of Canada. Ottawa: King's and Queen's Printer, decennial, 1901-81.

Chappell, Neena L. "The Future Impact of the Changing Status of Women." In *Canada's Changing Age Structure, Implications for the Future,* edited by Gloria M. Gutman. Vancouver: Simon Fraser University Publications, 1982.

———— and Nina L. Colwill. "Medical Schools as Agents of Professional Socialization." *Canadian Review of Sociology and Anthropology,* Vol. 18, No. 1, pp. 67-79, 1981.

Cicourel, Allen V., and John I. Kitsuse. *The Educational Decision-Makers.* Indianapolis: Bobbs-Merrill, 1963.

Clarke, H.D. et al. *Political Choice in Canada.* Toronto: McGraw-Hill Ryerson, 1979.

Clement, Wallace. *The Canadian Corporate Elite.* Toronto: McClelland and Stewart, 1975.

————. *Continental Corporate Power.* Toronto: McClelland and Stewart, 1977.

————. "The Corporate Elite, the Capitalist Class, and the Canadian State." In *The Canadian State,* edited by L. Panitch. Toronto: University of Toronto Press, 1977.

Clinard, Marshall B., ed. *Anomie and Deviant Behavior.* New York: The Free Press, 1964.

———— and Peter C. Yeager. *Corporate Crime.* New York: The Free Press, 1980.

Cochrane, Jean. *Women in Canadian Life — Politics.* Toronto: Fitzhenry and Whiteside, 1977.

Cohen, G.A. *Karl Marx's Theory of History.* Oxford: Clarendon Press, 1978.

Coleman, James S. *The Adolescent Society.* New York: The Free Press, 1961.

Collins, Randall. "Functional and Conflict Theories of Educational Stratification." *American Sociological Review,* Vol. 36, No. 6, pp. 1002-19, 1971.

———— and Michael Markowsky. *The Discovery of Society.* 3rd ed. New York: Random House, 1984.

Comte, A. *The Positive Philosophy.* New York: AMS Press, 1974.

Connor, Walter D. "The Manufacture of Deviance: The Case of the Soviet Purge, 1936-1938." *American Sociological Review,* Vol. 37, pp. 403-413, August 1972.

Conrad, Peter, and Joseph W. Schneider. *Deviance and Medicalization: From Badness to Sickness.* Toronto: C. V. Mosby Co., 1980.

Cooley, Charles H. *Human Nature and Social Order.* New York: Scribner, 1902.

————. *Social Organization.* Glencoe, Ill.: The Free Press, 1909, 1962.

Coulson, Margaret, and Carol Riddell. *Approaching Sociology.* 2nd ed. London: Routledge and Kegan Paul, 1980.

Cox, Oliver C. *Caste, Class, & Power: A Study in Social Dynamics.* New York: Doubleday, 1948.

Cuneo, Carl. "Class, Stratification and Mobility." In *Sociology,* edited by R. Hagedorn, pp. 237-77. Toronto: Holt, Rinehart and Winston, 1980.

————. "State, Class and Reserve Labour: The Case of the 1941 Canadian Unemployment Insurance Act." *Canadian Review of Sociology and Anthropology,* Vol. 16, No. 2, pp. 147-170, 1979.

Currie, Elliott P. "Crimes Without Criminals: Witchcraft and Its Control in Renaissance Europe." *Law and Society Review,* Vol. 3, No. 1, pp. 7-32, 1968.

Curtis, James and William Scott, eds. *Social Stratification: Canada.* Toronto: Prentice-Hall, 1979.

Dahrendorf, Ralf. *Class and Class Conflict in Industrial Society.* Palo Alto, Calif.: Stanford University Press, 1959.

Daniels, Arlene K. "Normal Mental Illness and Understandable Excuses: The Philosophy of Combat Psychiatry." *American Behavioral Scientist,* Vol. 14, No. 2, pp. 169-178, 1970.

Darroch, Gordon A. "Another look at ethnicity, stratification and social mobility in Canada." *Canadian Journal of Sociology,* Vol. 4, pp. 1-25, 1979.

———. "Early Industrialization and Inequality in Toronto, 1861-1899." *Labour/Le Travailleur,* Vol. 11, pp. 31-61, Spring 1983.

——— and Michael Ornstein. "Ethnicity and Class, Transitions Over a Decade: Ontario, 1861-1871." *Canadian Historical Association, Papers 1984,* pp. 111-137.

Davis, James A. *Elementary Survey Analysis.* Englewood Cliffs, N.J.: Prentice-Hall, 1971.

Davis, Kingsley. *Human Society.* New York: Macmillan, 1949.

———. "Sexual Behavior." In *Contemporary Social Problems,* edited by Robert K. Merton and Robert Nisbet, pp. 313-360. 3rd ed. New York: Harcourt, Brace, Jovanovich, 1971.

Dawe, Alan. "Two Sociologies." *British Journal of Sociology,* Vol. 21, pp. 207-218, 1970.

de Beauvoir, Simone. *Old Age.* Harmondsworth: Penguin Books, 1970.

———. *The Second Sex.* New York: Bantam, 1952.

Dentler, Robert A., and Kai T. Erikson. "The Functions of Deviance in Groups." *Social Problems,* Vol. 7, No. 2, pp. 98-102.

Denzin, Norman. *Childhood Socialization.* San Francisco: Jossey-Bass, 1977.

de Vries, John, and Frank G. Vallee. *Language Use in Canada.* 1971 Census of Canada, Catalogue 99-762E. Ottawa: Statistics Canada, 1980.

Donohue, George et al. "Gatekeeping: Mass Media Systems and Information Control." In *Current Perspectives in Mass Communication Research,* edited by G.F. Kline, pp. 49-69. Beverly Hills: Sage, 1972.

Doob, A., and G.E. McDonald. "Television Viewing and the Fear of Victimization: Is the Relationship Causal?" *Journal of Social Psychology and Personality,* Vol. 37, pp. 170-179, 1979.

Dranoff, Linda Silver. *Women in Canadian Life — Law.* Toronto: Fitzhenry and Whiteside, 1977.

Duberman, Lucile, and Clayton A. Hartjen. *Sociology.* Glenview, Ill: Scott, Foresman, 1979.

Durkheim, Émile. *The Division of Labour in Society.* New York: Free Press, 1933, 1965.

———. *The Rules of Sociological Method.* New York: Free Press, 1964.

Edwards, Lyford P. *The Natural History of Revolution.* Chicago: The University of Chicago Press, 1970.

Eichler, Margrit. *Families in Canada Today.* Toronto: Gage, 1983.

———. "Women as Personal Dependents." In *Women in Canada,* edited by Marylee Stephenson, pp. 38-55. Toronto: New Press, 1973.

Ekman, Paul, and Wallace V. Friesen. "The repertoire of nonverbal behaviour: Categories, origins, usage and coding." *Semiotica,* Vol. 1, p. 82, 1969.

Elkin, Frederick. "Communications Media and Identity Formation in Canada." In *Communications in Canadian Society,* edited by B. Singer, pp. 147-157. Toronto: Addison-Wesley, 1983.

———and Gerald Handel. *The Child and Society.* New York: Random House, 1978.

Ellis, Godfrey; Gary Lee; and Larry Petersen. "Supervision and Conformity: A Cross-Cultural Analysis of Parental Socialization Values." *American Journal of Sociology,* Vol. 84, No. 2, pp. 386-402, 1979.

Ellul, J. *The Technological Society.* Translated by J. Wilkinson. New York: Alfred A. Knopf, 1964.

————. *The Technological System.* Translated by J. Neugroschel. New York: Continuum, 1980.

————. *To Will and To Do.* Philadelphia: United Church Press, 1969.

Emerson, Richard M. "Power-Dependency Relations." *American Sociological Review,* Vol. 27, pp. 31-41, 1962.

Erikson, Kai T. *Wayward Puritans.* New York: John Wiley & Sons, 1966.

Ermann, M. David, and Richard J. Lundman. *Corporate Deviance.* New York: Holt, Rinehart & Winston, 1982.

Farrell, Ronald A., and Victoria L. Swigert. *Deviance and Social Control.* Glenview, Ill.: Scott, Foresman, 1982.

Firestone, Shulamith. *The Dialectic of Sex.* New York, Bantam, 1970.

Fischer, Linda, and J.A. Cheyne. *Sex Roles.* Ontario: Ministry of Education, 1977.

Fishman, Mark. *Manufacturing the News.* Austin: University of Texas Press, 1980.

Fishman, Pamela. "Interaction: The work women do." *Social Problems,* Vol. 25, pp. 397-406, 1978.

Freeman, Jo, ed. *Women: A Feminist Perspective.* Palo Alto, Calif.: Mayfield Publishing Company, 1975.

Freidson, Eliot. *Doctoring Together: A Study of Professional Social Control.* New York: Elsevier, 1975.

Frideres, James S. *Native People in Canada: Contemporary Conflicts.* 2d ed. Toronto, Ontario: Prentice-Hall, 1983.

Friedan, Betty. *The Feminine Mystique.* New York: Dell, 1963.

Gagan, David. "The 'Critical Years' in Rural Canada West." *Canadian Historical Review,* Vol. 59, No. 3, pp. 293-318, 1978.

————. *Hopeful Travellers: Families, Land and Social Change in Mid-Victorian Peel County, Canada West.* Toronto: University of Toronto Press, 1981.

Galbraith, J.K. *The New Industrial State.* 3d revised ed. New York: Mentor, 1978.

Gans, Herbert, J. *Deciding What's News.* New York: Vintage Books, 1980.

————. *The Levittowners.* New York: Pantheon Books, 1967.

————. "Symbolic enthnicity: the future of ethnic groups and cultures in America." *Ethnic and Racial Studies,* Vol. 2, pp. 1-20, 1979.

————. *The Urban Villagers.* New York: The Free Press, 1962.

Garfinkel, Harold. *Studies in Ethnomethodology.* Englewood Cliffs, N.J.: Prentice-Hall, 1967.

Gerber, Linda M. "The Development of Canadian Indian Communities: a two-dimensional typology reflecting strategies of adaptation to the modern world." *Canadian Review of Sociology and Anthropology,* Vol. 16, No. 4, pp. 404-421, 1979.

Gerbner, George. "The Dynamics of Cultural Resistance." In *Hearth and Home: Images of Women in Mass Media,* edited by G. Tuchman, A.K. Daniels, and J. Benet, pp. 46-50. New York: Oxford University Press, 1978.

———— and L. Gross. "Living with Television: the violence profile." *Journal of Communication,* Vol. 26, No. 2, pp. 173-199, 1976.

———— et al. "The Mainstreaming of America: Violence Profile No. 11." *Journal of Communication,* Vol. 30, No. 3, pp. 10-29, 1980.

Gerth, H.H., and C. Wright Mills. *From Max Weber: Essays in Sociology.* New York: Oxford University Press, 1958.

Giddens, Anthony. *Capitalism and Modern Social Theory.* London: Cambridge University Press, 1971.

————. *The Class Structure of the Advanced Societies.* London: Hutchinson University Library, 1973.

————. *Sociology: A brief but critical introduction.* New York: Harcourt, Brace and Jovanovich Inc., 1982.

Giedion, S. *Mechanization Takes Command.* New York: Norton, 1969.

Gillespie, Irwin. "On the Redistribution of Income in Canada." In *Structured Inequality in Canada,* edited by John Harp and John R. Hofley, pp. 22-53. Toronto: Prentice-Hall, 1980.

Gitlin, Todd. "Media Sociology: The Dominant Paradigm." *Theory and Society,* Vol. 6, pp. 205-253, 1978.

———. *The Whole World is Watching.* Berkely: University of California Press, 1980.

Glasgow Media Group. *Bad News.* London: Routledge and Kegan Paul, 1977.

———. *More Bad News.* London: Routledge and Kegan Paul, 1980.

Glaser, Barney A., and Anselm L. Strauss. *Awareness of Dying.* Chicago: The University of Chicago Press, 1965.

Glazer, Nathan, and Daniel P. Moynihan. *Beyond the Melting Pot.* Cambridge, Mass.: M.I.T. Press, 1970.

Glynn, Carroll, and Jack McLeod. "Public Opinion du Jour: an Examination of the Spiral of Silence." *Public Opinion Quarterly,* Vol. 48, pp. 731-740, 1984.

Goffman, Erving. *Behavior in Public Places: Notes on the Social Organization of Gatherings.* New York: The Free Press of Glencoe, 1963.

———. *Frame Analysis.* New York: Harper and Row, 1974.

———. *Gender Advertisements.* New York: Harper and Row, 1979.

———. *Interaction Ritual: Essays on Face-to-Face Behavior.* Garden City, N.Y.: Doubleday Anchor Books, 1967.

———. "The Moral Career of the Mental Patient." *Psychiatry,* Vol. 22, pp. 123-142, 1959b.

———. *Presentation of Self in Everyday Life.* Garden City, N.Y.: Doubleday, 1959a.

———. *Stigma: Notes on the Management of Spoiled Identity.* Englewood Cliffs, N.J.: Prentice-Hall, 1963.

Gold, David; Clarence Lo; and E.O. Wright. "Recent Developments in Marxist Theories of the Capitalist State." *Monthly Review,* Vol. 27, No. 5, pp. 29-43, 1975.

Golding, Peter, and Graham Murdock. "Ideology and the Mass Media: the Question of Influence." In *Ideology and Cultural Production,* edited by M. Barrett et al., pp. 198-224. New York: St. Martin's Press, 1979.

Gordon, Milton M. *Assimilation in American Life.* New York: Oxford University Press, 1964.

Gould, Stephen Jay. *The Mismeasure of Man.* New York: Norton, 1981.

Goulet, D. *The Uncertain Promise.* IDOC/North America, 1977.

Gove, Walter R., ed. *The Labelling of Deviance: Evaluating a Perspective.* New York: John Wiley & Sons, 1975.

Goyder, John C. "Social Mobility or status attainment, or social mobility and status attainment?". *Canadian Review of Sociology and Anthropology,* Vol. 21, No. 3, pp. 331-343, 1984.

——— and James E. Curtis. "Occupational Mobility Over Four Generations." *Canadian Review of Sociology and Anthropology,* Vol. 14, No. 3, pp. 303-19, 1977.

——— and Peter Pineo. "Social Class Self-Identification." In *Social Stratification: Canada,* edited by James E. Curtis and William G. Scott, pp. 431-447. Toronto: Prentice-Hall, 1979.

Grabb, Edward G. *Social Inequality: Classical and Contemporary Theorists.* Toronto: Holt, Rinehart and Winston, 1984.

Gramsci, Antonio. *Selections from the Prison Notebooks.* New York: International Publishers, 1971.

Grant, George. *Lament for a Nation.* Toronto: McClelland and Stewart, 1965.

Greer, Allan. "Wage Labour and the Transition to Capitalism." *Labour/Le Travail,* Vol. 15, Spring, pp. 7-22, 1985.

Griffin, John H. *Black Like Me.* Boston: Houghton Mifflin Co. 1977.

Grimes, Ruth-Ellen M., and Austin T. Turk. "Labeling in Context: Conflict, Power and Self-Definition." In *Crime, Law, and Sanctions: Theoretical Perspectives,* edited by Marvin D. Krohn and Ronald L. Akers, pp. 39-58. Beverly Hills: Sage, 1978.

Haas, Jack, and William Shaffir. *Shaping Identity in Canadian Society*. Toronto: Prentice-Hall, 1978.

Hagopian, Mark N. *The Phenomenon of Revolution*. New York: Harper and Row, 1974.

Hall, Edward T. *Beyond Culture*. New York: Anchor Books, 1977.

Hall, Stuart. "The Rediscovery of Ideology: Return of the Repressed in Media Studies." In *Culture, Society and the Media*, M. Gurevitch et al., pp. 56-90. London: Methuen, 1982.

Haralambos, Michael, and Robin M. Heald. *Sociology: Themes and Perspectives*. Slough, G.B.: University Tutorial Press, 1980.

Harvey, Edward B. *Barriers to Employer Sponsored Training in Ontario*. Toronto: Ministry of Education, 1980.

————. "The Changing Relationship Between University Education and Intergenerational Social Mobility." *The Canadian Review of Sociology and Anthropology*, Vol. 21, pp. 275-286, 1984.

————. *Educational Systems and The Labour Market*. Toronto: Longman, 1974.

Haskell, M. *From Reverence to Rape: The Treatment of Women in Movies*. New York: Holt, Rinehart and Winston, 1974.

Hauser, Robert M. et al. "Temporal Change in Occupational Mobility: Evidence for Men in the United States." *American Sociological Review*, Vol. 40, No. 3, pp. 279-97.

———— and David L. Featherman. *The Process Stratification*. New York: Academic, 1977.

Hawkins, Freda. *Canada and Immigration: Public Policy and Public Concern*. Montreal: McGill-Queen's University Press, 1972.

Heitlinger, Alena. *Women and State Socialism, Sex Inequality in the Soviet Union and Czechoslovakia*. Montreal: McGill-Queen's University Press, 1979.

Henley, Nancy. *Body Politics*. Englewood Cliffs, N.J.: Prentice-Hall, 1977.

Herberg, Will. *Protestant, Catholic, Jew*. New York: Doubleday, 1955.

Heron, Craig. "Labourism and the Canadian Working Class." *Labour/Le Travail*, Vol. 13, pp. 45-76, Spring 1984.

Hiller, Harry H. *Canadian Society: A Sociological Analysis*. Toronto: Prentice-Hall, 1976.

Hodge, Robert W.; P. Siegel; and Peter H. Rossi. "A Comparative Study of Occupational Prestige." In *Class, Status and Power*. 2d ed. Edited by R. Bendix and S.M. Lipset, pp. 322-334. New York: Free Press, 1966.

Horowitz, M., and I. Herrenstedt. "Changes in Skill Requirements of Occupations in Selected Industries." *The Employment Impact of Technological Change*, Vol. 2, Appendix. Washington: U.S. Government Printing Office, 1966.

Hughes, E.C. *French Canada in Transition*. Chicago: University of Chicago Press, 1943.

Hunter, Alfred A. *Class Tells: On Social Inequality in Canada*. Toronto: Butterworth, 1981.

Ingleby, David. "Mental Health and Social Order." In *Social Control and the State*, edited by Stanley Cohen and Andrew Scull, pp. 141-188. Oxford: Martin Robertson & Co., 1983.

Innis, Harold A. *The Bias of Communication*. Toronto: University of Toronto Press, 1951.

————. *Essays in Canadian Economic History*. Toronto: University of Toronto Press, 1956.

————. *The Fur Trade in Canada*. New Haven, Conn.: Yale University Press, 1930.

Isajiw, S.. "Multiculturalism and the Integration of the Canadian Community." *Canadian Ethnic Studies*, Vol. 15, No. 2, pp. 107-117, 1983.

Isajiw, W.W. *Identities: The Impact of Ethnicity in Canadian Society*. Toronto: Peter Martin Press, 1976.

Jackson, John D. "The functions of language in Canada: on the political economy of language." In *The Individual, Language and Society in Canada*, edited by W.H. Coons, D.M. Taylkor, and M. Tremblay, pp. 59-76. Ottawa: The Canada Council, 1977.

James, William. *The Principles of Psychology in Two Volumes*. New York: Holt, 1890.

Jencks, Christopher et al. *Inequality: A Reassessment of the Effect of Family and Schooling in America*. New York: Harper Colophon Books, 1972.

Jéquier, N. *Appropriate Technology: Promises and Problems*. Paris: Development Centre of the Organization for Economic Co-operation and Development, 1976.

Johnson, Laura. *Who Cares? A Report on the Project Child Care, Survey of Parents and Their Child Care Arrangements*. Toronto: Social Planning Council, 1977.

Johnson, Leo A. "The Development of Class in Canada in the Twentieth Century." In *Capitalism and the National Question*, edited by Gary Teeple, pp. 141-183. Toronto: University of Toronto Press, 1972.

———. "Land Policy, Population Growth and Social Structure in the Home District 1793-1851." *Ontario History*, Vol. 67, pp. 41-60, March 1971.

———. *Poverty in Wealth*. Toronto: New Hogtown Press, 1977.

Johnson, William. "The Gay World." In *Social Deviance in Canada*, edited by W.E. Mann, pp. 380-389. Toronto: Copp Clark, 1971.

Jones, Frank E., and Wallace E. Lambert. "Occupational rank and attitudes towards immigrants." *Public Opinion Quarterly*, Vol. 29, pp. 137-144, 1965.

Joy, Richard J. *Languages in Conflict: The Canadian Experience*. Toronto: McClelland and Stewart, 1972.

Kallen, Evelyn. *Ethicity and Human Rights in Canada*. Toronto: Gage, 1982.

Kallen, Horace M. "Functionalism." In *Encyclopaedia of the Social Sciences*, Vol. 3, edited by Edwin R.A. Seligman. New York: Macmillan, 1937.

Kanter, Rosabeth Moss. *Men and Women of the Corporation*. New York: Basic Books, 1977.

Katz, Elihu. "The Return of the Humanities and Sociology." *Journal of Communication*, Vol. 33, No. 3, pp. 51-52, 1983.

Kealey, Gregory S. *Toronto Workers Respond to Industrial Capitalism 1867-1892*. Toronto: University of Toronto Press, 1980.

Kealey, Linda, ed. *A Not Unreasonable Claim, Women and Reform in Canada, 1880s-1920s*. Toronto: Women's Press 1979.

Kehoe, Jack. "Ethnocentrism, Self-Esteem and Appreciation of Cultural Diversity." *Canadian Ethnic Studies*, Vol. 14, No. 3, pp. 69-78, 1982.

Kelner, Merrijoy; Oswald Hall; and Dan Coulter. *Chiropractors: do they help? a study of their education and practice*. Toronto: Fitzhenry and Whiteside, 1980.

Kennedy, Ruby Jo Reeves. "Single or triple melting-pot? Intermarriage in New Haven, 1870-1950." *American Journal of Sociology*, Vol. 58, pp. 56-59, 1952.

Kesterton, Wilfred. "The Growth of the Newspaper in Canada." In *Communications in Canadian Society*, edited by B. Singer, pp. 3-16. Toronto: Addison-Wesley, 1983.

Kimball, M. "Socialization of Women: A Study in Conflict." In *Marriage, Family and Society*, edited by S.P. Wakil, pp. 189-201. Toronto: Butterworth, 1975.

Klapp, Orrin E. *Collective Search for Identity*. New York: Holt, Rinehart & Winston, 1969.

Klapper, Joseph. *The Effects of Mass Communication*. New York: The Free Press, 1960.

Kopinak, Kathryn. "Polity." In *Sociology*, edited by Robert Hagedorn, pp. 429-473. Toronto: Holt, Rinehart and Winston, 1980.

Kuhn, Thomas S. *The Structure of Scientific Revolutions*. 2d ed. Chicago: The University of Chicago Press, 1970.

Landes, D.S. *The Unbound Prometheus*. London: Cambridge University Press, 1969.

Langness, L.L. *The Study of Culture*. San Francisco: Chandler & Sharp Publishers, Inc., 1974.

Lasswell, Harold. "The Structure and Function of Communication in Society." In *The Communication of Ideas*, edited by L. Bryson. New York: Harper, 1948.

——— and Abraham Kaplan. *Power and Society*. New Haven, Conn.: Yale University Press, 1950.

Lauer, Robert. "Socialization into Inequality: Children's Perception of Occupational Status." *Sociology and Social Research*, Vol. 58, No. 2, pp. 176-183, 1974.

Lautard, Hugh E., and Donald J. Loree.

"Ethnic stratification in Canada, 1931-1971." *Canadian Journal of Sociology,* Vol. 9, pp. 333-343.

Laxer, Gordon. "Class, Nationality, and the Roots of Foreign Ownership." In *The Structure of the Canadian Capitalist Class,* edited by Robert J. Brym. Toronto: Garamond Press, 1985.

Leacy, F.H., ed. *Historical Statistics of Canada:* Ottawa: Statistics Canada, 1983.

Lemert, Edwin M. *Human Deviance, Social Problems, and Social Control.* 2d ed. Englewood Cliffs, N.J.: Prentice-Hall, 1972.

Lennards, J. L. "Education." In *Sociology,* edited by Robert Hagedorn, pp. 475-514. Toronto: Holt, Rinehart and Winston, 1980.

Leslie, G.R. *The Family in Social Context.* 4th ed. New York: Oxford, 1979.

Levine, David. "Production, Reproduction, and the Proletarian Family in England, 1500-1851." *Proletarianization and Family History,* edited by David Levine, pp. 87-128. New York: Academic, 1984.

Levine, Robert, and Ellen Wolff. "Social Time: The Heartbeat of Culture." *Psychology Today,* pp. 28-35, March 1985.

Levitt, Cyril. *Children of Privilege: Student Revolt in the Sixties.* Toronto: University of Toronto Press, 1984.

Levitt, Kari. *Silent Surrender: The Multinational Corporation in Canada.* Toronto: Macmillan of Canada, 1970.

Levy, Robert I. "The Community Function of Tahitian Male Transvestism: A Hypothesis." *Anthropological Quarterly* Vol. 44, pp. 12-21, January 1971.

Lewis, Oscar. "The Culture of Poverty." *Scientific American,* Vol. 215, No. 4, pp. 19-25, 1966.

Li, Peter S. "A historical approach to ethnic stratification: the case of the Chinese in Canada, 1858-1930." *Canadian Review of Sociology and Anthropology* Vol. 16, pp. 320-332, 1979.

———. "Canadian immigration policy and assimilation theories." In *Economy, Class and Social Reality,* edited by J.A. Fry, pp. 411-422. Toronto: Butterworth, 1979.

———. *Social Research Methods.* Toronto: Butterworth, 1981.

——— and B. Singh Bolaria. *Racial Minorities in Multicultural Canada.* Toronto: Garamond Press, 1983.

Lichter, S. Robert, and Stanley Rothman. "Media and Business Elites." *Public Opinion Quarterly,* Vol. 45, pp. 42-60, 1981.

Lieberson, Stanley. *Language and Ethnic Relations in Canada.* New York: John Wiley & Sons, 1970.

Liebow, Elliot. *Tally's Corner.* Boston: Little, Brown & Co., 1967.

Lindell, Susan. "Role Expectations of Adolescent Women." *Canadian Women's Studies,* Vol. 4, No. 1, pp. 67-70, 1982.

Lindesmith, Alfred R.; Anselm L. Strauss; and Norman K. Denzin. *Social Psychology.* New York: Holt, Rinehart and Winston, 1977.

Linton, Ralph. *The Study of Man: An Introduction.* Englewood Cliffs, N.J.: Prentice-Hall, 1936.

Lipovenko, Dorothy. "Day Care Spaces for Infants Steadily Declining, Study Says." *Globe and Mail,* November 1984.

Lipset, Seymour Martin. *The First New Nation.* Garden City, N.Y.: Doubleday, 1963.

———. *Revolution and Counterrevolution.* New York: Anchor Books, 1970.

Liska, Allen E. *Perspectives on Deviance.* Englewood Cliffs, N.J.: Prentice-Hall, 1981.

Lofland, John. *Deviance and Identity.* Englewood Cliffs, N.J.: Prentice-Hall, 1969.

Luxton, Meg. *More Than a Labour of Love: Three Generations of Women's Work in the Home.* Toronto: Women's Press, 1980.

Lyell, Ruth G. "Adolescent and Adult Self-Esteem as related to Cultural Values." *Adolescence,* Vol. 8, pp. 85-92, Spring 1973.

Maccoby, Eleanor, and Carol Jacklin. *The Psychology of Sex Differences.* Stanford, Calif.: Stanford University Press, 1974.

Mackie, Marlene. *Exploring Gender Relations.* Toronto: Butterworth, 1982.

———. "Socialization: Changing Views of

Child Rearing and Adolescence." In *The Family, Changing Trends in Canada*, edited by Maureen Baker, pp. 35-62. Toronto: McGraw-Hill Ryerson, 1984.

———— and Merlin B. Brinkerhoff. "Measuring Ethnic Salience." *Canadian Ethnic Studies*, Vol. 16, No. 1, pp. 114-131, 1984.

Macpherson, C.B. *Democracy in Alberta: Social Credit and the Party System*. 2d ed. Toronto: University of Toronto Press, 1962.

————. *The Real World of Democracy*. Toronto: Canadian Broadcasting Corporation, 1965.

————, ed. *Property: Mainstream & Critical Positions*. Toronto: University of Toronto Press, 1978.

MacLellan, Margaret E., "The History of Women's Rights in Canada," in *Cultural Tradition and Political History of Women in Canada*. Studies of the Royal Commission on the Status of Women in Canada, #8, Information Canada, Ottawa, 1971.

Makabe, Tomoko. "The theory of the split labor market: a comparison of the Japanese experience in Brazil and Canada." *Social Forces*, Vol. 59, pp. 786-809, 1981.

Malinowski, Bronislaw. "Review of Six Essays on Culture by Albert Blumenthal." *American Sociological Review*, Vol. 4, pp. 588-592, 1939.

Mann, Michael. *Consciousness and Action among the Western Working Class*. London: Macmillan, 1973.

Mann, N.E., ed. *The Underside of Toronto*. Toronto: McClelland and Stewart, 1970.

Mannheim, Karl. *Ideology and Utopia*. New York: Harcourt, Brace and Company, 1936.

Marchak, Patricia. *Ideological Perspectives on Canada*. 2d ed. Toronto: McGraw-Hill Ryerson, 1981.

————. *In Whose Interests*. Toronto, McClelland and Stewart, 1979.

Marcuse, Herbert. *Counter-Revolution and Revolt*. Boston: Beacon Press, 1972.

————. *An Essay on Liberation*. Boston: Beacon Press, 1969.

————. *One-Dimensional Man*. Boston: Beacon Press, 1964.

Marsden, Lorna, and Edward Harvey. *Fragile Federation*. Toronto: McGraw-Hill Ryerson, 1979.

Martin, W.B.W. *The Negotiated Order of the School*. Toronto: Macmillan, 1976.

Marx, Karl. *Capital*, Vol. 1. Moscow: Foreign Languages Publishing House, 1954.

————. *A Contribution to the Critique of Political Economy*. Moscow: Progress Publishers, 1970.

————. "The German Ideology." In *The Marx-Engels Reader*, edited by R.C. Tucker, pp. 146-200. New York: Norton, 1978.

————. *Pre-Capitalist Economic Formations*. New York: International Publishers, 1965.

————. *Early Texts*. Edited by D. McLellan. Oxford: Basil Blackwell, 1972. *Selected Writings*. Edited by D. McLellan. Oxford University Press, 1977.

———— and Frederick Engels. "The Class Struggles in France." In *Selected Works*, 2 vols., K. Marx and F. Engels. Moscow: Foreign Languages Publishing House, 1950.

————. *The Communist Manifesto*. Edited by Samuel H. Beer. New York: Appleton Century-Crofts, 1955.

————. *The German Ideology*. New York: International Publishers, 1969.

Matthews, Ralph. "Regional Differences in Canada." In *Social Issues: Sociological Views of Canada*, edited by Dennis Forcese and Stephen Richer. Toronto: Prentice-Hall, 1982.

————. "The Significance and Explanation of Regional Divisions in Canada: Toward a Canadian Sociology." *Journal of Canadian Studies*, Vol. 15, No. 2, pp. 43-61, 1980.

Matza, David. *Becoming Deviant*. Englewood Cliffs, N.J.: Prentice-Hall, 1969.

Mayer, Arno. "The Lower Middle Class as Historical Problem." *Journal of Modern History*, Vol. 47, pp. 409-36, September 1975.

McCain, Garvin, and Erwin M. Segal. *The Game of Science*. Belmont, Calif.: Brooks/Cole Publishing Company, 1969.

McCallum, John. *Unequal Beginnings: Agriculture and Economic Development in Quebec and Ontario until 1870*. Toronto: University of Toronto Press, 1980.

McCoombs, Maxwell E., and Donald L. Shaw. "Structuring the Unseen Environment." *Public Opinion Quarterly,* Vol. 40, No. 1, pp. 18-22, 1976.

McGraw, Garet. "Wife Assault." *Canadian Forum,* Vol. 63, pp. 16-17, December 1983.

McLuhan, Marshall. *Understanding Media: The Extensions of Man.* New York: McGraw-Hill, 1965.

McQuail, Denis. *Mass Communication Theory.* London: Sage, 1983.

McRoberts, Hugh A. "Family of Origin and Social Mobility in Canada." pp. in Stephen Richer and Dennis Forcese (eds.)

———— et al. "Differences dans la mobilite professionnelle des francophones et des anglophones." *Sociologie et Societes,* Vol. 8, pp. 61-79, 1976.

———— and Kevin Selbee. "Trends in Occupational Mobility in Canada and the United States: A Comparison." *American Sociological Review,* Vol. 46, No. 4, pp. 406-21.

Mead, George H. *Mind, Self and Society.* Chicago: University of Chicago Press, 1934.

————. *The Philosophy of the Act.* Edited by Charles Morris. Chicago: The University of Chicago Press, 1938.

Meissner, Martin et al. "No Exit for Wives: Sexual Division of Labour and the Cumulation of Household Demands." *Canadian Review of Sociology and Anthropology,* Vol. 12, Part 1, pp. 424-439.

Melody, W., and Robin Mansell. "The Debate over Critical vs. Administrative Research: Circularity or Challenge." *Journal of Communication,* Vol. 33, No. 3, pp. 103-116, 1983.

Meltzer, B.N.; J.W. Petras; and L.T. Reynolds. *Symbolic Interactionism.* London: Routledge and Kegan Paul, 1975.

Mercer, Jane R. *Labeling the Retarded.* Berkeley, Calif.: University of California Press, 1973.

Merton, Robert K. *Social Theory and Social Structure.* New York: The Free Press, 1957.

————. *On Theoretical Sociology.* New York: The Free Press, 1967.

Michels, Robert. *Political Parties.* New York: The Free Press, 1962.

Miles, Robert. *Racism and Migrant Labour.* London: Routledge & Kegan Paul, 1982.

Milgram, Stanley. "The Experience of Living in Cities." *Science,* Vol. 167, pp. 1461-1468, 1970.

Miliband, Ralph. *The State in Capitalist Society.* London: Weidenfeld and Nicolson, 1969.

Millett, Kate. *Sexual Politics.* New York: Avon Books, 1970.

Mills, C. Wright. *The Power Elite.* New York: Oxford University Press, 1953.

————. *The Sociological Imagination.* London: Oxford University Press, 1959.

————. *White Collar: The American Middle Classes.* New York: Oxford, 1956.

Milner, Henry. *Politics in the New Quebec.* Toronto: McClelland and Stewart, 1978.

Miyamoto, Frank S., and Sanford M. Dornbusch. "A Test of Interactionist Hypotheses of Self-Conception." *American Journal of Sociology,* Vol. 61, 1956.

Mommsen, Wolfgang J. "Max Weber as a critic of Marx." *Canadian Journal of Sociology,* Vol. 2, No. 4, pp. 373-398, 1977.

Moore, Barrington Jr. *Social Origins of Dictatorship and Democracy.* London: Peregrine, 1969.

Moore, Joan W. "Colonialism: the case of Mexican Americans." *Social Problems,* Vol. 17, pp. 463-472, 1970.

Mortimer, Jeylan T., and Roberta G. Simmons. "Adult Socialization." In *Annual Review of Sociology,* Vol. 4, pp. 421-454. Palo Alto: Annual Review Inc., 1978.

Mumford, L. *The Pentagon of Power,* New York: Harcourt, Brace, Jovanovich, 1970.

Murdock, G., and G. Phelps. *Mass Media and the Secondary School.* London: Macmillan, 1973.

National Opinion Research Centre. "Jobs and Occupations: A Popular Evaluation." *Opinion News,* Vol. 11, pp. 3-13, 1947.

Naylor, R.T. "The Rise and Fall of the Third Commercial Empire of the St. Lawrence." In *Capitalism and the National Question,* edited by Gary Teeple, pp. 1-41. Toronto: University of Toronto Press, 1972.

Nett, Emily. "Canadian Families in Social-Historical Perspective." *Canadian Journal of Sociology,* Vol. 6, No. 3, pp. 239-260, 1981.

Neuman, W. Russell. "Television and American Culture: the Mass Medium and the Pluralist Audience." *Public Opinion Quarterly,* Vol. 46, pp. 471-487, 1982.

Newcomb, T.M. *Personality and Social Change.* New York: Dryden, 1943.

Newcomb, T.M. et al. *Persistence and Change: Bennington College and its students after 25 years.* New York: Wiley, 1967.

Newman, Oscar. *Defensible Space.* New York: Macmillan, 1972.

Newman, Peter C. *The Canadian Establishment,* Vol. 1. Toronto: McClelland and Stewart, 1979.

Niosi, Jorge. *Canadian Capitalism: A Study of Power in the Canadian Business Establishment.* Lorimer, 1981.

————. *Canadian Multinationals.* Ontario: Garamond Press, 1985.

————. *The Economy of Canada: A Study of Ownership and Control.* Montreal: Black Rose Books, 1982.

Nisbet, Robert A. "The Decline and Fall of Social Class." *Pacific Sociological Review,* Vol. 2, pp. 11-17, 1959.

————. *The Sociological Tradition.* New York: Basic Books, 1966.

———— and Robert G. Perrin. *The Social Bond.* 2d ed. New York: Alfred A. Knopf, 1977.

Noble, D. *America by Design.* New York: Knopf, 1979.

Noelle-Neuman, Elisabeth. *The Spiral of Silence.* Chicago: University of Chicago Press, 1984.

Nosanchuk, Terrance A. "A Note on the Use of the Correlation Coefficient for Assessing the Similarity of Occupational Rankings." *The Canadian Review of Sociology and Anthropology,* Vol. 9, No. 4, pp. 357-67, 1972.

Nunes, Maxine, and Deanna White. *The Lace Ghetto.* Toronto: New Press, 1973.

Oakley, Ann. *Subject Women.* New York: Pantheon Books, 1981.

O'Connell, Agnes. "The Social Origins of Gender." In *Female and Male: Psychological Perspectives,* R. Unger, pp. 146-166. New York: Harper and Row, 1979.

Ogmundson, Rick. "Party Class Images and the Class Vote in Canada." *American Sociological Review,* Vol. 40, pp. 506-512, 1975.

————. "Toward study of the endangered species known as the anglophone Canadian." *Canadian Journal of Sociology,* Vol. 5, No. 1, pp. 1-12, 1980.

O'Kelly, Charlotte G. *Men and Women in Society.* New York: Van Nostrand, 1980.

Ornstein, Michael D. "The Development of Class in Canada." In *Sociology: An Alternative Approach,* edited by Paul Grayson, pp. 216-259. Toronto: Gage, 1983.

Orwell, George. *Nineteen Eighty-Four.* New York: Penguin Books, 1984.

Osberg, Lars. *Economic Inequality in Canada.* Toronto: Butterworth, 1981.

Ossowski, S. *Class Structure in the Social Consciousness.* Translated by S. Patterson. New York: The Free Press, 1963.

Packard, Vance. *The Waste Makers.* New York: David McKay, 1960.

Palmer, Bryan D. *A Culture in Conflict: Skilled Workers and Industrial Capitalism in Hamilton, Ontario, 1860-1914.* Montreal: McGill-Queen's University Press, 1979.

————. *Working Class Experience: The Rise and Reconstitution of Canadian Labour, 1800-1980.* Butterworth (Canada) Ltd., 1983.

Pappert, Ann. "Today's Women, Yesterday's Dreams." *Homemaker's Digest,* pp. 166-180, October 1980.

Parai, L. *Immigration and Emigration of Professional and Skilled Manpower During the Post-War Period.* Ottawa: Queen's Printer, 1965.

————. *Race and Culture.* Glencoe, Ill.: Free Press, 1950.

Parkin, Frank. *Class Inequality and Political Order.* London: Macgibbon and Kee, 1971.

————. *Marxism and Class Theory: A Bourgeois Theory.* New York: Columbia University Press, 1979.

————, ed. *The Social Analysis of Class Structure.* London: Tavistock, 1974.

Parsons, Talcott. "Age and Sex Structure of the United States." *American Sociological Review,* Vol. 7, pp. 604-616, 1942.

———. "Culture and Social System Revisited." In *The Idea of Culture in the Social Sciences,* edited by L. Schneider and C. Bonjean, pp. 33-46. Cambridge University Press, 1973.

———. *The Social System.* New York: The Free Press, 1951.

Patterson, E. Palmer II. *The Canadian Indian: A History since 1500.* Toronto: Collier-Macmillan Canada, 1972.

Pelto, P.J. *The Snowmobile Revolution: Technology and Social Change in the Arctic.* Menlo Park: Cummings, 1973.

Pentland, Clare H. *Labour and Capital in Canada 1650-1860.* Toronto: University of Toronto Press, 1981.

Peters, John F. "Reciprocal Socialization." forthcoming, *Adolescence,* 1985.

Peterson, Richard A. "Revitalizing the Culture Concept." *Annual Review of Sociology,* pp. 137-166. Palo Alto: Annual Reviews Inc., 1979.

Phillips, D.P. "The Behavioral Impact of Violence in the Mass Media: A Review of Evidence from Laboratory and Nonlaboratory Investigations." *Sociology and Social Research,* Vol. 66, pp. 560-568, 1982.

———. "Suicide, Motor Vehicle Fatalities, and the Mass Media: Evidence Toward a Theory of Suggestion." *American Journal of Sociology,* Vol. 84, pp. 1150-1174, 1979.

Pickersgill, J.W., and D.F. Forster. *The Mackenzie King Record, Volume 4, 1947-1948.* Toronto: University of Toronto Press, 1970.

Pike, Robert M. "Education, Class and Power in Canada." In *Power and Change in Canada,* edited by Richard Ossenberg, pp. 106-145. Toronto: McClelland and Stewart, 1980.

Pineo, Peter and John Porter. "Occupational Prestige in Canada." *Canadian Review of Sociology and Anthropology,* Vol. 4, No. 1, pp. 24-40, 1967.

Porter, John. "Ethnic Pluralism in Canadian Perspective." In *The Measure of Canadian Society,* John Porter, pp. 103-138. Toronto: Gage, 1979.

———. *The Vertical Mosaic.* Toronto: University of Toronto Press, 1965.

———; Marion Porter; and Bernard Blishen. *Stations and Callings: Making it Through the School System.* Toronto: Methuen, 1982.

Portes, Alejandro. "On the Sociology of National Development: Theories and Issues." *American Journal of Sociology,* Vol. 82, No. 1, July 1976.

——— and John Walton. *Labor, Class, and the International System.* New York: Academic Press, 1981.

Posner, Judy. "From Sex role Stereotyping to SadoMasochism." *Fireweed,* Vol. 14, 1982.

Poulantzas, Nicos. *Classes In Contemporary Capitalism.* London: New Left Books, 1975.

———. *Political Power and Social Classes.* London: Verso, 1978.

Price, Charles. "The study of assimilation." In *Migration,* edited by J.A. Jackson, pp. 181-237. Cambridge: Cambridge University Press, 1969.

Prus, Robert C., and C.R.D. Sharper. *Road Hustler.* Toronto: Gage, 1977.

Quarentelli, E.L., and J. Cooper. "Self Conceptions and Others: A Further test of Median Hypotheses." *Sociological Quarterly,* Vol. 7, Summer 1966.

Real, Michael R. *Mass Mediated Culture.* Englewood Cliffs, N.J.: Prentice-Hall, 1977.

Reitz, Jeffrey G. *The Survival of Ethnic Groups.* Toronto: McGraw-Hill Ryerson, 1980.

Rejai, M. "Political Ideology: Theoretical and Comparative Perspectives." In *Decline of Ideology,* edited by M. Rejai. Chicago: Aldine and Atherton Inc., 1971.

Remmling, G.W. *The Sociology of Karl Mannheim.* London: Routledge and Kegan Paul, 1975.

Rex, John. *Race, Colonialism and the City.* London: Routledge & Kegan Paul, 1973.

———. *Race Relations in Sociological Theory.* 2d ed. London: Routledge & Kegan Paul, 1983.

——— and Robert Moore. *Race, Commu-*

nity, and Conflict: A Study of Sparkbrook. London: Oxford University Press, 1967.

———— and S. Tomlinson. *Colonial Immigrants in a British City.* London: Routledge & Kegan Paul, 1979.

Richardson, B. *Strangers Devour the Land.* New York: Macmillan, 1975.

Richardson, C. James. "Education and Social Mobility: changing conceptions of the role of the educational systems." *Canadian Journal of Sociology,* Vol. 2, No. 4, pp. 417-33, 1977.

Richardson, R. Jack. " 'Merchants Against Industry': An Empirical Study of the Canadian Debate." *Canadian Journal of Sociology,* Vol. 7, No. 3, pp. 279-295, 1982.

Richmond, Anthony H., and Warren E. Kalback. *Factors in the Adjustment of Immigrants and their Descendants.* Ottawa: Statistic Canada, Catalogue 99-761E, 1980.

Richta, R. *Civilization at the Crossroads.* New York: International Arts and Science, 1969.

Rinehart, James W. *The Tyranny of Work.* Toronto: Longman, 1975.

———— and Ishmael O. Okraku. "A Study of Class Consciousness." *Canadian Review of Sociology and Anthropology,* Vol. 11, pp. 197-213, 1974.

Ritzer, George. *Sociology: A Multiple Paradigm Science.* Boston: Allyn and Bacon, 1975.

Robert, Jean-Claude. "Urbanisation et population. Le Cas de Montreal en 1861." Revue d'Histoire de l'Amerique Francaise, 35 (Mar.) 1982.

Roberts, Lance W., and Rodney A. Clifton. "Exploring the ideology of Canadian multiculturalism." *Canadian Public Policy* Vol. 8: pp. 88-94, 1982.

Roberts, Wayne, and John Bullen. "A Heritage of Hope and Struggle: Workers, Unions and Politics in Canada, 1930-1982." In *Modern Canada: 1930-1980's,* edited by Michael S. Cross and Gregory S. Kealey, pp. 105-143. Toronto: McClelland and Stewart, 1984.

Roebuck, Julian, and Stanley C. Weeber. *Political Crime in the United States.* New York: Praeger, 1978.

Rogoff, Natalie. *Recent Trends in Occupational Mobility.* Glencoe, Ill.: Free Press, 1953.

Rosenham, D.L. "On Being Sane in Insane Places." *Science,* Vol. 179, pp. 250-258, January 19, 1973.

Rossi, Alice. "Gender and Parenthood." *American Sociological Review,* Vol. 49, No. 1, pp. 1-19, 1984.

————. "Transition to Parenthood." *Journal of Marriage and the Family,* Vol. 30, pp. 26-39, 1968.

Rowntree, John, and Margaret Rowntree. "The Political Economy of Youth." *Our Generation,* Vol. 6. Nos. 1-2, 1968.

Royal Commission on Newspapers, Ottawa: Supply and Services Canada, 1981.

Rubin, J.; F. Provenzano; and Z. Luria. "The Eye of the Beholder: Parents' Views on Sex of Newborns." *American Journal of Orthopsychiatry,* Vol. 44, No. 4, pp. 512-519, 1974.

Runciman, W.G. *Relative Deprivation and Social Justice.* London: Routledge and Kegan Paul, 1966.

Rybczynski, W. *Paper Heroes: A Review of Appropriate Technology.* Garden City, N.Y.: Anchor Press/Doubleday, 1980.

Sattel, Jack. "The Inexpressive Male: Tragedy or Sexual Politics?". In *Women and Work: Problems and Perspectives,* edited by Rachel Kahn-Hut, Arlene Kaplan Daniels, and Richard Colvard, p. 160, New York: Oxford University Press, 1982.

Scheff, Thomas J. *Being Mentally Ill: A Sociological Theory.* 2d ed. New York: Aldine, 1984.

Schneider, Joseph W., and Sally L. Hacker. "Sex Role Imagery and the use of generic man in Introductory texts: A case in the sociology of sociology." *American Sociologist,* Vol. 8, pp. 12-18, January 1973.

Schneider, L., and Charles M. Bonjean, eds. *The Idea of Culture in the Social Sciences.* Cambridge: Cambridge University Press, 1973.

Schwartz, Mildred. *Politics and Territory: The Sociology of Regional Persistence in Canada.* Montreal: McGill-Queen's University Press, 1974.

Seiber, Timothy R., and Andrew J. Gordon. *Children and Their Organizations.* Boston: G.K. Hall and Co., 1981.

Seidman, Steven. *Liberalism and the Origins of European Social Theory*. Berkeley, Calif.: University of California Press, 1983.

Shaffir, William. *Life in a Religious Community: The Lubavitcher Chassidim in Montreal*. Toronto: Holt, Rinehart and Winston, 1974.

Shapiro, Martin. *Getting Doctored: Critical Reflections on Becoming a Physician*. Kitchener, Ont.: Between the Lines Press, 1978.

Shibutani, Tamotsu. *Society and Personality: An Interactionist Approach to Social Psychology*. Englewood Cliffs, N.J.: Prentice-Hall, 1961.

Simmel, Georg. "The Metropolis and Mental Life." In *The Sociology of Georg Simmel*, edited by Kurt Wolff, pp. 400-427. New York: The Free Press, 1950.

———. *The Web of Group Affiliation (1908)*. Translated by K.H. Wolff. New York: The Free Press, 1955.

Simmons, J.L. *Deviants*. Berkeley, Calif.: Glendessary Press, 1969.

Simon, Roger. *Gramsci's Political Thought*. London: Lawrence and Wishart Limited, 1982.

Smigel, Erwin O., and H. Laurence Ross, eds. *Crimes Against Bureaucracy*. New York: Van Nostrand Reinhold, 1970.

Smith, Adam. *The Wealth of Nations*. London: Macmillan, 1894.

Smith, David, and Lorne Tepperman. "Changes in the Canadian Business and Legal Elites, 1870-1970." *Canadian Review of Sociology and Anthropology*, Vol. 11, No. 2, pp. 97-109, 1974.

Smythe, Dallas. "Communications: Blindspot of Western Marxism." *Canadian Journal of Political and Social Theory*, Vol. 1, pp. 120-127, 1977.

——— and Tran Van Dinh. "On Critical and Administrative Research: A New Critical Analysis." *Journal of Communication*, Vol. 33, No. 3, pp. 117-127, 1983.

Sobel, Michael E. "The Analysis of Occupational Mobility." *American Sociological Review*, Vol. 48, No. 5, pp. 721-27, 1983.

Soltow, Lee. *Men and Wealth in the United States: 1850-1870*. New Haven: Yale University Press, 1975.

Sorokin, Pitrim A. *Society, Culture and Personality: Their Structure and Dynamics*. New York: Cooper Square Publications Inc., 1969.

Spenner, Kenneth I. "Temporal Changes in Work Content." *American Sociological Review*, Vol. 44, pp. 968-975, 1979.

Statistics Canada. *Births and Deaths*. Cat. 84-204. Ottawa, May 1985.

———. *Canada Update*. Vol 2, No. 4 Ottawa, March 1984.

———. *Canada's Immigrants*. Cat. 99-936. Ottawa: Minister of Supply and Services, 1984.

———. *Canadian Yearbook*. Ottawa: Information Canada, various years.

———. *Charting Canadian Incomes. 1951-1981*. Ottawa: Supply and Services Canada, 1984a.

———. *Current Demographic Analysis: Report on the Demographic Situation in Canada 1983*. Cat. 91-209E. Prepared by Jean Dumas, Demography Division. Ottawa: Minister of Supply and Services, 1984.

———. *Education in Canada: A Statistical Review for 1982-83*. Cat. 81-229. Ottawa: Minister of Supply and Services, 1984.

———. *Historical Statistics of Canada*. 2d ed. Edited by M.C. Urquhart. Ottawa.

———. *Job Market Reality for Postsecondary Graduates, Employment Outcome by 1978 Two Years After Graduation*. Cat. 81-572E. By W. Clark and Z. Zsigmond, Ottawa, 1981.

———. *The Labour Force*. Cat. 71-001. Ottawa, April 1985.

———. *Life Tables 1980-82*. Cat. 84-522, Ottawa, 1984.

———. *Perspectives Canada III*. Ottawa: Minister of Supply and Services, 1980.

———. *Population. Labour Force-Occupation Trends*. 1981 Census of Canada. Cat. 92-920, Vol. 1, pp. 1-3 and 1-37. Ottawa, 1983a.

———. *Vital Statistics*. Vol. 1. *Births and Deaths, 1981*. Cat. 84-204. Ottawa, 1983.

———. *Vital Statistics*. Vol. 2. *Marriages and Divorces, 1982*. Cat. 84-205. Ottawa, 1983.

———. *Women in the Work World*. Chart 10(a). Ottawa: Supply and Services Canada, 1984.

Stebbins, R.A. *Teachers and Meanings: Definitions of Classroom Situations*. Leiden: E.J. Brill, 1975.

Stedman Jones, Gareth. "From Historical Sociology to Theoretical History." *British Journal of Sociology,* Vol. 27, No. 3, pp. 295-305, 1976.

Steinberg, Stephen, *The Ethnic Myth: Race, Ethnicity, and Class in America*. Boston: Beacon Press, 1981.

Stevens, Stanley S. "Mathematics, measurement and psychophysics." In *Handbook of Experimental Psychology,* edited by S.S. Stevens, pp. 1-49. New York: Wiley, 1951.

Stinchecombe, Arthur L. *Constructing Social Theories*. New York: Harcourt Brace Jovanovich, 1968.

———. "Some Empirical Consequences of the Davis-Moore Theory of Stratification." *American Sociological Review,* Vol. 28, pp. 805-808, 1963.

Stirling, Robert, and Denise Kouri. "Unemployment indexes—the Canadian context." In *Economy, Class and Social Reality,* edited by J.A. Fry, pp. 169-205. Toronto: Butterworth, 1979.

Strauss, Anselm et al. "The Hospital and its Negotiated Order." In *The Hospital in Modern Society,* edited by Eliot Freidson, pp. 147-169. New York: The Free Press, 1963.

Tanner, Julian. "Youth Culture and the Canadian High School: an Emperical Analysis." *Canadian Journal of Sociology,* Vol. 3, No. 1, pp. 89-102, 1978.

Taylor, D. Garth. "Pluralistic Ignorance and the Spiral of Silence." *Public Opinion Quarterly,* Vol. 46, pp. 311-335, 1982.

Teeple, Gary. "Land, Labour and Capital in Pre-Confederation Canada." In *Capitalism and the National Question in Canada,* edited by G. Teeple, pp. 43-66. Toronto: University of Toronto Press, 1972.

Terry, John. "The Gender Gap: Women's Political Power." Ottawa: Research Branch, Library of Parliament, October 1984.

Thio, Alex. *Deviant Behavior*. 2d ed. Boston: Houghton Mifflin, 1983.

Thomas, William Isaac, and Florian Znan-iecki. *The Polish Peasant in Europe and America*. New York: Dover, 1958.

Thompson, E.P. *The Poverty of Theory and Other Essays*. New York: Monthly Review Press, 1979.

Thompson, E.P. *Whigs and Hunters: The Origin of the Black Act*. New York: Pantheon, 1975.

Thompson, Edgar T. *Plantation Societies, Race Relations, and the South: The Regimentation of Populations*. Durham, N.C.: Duke University Press, 1975.

Thompson, Hunter S. *Hell's Angels*. New York: Ballantine, 1967.

Thompson, Paul. *The Nature of Work: An Introduction to Debates on the Labor Process*. Atlantic Highlands, N.J.: Humanities Press, Inc., 1984.

Thorsell, Bernard A., and Lloyd W. Klemke. "The Labeling Process: Reinforcement and Deterrent?". *Law and Society Review,* Vol. 6, No. 3, pp. 393-403., 1972.

Tienhaara, Nancy. *Canadian Views on Immigration and Population: An Analysis of Post-War Gallup Polls*. Ottawa: Manpower and Immigration, 1974.

Tilly, Charles. *As Sociology Meets History*. New York: Academic, 1981.

Toennies, Ferdinand. *Community and Society*. East Lansing: Michigan State University Press, 1957.

Toffler, Alvin. *Future Shock*. New York: Bantam, 1971.

Touraine, Alain. *The Post-Industrial Society*. New York: Random House, 1971.

———. *Workers' Attitudes to Technical Change*. Paris: Organization for Economic Co-operation and Development, 1965.

Treiman, Donald J. *Occupational Prestige in Comparative Perspective*. New York: Academic, 1978.

Tuchman, Gaye. *Making News*. New York: The Free Press, 1978.

———; and A.K. Daniels; and J. Benet, eds. *Hearth and Home: Images of Women in Mass Media*. New York: Oxford University Press, 1978.

Tumin, Melvin M. "Some Principles of

Stratification: A Critical Analysis." *American Sociological Review,* Vol. 18, pp. 387-393, 1953.

Turk, Austin T. "Criminology and Socio-Legal Studies." In *Perspectives in Criminal Law,* edited by Anthony N. Doob and Edward L. Greenspan, pp. 309-334. Aurora, Ont.: Canada Law Book, Inc., 1984.

———. "Organizational Deviance and Political Policing." In *Organizational Police Deviance,* edited by Clifford D. Shearing, pp. 111-125. Toronto: Butterworth, 1981.

———. *Political Criminality: The Defiance and Defense of Authority.* Beverly Hills, Calif.: Sage, 1982.

Turowetz, Allan, and Michael Rosenberg. "Exaggerating Everyday Life: The Case of Professional Wrestling." In *Shaping Identity in Canadian Society,* edited by Jack Haas and William Shaffir, pp. 87-100. Toronto: Prentice-Hall, 1978.

Tylor, Edward. *Anthropology: An Introduction to the Study of Man and Civilization.* London: Macmillan, 1924.

Urquhart, M.C., ed. *Historical Statistics of Canada.* 2d ed. Ottawa: Statistics Canada, 1983.

Vallee, Frank G. "Regionalism and ethnicity: the French-Canadian case." In *Perspectives on Regions & Regionalism,* edited by B.Y. Card, pp. 19-25. Western Association of Sociology and Anthropology Proceedings, 1969.

Vallieres, Pierre. *White Niggers of America.* Toronto: McClelland and Stewart, 1971.

Van de Berghe, Pierre L. "Race, perspective two." In *Dictionary of Race and Ethnic Relations,* E. Ellis Cashmore, pp. 216-218. London: Routledge and Kegan Paul.

Vanderburg, W.H. *Culture and Technique: I — The Growth of Minds and Cultures.* Toronto: University of Toronto Press, 1985.

Van Poecke, Luc. "Gerbner's Cultural Indicators." In *Mass Communication Review Yearbook,* Vol. 1, edited by Wilhoit and de Bock, pp. 423-431, 1980.

Vernon, Raymond. *Sovereignty at Bay.* New York: Basic Books, 1971.

Wallace, Joan, Commissioner. *Part-time Work in Canada.* Report of the Commission of Inquiry into Part-time Work. Ottawa: Labour Canada, 1983.

Ward, W. Peter. *White Canada Forever.* Montreal: McGill-Queen's University Press, 1978.

Ward, Robin, and Richard Jenkins, eds. *Ethnic Communities in Business.* Cambridge: Cambridge University Press, 1984.

Watkins, M.H. "A staple theory of economic growth." *Canadian Journal of Economics and Political Science,* Vol. 29, No. 2, pp. 141-158, May 1963.

Weber, Max. *The Agrarian Sociology of Ancient Civilizations.* London, New Left Books, 1976.

———. *The City.* Translated by D. Martindale and G. Neuwirth. New York: Free Press, 1958.

———. *Economy and Society.* New York: Bedminster Press, 1968.

———. *From Max Weber: Essays in Sociology.* Translated by H.H. Gerth and C. Wright Mills. New York: Oxford University Press, 1958.

———. *General Economic History.* New York: Collier Books, 1961.

———. *The Protestant Ethic and the Spirit of Capitalism.* London: George Allen and Unwin, 1974.

Weitzman, Lenore J. "Sex Role Socialization: A Focus on Women." In *Women: A Feminist Perspective,* edited by J. Freeman, pp. 157-237. Palo Alto: Mayfield Publishing Co., 1984.

Wesolowski, W. "Some Notes on the Functional Theory of Stratification." *Polish Sociological Bulletin,* Vol. 3-4, pp. 28-38, 1962.

West, Candace, and Don. H. Zimmerman. "Women's place in everyday talk: Reflections on parent-child interaction." *Social Problems,* Vol. 24, pp. 521-529, 1977.

Westergaard, John, and Henrietta Resler. *Class in A Capitalist Society: A Study of Contemporary Britain.* London: Heinemann Educational Books Ltd., 1975.

Whyte, William Foote. *Street Corner Society.* Chicago: The University of Chicago Press, 1961.

Willis, Paul. *Learning to Labour*. Farnborough: Saxon House, 1977.

Wilson, John. *Social Theory*. Englewood Cliffs, N.J.: Prentice-Hall, 1983.

Wilson, S.J. *Women, The Family, and the Economy*. Toronto: McGraw-Hill Ryerson, 1982.

Wilson, Seymour V. "The Role of Royal Commissions and Task Forces." In *The Structures of Policy Making in Canada*, B.G. Doern and P. Aucoin, pp. 113-129. Toronto: Macmillan, 1971.

Wilson, William J. *Power, Racism, and Privilege: Race Relations in Theoretical and Sociohistorical Perspectives*. New York: Free Press, 1973.

Winner, L. *Autonomous Technology*. Cambridge, Mass.: MIT Press, 1977.

Wiseman, Jacqueline. *Stations of the Lost: The Treatment of Skid Row Alcoholics*. Chicago: The University of Chicago Press, 1979.

Wolff, K.H. "The Sociology of Knowledge and Sociological Theory." In *Symposium on Sociological Theory*, edited by L. Gross. New York: Row, Peterson, 1969.

Worsley, Peter et al. *Introducing Sociology*. 2d ed. Harmondsworth: Penguin, 1977.

Wright, Charles R. *Mass Communication: A Sociological Perspective*. 2d ed. New York: Random House, 1975.

Wright, Erik Olin. "Class Boundaries in Advanced Capitalist Societies." *New Left Review*, Vol. 98, pp. 3-41, 1976.

Wrong, D.H. "The Oversocialized Concept of Man in Modern Sociology." *American Sociological Review*, Vol. 26, pp. 183-193, 1961.

Wuthrow, Robert et al. *Cultural Analysis*. Boston: Routledge and Kegan Paul, 1984.

Yancey, William L.; E.P. Ericksen; and R.N. Juliani. "Emergent ethnicity: a review and reformulation." *American Sociological Review*, Vol. 41, pp. 391-403, 1976.

Yankelovich, D. "New Rules in American Life: Searching for self-fulfillment in a World Turned Upside Down." *Psychology Today*, Vol. 15, No. 4, pp. 35-91, 1981.

Zeitlin, Irving M. *Capitalism and Imperialism*. Chicago: Markham, 1972.

_____. *Ideology and the Development of Sociological Theory*. ed. Englewood Cliffs, N.J.: Prentice-Hall, 1981b.

_____. *The Social Condition of Humanity*. New York: Oxford University Press, 1981a.

Zeitlin, Maurice. "Corporate Ownership and Control: The Large Corporation and the Capitalist Class." *American Journal of Sociology*, Vol. 79, pp. 1073-1119, March 1974.

Zimbardo, P. "The psychological power and pathology of imprisonment." Unpublished paper. Stanford University, 1971.

Zimmerman, Don, and Candace West. "Sex roles, interruptions and silences in conversation." *Language and Sex: Difference and Dominance*, edited by B. Thorne and N.M. Henley, pp. 105-129. Rowley, Mass.: Newbury House, 1975.

STUDY GUIDE

TABLE OF CONTENTS:

CHAPTER 1 SOCIOLOGY: THE SCIENCE OF SOCIETY

Key Terms

1. science

2. theories

3. social bonds

4. societies

5. paradigm

6. verification or validation

7. empirical

8. macrosociology

9. sociological imagination

10. normative expectations

11. determinism

12. negotiated meanings

a) the relationships that tie an individual into a group or society.

b) the behaviour society expects from an individual occupying a given role.

c) that which is grasped by the senses.

d) a form of solidarity found in modern societies in which citizens hold widely dissimilar roles, occupations, beliefs and world views.

e) imaginatively placing oneself in the place of another person in order to understand his/her thoughts and feelings.

f) the study of small-scale behaviour patterns within groups and institutions.

g) the totality of beliefs and sentiments common to the average citizens of a given society.

h) the recognition by members of a given economic or social class that their goals can best be achieved through collective action.

i) the construction and validation of theories about the real world based on observation, study and experimentation.

j) the ability to grasp how biography and history interact within a society.

k) the interpretations given to social acts through an interaction between the doer and the observer.

l) a solidarity present in primitive societies in which most people have similar occupations, lifestyles and world views.

13. role taking	m) the belief that our actions are shaped and triggered by forces beyond our control.
14. microsociology	n) tentative explanations of observable reality which can be used to predict future events.
15. mechanical solidarity	o) collections of relationships such as families, groups, clubs, organizations etc.
16. collective conscience	p) the study of large scale social interactions.
17. organic solidarity	q) evidence or social findings which are consistent with, and supportive of, a given theory.
18. structural functionalism	r) that which impedes the society's survival.
19. dysfunctional	s) a working model based on a particular theory that describes how a group or society functions.
20. class consciousness	t) the theory that a society's structure is shaped by the need to fulfill certain societal needs.

Pretest

1. Sociology is the study of:
   a) social change
   b) social disorder
   c) social order
   d) all of the above

2. Sociologists use history
   a) to predict the future
   b) to prove their theories
   c) at their own peril
   d) as a source of information

3. The Industrial Revolution led to the
   a) displacement of peasants from the land
   b) displacement of agricultural wage workers from the land
   c) destruction of long-distance trade

   d) reduced production of marketable commodities

4. The leaders of the Enlightenment defended
   a) the divine right of kings to rule
   b) the right of individuals to criticize the church
   c) traditional authority
   d) religion and mysticism

5. The Romantic Conservatives cherished the old order because
   a) it subjected imagination and feeling to rational ridicule
   b) it undermined the wisdom of established tradition and custom

c) they saw progress as something that should come about through slow and gradual reform
d) it de-emphasized morality

6. The founding fathers of sociology were interested in the themes of
a) social control and social deviance
b) economic development and underdevelopment
c) order and progress
d) capitalism and slavery

7. For Durkheim, mechanical solidarity is
a) restored by the development of modern society
b) undermined by the growth of a personal conscience
c) only possible under conditions of great social dissimilarity
d) opposed to the collective conscience

8. For Weber, bureaucratic domination is inescapable in
a) capitalist society
b) socialist society
c) feudal society
d) a and b above

9. The concepts of status, role and norm are central to a discussion of:
a) class struggle
b) social structure
c) bureaucratic domination
d) organic solidarity

10. To say that human beings are creatures and creators of society implies:
a) free will is available to all
b) societal forces determine individual behaviour
c) free will and determinism are zero-sum phenomena
d) free will and determinism are relative

11. Sociological insight is superior to common sense because it

a) relies on revelation and tradition
b) refuses to penetrate surface appearances
c) is quantitative in nature
d) is based on the logic of verification

12. The structural functionalist best known for his use of the concept social system is
a) Robert Merton
b) Talcott Parsons
c) Emile Durkheim
d) Seymour Lipset

13. Among the vital system needs of any society one must include
a) institutions of war
b) a social welfare system
c) integration of parts
d) an official state religion

14. When Marxists talk of social order, they assume it comes about as a result of:
a) coercion
b) consensus
c) shared goals
d) common values

15. Since humans construct and live within a world of meanings, symbolic interactionists feel that order must be:
a) coerced
b) impossible
c) pre-ordained
d) negotiated

Test

1. Sociologists study
a) human behaviour
b) human and animal behaviour
c) human behaviour in groups
d) human and animal behaviour in groups

2. The study of large scale social interactions is called

a) big-pictured sociology
b) macrosociology
c) political science
d) megasociology

3. The two founding fathers of sociology were
   a) Auguste Comte and Karl Marx
   b) Emile Durkheim and Karl Marx
   c) Emile Durkheim and Max Weber
   d) Auguste Comte and Henri de Saint Simon

4. As a source of truth Enlightenment thinkers embraced
   a) intuition
   b) introspection
   c) revelation
   d) reason

5. According to Karl Marx, the workers would overthrow Capitalism when:
   a) their lives became too miserable to bear
   b) they developed class consciousness
   c) both a and b occurred together
   d) hell froze over

6. Durkheim believed the basis for organic solidarity was:
   a) a common culture
   b) a shared love of the land
   c) a genetically based racial memory
   d) a mutual dependence caused by the division of labour

7. Max Weber focused his analysis of power in society on:
   a) the capitalist class
   b) trade unions
   c) bureaucracies
   d) the political system

8. The sociological imagination enables us to:
   a) see through the facade of history
   b) grasp the relationship between biography and history
   c) avoid the mistakes made by Marx and Durkheim
   d) appreciate the importance of bureaucratic rule.

9. Because our social behaviour is so highly patterned
   a) human beings are devoid of free will
   b) we are all prisoners of society
   c) we cannot deny the importance of social structure
   d) true freedom implies the destruction of established patterns of behaviour

10. Sociology can be a liberating science because
    a) it advocates critical and revolutionary change
    b) it helps reveal the hidden constraints on our behaviour
    c) it is devoid of theoretical disputes
    d) it is a non-empirical science

11. To recognize the importance of social structure in moulding behaviour
    a) denies the existence of free will
    b) confirms the existence of free will
    c) is more of a psychological than a social concern
    d) none of the above

12. Structural functionalism is most closely identified with
    a) Durkheim
    b) Marx
    c) Weber
    d) Darwin

13. Whereas functionalists stress order and stability, Marxists stress:
    a) social solidarity
    b) class conflict
    c) other-worldliness
    d) a and c above

14. Marxists think most people in a capitalist society live off:
    a) exploitation
    b) profits
    c) welfare
    d) wages

15. Symbolic Interactionism is primarily concerned with

a) the externally determined aspects of behaviour
b) the process of human conditioning
c) the interpretive understanding of human behaviour
d) the symbolic dimensions of poverty

16. A central concept in symbolic interactionism is
a) role confusion
b) role taking
c) role identity
d) role denial

17. The first Canadian University to establish an independent sociology department was
a) Toronto
b) Simon Fraser
c) McGill
d) Dalhousie

18. When people behave exactly as they are expected to in a given situation, they are meeting our
a) preconceived biases
b) stereotypical expectations
c) normative expectations
d) none of the above

19. Sociological explanations of the underlying causes of human behaviour are only useful if they are
a) consistent with common sense
b) subject to verification
c) politically and morally acceptable
d) formulated by social scientists

20. A tautological explanation is
a) tightly reasoned
b) applicable only in a laboratory setting
c) universally applicable
d) true by definition

21. Empirical data is gathered:
a) via sensory perceptions
b) via abstract reasoning
c) through intuition
d) from respected sacred and secular authorities

22. The social sciences include:
a) history, sociology, economics, anthropology
b) biology, anthropology, psychology and sociology
c) political science, medicine, sociology and history
d) psychology, anthropology, sociology and economics

23. A researcher's basic starting premise in tackling a research problem is his _____ assumption.
a) methodological
b) ideological
c) ontological
d) primary

24. Having "the sociological imagination" involves recognizing that:
a) a person shapes his/her own destiny
b) a person is shaped by history and social environment
c) neither a nor b is true
d) both a and b are true

25. The structural functionalist approach was first applied to the social science of
a) anthropology
b) economics
c) psychology
d) sociology

26. According to Marxists, the fact that most Canadians consider themselves middle class results from
a) an affluent society
b) Canadians tending to exaggerate their incomes
c) lying
d) false consciousness

27. In Marxist terms, being exploited means:
a) giving more in labour than one receives in wages
b) making maximum use of one's talents

c) working under harsh conditions
d) all of the above

28. Marxists view the state as an institution controlled by and operated for the benefit of
a) bureaucrats
b) the proletariat
c) all classes
d) the ruling class

29. The symbolic interactionists' perspective is
a) microsociological
b) macrosociological
c) none of the above
d) both a and b

30. According to symbolic interactionists, language is only one of many shared _____ human beings use to communicate with each other.
a) norms
b) roles
c) statuses
d) symbols

Posttest

1. Sociologists study:
a) families and small groups
b) entire societies
c) social institutions
d) all of the above

2. Microsociology is the study of:
a) small-scale behaviour patterns within groups and institutions
b) small countries or cities
c) any sociological phenomena so long as the study is a short one
d) an individual person's behaviour

3. History is important to sociologists because history:
a) reveals long-established social patterns
b) provides clues to future social developments

c) has shaped all aspects of society
d) all of the above

4. The social class that benefitted the most from the French Revolution was the:
a) aristocracy
b) peasantry
c) bourgeoisie
d) clergy

5. The Romantic Conservatives argued that:
a) many aspects of social behaviour are non-rational
b) science holds the key to understanding human behaviour
c) religion has no place in a modern society
d) men and women always act on the basis of reason

6. According to Emile Durkheim, modern societies produce a form of social cohesiveness called:
a) organic solidarity
b) mechanical solidarity
c) social solidarity
d) collective solidarity

7. Weber saw modern society as characterized by:
a) rational-legal authority
b) charismatic authority
c) traditional authority
d) military authority

8. Sociological knowledge is:
a) scientifically generated
b) empirically unsound
c) derived from untestable hypotheses
d) based on intuition

9. Unlike the natural scientist, the social scientist:
a) deals with absolutes
b) cannot predict the behaviour of his subject matter with 100% accuracy
c) does not deal with experimental situations
d) works only in the realm of theory

10. Because all individuals are unique:
    a) it is impossible to explain individual behaviour by studying groups
    b) sociologists try to explain all behaviour at the individual level
    c) sociological and psychological theories are identical
    d) sociological and psychological explanations of behaviour complement one another

11. The status of "girl" is an example of a(n) _____status.
    a) achieved
    b) ascribed
    c) attributed
    d) described

12. A person occupying a given status is expected to perform certain:
    a) deviant acts
    b) rituals
    c) norms
    d) roles

13. According to structural functionalists, a social practice or institution is more likely to survive if it:
    a) serves the interests of the ruling classes
    b) is compatible with the society's cultural traditions
    c) contributes to the overall survival of the social system
    d) is compatible with human nature

14. The leading structural functionalist was:
    a) Talcott Parsons
    b) Auguste Comte
    c) Max Weber
    d) Robert K. Merton

15. A social institution or social pattern that harms the society's ability to survive and be healthy is considered:
    a) deviant
    b) dysfunctional
    c) subversive
    d) illegal

Essay Questions

1. List some social conventions or customs that have died out in the past 50 years. How would a sociologist go about trying to explain these changes? How would the sociologist's approach differ from that of a(n) historian, economist, theologian or philosopher?

2. According to Durkheim, modern man is bound together by organic solidarity which is based on the division of labour. Which aspects of modern life seem to strengthen organic solidarity and which aspects weaken it?

3. Why does sociology contain so many different competing perspectives?

4. What are the points of agreement and disagreement between Marxists and structural functionalists?

5. Since all individuals are unique, how is it possible to explain any person's behaviour in terms of group attributes?

6. Why has structural functionalism been called inherently conservative? Is this assertion true?

ANSWERS TO CHAPTER 1

Key Terms

1. i	8. p	15. l
2. n	9. j	16. g
3. a	10. b	17. d
4. o	11. m	18. t
5. s	12. k	19. r
6. q	13. e	20. h
7. c	14. f	

Test

1. c	11. d	21. a
2. b	12. a	22. d
3. d	13. b	23. c
4. d	14. d	24. d
5. c	15. c	25. a
6. d	16. b	26. d
7. c	17. c	27. a
8. b	18. c	28. d
9. c	19. b	29. a
10. b	20. d	30. d

Pretest

1. d	6. c	11. d
2. d	7. b	12. b
3. a	8. d	13. c
4. b	9. b	14. a
5. c	10. d	15. d

Posttest

1. d	6. a	11. b
2. a	7. a	12. d
3. d	8. a	13. c
4. c	9. b	14. a
5. a	10. d	15. b

CHAPTER 2   SOCIOLOGICAL METHODS OF RESEARCH

Key Terms

1. research cycle

   a) the tendency of subjects to react to specific experimental conditions which might not exist in a real life situation

2. statistical regression

   b) a process that defines abstracts in such a way that they can be measured empirically

3. experimental mortality

   c) the aspect being studied; the variable that is (or may be) affected by changes in the independent variable

4. maturation

   d) the thing being studied (i.e. an individual, a group or an entire society

5. reactive effects

   e) descriptions of sociological relationships that have been found repeatedly to be accurate in many different studies

6. paradigms

    f) the tendency towards the average performance when subjects are selected on the basis of extreme scores on the dependent variable

7. operationalization

    g) natural changes in the subjects of an experiment over time (e.g. getting tired)

8. sociological laws

    h) subjects dropping out of an experiment before it is completed

9. theories

    i) the process in which theories are endlessly formulated, tested, modified, reformulated and retested

10. dependent variable

    j) the group that is exposed to the independent variable

11. independent variable

    k) the extent to which an experiment's results can be generalized to different situations and settings

12. the unit of analysis

    l) a quasi-experimental design that compares a dependent variable in two groups after an event (the independent variable) has occurred in only one of the groups

13. control group

    m) a sample created by selecting every n-th case in a population after the first case has been selected randomly

14. experimental group

    n) the research technique of gathering data about a group or organization by participating in the daily life of that group or organization

15. one-shot case study

    o) explanations of sociological laws

16. static-group comparison

    p) points of view expressed in schools of scientific thought

17. one-group pretest-posttest

    q) the factor that causes (hypothetically) changes in the dependent variable

18. internal validity

    r) the extent to which test procedures succeed in isolating the independent variable as the only plausible explanation for changes in the dependent variable

19. external validity

s) like an interval measurement but having an absolute zero

20. rival causal factors

t) a question that asks two questions at once

21. contingency table analysis

u) a quasi-experimental design that compares a single group before and after an event takes place

22. participant observation

v) the group that is not exposed to the independent variable

23. unobtrusive measures

w) a quasi-experimental design in which a single group is tested to see if some past event caused a change in a specific dependent variable.

24. random sample

x) the practice of collecting existing data from official statistics, public documents, private records etc.

25. systematic sample

y) a sample created purely by chance in that all elements in the group being studied had an equal likelihood of being selected

26. stratified sample

z) selecting a sample population in a way that ensures the sample will have certain characteristics (e.g. be 60% male or 30% Catholic)

27. cluster sample

aa) the use of numbers to identify qualitative categories (i.e. sex or religious affiliation)

28. quota sampling

bb) a sample created by dividing the general population into geographically based categories and then selecting a random or systematic sample from each area

29. availability sampling

cc) a scale of numerical categories in which the units are spaced at equal intervals (e.g. the Fahrenheit temperature scale). These scales have no absolute zero

30. snow-ball sampling

dd) a sample created by dividing the general population into subgroups and then selecting a random or systematic sample from within each subgroup

31. nominal level of measurement	ee) a question that does not ask a respondent to choose from among a limited number of answers
32. ordinal level of measurement	ff) a way of presenting and studying data so that the effects of two or more variables can be considered at the same time
33. interval level of measurement	gg) selecting a sample solely on the basis of willingness to participate in the study
34. ratio level of measurement	hh) the use of numbers to rank-order categories
35. open-ended question	ii) selecting a sample by having members of the sample refer other subjects to the researcher
36. double barrelled question	jj) variables which are competing explanations for changes in the dependent variable

Pretest

1. A theory that is inconsistent with the empirical evidence should be:
   a) modified
   b) rejected
   c) suppressed
   d) accepted

2. A sociological law is a theory that:
   a) has been proven right
   b) was formulated by one of sociology's founding fathers
   c) is consistent with the findings of repeated experiments
   d) is logically unassailable

3. Variables which cause changes in other variables are called _____ variables.
   a) dependent
   b) independent
   c) catalyst
   d) experimental

4. In a classical experimental design only the _____ group is exposed to the independent variable.
   a) control
   b) test
   c) independent
   d) experimental

5. The external validity of an experiment refers to the extent to which:
   a) results can be generalized to a larger population
   b) procedural sources of invalidity have been controlled
   c) the experimental findings appear to be conclusive
   d) none of the above

6. A researcher who goes into the field to live among the people she is studying is called a(n):

a) anthropologist
b) field worker
c) direct observer
d) participant observer

7. A researcher studying illegal immigrants who may not wish to reveal their status would likely have to use _____ sampling to create a sample population.
a) systematic
b) quota
c) random
d) availability

8. Creating a sample population by asking subjects to refer other subjects to the researcher is called _____ sampling.
a) word of mouth
b) referral
c) chain-reaction
d) snow-ball

9. Surveying public attitudes toward the military before and after it fights a war is an example of a(n) _____ experimental design.
a) static-group comparison
b) one-group pretest-posttest
c) one-shot case study
d) historical/comparative research

10. Unobtrusive measures are used to collect data:
a) through participant observation
b) without telling or asking the subjects being studied
c) from government statistics and private and public documents
d) all of the above

11. Dividing a population into groups based on geographic location and then drawing probability samples from each group is called _____ sampling.
a) geographic
b) cluster

c) quota
d) stratified

12. Which of the following is an example of probability sampling?
a) systematic sampling
b) quota sampling
c) snow-ball sampling
d) all of the above

13. "Do you think brutal criminals deserve the right to vote?" is an example of a(n) _____ question.
a) open-ended
b) closed-ended
c) double-barrelled
d) biased

14. The internal validity of an experiment is impaired by:
a) experimental mortality
b) selection biases
c) statistical regression
d) all of the above

15. Tentative answers to research questions which are tested in sociological experiments are called:
a) theories
b) hypotheses
c) biases
d) dogma

Test

1. Sociologists use _____ when designing experiments and interpreting findings.
a) biases
b) paradigms
c) experts
d) an open mind

2. The dominant paradigm in Canadian sociology today is:
a) structural functionalism
b) symbolic interactionism
c) dialectical materialism
d) none of the above; all three are dominant

3. The way to determine if a theory has a solid empirical base is to check it:
   a) for logical inconsistencies
   b) against concrete facts
   c) against established beliefs
   d) all of the above.

4. Defining an abstract concept in a way that allows a researcher to statistically measure its occurrence is called _____ the concept.
   a) quantifying
   b) objectifying
   c) concretizing
   d) operationalizing

5. The research cycle ends:
   a) when a theory is proved right or wrong
   b) when an experiment is concluded and its results published
   c) when a theory becomes a sociological law
   d) never

6. Many experiments are attempts to account for changes in the _____ variable.
   a) dependent
   b) independent
   c) research
   d) experimental

7. Sociologists cannot determine whether abortions should be available on demand because:
   a) more data is needed than now exists
   b) the question is a moral rather than a scientific one
   c) sociology is not a sophisticated enough science yet
   d) all of the above

8. In the classical experimental design, which group is *not* exposed to the independent variable?
   a) pure group
   b) dependent group
   c) test group
   d) control group

9. Trying to determine the effect of war on a country's economy by comparing the economy of a country at war to the economy of a country at peace is an example of a:
   a) one-shot case study
   b) static-group comparison
   c) one-group pretest-posttest design
   d) none of the above

10. The external validity of experimental findings depends on the:
    a) representativeness of the sample group
    b) experiment's internal validity
    c) extent to which the experimental conditions were like conditions in real life
    d) all of the above

11. Experimental mortality refers to:
    a) subjects dying in the middle of an experiment
    b) experiments being prematurely terminated
    c) subjects leaving an experiment before it is over
    d) all of the above

12. If young, single, professionals buy a lot of sports cars, then age, marital status and occupation are _____ in explaining sports car ownership.
    a) rival causal factors
    b) dependent variables
    c) contributing factors
    d) complementary factors

13. Bivariate and multivariate relationships are often made clearer when a researcher uses a _____ to cross tabulate different variables.
    a) contingency table
    b) survey sheet
    c) graph
    d) summary sheet

14. In his classic study of a black street corner group in Washington, D.C., Elliot Liebow used the research

technique of _____ to gather his data.
a) unobtrusive measures
b) cluster sampling
c) participant observation
d) snow-ball sampling

15. Creating a sample population by including every tenth name in the local telephone book is an example of _____ sampling.
a) stratified
b) cluster
c) systematic
d) quota

16. Creating a sample group by dividing the general population into subgroups and then surveying a portion from each subgroup is called _____ sampling.
a) simple random
b) stratified
c) snow-ball
d) availability

17. Which of the following is a form of non-probability sampling?
a) stratified sampling
b) simple random sampling
c) snow-ball sampling
d) cluster sampling

18. A researcher must ensure that the categories he puts his data into are both _____ and _____.
a) subjective . . . clearly defined
b) mutually exclusive . . . exhaustive
c) objective . . . open-ended
d) objective . . . of equal size

19. "Are you in favour of tougher gun control and anti-drunk driving legislation?" is an example of a(n) _____ question.
a) double-barrelled
b) closed-ended
c) open-ended
d) unobtrusive

20. Marx, Weber and Durkheim all used the _____ approach in formulating their main theories.
a) random sampling
b) classic experimental design
c) historical comparative
d) participant observation

21. A researcher who creates an unrealistic experimental situation faces the problem of _____ when trying to generalize his results to a larger population.
a) maturation
b) reactive effects
c) statistical regression
d) all of the above

22. Experimental designs that subject representative population samples to realistic, unextraordinary situations tend to produce findings with a higher degree of:
a) popular appeal
b) internal validity
c) external validity
d) experimental immortality

23. When subjects become tired or bored during prolonged testing, an experiment's internal validity is being threatened by:
a) reactive effects
b) experimental mortality
c) maturation
d) statistical regression

24. In participant observation studies, a researcher should tell her subjects that she is a sociologist:
a) always
b) only if such a disclosure will help the research
c) only if such a disclosure will not harm the research
d) there is no rule of thumb; it is an individual moral decision

25. Which of the following are unobtrusive sources of data?

a) diaries and novels
b) government reports
c) newspapers and motion pictures
d) all of the above

26. Which type of sampling technique enhances an experiment's external validity the least?
a) random sampling
b) cluster sampling
c) availability sampling
d) stratified sampling

27. A _____ sampling technique is used to ensure that a sample population will be 50% male or 30% Catholic.
a) quota
b) cluster
c) stratified
d) systematic

28. The _____ level of measurement uses numbers to classify but not rank subjects.
a) ordinal
b) nominal
c) ratio
d) interval

29. "What is Canada's greatest asset?" is a(n) _____ question.
a) historical/comparative
b) open-ended
c) closed-ended
d) unobtrusive

30. Before distributing a questionnaire, a researcher should:
a) pretest the group with a similar questionnaire
b) predict how the group will respond
c) review previous questionnaires to avoid duplicating questions
d) pretest the questionnaire on a similar group

Posttest

1. The problem of internal validity refers to the question of:
a) honesty in the reporting of research results
b) whether a study deserved the time and effort given to it
c) whether the independent variable actually caused changes in the dependent variable
d) generalizability

2. Theories:
a) cannot be proven or disproven conclusively
b) can only be proven when their concepts are clearly defined
c) can be disproven by empirical evidence
d) can be proven or disproven if concepts are operationalized into statistics

3. Randomization refers to the random:
a) reporting of data
b) assignment of subjects to groups
c) choice of questions used in a survey
d) selection of a quota sample

4. A nominal variable serves to _____ data.
a) classify
b) rank
c) name
d) none of the above

5. Participant observation studies differ from experimental research in that participant observation projects:
a) don't require any specific hypotheses
b) generate a smaller volume of data
c) usually don't require as much time to complete
d) none of the above

6. An experimental variable must have all but one of the following characteristics.
   a) a theoretical definition
   b) an operational definition
   c) a category that does not overlap with any other categories
   d) an interval parameter

7. Operationalization refers to:
   a) arriving at conceptual definitions
   b) deriving hypotheses from theories
   c) simplifying the random sampling process
   d) none of the above

8. An interval variable has the properties of:
   a) an ordinal variable but not a nominal one
   b) a nominal but not an ordinal variable
   c) an ordinal variable and a nominal one
   d) an independent and a dependent variable

9. Unanticipated events that affect subjects during the course of an experiment can become rival explanations for observed changes in the dependent variable. This threat to the experiment's internal validity is called a problem of:
   a) maturation
   b) history
   c) instrumentation
   d) statistical regression

10. A researcher studied why some families do long-term financial planning while others do only short-term planning. He found middle class families were more likely to engage in long-term planning than were working class families. The dependent variable in his study was:

a) long-term financial planning
b) social class
c) financial planning
d) middle class values

11. The research cycle is cyclical in that:
   a) research results must be checked by replications
   b) research is multi-disciplinary
   c) research moves back and forth between theory and facts
   d) no progress is ever made in resolving theoretical disputes

12. The independent variable in a hypothesis is:
   a) the variable that the researcher wishes to explain
   b) an irrelevant factor that can muddle research findings
   c) the expected outcome of other research variables
   d) the factor that explains changes in the dependent variable

13. Which of the following techniques is usually the best way to control extrinsic factors in an experiment?
   a) randomization
   b) precision matching
   c) self analysis to weed out the researcher's own biases
   d) frequency distribution matching

14. The choice of a particular research method depends on:
   a) the nature of the research topic
   b) the resources available
   c) the type of likely respondents
   d) all of the above

15. A quota sample is:
   a) similar to a cluster sample
   b) a probability sample
   c) a non-probability sample
   d) like a snowball sample

Essay Questions

1. Why can sociological research study moral issues but not resolve them?

2. Why are the results of quasi-experimental designs often inconclusive? What were the three kinds of quasi-experimental design described in the text?

3. What eight factors affect an experiment's internal validity? What two factors influence an experiment's external validity?

4. How do government statistics often reveal more about the statisticians than about the people the records are supposed to describe?

5. What are the four main types of probability samples? Why are these usually preferable to non-probability samples? In what kinds of situations would a researcher use a non-probability sample?

6. What are the drawbacks and benefits of including: a) open-ended and b) close-ended questions in a survey?

7. What kinds of projects are better suited to participant observation rather than survey research? Why?

   Research Suggestion: Go to your library and find back issues of all the sociological research journals carried there. This will probably involve first learning how to use your library's periodical index. Briefly flip through each journal and write a very short evaluation of each one, noting such things as: readability, any obvious biases, obvious strengths or weaknesses in specialized areas of sociology. Then get hold of a style guide for writing social science research papers and find out where the library keeps its books on sociological research and questionnaire design. All of this information should be useful to you later in the term.

ANSWERS TO CHAPTER 2

Key Terms

1. i	13. v	25. m
2. f	14. j	26. dd
3. h	15. w	27. bb
4. g	16. l	28. z
5. a	17. u	29. gg
6. p	18. r	30. ii
7. b	19. k	31. aa
8. e	20. jj	32. hh
9. o	21. ff	33. cc
10. c	22. n	34. s
11. q	23. x	35. ee
12. d	24. y	36. t

Pretest

1. a	9. b
2. c	10. c
3. b	11. b
4. d	12. a
5. a	13. d
6. d	14. d
7. d	15. b
8. d	

Test

1. b	11. c	21. b
2. d	12. a	22. c
3. b	13. a	23. c
4. d	14. c	24. d
5. d	15. c	25. d
6. a	16. b	26. c
7. b	17. c	27. a
8. d	18. b	28. b
9. b	19. a	29. b
10. d	20. c	30. d

Posttest

1. c	9. b
2. a	10. c
3. b	11. c
4. a	12. d
5. d	13. a
6. d	14. d
7. d	15. c
8. c	

CHAPTER 3   CULTURE, CHANGE AND AUTONOMY

Key Terms

1. material culture

a) the belief that the individual's interests must be subordinated to those of the state which is seen as a meritocracy

2. non-material culture

b) the importance a person attaches to his or her membership in an ethnic group

3. cultural capital

c) the tendency to rate one's own cultural or ethnic group higher than other groups

4. corporatism

d) the values, ideas and beliefs of a culture

5. Sapir-Whorf hypothesis

e) the physical artifacts produced by a culture

6. subcultures

f) the symbolic elements of culture that are valued by the society's dominant class (e.g. specific kinds of dress, speech, manners, attitudes, knowledge and experience)

7. ethnocentrism

g) a special vocabulary that identifies the speaker as a member of a specific subculture

8. argot

h) the theory that language shapes culture by organizing one's experiences according to linguistic terms and rules

9. stereotypes

i) groups whose norms, values and expressive symbols differ from ones more widely held

10. ethnic salience

j) the preconceived positive or negative images we assign to ourselves or others on the basis of membership in a particular group or category of people

Pretest

1. Which aspect of a person's life reflects the person's culture?
   a) one's morals
   b) one's habits and hobbies
   c) one's language
   d) all of the above

2. In a classic 1963 study, Lipset found Canadians are more _____ than Americans.
   a) conservative and authoritarian
   b) liberal and open minded
   c) tolerant and law abiding
   d) none of the above

3. Canadians have a _____ view of time.
   a) polychronic
   b) monochronic
   c) trichronic
   d) organic

4. Oscar Lewis suggested the culture of poverty could be ended by:
   a) bringing the poor into the middle class
   b) improving the schools in the ghettos
   c) fostering positive self images among the poor
   d) more community self-help projects

5. Marx, McLuhan and Innis all postulated _____ theories of culture in which cultural changes followed structural ones.
   a) materialist
   b) idealist

c) interdependence
d) autonomous

6. McLuhan described the generation gap of the 1960s as a clash between a _____ culture and a _____ culture.
   a) agricultural . . . industrial
   b) urban . . . rural
   c) print . . . electronic
   d) collective . . . individualistic

7. Bernard Blishen's 1978 study found Canadian regionalism was highest in:
   a) Quebec and Alberta
   b) British Columbia and Alberta
   c) Ontario and Quebec
   d) Quebec and the Maritimes

8. Marxists believe that a society's dominant culture:
   a) is imposed upon it by the dominant class
   b) depends on a society's ethnic composition
   c) results from a well developed sense of class consciousness
   d) evolves naturally from the interaction of individuals

9. Living in a slum can produce feelings of fatalism, helplessness, dependence and inferiority. Oscar Lewis said these feelings were part of the:
   a) welfare mentality
   b) culture of unemployment
   c) culture of poverty
   d) negative thinking syndrome

10. Which of the following can *not* be said to have a unique culture that could be studied by sociologists?
    a) General Motors
    b) Prince Edward Island
    c) the Montreal Canadiens hockey team
    d) Wayne Gretzky

Test

1. Discussions of culture usually focus on:
    a) norms, values, beliefs and expressive symbols
    b) norms, roles and values
    c) norms, beliefs and symbols
    d) none of the above

2. The kitchen sink is:
    a) not part of culture
    b) part of material culture
    c) part of non-material culture
    d) too universal to be culturally significant

3. Parsons described culture as one of four "action systems". The other three are the:
    a) gender, social class and religious systems
    b) biological, personality and social systems
    c) biological, personality and symbolic systems
    d) economic, educational and spiritual systems

4. Norms:
    a) govern appropriate behaviour
    b) are situation specific
    c) are learned in socialization
    d) all of the above

5. Marchak described the two major ideologies in Canada as:
    a) conservativism and liberalism
    b) conservativism and socialism
    c) socialism and liberalism
    d) nationalism and internationalism

6. A third major ideology emerging in the 1980s is:
    a) corporatism
    b) continentalism
    c) internationalism
    d) neo-facism

7. Expressive symbols include:
    a) language
    b) hair styles
    c) ritual behaviour
    d) all of the above

8. When Hall describes the Western orientation to time as monochronic he means that
    a) we compartmentalize our experiences
    b) we emphasize schedules and promptness
    c) we think of time as tangible
    d) all of the above

9. The Sapir-Whorf hypothesis assumes
    a) linguistic differences are slowly disappearing
    b) language is a way of organizing experiences
    c) the underlying structure of all language is similar
    d) none of the above

10. Generic terms like "he" and "man":
    a) are unique to the English language
    b) are understood by most people to refer to men only
    c) are understood by most people to refer to men and women
    d) are seldom used by well-educated people

11. North American televisions are turned on for an average of about:
    a) 3 hours a day
    b) 5 hours a day
    c) 7 hours a day
    d) 9 hours a day

12. What percentage of American homes have television sets?

a) 78%
b) 85%
c) 95%
d) 98%

13. Gerbner and his associates found that:
    a) television viewing decreases with age
    b) heavy viewers internalize the world view of television drama
    c) university students have little time for television
    d) most people reject the symbolic environment of television

14. According to Lewis, the culture of poverty:
    a) transcends national boundaries
    b) is handed down from generation to generation
    c) is characterized by feelings of fatalism and inferiority
    d) all of the above

15. Ethnocentrism refers to the universal tendency to
    a) want to learn about other cultures
    b) see the relative merits of all ways of life
    c) rate one's own group as superior
    d) none of the above

16. Style consists of:
    a) image
    b) demeanour
    c) argot
    d) all of the above

17. The description of British youth culture focused on their:
    a) values and beliefs
    b) expressive symbols
    c) ideologies
    d) norms of behaviour

18. Corporate culture refers to:
    a) the domination of multinational corporations
    b) the business ethic
    c) distinct norms and values within an organization
    d) all of the above

19. The electronic media, according to McLuhan:
    a) draw people together in a global village
    b) create rifts between subgroups
    c) are mind-numbing
    d) are mostly fantasy, so have little impact

20. Breton described symbolic changes in post-war Canada as:
    a) unimportant for most Canadians
    b) a response to cultural conflict
    c) breaking with British cultural determinism
    d) b and c

21. According to Ogmundson the central aspect of the Canadian experience is:
    a) our geography
    b) multiculturalism
    c) bilingualism
    d) Americanization

22. Ogmundson describes Canada as having:
    a) a strong culture
    b) a disappearing culture
    c) a culture of immigrants
    d) none of the above

23. The media mitigate against a strong Canadian identity because:
    a) much of our media consumption is of American products
    b) French and English Canada have separate media
    c) there are strong ethnic media in Canada
    d) all of the above

24. Canadians:
    a) have a stronger national than regional identity
    b) have a stronger regional than national identity
    c) have equally strong regional and national identities
    d) are indifferent about their regional and national identities

25. Ethnic salience:
    a) refers to the importance of one's ethnicity
    b) varies from one situation to another
    c) has increased with the universal tendency toward "ethnic rediscovery"
    d) all of the above

26. Mackie and Brinkerhoff's study of ethnic salience found:
    a) ethnicity is less salient than gender, citizenship or religion
    b) ethnicity is more salient for working class students
    c) ethnicity is more salient for women than for men
    d) all of the above

27. Porter felt that the price of upward mobility was a loss of:
    a) ethnic identity
    b) national identity
    c) both ethnic and national identity
    d) neither ethnic nor national identity

28. Some researchers feel that assimilation need not be at the price of ethnic identity because:
    a) the meaning of ethnic identity changes over time
    b) cultural change affects dominant groups as well as ethnic subcultures
    c) cultural identity can be strong even when individuals reject traditional life patterns
    d) all of the above

29. Critics of Canada's multiculturalism policy say that:
    a) not enough money has been allocated
    b) it does little more than appease non-charter groups
    c) multiculturalism is incompatible with a modern society
    d) all of the above

30. The study of culture is difficult because:

a) it is hard to tell material from non-material culture
b) we are all ethnocentric
c) culture is an all encompassing feature of life
d) all of the above

Posttest

1. People learn socially acceptable norms, values and beliefs through:
   a) education
   b) indoctrination
   c) socialization
   d) maturation

2. The ideology of corporatism advocates running society as a:
   a) corporation
   b) meritocracy
   c) place with as few rules as possible
   d) benevolent dictatorship

3. Latin American and Middle Eastern societies have a _____ view of time.
   a) mechanistic
   b) transcendental
   c) polychronic
   d) monochronic

4. A subculture's style is defined by its preferred form of:
   a) image
   b) demeanour
   c) argot
   d) all of the above

5. The _____ theory holds that cultural changes precede structural ones.
   a) materialist
   b) idealist
   c) interdependence
   d) autonomous

6. When free to choose, most Canadians prefer _____ produced books, movies, magazines and music.
   a) Canadian
   b) American
   c) locally or regionally
   d) internationally

7. John Porter thinks biculturalism and multiculturalism in Canada are now:
   a) long overdue
   b) out of place in a post-industrial society
   c) essential for social harmony and tolerance
   d) detrimental to national unity and harmony

8. The federal government replaced Canada's flag and national anthem with new expressive symbols to:

   a) appease non-British Canadians
   b) offend traditionalists
   c) reverse the Americanization of Canadian culture
   d) all of the above

9. Saying "Canada is the bread basket of the world" is a(n) _____ statement.
   a) racist
   b) ethnocentric
   c) factual
   d) nutritious

10. The blurring of cultural distinctions among nations is due to the:
    a) dominance of U.S. culture
    b) ease of international travel
    c) industrialization of most of the world
    d) all of the above

Essay Questions

1. Compare stereotypes of Americans and Canadians. Think of the stereotypes you hold of other cultural groups. Where do these ideas originate? How are they perpetuated?

2. Observe people in a public area of your university. How do differences in dress, demeanour and argot serve as symbols of inclusion and exclusion?

3. Consider the feminist claim that language is sexist. When answering the next few questions avoid using sexist terminology (i.e. the generic "he").

4. Gerbner feels the media create a symbolic environment which defines a world view and value system. While watching your favourite television drama, imagine what someone unfamiliar with Western culture would learn from it. List some of these "cultural indicators".

5. Discuss the issue of assimilation with a first-generation immigrant. How does he or she feel about the dilemma of maintaining cultural identity described by Porter.

6. Using Mackie and Brinkerhoff's study as a guide, do a mini-study to measure ethnic salience among your colleagues. Why do you think ethnic salience is greater for women and working class people? What factors would tend to increase ethnic salience and which would decrease it?

7. Do you agree with Porter that the speed of change in our society has made old cultural values useless? What traditional values, if any, do you think are likely to survive well into the next century?

Research Suggestion: Working with a group of students from different faculties (music, arts, business, etc.), develop an "inventory" of "style" differences which characterize members of different faculties in your school. Do members of the faculty implicitly encourage these differences?

ANSWERS TO CHAPTER 3

Key Terms

1. e	6. i
2. d	7. c
3. f	8. g
4. a	9. j
5. h	10. b

Test

1. a	11. c	21. d
2. b	12. d	22. b
3. b	13. b	23. d
4. d	14. d	24. a
5. c	15. c	25. d
6. a	16. d	26. d
7. d	17. b	27. a
8. d	18. c	28. d
9. b	19. a	29. d
10. b	20. d	30. c

Pretest

1. d	6. c
2. a	7. d
3. b	8. a
4. a	9. c
5. a	10. d

Posttest

1. c	6. b
2. b	7. b
3. c	8. a
4. d	9. b
5. b	10. d

CHAPTER 4   SOCIALIZATION

Key Terms

1. socialization

   a) the last of Mead's four stages of human development; the child has a sense of self and knows how to act in a socially approved way

2. primary socialization

   b) the process by which we learn to become members of society by internalizing cultural norms

3. the pre-play stage

   c) the theory that children usually categorize themselves as either boy or girl late in their second year and then begin acting in ways consistent with the category

4. play stage

d) the training in skills and values given to a person before he/she is allowed to assume a particular role

5. game stage

e) a way of classifying the human race on the basis of biology

6. generalized other

f) the second of Mead's four stages of a child's development; the child learns to see the viewpoints of others

7. sex

g) the first phase of socialization from birth to adolescence

8. gender

h) institutions that are responsible for nearly all aspects of a person's well-being and socialization

9. cognitive development

i) the adjustment period a person goes through when giving up one social role to take up another

10. disengagement

j) the first phase of Mead's four-stage theory of child development. Behaviour is guided by a combination of instinct and imitation

11. anticipatory socialization

k) the third stage in Mead's four stages of human development. The child learns to handle several stages simultaneously

12. resocialization

l) the adjustment a person makes to a new social environment

13. total institutions

m) a way of classifying people as male or female on the basis of different learned roles

Pretest

1. During childhood the greatest influence on our socialization is:
   a) family
   b) peers
   c) role models
   d) all of the above are equally influential

2. Thirty years ago sociologists usually thought of deviants as people who were:
   a) genetically inferior
   b) improperly socialized
   c) immoral
   d) all of the above

3. The third stage in Mead's four-stage theory of socialization is called the _____ stage.
   a) game
   b) generalized other
   c) play
   d) adolescent

4. Mead called the more conventional, controlled and socially conscious side of the self the:
   a) me
   b) I
   c) superego
   d) overseer

5. Studies of cross-cultural differences in socialization have found that hunting and gathering societies tend to value _____ while agricultural societies value _____ .
   a) conformity . . . individualism
   b) self-reliance . . . conformity
   c) individualism . . . piety
   d) brawn . . . brain

6. Freud was a:
   a) symbolic interactionist
   b) structural functionalist
   c) biological determinist
   d) all of the above

7. Cognitive development theory assumes that children usually begin to categorize themselves as either boy or girl after age:
   a) six months
   b) one year
   c) one and a half years
   d) two years

8. The latent messages people learn in socializing organizations include:
   a) accepted speech patterns, deportment and dress
   b) accepted procedures and routines
   c) who is who in the pecking order
   d) all of the above

9. Which of the following is a "total" institution?

   a) a university
   b) a boarding school
   c) a grade school
   d) a day care centre

10. A person who retires at 65 often goes through a period of _____ before he feels comfortable with his new role.
    a) disengagement
    b) anticipatory socialization
    c) cognitive development
    d) primary socialization

Test

1. The process of socialization:
   a) begins at birth and continues until adulthood
   b) begins when we are 4 or 5 and continues until adulthood
   c) begins when we are 4 or 5 and continues until death
   d) is lifelong

2. The agents of socialization include:
   a) the media
   b) the family
   c) schools
   d) all of the above

3. Sociologists have focused on:
   a) primary socialization
   b) secondary socialization
   c) both primary and secondary socialization
   d) neither primary nor secondary socialization

4. Reciprocal socialization can refer to:
   a) children's influence on their parents' attitudes
   b) students' influence on their teachers' attitudes
   c) both a and b
   d) socialization is not reciprocal

5. Two American sociologists who have influenced the Symbolic Interactionist perspective on socialization are:

a) Cooly and Mead
b) Cooly and Parsons
c) Parsons and Mead
d) none of the above

6. According to some sociologists, deviants:
a) disobey the law
b) are inadequately socialized
c) outnumber conformists
d) come from poor families

7. The oversocialized view of men and women:
a) was introduced by Wrong
b) emphasizes individual conformity
c) assumes that we are largely "moulded" by socialization
d) all of the above

8. The looking-glass self:
a) was introduced by George H. Mead
b) describes how we see ourselves as others see us
c) refers to the narcissistic tendencies in all of us
d) all of the above

9. The "generalized other" is the fourth of Mead's stages of self development. The other three are:
a) the pre-self, play and game stages
b) the pre-play, play and post-play stages
c) the pre-play, play and game stages
d) the pre-self, play and post-play stages

10. For Mead, the self consisted of:
a) the I and the you
b) the I and the me
c) the id, ego and superego
d) none of the above

11. Lewis said that poor children:
a) believe that money doesn't buy happiness
b) are socialized into a culture of poverty

c) are not influenced by their parents' poverty
d) have a good chance of escaping poverty

12. Studies of social class differences in socialization find:
a) white collar parents place a high value on conformity
b) blue collar parents place a high value on conformity
c) neither blue nor white collar parents value conformity
d) both blue and white collar parents value conformity

13. Alwin's Detroit study found over time:
a) parents place a higher value on autonomy
b) the most preferred value is "to think for himself"
c) obedience is less important than it was
d) all of the above

14. Children are able to accurately rank occupations (i.e. .9 correlation with national studies) by class when they are in:
a) grade 2
b) grade 4
c) grade 6
d) grade 8

15. Baldus and Tribe's study of Toronto area children found:
a) well dressed men were positively evaluated
b) primary school children had difficulty matching figures
c) the children's social class affected their ability to match
d) all of the above

16. Middle class parents:
a) stress gender appropriate behaviour
b) do not stress gender appropriate behaviour
c) have less influence on their children than upper class parents

d) worry about their children more than blue collar parents

17. Gender differences:
    a) are learned
    b) are best explained by biology
    c) are not well understood
    d) are greater than once believed

18. According to Freud:
    a) sex differences begin at the phallic stage
    b) boys fear castration
    c) personality differences are rooted in physiological differences
    d) all of the above

19. Freud suggested that girls have weaker superegos than boys because:
    a) they cannot easily resolve the Oedipal complex
    b) they have stronger egos
    c) they are socialized to be more passive
    d) Freud did not suggest this

20. Social learning theory suggests that gender roles are learned through reinforcement, but:
    a) the theory raises doubts because girls are usually more like their fathers than mothers
    b) there is no evidence that children are necessarily like their same sexed parent
    c) parents are only one among many influences on gender
    d) b and c

21. Androgenous individuals:
    a) have a balance of "male" and "female" characteristics
    b) are socially maladjusted
    c) are "feminine" men or "masculine" women
    d) have weak superegos

22. The social institution most responsible for traditional gender stereotyping is:
    a) education

b) the economy
c) the media
d) the family

23. Television is an important socializing agent because:
    a) its influence is pervasive
    b) we are introduced to television almost at birth
    c) television stereotypes social groups
    d) all of the above

24. Lyell's study of adolescence suggests that the feelings of ambivalence young people experience are due to:
    a) their lack of paid employment
    b) their parents' overprotectiveness
    c) the influence of the adolescent subculture
    d) the media's exaggeration of this notion

25. Campbell suggests the strongest evidence that a distinct adolescent subculture exists is:
    a) their distinctive dress code
    b) the anti-intellectual environment of the school
    c) the similarity of attitudes among all adolescents
    d) all of the above

26. The family remains a strong influence on adolescents because:
    a) parents continue to control scarce resources
    b) adolescents are basically conservative
    c) peer group values are not usually a significant challenge to parental values
    d) a and c

27. Adult socialization:
    a) is always a formal process
    b) is very much like childhood socialization
    c) is called secondary socialization
    d) stops with marriage and employment

28. The process of preparing to move into a new social role is called:
    a) secondary socialization
    b) preparatory socialization
    c) anticipatory socialization
    d) resocialization

29. That medical students share many attitudes and values is explained in part by:
    a) their high I.Q.s
    b) the male domination of the field
    c) selective recruitment
    d) all of the above

30. Resocialization:
    a) goes on in total institutions
    b) involves dramatic changes
    c) may be occasioned by personal crises
    d) all of the above

Posttest

1. Our socialization is influenced by our:
   a) social class
   b) religious affiliation
   c) sex
   d) all of the above

2. According to Cooly's "looking-glass self" theory, a positive self image comes from:
   a) accurately assessing one's own worth
   b) ignoring the opinions of others
   c) assuming that others think highly of you
   d) being one's own best friend

3. Mead called the impulsive and individualistic side of the self the:
   a) me
   b) I
   c) superego
   d) id

4. Erving Goffman believed impression management was a skill that people acquired:

a) genetically
b) easily
c) with difficulty
d) none of the above

5. Sex stereotyping begins:
   a) before birth
   b) at birth
   c) very early in life
   d) at puberty

6. Chappel and Colwill's 1981 study found that Canadian medical schools _____ attitudes in their students.
   a) instill radically new
   b) have no effect on existing
   c) usually reinforce existing
   d) instill elitist

7. Adjusting to prison life is made possible through:
   a) secondary socialization
   b) preparatory socialization
   c) anticipatory socialization
   d) resocialization

8. Canadian women who go to live in Arab countries often need a period of _____ to adjust to the different role women have in those societies.
   a) anticipatory socialization
   b) secondary socialization
   c) resocialization
   d) preparatory socialization

9. The last stage in Mead's four-stage theory of development is the _____ stage.
   a) play
   b) adult
   c) game
   d) generalized other

10. Oscar Lewis is best known for his study of
    a) youth cultures
    b) corporate cultures
    c) the culture of poverty
    d) total institutions

Essay Questions

1. Is socialization more effective when it is hidden, unconscious and covert or when it is explicitly taught? Justify your views and give some examples of overt socialization.

2. What is reciprocal socialization? Give some examples of the kinds of groups it occurs between. Besides using surveys, how else might a sociologist go about documenting evidence of reciprocal socialization?

3. Some sociologists see social values as a product of social structure. Others see social values being created by individuals interacting with each other. How does the latter, the symbolic interactionist perspective, account for changes in social values over time? Are these perspectives contradictory or complementary?

4. What is the empirical evidence to support Mead's theory that people see themselves the way they think others view them?

5. How are scientific debates on biological determinism versus socialization theories often a manifestation of political debates?

6. How does a person's social class affect her socialization process?

Research Suggestion: The text raised two interesting points about socialization that might, on the surface, appear to be contradictory. Firstly, it noted that socialization is a powerful, lifelong process in which several forces act to ensure that people develop the "proper" beliefs, habits and behaviour patterns. Secondly, we are told that Alwin's 1984 study found that parents value the ability of children to think for themselves above all other qualities they might try to instill in their children. And, Alwin says, the value placed on thinking for oneself is higher now than it was a generation ago. How do the pressures to conform to the socialization process jibe with the stated goal of learning to think for oneself? To examine this question further, you might interview a pre-selected group of students or others who claim to think for themselves. How many people, when asked, claimed not to think for themselves? Ask the group their views on social issues for which there is widely held consensus. You might use previous Gallup polls to identify such questions. Do the answers given by the free thinkers differ significantly from those given by the general public? If not, why not? If so, do the answers given by the free thinkers conform to another pattern of thought or ideology?

ANSWERS TO CHAPTER 4

Key Terms

1. b	6. a	11. d
2. g	7. e	12. l
3. j	8. m	13. h
4. f	9. c	
5. k	10. i	

Pretest

1. a	6. c
2. b	7. c
3. a	8. d
4. a	9. b
5. b	10. a

Test			Posttest	
1. d	11. b	21. a	1. d	6. c
2. d	12. b	22. c	2. c	7. d
3. a	13. d	23. d	3. b	8. c
4. c	14. c	24. d	4. c	9. d
5. a	15. a	25. b	5. a	10. c
6. b	16. b	26. d		
7. d	17. a	27. c		
8. b	18. d	28. c		
9. c	19. a	29. c		
10. b	20. d	30. d		

CHAPTER 5   CONTROL AND DEVIANCE

Key Terms

1. deviance

a) deviance that contributes to the survival and smooth running of society *more* than it detracts from society's survival and smooth running

2. norm

b) rule for distinguishing between acceptable right behaviour and unacceptable wrong behaviour

3. moral holidays

c) the third stage in the labelling process during which the alleged deviant is pressured to accept the label deviant

4. anomie

d) the second stage in the labelling process during which the controlling others begin to build a case against the deviant

5. functional deviance

e) special occasions on which the usual norms are suspended, e.g. New Year's Eve, Mardi Gras

6. labelling

f) people whose behaviour towards the deviant makes secondary deviance more possible

7. typification

g) exiled or killed

8. terminated

h) people who have the responsibility of rehabilitating and/or punishing a deviant

9. primary deviance

10. secondary deviance

11. facilitating others

12. controlling others

13. institutionalized deviance

14. underworld

15. underside

16. fringe

17. technological morality

18. justification

19. negotiation

20. enclosure

i) the subculture of criminals

j) the fourth stage in the labelling process during which the label is actually applied and action is taken against the deviant; he is ostracized, demoted, confined

k) behaviour that violates a norm

l) the initial identification of a deviant based on little information which is interpreted in light of existing stereotypes

m) the fifth and final stage in the labelling process; the deviant is either rehabilitated or terminated or institutionalized

n) deviance that has become a permanent part of a person's life so that his other activities are organized to facilitate the continued deviant behaviour

o) Jaques Ellul's term for the modern world's morality in which individual actions are judged according to how they contribute or detract from the collective interest

p) the initial act or acts of deviance committed by a person

q) the theory that deviance results from the gap between goals and the opportunities for achieving such goals

r) the five-stage process by which an individual acquires a particular identity or status in the eyes of the rest of society

s) the patterned behaviour of people after acquiring a deviant label

t) the subculture of chronically unsuccessful people i.e. "bums, dropouts, freaks and losers"—the chronically unemployed

21. disposition

u) the subculture of people in semi-respectable occupations, i.e. undertakers, carnival workers, executioners

Pretest

1. Sociology assumes knowing the difference between right and wrong is:
   a) learned
   b) innate
   c) irrelevant
   d) all important

2. The Ayatollah Khomeini, the Reverend Jerry Falwell and Pope John Paul II are moral:
   a) relativists
   b) absolutists
   c) moderates
   d) extremists

3. Deviance can contribute to social organization by:
   a) circumventing red tape
   b) providing a safety valve for pent up tensions
   c) uniting the group for or against a deviant
   d) all of the above

4. Moral boundaries are best clarified by:
   a) using precise language
   b) punishing transgressors
   c) passing laws
   d) all of the above

5. Moral relativism suggests deviance:
   a) can be curbed by strong family guidance
   b) is a subjective label and should not be punished
   c) depends on one's particular viewpoint
   d) all of the above

6. Labelling is more likely to deter future deviant behaviour when the:

   a) deviant has experienced a long career
   b) label can easily be removed
   c) deviant and the labeller are strangers to each other
   d) labelling occurs in a cross-group situation

7. The concept of "deviant place" refers to any place:
   a) where suspicious people may be seen
   b) regularly patrolled by official control agents
   c) more likely to facilitate than inhibit deviant acts
   d) in which deviant-smiths outnumber normal-smiths

8. A prostitute who says that her conduct helps to prevent rape is:
   a) stereotyping
   b) enclosing
   c) lying
   d) rationalizing

9. People who openly deviate from the prevailing norms of prosperity, appearance, competence and hopefulness inhabit the:
   a) fringe
   b) underside
   c) underworld
   d) dregs

10. Extremely fat persons are likely to inhabit which "deviant world"?
    a) underworld
    b) underside
    c) fringe
    d) closet

11. A person whose occupation is a barrier to normal social participation is what kind of deviant?
    a) secondary
    b) fringe
    c) professional
    d) primary

12. An example of organizational deviance is:
    a) a company president embezzles a million dollars
    b) a stockbroker sells stolen bonds
    c) a bank issues unsecured loans to politicians
    d) store clerks go on strike for higher wages

13. The causes of both organizational and individual deviant behaviour are most likely to be found in:
    a) interactions between actors and their environments
    b) generic factors
    c) imbalances between structural and processual forces
    d) social rather than psychological pathologies

14. In Ellul's view, the basic moral order of Western civilization is shifting to _____ morality.
    a) bourgeois
    b) technological
    c) Christian
    d) tribal

Test

1. People who insist that only what they believe is correct are called moral:
    a) constructionists
    b) absolutists
    c) conservatives
    d) entrepreneurs

2. Refusing to defend any one moral belief against others is:
    a) absolutism
    b) liberalism
    c) dogmatism
    d) relativism

3. Every human relationship has a pattern of:
    a) normative expectations
    b) deviations
    c) social controls
    d) all of the above

4. A social relationship is an:
    a) imposed order
    b) illusion of agreement
    c) ongoing joint accomplishment
    d) artificial construction

5. Deviation in a low-commitment relationship is unlikely to elicit:
    a) moral indignation
    b) control responses
    c) sanctioning
    d) interest

6. Because people tend to value that which is familiar to them, social order tends to become:
    a) invisible and unreal
    b) moral order
    c) only a construction
    d) weaker over time

7. The conception of social deviance as pathology is inconsistent with the view that deviance can be:
    a) functional
    b) non-behavioural
    c) eliminated or controlled
    d) adventurous

8. Simmons's 1969 research found that the tendency to stereotype deviants was correlated with:
    a) being deviant
    b) radicalism
    c) low education
    d) insecurity

9. All five deviant categories in Simmons's study were characterized as:
   a) irresponsible
   b) mentally ill
   c) insecure
   d) neurotic

10. Moral boundaries are:
   a) constructed in the interaction of deviation and control
   b) found only in traditional societies
   c) indefensible
   d) the same as norms

11. A norm is a:
   a) structural or organizational pattern
   b) rule for knowing right from wrong
   c) shared understanding
   d) statistical tendency

12. The decisions of specialists in classifying and processing mental illness, crime and other forms of social deviance are:
   a) highly accurate in distinguishing real deviants from normal people
   b) influenced mainly by personal observations of suspect behaviour
   c) interpretive and discretionary
   d) unrelated to the actual behaviour of the individuals being processed

13. Deviance can contribute to social organization by:
   a) dramatizing evil or abnormality
   b) blurring moral distinctions
   c) proving that anyone can fail
   d) helping to conceal serious structural problems

14. The crucial problem with Erikson's functionalist hypothesis about deviance quotas is that:
   a) religious conflict is not deviance
   b) every group needs a certain amount of deviance
   c) the forms and amounts of deviance are heavily influenced by political and economic factors
   d) crime waves far exceed the usual quotas

15. Treating a person in a rude manner is an example of:
   a) negotiation
   b) stereotyping
   c) labelling
   d) criminalization

16. An illustration of intra-group stigmatization is:
   a) parent disciplines child
   b) officer disciplines soldier
   c) manager disciplines employee
   d) dean disciplines student

17. Another term for stereotyping is:
   a) sanctioning
   b) typification
   c) classification
   d) labelling

18. The first phase in the labelling process is:
   a) enclosure
   b) justification
   c) negotiation
   d) identification

19. A police officer arresting a suspect illustrates:
   a) bourgeois morality
   b) cross-group stigmatization
   c) institutionalization
   d) termination

20. Justification in intra-group labelling relies mainly upon:
   a) common sense
   b) negotiation
   c) termination
   d) procedural norms

21. The phase of labelling in which opportunities for normal social participation are closed off is called:
   a) identification
   b) enclosure
   c) rehabilitation
   d) typification

22. An example of symbolic enclosure is:
    a) waiter spills water in customer's lap
    b) judge sentences criminal to prison
    c) woman refuses to go out with man
    d) instructor gives failing mark to student

23. Which of the following is less likely to occur in cross-group than in intra-group situations?
    a) negotiation
    b) justification
    c) rehabilitation
    d) enclosure

24. To be expelled from a college or university is to be:
    a) enclosed
    b) institutionalized
    c) terminated
    d) deposed

25. Lemert says that _____ deviation is essentially unpredictable because it arises out of a complex variety of causes.
    a) primary
    b) adventurous
    c) secondary
    d) defensive

26. Secondary deviation is a response to:
    a) primary deviation
    b) labelling
    c) temptation
    d) authority

27. Making the transition from primary deviation to a deviant identity is:
    a) inevitable
    b) non-behavioural
    c) irresponsible
    d) problematic

28. Among the factors affecting the transition to secondary deviation are:
    a) others
    b) hardware
    c) places
    d) all of the above

29. A person who encourages further deviation by denying that the actor is really deviating is a:
    a) normal-smith
    b) repressor
    c) secondary deviant
    d) moral entrepreneur

30. Control agents who clearly do not believe the deviant can be rehabilitated are:
    a) relativists
    b) secondary deviants
    c) deviant-smiths
    d) moral functionalists

Posttest

1. A neighbourhood that shields a popular criminal from the police may be performing a socially functional act by:
    a) giving the neighbourhood a moral holiday
    b) protecting the black market economy
    c) uniting the group around a common cause
    d) all of the above

2. The anomie theory of deviance suggests deviance is caused by:
    a) few opportunities for social advancement
    b) inadequate law enforcement
    c) inadequate moral training
    d) poverty

3. According to anomie theory, people who cannot achieve their life goals by either legitimate or illegitimate means often:
    a) set more realistic goals for themselves
    b) never stop trying
    c) blame society for their problems
    d) become alcoholics, drug addicts, suicides, mental patients or sexual deviants

4. Deviance is _____
   functional to society.
   a) never
   b) sometimes
   c) usually
   d) always in some sense

5. Which has the greatest functional
   payoff to society?
   a) child molesting
   b) terrorism
   c) prostitution
   d) it is impossible to measure this

6. The fifth and final stage in the
   labelling process is called the
   _____ stage.
   a) identification
   b) justification
   c) disposition
   d) enclosure

7. In cross-group labelling where
   population control is the ultimate
   goal, a deviant will most likely be:
   a) terminated
   b) rehabilitated
   c) socially institutionalized
   d) none of the above

8. Thorsell and Lein concluded that
   labelling someone a deviant _____
   further deviant behaviour.
   a) encourages
   b) discourages
   c) has no effect on
   d) all of the above can be true
      depending on when and how the
      label is applied

9. Which of the following is usually *not* a
   "facilitating other" in a deviant's life?

a) friends
b) judges
c) victims
d) accomplices

10. Telling your friend that shoplifting is
    not really such a bad thing to do
    makes you a(n):
    a) accomplice
    b) normal-smith
    c) deviant-smith
    d) quasi-criminal

11. Labelling is more likely to deter
    further deviance when the:
    a) labeller's opinion matters to the
       labellee
    b) label is fairly permanent
    c) deviant has been deviant for a long
       time
    d) all of the above

12. Chronically unemployed people
    belong to the _____ of
    society.
    a) underworld
    b) underside
    c) fringe
    d) marginal class

13. Mentally retarded people occupy
    which deviant world?
    a) underworld
    b) underside
    c) fringe
    d) marginal class

14. Deviance is a:
    a) social phenomenon
    b) constructed reality
    c) category of meaning
    d) all of the above

Essay Questions

1. What four factors comprise the opportunity structure of a deviant's environment?

2. Describe the five steps in the labelling process. Why is the labelling process a more effective deterrant for a young, middle class first-offender than it is for an older, repeat-offender from the working class?

3. Is it useful to look at opportunity structures in analysing organizational deviance at the nation-state level? If not, why not? If so, how might the various opportunity structures have contributed to the entrenchment of apartheid in South Africa or the killing fields of Cambodia?

4. Why does Jacques Ellul think individualism is dying out in the modern world? Give your reasons for agreeing or disagreeing with his analysis.

5. Why are so many apparently victimless crimes considered deviant?

6. How would an anomie theorist describe the relationship between crime and poverty? How would the same theorist see the media's role in promoting deviance?

7. Are deviants ever considered to be good people? If so, name some who were or are both deviant and widely admired during their own lifetimes.

Research Suggestion: Find out if any new forms of deviance have recently become a problem on your campus or in your neighbourhood. You might consider either nuisance or criminal behaviour. Focus on one specific form of deviance and see if its recent increased rate of incidence might be due to changes in the local opportunity structure. Suggest feasible, cost-efficient ways to make the opportunity structure in your area less conducive to this kind of deviance. Contact the appropriate authorities and find out what, if anything, they are doing about the problem. Ask them to evaluate your proposed solutions.

ANSWERS TO CHAPTER 5

Key Terms

1. k	8. g	15. t
2. b	9. p	16. u
3. e	10. s	17. o
4. q	11. f	18. d
5. a	12. h	19. c
6. r	13. n	20. j
7. l	14. i	21. m

Test

1. b	11. b	21. b
2. d	12. c	22. d
3. d	13. a	23. c
4. c	14. c	24. c
5. a	15. c	25. a
6. b	16. a	26. b
7. a	17. b	27. d
8. c	18. d	28. d
9. a	19. b	29. a
10. a	20. a	30. c

Pretest

1. a	6. b	11. b
2. b	7. c	12. c
3. d	8. d	13. a
4. b	9. b	14. b
5. c	10. c	

Posttest

1. c	6. c	11. a
2. a	7. c	12. b
3. d	8. d	13. c
4. b	9. b	14. d
5. d	10. b	

CHAPTER 6   ROLES AND INTERACTIONS

Key Terms

1. interactional patterns

2. social systems

3. institutions

4. perspective

5. negotiation

6. role

7. gender

8. multiple roles

9. role set

10. civil inattention

11. role taking

12. dramaturgical perspective

13. primary group

14. reference group

a) the way a person usually thinks, feels and acts about a particular situation

b) the structural or institutional relationships, groups and interpersonal bonds formed by people

c) what an individual actually does in a given situation

d) a group of roles that are all associated with having one particular status

e) a group characterized by close, extensive personal contacts and empathy

f) the cultural, social and psychological characteristics assumed appropriate to one's sex

g) the actual ways people behave towards one another in organizations

h) the view that sees people as actors who are trying to manage other people's impressions of them

i) roles which are enacted simultaneously but may be otherwise unrelated

j) a group that is influential in helping an individual form beliefs and values

k) the process of establishing rules of behaviour for a given situation

l) stable clusters of norms, values, roles and expectations

m) empathizing with others

n) the practice of deliberately ignoring the presence of strangers

Pretest

1. To a symbolic interactionist, social class is:
   a) static
   b) unimportant
   c) a process
   d) based on one's occupation

2. Perspectives on how to behave in a given situation vary:
   a) from culture to culture
   b) over time
   c) from social class to social class
   d) all of the above

3. Garfinkel had his students act as guests in their own parents' home:
   a) to demonstrate how much norms guide daily life
   b) for a joke
   c) to demonstrate that family ties are learned
   d) to demonstrate the effects of family deviance

4. Structuralists believe that the role a person plays depends mainly on her:
   a) ideology
   b) position in the social structure
   c) inherent predisposition
   d) social opportunities

5. A police officer whose job involves counselling young people, teaching at the police academy and catching criminals is engaged in:
   a) multiple roles
   b) ascribed roles
   c) a role set
   d) theatrical roles

6. Symbolic interactionists' analytical focus in any social situation is on:
   a) how social structure determines role enactment
   b) how group perspectives mesh together
   c) how multiple roles are juggled
   d) how role strains are handled

7. The results of Rosehan's experiment in which he and seven others pretended to be mentally ill suggests that:
   a) labels lose their strength if constantly reapplied
   b) people see what they expect to see
   c) mental illness is more apparent than real
   d) none of the above

8. Which of the following would not be considered a social group?
   a) the Toronto Maple Leafs hockey club
   b) an investment club
   c) a gang of bank robbers
   d) men

9. A group composed of three people is called a:
   a) dyad
   b) triad
   c) reference group
   d) primary group

10. We are more likely to choose a reference group that:
    a) treats us well
    b) offers upward social mobility
    c) is compatible with our own personality
    d) all of the above

11. Which of the following is not an example of a *secondary relationship*?
    a) mother-daughter
    b) boss-worker
    c) teacher-student
    d) dentist-patient

12. A *group* composed of two people is called:
    a) an intimate relationship
    b) an exchange
    c) a triad
    d) a dyad

13. Which of the following is one of the patterns a sociologist using a

structuralist perspective would look for in groups?
a) role taking
b) status climbing
c) role playing
d) status performance

14. *Role conflict* exists when:
a) an individual cannot meet role expectations
b) an individual performs two or more roles whose requirements are difficult to reconcile
c) an individual performs two or more roles whose requirements are complementary
d) an individual has severe personality problems

15. The Jonestown suicide has been explained using the following types of power exerted in the commune:
a) coercion, legitimate, referent, expert and consensual
b) coercion, misinformational, referent, expert and legitimate
c) coercion, informational, referent, expert and legitimate
d) consensual, illegitimate, referent, expert and irreverent

Test

1. Some sociologists examine the *macro-level* of social structure. On which of the following would they concentrate?
a) day-to-day interactions among friends
b) relationships between local communities
c) patterns in families
d) large social patterns that shape an entire society

2. *Micro-order* analyses focus primarily on:
a) the interactionist perspective
b) large scale patterns of roles and activities

c) the intricate web of minute, daily activities
d) a and c

3. *Social interaction:*
a) provides the basis of all social life
b) is continually negotiable
c) always involves interpretation
d) all of the above

4. *Social organization* includes:
a) societal values
b) patterns of relationships between people
c) collections of individuals
d) all of these

5. Sociologists use the term *social structure* to refer to the way individuals and groups relate to each other:
a) in an orderly or stable way
b) in an unpredictable or irregular way
c) collectively
d) individually

6. "Organizations make men into who they are." This statement is the viewpoint of:
a) the symbolic interactionist
b) the structuralist
c) the subjectivist
d) all sociologists

7. Which of the following statements agrees with the *symbolic interactionist's* view of social behaviour?
a) social behaviour is rigid and inflexible
b) individuals constantly evaluate others' behaviour and react accordingly
c) symbols are meaningful in themselves
d) behaviour is determined largely by the norms of social structure

8. The two main sociological views of roles are:

a) roles are seen as general or specific
b) roles are conflictual or complementary
c) roles are static and rehearsed or fluid and constantly constructed
d) both views agree roles are predetermined statuses that individuals fill

9. Which of the following statements is *false*?
a) roles are determined solely by choice
b) roles are based on expectations
c) we occupy many roles simultaneously
d) role performances are continually negotiable

10. Being born white, female and Canadian is part of a person's:
a) biological identity
b) achieved status
c) education
d) ascribed status

11. Most Canadians' occupational and marital roles are:
a) ascribed
b) achieved
c) inherited
d) expected

12. Doctors treat patients, publish books, work in the community and teach medical students. This complex of roles that accrues to a single status is called:
a) role bargaining
b) role conflict
c) achieved roles
d) a role set

13. Opposing demands which are built into a role engender:
a) role strain
b) role sets
c) theatrical roles
d) achieved roles

14. According to George Herbert Mead, to interpret the behaviour of others:
a) we usually act on impulse
b) we take the role of other people in our imagination
c) we respond in inflexible, stereotypical ways
d) none of the above

15. Nonverbal communication occurs through:
a) gender displays
b) manipulation of physical space
c) gestures
d) all of the above

16. According to George Herbert Mead, social acts take place through four stages including:
a) self-identification, appropriate enactment, interpretation of others' acts and evaluation
b) evaluation, manipulation, enactment and self-criticism
c) self-identification, role manipulation, self-interpretation and consummation
d) interpretation of others' acts, evaluation, appropriate enactment and evaluation

17. Goffman's term for the way we behave toward strangers, showing we are aware of their presence but avoiding eye contact with them, is:
a) dramaturgy
b) education
c) civil politeness
d) civil inattention

18. In which of the following situations is the learning of new role behaviour required?
a) a man becomes a househusband
b) a couple gets divorced
c) a young adult goes to university
d) all of the above

19. In all interactions, a certain amount of role bargaining occurs because:

a) roles are flexible
b) role enactment involves interaction between two or more people
c) role enactments are usually problematic
d) roles are achieved

20. A self-identity is closely linked to:
    a) what our parents taught us
    b) the roles we secretly wish to play
    c) the roles we enact and how we imagine others characterize us
    d) media images of appropriate behaviour

21. Being labelled mentally ill is a process in which:
    a) roles and situational expectations of mentally ill behaviour affect self-behaviour
    b) mental illness proceeds in a predictable way
    c) the labelling process is a set of standardized expectations imposed on all patients
    d) none of the above

22. The concept of *situational self* suggests:
    a) the self is presented in various ways depending on the situation
    b) we have no control over how the self will act
    c) self-behaviour results from inherited traits
    d) one never knows how selves will act

23. According to Zimbardo's mock prison research:
    a) most people are brutal and sadistic
    b) most people simply do what they are told
    c) most people will behave in ways consistent with situational expectations
    d) most people are reluctant to get involved in others' problems

24. Stanley Milgram conducted a series of experiments on people's willingness to obey authority. He found that:
    a) people were willing to obey cruel instructions from authority figures
    b) people were more harsh in giving out punishments than had been expected
    c) people obeyed authority figures only because they were told to do so
    d) all of the above

25. The sociologist who applied a *dramaturgical* approach to studying social interaction was:
    a) Anselm Strauss
    b) Erving Goffman
    c) George Herbert Mead
    d) Stanley Milgram

26. *Impression management* refers to:
    a) the fact that individuals don't worry about impressing others
    b) the fact that impressions are predetermined
    c) the fact that individuals attempt to control the impressions they make on others
    d) the fact that impressions are always believed

27. Goffman used the term "backstage behaviour" to refer to:
    a) out of role behaviour
    b) in role behaviour
    c) the covert, hidden side of the personality
    d) the open side of the personality

28. Which of the following would not be considered a *social group*?
    a) a swim team
    b) a family
    c) a bridge club
    d) redheads

29. Which of the following is not a structural characteristic of a *group*?
    a) the boundaries of the group

b) the group's relationships to other groups
c) the personality characteristics of its members
d) the size of the group

30. A *primary* group is characterized by:
a) infrequent, conflictual interaction
b) close, personal relationships and empathy
c) impersonal, goal-oriented exchanges
d) all of the above

Posttest

1. The "social construction of reality" refers to the way individuals and groups:
a) define a situation
b) build a society
c) avoid reality
d) all of the above

2. A symbolic interactionist thinks a person's acts are:
a) unpredictable
b) partly determined by social structure
c) difficult to describe objectively
d) completely a matter of choice

3. Who among the scholars is *not* associated with the structuralist approach to sociology?
a) Talcott Parsons
b) Erving Goffman
c) Robert Merton
d) Ralph Linton

4. The role of mental patients is:
a) achieved
b) ascribed
c) achieved and ascribed
d) inherited

5. Someone who is an amateur athlete, political activist, parent, daughter and wife is engaged in:
a) multiple roles

b) ascribed roles
c) a role set
d) theatrical roles

6. Erving Goffman described the practices of shaking hands and waving goodbye as forms of:
a) interaction rituals
b) civil inattention
c) theatricizing
d) role bargaining

7. According to Erving Goffman, we need to observe a person's _____ behaviour in order to really understand the person.
a) frontstage
b) backstage
c) internal
d) frontstage and backstage

8. Which of the following is a secondary group?
a) a street gang
b) a foster home family
c) an introductory sociology class
d) the Rolling Stones

9. A study of attitudes at Bennington College found that most students switched their primary reference group from their families to an identification with their:
a) boyfriends
b) classmates
c) teachers
d) favourite entertainers

10. The fact that a group of teenagers may start to dress alike illustrates the group's _____ function.
a) normative
b) standardizing
c) fashion
d) comparative

11. Sociologists define reference group as:
a) a research group
b) a group important in helping to define the individual's beliefs, values and opinions

c) the status group to which one belongs
d) a group important in helping a sociologist refer ideas and opinions

12. The rich, the audience at a rock concert and the people waiting for a bus are not examples of a social class because:
a) they are not constantly interacting
b) they have developed secondary relationships with each other
c) they lack awareness of their groupness
d) all of the above

13. *Symbolic interaction* suggests people learn:
a) by observation
b) by constant interaction
c) through imitation
d) through all these techniques

14. Barney Glazer and Anselm Strauss defined *awareness contexts* as:
a) the awareness of patients about their illness and that of others with similar illnesses
b) the combination of what each interactant knows about the identity of the other and his own identity in the eyes of the other
c) the combination of what non-interacting but physically close individuals know about each other's identity
d) the identities of dying patients in hospitals

15. Which of the following statements is false?
a) men talk more than women
b) men interrupt more than women
c) women gossip more about trivial matters
d) women do the shit work in keeping conversation going

Essay Questions

1. What is the difference between a role set and multiple roles?

2. Is there such a thing as one "true" or "real" self? If so, how can one identify one's true self?

3. What difference is there, if any, between role playing and acting in a phoney way?

4. What is role strain and what causes it?

5. How do politicians, celebrities and business executives make use of impression management techniques? How do you make use of these same techniques in your own daily living?

6. What makes people choose or change a reference group?

7. Are the structuralist and symbolic interactionist perspectives complementary or contradictory? Give reasons for your answer.

    Research Suggestion: Analyse a particular job in terms of the role strains it places on the people in it. Try to suggest economically feasible ways to reduce the role strains. Naturally, you will need to talk to several people actually working at the job you choose to study.

Key Terms

1. b	6. c	11. m
2. g	7. f	12. h
3. l	8. i	13. e
4. a	9. d	14. j
5. k	10. n	

Test

1. d	11. b	21. a
2. d	12. d	22. a
3. d	13. a	23. c
4. b	14. b	24. d
5. a	15. d	25. b
6. b	16. a	26. c
7. b	17. d	27. c
8. c	18. d	28. d
9. a	19. b	29. c
10. d	20. c	30. b

Pretest

1. c	6. b	11. a
2. d	7. b	12. d
3. a	8. d	13. c
4. b	9. b	14. b
5. c	10. d	15. c

Posttest

1. a	6. a	11. b
2. b	7. d	12. c
3. b	8. c	13. d
4. c	9. c	14. b
5. a	10. a	15. c

CHAPTER 7   GENDER AND GENDER RELATIONS

Key Terms

1. feminism

2. liberal feminists

3. socialist feminists

4. maternal feminists

5. sociobiologists

a) feminists who wish to expand the traditional, nurturing role of women in society

b) an ideology that argues men and women should have equal rights and that women's social contributions have traditionally been undervalued

c) theorists who emphasize that genetically based psychological traits influence social behaviour

d) feminists who see the abolition of class inequalities as a necessary prelude to the abolition of sexual inequalities

e) feminists who wish to reform the free enterprise system so that sexual inequalities are reduced or eliminated

Pretest

1. Studies of the innate differences between the sexes are usually performed on:
    a) human fetuses
    b) human infants
    c) very young children
    d) animals

2. In grade school, girls generally do better at _____ while boys are better at _____.
    a) science . . . art
    b) spelling . . . mathematics
    c) mathematics . . . social studies
    d) competitive games . . . co-operative games

3. Women's participation in the Canadian labour force exceeded 50% for the first time in about:
    a) 1980
    b) 1970
    c) 1965
    d) 1940

4. Women in _____ have the highest labour force participation rate in the world.
    a) Canada
    b) underdeveloped countries
    c) the Soviet Union
    d) the United States

5. Around the world, female labour participation rates are affected by:
    a) the availability of day care
    b) the availability of jobs
    c) public attitudes
    d) all of the above

6. For women, contributing economically to the family is:
    a) a fairly recent phenomenon
    b) a recent phenomenon in the working class
    c) a recent phenomenon in the middle class
    d) something they have always done

7. In developing countries, illiteracy is much more prevalent among:
    a) women
    b) men
    c) young people
    d) richer people

8. Men earn more than women because:
    a) women have inferior qualifications
    b) women are more likely to belong to unions
    c) of job ghettoization and the greater domestic duties of women
    d) women lack ambition

9. Marxists argue that participation in:
    a) production and financial independence are essential for equality between the sexes
    b) production and financial dependence are essential for equality between the sexes
    c) participation in reproduction and financial dependence are essential for inequality between the sexes
    d) none of the above

10. Men teachers were paid twice as much as women teachers in the early 19th century because the men:
    a) worked longer hours
    b) all had families to support
    c) were better teachers
    d) were professionally trained while the women weren't

11. Studies of interpersonal relations between the sexes show:
    a) men interrupt women more in conversation than women interrupt men
    b) sexual harassment in the work place is no longer a problem
    c) men earn more money than women
    d) people now see women as just as authoritative as men

12. People who argue against the validity of biological explanations for gender roles point to:

a) cultural variations in gender roles
b) historical variations in gender roles
c) both of the above
d) none of the above

13. A major stumbling block to equality between the sexes is that:
a) women bear the responsibility for child care and housework
b) women are underrepresented in the Senate
c) too few men work as homemakers and office workers
d) women are reluctant to take entrepreneurial risks

14. The movement to change male roles has been smaller and weaker because:
a) male roles are more healthful
b) male roles are more powerful and lucrative
c) men are taught not to question their socialization
d) all of the above

15. International feminist groups have been actively involved in:
a) pro-life lobbies
b) anti-war protests
c) promoting equality in the workplace
d) b and c

Test

1. Research concerning whether gender differences are innate or culturally induced is inconclusive because:
a) the research methods and basic concepts have been challenged
b) we cannot do intensive research on human infants
c) we cannot control socialization experiences
d) all of the above

2. The value of education on the labour market is:
a) higher for females than males

b) higher for males than females
c) equal for both sexes
d) irrelevant—there's no relationship

3. Employment equity is a difficult goal because it involves:
a) hiring women and minorities in proportion to their availability for work
b) equal pay for work of equal value
c) encouraging women and minorities to seek job advancement
d) all of the above

4. The labour force participation rate of married women has increased because:
a) the service sector of the labour force expanded creating a demand for labour
b) they can now control their fertility
c) they wanted to use their education and families needed the money
d) all of the above

5. The participation rate of married women in the labour force is now about:
a) 22%
b) 53%
c) 65%
d) 35%

6. Equal pay for work of equal value legislation has been ineffective because:
a) women's work is less important
b) women have a fear of success and don't want higher wages
c) men and women do different jobs and judging equivalence is difficult
d) a and b

7. Since the beginning of this century:
a) men's labour force participation rate has increased
b) women's labour force participation rate has increased
c) neither sex's participation rates have increased
d) both sexes' participation rates have increased

8. Having school-aged children used to keep women out of the labour force. Now:
   a) women of prime childbearing ages are still least likely to work for pay
   b) women of prime childbearing ages are most likely to work for pay
   c) day care centres are readily available and widely used by working mothers
   d) older women are least likely to be out of the labour force

9. People who want to reform the existing system to grant equality to women are called:
   a) socialist feminists
   b) maternal feminists
   c) liberal feminists
   d) conservative feminists

10. Members of 19th century feminist groups were largely:
    a) poor single women
    b) very rich women
    c) poor socialist men and women
    d) middle class educated women

11. Feminist ideas originated:
    a) in the 1960s with the civil rights movement
    b) during World War II when women took over men's jobs in the munitions factories
    c) at least as far back as the American and French Revolutions
    d) in 1918 when women won the right to vote

12. Co-education at the university level was:
    a) resisted until proven financially necessary
    b) initiated by the elite schools
    c) resisted for fear of lowering the standards
    d) a and c

13. The anti-suffrage lobby was:
    a) against women suffering from poverty
    b) led by the brewers and distillers
    c) worried about rising birth rates
    d) in favour of votes for women

14. Canadian women were given the vote in 1917 because:
    a) the Conservatives expected women to vote for conscription
    b) the Conservatives believed in equality for all people
    c) the Liberals expected women to vote against conscription
    d) the Liberals believed in equality for all people

15. Men have been overrepresented in politics because:
    a) they represent the interests of the population more accurately than women
    b) they are more likely to be doctors and dentists, from among whom most politicians are drawn
    c) they are better educated than women
    d) they are more likely to be lawyers and businessmen, from among whom most politicians are drawn

16. Women have historically fared better in:
    a) competitive, militaristic societies with high birth rates
    b) capitalist rather than socialist societies
    c) agricultural compared with horticultural societies
    d) non-competitive, non-militaristic societies with low birth rates

17. Development projects have often favoured male workers because:
    a) women have not worked in most developing countries
    b) consultants often brought their biases to developing countries
    c) both a and b
    d) neither a nor b

18. Reasons given for not promoting equality of the sexes include:

a) children need their mothers at home
b) the customer or client would not accept a woman in a position of authority
c) equality would be too costly
d) all of the above

19. Despite increases in higher education for women:
a) education no longer guarantees a job
b) unemployment rates are high even for educated people
c) women tend to specialize in those areas with higher unemployment rates
d) all of the above

20. After Canadian women won the vote:
a) their representation in government quickly increased
b) their representation in corporate management quickly increased
c) a and b
d) neither a nor b

21. During World War II, the federal government provided:
a) subsidized child care for workers in Ontario and Quebec
b) equal pay for work of equal value
c) affirmative action programs in all of Canada
d) no incentive for women to enter the work force

22. Cross-cultural comparisons of the relative status of men and women usually involve:
a) comparisons of educational attainment
b) comparison of occupational status
c) an analysis of legal equality
d) all of the above

23. When partners divorce in any part of Canada:
a) the economic value of unpaid work might be considered in property settlements

b) the economic value of unpaid work is always considered to be equal to paid work in property settlements
c) only paid work and property are considered in property settlements
d) the woman always gets more than an equal share of property

24. Theories which focus on socialization differences to explain the higher status of men:
a) cannot always explain the origin of the ideology of male dominance
b) usually ignore vested interests in perpetuating male dominance
c) both a and b
d) neither a nor b

25. Economic theories of the relative status of men and women emphasize:
a) the different jobs men and women have been socialized to choose
b) the fact that women must leave work when they have babies
c) the monetary value attached to the work men and women have historically done
d) that men have been encouraged by their families to strive for top paying positions

26. Women's vote has become politically important in the 1980s because:
a) of their increasing financial independence and presence in public life
b) over one quarter of politicians are now women
c) no other important political issue has surfaced
d) the women's lobby was ineffective in rallying support for women's issues

27. Over the past 20 years in North America, attitudes towards gender equality have changed considerably:
a) but behaviour has changed more slowly
b) so that there are no longer any barriers to women's participation in public life

c) but women's place is still in the home
d) none of the above

28. Maternal feminists argued that:
    a) equality is not possible without vast changes in the distribution of wealth
    b) women's contribution to society would make the world more peaceful and humane
    c) mothers should all have maternity leave with full pay
    d) working mothers with young children are depriving their children of important early experiences

29. Compared to women in capitalist countries, women in socialist countries usually are:
    a) better represented in political positions
    b) better represented in the labour force
    c) provided with government-subsidized child care
    d) all of the above

30. Rising expectations of an improved life, along with increased education:
    a) led to a resurgence of interest in feminism in the 1960s
    b) encouraged women to join feminist groups in the 1930s
    c) led to a women's rights movement in the 1940s
    d) encouraged women to produce more children during the post-war baby boom

Posttest

1. Job ghettoization is least pronounced for women in the _____ economy.
    a) Canadian
    b) Japanese
    c) Soviet
    d) American

2. Most Canadian government legislation and policy changes concerning women were influenced by the ideas of _____ feminists.
    a) socialist
    b) liberal
    c) conservative
    d) maternal

3. The University of Toronto admitted its first women students in:
    a) 1867
    b) 1884
    c) 1899
    d) 1907

4. Margaret Sanger is best known as an early advocate of:
    a) birth control
    b) free love
    c) temperance
    d) voting rights for women

5. The Toronto Women's Suffrage Association was founded in 1883 by _____ , Canada's first female medical doctor.
    a) Margaret Sanger
    b) Nellie McClung
    c) Emily Howard Stowe
    d) Agnes Macphail

6. Women's parliamentary representation rates are highest in _____ countries.
    a) North American
    b) wealthy capitalist
    c) developing
    d) socialist

7. Women could not be appointed to Canada's Senate until 1929 when a lengthy court battle established that women were legally:
    a) citizens
    b) adults
    c) persons
    d) competent

8. During the 1950s baby boom, the proportion of married women who worked for pay outside the home:

a) increased
b) decreased
c) stayed constant
d) fluctuated erratically

9. After the 1984 federal election, about _____ % of Canada's MPs were women.
   a) 9
   b) 16
   c) 3
   d) 25

10. By the end of 1984, about _____ % of Canadian Senators were women.
    a) 6
    b) 11
    c) 20
    d) 28

11. Sociobiologists believe social behaviour is primarily shaped by:
    a) the physical and social environments
    b) individual will-power
    c) genetics
    d) all of the above

12. According to Engels, women's economic role _____ after the Industrial Revolution.
    a) expanded
    b) shrank
    c) stayed the same
    d) became more independent

13. Theories which explain the subordination of women by emphasizing cultural tradition and socialization are:
    a) biological
    b) psychoanalytical
    c) idealist
    d) based on a form of dialectical materialism

14. According to economic theories on the subordination of women, housework is often not recognized as work because housework is:
    a) unskilled
    b) unpaid
    c) done by non-unionized women
    d) all of the above

Essay Questions

1. What differences in aptitude have shown up between girls and boys in studies of North American grade schools?

2. Why do men generally earn more money than women?

3. Why were females excluded from higher education in the 19th century but allowed to study with males in the lower grades of school?

4. What factors have contributed to the increased involvement of women in public life? What barriers to further involvement still exist?

5. Why do socialist feminists believe that equality between the sexes is not possible in a class society?

6. What are the arguments for and against using affirmative action programs to raise the status of women?

Research Suggestion: Look into the question of whether giving women the right to vote has, historically, been a first step towards giving women a higher status in other areas. Compare three capitalist countries that gave women the vote relatively early (i.e. Australia, Finland, Norway) with three capitalist countries that gave women the right to vote fairly late (i.e. Italy, Greece, Switzerland). Is there a positive correlation between granting the vote early and having:
a) a higher proportion of women elected to parliament
b) a smaller wage gap between men and women
c) a higher work force participation rate for women?
Account for your findings and suggest other factors that might correlate more positively with a, b and c.

ANSWERS TO CHAPTER 7

Key Terms

1. b	4. a
2. e	5. c
3. d	

Pretest

1. d	6. d	11. a
2. b	7. a	12. c
3. a	8. c	13. a
4. c	9. a	14. b
5. d	10. d	15. b

Test

1. d	11. c	21. a
2. b	12. d	22. d
3. d	13. b	23. a
4. d	14. a	24. c
5. b	15. d	25. c
6. c	16. d	26. a
7. b	17. b	27. a
8. b	18. d	28. b
9. c	19. d	29. d
10. d	20. d	30. a

Posttest

1. c	8. a
2. b	9. a
3. b	10. b
4. a	11. d
5. c	12. b
6. d	13. c
7. c	14. b

CHAPTER 8   FAMILIES

Key Terms

1. family

a) a family in which a husband and wife live together

2. extended family

b) the theory that people are attracted to others of a similar background, race, ethnic and age group, social class and educational level

3. census family

c) a group of people related by blood or marriage who may or may not live together

4. nuclear or conjugal family

d) having more than one spouse at a time

5. household

e) the government definition of a family in which at least one parent lives with his or her dependent children

6. monogamy

f) an early Roman law that gave a father the right of life or death over his children

7. polygamy

g) having more than one husband at a time

8. polygyny

h) all the people who share in a home, regardless of whether they are related

9. polyandry

i) having one spouse

10. social homogamy

j) having more than one wife at a time

11. patria potestas

k) a family in which several generations live together

Pretest

1. More than _____ % of Canadians marry at least once.

   a) 80
   b) 85
   c) 90
   d) 95

2. Nearly _____ % of Canadians who get a divorce later remarry.

   a) 50
   b) 60
   c) 75
   d) 90

3. One former family function now carried by the state is:
   a) helping the unemployed
   b) having children
   c) providing companionship
   d) all of the above

4. The theory of social homogamy suggests people are attracted to other people who have:
   a) similar experiences, ethnicity, race, religion, age, education or social class
   b) different experiences, backgrounds and personality strengths
   c) higher statuses
   d) all of the above

5. About _____ % of Canadian women with children under age 6 now work outside the home.
   a) 25
   b) 40
   c) 50
   d) 75

6. Frontier areas and large urban centres tend to have _____ divorce rates compared to established rural areas.
   a) higher
   b) lower
   c) similar
   d) unpredictable

7. In the 1971 Murdoch case, a woman who divorced her husband after 25 years of living together on the same farm was judged to have _____ % ownership in that farm.
   a) 0
   b) 25
   c) 50
   d) 100

8. During the post-war baby boom:
   a) family size increased
   b) women's labour force participation continued to increase

   c) public attention focused on the joys of family living
   d) all of the above

9. Common-law relationships:
   a) are more stable than legal marriages
   b) are happier than legal marriages
   c) are less stable than legal marriages
   d) are less happy than legal marriages

10. The life cycle approach to the family may be outmoded because:
   a) people don't necessarily marry before having children
   b) husbands and wives might be at quite different stages in their lives
   c) we can no longer assume that marriage means the same to husbands and wives
   d) all of the above

11. Recent trends in the family indicate that:
   a) legal marriage is dying out
   b) the institution is very adaptive and can survive enormous change
   c) the family as an institution is no longer viable for most people
   d) childbearing and child rearing are no longer goals for most young people

12. With increasing education:
   a) women's divorce rate rises
   b) women's fertility declines
   c) women's probability of marriage declines
   d) all of the above

Test

1. In the last 20 years, the popularity of marriage and the desire for permanent relationships has:
   a) declined considerably
   b) remained high
   c) remained low
   d) increased considerably

2. The proportion of childless couples in Canada has remained relatively stable because:
   a) few couples really want to remain childless
   b) medical technology has enabled more involuntary childless couples to reproduce
   c) pressure to have children remains strong
   d) all of the above

3. The "census family" used in government documents includes:
   a) a married couple with or without dependent children or a single parent with never-married children
   b) all related people sharing a household
   c) a married couple with or without dependent children and any other relative living with them
   d) none of the above

4. Increasingly, the state has taken over some of the functions of the family. These include:
   a) reproduction
   b) socialization of children
   c) companionship
   d) all of the above

5. The family remains an important institution in society because:
   a) family members provide important services such as housework, babysitting and financial assistance
   b) the family is still involved with "values education"
   c) it still provides companionship
   d) all of the above

6. In the conjugal family, the ties between _____ are most important:
   a) father and son
   b) parents and children
   c) husband and wife
   d) grandparents and grandchildren

7. The extended family was:
   a) more prevalent than the nuclear family in the 19th century in North America
   b) always unusual in North America because of short life expectancies and migration
   c) more prevalent than the nuclear family in 19th century Europe
   d) none of the above

8. Having more than one wife at a time is called:
   a) polygamy
   b) polyandry
   c) polygyny
   d) monogamy

9. In countries where men can have more than one wife:
   a) men have a higher sex drive
   b) wives often become symbols of their husband's wealth and status
   c) the wives are always jealous of each other
   d) a surplus of women is necessary in the population

10. Virginity is usually more important for brides than grooms because:
    a) women are not supposed to have strong sex drives
    b) knowledge of paternity is important for inheritance and naming
    c) men prefer inexperienced and younger wives
    d) all of the above

11. Societies which practise arranged marriages often have the idea that:
    a) divorce is not possible under any circumstances
    b) romantic love is an unsound basis for marriage
    c) young people are capable of making valid marital choices
    d) marriage should be based on a solid love relationship

12. The theory of complementary needs states that people choose as marital partners someone:
    a) who fulfills their psychological needs
    b) who compliments them a lot
    c) with a similar social background
    d) whom they think will best fulfill their psychological needs

13. "Patria potestas" referred to:
    a) a powerful love of one's native land
    b) a man with a powerful sex drive
    c) a father who desired a large family
    d) the right of life or death which a father had over his children

14. With large-scale industrialization in Central Canada in the 19th century:
    a) rural sons left home to seek wage labour in the cities
    b) rural sons left home to seek domestic service with other families
    c) daughters usually left to do factory work in the cities
    d) daughters left to perform domestic work in the cities

15. Large families used to be an asset because:
    a) children contributed unpaid work to the household
    b) children could support their elderly parents who could no longer work
    c) a and b
    d) neither a nor b

16. Prior to 1872 in Canada, married women could not:
    a) work outside the home
    b) retain their own wages
    c) own property separately from their husbands
    d) b and c

17. Working for pay outside the home by the wife and children gradually:
    a) reduced patriarchy within the home
    b) raised the divorce rate
    c) led to the dissolution of the family unit
    d) none of the above

18. Engels argued nearly a century ago that the practice of monogamy arose when:
    a) knowledge of maternity became important for inheritance
    b) knowledge of paternity became important for inheritance
    c) nomadic people became sedentary and concerned with private property, inheritance and paternity
    d) all of the above

19. Quebec now has the _____ birth rate in Canada.
    a) highest
    b) lowest
    c) fastest growing
    d) none of the above

20. According to Statistics Canada, most working parents with preschoolers:
    a) send their children to day care centres
    b) hire baby sitters to care for their children
    c) can find subsidized day care
    d) can deduct day care expenses from their income tax

21. Canadian divorce rates:
    a) are much higher than other industrialized countries'
    b) indicate that the family is a dying institution
    c) become lower as you move West
    d) have increased substantially since 1968

22. One-parent households are often poor because:
    a) inflation has made two incomes increasingly necessary
    b) they are headed by women, who earn lower wages than men
    c) men frequently default on their support payments
    d) all of the above

23. Since the Law Reform Commission:
    a) there has been little change in the proportion of fathers receiving custody of their children
    b) there has been a substantial increase in the proportion of fathers receiving custody of their children
    c) custody is supposed to be granted to either parent
    d) a and c

24. After divorce, about:
    a) two thirds of men remarry
    b) three quarters of women remarry
    c) half of both sexes remarry
    d) two thirds of women and three quarters of men remarry

25. American studies show that people who have already been divorced:
    a) have less chance of a second divorce
    b) have more chance of a second divorce
    c) claim to be unhappy in their second marriages
    d) none of the above

26. Marriage dissolution is most likely among:
    a) couples with only one wage earner
    b) couples with more than two children
    c) couples who married as teenagers when the woman was pregnant
    d) all of the above

27. The creation of temporary shelters and transition houses for abused women and their children indicates:
    a) a rise in public concern about family violence
    b) the public's dissatisfaction with the police's treatment of family violence
    c) a rise in family violence
    d) a and b

28. The Canadian state is now more

involved than it used to be with:
    a) monitoring child rearing
    b) settling marital disputes
    c) protecting the rights of children
    d) all of the above

29. The age of marriage in Canada:
    a) has been gradually increasing
    b) has been gradually falling
    c) fell from the 1940s to the 1970s and is rising again
    d) increased from the 1940s to the 1970s and is now falling

30. Experiments in alternatives to the nuclear family indicate that:
    a) most people conform to our traditional family patterns
    b) increasing the complexity and size of households leads to considerable problems
    c) communal living is clearly preferred by a minority of people
    d) all of the above

Posttest

1. "Sequential polygamy" is having:
    a) several spouses at the same time
    b) different spouses at different times
    c) one spouse for an entire lifetime
    d) none of the above

2. Having more than one husband at a time is called:
    a) polygamy
    b) polyandry
    c) polygyny
    d) monogamy

3. The _____ theory says people try to select mates whom they think will fulfill their psychological needs.
    a) social homogamy
    b) residential propinquity
    c) complimentary needs
    d) complementary needs

4. After compulsory education was introduced, the value of children became primarily:
   a) economic
   b) educational
   c) emotional
   d) social

5. The highest birth rate in Canada is now in:
   a) Quebec
   b) the Maritimes
   c) the Northwest Territories
   d) Manitoba and Saskatchewan

6. The 1984 Badgley Report found most child abuse is done by:
   a) strangers
   b) babysitters, teachers and childcare workers
   c) female relatives
   d) male relatives

7. Birth rates tend to rise when:
   a) a formerly nomadic people settles on a piece of land and develops large-scale agriculture
   b) a nomadic people is involved in hunting and gathering
   c) a nomadic people becomes involved in horticulture
   d) people learn how to control fertility

8. In many industrializing countries, infant mortality and maternal death rates fell with the introduction of:
   a) modern medical technology
   b) "the pill"
   c) improved nutrition, sanitation, accommodation and health facilities
   d) improved maternity leave provisions

9. The 1984 Badgley Report on sexual abuse of children concluded:
   a) child abuse is increasing dramatically
   b) half of women and one third of men have experienced some form of sexual abuse in their youth
   c) strangers most frequently abuse children
   d) the state will only intervene if a child is severely abused

10. Living together instead of legal marriage:
    a) has become a new "courting" pattern
    b) is replacing marriage
    c) shows people's dissatisfaction with marriage as an institution
    d) is becoming less popular

11. Family instability is a part of our history because of:
    a) high rates of immigration and migrant labour
    b) high maternal death rates
    c) high male death rates in frontier industries
    d) all of the above

Essay Questions

1. Why do more men than women remarry after a divorce?

2. Why do abused wives wait, on average, until they have been beaten 35 times before going to the police? How could society help wives feel freer to act sooner?

3. What is the difference between a family and a household?

4. According to Marxists, why does the state place such an emphasis on the importance of the family as an institution?

5. Why do modern industrial, urban societies have higher divorce rates than traditional, rural, agricultural societies?

6. What are the potential benefits and drawbacks of the state becoming more involved in questions of divorce, family violence, childbearing and child rearing?

7. What is the rationale for splitting all family assets 50-50 upon divorce? Suggest why this is fair or offer an alternate formula that you think would be fair.

8. Is there any way in which sex discrimination, child abuse and wife battering can be considered functional for society?

   Research Suggestion: Try to find some statistics on occupation and divorce or family violence. Which jobs produce the highest divorce rates? Is there any correlation between high divorce rates or high incidence of family violence and a) job stress, b) low pay, c) low job status, d) prolonged periods of unemployment? If you find a strong positive correlation, design a questionnaire and distribute it to some people working in that job to have them explain why they think such a correlation exists. Ask them to suggest ways their jobs could be changed to reduce these apparent negative effects on family life. Note: Always try to think of plausible, competing cause-and-effect explanations for the family problems.

ANSWERS TO CHAPTER 8

Key Terms

1. c	7. d
2. k	8. j
3. e	9. g
4. a	10. b
5. h	11. f
6. i	

Pretest

1. b	7. a
2. c	8. d
3. a	9. c
4. a	10. d
5. c	11. b
6. a	12. d

Test

1. b	11. b	21. d
2. d	12. d	22. d
3. a	13. d	23. d
4. b	14. a	24. d
5. d	15. c	25. b
6. c	16. d	26. c
7. b	17. a	27. d
8. c	18. c	28. d
9. b	19. a	29. c
10. d	20. b	30. d

Posttest

1. b	7. a
2. b	8. c
3. d	9. b
4. c	10. a
5. c	11. d
6. d	

CHAPTER 9   RACE AND ETHNIC RELATIONS

Key Terms

1. subjective identity

a) Park's theory that racial groups first meet, then compete, then accommodate each other and finally form one homogeneous group

2. race

b) social boundaries which separate a group from outsiders

3. ethnicity

c) a way of grouping people based on socially selected physical traits

4. closure

d) the first language one knows

5. social race

e) a form of structured inequality that denies some groups equal access to, and benefits from, social institutions

6. assimilation

f) an ascribed identity (usually based on physical characteristics and/or cultural traits)

7. race relations cycle

g) the American assimilationist view that sees all ethnic cultures contributing to the general culture

8. Anglo-conformity

h) the bottom stratum of society; the stratum below the working class

9. melting pot thesis

i) a way of grouping based on socially selected cultural traits (usually ancestry, language, religion and traditions)

10. triple melting pot thesis

j) racial groupings which are not based on physical appearances

11. cultural pluralism

k) the view that assimilation in the U.S. takes place within the Catholic, Protestant and Jewish religious groups

12. structural pluralism

l) the American assimilationist view that all immigrant and ethnic minority groups should conform to the dominant Anglo-Saxon culture

13. underclass

m) relatively superficial part-time expressions of ethnicity which do not interfere with full participation in the mainstream culture

14. internal colonization

n) the practice of marrying within one's own group

15. split labour market

o) the language one speaks at home

16. home language

p) the existence of subsocieties separated from the mainstream culture

17. ancestral language shift

q) the process by which linguistic minorities come to adopt English as their mother tongue and/or home language

18. mother tongue

r) the practice of retaining cultural traditions in primary groups while participating with other cultural groups in secondary relations

19. current language shift

s) the process whereby people of diverse origin become similar

20. Anglicization

t) a lack of correspondence between one's home language and one's mother tongue

21. endogamy

u) a lack of correspondence between someone's ethnic origin and his/her mother tongue

22. institutional racism

v) the political and economic domination of ethnic minorities within the same country

23. symbolic ethnicity

w) the phenomenon of different racial groups being paid different wages for the same kind of work

Pretest

1. Physical traits are important in defining race because they are:
   a) caused by genetic variations
   b) results of differential adaptive capacity
   c) socially recognized
   d) correlated with social achievements

2. Park's "race relations cycle" takes the form of:
   a) identity, culture, language and religion
   b) contacts, competition, accommodation and assimilation
   c) discrimination, acculturation and melting pot
   d) pluralism and assimilation

3. The assimilationist perspective has been criticized because:
   a) Park's race relations cycle is mechanical
   b) assimilation is loosely defined
   c) it is ethnocentric
   d) all of the above

4. The "triple melting pot" refers to assimilation within the three groups of:
   a) blacks, whites and orientals
   b) Anglo-Saxon, French and native people
   c) upper class, middle class and working class
   d) Catholics, Protestants and Jews

5. All but one of the following is not part of the colonization process:
   a) incursion of the colonizing group
   b) external political control
   c) economic dependence of the colonized people
   d) pluralism

6. According to Bonacich's "Split Labour Market Theory", the source of racial antagonism is differential:
   a) price of labour between two groups

   b) technological level
   c) cultural development
   d) resources

7. The emergence of a split labour market is related to:
   a) the rise in labour cost of white workers
   b) the availability of non-white labour from peripheral countries
   c) the rise of racism
   d) a and b

8. Ancestral language shift occurs when the mother tongue of a person, or the language that a person learns in childhood, does not correspond to the person's:
   a) culture
   b) home language
   c) ethnic origin
   d) country of birth

9. Porter uses the term "charter group" to refer to:
   a) English and French
   b) native people
   c) immigrants
   d) all Canadians

10. The main thesis of Porter's *Vertical Mosaic* is that a relationship exists in Canada between:
    a) race and ethnicity
    b) ethnic origin and social class
    c) social achievement and ascription
    d) resource development and regional disparity

11. When the mother tongue of a person does not correspond to the home language, it is referred to as:
    a) current shift
    b) ancestral shift
    c) mother tongue shift
    d) ethnic shift

12. Which of the following points was *not* made by John Porter in *The Vertical Mosaic?*

a) English and French origin Canadians enjoy a privileged status
b) there is no link between ethnicity and occupational structure
c) the English are overrepresented in the economic elite
d) the English are doing much better than the French

13. According to the colonial model, the modern economic function of racism is to:
a) justify slavery
b) create a market for armaments companies
c) reduce labour costs
d) divert Third World countries from the more important tasks of economic development

14. The area of Canada (excluding the territories) that has the highest percentage of neither French nor English origin is:
a) the Maritimes
b) Ontario and Quebec
c) the Prairies
d) British Columbia

15. The ethnic group with the highest average annual income is the:
a) English
b) Jews
c) Scandinavians
d) Germans

Test

1. Canada's race relations:
a) have always been unusually harmonious
b) hit a low due to the increased immigration after World War II
c) have always been unusually violent
d) have become antagonistic at various points throughout our history

2. Racial and ethnic divisions in Canada have been highlighted in the past by:

a) England's conquest of New France
b) the conquest of the native people
c) the internment of Japanese Canadians in World War II
d) all of the above

3. The concept of social races points out that definitions of race are *not* necessarily based on:
a) superficial physical characteristics
b) socially defined relevant characteristics
c) laws and convention
d) all of the above

4. Park sees the race relations cycle as:
a) destructive and unfair to minorities
b) progressive and reversible
c) an inefficient process with few lasting effects
d) none of the above

5. According to Park, immigration restrictions and racial barriers will _____ the race relations cycle.
a) stop
b) reverse
c) accelerate
d) slow down

6. The view that all immigrants to the United States will learn to speak English, adopt Christianity and believe in liberal democracy is part of the _____ assimilation theory.
a) melting pot
b) cultural mosaic
c) Anglo-conformity
d) pluralistic

7. Which group is among the three groups referred to in the triple melting pot theory of assimilation?
a) Moslems
b) Buddhists
c) atheists
d) none of the above

8. A Canadian who speaks German at home but English or French outside it is practising:
   a) Anglo-conformity
   b) cultural pluralism
   c) structural pluralism
   d) none of the above

9. Pluralists believe that North American ethnic groups that participate in mainstream life can retain their unique aspects:
   a) in their social networks, churches, home language etc.
   b) only by dropping out of the mainstream
   c) for only a limited time
   d) only by living in cultural enclaves

10. A person who preserves his culture and ethnicity by having little or no contact with the dominant culture is experiencing:
   a) cultural pluralism
   b) cultural isolation
   c) structural pluralism
   d) cultural deprivation

11. The pluralist perspective has been criticized for:
   a) overemphasizing the old world culture
   b) downplaying ethnic and racial inequality
   c) overemphasizing superficial expressions of ethnicity
   d) all of the above

12. Some theorists have labelled the second-class status imposed on Canada's native people a form of:
   a) internal colonization
   b) structural isolation
   c) neo-racism
   d) cultural isolation

13. In 1967, Canada's Department of Immigration adopted a universal points system to judge potential immigrants to Canada. This system:
   a) led to a decrease in immigration
   b) penalized non-whites

   c) led to an increase of non-white immigrants
   d) had little effect on the kinds of people admitted to Canada

14. The fact that during hard times native-born Canadians often view immigrants as competitors for jobs supports the _____ theory.
   a) triple melting pot
   b) cultural pluralism
   c) split labour market
   d) structural pluralism

15. Approximately what fraction of Canada's population was of neither British nor French ancestry in 1981?
   a) one tenth
   b) one third
   c) one half
   d) three quarters

16. After the English and French the third largest ethnic group in Canada is the:
   a) native peoples
   b) Italians
   c) Germans
   d) Chinese

17. One major reason that Canada, in 1967, began admitting more immigrants from non-traditional sources is that Canada wanted:
   a) to build a huge home market
   b) to relieve population pressures in the Third World
   c) a more skilled labour force
   d) all of the above

18. The 1981 census found that about _____ % of Canadians were officially bilingual.
   a) 5
   b) 15
   c) 25
   d) 35

19. The French peasantry began to shed their conservative, fatalistic and passive world view:

a) after the conquest of 1759
b) after the influx of United Empire Loyalists in 1776
c) during the Quiet Revolution of the 1960s
d) with the election of the Parti Québécois in 1976

20. Vallee has postulated that a Canadian's ability to retain French as his/her home language deteriorates:
a) the further away from Quebec that he/she lives
b) the older he/she gets
c) whenever French is not used as the main language of business
d) all of the above

21. Outside of Quebec, language maintenance for French is strongest in _____ and weakest in _____.
a) Ontario . . . the Maritime provinces
b) Manitoba . . . Newfoundland
c) Ontario . . . Alberta
d) New Brunswick . . . the Western provinces

22. Among the major linguistic groups in Canada, the _____ have the lowest rates of language retention.
a) Italians and Greeks
b) Chinese and Portuguese
c) Native peoples
d) Dutch and Germans

23. An Italian family living in Montreal speaks only French. What form of language shift is this?
a) mother tongue shift
b) current shift
c) ancestral shift
d) ethnic shift

24. John Porter placed all of Canada's ethnic groups in one of two categories. Those two categories were:
a) white or non-white
b) upwardly mobile or downwardly mobile
c) entrance status or charter status

d) independent or assimilationist

25. In 1975, Wallace re-examined the ethnic backgrounds of Canada's corporate elite and found that in the elite:
a) more than 85% were of English origin
b) the percentage of French origin members had dropped
c) people of Jewish origin were underrepresented
d) all of the above

26. "Visible minorities" is the term used to describe:
a) legal immigrants
b) non-whites
c) unassimilated minorities
d) members of ethnic minorities working outside the home

27. Multiculturalism has been officially embraced by the Canadian government since:
a) 1867
b) 1950
c) 1967
d) 1971

28. Gallup polls have found that Canadians prefer that their government admit immigrants:
a) only for humanitarian reasons
b) from Northern Europe rather than from Asia
c) in very large numbers
d) in equal numbers from all regions of the world

29. Institutional racism occurs when:
a) individuals in social institutions become bigoted
b) members of racial minorities are put in institutions
c) social institutions systematically discriminate against a racial group
d) all of the above

30. The French and English have had an advantage over other groups because these two charter groups were able to:

a) dominate the economy
b) control immigration
c) dictate which languages would be used by governments and schools
d) all of the above

Posttest

1. The view that all groups contribute to the making of American culture is called the _____ view.
   a) melting pot
   b) cultural mosaic
   c) Anglo-conformity
   d) pluralistic

2. The assimilationist perspective has been criticized for defining assimilation:
   a) as losing one's mother tongue
   b) as adopting aspects of the mainstream culture
   c) too vaguely
   d) too rigidly

3. The concept of internal colonization has been used to describe:
   a) British colonies in Africa
   b) the dominance of men over women
   c) black ghettos in the United States
   d) all of the above

4. The term "underclass" refers to:
   a) the social stratum below the working class
   b) any class that is subordinate to another
   c) the proletariat
   d) none of the above

5. The split labour market theory has been used to explain conflicts between:
   a) age generations
   b) blue and white collar workers
   c) management and labour
   d) different racial groups in the same job category

6. Until 1967, Canada's immigration policy favoured immigrants:
   a) who were highly skilled
   b) from Britain, the U.S. and Northern Europe
   c) who faced oppression in their home countries
   d) all of the above

7. Most developed countries, including Canada, tailor their immigration policies to:
   a) keep their racial balance constant
   b) meet their labour market needs
   c) avoid a "brain drain" out of the Third World
   d) make their populations grow faster

8. The relatively low rates of language retention by Canadians of Dutch and German origin is partly explained by the fact that these groups:
   a) speak languages similar to English
   b) usually live in the same areas as dominant linguistic groups
   c) tend to be less committed to the principle of multiculturalism
   d) none of the above

9. If my mother tongue was Chinese, but my home language is now French, what kind of shift have I experienced?
   a) mother tongue shift
   b) current shift
   c) ancestral shift
   d) ethnic shift

10. Sociologists measure the degree of ethnic segregation by examining:
    a) language retention rates
    b) residential segregation
    c) in-group marriage rates
    d) all of the above

11. Which of the following groups is not considered a visible minority?
    a) blacks
    b) Chinese
    c) Jews
    d) native people

12. Members of visible minorities are usually doubly handicapped in the labour market because of their:
   a) immigrant status and the racial prejudice against them
   b) inadequate education and the racial prejudice against them
   c) language barrier and poor training
   d) lack of contacts and inferior education

13. Official multiculturalism has:
   a) not effectively combated racism
   b) made Canada more multi-lingual
   c) made the concepts of charter status and entrance status obsolete
   d) none of the above

14. Sociologists usually define race and ethnicity in one of two ways. They see racial and ethnic groups as either:
   a) biological groupings or social constructs
   b) cultural groups or conflict groups
   c) socially relevant or forms of false consciousness
   d) upwardly mobile or downwardly mobile

15. Ethnic groups can help to preserve their culture by:
   a) living in cultural enclaves
   b) keeping their mother tongues as their home tongues
   c) marrying within their own group
   d) all of the above

Essay Questions

1. Why hasn't Canada's official policy of multiculturalism been more effective in reducing racism? How could the policy be made more effective?

2. In what sense are Indian reservations and ethnic ghettos like "internal colonies" according to the colonial model? In what ways are the reservations and ghettos not analogous to Third World colonies?

3. Using the experiences of specific ethnic groups in Canada, argue for or against the notion that cultural assimilation, a high degree of language shift and being an "invisible" minority all increase an ethnic minority group's chances for success in this country.

4. At what point does an individual become assimilated into the mainstream culture? What are the costs and the benefits, on both an individual and societal level, of resisting pressures to assimilate?

5. How do events which happened long ago, such as slavery and colonialism, exert an influence on race relations today?

6. What advantages, if any, do the English and French enjoy over other ethnic groups in Canada? Is ethnicity becoming a less relevant indicator of a person's chances for success in Canada? Give reasons for your answer.

7. Do you think the United States is more accurately described as a melting pot or as a culturally pluralistic society? Why?

8. Why are certain ethnic groups congregated in certain jobs?

Research Suggestion: Consider the question of whether our Immigration Department practises a form of institutional racism. Get a copy of the criteria that the Department of Immigration uses to award points to potential immigrants to Canada. Find which countries have had the highest rates of acceptance since the points system was introduced. To calculate this you will have to calculate the number of acceptances as a percentage of the number of applicants from each country. Examine the points system criteria closely to see if there are any biases which might account for the differential success rates of applicants from different countries.

ANSWERS TO CHAPTER 9

Test

1. d	11. d	21. d
2. d	12. a	22. d
3. a	13. c	23. c
4. b	14. c	24. c
5. d	15. b	25. a
6. c	16. c	26. b
7. d	17. c	27. d
8. b	18. b	28. d
9. a	19. c	29. c
10. c	20. a	30. d

Key Terms

1. f	9. g	17. u
2. c	10. k	18. d
3. i	11. r	19. t
4. b	12. p	20. q
5. j	13. h	21. n
6. s	14. v	22. e
7. a	15. w	23. m
8. l	16. o	

Pretest

1. c	6. a	11. a
2. b	7. d	12. b
3. d	8. c	13. c
4. d	9. a	14. c
5. d	10. b	15. b

Posttest

1. a	6. b	11. c
2. c	7. b	12. a
3. c	8. b	13. a
4. a	9. b	14. b
5. d	10. d	15. d

CHAPTER 10   CLASS AND STRATIFICATION

Key Terms

1. social mobility

    a) any social process that a group uses to prevent outsiders from having equal access to resources and opportunities

2. stratification theories

    b) historically distinct ways of organizing productive activities so that a particular way of life is produced and maintained

3. class theories

    c) the movement of people out of one economic class and into another

4. surplus value

d) the process by which more and more people come to be increasingly dependent on wages or salaries for their main or sole source of income

5. modes of production

e) a system in which society's top privileged positions are earned in a fair and open competition

6. bourgeoisie

f) theories which focus on social mobility and the forms of social rankings

7. social closure

g) the capitalist class of employers whose main income comes from extracting the surplus labour of their employees

8. meritocracy

h) the value of production minus the cost of production

9. cultural capital

i) theories that focus on relations of exploitation, dominance and dependence between groups in society

10. proletarianization

j) values, attitudes and ideologies that are useful in achieving material wealth and social status

Pretest

1. Marx thought the three major classes in 19th century England were the:
   a) aristocracy, clergy and peasantry
   b) landlords, peasants and proletariat
   c) landlords, capitalists and wage labourers
   d) proletariat, clergy and bourgeoisie

2. Marxist theory sees social classes in terms of:
   a) income levels
   b) self perceptions
   c) ownership of means of production
   d) ascribed social status

3. Critics of Marxism argue that progressive proletarianization was halted by the:
   a) creation of the modern welfare state

   b) raising of living standards for all social classes
   c) growth of the white collar sector of the work force
   d) all of the above

4. Max Weber thought _____ caused people to lose control of their own work and to become dominated by others.
   a) capitalism
   b) socialism
   c) bureaucracy
   d) the Protestant work ethic

5. Which of the following is a tool of social enclosure?
   a) private property
   b) a university degree
   c) mandatory retirement laws
   d) all of the above

6. A 1979 *Financial Post* story reported that more than half of all Canadian sales were made by just _____ % of Canadian companies.
   a) 17
   b) 10
   c) 7
   d) 3

7. A stratified society is produced by which two social institutions?
   a) the educational and legal systems
   b) private property and the labour market
   c) the mass media and the school system
   d) private property and the family

8. Progressive taxation, unemployment insurance and other social programs have, over the past 30 years:
   a) had little effect on Canada's income distribution structure
   b) substantially reduced the proportion of Canadians living below the poverty line
   c) failed to prevent the wealthy from claiming an even larger share of the national income pie
   d) none of the above

9. Studies have found that as increasing numbers of women enter the paid labour force:
   a) most women remain within a small range of poorly paid jobs
   b) women are rapidly spreading through all kinds of white collar work but are still underrepresented in managerial positions
   c) women are becoming increasingly overrepresented in law and dentistry
   d) the range of occupations that are widely held by women is actually shrinking

10. If proletarianization occurs when people lose control of the means of production and are forced to rely on wages or salaries as their only source of livelihood, then proletarianization:
    a) was common in the 19th century but is now very rare
    b) happened in Europe but not in North America
    c) is just starting to affect large numbers of Canadians
    d) has been proceeding in Canada for more than a century and now affects the great majority of Canadians

11. The spread of commodity markets and middle class lifestyles has been accompanied by inequalities in the distribution of incomes. This trend:
    a) has stayed virtually unchanged since World War II
    b) is effectively counter-balanced by progressive taxation laws
    c) is ending as income gaps begin to shrink in the 1980s
    d) has only been documented in Europe and North America

12. The fact that real incomes have risen recently while income inequalities have remained stable indicates that:
    a) some of the data must be wrong; the trends are incompatible
    b) the working class will not exist soon because almost everyone will be affluent
    c) people can begin to think of themselves as upwardly mobile without gaining any ground on people who are richer
    d) none of the above

Test

1. Stratification theories are largely debates with Marxist class theory because class theory:
   a) developed first
   b) provides the basic concepts for analysing inequality

c) is more systematic and historically based

d) poses provocative questions that cannot be ignored

2. Although Marx saw English society as divided into three great classes, Marxist theory depicts capitalist society as divided into only two hostile classes. This is because:
   a) Marx saw England as an exceptional case
   b) one of the three English classes is now extinct
   c) Marx distinguished between historically specific social forms and general tendencies
   d) Marx thought a two-class model was too simplistic

3. In Marxist theory, exploitation:
   a) is universal and inevitable in all societies
   b) takes a different form in different kinds of societies
   c) has been progressively reduced with modernization
   d) is unique to capitalism

4. Marxist theory distinguishes between "labour", which is the way work is organized in a specific historical setting, and "labour power", which is:
   a) a universal capacity of human beings to do work
   b) any source of power, inanimate or otherwise, that can be used to do work
   c) the name given to the alliance of unions and social democratic political parties
   d) the capacity for revolution that could be tapped if the workers developed class consciousness

5. To Marxists, the basic source of class conflict lies in the fact that:
   a) workers want to establish a dictatorship of the proletariat
   b) the workers lack a decent standard of living

c) the capitalists are unwilling to compromise

d) capitalists exploit workers

6. Proletarianization is the process by which increasingly large numbers of people:
   a) lose their jobs
   b) become dependent on wages for their livelihoods
   c) begin thinking of themselves as working class
   d) fall below the poverty line

7. Weber's theory of stratification is based on the idea that:
   a) bureaucracy stifles individuality
   b) the growth of the middle class offsets proletarianization
   c) people are different in social status but not in social class
   d) social groups have different capacities to control markets

8. The dominant Canadian ideology, as expressed in our mass media, political rhetoric, schools and everyday speech, most closely corresponds to the _____ view of social stratification.
   a) functionalist
   b) Marxist
   c) Weberian
   d) none of the above

9. Weberians argue that classes rarely become politically organized because:
   a) people do not really share common economic positions
   b) most people are apolitical
   c) racial mistrust outweighs shared economic interests
   d) there is no obvious transition from sharing an economic position to sharing a political goal

10. Social closure is a Weberian concept that refers to:
    a) a process of monopolizing opportunities

b) racial and ethnic conflicts

c) a process of expanding class boundaries

d) the way public debates are stifled

11. Functionalists say class conflict is no longer relevant since:
    a) poverty is disappearing from our society
    b) Marxist theories are just political propaganda
    c) bureaucracy is a greater danger than class conflict
    d) social classes are not in conflict with one another

12. Functionalists argue that inequality is a necessary feature of all societies because:
    a) inequality helps a society run more efficiently
    b) some people are more talented than others
    c) wealth is inherited in all societies
    d) human nature makes people exploit each other

13. Functionalism argues that social class divisions faded in the 20th century because:
    a) of a more sophisticated analysis of social data
    b) material and social improvements have minimized conflicts of interest
    c) civil rights laws now guarantee opportunities for everyone
    d) wealth is no longer distributed unfairly

14. Functional theory is based on a market metaphor that suggests society needs to protect its supply of skilled labour by:
    a) attaching high status and high incomes to key jobs
    b) letting the market determine wages for all jobs
    c) teaching skilled trades in the public school system
    d) all of the above

15. The process of proletarianization involves a decrease in _____ and an increase in _____ in the population.
    a) standard of living...unemployment
    b) the number of farm workers...the number of factory workers
    c) the number of corporations...the level of class conflict
    d) the number of small-property owners...wage earners

16. The most recent studies on the occupational changes of Canadian men between 1861 and 1871 show that in that decade:
    a) there was little social mobility or changing of jobs
    b) large numbers of people moved into family farming
    c) a great many people left farming to take jobs in the cities
    d) good farmland became too expensive for most people

17. Farmers were the core of the Canadian bourgeoisie until _____ . Now this group consists mainly of self-employed businessmen and professionals.
    a) late in the 19th century
    b) the middle of the 19th century
    c) after World War II
    d) World War I

18. Some studies suggest that the issue of foreign control of the Canadian economy is a less important issue than the increase in the concentration of ownership of Canadian business in the hands of a small group of Canadian capitalists. This is because:
    a) foreign ownership is decreasing
    b) Canadian ownership is and has been the most important characteristic of our economy
    c) foreign capitalists have demonstrated a greater social responsibility
    d) all of the above

19. Over the past 30 years, mobility into the key positions on boards of Canada's largest corporations and financial institutions has:
    a) become increasingly restricted to a narrow circle
    b) become much more accessible to highly educated people
    c) stayed about the same although there has been some turnover
    d) been similar to elite mobility patterns in other countries

20. The best available evidence suggests stock ownership has:
    a) been restricted to about 10% of all Canadian families
    b) become widespread since World War I
    c) been too expensive for the average Canadian
    d) been limited to an increasingly small group of wealthy families

21. About 10% of Canada's families control about 50% of all the wealth (total assets) in this country. This degree of concentration of wealth _____ compared to inequalities in other Western countries.
    a) is mild
    b) is extreme
    c) cannot be accurately
    d) is normal

22. Class and stratification are:
    a) different terms for the same thing
    b) unique products of capitalism
    c) different forms of inequality and power
    d) concepts that will not apply in a post-industrial society

23. The growth of white collar, technical, clerical and professional work has offset the decline in farming and other primary work over the past few decades. This trend seems to explain:

a) how proletarianization and an increase in middle class lifestyles can occur at the same time
    b) the demise of class-divided society
    c) why the working class is shrinking
    d) why the ruling class is growing

24. Some recent studies question the idea that the shift to a white collar economy has involved a broad upgrading of skills and responsibilities. These studies note that:
    a) white collar workers are often women and women tend to have less education than men
    b) many of the new white collar workers graduated from a modern, inferior school system
    c) blue collar tradesmen train longer than secretaries do
    d) much white collar work is simple, routine and highly supervised

25. The _____ come closest to using the term "middle class" the same way most Canadians do in their everyday speech.
    a) highly class conscious neo-Marxists
    b) functionalists who see class as largely irrelevant
    c) neo-Weberians
    d) classical Marxist theorists

26. The widespread emergence of middle class lifestyles, characterized by a steady increase in real incomes, consumerism and leisure activities began in Canada:
    a) after World War II
    b) in the middle of the 19th century
    c) in about 1920
    d) during the Great Depression of the 1930s

27. The recent rise in the number of families with two income earners appears largely to be due to:
    a) housewives beginning to realize they have marketable skills

b) families needing two incomes to support a middle class lifestyle
c) couples having fewer children
d) employers hiring large numbers of women for new kinds of jobs

28. Many recent mobility studies have tried to determine how many changes in social mobility are due to structural changes in the economy and how many are due to actual changes in the opportunities for advancement. These studies indicate that:
    a) it is impossible to determine the cause of mobility
    b) structural changes account for almost all of the mobility
    c) structural changes had little effect on mobility
    d) decreased prejudice and structural changes contributed equally to mobility

29. The claim that rising living standards have masked the persistence of economic and social inequalities in Canada:
    a) is a basic assumption of functionalist theory
    b) has not been supported by empirical evidence
    c) is supported by a growing body of empirical evidence
    d) is plausible only when it is applied to the Maritimes

30. The notion of the middle class has been:
    a) systematically explored in social theory
    b) rendered obsolete by the emerging post industrial society
    c) central only to Weberian theories of stratification
    d) poorly developed in all major theories of class and stratification

Posttest

1. In everyday speech, _____

is often substituted for the Marxist term "surplus value".
   a) profit
   b) overpricing
   c) underpricing
   d) none of the above

2. According to Marxist theory, every society contains:
   a) one dominant mode of production
   b) two competing modes of production
   c) several modes of production, all struggling for dominance
   d) several modes of production

3. Most Canadians consider themselves to be in the _____ class. According to the Marxist definition of class, most Canadians are in the _____ class.
   a) working...middle
   b) middle...upper
   c) middle...working
   d) middle...middle

4. Weber thought _____ caused people to lose control of their own work and to be dominated by others.
   a) capitalism
   b) socialism
   c) bureaucracy
   d) religion

5. The core of the Canadian petit-bourgeoisie now consists of:
   a) independent farmers
   b) white collar employees and independent farmers
   c) self-employed professionals and small business owners
   d) managers of large multi-national corporations

6. One study concluded that about _____ % of Canadian families owned stock worth $5000 or more in 1970.
   a) 20
   b) 13

c) 9
d) 3

7. If a working class person is defined as someone whose main income is derived from working as somebody else's employee, more than _____ % of Canadians are in the working class.
   a) 45
   b) 60
   c) 75
   d) 80

8. Since 1976, the average real income in Canada has:
   a) doubled
   b) tripled
   c) fallen
   d) stagnated

9. The fact that the average Canadian has much more formal education than her counterpart of a generation ago does not necessarily mean that educational barriers to opportunities have been reduced. This is because:
   a) more education is needed just to maintain one's ranking relative to other people who also have more education
   b) the most lucrative jobs don't require a formal education
   c) the school system today is less demanding than it used to be
   d) all of the above

10. The functionalist theory on stratification is supported by national studies of occupational prestige that show:

a) occupational prestige rankings differ from place to place
b) people agree on the prestige rankings of very few jobs
c) a widespread consensus on the prestige rankings
d) no consensus anywhere on which jobs are the most prestigious

11. Although few Canadians now expect to inherit substantial amounts of property, coming from an affluent background is still considered an asset because affluent parents can provide their children with:
    a) moral support
    b) cash, stocks and bonds and sound financial advice
    c) a university education, meritocratic values, a high social status, useful personal connections and other cultural capital
    d) a positive role model

12. Social mobility and status attainment research have focused on how the status of parents is transmitted to children in contemporary Western societies. Many of these studies have found:
    a) status is not transmitted from one generation to another
    b) most people are not status conscious
    c) a parent's status directly affects the kind of job that his children are likely to get
    d) a parent's status directly affects the amount of formal education his children are likely to attain

Essay Questions

1. How is civil rights legislation often an attack on different forms of social closure? What forms of social closure do these laws leave unchallenged?

2. Argue for or against the idea that equality of opportunity is possible without equality of condition.

3. Explain the difference between apparent upward social mobility due to structural changes in the economy and "real" upward social mobility.

4. Why did Marx consider the hiring of one person by another to be exploitive?

5. Why does the Canadian working class lack class consciousness? How big is the Canadian working class?

6. What is cultural capital? What kinds of cultural capital have you received from your family and friends? How is cultural capital transformed into real capital?

7. Does the widespread consensus on occupational prestige rankings indicate that functionalists are right in asserting that social stratification is beneficial to society? Why or why not?

   Research Suggestion: Considering that occupational prestige rankings have demonstrated a remarkable stability over several decades, is it possible for people to improve their status without changing their jobs? Compare recent prestige rankings with rankings done several decades ago. Choose, for further study, an occupation that showed the greatest upward or downward movement in the rankings over time. Try to account for this movement. Is there a relationship between a change in status and a relative change in:
   a) income
   b) degree of professional organization and the use of social closure
   c) working conditions
   d) educational requirements needed for the job
   e) some other factor.
   If you do find a relationship, how does it work? Did the status change cause a change in the other factors or did it happen the other way around?

ANSWERS TO CHAPTER 10

Key Terms

1. c	6. g
2. f	7. a
3. i	8. e
4. h	9. j
5. b	10. d

Test

1. d	11. d	21. d
2. c	12. a	22. c
3. b	13. b	23. a
4. a	14. a	24. d
5. d	15. d	25. b
6. b	16. b	26. c
7. d	17. c	27. b
8. a	18. b	28. b
9. d	19. c	29. c
10. a	20. a	30. d

Pretest

1. c	7. b
2. c	8. a
3. d	9. a
4. c	10. d
5. d	11. a
6. d	12. c

Posttest

1. a	7. d
2. d	8. d
3. c	9. a
4. b	10. c
5. c	11. c
6. d	12. d

CHAPTER 11   ECONOMIC INSTITUTIONS AND POWER

Key Terms

1. institution

2. economic institutions

3. mode of production

4. relations of production

5. instrumentalist view

6. structuralist view

7. extraterritoriality

a) the neo-Marxist theory that the state has a limited autonomy to act in matters that do not threaten the capitalist class's long-term interests

b) the Marxist term for a set of interrelated economic institutions which includes both the forces and relations of production

c) the neo-Marxist theory that the capitalist class exercises nearly total control over the state

d) the application of laws made in a multi-national enterprise's home country to the countries where the MNE has branch operations

e) the set of organizations which produce and distribute goods and services

f) the central elements of social organization which mobilize people and resources in ways consistent with society's values

g) the class, property and power relationships involved in a mode of production

Pretest

1. The form an economic institution will take depends on the society's:
   a) basic mode of production
   b) available technology
   c) central values
   d) all of the above

2. When it comes to studying economic institutions, economists tend to focus more on _____ than sociologists do.

   a) market factors
   b) the power structure
   c) class inequalities
   d) cross cultural analysis

3. According to the doctrine of laissez-faire, an economic system which allowed individuals to pursue their own selfish interests would result in:
   a) economic chaos

b) high levels of pollution and concentration of ownership
c) general prosperity
d) all of the above

4. Marx thought _____ would eventually lead to ownership of the means of production being concentrated in fewer and fewer hands.
a) technological improvements
b) international stock exchanges
c) trade tariffs
d) trade unionism

5. Which of the following practices is *not* an example of planned obsolescence?
a) changing the trim on North American automobiles each year
b) holding seasonal fashion shows
c) marketing a medical drug that may soon be improved upon
d) selling panty hose which get runs easily

6. The two world wars were largely a struggle:
a) over political ideals
b) over access to markets
c) over human rights
d) between classes

7. The _____ view of some neo-Marxists argues the state will occasionally meet working class demands if the long-term interests of capitalism are not threatened.
a) structuralist
b) instrumentalist
c) reformist
d) situational

8. The degree of foreign control of the Canadian economy:
a) is rising rapidly
b) is highest in the banking sector
c) is among the highest in the industrialized world
d) all of the above

9. The "staples trap" refers to:

a) recurring "busts" in the demand for raw materials
b) Canada's inaction in breaking its dependence on the export of raw materials
c) the need to constantly find technological innovations for extracting raw materials
d) the gradual depletion of Canada's non-renewable resources

10. Contrary to the Merchant Against Industry thesis, one 1982 study found that Canadian merchants were:
a) strong supporters of industrialization
b) strongly opposed to industrialization
c) often industrialists too
d) indifferent to the issue of industrialization

11. The relationship between economic power and the state was:
a) largely ignored by Marx and Modern Marxists
b) seen by Max Weber as very complex
c) seen by Max Weber as a reflection of the class struggle
d) largely ignored by Max Weber

12. Many sociologists are concerned that multinational enterprise:
a) threatens national sovereignty
b) exports political and economic power
c) exports jobs
d) all of the above

13. Canada's low ratio of tradition carriers to new arrivals is one explanation for:
a) the "boom-bust" nature of the Canadian economy
b) the value of changes of the 1960s
c) our weak sense of national identity
d) all of the above

14. Regional specialization of economic activity in Canada has been attributed to:

a) geography
b) political action
c) the high degree of foreign control of Canadian manufacturing
d) all of the above

15. Canadian sociologists:
a) have developed several competing explanations of the nature of the Canadian economy
b) generally agree on the nature of the Canadian economy
c) tend to ignore the relationship between economy and society, in contrast to their American counterparts
d) are reluctant to search for answers to complex puzzles

Test

1. Social institutions are:
a) organizations
b) collections of organizations
c) concerned only with mobilization of people and resources
d) concerned only with values

2. Every society contains:
a) economic institutions
b) political institutions
c) family institutions
d) all of the above

3. Economic institutions perform the basic material processes of:
a) production and distribution
b) capital and labour
c) technology and organization
d) none of the above

4. To a sociologist, power is:
a) an attribute
b) a relationship
c) the inverse of dependence
d) both b and c

5. The disparity in economic power between the prairie wheat farmer and the central Canadian manufacturer occurs because:
a) wheat farming is inherently unprofitable
b) manufacturing is inherently profitable
c) of differences in their ability to withhold production from the market
d) all of the above

6. In tribal societies, production is generally based on:
a) an extensive division of labour
b) a formal occupational structure
c) private ownership of the means of production
d) the kinship unit

7. In capitalist industrial society, the distribution of wealth generated by economic activity is determined by:
a) economic criteria, such as ownership of the means of production
b) non-economic criteria, such as kinship obligations
c) people's needs
d) tradition

8. In socialist industrial society, productive decisions are based upon:
a) profit maximization
b) the law of supply and demand
c) centralized planning to meet consumer demand and political objectives
d) all of the above

9. According to Emile Durkheim:
a) economy shapes society
b) economic institutions change in response to population pressures
c) organic solidarity results from a complex division of labour
d) all of the above

10. Which of the following is *not* true of Karl Marx's concept of the *mode of production*?
a) it comprises the *forces of production* and the *relations of production*

b) friction between the forces and relations of production inevitably produces social change
c) the relations of production are relatively static in a given epoch
d) the forces of production are constantly changing

11. In Max Weber's analysis:
    a) economy shapes society
    b) society shapes economy
    c) the causal direction is unclear
    d) population pressures are the underlying causal element

12. Max Weber's analysis showed:
    a) the disintegration of the Roman Empire resulted from the decline of commerce
    b) capitalist agriculture developed in England because England needed to maintain a large army
    c) tension between the forces and relations of production produces economic change
    d) all of the above

13. Which of the following did *not* contribute to the rise of capitalism in the analyses of *both* Marx and Weber?
    a) the separation of the labourer from the means of production
    b) the rise of rationality
    c) the expropriation of the English agricultural producer
    d) European inflation resulting from Spain's gold imports

14. Karl Marx analysed capitalism as a process producing:
    a) commodities
    b) surplus value
    c) the continuing reproduction of the relation between capitalist and wage labourer
    d) all of the above

15. According to Max Weber, which of the following did *not* contribute to the rise of capitalism?

a) the rise of rationality
b) the influence of ascetic Protestantism
c) conspicuous consumption by the rich
d) the development of bureaucracy

16. According to Karl Marx, the ultimate result of capitalist competition will be:
    a) a more equitable division of surplus values
    b) the doctrine of "laissez-faire"
    c) a growing number of competitive firms
    d) the overthrow of capitalism

17. One reason Marx's anticipated revolution by the working class has not occurred in advanced capitalist societies is:
    a) reduced price competition has permitted increased wages
    b) the rate of surplus value has declined
    c) unions have become too powerful
    d) the re-emergence of Adam Smith's "laissez-faire" philosophy

18. Sociologists have found that unemployment breeds deviance because:
    a) deviants don't make good workers
    b) unemployed workers face financial ruin and starvation
    c) unemployed workers are robbed of their raison-d'etre
    d) all of the above

19. The North American auto industry has been a good example of industrial success in promoting the "throw away" society because:
    a) it promoted the idea of "keeping up with the Joneses"
    b) it increased the demand for automobiles
    c) it permitted cars to be made more cheaply
    d) all of the above

20. The overthrow of the values of the "throw away society" would likely cause:
    a) increased employment
    b) increased unemployment
    c) a more equitable distribution of wealth
    d) lower quality goods to be produced

21. It has been found that multinational enterprise:
    a) is always guided by the laws of its home society
    b) is always guided by the values of its home society
    c) is always guided by the values of its host society
    d) may be guided by the values of either its home society or its host society

22. Which of the following is *not* claimed to be a benefit of management control of large corporations?
    a) it breaks down the rigid class system
    b) economic power becomes based on achievement rather than inheritance
    c) it reduces the economic power of large corporations
    d) it enhances social mobility

23. The rise of management control:
    a) has been conclusively demonstrated
    b) has been conclusively rejected
    c) seems to be a sporadic long-term process
    d) has been found to threaten national sovereignty

24. Canadian society can be differentiated from other industrial capitalist societies by:
    a) the degree of foreign control of our economy
    b) the degree of regionalism
    c) our weak sense of national unity
    d) the combination of all of the above

25. Canadian and American sociology differ in explaining the nature of our respective societies. Explanations are usually based on:
    a) race in the U.S. but on ethnicity in Canada
    b) social structures in Canada but on individual traits in the U.S.
    c) social structure in America but on individual traits in Canada
    d) social structures in America but on values in Canada

26. The *staples perspective* has been used to explain:
    a) Canada's high standard of living
    b) Canada's low standard of living
    c) Canada's "boom-bust" economy
    d) the growth of Canadian multinationals

27. The *staples perspective* has been used to explain:
    a) Canada's retarded industrialization
    b) Canada's high degree of regionalism
    c) Canada's pattern of immigration
    d) all of the above

28. The "Merchants Against Industry Argument" proposes that:
    a) Canadian manufacturers could not expand because the ruling merchant class would not allow them to
    b) Canadian merchants could not survive because the ruling industrial class would not allow them to
    c) Canada is a passive hinterland, unable to control its economy
    d) Canada has moved from colony to nation

29. Ontario personal per capita income is currently double the personal incomes in P.E.I. and Newfoundland. This ratio:
    a) has remained constant over the last 50 years

b) has increased over the last 50 years

c) has declined over the last 50 years

d) illustrates how society shapes economy

30. Canadian regionalism can be effectively analysed in terms of:
a) the distributive function of economic institutions
b) dominance and dependency
c) the "Merchants Against Industry Argument"
d) all of the above

Posttest

1. In tribal societies an economic surplus is usually distributed on the basis of:
a) need
b) tradition and military prowess
c) equal shares for each
d) chance

2. According to Marx, the forces of production are constantly changing because of:
a) population pressures
b) technological developments
c) the division of labour
d) all of the above

3. According to Weber, the Protestant prohibition of _____ contributed to the growth of capitalism.
a) gambling
b) individualism
c) conspicuous consumption
d) competition

4. Laissez-faire capitalism has gradually evolved into:
a) state socialism
b) the welfare state
c) mercantilism
d) free trade

5. Duberman and Hartzen concluded that so many people get into debt problems because of:

a) ignorance about personal finances
b) the ease of getting credit
c) the effectiveness of modern advertising
d) all of the above

6. The positive aspect of planned obsolescence is that it:
a) stimulates sales and employment
b) encourages research and development
c) rewards high quality workmanship
d) helps to conserve our non-renewable resources

7. A 1985 study by the Canadian Bankers' Association concluded that nine Canadian families control _____ of the 300 most important companies on the Toronto Stock Exchange.
a) about one quarter
b) about one third
c) nearly one half
d) almost two thirds

8. The staples perspective was developed by:
a) Max Weber
b) Harold Innis
c) David Staples
d) Marshall McLuhan

9. Sociologists are more interested than economists are in explaining the relationship between:
a) economic systems and the creation of wealth
b) competition and profits
c) the economy and society
d) labour and productivity

10. Which of the following is *not* an example of the kind of staples referred to in Innis' staples perspective?
a) oil extracted in Alberta
b) gold mined in Timmins
c) trees felled in British Columbia
d) cars built in Oshawa

11. Many scholars believe the pervasiveness of multinational enterprises:
    a) threatens Canadian sovereignty
    b) creates barriers to social mobility for Canadian executives
    c) has been greatly exaggerated
    d) none of the above

12. The concept of extraterritoriality refers to the fact that multinational enterprises often:
    a) must break the law of one country to obey the law in another
    b) expand their operations beyond an efficient size
    c) act as agents for their home country's government
    d) all of the above

13. Canada's low ratio of tradition carriers to new arrivals is one explanation for:
    a) the "boom-bust" nature of our economy

    b) the multicultural nature of Canadian society
    c) our weak sense of national identity
    d) the slow pace of Canada's industrialization and urbanization

14. The various explanations of the nature of Canadian economy outlined in the text all illustrate:
    a) how the economy shapes society
    b) how society shapes the economy
    c) the complex relationships between economy and society
    d) that there is no relationship between economy and society

15. Canadian regionalism is:
    a) primarily a social phenomenon
    b) primarily an economic phenomenon
    c) both an economic and a social phenomenon
    d) primarily a geographic phenomenon

Essay Questions

1. How does a person's job affect the way he or she sees the world? Illustrate your points with specific examples.

2. What are the arguments for and against limiting the amount of foreign control of Canadian corporations? Is the ownership question more important in some economic sectors than in others? Which sectors, if any, do you think should be Canadian owned? Justify your choices.

3. What is the staples trap? Suggest some ways of escaping from this trap. Why haven't these ways already been tried?

4. Is Canada's social structure conducive to building a strong national identity and sense of unity?

5. What are the costs and benefits of the "throw away society"? Why might the throw away society be fading out of existence? What will (or should) replace it?

6. How does laissez-faire capitalism differ from corporate capitalism? What forces caused this evolution? How, if at all, is corporate capitalism likely to change in the coming decades?

7. What sorts of factors should the federal government consider when deciding whether or not a foreign corporation should be allowed to invest in Canada?

8. What are the chief differences between a corporation in a capitalist society and a corporation in a state socialist society? What are the chief similarities between the two corporations?

Research Suggestion: To better understand the relationship between occupation and world view, consider the case of farmers. Find some statistics on the declining number of farms in North America and Europe. Note that the trend is both widespread and persistent. Talk to some farmers to find out why they like their jobs and try to find some ex-farmers who were forced into new lines of work because of financial problems. How are the ex-farmers adjusting to new jobs? How have their lifestyles been changed by changing their jobs? Try to suggest some ways to make the transition out of farming as smooth as possible.

ANSWERS TO CHAPTER 11

Test

1. b	11. c	21. d
2. d	12. a	22. c
3. a	13. b	23. c
4. d	14. d	24. d
5. c	15. c	25. b
6. d	16. d	26. c
7. a	17. a	27. d
8. c	18. c	28. a
9. d	19. d	29. a
10. b	20. b	30. b

Key Terms

1. f	5. c
2. e	6. a
3. b	7. d
4. g	

Pretest

1. d	6. b	11. b
2. a	7. a	12. d
3. c	8. c	13. c
4. a	9. b	14. d
5. c	10. c	15. c

Posttest

1. b	6. a	11. d
2. d	7. c	12. a
3. c	8. b	13. d
4. b	9. c	14. c
5. c	10. d	15. c

CHAPTER 12   MASS MEDIA AND INFLUENCE

Key Terms

1. administrative research

a) the shaping of a common outlook or world view among heavy consumers of television

2. critical research

    b) a content analysis of the cultural messages implicit and explicit in the media (such as American television dramas)

3. consciousness scale

    c) the special salience a television feature has for a specific group

4. gender display

    d) the science of signs which studies media messages as structural wholes

5. message system analysis

    e) the tendency to voice only opinions that we think others will agree with

6. cultivation analysis

    f) studies which use the "who says what, through what channel, to whom with what effect" approach

7. mainstreaming

    g) studies which analyse communications phenomena in terms of how they fit into and support a given social system

8. resonance

    h) the process of making some social issues more salient than others to the public

9. cultivation theory

    i) a way of measuring how women are portrayed in advertising

10. semiotics

    j) the editorial function of deciding what should get into the media and how much prominence it should be given

11. gatekeeping

    k) survey research that studies how recurrent television images affect viewers' perceptions of the world

12. agenda setting

    l) the view that media content affects the way regular media consumers see the world

13. spiral of silence

    m) conventionalized portrayals of people performing gestures or behaviours that have been traditionally linked with one sex

Pretest

1. The stimulus response model of the mass media assumed the media could effectively:
   a) shape public opinion
   b) set the political agenda
   c) educate the bulk of the population
   d) preoccupy the public with shallow entertainment

2. Critical theorists study the media's ideological role of:
   a) defining reality
   b) setting political agendas
   c) legitimizing the status quo
   d) all of the above

3. Wallace Clement thinks the dominant capitalist interests in Canadian society control:
   a) most of the private media
   b) private broadcast and some print media
   c) the public media
   d) the private and public media

4. Ethnic minorities are _____ in the Canadian media.
   a) portrayed fairly accurately
   b) almost always of European ancestry
   c) underrepresented
   d) overrepresented

5. In the 1970s, the women's movement focused mainly on how the media _____women.
   a) misinform, stereotype and degrade
   b) stereotype, underrepresent and trivialize
   c) exploit, flatter and educate
   d) all of the above

6. The media-created image of feminists as "bra burners" is an example of how the media have _____ the women's movement.
   a) sensationalized
   b) popularized
   c) lied about
   d) trivialized

7. American elite journalists rank which group as the most powerful?
   a) themselves
   b) the business elite
   c) labour and consumer group leaders
   d) intellectuals

8. Agenda setting refers to the process of:
   a) choosing a line-up for a news broadcast
   b) rating television by popularity
   c) stereotyping ethnic or other groups
   d) making some social issues more salient to the public than others

9. Elisabeth Noelle-Neuman thinks that people who avoid voicing opinions that may be controversial or unpopular reinforce:
   a) cultural stereotypes
   b) public opinion
   c) the spiral of silence
   d) conservative ideologies

10. "Copycat" crimes that imitate crimes seen in the media:
    a) have never been documented
    b) would probably happen without media prompting
    c) illustrate the effects of the spiral of silence
    d) rarely happen

Test

1. The empirical approach to the study of mass communication:
   a) is a North American approach
   b) is primarily concerned with effects
   c) lacks a unifying body of theory
   d) all of the above

2. The phrase: "who says what, through what channel, to whom with what effect" was introduced by:
   a) Lasswell
   b) Longwell
   c) Lassman
   d) Smith

3. Wright described the functions of the media as:
   a) surveillance, correlation and cultural transmission
   b) surveillance, correlation, cultural transmission and entertainment
   c) cultural transmission, relaxation and entertainment
   d) news, entertainment, vicarious pleasure and companionship

4. According to Smythe the main function of the media is:
   a) mobilization
   b) entertainment
   c) socialization
   d) creating audiences for advertisers

5. The major difference between the critical and empirical approaches is that the critical approach emphasizes:
   a) the audience
   b) the ideology
   c) communicators
   d) advertisers

6. One study found newscasts show an anti-union bias in:
   a) their emphasis on particular kinds of industrial disputes
   b) the structure and placement of interviews
   c) both a and b
   d) none of the above

7. "Black Wednesday" refers to:
   a) race riots in Detroit
   b) the closing of two Canadian newspapers in Canada in 1980
   c) the low point of the 1982 recession
   d) none of the above

8. The Kent Commission recommended that:
   a) media ownership be restricted
   b) media content be improved
   c) the media should be publicly owned
   d) all of the above

9. Hard news:
   a) is difficult to report
   b) requires immediate coverage
   c) is seldom reported
   d) is seldom reported in electronic media

10. The "consciousness scale" measures:
    a) our attitudes to advertisers
    b) images of women in advertising
    c) our receptivity to advertising
    d) how aware of their surroundings people are

11. Symbolic annihilation refers to the:
    a) distortion of cultural symbols by the media
    b) amount of violence in the media
    c) threat of nuclear war
    d) media's treatment of women

12. Message system analysis:
    a) is used to analyse the content of American television dramas
    b) is the study of network news
    c) compares newspaper coverage to television reporting
    d) is also called cultivation analysis

13. What percent of leading characters are involved in violence in television drama?
    a) over one quarter
    b) over one third
    c) over half
    d) over three quarters

14. The amount of violence on television:
    a) has declined in response to public complaints
    b) is relatively stable year to year
    c) has increased in the 1980s
    d) has no effect on viewer perceptions

15. The fact that "heavy" television viewers share a common outlook is called:
    a) mainlining
    b) homogenizing
    c) mainstreaming
    d) standardizing

16. "Heavy" television viewers share a common outlook:
    a) but there are important differences between men and women
    b) but level of education makes a difference
    c) but race is an important differentiating factor
    d) despite differences in race, income and education

17. Gerbner found that "heavy" television viewers:
    a) were mostly housewives
    b) were between the ages of 20 and 40
    c) expressed feelings of mistrust and anger
    d) had a strong sense of reality

18. That soap opera viewers exaggerate the extent of social problems in the "real" world:
    a) refutes the cultivation theory
    b) supports the cultivation theory
    c) is cause for alarm
    d) is unimportant since a large number of viewers are students

19. What percent of children's television programs contain some violence?
    a) over 60
    b) over 70
    c) over 80
    d) over 90

20. Content analysis involves:
    a) the quantitative anlysis of media content
    b) the analysis of communicators' intentions
    c) the analysis of the effects of media content
    d) all of the above

21. Semiotics differs from content analysis in that semiotics:
    a) is not quantitative
    b) is not generalizable
    c) concentrates on latent messages
    d) all of the above

22. The structure of news reports:
    a) varies widely over time
    b) differs a great deal from culture to culture
    c) demonstrates few consistent patterns
    d) none of the above

23. Journalists see themselves as:
    a) an endangered profession
    b) very powerful
    c) pawns in the system
    d) victims of circumstance

24. Getlin thinks that trying to measure the effects of the media:
    a) is not as hard as sociologists make it out to be
    b) is a waste of time
    c) is like expecting a fish to discover the effects of water
    d) should be the most important focus of study

25. The process whereby social issues become salient is called:
    a) issue setting
    b) salience setting
    c) agenda setting
    d) none of the above

26. The spiral of silence refers to:
    a) the media cover-up of political scandals
    b) the uncritical nature of media content
    c) the fact that television has replaced family interaction
    d) the media's influence on public opinion

27. People who think their opinions are not widely held will:
    a) avoid voicing those opinions
    b) try to convert others to their ideas
    c) change their opinions
    d) all of the above

28. The study of effects of the media:
    a) is the greatest preoccupation in this field

b) has been dominated by laboratory experiments
c) is a controversial issue
d) all of the above

29. Phillips' studies of imitative behaviour found:
a) suicides increased following media reports of suicide
b) suicides declined following media reports of suicides
c) no relationship between the incidence of suicide and news reports of suicide
d) none of the above

30. Soap opera suicides:
a) have no effect on suicide rates
b) are followed by an increase in suicide rates
c) suppress the tendency to commit suicide
d) none of the above

Posttest

1. The media's influence on shaping definitions of social reality is now thought to be:
a) fairly weak
b) strong and direct
c) indirect, cumulative and powerful
d) powerful but temporary in its effects

2. Television reporters often "encode" their news stories by:
a) lying
b) reporting the story in a biased way
c) using subliminal seduction
d) all of the above

3. On any given day, more than half the daily newspapers sold in Canada are published by one of _____ newspaper publishing companies.
a) two
b) three
c) five
d) eight

4. According to Pierre Berton, one of the biggest purveyors of misleading stereotypes about Canada has been the:
a) Canadian school systems
b) Hollywood movie industry
c) American-owned book publishing companies
d) advertising industry

5. Soft news:
a) requires immediate coverage
b) usually makes for action-filled television
c) is often about trends rather than single events
d) usually takes precedence over hard news

6. The structure of a Canadian television news show from 1965 would differ from a Japanese news broadcast in 1985
a) very little
b) mainly in the pace and overall length
c) in a great many ways
d) none of the above

7. An editor who puts a story about a housing shortage on the back pages of the newspaper is exercising her role as a media:
a) censor
b) gatekeeper
c) regulator
d) distorter

8. Public opinion surveys found that before the Watergate hearings were televised only about _____ % of Americans knew about the story.
a) 10
b) 35
c) 50
d) 60

9. Which of the following cannot be considered a product of the spiral of silence?

a) standardized news lineups
b) the concentration of media ownership
c) the success of political "bandwagons"
d) an apparently large degree of social consensus

a) the media are omnipresent
b) the effects are temporary
c) the media are a powerful interest group
d) effects are qualitative, not quantitative

10. Media effects are difficult to measure because:

Essay Questions

1. What causes a culture of silence? Does this theory adequately account for shifts in public opinion?

2. How does the need to make a profit influence and limit the kind of product the privately owned mass media produce?

3. What are some arguments for and against allowing greater concentration of ownership of the Canadian mass media?

4. Why is semiotics "unscientific"? Does that label mean it is not a proper area for sociologists to study?

5. Given the fragmentation of the marketplace for the consumers of media products (i.e. the proliferation of specialty magazines and radio stations, pay television, cable TV, VCRs etc.), does it make sense to speak of a "mass media" any longer? If not, what are the wider, societal implications of the decline of mass society?

Research Suggestion: Consider the question of who has the most access to the media. Do a content analysis of the news section of your local newspaper for one week (or a local television or radio news broadcast) and record who gets quoted and asked to comment on issues. Also, take note of the slant (i.e. positive or negative or neutral) and the prominence (i.e. length and positioning in the paper or broadcast) given to each story. Note any obviously biased reporting. See if you can find any similarities among the people whose views appear most (or least) often in the media. Try to account for why some kinds of people appear more often than others in the media.

ANSWERS TO CHAPTER 12

Key Terms			Pretest	
1. f	6. k	11. j	1. a	6. d
2. g	7. a	12. h	2. d	7. b
3. i	8. c	13. e	3. d	8. d
4. m	9. l		4. c	9. c
5. b	10. d		5. b	10. d

Test

1. b	11. d	21. d
2. a	12. a	22. d
3. b	13. c	23. b
4. d	14. b	24. c
5. b	15. c	25. c
6. c	16. d	26. d
7. b	17. c	27. a
8. a	18. b	28. d
9. b	19. d	29. a
10. b	20. a	30. b

Posttest

1. c	6. a
2. b	7. b
3. a	8. c
4. b	9. b
5. c	10. a

CHAPTER 13   TECHNOLOGY AND SOCIAL CHANGE

Key Terms

1. hardware

   a) the four-stage research process consisting of 1) studying a problem 2) building a theory 3) testing the theory 4) using the test results to fully or partially solve the original problem

2. software

   b) physical objects which can be used as tools i.e. machines, bridges etc.

3. technostructure

   c) concepts, theories, ideas, attitudes which can be used as tools

4. technical operation

   d) Galbraith's term for the "brain of a corporation" in which formally educated people co-ordinate the company's many activities

Pretest

1. Before a traditional society can begin to effectively utilize modern technology, that society must:
   a) sell the idea of modernization to most of the citizens
   b) fundamentally change its culture and organization
   c) rebuild a transportation and communications structure
   d) all of the above

2. The technical mentality uses rationality to try to maximize:
   a) efficiency
   b) power
   c) profits
   d) all of the above

3. The first social class to fully embrace the cultural values of modern capitalism was the:

a) bourgeoisie
b) aristocracy
c) peasantry
d) urban working class

4. The technical revolution and the accompanying cultural transformation:
   a) was led by the technical revolution
   b) reinforced each other
   c) worked at cross purposes
   d) was led by the cultural transformation

5. Underdevelopment in the Third World typically divides societies by pitting:
   a) the rich against the poor
   b) tribe against tribe
   c) modern elements against traditional elements
   d) the young against the old

6. Auguste Comte saw social progress and social evolution as:
   a) inevitable
   b) illusory
   c) a mixed blessing
   d) incompatible

7. Auguste Comte advocated directing all thought and action towards the establishment of a(n) _____ society.
   a) theocratic
   b) just
   c) industrial
   d) classless

8. Before the late nineteenth century, knowledge was acquired:
   a) mainly through apprenticeship systems
   b) in a haphazard, inefficient way
   c) mainly through formal school systems
   d) mainly by reading books

9. Twentieth century corporations have typically reduced the risks of

spending a lot of time and money on developing new products that may not sell well by:
   a) developing fewer new products
   b) diversifying their product lines
   c) establishing market monopolies
   d) all of the above

10. The technical operation could not be used effectively to:
    a) increase productivity on a farm
    b) solve someone's moral dilemma
    c) improve the sexual satisfaction of a husband and wife
    d) help a hockey team to win more games

11. Applying technical solutions to problems often creates new problems because:
    a) of Murphy's law
    b) most problems are non-technical
    c) technical experts are often ignorant of other fields
    d) workers often sabotage automation projects to avoid losing their jobs

12. The tendency to technically analyse more and more aspects of life is difficult to slow down because:
    a) technocrats are gaining in social power
    b) our social and economic planners think unidimensionally
    c) consumers expect better gadgets every year
    d) technical innovations produce economic rewards

13. The third primary milieu that humans have experienced, the technique milieu, began:
    a) when the first human tools were built
    b) with the arrival of the post-industrial society
    c) with the industrial revolution
    d) after World War II

Test

1. In the 20th century the impact of technology is:
   a) severely restricted by cultural boundaries
   b) increasingly universal
   c) contributing to the diversity of human culture
   d) helping to strengthen the indigenous knowledge base of different countries

2. The transfer of modern technology to traditional Third World societies is problematic because it:
   a) yields different results from those observed in the industrialized nations
   b) requires vast amounts of capital, a high degree of planning and special resources
   c) fundamentally alters the culture and social structure of the recipient society
   d) all of the above

3. The concept of an Industrial Revolution is useful because:
   a) it reminds us of a set of theories which gave too narrow an account of what was happening at that time
   b) it focuses our attention on where the real revolution took place, namely in industry
   c) similar changes in other areas of society were relatively insignificant compared to the changes in industry
   d) it focuses our attention on the decisive role machines played in the transformation of society

4. The technical orientation of the Western European societies, where industrialization began, is not characterized by:
   a) a mechanistic world view
   b) customs and traditions rooted in technology
   c) a rational conception of human life and society
   d) a sense of the possibility of human progress

5. The putting-out system of textile making was *not* a system:
   a) in which people produced textiles at home
   b) in which people used spinning wheels and hand looms
   c) which employed rural people when they were not working on the land
   d) that gave entrepreneurs effective control over the production process

6. The traditional putting-out system of production in England:
   a) was incompatible with rural life and subsistence farming
   b) responded effectively to changes in the demand for textiles
   c) illustrates the highly interrelated character of a society as reflected in the network of the flow of goods
   d) was ideally suited to experimentation with the mechanization of textile making

7. The new factory-based system of production that arose in England in the first half of the 19th century did *not* involve:
   a) a highly developed technological division of labour
   b) a high level of control over the production process
   c) the application of science to any significant degree
   d) the accumulation of large amounts of capital

8. As industrialization advanced, the change from a rural to an urban society did *not* involve the:
   a) hiring of wage earners who had to buy basic necessities
   b) emergence of a powerful dominant class who controlled capital

c) weakening of the family unit
d) gradual emergence of a group morality to offset the weakening of the family

9. The large cities which emerged as a result of industrialization did *not* create a need for techniques:
a) for city planning
b) for sewage disposal
c) of amusement
d) of commerce

10. A so-called underdeveloped society:
a) is poorer and less progressive than other societies
b) lags behind the industrial nations because of colonialism
c) contains incompatible modern and traditional elements which cannot be integrated into a coherent way of life
d) wishes to industrialize but lacks resources to do so

11. Who advocated applying scientific and technical reason embodied in a new science that he called sociology, to ensure the transformation from a military and theological past to a scientific and industrial future?
a) Max Weber
b) Henri de Saint-Simon
c) Auguste Comte
d) Karl Marx

12. Which of the following is *not* an aspect of alienation in the capitalist system as described by Karl Marx?
a) workers being bought and sold as merchandise in the form of a mobile working force
b) the poverty of the proletariat
c) people being valued only for their money and possessions, such as their labour power
d) the false consciousness of the proletariat

13. According to Durkheim, the mechanical solidarity of earlier societies was characterized by:
a) intense social differentiation and complex division of labour
b) a high degree of individual choice
c) a strong collective consciousness and a high level of integration of the individual into the community
d) widely varying values, experiences and emotions

14. Max Weber believed the rationalization of society:
a) can become an end in itself, undermining all other goals and values
b) could make an individual powerless to direct her affairs
c) could create a whole range of new problems that cannot be resolved by industrialization
d) all of the above

15. Organic solidarity as defined by Durkheim is *not* characterized by:
a) a relationship of complementarity between members of society
b) a collective consciousness which is weaker than that of a society characterized by mechanical solidarity
c) an absence of anomie
d) the absence or disintegration of norms

16. The latter part of the 19th century saw a complete transformation of the technological knowledge base in industrial societies. This new knowledge base:
a) was founded on empirical knowledge passed on from one generation to the next
b) led to knowers and doers increasingly becoming the same persons
c) depended on formal education and specialized training
d) none of the above

17. The process of restructuring the large corporation during the 1950s and 60s involved:
    a) many people with complementary types of empirical knowledge collaborating
    b) highly advanced factories that can produce a diversity of products
    c) the creation of a technostructure
    d) a decrease in the time needed to design a new product

18. The newly developed technical knowledge base did *not* force the large corporation to:
    a) increase its reliance on the market to supply the specialized materials needed for its new products
    b) manage consumer demand through such techniques as advertising
    c) rely on the state to provide the specialists for its technostructure through the funding of educational institutions
    d) diversify its product line to minimize risk

19. The widespread application of the new technical knowledge base during the first half of the 20th century did *not* contribute to:
    a) the creation of a mass society
    b) an increase in consumer sovereignty with respect to the large producers
    c) the need to create equal educational opportunities for all
    d) the creation of a public sector in the economy

20. Increasingly, modern societies are best characterized by:
    a) high technology industries
    b) the phenomenon of technique
    c) a wide range of activities based on custom or tradition grounded in a technical culture
    d) a belief that the quality of life cannot be improved merely by making the means of existence more efficient

21. Much of the present speculation about the possibilities of computer technology fails to take into account the:
    a) socio-cultural context in which the computer was invented and continues to be applied
    b) fact that information techniques are not culturally neutral
    c) potential negative social effects making information and knowledge-related activities more efficient
    d) all of the above

22. In traditional, non-technicized work:
    a) workers must, to a considerable extent, suppress their personality, state of mind and past experiences
    b) a high level of nervous fatigue is often experienced
    c) the work is performed on the basis of the person's mental map
    d) the mind makes it impossible to live each work experience holistically

23. Modern advertising is:
    a) an example of the way techniques mediate between producers and consumers in a non-neutral fashion
    b) a neutral diffusion of information about the products
    c) a form of symbolic manipulation which affects people in ways of which they are fully conscious
    d) a way of using information to undermine consumer sovereignty

24. Once most of the relationships engaged in by the members of a society become technically mediated:
    a) human consciousness stops being affected by the primary milieu
    b) technique becomes the primary milieu
    c) the social milieu disappears
    d) alienation is reduced

25. A relationship mediated by the telephone is:
   a) culturally neutral because it allows members from different cultures to communicate with one another
   b) not culturally neutral because it is indirect communication
   c) not culturally neutral because communication is much more than the exchange of the spoken word
   d) none of the above

26. The milieu of technique appears to be:
   a) taking over from culture as the social foundation
   b) changing the way we symbolically mediate all our relationships
   c) affecting the very nature of individual and collective existence
   d) all of the above

27. The technicization of life has generated a wealth of information which greatly increases individual autonomy because:
   a) people use this information to become better informed about an ever greater range of activities
   b) a greater diversity of experts can be consulted about areas where people are not knowledgeable
   c) all of the above
   d) none of the above

28. The main problem associated with technique having become the primary milieu of human life is:
   a) the arms race threatens human existence
   b) it is impossible for people to fully participate in technicized relationships
   c) the destabilization of the ecosystem and economic alienation
   d) a growing anomie due to the decline of traditional values

29. The "cure" for the alienation produced by an overly technicized society is, according to Chapter 13:
   a) a return to traditional values
   b) retraining workers who lose their jobs to automation
   c) the creation of a culture not based on technique
   d) better forms of escapism

30. In the post-industrial society, the most important resource is expected to be:
   a) information
   b) people
   c) energy
   d) capital

Posttest

1. The modern state emerged as a product of:
   a) urbanization
   b) capitalism
   c) the French Revolution
   d) mercantilism

2. Most analyses of the effect of technology on society have focused on the technologies':
   a) hardware
   b) software
   c) achievements
   d) problems

3. The major reason for putting several looms in one textile factory was that this allowed the factory owner to:
   a) compare the efficiency of different loom designs
   b) compare the efficiency of different work crews
   c) fully utilize a central power source
   d) increase the total output of the looms

4. Many analysts argue that it was easier for Western Europe to modernize in the past than it is for the Third World countries to modernize today because Europe:

a) was not colonized
b) had abundant natural resources
c) did not have to compete with nations that were economically stronger than itself
d) all of the above

5. Auguste Comte and Henri de Saint-Simon agreed that the key to human progress lay in developing and applying:
    a) steam power
    b) scientific and technical reason
    c) moral rigour
    d) ways of accumulating capital

6. Durkheim thought the absence or weakening of norms in modern societies creates a sense of _____ in people.
    a) alienation
    b) anomie
    c) rebelliousness
    d) joy

7. Max Weber believed industrialization was part of the larger phenomenon of the _____ of society.
    a) modernization
    b) urbanization
    c) democratization
    d) rationalization

8. The growth of formal education in the late 19th century accelerated the separation between:
    a) white collar and blue collar workers
    b) intelligent and unintelligent people
    c) knowers and doers
    d) the arts and the sciences

9. Galbraith used the term _____ to describe a corporation's brain, the body of formally trained specialists who co-ordinate the company's diverse functions.
    a) superstructure
    b) executive branch
    c) technostructure
    d) data processing group

10. In the 20th century, governments have supported the efforts of corporations by:
    a) expanding the educational system
    b) regulating the economy
    c) stimulating scientific and technical research
    d) all of the above

11. The three primary milieus human beings have experienced were described in this chapter as:
    a) natural, social and technical
    b) nomadic, rural and urban
    c) prehistoric, religious and scientific
    d) nomadic, agrarian and urban

12. The technicization of life produces a kind of alienation in:
    a) consumers
    b) all social classes
    c) primarily the working class
    d) artistic people

13. Technical solutions to problems created further problems when:
    a) pesticides were used to kill insects
    b) weapon systems were built to defend countries
    c) factories automated to improve productivity
    d) all of the above

Essay Questions

1. How does technological change itself create the need for more technological change? Give some examples of the process in your answers.

2. Is economic efficiency possible in an economic system that is humane and non-alienating? Why or why not?

3. What is the difference between being alienated from one's work and being exploited in one's work?

4. Why are people in a highly technicized society unable to escape from alienation even in their leisure time?

5. In what sense was the Industrial Revolution only one aspect of a more widely reaching phenomenon? What were the other aspects of the larger phenomenon?

6. How does a competitive marketplace influence the pace of technological change?

7. How have governments tried to both promote technological change while limiting the dangers of researching and developing innovations?

8. In what sense is the ascendancy of specialized formal education largely responsible for both the biggest strengths and the biggest weaknesses of a highly technicized society?

Research Suggestion: In order to try to determine the appeal and pervasiveness of the technical milieu when economic considerations are minimal, consider the phenomenon of computer dating. This is still a relatively new kind of business and is showing no signs of replacing earlier forms of dating as the dominant way of finding a mate. Why is this? Is it because there is no economic incentive for people to use this new technology? Is it because cultural traditions about dating are still strong? Or are there simpler reasons such as prohibitive fees or a lack of confidence in the technology's efficiency? Try to find some statistics on the computer dating industry or computer matchmaking. How fast is it growing or shrinking? Survey some single people to find out why they do, would or wouldn't use such services. Try to draw some conclusions about what kinds of people use this kind of technology.

ANSWERS TO CHAPTER 13

Key Terms
1. b
2. c
3. d
4. a

Test

1. b	11. c	21. d
2. d	12. b	22. c
3. a	13. c	23. a
4. b	14. d	24. b
5. d	15. c	25. c
6. c	16. c	26. d
7. c	17. c	27. d
8. d	18. a	28. b
9. d	19. b	29. c
10. c	20. b	30. a

Pretest

1. b	6. a	11. c
2. d	7. c	12. d
3. a	8. a	13. d
4. b	9. b	
5. c	10. b	

Posttest

1. c	6. b	11. a
2. a	7. d	12. b
3. c	8. c	13. d
4. d	9. c	
5. b	10. d	

CHAPTER 14 IDEOLOGY, SOCIAL ORDER AND SOCIAL CHANGE

Key Terms

1. ideology

   a) ideology at the micro or individual level

2. interventive control

   b) ideology at the macro level of entire civilizations or epochs

3. complementary conditions

   c) physical coercion

4. routinization

   d) a body of systematic beliefs and ideas that claims to describe reality while suggesting certain actions to take

5. particular conception of ideology

   e) the process of building institutions to carry on the movement started by a charismatic leader

6. total conception of ideology

   f) pre-existing trends and aspects of social life that can be manipulated for ideological purposes

Pretest

1. According to Weber, the Protestant doctrine that contributed most to the development of capitalism was the:
   a) Baptist prohibition against alcohol and gambling
   b) Mennonite emphasis on hard work
   c) Lutheran idea that priests could marry
   d) Calvinist doctrine of predestination

2. According to Mannheim, the ruling class in any society tends to dismiss the ideas of the ruled class as:
   a) illogical and unjust
   b) utopian and unrealistic
   c) self-serving and boring
   d) ideological and subversive

3. Which of the following factual statements is free of an ideological component?
   a) Canada has one of the highest living standards in the world
   b) men are usually stronger than women
   c) Wayne Gretzky earns more than $500,000 per year
   d) none of the above

4. According to Marx and Engels, the ruling class in any era will try to present its interests as:
   a) paramount
   b) subordinate to the general interest
   c) everyone's interests
   d) irrelevant

5. The Falkland Islands war in 1982 demonstrated how the governments of the United Kingdom and Argentina used the ideology of _____ to divert public criticism away from their own domestic affairs.
   a) militarism
   b) imperialism
   c) nationalism
   d) racism

6. Using lotteries to entertain poor people by giving them an unrealistic hope of sudden riches is an example of using _____ to keep people's minds off social problems.
   a) bribes
   b) complementary conditions
   c) coercion
   d) persuasion

7. The man who postulated that a typical revolution will pass through three distinct phases was:
   a) Robert Michels
   b) Crane Brinton
   c) Herbert Marcuse
   d) Vilfredo Pareto

8. In the 1960s the North American student and youth movements were drawn to Marxism mainly by the ideology's _____ content.
   a) analytical
   b) feminist
   c) deterministic
   d) humanistic

9. A *liberal* democracy is one that:
   a) usually elects the Liberal party in national elections
   b) tolerates dissent
   c) defines democracy in a vague, non-rigid way
   d) evolved in a capitalistic free market economy

10. Generally speaking, ideologies:
    a) are unrelated to the economic structure of society
    b) are always neutral in advancing class claims
    c) mask certain aspects of social reality
    d) reveal the true nature of social reality

11. The aspect of an ideology which best speaks to the translation of values into practice is its:
    a) cognitive dimension
    b) evaluative dimension
    c) programmatic dimension
    d) none of the above

12. According to Weber, the term routinization describes the process by which:
    a) the ordinary becomes extraordinary
    b) the extraordinary becomes ordinary
    c) the ordinary never changes
    d) the extraordinary never changes

13. According to Crane Brinton's analysis of revolutionary processes, the Thermidorian reaction begins with:
    a) the topmost levels of the radical movement
    b) the reign of terror
    c) the young, enthusiastic revolutionaries
    d) b and c above

14. The FLQ movement in Canada:
    a) attempted to bring English Canadians up to the same economic level as French Canadians
    b) was the militant wing of the federal Liberal party
    c) was unaffected by any radical ideology
    d) none of the above

15. Ideologies describe themselves as:
    a) arguments
    b) emotional appeals
    c) the truth
    d) all of the above

Test

1. In everyday speech when someone is called ideological it means that she:
   a) has all the facts at her disposal
   b) deals largely in the world of ideas
   c) does not have any preconceptions about the world
   d) is overly narrow in outlook

2. Ideology is similar to charisma because:
   a) they are always found in the same individuals
   b) they are both taught systematically and explicitly
   c) examples of them are easier to come by than definitions
   d) they are limited to politicians

3. For Thomas Kuhn, a paradigm is:
   a) an inherently conservative view of the world
   b) a well-defined and coherent set of beliefs and practices
   c) a synonym for "scientific revolution"
   d) an essentially religious view of reality with smatterings of scientific insight

4. If normal science is conservative and scientific revolutions are radical, we can expect each to advance its own:
   a) ideological justifications and defences
   b) charismatic leaders
   c) ideological assaults on religion
   d) b and c above

5. For Marx, the basis of ideology is primarily:
   a) cultural
   b) political
   c) educational
   d) economic

6. Marx viewed ideology as:
   a) a system of beliefs that justifies the rule of the few over the many
   b) the salvation of the workers from capitalist oppression
   c) the opposite of false consciousness
   d) a direct consequence of religion

7. In discussing power, Marx:
   a) borrowed many of Weber's ideas
   b) overestimated the role of ideology in social exchanges
   c) focused on the struggle between feudal lords and serfs
   d) underestimated the autonomous role of ideas in everyday life

8. Weber was critical of Marx because the latter:
   a) paid too much attention to revolution
   b) failed to define social class
   c) did not fully appreciate the non-economic bases of action
   d) did not practise what he preached

9. For Weber, psychological states:
   a) are unimportant for shaping behaviour
   b) are as important as material interests for shaping behaviour
   c) are related to material interests
   d) a and c

10. According to Weber, the Protestant ethic:
    a) complemented the moving forces of early capitalism
    b) caused the development of capitalism
    c) retarded the early development of capitalism
    d) none of the above

11. In "The Protestant Ethic and the Spirit of Capitalism" Weber:
    a) was interested in refuting Marx's ideas
    b) was able to prove that religion corrupted people
    c) argued that ideas can become effective forces in history
    d) was clearly biased against capitalism

12. Where Marx identified an almost one-to-one correspondence between ideas and material interests, Weber:
    a) was in full agreement with him
    b) paid no attention to material forces
    c) was not in the least concerned with economics
    d) was anxious to recognize possible tensions between them

13. The sociology of knowledge tradition associated with Weber and Mannheim:
    a) has nothing in common with the Marxian tradition
    b) arrives at similar class-theoretical conclusions as Marxism
    c) is rooted in structural-functional sociology
    d) b and c above

14. Mannheim did not limit himself to a program of study inherited from Marx because:
    a) he felt that ideas were not related to social class
    b) he was opposed to proletarian revolution
    c) he was more sensitive to the non-material bases of action
    d) he disagreed with Marx's definition of social class

15. Situationally transcendent ideas are unreal because:
    a) they fit too neatly into the prevailing social order
    b) they are religiously inspired
    c) they do not fit the prevailing social order
    d) they are economically unsound

16. Situationally transcendent ideas are of two types: either they are ideological or they are:
    a) utopian
    b) practical
    c) real
    d) true

17. When discussing the thought of an epoch or civilization we are dealing with the _____ conception of ideology.
    a) Weberian
    b) Durkheimian
    c) particular
    d) total

18. Both ideology and science lay claim to the truth, but science alone:
    a) pursues truth in a readily demonstrable fashion
    b) is clearly non-empirical
    c) is free of theoretical distortion
    d) all of the above

19. Ideology can be equated with:
    a) science
    b) dogma
    c) truth
    d) fact

20. The cognitive dimension of ideology refers to the fact that ideology embodies a significant element of:
    a) passion
    b) emotion
    c) myth
    d) a and b above

21. The ideology of individualism insists that individuals:
    a) take the blame for their actions
    b) take the praise for their actions
    c) are at odds with society
    d) a and b above

22. The evaluative dimension of ideology concerns:
    a) the lack of moral principles in modern society
    b) the opposition between monarch and democracy
    c) the question of human rights
    d) the idea of the good society

23. Along with the promotion of social

order, the other major functions of ideology concern:
a) social change
b) social satisfaction
c) social rehabilitation
d) two of the above

24. Bureaucratic organizations are noted for:
a) their lack of leadership
b) making speedy decisions
c) their ability to combat routinization
d) concentrating decision-making in few hands

25. The expression "iron law of oligarchy" is associated with:
a) Max Weber
b) Robert Michels
c) Vilfredo Pareto
d) Gaetano Mosca

26. The student and youth movements in particular attracted:
a) people from the least privileged sectors of society
b) those who wanted to grow up in a world free of communism
c) idealistic people of middle-class origin
d) individuals who were unconcerned with alienated conditions of existence

27. Within the student movement:
a) there was only a superficial understanding of Marxism
b) the vast bulk of the supporters had a profound understanding of Marxism
c) Marxism was a discredited ideology
d) most adherents were ideologically pure

28. The demands of the FLQ leadership:
a) were unequivocally anti-socialist
b) were only superficially informed by Marxism

c) were in favour of retaining Anglo-capitalism in Quebec
d) clearly called for the abolition of capitalism as an economic system

29. According to the scientific meaning of the term democracy:
a) the Western countries and their allies are the only ones with true democracy
b) the socialist and communist countries could never be democratic
c) socialism and democracy are not contradictory
d) all capitalist countries are by definition democratic

30. The ideology of liberal democracy:
a) rids people of false consciousness
b) masks the real inequalities in the system
c) is less pernicious than the ideology of communism
d) is rooted in the religious teachings of Christianity

Posttest

1. Mannheim says radicals usually dismiss upper class ideas about the sanctity of tradition or the natural order of things as:
a) silly
b) utopian
c) ideological
d) irrational

2. In Mannheim's terms, when we exhibit "the special formulation of the total conception of ideology" we are able to see:
a) the ideological content in our opponent's arguments
b) the ideological content in our own arguments
c) the ideological content in everyone's arguments
d) that ideology will not help us understand the matter at hand

3. Ideology is *primarily* a body of:
   a) beliefs
   b) ideas
   c) rituals
   d) traditions

4. A value-neutral ideology is:
   a) one that only lists facts
   b) a contradiction in terms
   c) possible only on a non-controversial topic
   d) one that gives equal weight to all relevant opinions

5. Ideology can be used to support the existing order by:
   a) defining reality
   b) diverting attention away from social problems
   c) discrediting critics
   d) all of the above

6. One product of routinization as described by Weber is:
   a) a mid-life crisis
   b) an automobile assembly line
   c) the Roman Catholic Church
   d) the Dewy decimal system

7. Weber considered routinization to be a(n):
   a) necessary evil
   b) negative development
   c) positive development
   d) unimportant development

8. In the 1960s, Rowntree and Rowntree argued that the U.S. government had kept youth unemployment to acceptable levels by:
   a) expanding the school system and the military draft
   b) padding government payrolls with unnecessary workers
   c) doctoring the unemployment statistics
   d) all of the above

9. The FLQ's Manifesto called for an independent Quebec that would be:
   a) virulently anti-communist
   b) Marxist
   c) free of Anglo-Saxon capitalism
   d) economically linked to the United States

10. As a mechanism of social control, ideology is:
    a) less efficient and more costly than coercion
    b) more efficient and less costly than coercion
    c) unlikely to have positive long-term consequences
    d) more likely to lead to social unrest than is coercion

11. In discussing the functions of ideology, social control and freedom are:
    a) zero-sum phenomena
    b) matters of degree
    c) contradictory phenomena
    d) mutually exclusive

12. In discussing power and leadership, Weber felt that charismatic leaders are:
    a) politically impotent
    b) cautiously conservative
    c) truly revolutionary
    d) unlikely to have a mass following

13. The ideology of change that characterized social movements in the 1960s was:
    a) inspired by the work of Max Weber
    b) informed by a general sympathy for Marxism
    c) more critical of government than big business
    d) more critical of big business than government

14. As a political system, liberal democracy is:
    a) the best possible form of government
    b) premised on absolute equality among individuals

c) stronger in the United States than in Canada

d) incompatible with socialism

15. Which of the following kinds of governmental systems would describe itself as democratic:

a) the South African system of apartheid

b) a one-party structure

c) a country which will not let women vote

d) all of the above

Essay Questions

1. Define democracy in your own words. How does your definition differ (at least in its specific applications i.e. governmental procedures) from other definitions? Why do so many widely different forms of government all claim to be democratic?

2. What are the three stages of a revolution according to Crane Brinton? Do you think his theory is an accurate description of all revolutions? If not, which ones didn't fit the pattern he describes?

3. Keeping in mind that ideology is primarily a system of beliefs rather than ideas, how are ideologies changed?

4. If you were the head of your country's secret service, how would you make use of specific complementary conditions to undermine the efforts of nations and organizations of which you disapproved?

5. Argue either for or against the notion that scientists can be free of ideology.

6. Why did Weber call routinization a "necessary evil"? Construct an argument to either agree or disagree with him on this point.

7. Why did the FLQ (or the student youth movement) eventually peter out?

8. What are the five main functions of all ideologies?

   Suggested Research: To study the ideological content of language, collect several news items from your local newspaper. Go through the text and pick out all the words or phrases that have negative or positive connotations. Then, without changing any of the facts or structure of the story, replace the words and phrases that have negative connotations with positive or neutral words and phrases. Reverse the process for words that have positive connotations in the original news items. Compare your stories to the originals to see how the facts can be given vastly different slants. Try to account for the writer's choice of words. What ideological assumptions shaped the writing of the original stories.

ANSWERS TO CHAPTER 14

Test

1. d	11. c	21. d
2. c	12. d	22. d
3. b	13. b	23. a
4. a	14. c	24. d
5. d	15. c	25. b
6. a	16. a	26. c
7. d	17. d	27. a
8. c	18. a	28. b
9. b	19. b	29. c
10. a	20. c	30. b

Key Terms

1. d	4. e
2. c	5. a
3. f	6. b

Pretest

1. d	6. b	11. c
2. b	7. b	12. b
3. d	8. d	13. a
4. c	9. d	14. d
5. c	10. c	15. c

Posttest

1. c	6. c	11. b
2. a	7. a	12. c
3. a	8. a	13. b
4. b	9. c	14. b
5. d	10. b	15. d

INDEX

Groups:
    characteristics of, 150–51; individuals in, 150; primary, 151–52; reference, 153–54; secondary, 152

Haas, Jack, 153
Hagopian, Mark N., 358
Hall, Edward T., 67, 70
Haralambos, Michael, 30
Haskell, M., 53
Hegel, Georg, 322
Henley, Nancy, 148
Hiller, Harry H., 33
Historical/comparative research, 44–45
History:
    of sociological thought, 10–11; and sociology, 9–10; as source of internal invalidity, 43
Hobbes, Thomas, 59
Household, defined, 190
Hughes, Everett C., 32

Idealism, 75
Identification theory, 96
Ideological power, 324–25
Ideology, 26, 67, 69, 357–379
    classical views on, 357–361; contemporary views on, 361–363; and democracy, 376, 378; five dimensions of, 362–63; functions of, 364–376; power, belief, and change, 324–25; routinization, change and, 371–376; a working definition of, 363
I-feeling (Cooley), 92
Illiteracy, 165, 166
Imitative behaviour, 317, 318–19
Immigration into Canada, 79, 81, 217, 218–19, 223, 228
    changing sources of immigrants, 219, 221, 222; and the staples economy, 298
Impression management (Goffman), 93, 146–47, 149
Income stratification in Canada, 265–68
Independent variables, 39, 41, 42
Indian women, rights of, 171
Individuals in groups, 150
Individual uniqueness, and sociological explanation, 17–18, 21, 122
Industrialization, 300
Industrial Revolution, 5, 10, 329–39
    cultural transformations, 334–39; technical revolution, 331–34
Inequality:
    in functional theory, 247–48; racial and ethnic, 228–32
Infant mortality rates, 197
Information revolution, 323

Inkeles, Alex, 60
Innis, Harold A., 31, 75, 297–98, 299
Institutional racism, 232
Institutions, *see* Social institutions
Instrumentalist views in neo-Marxist theory, 294
Instrumentation, as source of internal invalidity, 43
Integration, as process in social change, 323
Interactionism, *see* Symbolic interactionism
Interaction rituals, 143
Interactions, roles and, 126
Interdependence, 75
Internal colonies, 217–18
Internal validity, 43
Interval level of measurement, 55
Interviewing, 19
Invalidity, sources of, 43–44
Isajiw, W.W., 83

James, William 145
Japan, 77–78
Johnson, Leo A., 51
Jonestown mass suicide, 155–56

Kallen, Evelyn, 23, 232
Kanter, Rosabeth Moss, 152
Katz, Elihu, 316
Kehoe, Jack, 74
Kimball, M., 97
Kohlberg, Lawrence, 97
Kuhn, Thomas S., 37, 357–58

Labelling processes, 112, 113
    effects of, 144; responses to (secondary deviance), 113–116
Labour force, 167
Laissez-faire, 290
Landes, D.S., 332
Language:
    and culture, 70–71; and interaction between men and women, 148–49; *See also* Bilingualism.
Language maintenance and shift, 225–28
Lasswell, Harold, 305–306
Latent functions, 26
Lauer, Robert, 94
Lautard, Hugh E., 229
Laxer, Gordon, 300
Learning, 28–29. *See also* Education.
Lemert, Edwin M., 113–14
Lewis, Oscar, 73, 93
Liberal democracy, 378
Liberalism, 69
Liebow, Elliot, 50
Life expectancy, 196
Lindell, Susan, 98

Sociological imagination (Mills), 15–16
Sociology:
    Canadian sociology, 31–33; contending
    perspectives within, 22–31, 37; con-
    trasted with other disciplines, 3–4,
    9; as a science, 19–22; subject matter
    of, 4–5, 20
Sorokin, Pitrim A., 21
South Africa, 233
Spencer, Herbert, 321
"Spiral of silence," 317
Split labour market model, 218–19
Staples perspective (Innis), 297–99
State and social structure, 342
Static-group comparison, 42
Statistical regression, as source of internal
    invalidity, 43
Statistics, official, 51–52
Statuses, 16–17, 25, 137
Status groups (Weber), 246
Stereotypes, 81, 95, 98, 108–109
    sex-role stereotyping, 148, 149, 183
    312–13
Stigmatization, *see* Labelling processes.
Stirling, Robert, 51–52
Stowe, Emily Howard, 172
Stratification:
    in Canada, 252, 255–56, 258; distin-
    guished from class, 239–40; func-
    tional theory of, 247–49; by income
    (Canada), 265–68; Weberian theory of,
    244–47
Stratified sampling, 53–54
Strauss, Anselm, 135, 136, 144
Structural functionalism, 23–26
    approach to roles, 137–39, 141; ap-
    proach to study of organizations, 134,
    135; criticisms of, 30; interpretation
    of group behaviour, 150; view of
    culture, 67, 68, 69; view of socializa-
    tion, 91
Structuralist views in neo-Marxism, 294
Structure, concept of, 25
Student/youth movement, 373–75
Subcultures, 68, 73–75
    deviants, 116–18; youth, 74, 99–100
Substructure and superstructure of society
    (Marx), 358
Suffrage for women, 172–74
Suicide, Durkheim's study of, 38, 45
Surplus value (Marx), 240–41
Survey research, 45–49
    bivariate analysis, 46–47; logic of,
    45–46; multivariate analysis, 48–49
Symbolic change, 78
Symbolic ethnicity, 232
Symbolic interactionism, 28–30
    approach to study of organizations,

134–35; criticisms of, 31; interpretation
of group behaviour, 150, 153; perspective on roles, 141–45; view of
culture, 67–68; view of socialization,
91–93
Symbols, 28
    expressive symbols, 67–68, 69–73
Systematic sampling, 53

Tanner, Julian, 99–100
Tautological theories, 2
Technical knowledge base, transformation
    of, 339–43
Technical revolution, 331–34
    views of Marx, Durkheim, and Weber
    on, 336–39
Technicization of life, consequences of,
    345–49
Technological determinism, 75, 77
Technological morality, 122
Technology:
    and change, 75, 77, 323, 329–52
Technostructure (Galbraith), 340–42
Teleological approach to understanding
    society, 23
Television, 71–73
    influence of, in socialization, 98;
    McLuhan's ideas on, 77
Test variable, 41, 42
Theoretical definition of variables, 54–55
Theories, sociological, 2–3, 4
Thomas, W.I., 52
Throw-away society, 291–92
Tiger, Lionel, 180
Time, and cultural differences, 70
Toffler, Alvin, 77, 291, 324
Top-down, bottom up, 127–28
Total institutions (Goffman) 102
Tradition-carriers, 298
Tribe, Verna, 61, 94
Tsigoloicos, 74, 76–77
Tylor, Edward B., 67

Unanticipated consequences, 5, 6
Underclass, 217
Underside world, 118
Underworld, 117
Unemployment, 291
Unions and women workers, 166–67
Unit of analysis, 40
Unobtrusive measures, 51–53
Urbanization and industrialization,
    332–33

Values, *see* Cultural values and norms.
Variables, 39, 41, 42
    operational and theoretical definitions
    of, 54–55

Verification of theories, 2, 18
Vernon, Raymond, 294
Vertical Mosaic, The, 228–29, 232
Violence:
    in the family, 207–208; in the media, 314, 317–18; in the underworld, 117–18
Visible minorities, 230–32
Voluntarism, 18

Wage labour, 241–42
War, transformed by technology, 349
Wealth distribution in Canada, 254–56
Weber, Max, 19, 26, 28, 60, 278, 284, 371
    on bureaucracy, 15, 128; on economic institutions, 288–89, 290, 293; on the Protestant ethic, 44, 75, 290; on the rationalization of social life, 338–39; on social change, 322, 325; theory of stratification, 244–47; views on ideology, 358–60
Welfare state, 291
West, Candace, 148
Westhues, Kenneth, 3

Whyte, William Foote, 152
Wife battering, 208
Wolff, K.H., 70
Women:
    explanations for subordination of, 180–84; history of women's rights, 170–78; images in the media, 183, 312–13; in the labour force, 165–70, 179–80, 182–83, 199, 260, 267; major issues, 184; movement in Canada, 177–78; payment of, 166–67, 168–69; recent changes, 178–80; voting rights for, 172–74. *See also* Gender relations; Sex-role stereotyping.
World Wars, 293
Wright, Charles R., 306

Yankelovich, Daniel, 103
Youth cultures, 74, 99–100

Zeitlin, Irving M., 288, 358–59
Zeitlin, Maurice, 297
Zimbardo, Philip, 145–46
Zimmerman, Don, 148